FROM SHOCK TO THERAPY

UNU WORLD INSTITUTE FOR DEVELOPMENT ECONOMICS RESEARCH (UNU/WIDER)

was established by the United Nations University as its first research and training centre and started work in Helsinki, Finland in 1985. The purpose of the Institute is to undertake applied research and policy analysis on structural changes affecting the developing and transitional economies, to provide a forum for the advocacy of policies leading to robust, equitable, and environmentally sustainable growth, and to promote capacity strengthening and training in the field of economic and social policy-making. Its work is carried out by staff researchers and visiting scholars in Helsinki and through networks of collaborating scholars and institutions around the world.

FROM SHOCK TO THERAPY

The Political Economy of Postsocialist Transformation

GRZEGORZ W. KOLODKO

A study prepared for the World Institute for Development Economics Research of the United Nations University (UNU/WIDER)

OXFORD

UNIVERSITY PRESS

OXFORD
UNIVERSITY PRESS

Great Clarendon Street, Oxford OX2 6DP

Oxford University Press is a department of the University of Oxford.
It furthers the University's objective of excellence in research, scholarship,
and education by publishing worldwide in

Oxford New York

Athens Auckland Bangkok Bogotá Buenos Aires Calcutta
Cape Town Chennai Dar es Salaam Delhi Florence Hong Kong Istanbul
Karachi Kuala Lumpur Madrid Melbourne Mexico City Mumbai
Nairobi Paris São Paulo Singapore Taipei Tokyo Toronto Warsaw
with associated companies in Berlin Ibadan

Oxford is a registered trade mark of Oxford University Press
in the UK and in certain other countries

Published in the United States
by Oxford University Press Inc., New York

UNU/WIDER: World Institute for Development Economics
Research of the United Nations University, Katajanokanlaituri 6 B,
00160 Helsinki, Finland

British Library Cataloguing in Publication Data
Data available

Library of Congress Cataloging in Publication Data
Data available

ISBN 0-19-829743-2

1 3 5 7 9 10 8 6 4 2

Typeset in Plantin
by Graphicraft Limited, Hong Kong
Printed in Great Britain
on acid-free paper by
T.J. International Ltd
Padstow, Cornwall

For the next generation

I know there is truth opposite to falsehood
that it may be found if people will
and is worth seeking.

John Locke (1632–1704)

FOREWORD

The transition of the former socialist countries of Europe and Asia to the market economy is certainly the most momentous event of the last two decades of this millennium. Its onset has been unpredictable, and most of its outcomes contrast sharply with the initial expectations. While generating an extensive—and still rapidly growing—literature, many aspects of the transition process—such as the huge cross-country differences in economic and social performance—broadly remain unexplained and poorly understood.

Until recently, most of the transition debate has placed greater attention on some aspects of this great transformation, e.g. on rapid macroeconomic stabilization, liberalization, and privatization. It has given less emphasis to the role of initial institutional conditions, the political economy of transition, and the role of external advice in this process. In this highly original single-author study on the economics of postsocialist transition, Grzegorz Kolodko attempts to fill this gap. He recognizes the need for sound economic fundamentals but, at the same time, emphasizes the long-term multifaceted nature of the transition process, the influence of historical factors on the outcomes of the reform process, and the crucial need for developing gradually but steadily those institutional arrangements which are the best guarantees of successful transition.

While not all readers may agree with his interpretation of the transition or his policy approach, they will no doubt benefit from this well-researched and provocative analysis, which challenges many of the simple ideas of the 'Washington consensus'. Indeed, Kolodko places his analysis of the transition in a broader social and political-economic context, and strongly emphasizes the need for a gradual build-up of institutions. This book has been written by a scholar who played a key role in the formulation of the successful policies adopted in Poland from 1994–7, the most successful transitional economy of Europe. As such it does not suffer from the lack of credibility and empirical support that affects some of the current literature on the transition process.

Kolodko's book is therefore essential reading for anyone interested in a critical assessment of the transition process. It is an invaluable guide for those seriously interested in understanding the great transformation still under way in most of the former socialist bloc. As such, I warmly recommend it to academics and practitioners alike, as well as to investors, economists from international agencies working on the transition, and, of course, the enlightened general reader.

Giovanni Andrea Cornia
Director, UNU/WIDER

CONTENTS

ACKNOWLEDGEMENTS

The central thrust of this book took shape when the author held the Distinguished Sasakawa Chair and was research professor in development policy at the World Institute for Development Economics Research of the United Nations University (UNU/WIDER) in Helsinki in 1997–8 and senior visiting fellow at the Policy Research Department of the World Bank in Washington, DC, in 1998.

The author has benefited greatly from discussions with many colleagues, but especially from the critical comments and useful suggestions of UNU/WIDER Director Giovanni Andrea Cornia. Without his help it would have been difficult to complete this work.

The author is also indebted to Marie Lavigne of the Sorbonne, Kaz Poznanski of the University of Seattle, Vladimir Popov of the Universität Kaiserslautern, and Jerzy Hausner of Cracow Economics University for their observations, comments, and suggestions.

The author is most obliged to D. Mario Nuti of the London Business School and the Università di Roma 'La Sapienza'—a great economist and a great friend—for his constant support. He acted as a reliable advisor when the author was serving as first deputy premier and minister of finance in Poland in 1994–7, and he has been a demanding witness of the creation of this text. Now that it has been completed, the reader may judge the results.

The author is especially grateful to Robert Zimmermann for his patience and outstanding editorial assistance.

Washington, DC
Thanksgiving Day, 1998

Introduction

On the eve of the 21st century one of the most important features of the global economy is the comprehensive process of postsocialist transformation. Altogether over 30 countries in Europe and Asia, with a population of one and a half billion people, one-fourth of all mankind, are involved in these dramatic changes. The implications are vital not only for these nations, but also for the entire world.

An indispensable part of the transition to a market system is the opening up of former socialist countries and their integration into the global economy. What we are observing in this historical endeavour is not the abandonment of communism, but the abandonment of state socialism, that is, the statist centrally planned economy. The notion 'communism' has been widely used in the West to describe systems which should be called 'socialist'. When, in China and in the former Soviet Union, party leaders referred to 'communism', they meant this more as a target, a final (if not utopian) outcome, but never the current reality.

Eastern European nations let go of this dream during the period of de-Stalinization after 1956. The agenda then became focused on the socialist political and economic system. For this reason, the current wave of spectacular changes—the most wide-ranging since the attempt to introduce the socialist regime—must be called 'postsocialist'. Actually, there are several transformations, since the paths and the pace by which particular countries are reforming the socialist economy, like China, or moving away from it, like Russia, are different everywhere.

Transition is a process involving a fundamental shift leading from the late socialist centrally planned economy based on the dominance of state ownership toward a free market, with the private sector in the key role. Thus, unlike the process of the reform of socialism, which aimed at the improvement of the existing socialist system through alterations rather than through a general overhaul of the basic institutional framework, the transition entails the introduction of entirely new arrangements. This is a process of replacing an old system with a new one. It is not simply another attempt to refurbish the old system by tinkering with the way it performs.

Whereas some of the former 'traditional state socialist' countries are engaged in this transition, certain other nations have undertaken comprehensive reforms and restructuring. Although these nations are no longer classical command economies, they are not all experiencing a transition from socialism. Nonetheless, the vast reforms taking place in these nations mean that institutions, structures, policies, and behaviours are changing, too. Thus,

reforms are being implemented and the transition from socialism is occurring in a large part of the world.

The 'postsocialist transition' was initiated after 1989, and two events were
of paramount importance in this process. The first centred on the roundtable
negotiations between the government and the opposition in Poland from
February to April 1989 (in which the author took part). The second was the
decision of Mikhail Gorbachev, the Soviet leader, to bring down the Berlin
Wall. Surely, if not for the historical compromise accomplished in Poland,
this second event would not have taken place, or at least it would not have
taken place when it did. If the decision to demolish the Berlin Wall was of
a strictly political nature, albeit one with significant economic implications,
the negotiations in Poland represented a momentous turning point in a long
process of gradual economic liberalization.

Hence, whenever there is discussion about the reforms and the transition
(the 'transformations'), it is indispensable that one take a retrospective look
at the causes of the systemic changes and the reasons why they happened
when they did. Yet, one should also take a prospective look at what the coming years may bring and at how to manage the process of development so
that the future becomes an improvement on the past. Whenever necessary
this book therefore refers to the causes in the past and the aims for the future.
In searching for an answer to the question 'What triggered the transition?',
one must go at least as far back as 1950, and, in looking for ways to manage long-term sustainable development, one must look at least as far forward
as the first two decades of the next millennium.

However, the considerations are centred mainly on the 1990s, and the
economies of Eastern Europe, the former Soviet republics, China, Indochina,
and Mongolia, as well as Cuba and North Korea, are all examined. Yet,
the comparative analysis does not cover all of these nations equally. There
is no need to do so since this is not a compendium of country studies, but a
general discussion of the postsocialist transition. Nonetheless, one may find
here many country-specific examples and many country case studies, but
only for the sake of providing the background for the general analysis and
conclusions.

To present a connected series of observations on this subject is not easy,
since there is still some doubt about exactly what the transition is and what
it is not, so that the topic coverage in the relevant literature is not always
consistent. For the purposes of this book, the transition is defined clearly
now: *the postsocialist transition is the process of the replacement of the centrally
planned economy by a market economy.*

The course of events has yet to determine whether China, Vietnam, and
some of the former Soviet republics are involved in reforming the old regime
or are already on the transition path. Considering the logic and the mechanisms of market-oriented reform and the transition to a market economy,
it seems quite likely that these countries, for various reasons, are at least

'transitioning' from a centrally planned to a full-fledged market economy. However, this is not absolutely certain. There is no doubt that in China and Vietnam the scope of the current changes in economic arrangements and in the tools of development policy is beyond that of any adjustments which have been made since the introduction of the socialist order. Nonetheless, though there is an opportunity for more radical alterations, there is yet no guarantee that this opportunity will be embraced, and these countries are not as advanced in the process of change as are the majority of the Eastern European nations, where there is no doubt that a definite decision has been taken in favour of capitalism.

By example, the successful transformations in some countries influence positively the reasoning in others, including all post-Soviet emerging markets and the Asian reformed socialist economies. This 'demonstration effect' is playing an important role in postsocialist transformation. The transition was initially launched only in a few countries (mainly because of the growing inefficiency of the central planning system and its inability to compete in a world economy undergoing vast globalization), but later the phenomenon became widespread because of this demonstration effect. It is only a matter of time before Belarus and the new Yugoslavia (Serbia and Montenegro) initiate the same sort of historic evolution which has been taking place elsewhere with such great dynamism in an irreversible way. Even nations as remote from the market and from democracy as Cuba and North Korea will eventually adopt the course of transformation.

Postsocialist transformation consists of a spectrum of changes in many areas of political, social, and economic life. There are various groups of important interactions: between political and economic adjustments, between the way the economy begins to perform under the new circumstances and the way society adapts, between the way people work and the methods through which governments rule, and, finally, between the means used by the partners acting on the international scene and the results of economic integration.

Thus, without proper attention to the non-economic aspects of transition and to the interplay between political life and the economic sphere, the economic dimension of the process will not be understood, and the shift to the market economy and civic society will not be carried out correctly. This is so because of the political struggle accompanying transition. The process of marketizaton goes hand-in-hand with democratization, which renders the whole evolution easier in the long term, but which may cause additional stress and more political hurdles in the short term. Attempts to achieve improvements in allocative efficiency or competitiveness are being accompanied by skirmishes over the new patterns in the redistribution of income and wealth. The tug-of-war is all the more dramatic because it is occurring in parallel with the most extensive privatization of state assets in history.

The transition to the market involves much more than liberalization and privatization, since it encompasses complex structural and institutional adjustments, as well as social and political changes. So, while attempting to establish the new economic order which is supposed to be for the benefit of all (if this is possible), various groups in society are also trying to achieve for themselves lofty positions within the new order. There are winners, but there are also losers. Consequently, there are conflicts, and ways must be found to resolve these conflicts while supporting economic growth and social development.

A compelling feature of the transition is the process of recession and growth. The transition was initiated in response to the urgent need to boost the ability of the economy to expand. However, contrary to expectations, economic output shrank by a very large margin during the early transition, and only later did countries begin one-by-one to gain economic momentum and return to the path of growth. In 1998, after almost a decade of transition, the average national income, or GDP, of the 27 countries of Eastern Europe and the Commonwealth of Independent States (CIS) was still below three-quarters of the pre-transition level in 1989, the year most often employed as a benchmark.[1]

This raises questions. Why was the transitional recession so severe? Why did it last so long? Were the early expectations too optimistic, or does the fault lay with poor strategies and policies? Why did some countries experience output decline for ten straight years and lose over half the value of GDP?

One question is most crucial, namely: What is the nature of a proper development strategy to recover production and sustain high-speed growth? Among the many reasons why economic growth is necessary is the political support it can generate so that the momentous changes involved in the transition process can continue. Otherwise, electorates may begin to wonder if all their sacrifices have been in vain.

Leading transition countries are already enjoying rapid economic growth, though this has come at the cost of a profound initial decline in output, spreading poverty, and intense social stress. Could recovery have occurred earlier and growth been more rapid? More importantly for future development: Is there a chance for a turnaround in the nations still suffering from transitional recession?

---

[1] The CIS includes all former Soviet republics, except the Baltic States, and consists of 12 economies: Armenia, Azerbaijan, Belarus, Georgia, Kazakhstan, Kyrgyzstan, Moldova, Russia, Tajikistan, Turkmenistan, Ukraine, and Uzbekistan. 'East-Central Europe' consists of 15 countries: Albania, Bosnia-Herzegovina, Bulgaria, Croatia, the Czech Republic, Estonia, Hungary, Latvia, Lithuania, FYR ('Former Yugoslav Republic of') Macedonia, Poland, Romania, Slovakia, Slovenia, and the new Yugoslavia (Serbia and Montenegro). However, if the distinction is between 'the former Soviet Union' (or the 'former Soviet republics') and 'Eastern Europe', then the former counts 15 states, and the latter 12 because of the shift in the classification of the Baltic States, which are former Soviet republics, but not part of the CIS. The former German Democratic Republic (GDR), though referred to from time to time, is not counted here. Several other countries are mentioned, too: Mongolia, which belongs to the category of transition economies, China and Vietnam, Cambodia and Laos, and Cuba and North Korea. Altogether, with the former GDR, this makes 35 countries.

The answers to these questions reside in the effectiveness of policy-making. High-quality growth must be firmly based on high-quality policy. Transformation is a process of systemic redesign, and this requires that a distinction be made between transition policy and development strategy. The one is not a substitute for the other. Transition policy aims to enhance the ability of the economy to grow by changing the economic and political system, while development strategy aims to use the advantages provided by the existing system, whatever its limitations, so as to improve the standard of living and the quality of life in society. No matter what the system, there is always room for good policy, just as there is always the possibility of policy errors. Sound development strategy and the active role of the state are the necessary ingredients in any recipe for economic success. Only when these are present will it become feasible to meet the growing expectations of societies and of the international community.

Likewise, the transition ought to be seen as an instrument of long-term development strategy. Transition should not be treated as an isolated goal. Ongoing change makes sense only if productivity eventually grows and competitiveness and efficiency advance so that the standard of living—including the quality of consumption, of social capital (that is, education, research, health care, and social security), and of the natural environment—is bound to rise.

Nonetheless, many rival policy targets always find their way onto the agenda. Policies are frequently in danger of being weakened because of the clashing preferences of different interest groups. Transition is thus as much a political process as an economic one. Indeed, the politics may be even more challenging than the economics. The experience of the first decade of transition shows clearly that the major difficulties occur not because of a lack of the theoretical knowledge required to tackle the issues, but because of the inability of governments to carry out sound policies based on this knowledge. What seems to be necessary from the economic viewpoint often turns out to be impossible from the political perspective. This is the core contradiction and the nightmare facing policymakers involved in the transition.

A better understanding of the connections between the economic and the political factors is necessary to facilitate the implementation of policies which may be able to make the transition less harsh and more fruitful. As Douglass C. North (1997, p. 16), the 1993 winner of the Nobel Memorial Prize in Economic Science, has observed, 'The interface between economics and politics is still in a primitive state in our theories, but its development is essential if we are to implement policies consistent with intentions.'

This is all the more true of the postsocialist transition, since policies are being applied in a context of profound economic and political change. The political economy of the entire process of recession, recovery, growth, and development should therefore be of special interest on the long and winding road to the market and to democracy. 'Political economy' indicates an emphasis on conflict resolution (which markets are not very good at) and by definition focuses on issues relevant for political discussion and amenable to political compromise. Likewise, the well-being of the nations establishing a market economy and a civic society depends on the ability of these nations to achieve economic growth without burdening their neighbours. The expansion of production and trade and the improvement in standards of living should create a sound foundation for regional cooperation and good cross-border relations.

Only those nations capable of achieving sustainable growth and development have a chance of catching up with the most advanced economies in due time. However, this will require a generation or two of hard work, wise government, and strong international support.

The experience of the early reforms under socialism and of a decade of postsocialist transformation has taught that the key element for successful transition is good macroeconomic management. The discouraging results of transition so far, especially the 'great slump' in economic growth, are the evident consequences of wrong policies. The government's role has been neglected. The state should not retire from economic activity, but should take a firm position in terms of the regulatory environment, infrastructure development, and investments in human capital.

The new institutional arrangements must facilitate growth. Liberalization, stabilization, and privatization are indispensable, and sound fundamentals are required, but these will not work without institutional backing. A strong fiscal position, balanced budgets, balance in current accounts, low inflation, liberal regimes toward international trade and capital flows: all these will help growth only if they are supported by adequate organizations, good institutions, and market rules which are respected. Nations which have been able to act in these areas wisely have grown more, and their peoples are enjoying a gradual rise in living standards.

The postsocialist transition will last for at least several more years. There are going to be fresh success stories and more failures. The process is not a steady one. History and geopolitics are also influencing outcomes and future prospects. But policymaking is the most important element. For transition countries policymaking is crucial to the course of change, critical for integration with the world economy, and decisive for the accumulation of social capital. We do not know all the answers to all the urgent and difficult questions, but we already possess a great deal of experience. This experience may help us find the answers, and there is good reason to hope that ultimately we may succeed.

Departure

1

Transition from Socialism: Where To?

1.1. WHAT TRIGGERED THE TRANSITION?

The transition was triggered by a conviction that the centrally planned economy had reached its limits. The fact that the socialist system was so close to exhaustion was being taken as proof of its inability to adapt.

However, some experts have stressed with considerable argument that in the Soviet Union, when Gorbachev came to power, the centrally planned economy had the prospect of at least another 15 years or so of relatively good performance without recession. Growth was not expected to be significant, but this was not anticipated to matter much for the sustainability of the government because there was no major social unrest—as in Poland—and the political system was quite strong. According to this view, in other countries like Czechoslovakia and the GDR in the mid-1980s the centrally planned economy and the political regimes were far from having used up their full potential (Popov and Shmelev 1990).

Some have even voiced the opinion that the fall of communism is a 'myth', at least for Russia, and this myth is 'one of the greatest errors of our century' (Shevtsova 1995). Luckily, the century is coming to an end.

Within each particular economic system and institutional framework there are always policy alternatives for combining the factors of production, allocating them, and sharing out the resulting output. Yet, progress can be achieved only if there is growth. Owing to serious financial, economic, social, and ultimately political imbalances, the socialist economies were losing the ability to expand (Stiglitz 1995). Vast shortages, persistent inflationary pressure, structural weaknesses, and poor macromanagement were generating and intensifying microeconomic inefficiencies. Social needs could no longer always be satisfied. Growth was slowing due to shrinking investment and declining productivity. The people were becoming more and more disillusioned with economic policies and ultimately with the system itself.

Before the system could collapse under its own weight, attempts were made at reviving it. The notion of 'reform' was employed from time to time in centrally planned economies. The common denominator of the 'reforms', whatever their features and characteristics, was an effort to sustain and improve the system by enhancing efficiency and boosting standards of living. The reforms which had been carried out in the late 1950s and then in the late 60s and again in the early 70s always delivered some improvements in economic performance, though these could never be sustained. Now, once more in the 80s, the positive results of attempts at reform were evaporating.

In no case were the reforms able to secure rapid and durable economic growth. After a certain amount of initial progress, economies slowed and then entered another round of deterioration in economic equilibrium (Kolodko 1986a). Again and again shortages reappeared, and repressed inflationary pressures re-emerged, with all the accompanying inefficiencies (Kornai 1980). The bigger the disequilibrium, the slower the long-run rate of growth. The bigger the shortages, the wider the fluctuation in the rate of growth. This was the case to varying degrees throughout Eastern Europe from 1950 until the end of the 80s.

A laboratory for reform in the centrally planned economy in Europe happened to be Poland. This country can therefore be considered as a special case offering general insights into the overall process of the break-down of the socialist system. In Poland, as in Hungary, the efforts to reform the traditional Soviet-style economy were more serious than elsewhere. In the late 1950s the management of state companies was decentralized, and worker-led management initiatives were exercised more widely. The reforms of the late 1960s were inconsistent and superficial and lacked the adequate support of the political leadership, and there was another grim economic and political crisis in 1970.

Then, after a few years of remarkable improvement in 1971–4, the economy was driven back into huge imbalances and—the beginning of the end—excessive foreign debt. Because of faulty policies, the economic openness which had been instituted by the reforms and which was sup-posed to be a means to growth, led to a debt burden which was strang-ling the economy. Ultimately, this caused another severe crisis and the near collapse of the system. A further staunch effort at reform was initi-ated in the course of the 80s, but the task this time was even more urgent. This was so because of the existence of a strongly distorted financial environment.

Despite all the drawbacks, the market-oriented reforms undertaken during these years eventually contributed, though only to a degree and only for short periods, to higher growth rates and more competitiveness. The new institutional arrangements which were established rendered economic entities, especially state enterprises, a little bit more flexible and able to respond positively to market signals. However, the lack of other organiza-tions and institutions crucial for economic development caused various con-tradictions and tensions. The logic of these processes was such that the economic tensions were transmitted—after a time-lag, but unavoidably—into the social and ultimately the political spheres.

In other countries the pre-transition economic reforms implemented in the 1980s were likewise preceded by numerous false starts.[1] Attempts at reforming socialist economies were being undertaken as early as 1956–8. At that time the reforms were a reaction to the compromised and utterly bureaucratic Stalinist system.

Stalinism had caused fundamental changes in Eastern European economies after the Second World War. It engineered essential adjustments in economic structures, mainly through rapid industrialization and the establishment of the groundwork for additional expansion, especially in heavy industry. The new structures, because of overindustrialization and the underdevelopment of the service sector, gradually became rigid and inflexible, and they were unable to keep pace with the quickly rising aspirations of populations for a better quality of life. The need for far-reaching changes became increasingly pressing. However, the efforts failed because the political leadership lacked the determination to carry out sufficiently profound reform. Meanwhile, economic structures and institutions, though unyielding, were proving quite stable. Several years went by; reforms failed and, not surprisingly, were abandoned.

Drawing lessons from the earlier experiences in Poland, Hungary recorded some achievements beginning in the late 1960s.[2] Hungarian 'goulash socialism' was often pointed to as the best example of an alternative centrally planned economy. During this period, learning by doing— or by seeing the mistakes of others—became more common. Thus, both Hungary and Poland observed the experiments in self-management and decentralized socialism in Yugoslavia, which remained outside the Soviet bloc. Other countries fiddled with specific elements and mechanisms in their economic systems, but this was never as comprehensive as the efforts in Hungary, Poland, and Yugoslavia.

1.2. THE CONDITIONS FOR MARKET REFORM UNDER SOCIALISM

The history of economic reform, including its achievements and its failures, shows that at least four conditions must be satisfied if any reform is to succeed. First, society must be willing to carry out the reform and bear the relevant costs. Second, the political authorities must be firmly committed to push the reform through. Third, knowledge is required to provide a theoretical foundation for the new system. Fourth, the reform must be

---

[1] For more on this issue, see, inter alia, Brus 1988, Kolodko 1989a, Kornai 1986, Nove 1992, Poznanski 1996, Wilczynski 1972, Wiles 1977.

[2] In turn, Hungary was frequently cited as a model during the Polish reforms in the 1970s and 80s.

supported with sufficient resources to facilitate ongoing change. One is hard pressed to find a good example of a case in which all these conditions were met.

The market reforms were quite difficult for the people. The argument that a lack of reform would be even dearer was never heard. Support for the reforms varied, depending on the particular concerns of society during the period of implementation. For instance, while the Polish people displayed much interest in and backing for economic reform in the 1980s, though not as much as they had shown earlier, especially in 1956–8 and 1971–4, they also demonstrated a reluctance to bear the inevitable costs of systemic and structural change. While Hungarians were keen to accelerate the reform process in the early 1980s, by the end of the decade they had become much less determined to see it through. In Czechoslovakia there was much enthusiasm for reform in the spring of 1968, but later, after the Soviet-led military invasion, this petered out and was replaced by something quite at the other extreme, namely, apathy.

Feelings were often contradictory. While societies were eager to test the new solutions proposed within the framework of reform, they were soon passively—or sometimes even actively—resisting the steps necessary to realize them. When it came to concrete action which, at least initially, would generate only greater costs, the people wanted to have their cake and eat it, too. Public opinion surveys in Poland during the 1980s provided clear evidence of this, especially in regard to price adjustments and income policies. The people regularly declared that they preferred price levels and price structures based on market categories. This meant that they welcomed the idea of bringing prices to the market clearing level, but they also protested loudly, even through strikes, whenever the authorities raised prices significantly.

The reasons for the resolve shown by political leaders to implement systemic reform are more complex. People in government were not always an homogeneous group, no matter what outsiders may have thought. They were struggling against contradictions similar to those being experienced by the wider society, though this fact was never aired publicly.[3] Often, what one faction within government accepted as obvious, another found troublesome. What the military-industrial complex preferred, the agro-business sector could not support. Under such circumstances, without a clear mechanism of political arbitration among alternative viewpoints and contradictory interests, it was quite difficult—if not impossible—to reach a workable consensus.

Likewise, the approach (or lack thereof) of the authorities and of interest groups toward reform was not the same in every country nor from one

---

[3] With the exception, of course, of open political crises, such as in the GDR in 1953, Hungary and Poland in 1956, Czechoslovakia in 1968, and again Poland in 1970–1 and 1980–1.

period to the next. In the 1980s there was institutional stagnation in Bulgaria, Czechoslovakia, and the GDR. Albania and Romania were more rigidly oriented than reform-minded. They tried to centralize their economies still further and to close them even more. In the Soviet Union Mikhail Gorbachev introduced 'glasnost' and 'perestroika', but the lack of a comprehensive programme and the Soviet involvement in a losing war in Afghanistan doomed these reform efforts. Nonetheless, some Soviet republics achieved progress with market reform. For example, Estonia continued to experiment with partial liberalization, although within the strict limits of the predominance of state ownership and central government control. In more 'remote' socialist countries, like Cuba, Mongolia, and North Korea, traditional central planning was exercised, but in the context of a certain dependence on heavy subsidies from China and the Soviet Union. Meanwhile, Vietnam—at the behest of no one, but definitely encouraged by Gorbachev's perestroika—launched its own reforms, known as 'doi moi'. In Eastern Europe only Hungary and Yugoslavia continued to favour gradual decentralization and liberalization, although these efforts were losing momentum.

Also in the 1980s the Polish leadership—like no one before—exhibited real determination to push ahead with sound market reform. This determination had many roots, including bitter experiences with central planning and, indeed, the conviction that the economy would never perform efficiently or achieve sustainable growth without a major overhaul. But this authentic commitment of the authorities was not backed by crucial social partners. Moreover, because of political infighting and against the backdrop of a deteriorating economic and financial situation, important pro-reform groups turned against the government in its attempts to execute otherwise uncontroversial changes.[4]

For reform to succeed, the interests of government authorities and of society had to be compatible. A firm coalition in favour of change should have been sought. Such a coalition could have stimulated the reform process. In Poland in the 1980s this did not occur, more for political reasons than for purely economic ones. Indeed, especially after the declaration of martial law at the end of 1981, the opposition followed quite a destructive political approach, which may be called 'the worse, the better' and which supposed that economic and social hardship would generate an opportunity to restructure the political system along the lines desired by the opposition, both domestic and foreign. Thus, according to this rather bizarre view of the political struggle, the situation seemed 'promising' when, after some

---

[4] It turned out that a large share of the blocked structural reforms was reintroduced by these same groups as soon as they had the political wherewithal. Unfortunately, their earlier opposition to price adjustments in the late 1980s meant that prices jumped in the second half of 1989 by about 2,000% (on an annual basis). In 1990 the consumer price index (at year-end) was around 250%.

improvement in 1983–5, the economy started to decline again. There were attempts to introduce democratic institutions and practices, but the lack of wide-ranging political change weakened the government's ability to undertake economic reform. The effort to turn the economy around by exclusively economic means had reached a limit, proving that economic reform had to be accompanied by political reform.[5]

Before the transition the understanding of these linkages was quite modest, as was the familiarity with the quirks of a market economy. Though more and more was being learned about reforming a socialist economy, the target system was never very clear, and something odd and unexpected always seemed to occur to influence and complicate the course of change. Most often this had a rather negative effect, making the reform process even more challenging. During the most difficult times the number of theoretical and pragmatic policy questions seemed to grow exponentially, while the ability of economists and politicians to answer them improved only at the pace of an arithmetic series. Thus, the gap between the questions and the answers widened. Moreover, aside from the lack of knowledge about the way to improve the system and raise efficiency, there was never a mature intellectual and political consensus—be it in Moscow or Prague, Warsaw or Belgrade, Budapest or East Berlin—on the policy programme to be adopted in order to move forward.

In any case, none of the former socialist countries, not even the Soviet Union with all its vast natural wealth, had sufficient financial and material resources for successful, profound reform. The capital needs of these countries were huge. How huge became obvious only later during the post-socialist transition, when these nations were entirely exposed in their dealings with the international community.

Thus, even if Hungary and Poland were committed to sound reform, they were in no position to achieve it easily. The situation was rendered more difficult by the burden of foreign debt, which in Poland was extreme (Table 1). The debt in Poland was the result of the attempts to open up

---

[5] Of course, the true reformers in the political opposition were aiming for a sound overhaul and improvements in the performance of the system, though they doubted that the situation could become better before a high price had been paid. For this reason, for some time already, but especially when the economic reforms introduced under the umbrella of martial law had started to lose momentum in the mid-1980s, a segment of the political opposition, including several influential economists, ceased to support the reform-oriented policies of party leaders, the government, and the central bank. They realized that these policies tended in the proper direction, but they did not wish to be associated in the exercise. This made the implementation of the necessary reforms still more difficult. Simultaneously, nonetheless, an intellectual and political debate about the future course of reform was going on within opposition circles. Because of this debate, as well as the discussion on economic matters that was taking place among government reformers, an understanding of the future course of reform was emerging. Indeed, the intellectual and technical debate, if not the political one, between the leading economists within both groups was always lively and constructive. Later this bore fruit in the newfound health of the Polish economy.

Table 1 Poland's gross foreign debt in convertible currencies, 1971–1988

Year	Foreign debt[a]	Year	Foreign debt[a]	Year	Foreign debt[a]
1971	1.3	1977	15.4	1983	26.4
1972	1.7	1978	18.5	1984	26.8
1973	3.1	1979	21.9	1985	29.3
1974	5.3	1980	25.0	1986	33.5
1975	8.4	1981	25.5	1987	39.2
1976	12.1	1982	25.2	1988	40.1

[a] In billions of dollars, end-year.
Source: GUS 1988a.

the economy to closer ties with the West in the course of the 1970s and 80s. By the end of the 80s it was seriously limiting the room for man-oeuvre required for the successful implementation of reform. The most favourable opportunities seemed to come only during periods when the economy was in relatively good condition and able to furnish enough resources to cover the costs of adjustment (say, in Poland in the first half of the 1970s). At such times, the desire to reform seemed to evaporate. If the economy was working, why fix it? The endeavour to overhaul the economy therefore failed precisely because of the waning support for a con-tinuation of the difficult reform process at moments when improvements were occurring due principally to inflows of foreign loans.

Gradually, in the course of the intensive reforms implemented in numerous countries in the 1960s and 70s, the awareness grew that bureau-cratic planning and centralized management were losing their effectiveness. The system of 'real socialism' was unable to guarantee the efficient alloca-tion of labour, capital, and material resources.[6] This inability was creating even more economic, commercial, financial, and technological difficulties and leading to worsening overall performance. Moreover, the economic malaise was causing social and political tensions which were adding to the pressure for market reform, particularly because of the remarkable progress being accomplished at that time, mainly after the energy crisis of 1972–4, in the developed capitalist economies and in the East Asian high-performing economies. Hence the countries which were already on the road to reform, especially Hungary and Poland, took fresh steps to introduce comprehensive market arrangements, though still within the socialist institutional framework. The idea was to change economic and financial mechanisms extensively, but to alter state ownership and property rights only slightly.

[6] Often referred to as 'directively distributory management' in order to emphasize the role of the central rationing of the scarce means of production.

1.3. 'SOCIALIST FRIEDMANISM' OR 'GALBRAITH'S SOCIALISM'?

The best example of the approach was the Polish reform of the 1980s that was based on the introduction of market mechanisms on a far broader scale than ever before. Sometimes these mechanisms were important, other times less so, but the aim was to use them for the purpose of realizing the central plan. Thus, they were kept under the control of the government authorities, but, depending on the strength of the trend toward decentralization, they were employed more or less freely. Later, the role of money, prices, credit, interest rates, exchange rates, and so on was gradually, though significantly, enhanced. The same could be said about some market organizations and the related institutional links, such as banks, commodity exchanges, chambers of commerce, and antitrust bodies.

The conviction that these market instruments and institutions were necessary was derived from several premises. First, *the market was assumed to foster financial discipline by curbing any excessive expansion drives.* Typical of bureaucratized central management, such drives had previously led to overinvestment, with all the adverse consequences for performance, especially widening imbalances and lower productivity. The earlier passive role of money meant that it had only secondary importance, complementary to physical manufacturing processes. In contrast to the usual situation in a free market economy, the biggest units in any factory were usually the planning and procurement divisions, whereas the smallest were always the marketing departments. There was no problem in selling products; the problem arose in purchasing them. So, the economic reforms were designed to inverse these relationships, that is, to subordinate the material processes to the financial ones. This was supposed to favour a balance between input and output and, through increasing competitiveness and enforced equilibrium, contribute to higher efficiency.

Second, *the market instruments and dear money policy were intended to create systemic conditions allowing for the imposition of demand constraints vis-à-vis both companies and households.* Previously, only households had known the true meaning of 'hard' budget constraints.[7] All efforts to apply such constraints to state firms had failed, precisely because of the overly passive position of money and the market. The inability to impose these constraints was the biggest failure of the socialist economic system, including the reformed one. Now, the idea was to create market competition by offering economic entities a free choice in the activities they undertook. For

---

[7] Budget constraints are 'hard' if the only source of expenditure is earned income (including commercial credit which must be financed and paid back from future income), while the only source of income is revenues from the sale of products and services on the market. If subsidies or any other transfers from the state budget are provided, then the budget constraints are 'soft'.

the sake of stabilization this had to be based on hard budget constraints, without any guarantee that state subsidies would become available in the case of loses.

Third, it was believed that *a regulated market could become an efficient allocative mechanism through which the output structure (in the short term) and the investment structure (in the long term) could adapt themselves to market demand and social needs.* The architects of the reforms came to the conclusion that, except for certain strategic infrastructure projects to be determined by the government, central planning was no longer able to determine the volume and structure of output and to balance the flows of aggregated supply and demand. This was so despite major advances in planning methods and computing techniques. The shortcomings of central planning were especially visible in regard to the consumer goods and services provided by the public sector, including consumption in kind. Deterioration in these areas was having a severely negative influence on the social climate and tended to erode any political support there might be for reform.

The identification of the role of the market and the way to implement the market turned out to be the fundamental problem in the theory and the practice of systemic reform under socialism. It was no coincidence that the evolution in the discussions on these subjects was similar in many countries which experimented with reforms and sooner or later tried to introduce them (Brus and Laski 1989). One must remember that *socialism was originally conceived as the antithesis, the negation of capitalism based on free market forces.* Whereas under capitalism the driving force of expansion is the effort to maximize profits, under socialism it was supposed to be the 'satisfaction of social needs'. Whereas in the market economy tough competition is seen as a means of improving quality, under the planned economy so-called 'socialist cooperation' was supposed to achieve this. Whereas price-setting under the free market is left to the market clearing mechanism, under the centrally planned economy prices were assumed to be more efficiently fixed by government. Whereas in the capitalist system the allocation of the means of production is conducted through the spontaneous interactions of supply and demand, in the socialist system it was managed through the bureaucracy. Last but not least, whereas the market economy is founded on private property, the planned economy was based on state and cooperative ownership.

However, the reforms were not aimed at overturning the socialist economic system, but only at adapting it to the new circumstances. They were an effort to 'escape forward', an attempt to make a leap in development toward the institutional arrangements in a modern market resulting from the ongoing evolution of the capitalist system. Thus, the market-oriented reforms under socialism were a sort of 'negation of the negation'.

In the beginning, socialism in these countries had stood for a total rejection of capitalism, and almost everything involved in economic management and performance had been set on its head or, at least, profoundly altered. Later, all these revolutionary institutional arrangements were challenged by the mere fact of the gradual reintroduction of some market elements. Yet, many of these fresh elements were not the same ones that had been rejected earlier, because in the meantime capitalism itself had changed tremendously, not least because of the strong demonstration effect of socialism (Cassidy 1997).

Thus, the attempts at reform, including Yugoslavia's self-management system, Hungary's goulash socialism, the Polish market socialism of the 1980s, the Vietnamese doi moi, and Gorbachev's perestroika, were undertaken only for the sake of grafting limited features of the market onto the socialist system. At the time the intention was definitely not to replace this system by a market economy, not even in the very long term. Whatever was changed was changed only so as to perfect the old system, not to create an alternative one.

So, in Eastern Europe and the former Soviet Union (and it seems also today in China and Vietnam) two obvious questions were finally being confronted: first, what are the limits of market mechanisms in the context of a reformed socialist economy?, and, second, where is the border between 'reformed socialism' and the abandonment of the socialist system altogether?

There were conflicting views on these matters. Janos Kornai (1986) referred to a thoroughgoing introduction of market instruments as 'socialist Friedmanism'. (This would presumably have been the case in Hungary and Poland if the radical reform plans had been fully realized, which they were not.) For a system based on moderate changes and an active role for the state in economic matters, especially in resource allocation, Kornai used the term 'Galbraith's socialism'. Kornai's observations drew mainly on the Hungarian experience at the time. They were not relevant for other socialist countries.

The exception was Poland, where already in the second half of the 1980s more radical ideas about the way the system must be reformed were gaining ground even more quickly than they were in Hungary. The Polish debate during this period revealed an interesting shift in opinion. This is all the more important because, with a natural time-lag, the evolution of theoretical concepts was followed by significant alterations in the outlook of politicians and, eventually, an adjustment in the policy toward systemic and institutional change.

Previously, the reforms in Poland were expected to consist mostly of a narrow application of certain market mechanisms. Then it was decided that the scope of the market must be expanded. An auxiliary and corrective role for the market came to be discussed in the same breath with the dominant role of central strategic planning. Subsequently, there was yet another enhancement of the role of the market. This was evident in the ever widening field of play for market instruments, which were applied at first only in the consumer sector, but then also in the production sector, this being reflected, inter alia, in the relaxation of price controls. In the next stage there was more talk about the creation of money markets and capital markets and about the necessity of launching a true labour market. The suggestion could also be heard that the market mechanisms must be made stronger and more far-reaching, albeit still within the inviolable limits of socialism.

Hence the institutional arrangements of the market were no longer talked about only as corrective tools, but also as an 'equal partner' of the central plan. Economic processes were no longer to be guided exclusively by the visible hand of the central planner, but also—and step-by-step to a greater degree—by the invisible hand of the market. In Poland by the end of the 1980s one could anticipate that in the next stage of discussions the emphasis would finally be put on the market model first and, only afterwards, on the central planning model. In reality, for several years already the central plan had become a secondary matter, and an ever greater portion of the economy was in effect subject to market forces. The introduction of a full-fledged market economy had already been decided upon in the 1980s. The only and, indeed, the very crucial issue that had been left open was when and how to accomplish this.

The moment was approaching when the reformed socialist economies would have to come to grips with a complete reversal of their fundamental ideological and political options. Previously, at most the market had seemed to be required only to correct the shortcomings and inconsistencies of central planning. Now, under the new approach—on the heels of both the successes and the failures of the reforms—central planning was to be employed only to correct the negative effects of the powerful market machine. The driving force of economic growth was being shifted from the plan, which was moribund, to the market, which was emerging. Socialism was ceasing to be the antithesis of capitalism and had started to evolve toward the incorporation of the institutional arrangements and behaviours of the market economy.

1.4. THE LAST EXPERIMENT: THE POLISH
REFORMS OF THE 1980s

In Poland in the late 1980s the organizational framework and institutional arrangements were following a development path from 'planned market-type socialism' to a 'market-type planned economy', that is, regulation through the market was gradually taking over from centrally planned allocation. At the beginning of 1989 the still mighty Planning Commission was abandoned and replaced by the Central Planning Agency, which was more compatible with market regulatory needs. The nature of the new agency

was influenced by French and Japanese experiments with indicative planning rather than by early Soviet-style directive planning.[8] The logic of this
evolutionary process appeared to be quite clear. The new challenges required
new instruments and new institutions.[9]

Nonetheless, the system established in the 1980s was a hybrid combining the relics of old arrangements with elements of the new. In a non-
performing way, it still mixed centralized bureaucratic rationing with
market allocation methods. Even solutions typical of wartime economies,
such as coupons for certain kinds of meat, existed side-by-side with free
market mechanisms, such as foreign exchange auctions. Both heterogeneity
and incoherence in the instruments introduced by the reforms were characteristic of the system. This had an adverse impact on economic processes
and led to many poorly conceived policy initiatives, especially in regard to
financial stabilization.

The gradual shift away from central planning made room for prepara-
tions for the birth of a capital market, a true labour market, and the commercialization of the banking system. When the conviction that the capital
market was indispensable had matured, a banking reform was implemented.
This reform would not have made much sense earlier in the traditional
statist set-up since it could not then have provided any benefits. But in
1987–9, after liberalization had somehow advanced, a network of commercial
banks was established.[10] In turn, the commercialization of the banking
system served as a systemic tool to promote further marketization, especially market-based capital allocation and the balancing of aggregate supply
and demand. It also aimed at the enhancement of efficiency in production and investment through the imposition of hard budget constraints on
state and cooperative enterprises. However, the creation of the two-tier
(commercial and central) banking system also had a deeper significance.
It was the institutional confirmation of the increasing role of money and
the market in the socialist economy, which was already being led more by
market forces than by the central plan. Within this banking system it was
possible for money to play an active part and influence production and
distribution.

After these reforms it was also necessary to exercise responsible monetary policy, which previously had been subordinated to the planning in
physical units. The evolution in microeconomic management was evident

---

[8] This 'quasi-ministry' was dismantled only in 1996, when it was replaced by the
National Strategic Studies Centre, which is not a bureaucratic entity, but rather a 'think tank'
with no administrative prerogatives.

[9] Similar observations can be made about Hungary, Yugoslavia, and, to some extent, China
at the time. On the economic reforms in the 1980s in China, see, for example, Ellman 1986,
Feuchtwang and Hussain 1983, Fan 1997, Harding and Hewett 1988, Kosta 1987, Perkins
1988, Quassier 1987, Zhang 1989.

[10] On the structural reforms and institutional arrangements in Poland in the 1980s, see
Kolodko 1989a.

in the move from separate financial planning and input-output planning in physical units to an integrated system of 'material and financial planning' that was created in 1989. Integrated material and financial planning aimed at accelerating the shift from directive-type planning to the model of market-related planning. This radical (for that time) systemic change, as well as the policies in the programme for the second stage of economic reform (Wydawnictwo 'Rzeczpospolita' 1988), was the natural outcome of the general overhaul of the economic system.

The nationwide referendum which preceded the adoption of the programme for the second stage of reform demonstrated another fundamental feature of the changes in Poland: the gradual democratization of the political process. Official party documents, research papers, and press statements had already begun to reflect the fact that the 'democratization' of the economy through the introduction of market forces was not possible without democratization in a broader political sense. This conviction was emerging not simply because democracy was coming to be considered a value in itself. It was also well understood that in an environment of political democratization the market would not be so susceptible to the pressures of various interest groups, which could therefore be more readily resisted.

There was another reason as well. Serious inconsistencies had emerged between the determination to enforce market rules and liberalize economic policies on the one hand and the commitment to move forward with political liberalization on the other. *The reform measures lacked comprehensiveness.* The reformers hesitated to abandon central planning completely. Each of these factors weakened the reform process. The old system did not work well anymore, but the new one could not yet eliminate the growing economic inefficiencies and relieve the social hardships. It was clear that more was needed from reform.

Unfortunately, people were becoming dissatisfied and impatient with reform. It was becoming obvious that the reform process could not continue without somehow garnering more social support.

Poland had experienced recession only once under the socialist order. In 1979–82 output contracted significantly, and reforms were undertaken as production bottomed out in 1982. The standard of living was actually improving thereafter. Thus, the causes of the growing discontent must be sought elsewhere.

In fact, two psychological factors had come into play. First, there is always a substantial difference between social aspirations and the degree to which they can be satisfied. Consumers tend to believe that the economy is going badly whenever the gap between their expectations and actual consumption is widening, even if the absolute level of consumption is increasing. Such a situation has elsewhere been referred to as the 'paradox of a low degree of satisfaction at a high level of consumption' (Kolodko 1987). It arose in Poland between 1983 and 1989. This was evident in the way

Table 2 Economic growth in Poland, 1983–1998 (%)

	1983	1984	1985	1986	1987	1988
Net national income	6.0	5.6	3.4	4.9	1.7	3.8
National income distributed	5.6	5.0	3.8	5.0	1.6	3.3
Investment	9.5	12.3	4.9	5.9	5.1	4.1
Consumption	5.8	4.4	2.9	4.8	2.9	2.9
Industrial output	6.0	5.6	4.1	4.4	3.5	4.0
Exports	10.3	9.5	1.3	4.9	4.8	5.5
Imports	5.5	8.6	7.9	4.9	4.5	4.0

Source: GUS 1988b.

people were claiming that economically they were worse and worse off, although political leaders could point to improvements in the standard of living, and real income and household consumption were both expanding in absolute terms (Table 2).

The declining support for market reforms was closely related to the existence of inflationary pressure, of which Poland was the most spectacular case (Kolodko 1989b). In some other countries, especially Czechoslovakia and the GDR, there was no inflation, and there were no general shortages (as opposed to sectoral ones). In Hungary and Yugoslavia there was open inflation, but the shortages were at most only very limited. In contrast, in Poland inflation existed in both forms characteristic of a destabilized reformed planned economy: as open (price) inflation and as repressed inflation.[11]

Facing high inflation, a population tends to evaluate the economic situation in the light of the real purchasing power of disposable income rather than through the prism of indicators illustrating the rate of real economic growth. Inflation invariably leads to currency depreciation and, in a country with a weak and inconvertible currency, like Poland in the 1980s, also to far-reaching devaluation (Table 3). Given the intensive inflationary processes, it is little wonder that the population was sceptical of or even against the economic reforms. There was a direct link between the reforms and parallel stabilization measures. Because of the inflationary implications, the measures were not accepted at all; the attitude of the public was hostile.

Inflation became one of the most difficult barriers to the introduction of new arrangements. Initially, open inflation—unavoidable during price

---

[11] 'Repressed inflation' is reflected in the existence of persistent shortages, rationing schemes, forced substitution, and unofficial parallel markets. 'Open inflation' is typified by price rises. Repressed inflation results in involuntary saving by households due to the shortages of consumer goods, rather than the growth in price levels (Portes 1981, Kolodko 1986b, Nuti 1989).

Table 3 The inflation, depreciation, and devaluation of the Polish zloty, 1981–1998 (%)

	1981	1982	1983	1984	1985	1986	1987	1988
Inflation[a]	24.4	101.5	23.0	15.0	15.1	17.7	25.7	60.0
Depreciation[b]	17.5	51.1	17.6	12.9	13.1	15.0	20.5	37.5
Nominal devaluation[c]	23.7	55.0	13.8	28.3	17.2	33.6	59.7	61.6

[a] Consumer price index (CPI). [b] Drop in purchasing power. [c] Fall of the zloty relative to the dollar.

Sources: National statistics and author's calculations.

liberalization in a context of severe shortages—was a major condition for the implementation of reform. The trick was to balance aggregate supply and demand by enforcing market clearing prices. It was vitally important for efficiency that the shortages and the price distortions be quickly eliminated. However, the inflation was caused by deep structural and systemic factors. Some of the recently introduced elements of the new financial mechanisms also appeared to be inflationary. A substantial complex of new systemic arrangements was envisaged to achieve a balanced economy with market clearing prices, since only in such an environment can market mechanisms perform well. Within the context of a shortage economy, a two-digit inflation rate (the rate in Poland in 1981–8 was 35 per cent on average) can kill any economic and financial incentives, and one cannot expect reform to succeed under such circumstances.[12] Moreover, the rate of inflation was not only high, it was accelerating.

So, the persistent and occasionally even growing imbalances were creating fundamental obstacles to the broader application of the so-called 'three-S formula' associated with reform. The triple 'S' stood for 'self-management', 'self-dependence', and the 'self-financing' of state companies. Despite a commitment to enforce these principles, the weight of structural distortions generated constant pressure for the transfer of resources from efficient enterprises to less profitable ones. To compensate for the unprofitable production there were many grants and subsidies, as well as a strong dose of fiscalism, which was expressed in the relatively heavy taxation of enterprises.[13] Despite reform, there was still a fair proportion of unprofitable

[12] In certain situations, when the market clearing mechanism is functioning, inflation may be compatible with growth. Turkey in the 1980s and some transition economies offer examples. The critical point at which the relationship between growth and inflation definitely becomes negative is relatively high. Even the International Monetary Fund (IMF) and the World Bank have learned to live with two-digit inflation as long as it is less than 20% or 25% and is falling, and as long as the rising prices are clearing the market (World Bank 1996).

[13] This taxation was driven even higher because direct taxes on households played only a marginal role at the time.

products, and this imposed a significant burden on the state budget. For many years the budget was running a deficit, though a limited one, due to the fact that tax collection was insufficient to offset growing state expenditures. The budget deficit, a major contributor to the demand-induced inflation, was from 3 to 5 per cent of overall expenditures, or less than 1 per cent of GDP (Kolodko 1992a).

However, given that there were no government bonds and that the public debt was not managed on the open market, the breach was filled by the monetary expansion of the central bank, with all the inflationary implications this entailed. The policy was unable to solve the difficulties in financing government outlays in the long run. As a result, aggregate demand, which was always outstripping supply, created even more severe inflationary pressures. Together with the effort to liberalize prices, this led to higher price inflation.

For these reasons, despite the fairly solid rate of growth and despite rising household consumption, the public started to turn against the reform programme.[14]

The stabilization policy exercised during the reforms involved sharp contradictions. It was necessary to liberalize the rules for price-setting, but this accelerated the rate of price and wage inflation. After three years of falling inflation (from 101.5 per cent in 1982 to 15 per cent in 1985), the consumer price index rose back up to 60 per cent in 1988 and then to about 160 per cent in the first semester of 1989. In 1988 there was a serious attempt to liberalize prices, but the government did not have the political leverage to succeed with this step.

Price policy is a very sensitive issue under any circumstances, but particularly so when open inflation is accompanied by repressed inflation. This was precisely the case in Poland in the 1980s: everything was getting increasingly expensive, and there was not much that could be bought without queuing or without special rationing coupons. The parallel existence of open inflation and repressed inflation is known as 'shortageflation' (Kolodko and McMahon 1987). *Shortageflation deeply eroded the efficiency of the centrally planned economy and was behind its inability to compete on world markets.*

Against such a backdrop, the endeavour to adjust relative prices to the structure of costs and market demand failed to yield the desired effects. The price structure considerably differed from the structure of production costs, and thus it could not properly inform producers and consumers about the actual scarcity of particular goods and services. This also prevented a share of input from being allocated according to efficiency requirements because, given the lack of a market-clearing mechanism, input had to

---

[14] The gross national product had grown by 3.8% per year on average between 1983 and 1989.

be distributed through administrative methods. A specific feature of the socialist economies was the relatively low prices for subsistence goods and services, such as food, some types of clothing, housing rents, public transportation, and medical services. Efforts to raise these prices in order to cut the subsidies were strongly opposed, including through strikes, and were accompanied anyway by almost automatic compensations for the increase in the cost of living.

This was the case, for example, when the inflation spiral started up again in 1988. During the first half of the year the consumer price index stood at around 49 per cent, and average nominal wages were indexed at about 53 per cent owing to strong political tensions and inconsistent regulation. At the same time, there was an increase in pensions and other social transfers provided by the state budget. Since the growth of these was not matched on the revenue side, this generated additional inflationary pressure. The changes accomplished vis-à-vis relative prices were modest, but income redistribution was substantial, and, contrary to the policy intention, inflation was accelerated. Still worse, shortages became more serious than they had been before the whole endeavour. In the late 1980s it became clear that the easiest way to overthrow the socialist regime was to play the inflation game. So, it was played. The government's ongoing attempts to reform the system were doomed to failure because the system had already started to fall apart.

It must be emphasized that, in a context of imbalances, price increases are not automatically or entirely equivalent with lowering the consumption level. While the average real wage dropped in Poland in 1987 by 3.7 per cent, consumption (at fixed prices) went up by 2 per cent. This was an effect of the restraints on the excessive liquidity of households or an effect of the removal of shortages. Therefore, in certain circumstances, while official statistical data may suggest that real income (in money terms) is falling, consumption may not actually be decreasing; indeed, it may even be rising. It is also possible that statistics show growth in real incomes, but that de facto consumption is not expanding due to shortages in consumer markets.

The public was tired of the persistent structural crisis and of the way the reforms were being implemented. This was a vicious circle. In reform-oriented economies like Hungary, Poland, and Yugoslavia, the public identified reform with its most painful symptoms, mainly with constant price rises. For this reason, many households preferred the rationing of meat, for example, rather than more realistic pricing. In political language, this meant that the public did not accept the reforms nor the policies by which the government was trying to implement them. As long as politically sensitive groups were unwilling to accept such redistributions, they remained a barrier to the implementation of the necessary changes. Neither rational arguments, nor theoretical accuracy make it possible to introduce a desired system or an adjustment programme. Only the actual balance of political forces interested (or not interested) in pushing through a particular reform can accomplish this (or render it impractical). In Poland the balance started to become favourable only at the end of the 1980s.

Meanwhile, it was already obvious after the crisis of 1979–82 that Poland would not be able to pay off all the debt the country owed to foreign governments and commercial banks. This was even more apparent at the end of the 1980s. It was also increasingly clear that there was not going to be any important foreign debt reduction, restructuring, or rescheduling without an overhaul of the economic and political system. From this per- spective, *the unmanageable load of outstanding foreign debt was another key reason for the breakdown of market reform in Poland.* This was also the case in Hungary to a certain extent.[15]

The outstanding debt was used as a lever of political persuasion to inch both Hungary and Poland toward the full-fledged market and, later, toward Western-style capitalism. Paradoxically, the two most reformed social- ist economies were the ones most affected by the dependency stemming from their financial obligations to the world economy, especially to inter- national creditors. The debt hampered the success of reform primarily because it prevented the more timely establishment of convertibility and trade liberalization. It also caused additional budgetary burdens and inflationary pressures.

In the case of Poland, unlike the experience in Hungary, the major share of the foreign debt was owed to Western governments, hence their eager- ness and their ability to influence institutional change behind the 'Iron Curtain'. Actually, at the time, the Iron Curtain was as much a fiction as central planning, at least with respect to these two most-reformed nations. Nonetheless, the insistence on far-reaching liberalization so as to be able to meet financial obligations was tremendous. This is why Poland attached so much importance to collaboration with the World Bank and the International Monetary Fund in the mid-1980s, rejoining these Bretton Woods institutions in 1986.[16] Membership had been linked to the implementation of economic stabilization and structural adjustment pro- grammes, reflecting a real desire on the part of the political leadership to execute proper institutional reform. These international organizations could provide assistance in the preparation of the required adjustment

---

[15] Owing to the faltering transition process in Russia over the course of the 1990s, this has also been the situation in that country. By the end of the decade, Russia had become virtually insolvent, and its foreign debt must be restructured. Part of the debt must be writ- ten off; otherwise, the debt can no longer be serviced. A special programme of 'debt for reform' and 'debt for equity' must therefore be worked out for the sake of surmounting the immense crisis in Russia's economic and political system.

[16] Poland had belonged to the Bretton Woods institutions in the late 1940s, but it with- drew soon after the introduction of the centrally planned regime.

measures and supply some financial relief and aid. By the late 1980s it was very well known that, unless such assistance could be secured, even the most ambitious and relevant reform scenarios would underperform. Of course, such assistance was not provided to Poland (nor to Hungary) because it was clear that the most painless (for the West) way to overthrow the socialist regime was to play the foreign debt game. So, it was played.

Thus, the lack of a comprehensive approach toward economic and social challenges, the neglect of political measures supporting the economic overhaul, growing inflationary pressures, the expanding gap between expectations and actual development, and the unbearable burden of foreign debt were the main factors explaining the failure of the early market reforms in Poland.

By the late 1980s the Polish economy and other socialist economies were suffering from a serious case of 'growth fatigue' (Poznanski 1996). *People in these societies were disappointed as producers* because of the mounting conviction that part of their effort was being wasted owing to policy mismanagement, which was leading to stagnating output and a lack of competitiveness. *They were irritated as consumers* because of the inefficiencies of the distribution system and the time they had to spend queuing. *They were dissatisfied as citizens* because of their inability to affect the course of the economic, social, and political changes in a way that would better serve their own interests. The combination of these three motives was strong enough to spark another push away from the centrally planned economy toward the market system.

However, not surprisingly, in Poland the public and the political leadership were tired of repeated and fruitless attempts at reform and were ready to give it up. This was the real turning point and the true beginning of the end of the socialist system throughout the region. Instead of yet another stab at reforming the socialist planned economy, the time had come to transform it completely and adopt another system.

The transition to a 'social market economy' was launched at the end of the 1980s and the beginning of the 90s. There would not have been such an historic shift if not for the early market reforms, with all their merits and drawbacks. The experience gained through these reforms made it easier now to undertake fundamental change. At least a few lessons had already been learned well.

It is no longer very relevant whether the early reforms might have succeeded somehow. If it had been possible, it should have happened, but this was not to be the case (Nuti 1992a). Consequently, Poland was the first country among the socialist centrally planned economies to take the step in a definite and irreversible manner away from the reform of the old system and toward the complex process of building an entirely new system.

1.5. THE POLITICS OF 'THE WORSE, THE BETTER'

In economic reform, policy questions about direction and pace, as well as about the costs and the results of reform, are always supposed to be at the top of the agenda. In stable, traditionally democratic systems it is usual to think that worsening performance is a matter of serious intellectual and political concern, and policies which generate such problems face appropriate criticism and are quickly corrected. Nobody would propose to change the entire system, since there is a strong and proper conviction that policy modifications will do the job.

Yet, this was not the case in European socialist states because, unlike the situation in modern capitalist nations, the issue of doing away with the system was already very much on the agenda. Any sign of crisis was welcomed by dissidents within the states and by their foreign supporters. Indeed, crisis was better than prosperity, and difficulties were more appreciated than the ability to tackle them.

Recently, despite high rates of growth, there have been signs of structural crisis in the Chinese and Vietnamese economies. The perception that there could be crisis is often swiftly followed by the hope that unfavourable circumstances might trigger comprehensive changes which might not otherwise be possible. 'A crisis is an opportunity for the reforms. It'll make people see the current situation [as] untenable' (Grant 1997). Hence, as in the case of European socialism, the idea is that, before things can get better, they will probably have to get worse. One person's pain is someone else's gain.

This was a familiar refrain in at least a few of the Eastern European countries in the 1980s, when economic deterioration was being considered by some economists and political antagonists as a favourable turn of events since it could facilitate reform and ultimately lead to the end of the socialist order. However weird it may sound today, the truth is that the idea of 'the worse, the better' was widely exploited, especially in Poland by the opposition led by Solidarity and its trade unions. At the time, vast strikes, constant pressure for inflationary wage indexing, demands for heavy subsidies for state companies, and even encouragement for foreign financial sanctions were used to make the economic situation worse (that is, 'better').

It was rightly assumed that the shift from the socialist economy could not occur without the strong commitment of the people for such a move. Consequently, the logic behind this otherwise bizarre approach was that any improvement in the social or political climate might hamper the chance for more reform: it is better if the people firmly desire change, and the more unbearable the situation is, the more the people will firmly desire change. Thus, living standards and working conditions should first become worse, so that they will become more unacceptable. All this, of course, in favour of a 'better' future. By the same token, it would be 'worse' if conditions improve under the aegis of the old regime. In other words, 'better' or 'worse' economic performance was no longer merely an economic reality; it had become a political concept. A stronger economy could mean a weaker political position, and falling output might mean rising political prospects. Certainly, this attitude contributed to the crisis which led to the collapse of 'real socialism' and to the severe economic contraction, the 'great slump', during the early stages of transition.

The true impetus behind the reforms undertaken by the various socialist governments was the wish to boost efficiency and raise the standard of living. Yet, from the political perspective, there should be no doubt that the reforms also served as a means of protecting and upholding the socialist system. So, the political opposition hoped to use reform failure for the opposite aim, that is, to overthrow the order it did not like. What was supposed by some to be a remedy, was seen by others as a poison. The authorities saw economic matters partly as an instrument to prolong the existence of 'real socialism', while the opposition saw the economy as an instrument to bring 'real socialism' down.

The easier it was to bring 'real socialism' down (in other words the worse the economic situation), the more readily the situation could get out of hand for government policymakers. Awareness of this danger led to different reactions. While some countries, like Hungary, Poland, and the Soviet Union under Gorbachev, tried to move decisively forward with economic reform, seeing it as an antidote for social unrest, other countries, like Albania, Czechoslovakia, and Romania, pulled back from the attempt at any liberal reform, preferring instead to strengthen the hold of the authorities on political life and counteract any tendency toward political liberalization.

The lessons of this tug-of-war appear to have been learned by the leaders of China and Vietnam. They have decided to assign a clear priority to sound reform of the economic system and maintain for the time being a rather orthodox vision toward political change. Yet, an approach like this can work only for a certain amount of time. Paradoxically, the more the economy becomes developed, the more society becomes educated. The more countries are open to vigorous contacts with the outside word, the more difficult it is to reduce the temptation of the political opposition to take advantage of a tactic of 'the worse, the better'.

A similar situation exists in Cuba. Undoubtedly, the economic hardships which Cuba has been experiencing since the collapse of the Soviet bloc are being augmented by the political opposition. Domestic opponents, but especially Cuban exile groups, definitely see this as a good time to redouble efforts to render the economic hardships even worse, so that—they believe —a general economic and political transformation becomes even more likely: once more, 'the worse, the better'.

The ideological and political arguments favouring the economic sanctions imposed occasionally on socialist countries (and others) by the US-led

coalition of rich nations and the international organizations which are sometimes dependent on their will have evolved precisely from these same roots.
Unfortunately, sanctions—whether the political regimes are harmed or
remain indifferent, as was the case for so long in Cuba and North Korea—
always increase the misery among ordinary people, be they Soviet citizens
in the past or Indians and Pakistanis more recently.

Poland was subjected to sanctions in the 1980s, and they did add
significantly to the worsening economic performance at that time and, consequently, in keeping with 'the worse, the better', to the improvement in
the political climate required for a final breakthrough.[17] Vietnam experienced this type of pressure, especially through the American restrictions
which were lifted only a short time ago. Even during the postsocialist era
tough sanctions have been used, for different political motives, against
Belarus, Croatia, and the new Yugoslavia. As recently as 1997–8 there
was support, particularly in the US, for economic sanctions against China,
even on the eve of Sino-American summits. Nonetheless, the pragmatic
alternative has not always been rejected, and the conviction that 'worse'
does not always mean 'better' has sometimes won the day. Geopolitical
considerations sometimes signify that there is much more to lose than there
is to gain from efforts to achieve 'improvement through deterioration'.

1.6. FROM MARKET SOCIALISM TO CAPITALIST RESTORATION

At the end of the 1980s and the beginning of the 90s the socialist countries became determined to get rid of the old system, which was no longer
adaptable to the challenges of the world economy. At the same time, they
chose to install a market economy. (They assumed, of course, that it would
be a richer economy and that it would become a reality rather sooner than
later.) The transition from socialism was inevitable the instant the political situation permitted it to be a possibility. This was so because under
the old system there had been no room to accommodate new circumstances
and exercise adequate policies. Now, adequate policies and medium- and
long-term growth strategies meant that a fresh set of measures had to be
adopted. However, the socialist system was not up to the task.

There were few doubts that the new system would involve a market
economy of some sort, but there was much hesitation concerning how to
start off on this journey and what sort of market economy should be the

---

[17] On the other hand, having chosen the path of transition, Poland has benefited greatly
from foreign assistance, particularly the forgiveness of foreign debt; altogether about half of
the outstanding debt has been written off. It is difficult to evaluate precisely how the scale
tips in terms of the cumulative economic effect of the sanctions and the aid. Overall it seems
that the negative impact of the sanctions in terms of stagnation and recession has been greater
than the positive impact of the assistance in terms of recovery and growth.

goal. If it was clear to both political leaders and society as a whole that the time had come to abandon the old system, at the outset of the transition it was not so clear that the future lay in the restoration of capitalism. Despite claims to the contrary, in late 1989 in the Czech Republic, Hungary, and Poland, as well as in 1990–2 in several other countries, including the former Soviet republics, the conviction became dominant that it was time to search for a sort of 'socialist market' economy. In some cases (and not only for tactical reasons, despite the assertions heard ex post) the aim of the changes was even openly declared to be a 'social market' economy. This was the case of the programme of the first postsocialist government in Poland in September 1989. At the time the government meant what it said, and only later was there a more widely accepted opinion that the liberal free market economy—no matter what the social features might be—had to be a capitalist economy.

Four circumstances turned out to be crucial. First, *almost from the beginning of the transition, politicians and leading economists firmly believed that the introduction of a market economy requires not only a market for products, but also sound labour and capital markets.* These last were to be established through an emerging private sector, with a fundamental role for private ownership. The initial process of the expansion of private capital, somehow limited at first by the legacy of the old ideological constraints, eventually gained momentum and led to a mushrooming core of capitalism even in countries which had chosen a more gradual path toward privatization. Thus, capital markets evolved at the start more by chance than by design and in a chaotic rather than an organized way.

In Poland influential politicians thought that a utopian 'people's capitalism' could be established through the free distribution of state assets. This was the case of Solidarity and Lech Walesa, its leader and later the president of the country. Workers, politicians, and others who were the early benefactors of denationalization were soon staunch advocates of privatization and were demanding the enhancement of market institutions. Especially among workers there were many people who sometimes seemed almost ready to take up arms for privatization and therefore against socialism.

Only when it was already too late to turn back the wheel of history did they realize that what they had actually supported and toiled for was a 'capitalist restoration' and not some sort of 'socialist market', 'market socialism', or 'socialism with a human face'.[18] Indeed, Solidarity had been born in 1980–1 on a platform dedicated to changing socialism, not replacing

[18] According to Poland's new constitution, which was adopted in mid-1997, eight years after the transition was initiated, the state is based on a 'social market economy'. Whatever the words may mean this time around, the notion is inclusive enough to fit almost all expectations ('one size fits all'), while it is not as ideologically sensitive as 'capitalist market economy'. So much for names.

it. This same platform was adopted later by Mikhail Gorbachev in the Soviet Union and, at least at the beginning, by Boris Yeltsin in Russia, as well as by a number of other former Soviet republics. In Azerbaijan, Belarus, Turkmenistan, and Uzbekistan the struggle is still focused rather more on reforming the old system than on commencing a transition toward full-fledged capitalism.

Second, *it was clear from the start that in the contemporary world the introduction of a market system in a particular country means the country must become integrated with the global economy.* Hence openness and liberalization were not matters of preference, but matters of necessity. Before long the new leaders left off being opponents of too much involvement in international economic affairs. They quickly opened up the economies of their countries to the world market, and soon this step had become irreversible. Thus, they discovered that an open market economy and capitalism must go hand-in-hand (Csaba 1995).

Third, *other nations followed rapidly on the heels of the forerunners.* Before long, the deep commitment to an acceleration in reform and in the transformation to a market (had the words yet come to mean the 'restoration of capitalism'?) seemed to be shared nearly everywhere. Some nations, like the Baltic States or Kyrgyzstan, took less time to follow the trail than did others, like Mongolia or Ukraine. In Bulgaria and Romania only the crisis within a crisis, namely, the dire financial situation in the mid-1990s, sparked the shift toward the market transformation. In most countries the domestic pressure to alter the system was growing. However, the specific shift to a capitalist restoration was catalysed by the very convincing demonstration effect of the emerging liberal markets in neighbouring nations. The encouraging examples of the Czech Republic, Estonia, Hungary, Poland, and Slovenia were not overlooked in the Balkans or in the former Soviet republics. People were discovering a desire to change.

Fourth, *no matter what political leaders may have had in mind at the end of the 1980s and the beginning of the 90s vis-à-vis the overhaul of the economic system, they could not succeed without the active support of the wealthier part of the world*, and without a doubt the Bretton Woods institutions and the governments in the rich developed market nations supported the drive toward a Western-style economy. Only changes which guaranteed that at the end of the transition a free market economy (that is, full-fledged capitalism) would emerge were going to be backed politically and financially by the West. In a sense, the early transition from state socialism to a 'social market' economy had made it easier to persuade the transition countries to go a bit further and seek free market capitalism.

So, the next step toward capitalism was taken, and the world capitalist economy became directly involved in the transition, which seemed to offer it a tremendous chance to expand. This opportunity has been pursued to the limits ever since. Step by step and year by year foreign capitalist market institutions and international organizations have managed some-how to facilitate and accelerate the process of transition from socialism to capitalism, whatever the costs for the transition countries. Thus, quite quickly the problem for them became not how to put capitalism on top of the agen-das of the transition countries, but how to realize the capitalist system.

Both in theory and in practice there is still a great deal of confusion about the nature of market reform and the transition to a market economy. It is not always clear what is to be understood by the concepts. We are involved in a very dynamic historical process. Vast changes are taking place on the economic, as well as on the political levels. They are being carried forward in a gradual manner or in a more radical way. One can still talk about only reforming the old regime or about a transition to an entirely new system. There are possible successes, but possible failures as well. So, it would be useful to clarify some notions and interpretations, since they are important in any further considerations.

One must distinguish between market-oriented reform and a transition to a market economy. Whereas reform focuses on adjustments and the upgrad-ing of an existing system, transition involves the establishment of new systemic foundations. One 'reforms' an economic system not by eliminat-ing it, but by seeking to give it new life. In transition, the aim is to replace the old system with entirely different institutional structures and new types of economic relationships.

Thus, in Eastern Europe there was a series of reforms before 1989, and it is obvious that these particular reform efforts came to an end around 1990, when the whole region began to take up the challenge of replacing the old system with a new one.

How should one qualify the changes in China and Vietnam? Do they represent simply an advanced process of market reform within a socialist economy, or are they the onset of a transition from socialism to capitalism?[19] The answers to these questions are even more difficult given the confus-ing experiments with various combinations of socialism and the market in Eastern Europe during early reform programmes. However, though these experiments were generally fruitless, this should not be taken as a sign that similar experiments cannot bear fruit elsewhere. Thus, the case of China is important not only because of the significance of this mighty country and its economy, but also because of the new path taken in the introduc-tion of so-called 'market socialism'.

---

[19] The author was invited to a conference in Beijing in the summer of 1997 that was organized by the Chinese government and the China Reform Foundation. He was asked to present a paper on the causes of the failure of the economic reforms in Poland before the transition, that is, before the end of the 1980s. He was not asked to speak about the causes of the successes accomplished later in the course of the transition during the 90s. This may suggest that the conference organizers were seeking a good recipe for avoiding failures in market-oriented reform rather than for pushing ahead with a transformation to a full-fledged market.

The profile of the system of the future is not yet as clear in China as it appears to be in Eastern Europe and the former Soviet republics, but there have been several hints that transition is around the corner. The Chinese and the Vietnamese have come much closer than ever before to the establishment of a market economy, or rather they are further from the traditional socialist system than ever before. The economic system seems to be evolving toward the market, while the political system is lagging behind. Especially in textbooks on comparative economic systems, China is already being referred to as a market economy (Gregory and Stuart 1992, 1994, Gardner 1998).[20] Some experts believe that within the next 10 years China will be no less 'capitalist' than, say, Indonesia, and they may be correct.

On the eve of the 15th communist party congress in September 1997, Wu Jinglian, one of the most influential Chinese economists, defined socialism as 'social justice plus [the] market economy' (quoted in Walker 1997). This description is bold enough to fit not only the reforming socialist and postsocialist economies, but also a number of other countries which would hate to admit they have anything in common with socialism, such as Great Britain during the Margaret Thatcher tenure or the United States during the Reagan Administration.

But this is not merely a linguistic exercise, because sometimes the words come first, and later come the deeds, especially in the case of China. This can be read clearly in the recent history of two decades of reform (Fan 1997): the new terms and definitions have served the purpose of expressing the intentions behind the fresh policies, especially during the political climax represented by the party gatherings.

This may once again be the case, although another author claims that 'We [had] two banners hanging in front of the socialist house: one read "egalitarianism", and the other "state ownership". Deng tore down egalitarianism, and now his successors are removing state ownership. It is a deep change' (Wang 1994). In fact, this time the crucial issue is the change in property rights.

Neither the Chinese reforms, nor the ones in Vietnam have eliminated the monopoly of the communist party, which, together with the army, is actively involved in economic activities. The state sector continues to dominate the economy, despite some decentralization and the rapid growth of township and village enterprises. Whatever may be their label as non-state companies, these are definitely not private. Aside from deregulation and the easing of the bureaucratic hold over the economy, there is still a great deal

---

[20] Some authors, for example Popov and Shmelev 1990, argue that even the Soviet New Economic Policy (NEP) of the 1920s was essentially an effort to undertake a transition to the market, albeit based on the existence of state property in industry and without any democratization. However, the NEP episode was an attempt to sustain the system, not to replace it, so the analogy between recent transformations and the old NEP is not really justified.

of central control over prices, labour migration, investment, capital transfers, and credit allocation.

Nonetheless, it is often stressed that these nations, while not yet abandoning the socialist system, are even more advanced in terms of some market-oriented changes than are the post-Soviet transition economies. Nuti (1997a) has observed that 'Both countries have gone further than a "reformed" Soviet-type economy, in particular eliminating shortages, thereby creating a proper market environment; in some respects, such as market competition and the building of financial institutions, at least China may be ahead of even some transition economies.'

Though it is true that these two countries have gone further in reforming the socialist system than has any other country, it also remains true that if it had not been for the transition to a market economy in Eastern Europe and the former Soviet republics, one would hardly be tempted to describe what is happening in China and Vietnam as a 'transition' to capitalism. This is so because of another aspect of transition, namely, economic versus political changes. On the basis of strictly economic analysis, economic factors alone should determine the nature of reform and of transition. However, the situation is actually more complicated. Economic activities are usually much more tied to political developments and to the institutional framework than is admitted.

A fundamental question therefore appears: Is it practical to transform a socialist economy into a market economy without a parallel transformation of the political system? History offers many examples of cases in which it was possible to achieve robust growth and successful economic reform—including liberalization and openness to the world economy—without much political freedom or democracy.

Nonetheless, the logic of development during the era of globalization suggests that there are limits to the speed of growth if progress on the political front has not gone far enough. The argument that the market can perform well and that, whatever the political regime, growth is sustainable is perhaps correct for a while when a country is still underdeveloped. But in due time—the amount of time depends on the overall level of development, the nature of the technological advances achieved, and the scale of integration with the world economy—further growth and development become strongly allied to political liberalization. Sooner or later this turns out to be a hurdle or a catalyst for economic progress.

One may argue that in the last decade the level of development and the technological linkages forced political liberalization on countries like Indonesia, South Korea, and Taiwan, but not on the backward economies of China and Vietnam. Therefore, one might expect a democratization process to take place in China and Vietnam in the near future, although in a more gradual manner than has been the case in Eastern Europe and some former Soviet republics. Economic growth and social development seem to be unsustainable in the long run if they are not supported by democratic institutions. In the very long run, say, a couple of generations, the well-performing market economy will invariably be combined with a democratic political system.

Transition is always associated with a mix of economic and political changes, while reform is tied exclusively to economic changes. Thus, there was no expectation of extensive political shifts during the early reforms in the economic system in Eastern Europe and the former Soviet Union. Indeed, when the early economic reforms were able to deliver positive results in terms of higher standards of living and improvements in welfare, the pressure for political change eased, and the drive for democratization was abandoned. In contrast, the process of transition to a market system is supposed to take place in parallel with steps to establish parliamentary democracy and civic society. Since this is not the case in some countries, the question reappears: Have these nations only undertaken market reform, or has a transition already been initiated?

There is also a shadowy area when a reform or transition process is not clearly gradual or radical. This may be a matter of definition: what one person considers a gradual transition may be viewed as a radical reform by someone else. A number of Chinese politicians and economists claim that their reforms are a sort of gradual transition, and from such an angle they refer to the changes in Eastern Europe as radical reforms or so-called 'shock therapy' (Fan 1997). But there are at least two problems here. First, in the long run is the process of change in China the same as the transition in Eastern Europe? Second, can one accurately refer to the changes in Eastern Europe as radical reform, since, as has been argued already, the aim of the transition is the replacement of the old system by a new one?

These questions can be answered only ex post, because the criterion is the ultimate outcome of the changes, and this is not yet known in every case. While in Eastern Europe, as well as in the majority, if not all, of the former Soviet republics, it seems obvious that the socialist centrally planned economy is giving way to a capitalist market economy, the direction China or Vietnam is taking is not yet clear.[21] It will be obvious only in years to come whether already in the 1990s Cambodia, China, Laos, and Vietnam were in the midst of a transition to the market economy and the capitalist system or merely a comprehensive and effective reform of socialism.

The problem of the radical versus the gradual approach must also be examined from another perspective. The transition to the market is a complex process of modifications on various levels of the economic and political life of a country. In the economy, one can point to three differ-

---

[21] Nuti (1997a) claims that 'Clearly the "Market Socialism" project is nowhere near completion in either country, but is still a credible undertaking whose success cannot be ruled out on the basis of experience to date.'

ent, though interacting, spheres through which the alterations are moving. First are economic liberalization and macroeconomic stabilization; second are structural reform and institutional change, and third is the microeconomic restructuring of industrial capacity.

Though it seems obvious that liberalization is at the core of the transition to the market, it is also very well known that this sort of liberalization is initially followed by destabilization owing to upward price adjustments and the neutralization of so-called 'inflationary overhang'.[22] Thus, liberalization must be accompanied by sound efforts to stabilize the economy, especially by constraining the fiscal deficit and controlling inflation, which at the outset accelerates significantly, in some instances to the point of becoming hyperinflation. These parts of the transition exercise can therefore be executed in a radical or in a gradual manner. Which track to take depends on the amount of monetary and financial instability there is prior to stabilization, as well as the scope of price and trade controls before transition. The more the economy has been controlled and the greater the financial instability at the start, the more reasonable it is to take advantage of the radical approach toward liberalization and stabilization.

The second sphere, that is, the structural reform and institutional arrangements, including privatization and corporate governance, always involves a gradual process. With the unique exception of the former German Democratic Republic, the nature of these changes is such that they take a long time and are costly in both financial and social terms. It takes years to develop a proper institutional framework and to alter the way the actors behave on the economic and political scene. Hence structural reform and institutional change may be carried out more or less efficiently and may be enforced more quickly or more slowly, but none of this ever occurs in a radical way.

The microeconomic restructuring of existing capacity, the third sphere of transition, must be gradual. This time even the former GDR was no exception. New investments, the closing of old factories, the redeployment and retraining of labour, the effort to raise the competitiveness of industries, and the absorption of inflowing capital all take time and cost a great deal of money. Even to spend that much money—if one has it—takes time. The restructuring requires sound intervention by government and wise industrial policy. To counteract the social stress caused by restructuring calls for political acumen and consensus and a lot of capital. Actually, political

---

[22] 'Inflationary overhang' is created by the stock of forced savings that has been accumulated without regard to any voluntary propensity to save of households. Residual money balances are retained, although households may be keen to spend this money, because spending is inhibited due to the short supply of consumer goods. In other words, excessive aggregate demand is not matched by aggregate supply and is therefore involuntarily converted into 'inflationary overhang' because price adjustments are suppressed and prices are not allowed to reach the market clearing level.

consensus and capital become a little bit interchangeable if there is enough of both. Unfortunately, this has not been the case except in the former GDR.

Hence the picture is quite complex, and it cannot be simply claimed that there is a clear alternative between two options, between, for instance, the often (and indeed mistakenly) cited choice of either gradualism or shock therapy. The only thing that is sure is that so-called 'shock therapy' is not at all feasible with respect to the complex transition process; this process cannot be carried out in a radical way. At most, a radical approach is practicable in the case of liberalization and macroeconomic stabilization, and some aspects of the new institutional arrangements and structural reforms can be implemented in a radical manner if political and financial conditions permit. Otherwise, all this takes a lot of time. A revolutionary push for change might be able to create appropriate initial conditions for an eventual gradual transition, but under no circumstances can it be a substitute for such a transition.

Thus, a more realistic policy problem is the choice between economic transformation carried out through an organized set of policy measures or through a scattershot one. In other words, is transition to be executed by design or by chance? If one reconsiders from this angle the case most often (and most wrongly) mentioned as an example of 'shock therapy', namely, Poland in 1989–92, one sees that a radical thrust toward additional liberalization only accelerated the progress of reforms which had already been launched. This was followed, first, by a rather chaotic situation in which developments occurred by chance and, only later, especially in 1993–7, by a planned approach implemented in an organized way.

The observations of this shift offered by John Williamson, a leading Washington-based economist, are interesting.[23] He claims that

I was particularly pleased that you have tried to define an alternative [in Kolodko and Nuti 1997, as well as in actual policy] to big bangery in terms of a more careful design of individual policy components rather than generalized go slow ['gradualism']. On just about all the individual items you identify, certainly including protection and privatization, I agree with you in retrospect, and indeed I would have agreed with you at the time. . . . But in all honesty I have to confess that I still worry that had I been in the place of Balcerowicz [Poland's deputy prime minister and minister of finance in 1989–91] I might not have put together the decisive package that I think in retrospect Poland needed at the time and that laid the foundation for your successful period in office. Perhaps one needed a little bit of overkill to make it emotionally possible for your allies to accept that the world had changed, and even to give you the opportunity of correcting their excesses and in the process winning their acceptance of the new model? It reminds me of the situation in my home country: I am much more comfortable with Tony Blair than with Mrs Thatcher, but I am not sure that we could have had him without her.

[23] Personal communication with the author.

So, the psychological rather than the economic argument is brought to the fore as a decisive factor in favour of the 'radical' set of policies ('big bangery') undertaken unsuccessfully at the beginning of the 1990s. However, it seems that we still differ in our evaluations of the scope and the costs of the 'overkill'. Was the overkill only 'a little bit', as some may still believe, or was it 'too much', as others seem to have demonstrated (Kolodko 1991, Rosati 1994, Poznanski 1996)?

There is still a great deal of confusion in terminology, however. In considering quite a wide range of conditions and their influence on actual transition strategies, from the year of the start of central planning to the scope of trade liberalization, from the structural distance to be travelled to achieve the most rudimentary market economy to the relations between Catholics and Lutherans, Wolf (1997) argues that even in Poland in 1989–90 there was a gradual approach, and the radical one was undertaken only in 1991.

Other countries with a radical transition strategy have been Albania, the Czech Republic, Estonia, Hungary, Lithuania, and Slovakia since 1992, and Kyrgyzstan since 1993. According to this classification, none of these nations abandoned the radical path for a gradual one, or a gradual one for a 'lagging' one (where countries like Armenia, Azerbaijan, Belarus, Bulgaria, Georgia, Kazakhstan, Moldova, Russia, Tajikistan, Ukraine, and Uzbekistan are counted). Cornia and Popov (1998) consider Vietnam a typical case of the shock approach, pointing to the 'immediate deregulation of prices and macro-stability'. Consequently, they refer to Russia and Ukraine as cases of a strategy of 'inconsistent shock', that is, the immediate deregulation of prices, but failure to ensure macroeconomic stability.

None of these debates lacks significance. The term 'shock therapy' may seem to some to have a nice touch, since the notion 'shock' has been wedded to the somewhat opposite notion 'therapy'.[24] The divorce of an alliance with such a good ring to it is not so easy, but, in fact, if the 'shocks' introduced while a country is engaging in transition are too thoroughgoing, there may be no therapy, as the case of Poland in 1989–92 shows. Thus, if there can be a 'shock therapy' according to this line of reasoning, then by the logic of symmetry there must also be a 'shock failure'. Moreover, if there is 'shock therapy' and consequently 'shock failure', then all the more reason there can be 'gradual therapy' and 'gradual failure' (Table 4).

Having clarified somewhat the taxonomy and the terminology, as well as some of the characteristics of the early reforms and the first decade of transition, one can now examine particular cases in order to understand better these terms.

[24] In contrast, the term 'inconsistent shock' has not been thriving and has not been bandied about worldwide.

Table 4 Market reforms and the transition: gradualism versus radicalism and success versus failure

Market reform	Transition to a market
Gradualism versus radicalism	
By design (organized)	*By design (organized) or by chance (chaotic)*
	1. Liberalization and macroeconomic stabilization
Gradual: Yugoslavia from the 1950s to 1990. Hungary and Poland in the 70s and 80s. China and Vietnam in the 80s and 90s.	Gradual: CIS, all Eastern and Central Europe in the 1990s, except Poland in 1989–91.
	Radical (shock): Poland in 1989–91. Russia in 1996–7. Bulgaria and Romania in 1997.
	2. Institutional changes
	Gradual: all, except for former GDR.
	3. Microeconomic restructuring of capacity
	Gradual: everywhere.
Economic and political changes	
Limited economic changes/restricted political changes	Fundamental economic/political changes
Eastern and Central Europe in the 1970s and 80s and China and Vietnam in the 80s.	Eastern and Central Europe and the CIS in the 1990s, with the exception of Belarus and countries involved in war, like Bosnia and Tajikistan.
Success (therapy) or failure	
Gradual reform success: China and Vietnam in the 1980s and 90s.	Gradual success: Czech Republic, Estonia, Hungary, Kyrgyzstan, Latvia, Poland, Slovenia in the 1990s.
Gradual reform failure: Eastern and Central Europe in the 1980s.	Gradual failure: Moldova, Russia, Ukraine in the 1990s. Radical failure: Albania in 1996–7.

Source: Compiled by the author.

Market-oriented reforms were undertaken in Russia in the 1980s, when the country was still the core of the former Soviet Union. These reforms were limited and involved no fundamental political changes. They were part of a gradual process which ultimately turned out to be a big failure. Later, after 1990, the transition to a market was launched, and all three spheres of the process—that is, liberalization and macroeconomic stabilization, structural reform and institutional change, and the microeconomic restructuring of industrial capacity—were implemented in a gradual manner, although some may still call this 'a radical reform in Yeltsin's Russia' (Nelson and Kuzes 1995). However, whether gradual or radical, this transition should be considered a failure, too. The economic performance has been extremely weak throughout the 1990s, and the financial collapse in 1998 is evidence that the transition effort has led to a severe crisis and systemic confusion.[25]

In China there has been a determined effort over the last two decades to carry forward sound market-oriented reforms with only limited, albeit not negligible, political liberalization. This is a gradual process, and it should not be referred to as a 'transition' in the post-Soviet and Eastern European sense of the 1990s. These reforms—which may or may not turn out to be part of a transition to a full-fledged market economy and democracy—have been the most successful in the history of socialism, especially if one considers the outcomes of the early attempts at reform in the Soviet Union and other countries of the Council of Mutual Economic Assistance (Comecon).[26] There is no doubt that the remarkable growth of the Chinese economy—and the same is true in the case of Vietnam—is due to these reforms, just as there is no doubt that the collapse in the 1990s of the economies of Russia and Ukraine must be associated with mismanagement of the transition process. China and Vietnam are the best examples of successful gradual market-oriented reforms, whereas Russia and Ukraine, at least for the time being, are the most spectacular examples of the failure of a gradual transition to a market economy.

In Poland, although the early reforms of the socialist economy eventually made a positive contribution to the successful transition, from the historical perspective they were a disappointment. Indeed, the transition to a market was first launched in this very country precisely because of the failure of the previous attempts to reform the old system. Subsequently, there was a radical approach toward liberalization and macroeconomic stabilization in 1989–92, and this was at least a partial failure, too, especially if one compares the expected contraction of 3 per cent of GDP with

---

[25] Nonetheless, Åslund (1995) claims that Russia had already become a market economy after only four or five years of transition. This is, of course, a matter of definition, but, according to the reasoning here, even the countries which are most advanced in transition (such as the new members of the Organization for Economic Cooperation and Development) are not yet true market economies, and Russia is definitely much further from this target than are the majority of the postsocialist nations.

[26] Prior to its dismantling in 1990, the CMEA (known more widely in the West as 'Comecon') included Cuba, Mongolia, the Soviet Union, Vietnam, and all the Eastern European socialist economies except Albania and the former Yugoslavia.

the severe recession of 20 per cent between mid-1989 and mid-1992.[27] Later, under the 'Strategy for Poland' programme, the policies of liberalization and macroeconomic stabilization were shifted toward gradualism (Kolodko 1996). These were successful. They brought inflation down by more than two-thirds in 1994–7 and simultaneously boosted GDP by over 28 per cent. Meanwhile, institutional changes were implemented from the very beginning of the transition in a gradual manner. Of course, these changes should also be seen as a significant acceleration of the changes introduced during the reforms of the 1980s. Thus, the transition process, after some turbulence and mismanagement in the early 1990s, became quite healthy after 1993 in terms of the advances in market institutional arrangements and the achievement of the highest medium-term rate of growth not only among transition economies, but also in the whole of Europe.

In Romania there were hardly any true market-oriented reforms in the 1970s and 80s, and the early transition—with the political reforms lagging behind—was a flop. Owing to mounting difficulties and the growing conviction that the changes must be accelerated, only since 1997 has there been an attempt to 'radicalize' the transition exercise.

Other characteristics can be observed in other specific cases, which are difficult to qualify clearly.

There are still countries in which the legacy of the old system is more evident than the features of the new. This is the case in Belarus, Tajikistan, and Turkmenistan, which—according to the transition scoreboard of the European Bank for Reconstruction and Development (EBRD 1996, 1997a)—have not accomplished much in recent years. In Belarus economic adjustment slowed and then was postponed, and the economy is managed in a manner somewhat similar to that typical under Soviet-style policies. In Tajikistan and Turkmenistan the private sector accounts for only about 15 per cent of GDP, so the process of market-oriented change must mature appreciably before one can consider these as true transition economies.

As time passes and the situation evolves, a country which is successful today may become a failure tomorrow, and what appears only to be a set of reforms now may yet turn out to be a transition. (Hopefully, not the other way around.) Likewise, the effort to upgrade the efficiency of a centrally planned economy may become a search for market socialism. For the time being, China and Vietnam seem to be at this stage. Meanwhile, though the former Soviet republics and the Eastern European economies are involved to a greater or lesser extent in the transition from socialism to capitalism, Cuba and North Korea have been delaying even limited market reform. Overall, a significant portion of the world economy is engaged

<hr>

[27] The Polish government, backed by international organizations and Western governments, anticipated only a mild contraction lasting about one year and followed by rapid recovery and growth. Even more inaccurate were the expectations vis-à-vis the inflation rate, which turned out to be several times the officially predicted rate.

in the challenging task of implementing market socialism or a capitalist restoration. What sort of capitalism this will be is another matter.

1.7. TRANSITION TARGETS: VISIONS AND ILLUSIONS

The transition process is still going on, and the attitudes toward it are shifting. Unlike the very familiar 'point of departure', the goal of transition has not always been clear. From a psychological and political perspective, it seems as though societies were keen simply to break through the limitations of the old system, naïvely assuming that this would be sufficient to deliver progress. While the known but 'worse' was being rejected, the unknown but 'better' was being accepted. It was believed that sooner or later the future would be an improvement on the past, and this would become true because of the establishment of a market economy. However, this vision was never drawn out in detail.

Catchwords like 'social market economy', 'people's capitalism', 'enfranchisement', 'mass privatization', 'improvement of efficiency and competitiveness', 'fast growth', and 'higher standards of living' were used as substitutes for a comprehensive blueprint of the new system which was to emerge from the transition. Visions about the outcome were fuelled more often by the experiences of somebody else, especially the developed market economies, rather than by critical analyses of one's own abilities and constraints. The demonstration effect of what neighbouring countries were doing had a particular impact in shaping the expectations and influencing the attitudes of the people in transition nations. The lack of pragmatic programmes, realistic scenarios, and a consistent vision of the goal of transition, together with the general ignorance concerning the historical evolution in developed market countries, seemed not to matter given the pleasant possibilities which the current situation in advanced capitalist nations and mature civic societies appeared to promise.

A misconception about the amount of time which would actually be required for transition dominated the way the targets of transition were set. Though psychologically understandable, this is not scientifically adequate, and politically it is plain risky. The early negative experiences, owing to the hardships imposed by the crisis at the onset of transition, eventually provoked heated political disputes and led to reassessments. For several years the intellectual debate was overshadowed by these political disputes. The resulting atmosphere has not always been conducive to calm and to rational reflection. Even the majority of scholars and intellectuals found themselves deeply engaged in the political fights. It is no coincidence that so many distinguished writers, professors, and lawyers have got involved in politics and become ministers and even heads-of-state, for instance in the Czech Republic, Georgia, FYR Macedonia, and Romania. In Poland in 1994–7 there were more professors in the government than there had been generals in the martial law governments of the 1980s. The bigger the disappointment with the initial results of the systemic changes, the more deliberation and educated debate seemed essential.

The vision of what the future had in store was unrealistic for three main reasons. First, *the expected growth in production never materialized*. Quite naturally, the new reality which was anticipated based on the fresh political circumstances was imagined as healthier, and rapid growth was thought to be just around the corner. However, this did not turn out to be the case even in the best performing countries. This promptly caused political frustration. The exaggerated expectations were not derived from able and responsible projections. Often they were simply illusions; sometimes they were reactions to the chaotic events and were supported by no particular plans for the future.

In the nations which had already come to grips with reform during the socialist era, the expectation that the transition would accelerate the reshuffling already under way was somewhat justified. In countries surprised by the dynamism of the transition, the atmosphere was more revolutionary: what mattered most was to get rid of the old system immediately; then one would gain a better idea of what else had to be done.

The illusion that merely dismantling 'real socialism' would by itself quickly solve the problems which had appeared under the outgoing system was encouraged by the new political leaders. They used this exaggerated expectation as a means to push through otherwise less acceptable measures. Unfortunately, despite early warnings about such naïveté, this was a common occurrence. It was even a popular belief in some important Western intellectual and political circles and thereby had a major impact on the responses of these circles to the transition.

For example, already in 1989 the ill-advised utopian dream about a coming 'leap' into the free market was thriving in Poland. In the early 1990s excessive optimism about growth could be seen among German authorities, who were expecting to be able to turn five eastern Länder (the former GDR) into an integrated market economy much sooner and at substantially lower cost than has actually been the case. Excessive optimism could still be observed in the mid-1990s, when the Bretton Woods institutions were anticipating a resurgence in growth in Russia and Ukraine. Despite all the negative experiences with 'shock therapy', in 1997–8 the sin of excessive enthusiasm and of underestimating the time horizons reasonably required for adjustment and the resurgence of growth was committed again, this time in Bulgaria and Romania. International organizations and liberal financial newspapers and magazines were fervently supportive of the radical plans of the governments and central banks in these countries, although these governments and banks were making quite unrealistic assumptions, especially vis-à-vis privatization and stabilization.

Across the entire transition region unrealistic expectations and baseless promises were evident in the programmes of various political alliances. Populist and pragmatic parties alike have been inclined to offer much more than they can deliver, even under the most favourable circumstances.

The second main reason for the unrealistic vision of the future was that *the expectation that economic systems and the overall level of development would soon be similar to those in advanced countries was mistaken.* This illusion still seems to be quite prevalent in Eastern Europe, where a mirage of wealth from the rapidly approaching integration with Western Europe has seemed to be maintained on the horizon. The transition was initially seen not as the difficult process of building a new economic system, with distinct financial mechanisms of allocation and new income distribution patterns, but simply as a way to become a rich country quickly. Instead of being told the truth that the process of change would be long and costly, people were allowed to go on believing that a rapid transition would make them wealthier sooner. While the determination to close the development gap between advanced market countries and postsocialist nations was rightly embraced, it was accompanied by the conviction that this could be accomplished in a couple of years. Only when it became evident that wealth is for the few and poverty for the many during transition even more than under socialism did this early naïveté begin to disappear, though it has not vanished entirely.

On the strictly economic side, it was assumed that financial distortions could be removed by getting rid of 'shortageflation' through rapid price liberalization backed by tough fiscal and monetary policies. This was supposed to happen without severe contraction. There has not been a single instance in which a government and the international organizations and prestigious research entities supporting its policies have correctly foreseen the scope of the recession following on the heels of the application of the liberalization and stabilization measures applied along the lines the organizations and entities have advised. Unfortunately, instead of moving from shortageflation to dynamic equilibrium and market clearing prices, first there was a shift to 'slumpflation' and then, after some recovery and growth, to 'stagflation'. The misery index of shortages and of inflation has been replaced by the misery index of even higher inflation and unemployment. Thus, the outcome of the early stage of transformation was the shift from 'shortageflation' to 'stagflation'.

Deep contraction accompanied by mass unemployment has been a harsh experience for all transition economies. Yet, in many of them this negative shock (definitely without any therapy) was still more negative because for at least two generations the people had never witnessed open inflation or unemployment. The impression of people that their countries have been exiting from one sort of crisis to enter another is therefore quite justified. The distorted centrally planned economy has been replaced by a distorted market economy, and the imbalances associated with the socialist system have been replaced by the imbalances linked to the capitalist order.

Third, *transition policies were misguided*. Societies have been forced to pay a heavy price for adjustment. Severe impoverishment and a deterioration in standards of living were the direct and otherwise unnecessary result of these mistakes. Output shrank, and consumption fell; the proportion of people living below the poverty line increased, and mass unemployment emerged. Now, most transition countries are finally on the path of recovery, and some leading nations are already on the road to sustainable development.[28] But there is still a question: Have the relevant lessons been learned? If the answer is 'yes', then there is room for optimism.

It is extremely difficult and perhaps impossible to solve the problems inherited from the statist central planning system on the basis of liberal market policy guidelines, just as it was virtually impossible to tackle these problems within the framework of the socialist economy. This seems now to be more widely understood and accepted in countries like Hungary and Slovenia, where market institutions already have a dominant position, as well as reformed socialist economies like China and Vietnam and nations like Moldova and Uzbekistan, where market forces are relied on only to support statist arrangements and policies which are administered by bureaucracies. The way to resolve challenging economic and social issues seems to be to contain excessive expectations and take gradual steps to improve economic efficiency and the standard of living. Only a well-designed transition which is managed through properly tailored long-run policies offers a chance to achieve this sort of balance. This can in due course turn the vision of a well-performing market economy into a reality.

The disappointment was great when the scenario of the overnight transformation of a crisis-ridden socialist economy into a flourishing market economy was revealed to be an illusion. But there is more bad news. After several years of transition, despite the significant progress in structural adjustment and stabilization, recovery and growth are still sluggish. Stability has not yet been attained. The social support for transition is weak and may not hold up. If the transition is to succeed, economies must be turned around so that there is durable growth. Only then will it be possible to guarantee higher living standards.

It has been possible to manage the collapse of the socialist system (almost) peacefully. There have been exceptions: in the former Yugoslav republics, especially Bosnia-Herzegovina and the new Yugoslavia, and at various times in the former Soviet republics of Armenia, Azerbaijan, Georgia, Moldova,

---

[28] The notion 'sustainable' is used here to refer to stable and durable growth, although this growth should be compatible with sustainable development in a wider sense, that is, development which includes improvement in the natural environment and the protection of non-reproductive resources (OECD 1997a).

and Tajikistan and, of course, in Chechnya. The regional conflicts have been caused by non-economic factors. In any case, the (mostly) peaceful course of the first decade of postsocialist transition is a great achievement in itself. This is a bit of good news. Given the paramount challenge represented by the whole process, the situation could have got out of control, and the cost of the dismantling of socialism could have been even higher.

Yet, on the economic side, considering the challenges ahead, there is still a long way to go before a well-working market and a performing democracy can rise from the ashes of the socialist system.

2

Different Points of Departure

2.1. GEOPOLITICS: INITIAL POSITION AND FINAL OUTCOME

Though the general picture of the transition economies looks much healthier at the end of the 1990s than it did a couple of years ago, many major obstacles remain. Most of these are related to the geopolitical dimension of transformation, which is evolving within the wider context of the global economy and international political relations.

In 1997, on the eve of the annual gathering of the EBRD, the financial organization specially established to facilitate postsocialist modernization, it was being stressed that

The continent as a whole, whatever the disappointments that have followed the fall of communism, is slowly becoming safer, richer, and more hopeful. Even countries as rough as Russia, Romania, and Bulgaria are moving in the right direction. The Balts look a bit less vulnerable, the Caucasus a bit less chaotic, the Balkans a bit less bloody. (*The Economist* 1997a)

And, obviously, the Eastern European members of the Organization for Economic Cooperation and Development look to be much more open and integrated within the world economy than ever before. So, despite all the hardship, the situation does seem to be 'moving in the right direction'.

Although the circumstances are quite diverse, there have been various attempts to categorize particular countries into well-defined groups. In the case of transformation, this is not easy. Such a classification becomes still more difficult if one looks not only for common denominators, but also searches for more detailed descriptions.

The geopolitical dimension matters. In today's world economy—with the free trade of goods, record capital flows, huge migrations of labour, rapid transfers of technology, worldwide television, the global Internet village, and so on—the location of particular nations on the world map is not so important as it used to be during the period of colonization, the industrial revolution, the birth of the socialist system, or the cold war. Nonetheless, it still does mean a lot from the angle of local, regional, and global economic and political relations. The geopolitical position of postsocialist markets is an inflexible factor which influences other major factors. Especially from the point of view of investment links, trade patterns, and membership in regional organizations, the past, present, and future of nations depend not only on what they have done and what they will do, but also on where they are.

Some authors believe that geographical position matters significantly for growth. They try to use it to explain the ability to expand (Gallup and Sachs 1998). Since policy cannot change geography, several countries said to be in a relatively unfavourable geographical location are supposedly doomed to do more poorly than others. If this were true, Albania should be thriving, whereas Kyrgyzstan ought to be decaying; Cuba should be prospering, while Mongolia must be stagnating. However, this is not the case. One should therefore be wary of exaggerating the importance of location. Moreover, the political aspects of geography matter as well. The best players from this angle seem to be the three tiny Baltic States, Estonia, Latvia and Lithuania, which are trying to take advantage of their location interpreted in a political sense rather than in a strictly geographical one.

Of course, integration in the world economy is more reasonable for a nation which is close to developed markets, such as the Czech Republic or Hungary, than it is for a nation with a less favourable geographical location in this sense, such as Kazakhstan or Laos.[1] A location which was unfavourable for many centuries in terms of the problems and challenges for economic development has sometimes turned out to be a favourable one today. This is the case of Poland, for example, which has had the misfortune (at times) and the fortune (at times) to lie between Germany and Russia, or of Slovenia, which is wisely taking advantage of its vicinity to Austria and Italy. The collapse of the socialist order has created geographical problems for other countries, such as FYR Macedonia in Europe or Tajikistan in Asia.

Nonetheless, this type of constraint should not be seen as an excuse for a lack of comprehensive structural reform or the postponement of institutional change. Rather, it should facilitate serious attempts to open up an economy to extensive ties with the outside world. This is precisely the case of Mongolia, which has made considerable progress in liberalization, in contrast to the experience of several other nations in Central Asia, like Turkmenistan, that are also affected by relatively less attractive location. An unfavourable geopolitical position has to be offset by still more determined attempts to achieve sound market reform and postsocialist modernization. As an individual can compensate for the lack of a pleasing figure or physique by wearing a well-tailored dress or suit, awkward geopolitical position can be offset by well-designed policies, just as a relatively

---

[1] What once was a favourable location may become of no significance. For example, Uzbekistan used to lie on the transcontinental silk road and Romania at the European crossroads of the silk and the amber roads. Both countries are very central in terms of their respective continents from a geographical viewpoint, but from an economic perspective they are in peripheral regions. So, a possible question is: What are the silk and amber roads of the future going to be?

favourable geographical position may be neutralized by poorly adjusted policies. This is the case of Slovakia, which, unlike its neighbour, the Czech Republic, has not been invited to take part in the first round of the negotiations with the European Union, or especially of Belarus, which has received very little foreign aid and, although much bigger than its small northern neighbours, Estonia, Latvia, and Lithuania, has absorbed two or three times less foreign direct investment.

It is natural that integration with near neighbours is easier than the expansion of ties with distant partners. In general, proximity should facilitate close economic links, but this does not always occur. A radical westward shift in trade patterns, sometimes motivated more by political preferences than by comparative advantage, led to the collapse of trade connections between the nations of Eastern Europe and the former Soviet republics. Thus, Belarus and Poland share a long border, but Belarus sells only a meagre 1–2 per cent of its exports to Poland. The trade among the former Soviet republics has been in disarray for several years. Traditional markets were given up to foreign competitors during the period of output contraction. Later, it was difficult if not impossible to recover trade levels and regain access to these markets.

Under some circumstances it may be more feasible to cement a closer bond with a distant country than with a direct neighbour. This used to be the situation in the relations between Cuba and the Soviet Union (Roca 1988). It is the case in the involvement of Japan in trade and investment in Brazil, China's growing activity in Southern Africa, and the progress by Chile and the US under the free trade regime of the American Free Trade Agreement. Some transition economies are becoming involved in various activities (such as trade, but also direct investment) with more developed economies, often despite great distances. The expanding East Asian trade and investment in some Eastern European nations are a good example.

The collapse of the socialist economic system and the political aftermath led to the end of Soviet-era patterns of international cooperation. The vacuum is being filled by capital from the advanced economies of Western neighbours (and now also political friends), but also from more distant countries which are rich enough to invest and also happen to see the transition as an opportunity for business expansion.

Yet, despite globalization and the increasing participation of transition countries in the world economy, constraints and limitations are imposed by location. Because of current global trends and the peculiarities of post-socialist change, the geopolitics of transition is contributing to a fundamental restructuring in international ties. This is acting as a catalyst in the pace of transition and is shaping the outcomes. Eventually, it will have an effect in the diversification of the emerging postsocialist markets.

Within the centrally planned system a sort of structural uniformity was enforced. The tendency to render institutional arrangements homogeneous and the attempts to coordinate development policies ultimately had an impact after several decades of policy-led change. Economies as distant as Cuba and Vietnam, Bulgaria and Mongolia, or Romania and Uzbekistan that had been quite different in terms of history, culture, and geopolitics gradually came to rely on quite similar structures, and the socialist nations, due to their special mechanisms of cooperation and the trade ties exercised within Comecon, became quite similar.

This was also true of industrial structures, which, instead of becoming supportive of and compatible with each other, became more competitive only in the sense that they were often involved in manufacturing the same or similar goods. There was insufficient specialization in production. Owing to persistent shortages, which eroded the ability of consumers to exert pressure for upgrading, this sort of competition, unlike that in a market economy, did not encourage improvements in quality. The central plan failed to diversify economic structures in the ways envisaged and expected by its advocates. During the late stages of the socialist system, the ability of industries to compete within the world economy and even within Comecon was declining. Hence the inter-country integration orchestrated under the socialist command system, especially during the early phase of industrialization and the following period of remarkable growth in heavy industry, was no longer so welcome; indeed, it was becoming a real burden.

The postsocialist nations therefore set out early in search not only of alternative paths toward development, but also of new partners they could deal with on a more equal basis. Several Eastern European countries established a free trade area, the Central European Free Trade Agreement, while actively working to create a strong relationship with developed market nations.[2] It was natural for Eastern Europe to look initially toward the western part of the continent.

For the Caucasus republics, it made sense to seek new allies in their vicinity, including the Middle East, whereas, in the case of Cambodia, Laos, and Vietnam, the Association of South East Asian Nations (ASEAN), Japan, and, of course, China seemed to be the logical partners.

For some countries the closest allies were to be found just across the border, for example Austria for Hungary and Slovenia, Finland for Estonia and Latvia, or Thailand for Laos and Vietnam.

Some former Soviet republics seemed to be doomed to dealing mainly with Russia and among themselves, though under new rules. This has been the case of all members of the CIS. The challenges are similar to those for Eastern Europe. Yet, to overcome them is more difficult from the perspective of mutual relations among the former Soviet republics,

[2] The Central European Free Trade Agreement was initially constituted of the Visegrad Group, that is, Czechoslovakia (after the split, the Czech Republic and Slovakia), Hungary, and Poland. In 1996 Romania and Slovenia joined, and in 1998 Bulgaria. Lithuania has been seeking to join as well.

as well as from the angle of contacts between this group and more remote nations.

Under the central planning regime in the Soviet Union, trade ties with other socialist economies were handled by state entities and were managed from Moscow. Whereas there was some direct economic cooperation between the Soviet Union and Yugoslavia, there was none between, for instance, Moldova and Slovenia. While there was direct trade between Mongolia and Romania, there was none between Romania and Turkmenistan. Thus, today, unlike in Eastern Europe, new outward-oriented relationships must often be created from scratch in the emerging markets of the postsocialist economies of the former Soviet republics. Except for Russia, the CIS members are as trapped as a recently divorced individual. Even if he (or she) feels free and is ready to commit to some new type of institutional arrangement, for the time being he can hardly afford such a luxury, for he is encumbered by the heavy burden of familiar habits, fresh financial problems, and, after all, the same old address.

Liberalization and privatization have opened up new opportunities for involvement in various financial, investment, trade, and technological relationships with neighbours which have had the market economy for a long time. While one must acknowledge the obvious, that the emerging markets are being penetrated by transnational corporations headquartered in the leading economies, like Germany, Japan, and the US, nonetheless the bulk of foreign direct investment in Hungary now comes from Austria, in Latvia from Sweden, in FYR Macedonia from Greece, in Slovenia from Italy, in Turkmenistan from Turkey, and in Vietnam from Australia. To get an injection of capital and technology from North America or Japan, Hong Kong or Taiwan, Great Britain or Spain seems to be as difficult for Croatia as it is for Poland. The problem for the smaller countries of FYR Macedonia and Moldova is not so different from that of the bigger countries of Kazakhstan and Ukraine. It is much easier to import goods from Iran to Armenia than to Bosnia-Herzegovina, to bring Finnish money and expertise to Estonia than to Albania, or to receive Austrian investment in the tourist sector in Slovakia than in Kyrgyzstan.

Clearly, trade and investment are leaving imprints on the path of transition, but so also are the flow of ideas and cultural exchanges. Geopolitical position is important in this area, too. It is much easier for the Czech Republic to become integrated with the European Union than it is for Ukraine not only because the output level of the Czech Republic is more comparable to that of any Western European country, but because the Czech Republic is a neighbour of Austria and Germany, with all this means in terms of cultural and historical linkages. For exclusively geopolitical reasons it has been easier for Vietnam to join ASEAN than it would have been for Mongolia to do so, since, although Mongolia has a much more liberalized economy, Vietnam is in Southeast Asia. For similar reasons Cuba,

Kyrgyzstan, Poland, and Vietnam, all of which used to be members of Comecon, already belong, or eventually will belong, to separate regional organizations such as the North American Free Trade Agreement (NAFTA), CIS, the European Union, and ASEAN. Mongolia may yet apply to join ASEAN, but it will not be joining NAFTA any time soon; Bulgaria may try again to negotiate entry into the EU, but it is not likely to consider membership in the CIS. This geopolitical dimension is quite important for the final outcome and the development implications of the transformation. That's the geopolitics of transition.

2.2. ECONOMIC SYSTEMS AND STRUCTURES

Despite the institutional uniformity and the persistent efforts to tailor the various socialist political and economic systems out of the same cloth, each socialist economy had its own character. The political drive toward uniformity was opposed by cultural heritage, geopolitical position, individual visions of the socialist future, and the conflicting ambitions of political leaders.

Yet, both in the East and in the West attempts were made to lump the socialist nations together or, at most, into two groups, one led by the Soviet Union, and the other by China. In the East this sort of taxonomy was used to emphasize the general merits of the common socialist system, while in the West it was pointed to as evidence of the evil tendency of socialism to stifle individuality.

A clear example from the East was the concept of the so-called 'advanced socialist society' that was promulgated by the Soviet Union in the 1970s. The idea was to propagate a model for state socialist institutions and through it to bind more tightly together the members of Comecon, especially those in Eastern Europe. With the exception of Romania, the members of Comecon were all anxious to comply and competed among themselves to prove that they deserved to be included. The model also had a policy aspect, and this influenced the way institutions were designed and structures were formed. Thus, the model was used not only as a means of advancing the Soviet system, but also as an instrument to homogenize the system through organizations, structures, and policies.

In general, one can point to many types of socialist economies *sensu largo* (Table 5), but, in the context of the shift from the planned to the market economy, attention is usually focused on a particular kind of socialism, known as 'state socialism' (or 'communism', as it is often called in the West). The term 'postsocialist transition' therefore refers to the transformation of a statist economy characterized by the dominance (or monopoly) of state ownership and a leading role for central planning in resource allocation and income distribution.

Table 5 Types and degrees of socialism

Dominant public ownership	Equality, social consumption	Participation, economic democracy	Social control over economic processes (plan)	Examples
Yes	Yes	Yes	Yes	Maximalist socialist ideal. Chinese Cultural Revolution in theory.
Yes	Yes	Yes	No	Full communist ideal: collective ownership, 'from each according to ability, to each according to need', the state 'withers away'.
Yes	Yes	No	Yes	China after 1978: 'socialism with Chinese characteristics', 'growth with equality', 'market socialism', state and township and village enterprise ownership, moderate equality, macroeconomic control.
Yes	No	Yes	Yes	Yugoslavia in theory: 'social' ownership, interregional and inter-enterprise inequality, self-management and associations, macroeconomic control.
Yes	No	No	Yes	Soviet-type central planning, state, local and cooperative ownership, no 'uravnilovka' ('income levelling'), 'democratic centralism' (that is, the political monopoly of the Communist Party).
Yes	No	Yes	No	Yugoslavia in practice: lack of macroeconomic control: unemployment, inflation and economic fluctuations.
Yes	Yes	No	No	Taiwan in the 1960s (60% state sector), some less developed countries: Chinese Cultural Revolution in practice (loss of state control, famine, authoritarianism).

Description				
Postcommunist transitional economies in 1989–92: dominant residual state sector, inequalities, no economic democracy, mass unemployment, inflation and deep recession.	No	No	No	Yes
Social democratic ideal: private ownership and enterprise, egalitarianism, collectivization of risk, economic democracy, high and stable employment.	Yes	Yes	Yes	No
Austrian-type neo-corporatism: private ownership and private enterprise, no concern for equality, interest group representation, income policy and Keynesian macropolicies.	Yes	Yes	No	No
Nazi/fascist model: private property and enterprise, some equality, authoritarianism, state interventionism.	Yes	No	Yes	No
Weaker version of the social democratic model, with deregulation and blander state intervention in the economy.	No	Yes	Yes	No
The Welfare State, Scandinavian social democracy since the late 1980s: nominal participation, emergence of large-scale unemployment.	No	No	Yes	No
German-type 'codetermination' ('Mitbestimmung'), that is, the minority participation of employees in some sectors, 'social market economy' stressing market competition.	No	Yes	No	No
French-type indicative planning: ordinary public policy, plus state economic forecasting based on consensus, transparency, incentives conditional on the implementation of quasi-contracts.	Yes	No	No	No
Capitalism *tout court* (including managerial capitalism and the mixed economy).	No	No	No	No

Source: Nuti 1993.

The economic model under consideration here is limited to socialism as practised in Albania, the Asian socialist nations, the Eastern European Comecon members, Soviet-style economies, and Yugoslavia. When relevant, reference is made to Cuba (which was a member of Comecon) and North Korea (which was not). The criteria of classification are the systemic characteristics, not geographical location, whatever may have been the importance of the latter at various stages of the evolution of the world socialist system or the cold war. After all, Albania, Cuba, and North Korea had more in common at the end of the 1980s and the beginning of the 90s, despite the fact that they are located in three different continents, than did Albania with neighbouring Yugoslavia or North Korea with Vietnam, another Asian socialist economy. What mattered at the time was not so much geography, but the dominant ideology and the actual policy orientation.

For numerous ideological, political, cultural, and economic reasons the 'point of departure' from socialism was different in different countries (Cornia 1997). The development level, institutional setting, relations with the world economy, political system, culture, and climate for change were not identical. Of great importance were the distortions in industrial structures and in trade patterns.[3]

Though the socialist economies have frequently been analysed as though they were all more or less the same, they varied significantly. Actually, these countries were often all put in the same basket because of their political rather than their economic features. On the eve of the transition the 'socialist' or 'communist' countries were still being viewed as a group, although, from an economic perspective, Hungary and Poland, for example, seemed to fit more the mould of the (capitalist) market economy of Argentina or Malaysia than they did that of the more traditional socialist economy of Albania or Mongolia. Thus, in Eastern Europe, Hungary and Poland were reformed economies, and Yugoslavia exercised a distinct system of self-governance and decentralization, but there were also the rigid centrally planned economies of Albania, Bulgaria, Czechoslovakia, Romania, and the GDR, though this last enjoyed special links to the Federal Republic of Germany. The Soviet-style economies were not identical either. Whereas the Central Asian republics and Mongolia had some of the structural features of both the command economies and the less-developed countries, the Baltic States were more advanced. Likewise exceptional were the system and development level of the Asian socialist economies of China and—the poorest of them all—Cambodia, Laos, and Vietnam (Dodsworth *et al.* 1996).

Therefore, the burden imposed by the structural, institutional, and political features of the old economic system was not the same for these

---

[3] Popov (1998a) claims that up to two-thirds of the subsequent variation in the performance of transition economies is to be explained by these two factors.

countries, nor was the positive legacy of relatively high levels of education, labour skills, and income equality identical. The ability to adjust to new circumstances was not the same either.

Paradoxically, in some cases, factors which were supposed to become advantages in the process of marketization turned out to be hurdles. For instance, in Poland, unlike in other countries, collectivization had not succeeded, and the agricultural sector had remained predominantly a private one throughout the socialist episode. In 1989 about 80 per cent of the farmland in Poland was privately owned. However, soon after the onset of the transition, it became apparent that other nations were in relatively better shape in this area because socialist nationalization and forced collectivization in these nations had led not only to the dominance of state and cooperative farms, but also to the consolidation of farmland and, consequently, to more scope for efficiency. The size, structure, and capitalization of farms, as well as the way they are managed, have been more important in terms of efficiency and labour productivity than has the form of ownership.[4]

For the positive legacy, the financial and economic mechanisms used in the outgoing system were of primary importance. There was substantial variation in the specifics and in the solutions adopted in allocation decisions in the central planning machinery. The specifics and the solutions were never uniform anyway, and they became even more diversified as the market-oriented reforms progressed. In some countries they went quite far, albeit never and nowhere far enough. China is depending on allocation through the market much more today than ever before and is more advanced in the process of market reform than the Soviet Union ever was.

From this angle, one is justified in claiming that a decade ago, prior to transformation, the distance was shorter from, for instance, FYR Macedonia (then still a republic of socialist Yugoslavia) to capitalist Greece than it was from FYR Macedonia to its other nearest neighbour, orthodox socialist Albania.

By the same token, the Poland of the late 1980s was more like the distorted market economies of South America or North Africa than it was like Romania during the last years of Ceauçescu. Whereas the Polish economy was actually a mixed one with a growing private sector, in Romania the monopoly of state ownership was absolute. In Poland in 1989 over 50 per cent (in terms of value) of all prices were already free market prices, while in Romania all prices were fixed by the central authorities. In Poland there was a government antitrust agency and a policy of competition; in Romania the rigid state monopoly reigned. In Poland in the 1980s some

---

[4] This explains why, as late as the mid-1990s, though Hungary and Poland were structurally and institutionally so similar and though the share of agriculture in GDP was almost the same (6% and 6.6%, respectively), the share of labour employed in agriculture in Poland was still almost twice that in Hungary.

industries began to benefit from foreign direct investment, while the Romanian economy was tightly closed off from the outside world. In Poland in early 1989 the first decisions were taken in favour of exchange rate liberalization, and the black market in foreign currency ceased to exist; in Romania the state control over all currency transactions was tough and unbending.

These examples support a broader observation about the qualitative scope of diversity among socialist economies. One should not look at them in an oversimplified way as a uniform group, which they never were.

In some countries, such as Bulgaria, Hungary, Poland, or Yugoslavia, there was already a two-tier banking system in the 1980s, whereas in others a 'mono-bank' dominated (that is, the central bank also performed commercial banking functions). In these latter countries, networks of commercial banks were established apart from the central banks only in the early 1990s. While in most reformed economies some flexibility in currency regimes was introduced early on, in others this occurred when the transition was already under way.

The biggest differences, however, existed vis-à-vis the management and corporate governance of the state sector. In most reformed economies, like Hungary and Poland, but to an extent also in Bulgaria and the GDR, companies were rather independent from the influence of state authorities and managed their own businesses. This was very important in terms of the economics and politics of transformation. The more the economy had been decentralized and liberalized under the central planning regime, the more easily managed was the initial stage of the transition and the more favourable was the path toward a full-fledged market system.

This line of reasoning can be carried even further. For some time it had been apparent among at least some segments of the intellectual and political leadership of the former socialist states that 'real socialism' was doomed. Though it would be ridiculous to claim that this view was widely held in Albania under the Hozxa dictatorship or even among key economic experts and professionals in Czechoslovakia as late as the spring of 1989, it was surely widely held in Hungary and definitely widely held in Poland. In this sense, intellectuals (we include here leading economists) and reform-minded policymakers were preparing for a safe landing for the outgoing system and a smooth takeoff for the market regime, though this was never admitted publicly.

On both theoretical and pragmatic grounds, especially in Hungary and Poland, reformist political leaders and economists were preparing the way for the beginning of transition, and without this sort of commitment the vast changes would not have taken place. No wonder that, from a bird's eye view, the continuity between the early reforms and the recent stages of transition seems significant in certain countries (Kolodko 1989a, Csaba 1995, Poznanski 1997). It must be obvious that the more continuity there is, the better a country has performed during the transformation. The more firmly the intellectual and political foundations were laid for transition policies and management, the more the entire process of systemic change has gone forward smoothly. This is not only a theoretical conclusion stemming from the experience of the leading nations in the reform process, but also a piece of policy advice for nations currently lagging behind in transition. Some of them, like China and Vietnam, seem to have got the message on time.[5] Others, like Cuba and North Korea, have thus far failed to do so. Still others, like Belarus and Turkmenistan, now have a great chance to learn.

2.3. FINANCIAL DESTABILIZATION AND THE SHORTAGEFLATION SYNDROME

In the centrally planned economy the financial system played a secondary role. The direct mechanism of allocation typical of the command system was preferred, and financial arrangements were adjusted to it, not the other way around. Yet, here, too, conditions were far from uniform. In the nations which were further along on the road of market-oriented reform, financial intermediaries and instruments did not act exclusively as passive tools in planning procedures, but were having a growing impact on the economy. Because fiscal and monetary processes were more autonomous, financial equilibrium was put higher on the list of policy targets. The reforms introduced in some countries aimed only at the limited financial liberalization of the state sector. A more active part was to be played by credit redistributions and cash flows, within, however, the boundaries of central planning, which was still the leading actor. It was assumed that these reforms would improve efficiency and competitiveness. And this was so for a while, that is, until these processes started to fall out of control.

Contrary to the will and expectations of the authorities, the financial mechanism worked in such a way that there was a permanent inclination toward disequilibrium. This was reflected in various imbalances which spread throughout the economy. When it became obvious that the central plan was not going to be able anymore to remedy this systemic bias, a partial and managed liberalization was undertaken.

Initially, there was an improvement in efficiency due to the increasing flexibility and capacity to adjust to market signals and external shocks. This contributed to the healthier allocation of resources and to medium-term

---

[5] These countries have also learned from the so-called 'Asian economic miracle' (Stiglitz 1996). Despite the recent crisis (or maybe because of it), there are still policy lessons to be drawn from the East Asian region.

expansion. Later, owing to policy mistakes and the incompatibility between command and market instruments, imbalances reappeared, and inflationary pressure began to rise. There were shortages not only of consumer goods and services, but also of intermediate production goods, capital goods, labour, and foreign exchange. This affected both the domestic market and the export sector. Fiscal deficits started to become a subject of serious concern. In 1990 the deficit (central government balance) of Eastern Europe and the Soviet Union was estimated by the IMF at about 5 per cent of GDP. Public debt, including the foreign one, was on the ascent, too. The total foreign debt of the entire group increased from $154 billion in 1989 to $170 billion in 1990. Debt servicing obligations rose from $22 billion to $34 billion, and the ratio of debt service to export revenue climbed from 10.9 to 18.1 per cent. Total debt grew from 77 to 89.8 per cent of the value of exports. Because of a severe contraction in exports, this ratio jumped to 122.3 per cent in 1991, and these economies were brought to the edge of default. Poland especially was extremely close to defaulting.

In the late stages of the centrally planned economic regime in Eastern Europe and the former Soviet Union there were two significant groups of nations. First were the rigid, traditional command economies in which rather unsuccessful attempts were undertaken to adjust the flow of money to the flow of goods through administrative measures. Because prices were inflexible, this resulted in cumulative imbalances and growing shortages. Second was the group of countries which were aiming at the implementation of market mechanisms, though still within the limits imposed by the statist economy, and which were becoming susceptible to open inflation.

Governments had tried for a long time to achieve a balance through a positive supply response (that is, in terms of quantity growth). When this failed and price repression began generating mounting shortages, upward price adjustments became unavoidable. (Clearly, effective demand should have been contained by cutting real income, especially that of households, rather than by attempting to boost supply, which was futile given the severity of the imbalances.)

A sharp price jump was therefore implemented. This was intended as a once-and-forever measure, but after a while the cycle began to repeat itself. This was due to the residue of the structural roots of the disequilibria, mainly excessive demand, and was quite unlike the situation in a market economy. So, reform-oriented policymakers decided to abandon this sort of pricesetting in favour of market-like adjustments. However, the adjustments were very limited and modest, so that inflationary pressure started becoming a permanent factor. The strength of this pressure fluctuated, but it never disappeared completely. The more the economy was reformed (and a crucial segment of the reforms was focused on further price liberalization), the greater the acceleration in open price inflation (Table 6).

Table 6 Open inflation in centrally planned economies: CPI 1974–1990 (%)

	1974–83	1984	1985	1986	1987	1988	1989	1990
Centrally planned economies	3.0	3.5	4.4	5.4	5.8	7.3	18.3	21.2
Soviet Union	0.8	−0.1	0.7	2.1	1.5	0.3	2.3	5.4
Eastern and Central Europe	10.0	14.6	16.1	16.9	23.6	41.8	130.6	142.2

Source: IMF 1992.

On the eve of the postsocialist transformation, some countries still belonged to the first group of traditional command economies with relatively rigid prices, but also with vast and growing shortages resulting from repressed inflation. The second group of countries was already well on the road toward open inflation, though these countries were making progress in the introduction of market pricing, that is, the market clearing mechanism.

Of course, circumstances were not identical within either group. In the first group, Bulgaria, Czechoslovakia, and the GDR were less troubled by repressed inflation, and the shortages were not as severe or counterproductive as they were in Albania, Romania, or the Soviet Union. Within the second group, with partly liberalized prices, there were two patterns. In Hungary and Yugoslavia an ex-post balance between supply and demand was achieved by the classical market method (which, however, was unusual in a planned economy) of open inflation and upward price adjustments, which significantly contained the shortages. In Poland macroeconomic mismanagement caused by growing political tensions led to mounting shortages accompanied by accelerating price inflation.

Meanwhile, China and Vietnam have been quite successful (and for much longer) in executing gradual price liberalization. Though similar to those in the second group of countries in Eastern Europe, the policies in both these nations have restrained price inflation without causing shortages. This has been mainly due to a sound combination of development policies and systemic reforms. The reforms have aimed at boosting the supply side while achieving managed price liberalization. There has been remarkable growth in the supply of food products and other consumer goods, and the market for consumer goods has been by and large in equilibrium. Thus, inflation has seemed to be under control.

In contrast, in Eastern Europe the 'shortageflation syndrome' eroded efficiency and, owing to the queues, led to forced substitution and irritating rationing schemes which tended to wipe out the positive results of growing real consumption. Some nations experienced relatively significant price inflation, but limited shortages. This was the case in Hungary and Yugoslavia in the 1980s and in China and Vietnam in the first half of the 90s. Other economies exhibited huge shortages, but marginal open inflation, like Romania and the Soviet Union in the 1980s and Cuba and North Korea in the 90s.

And there was Poland, which suffered both severe shortages and high and accelerating price inflation, that is, severe shortageflation syndrome. In Poland at the end of 1989, inflationary overhang was estimated to be in the range of 25–35 per cent of the overall household money balance, or about 10–12 per cent of annual disposable household income (Gorski and Jaszczynski 1991, Kolodko 1991).

The course of events in Poland in the late 1980s was partly repeated by the Soviet Union at the beginning of the 1990s. In the Soviet Union forced savings had started to increase at an accelerated rate in 1985. The European Commission estimates that, whereas disposable household income that year was 371.1 billion roubles, forced savings stood at only 4.1 billion roubles, or only 1.1 per cent of total savings (EC 1990).[6] By 1990 this ratio had shot up to 20.4 per cent: disposable household income was 562.5 billion roubles, but forced savings had reached 114.5 billion roubles. These figures were still more important since they were used as the basis for a programme aiming at achieving a market economy in just 500 days.

Market clearing prices were essential for the proper functioning of central planning, and so they were all the more indispensable in the reformed system. Thus, even a partial price liberalization executed under the centrally planned economy must be seen as a positive factor later in the postsocialist transformation. If, in the aftermath of failed attempts to achieve partial liberalization and stabilization under the socialist regime, economic disequilibrium was still serious during the initial phase of transition, balancing it became more difficult. In turn, structural reform and the implementation of the market clearing mechanism could more readily go forward if the system had been liberalized, even if only partially, prior to transition. Sometimes, such as in the case of Hungary and Poland, early reforms aiming at liberalization were accompanied by destabilization and inflation, but the effort was nonetheless decisive in future developments, including the relatively short time needed for recovery. For countries with only modest price inflation (but with rigid price-setting), the situation was not as good because the inflation which then occurred during the early transition created additional hurdles, further delayed structural reform, and therefore also contributed to the postponement of recovery and growth.

---

[6] In 1998 the rouble was denominated by a factor of 1,000. 'Forced savings' are defined as the stock of inflationary overhang. Here, forced savings are calculated as actual savings, minus the savings that would have occurred (the flows) had the 1970–84 average savings rate applied (EC 1990, Shatalin et al. 1990).

2.4. GROWTH CYCLES AND STAGNATION
IN THE SOCIALIST ECONOMY

Contrary to a recently popular yet false belief, the centrally planned economies experienced a long period of sound growth, in some countries reaching from the late 1940s until the end of the 80s. Especially early on, rates of growth were relatively high. This was facilitated mainly by a remarkable expansion in investment, although the investment drive was periodically undermined because of the need for growth in consumption. Due to the constant absorption of labour (unlike in the market economies), there was full employment. However, this full employment was a by-product of excess demand and low labour productivity; indeed, employment was actually too full and thus rather a mixed blessing. So-called 'extensive'-type growth was dominant, meaning that priority was assigned to growth which was high speed in quantitative terms, while there was less concern about quality, efficiency, and a healthy relationship between input and output.

Because of their peculiar characteristics, the same factors which encouraged the acceleration in the growth in production also led in the long run to a creeping deterioration in competitiveness and in the ability to meet social needs. From this perspective, the growth of the socialist economies eventually came to be seen by many as vain, since it was believed that the rise in overall input could be even more rapid than the expansion in total output. This disharmony was reflected in the fact that indebtedness was increasing more quickly than was production. This indebtedness took the form of foreign debt, or, in light of the lack of a bond market, the forced savings of households, or both. As a result, because of mounting inefficiencies and imbalances, the potential for further growth was shrinking.

It had once been assumed that the central allocation of investment and of the means of production would foster economic expansion, which under socialism, unlike under capitalism, would not only be rapid, but would also continue smoothly. The business-cycle fluctuations typical of a market economy were not expected to appear. The theoretical arguments and official policy documents all predicted that the rate of growth would be relatively high, definitely higher than that under the alternative circumstances of a market economy. It was also believed that this higher rate of growth would be quite stable and would exhibit no significant ups and downs. The principal aim of macroeconomic policy was quick and steady output growth, which, it was anticipated, would lead to better standards of living. Investment outlays were treated as the main strategy tool to facilitate the accomplishment of this target. The absolute level of investment and the fluctuations in the investment rate were not only tolerated, but were used as a cushion for the otherwise less steady rate of growth. This explains why the breadth of the growth in investment or the fluctuations in capital formation were so substantial relative to the slower pace in the growth of consumption and to the still less volatile oscillations in the GDP growth rate.

If there was a slowdown, as happened for the first time after the initial phase of accelerated industrialization in the late 1950s, it was blamed on fortuitous occurrences, or new political leaders said their predecessors had made policy errors. For ideological and political reasons, the idea was rejected that the endogenous mechanism of policy-induced investment expansion and contraction could produce regular fluctuations in growth rates. If the economy was centrally planned, it was not supposed to develop cyclical processes which were indifferent to the will of the government.[7]

Nonetheless, under socialism, growth followed a pattern of quasi-regular cycles of acceleration and slowdown (Bauer 1978, Gruszczynski and Kolodko 1976, Kolodko 1976, 1987). Unlike national income, from time to time investment contracted, though the usual course of events was an acceleration followed by a deceleration in the long-term growth of investments. With some exceptions, the absolute level of GDP grew steadily over the medium and long term. It was the rate of growth that fluctuated. The rather regular growth cycle, usually lasting about four years, was quite evident (Table 7).

Whenever there was a risk (or was it an opportunity?) of a shift from socialism, be it Hungary after 1956, Czechoslovakia after 1968, or Poland after 1981, it was avoided not solely by the use of force. Force was a short-term instrument which could contain problems for a while, but which could not attack the structural roots of the problems. The only way to tackle the long-run challenge was to improve living standards. Yet, this was attainable exclusively through rapid growth. In fact, an acceleration in economic growth was evident during the periods following these political crises.

The other feature of the pace of long-term growth was a tendency to decelerate. Over a period of decades, the economy grew, but the long-run rate of growth was falling. Obviously, there is a causal relationship between the existence of growth cycles and the ability to maintain high-speed growth. The expansion drive eroded, with all the negative consequences for sustainable development. Growth was gradually losing momentum. In 1989–90 there was already a tendency toward stagnation. In each of the seven European members of Comecon there was a deceleration in the growth of national income in 1989, of which the most remarkable cases were Bulgaria, Poland, and Romania. Even more important, this time there was little possibility to rekindle growth, as had occurred so often before.

---

[7] When the author published his first research paper on this topic in 1979 in *Gospodarka Planowa* (*Planned Economy*), a leading periodical in Poland, the government censor changed the expression 'growth cycles' in the title of the paper to 'stages of growth' (Kolodko 1979).

Table 7 Economic growth cycles in centrally planned economies, 1950–1989

Years/Growth rate in net material product (%)

Bulgaria	—		1953–6 6.5 −	1957–9 14.0 +	1960–3 6.0 −	1964–7 9.1 +	1968–71 7.4 −	1972–5 8.3 +	1976–80 6.4 −	1981–5 3.5 −		1986–8 5.2 +	1989 0.5 −
Czechoslovakia	—	1950–2 10.0 −	1953–6 6.5 −	1957–61 7.4 +	1962–5 0.8 −		1966–9 7.2 +	1970–5 5.3 −	1976–8 4.7 −	1979–84 1.8 −		1985–8 2.4 +	1989 1.9 −
GDR	—	1950–2 18.0 −	1953–6 6.7 −	1957–9 8.7 +	1960–3 2.2 −	1964–9 5.0 +	—	1970–5 5.7 +	—	1976–86 4.4 −		1987–8 3.3 −	1989 2.5 −
Hungary	—	1951–3 9.3 −	1954–6 2.0 −	1957–60 11.0 +	1961–5 5.4 −		1966–9 7.2 +	1970–4 6.2 −	1975–8 5.0 −	1979–85 0.9 −		1986–8 1.6 +	1989 0.4 −
Poland	—	1950–3 9.8 −	1954–7 9.1 −	1958–63 5.4 −	—	1964–8 7.1 +	1969–70 3.7 −	1971–5 9.8 +	1976–8 4.9 −	1979–82 6.5 −	1983–5 4.9 +	1986–8 3.9 −	1989 0.2 −
Romania	—	1951–3 17.0 −	1954–6 5.0 −	1957–9 10.6 +	1960–2 7.6 −	1963–6 10.5 +	1967–70 7.0 −	1971–6 11.5 +	1977–9 7.7 −	1980–4 4.0 −		1985–8 5.4 +	1989 4.0 −
Soviet Union	1950–1 16.0 −	1952–3 8.2 −	1954–6 11.6 +	1957–63 6.0 −	—	1964–8 8.2 +		1969–73 6.5 −	1974–8 5.0 −	1979–88 3.3 −		—	1989 2.6 −

+ = acceleration; − = slowdown.

Sources: GUS various years and author's calculations.

The old system had reached its limits. This sparked the transition and a search for a new system able to speed up growth.

There would not have been such a severe recession in the early 1990s if the transformation had not been launched. If not for the political decision to shift radically toward the market economy, whatever the costs of adjustment, or, more simply, if not for the fact that in some instances, owing to the political climate, the authorities were losing control of the situation, the sluggish economic growth of the late 1980s could have continued for a number of years. There was no chance for a fundamental turnaround within the centrally planned economy, but there was a possibility to push ahead with the old methods of macroeconomic management. Consequently, there was also an opportunity to maintain growth, which, however, would have occurred at an ever slower pace. In any case, political factors, together with the economic ones (since neither set of factors alone would have spawned the transition toward a new system), meant that the continuity in the growth achieved through the old system was interrupted. There was a definite split: the old had ceased to exist, but the new was still only emerging.

The sharp decline in GDP in North Korea (by one-third in 1990–7) and the Cuban crisis in the 1990s may imply that the situation is similar in economies which have retained the old system and the old policies. But the North Korean and Cuban recessions have been due less to the features of these economic systems and more to the isolation of these systems from the world economy, an isolation which has been self-imposed in the former country and imposed from without in the latter. However, one might also say that the truth is in the opposite direction and that these economies are in crisis because of their recent inclusion in the world economy, that is, their significant exposure—caused by the collapse of Comecon and the dismantling of the old trade scheme with the former Soviet Union—to external shocks due to the withdrawal of subsidies and the shift to world prices.

If the economies currently in transition had not abandoned the old system at the beginning of the 1990s, output would not have increased much and might even have fallen somewhat in subsequent years. But if they had persisted along old lines, the duration of the period of stagnation and the scope of the recession would have been a function of the reforms carried out and the policies selected. If these hypothetical reforms had been executed in a comprehensive fashion, output might have soared, as happened in Hungary after 1968, in Poland after 1971, or in China and Vietnam more recently. If the hypothetical reforms had not been implemented, output would have shrunk, as indeed it started to do. But such considerations are nothing but pure speculation. The fact is that the transition was undertaken.

Detours

3

Systemic Change and
Economic Performance

3.1. ECONOMIC REFORMS AND GROWTH:
CHINA AND VIETNAM

High rates of growth might have been possible under socialism and the centrally planned economy. Growth could have been rapid and could have been sustained for long periods if only economic systems had been adequately reformed on time and development policies had been reasonable. This combination—reform and development policies—would have been necessary. There would have to have been the correctly fashioned reform of institutions, and there would have to have been appropriate development policies in line with the limitations and opportunities characteristic of the institutional system. A good system alone cannot offset a lack of sound development policy, just as sound development policy alone cannot compensate for a bad system. They are two sides of the same coin, namely, the long-term ability to expand.

It seems that in China and Vietnam, in contrast to pre-transition Eastern Europe and the former Soviet Union, this has not been overlooked. However, there are several questions: To what extent will these nations be able to maintain such high rates of growth while policy and the economy are being forced into the strictures of a mix of socialism and the market? Are they still implementing market reforms aimed only at improving the old socialist system, or are they already on the road from reform to postsocialist transition? If they are on the road to transition, does this mean that there has already been a shift toward a restoration of capitalism, though there has obviously not yet been a total rejection of socialism a priori? It may be too early to tell (Fan 1997).

China and Vietnam are the best examples in the history of the socialist economic system of a working combination of development policy and systemic reform. There seems to be no commitment, nor any alternative plans among the authorities in these two countries to abandon the socialist system, and such a turn of events should not be expected soon. Indeed, the leaders of these countries appear determined to save the system, and the majority of people seem to support them in this goal.

Anyway, time is short. Experience suggests that the socialist system cannot endure if one relies on the old structures, institutions, and policies. If the socialist system is to be maintained at all, this can only be accomplished through far-reaching change and sound adjustment to the new circumstances in the world economy and through a compromise with the expectations and the needs of society. The only possible way to protect socialism is to alter how it works without destroying its foundations. This will require further decentralization and liberalization within the limits imposed by the statist economy.

Though it may not yet be fully capitalist, the economic system of China has already changed to an incredible extent. The ruling party is quite pro-capitalist—or so it seems to be at least since the 15th party congress, which was held in the spring of 1998—and should not really be called 'communist' at all.[1] Can a party which has promised a policy shift from reform to transition and vast privatization, which has introduced a true labour market and allowed unemployment, which has downsized the state sector and closed loss-making enterprises, and which has encouraged mounting foreign direct investment and supported the expansion of capital markets really be called 'communist'?

There is another lesson the governments of the rapidly growing Asian socialist economies seem to have learned, too. Only if the economy is expanding quickly is political support forthcoming for the reform of the system, or at least only then can the active opposition against reform be neutralized. If in the 1980s the Eastern European countries and the former Soviet republics had shown the remarkable rate of growth of China and Vietnam, it is doubtful that they would be experiencing the sort of transition we are witnessing there now. A system evolves peacefully not because change is desired by intellectuals, suggested by the news media, welcomed by foreign investors, pushed through by international organizations, or insisted on by the governments of other nations. All these factors can only act as a catalyst for such a process if that process has already become inevitable within the country because real change is sought by the political leaders and backed by the aspirations of the people. If the expectations of the people can be met and social needs can be satisfied within the framework of the development attained through one system, then few will be keen to replace it with another system. According to the apparent logic of the Chinese and the Vietnamese, there is no such urgent compulsion to replace the system. Rather, there seems to be a conviction based on the observation of occurrences elsewhere that, rather than solve old problems, any drastic step may cause serious new ones.

---

[1] Likewise, there are political parties in all parts of the world that dare to call themselves 'democratic', 'liberal', or 'popular' when in fact they are autocratic, conservative, or elitist. The names seem to mean nothing.

The Eastern European and post-Soviet experience during the first decade of transition is indeed discouraging. Between 1990 and 1998 the GDP in Russia and Ukraine was halved, while the GDP in China and Vietnam doubled. One therefore really finds it impossible to conclude that the approach undertaken in Russia and Ukraine serves the purposes of development and progress better than the approach in China and Vietnam. This time there has been a negative demonstration effect arguing against a full-fledged transition to a market economy and Western-style democracy.

The Chinese and Vietnamese economies have not experienced any 'growth fatigue'. Their capacity for fast growth and sustainable development, led by active state policies within socialist-style institutional arrangements, is far from exhausted. But if the situation deteriorates, which may happen because of the external shocks, then the conservative attitude toward profound systemic transformation could rapidly lose support. Much more thoroughgoing liberal reform or even a transition to postsocialist institutional arrangements could be pushed to the fore by financial instability and a deceleration in growth. Thus, during the East Asian crisis in 1997–8, there was serious concern in China and Vietnam about the course of the reforms and of development. The impact of this crisis on the course of reform and the path of growth may even be greater than the influence of the Eastern European postsocialist transition. It has been pointed out that, in the case of Vietnam, the discussion now centres on the fact that

there are costs of reforms, but then also costs of not reforming, and as the East Asian crisis gets more difficult, the costs of not reforming rise. . . . Highlighting tough times ahead for Vietnam, the IMF said the government was working on economic reform initiatives but that some of the issues were overwhelming. . . . Vietnam's economy is being buffeted from all sides. Many donors urged the government to develop a two- or three-year road map in banking, state-owned enterprise, and foreign trade reform, with specific milestones for each year. (*Development News* 1998a)

There are three other questions which are quite important, especially since over 1.3 billion people live in China and Vietnam and this is four times more than the populations of the 27 countries of Eastern Europe and the CIS.

First, is there a limit to economic growth without a comprehensive transition to a full-fledged market economy? The answer is that it is feasible to sustain long-term high-speed growth under socialism, but only if reform becomes an ongoing effort to upgrade the economic and financial system, rather than simply a sporadic response to immediate situations. Given the complexity of today's technological, trade, and financial relationships, such dynamic growth would not be feasible in a traditional command economy, but it is compatible with market-oriented socialism, and this is being most clearly demonstrated by China and Vietnam. Moreover, rapid and long-lasting growth is possible, but only if proper attention is paid to development policy, which must not be viewed merely as a substitute for necessary systemic reform. Structural reforms and development policy must support each other.

The second question is: To what degree is a liberalized and partly free economic system compatible with a non-democratic political regime? The answer is difficult. The mixed results of the Eastern European reforms and the failure of glasnost and perestroika in the Soviet Union seem to suggest that such a system is incompatible with such a regime. At some point, which is not easy to identify ex ante, further economic expansion cannot occur without political liberalization. The free flow of information, the liberalization of capital transfers, vast labour migration, and the technological and financial linkages essential for international business activities: nowadays all these important components of growth require steady progress in the political arena. In an era of economic openness, the flow of capital and the related international linkages are such that they can be employed more efficiently within a framework of political freedom.

During the early stages of socialist industrialization and collectivization, especially in poor countries like China and Vietnam, it was easier to mobilize savings and labour under a central plan backed by a strong authoritarian regime. Today, it is easier to achieve economic progress within a democracy. The shift to more democracy is only a matter of time and a matter of the methods to be used to make it happen. In a sense, it is happening already, albeit rather gradually. Between the early and the late 'Deng-period' in China not only the economy, but also the political system and society were extensively reshaped, and there has continued to be qualitative change since then. Despite the greater speed and depth of the course of reform since the 15th party congress, the shift is still evolutionary. While it may not seem so spectacular as the shift in the postsocialist nations, it may be more effective from the standpoint of development.

Whatever its shortcomings, the Chinese political regime of the late 1990s shows signs of liberal change, at least relative to the 70s, though not necessarily to the 50s. The Chinese political system is non-democratic in comparison to the current system in Russia, but it is certainly mild in comparison to the harsh Soviet regime of only 10 or 20 years ago.

The evolution of change in Asia has been fundamentally different from that in Eastern Europe and the former Soviet republics. In Asia economic reform has led the way, with a significant time-gap, for political liberalization. In Europe, even among the frontrunning countries, economic reform is lagging behind the political changes which are occurring at revolutionary speed.

The third question which must be asked is: Aside from socialism and capitalism, is there a 'third way'? Certainly, a third way, no matter what it might be, no longer has any practical meaning for the Eastern European economies, including the poorest of them, like Albania and FYR Macedonia. Even the footdraggers like Belarus and the new Yugoslavia will in due time join the postsocialist mainstream in the region.

For the Central Asian countries of the CIS that are not so far along in the transition process there appears to be no third way either. However, though not entirely relevant for them, these nations probably have much more to learn from the experience of China and Vietnam than they do from advanced capitalism or Russian postsocialism (Simonia 1997). The components of the Chinese and Vietnamese reforms—such as the new institutional arrangements, the unorthodox approach toward macroeconomic stabilization, stepwise trade liberalization, limited currency control, the managed deregulation of capital flows, gradual privatization, openness to monitored foreign direct investment, decentralization in the administration of the state sector, support for joint ventures, and the transfer of power to local governments—are good examples of policies which may be more meaningful in Central Asia than are the experiences of more institutionally mature Eastern European transition countries.

Sometimes it may be better to arrive for a party late rather than early. Nations like Cuba and North Korea must learn the relevant lessons from the mixed results of the postsocialist transition in the CIS, as well as from the successful reforms in the socialist economies of Asia. Still practising orthodox socialism with only minor attempts at reform, Cuba in the late 1990s would be wise to learn as much as it can about the successes and the failures elsewhere and draw appropriate conclusions.

Cuba and North Korea have already been affected by a severe contraction in the 1990s. But there is an important difference between the recessions in the postsocialist economies and the ones in the unreformed socialist economies. In the postsocialist economies, the fall in output has occurred owing to demand constraints imposed for the sake of macroeconomic stabilization. In the unreformed socialist economies, the contraction has been due to supply constraints and the shortage phenomenon. So, if Cuba and North Korea can eventually follow the Chinese example or, even more relevant, the Vietnamese example, then they may have a chance of implementing a successful transition without further contraction. If a contraction takes place nonetheless, it should be a modest one, and one caused this time by demand constraints and not because of a crisis in supply. Thus, given the point of departure and the policy options, these economies are not doomed to further recession. It is a matter of policy choice.

However, given the political and geopolitical factors, we will likely see quite different patterns of development in these two specific cases. For Cuba one may expect an initial period of turmoil and destabilization, followed only later by an inflow of capital from the Cubans in the US and subsequent recovery and growth along the lines of other Latin American and Caribbean economies (Pastor 1997). For North Korea, there will be a gradually managed transition to an Asian-style market economy (Lee 1997). This process will last much longer than the German reunification. Hence the geopolitical aspect is going to be decisive. The future course of these two countries depends very much on decisions in Miami and Seoul, and these will restrain the policy alternatives.

3.2. TRANSITION AND CONTRACTION: EASTERN EUROPE AND THE FORMER SOVIET REPUBLICS

A long and complicated series of political and social, psychological and behavioural, structural and institutional, economic and financial events separate the postsocialist transition countries of today from the socialist economies, even the leading reforming ones, of a decade ago. Yet, many linkages are still intact, and the stronger they are, the more the outgoing system and the incoming one will possess features in common.

More linkages appear to have been broken in the countries in which, before transition, only tiny steps were taken toward a market-based economy. These countries have tended to suffer more shocks (not necessarily followed by therapy). Thus, for them, the whole process of postsocialist change has been more volatile.

Clearly, special attention must be paid to the continuity-discontinuity tradeoff. It is certainly wiser to try to orchestrate policies than simply to allow events to unfold willy-nilly. Discontinuity by design is less costly than discontinuity by chance. In this sense, ideological misgivings and political conservatism must sometimes be abandoned in favour of the tackling of problems head-on through government interventionism.

There is another consideration as well. In several countries where neither the reforms under socialism, nor the changes during the postsocialist era have been very far-reaching, either the transition recession has been relatively mild (Belarus and Uzbekistan), or the subsequent recovery has been quite robust (Kyrgyzstan and Latvia). We are dealing here also with continuity, but this time not with continuity in reform, but with continuity in the postponement of reform. Uzbekistan has experienced the mildest recession among all former Soviet republics. Its GDP in 1997 was 86 per cent of that in 1989.[2] In nearby Kyrgyzstan, Uzbekistan's more reformed neighbour which is also more advanced in transition, output had recovered only to 59 per cent of the pre-transition level. Yet, while the rate of growth in Uzbekistan in 1996–7 was only 2 per cent, in Kyrgyzstan, after a very severe contraction in 1991–5, the average rate was 8 per cent.

Likewise, while the GDP of Belarus in 1997 had already bounced back to 71 per cent of the 1989 level, in neighbouring Lithuania, which was

---

[2] The source of the statistics quoted in this section is EBRD 1998.

further along in transition, the corresponding figure was only 43 per cent. This does not mean that a lack of reform or a slow transition is better; it only goes to show that countries like Kyrgyzstan and Lithuania have been much more affected by discontinuity in these processes. In other words, the more profound the systemic change, the more severe the fallout in terms of a slowdown in manufacturing activity and losses in output.

Always cited as the country lagging behind the most with respect to institutional overhaul, Belarus is doing much better economically than some of the most radical reformers. It would nonetheless still be quite difficult to argue in favour of this model rather than, say, the model of the Czech Republic, where in 1997 there was only meagre growth of 1 per cent, despite the fact that in Belarus real GDP expanded by an impressive 10 per cent, one of the highest rates in the region. Of course, a one-year success does not mean that Belarus is doing well, just as the earlier sluggish growth in that country did not prove much. While it would certainly be difficult to convince the Belarusians that another country's 1 per cent growth is better than their own 10 per cent growth, the long-term tendency will tell the tale.[3]

There are still more depressing examples. In Ukraine the 1997 output was equal to a meagre 38 per cent of the 1989 GDP, and in Turkmenistan to 43 per cent. Unlike Bosnia-Herzegovina or Moldova, neither of these two countries has been involved in a civil war or a local conflict. This only points up the fact that, if there is significant continuity in institutional arrangements, if true institutional reforms fail, and if there are simultaneous policy fluctuations and inconsistencies, then production may shrink by a very big margin.

In advanced transition economies the medium-term pace of growth is climbing, whereas in the lagging countries it is falling. The prospects for growth are thus surely brighter in those nations which have already paid the price (albeit often excessive) for the shock of a break in continuity and which also have been able to introduce appropriate reform packages and exercise sound development policies. Such a sequence may change in the long run when the postsocialist economies which are now lagging behind in structural and institutional reform eventually take off toward full-fledged markets (De Melo, Denizer, and Gelb 1996).

However, future growth and development cannot always be seen as a substitute for past recession and policy failure, especially if an alternative path is available that might have led to a faster rate of growth in the long term. If deeper recession in the past has been a precondition for a higher rate of future growth, then there is certainly an economic and political dilemma. But if, as many examples clearly show, a severe slump does

[3] The EBRD (1998) has predicted growth of 2% for 1998 in both cases. PlanEcon (1997a, 1997b) has forecast an average of minus 0.7% for Belarus and an average of 4.7% for the Czech Republic for 1998–2001. (See the Statistical Appendix.)

not necessarily eventually enhance recovery and growth, then the slump should definitely be marked up to the account of policy error.

Of course, when huge recession is followed by sound growth, as in Poland, where there was an output collapse of about 20 per cent at the beginning of the 1990s and a remarkable GDP expansion of over 28 per cent in 1994–7, then arguments may be put forward that the former fostered the latter. Yet, in fact, this was not the case in Poland, because the contraction was mainly due to earlier policy mistakes, while the later success stemmed from quite different, even opposed, policies. Such a sequence— a dropoff followed after a time-lag by sound growth—is nonetheless likely to be repeated in other countries, including those still experiencing recession or early recovery, such as Bulgaria, Romania, Russia, and Ukraine. These economies are eventually going to turn around and will achieve durable growth, too.

It will still be difficult to claim that high-rate growth (where it occurs) has been achieved because of serious policy mistakes. This would be as bizarre as trying to explain a hypothetical expansion of Russian GDP of 30 per cent in, say, 2000–4 on the basis of the recession of 20 per cent in 1994–6 or of the current financial and political crisis. There are no historical cases in which there has been a causal relationship, after such a time-lag, between recession and growth, especially because one set of factors has led to the recession and another has led to the rise in production. Thus, *the postsocialist slump does not reflect any sort of 'investment' in the future, but has simply been a waste of precious time and energy*. Many countries could have done with a much milder contraction, if only because they would have been more quickly able to adopt a policy course similar to that of Poland after 1993.

One must add that, for recovery and growth, what has happened since the transitional contraction is important, but so is what happened before it. The reforms realized under socialism provided more flexible structures, organizations, and institutions. Hence, owing to the early introduction of certain market-type allocation mechanisms and private sector activities, it was easier to reach the stage of positive supply responses and initiate economic recovery after the fall of output. *The more extensively socialist centrally planned economies were reformed, the shallower and shorter was the transitional recession.* If this is true—and it is true—then the drive toward market-oriented reforms, not the commitment to the policy of 'the worse, the better', should be valued more ex post. The experiences of Croatia, Estonia, Hungary, Poland, and Slovenia have proved that the reforms under the old system have paid off and have contributed not only to the relatively faster implementation of the new system, but also to the milder recession and the more rapid recovery.

In Poland, the transitional contraction lasted 'only' three years, from mid-1989, when the Solidarity-led government took over, until mid-1992. If not for the previous reforms, this contraction would have lasted longer, as indeed occurred in a number of other countries which had not been keen to undertake systemic reform. By the same token, the decrease in output would have continued longer if not for the fundamental policy shift executed after 1993 vis-à-vis both development and systemic change.[4] Only an appropriate combination of initiatives in these two policy areas— development and systemic change—can solve the two problems of transition and growth. These are the two problems, and they require two suitable policy approaches which must be linked within a consistent strategy.

So, the lack of sound reform and adjustment, together with wrong policies, led to severe, long-lasting recession. The severity of the recession can be explained to some extent by what happened before the transition, not simply by what occurred during transition. Thus, some authors (Blasi, Kroumova, and Kruse 1997) assign Mikhail Gorbachev, the president of the former Soviet Union, at least part of the blame for the tremendous Russian crisis. They claim that he failed to introduce gradual market reforms. Therefore, he 'deprived the country of the crucial headstart which has made the capitalist transformation easier in countries such as Poland, Hungary, and China' (Freeland 1997a). Such a conclusion has more than merely historical significance, since *in several postsocialist (mainly post-Soviet) economies there is still room for an acceleration of certain reforms not in place of transition, but together with it.* It is precisely a matter of managing the continuity-discontinuity tradeoff. This is not easy, but it is feasible, as several countries, particularly Hungary, Poland, and Slovenia in Europe and China and Vietnam in Asia, have shown.

In 1998, after nine thorny years of recession, the average weighted GDP of the postsocialist countries was only 67 per cent of the pre-transition level. For 13 Eastern European countries, this figure stood at 98 per cent.[5] Thus, it took altogether nine years to recover (almost) the 1989 GDP level in Eastern Europe. In the case of the 12 members of the CIS, the situation was much worse because output in 1998 was equal to only 53 per cent of the pre-transition level (Table 8).[6] For this group of countries it will take at least a dozen or so years to recover the production levels reached before the Soviet Union collapsed. Altogether, the amount of time required for the great slump and the recovery to the pre-transition level of GDP is going to be close to an entire generation.

---

[4] In fact, some important changes had also been introduced in 1991 and especially in 1992–3. At least two crucial initiatives undertaken by three consecutive Solidarity-led governments must be mentioned. First, in May 1991 the fixed zloty-dollar exchange rate used as a nominal anchor in the stabilization programme was replaced by a more flexible crawling-peg mechanism. Second, in 1992–3 the government launched the so-called 'Enterprise Pact', which was designed to improve the relationship between employees and employers in the state sector and which was significant in the effort at structural reform.

[5] Bosnia-Herzegovina and the new Yugoslavia (Serbia and Montenegro) are not included in this accounting. The three Baltic States, Estonia, Latvia, and Lithuania, are included.

[6] The EBRD (1998) provides a slightly different index: 99% for Eastern Europe, 57% for the CIS, and 73% for this whole group of 25 transition economies (that is, excluding Bosnia-Herzegovina and the new Yugoslavia).

Table 8 Growth in real GDP in transition economies, 1990–1998

	1990	1991	1992	1993	1994	1995	1996	1997	1998	1997	1998
										(1989 = 100)	
Albania	−10.0	−27.7	−7.2	9.6	9.4	8.9	9.1	−8.0	10.2	79.1	87.2
Armenia	−7.4	−10.8	−52.6	−14.8	5.4	6.9	5.8	3.3	6.6	41.1	43.8
Azerbaijan	−11.7	−0.7	−22.6	−23.1	−18.1	−11.0	1.3	5.0	7.1	40.5	43.3
Belarus	−3.0	−1.2	−9.6	−7.6	−12.6	−10.4	2.6	10.0	−7.1	70.8	65.7
Bulgaria	−9.1	−11.7	−7.3	−1.5	1.8	2.1	−10.9	−7.4	3.5	62.8	65.0
Croatia	−6.9	−20.0	−11.7	−0.9	0.6	1.6	4.3	5.5	5.5	73.3	77.3
Czech Republic	−0.4	−14.2	−3.3	0.6	3.2	6.4	3.9	1.0	1.4	95.8	97.1
Estonia	−8.1	−7.9	−14.2	−8.5	−1.8	4.3	4.0	10.0	6.4	77.9	82.8
Georgia	−12.4	−13.8	−44.8	−25.4	−11.4	2.4	10.5	10.0	10.2	34.3	37.8
Hungary	−3.5	−11.9	−3.1	−0.6	2.9	1.5	1.3	4.3	5.4	90.4	95.2
Kazakhstan	−0.4	−13.0	−2.9	−10.4	−17.8	−8.9	1.1	1.8	3.8	58.1	60.3
Kyrgyzstan	3.0	−5.0	−19.0	−16.0	−20.0	−5.4	5.6	10.4	6.8	58.7	62.7
Latvia	2.9	−8.3	−34.9	−14.9	0.6	−0.8	2.8	6.0	6.0	56.8	60.3
Lithuania	−5.0	−13.4	−37.7	−17.1	−11.3	2.3	5.1	5.7	5.0	42.8	45.0
FYR Macedonia	−9.9	−12.1	−21.1	−8.4	−4.0	−1.4	1.1	1.0	2.8	55.3	56.9
Moldova	−2.4	−17.5	−29.1	−1.2	−31.2	−3.0	−8.0	1.3	1.2	35.1	35.5

Poland	−11.6	−7.0	2.6	3.8	5.2	7.0	6.1	6.9	6.5	111.8	119.0
Romania	−5.6	−12.9	−8.7	1.5	3.9	7.1	4.1	−6.6	−2.1	82.4	80.7
Russia	−4.0	−13.0	−14.5	−8.7	−12.6	−4.0	−4.9	0.4	−0.4	52.2	52.0
Slovakia	−2.5	−14.6	−6.5	−3.7	4.9	6.8	6.9	6.5	4.0	95.6	99.5
Slovenia	−4.7	−8.1	−5.5	2.8	5.3	4.1	3.1	3.3	4.1	99.3	103.4
Tajikistan	−1.6	−7.1	−29.0	−11.0	−18.9	−12.5	−4.4	2.2	4.5	40.0	41.9
Turkmenistan	2.0	−4.7	−5.3	−10.0	−18.8	−8.2	−8.0	−15.0	4.7	48.3	50.6
Ukraine	−3.4	−9.0	−13.7	−14.2	−23.0	−12.2	−10.0	−3.2	1.2	38.3	38.8
Uzbekistan	1.6	−0.5	−11.1	−2.3	−4.2	−0.9	1.6	2.4	5.8	86.7	91.8
GDP-weighted average[a]											
25 countries of EBRD	−5.0	−11.5	−10.5	−5.5	−7.1	−1.1	−1.3	1.6	2.5	71	73
Eastern/Central Europe	−6.8	−11.0	−4.1	0.7	3.5	5.3	4.2	3.5	3.9	95	99
CIS	−3.7	−12.0	−14.3	−9.3	−13.5	−4.9	−4.6	0.5	1.7	56	57

[a] Weights used are EBRD estimates of nominal dollar-GDP for 1996.

Sources: EBRD 1998. Projections for 1998 from PlanEcon 1998a, 1998b.

Similar quantities of the same goods delivered during the era of the state planning bureaucracy and now in response to consumer demand and market signals may be extremely different in quality, and this is important (Pinto, Belka, and Krajewski 1992). Thus, one may distinguish among different transition economies according to shifts in the level of production, but also according to the quality of production. There is currently strong market pressure for quality improvements because shortages are being eliminated (Kornai 1993). Production in the countries which are more advanced in recovery and transition is expanding, but the structure of output has also become substantially different (Estrin and Urga 1997).

If it is delivered in different times and under different systems, the same amount of production is not identical. For instance, GDP in Romania in 1998 was expected to recover to 86 per cent of the 1989 level, while GDP in Latvia was expected to reach only 58 per cent of this level. Nonetheless, Latvia—more advanced on the transition path—enjoys a more competitive output structure and therefore a higher quality of goods and services, though these welcome results are not always or entirely reflected in official statistics on production or in national accounts. The GDP produced in Poland in 1996 statistically matched the GDP produced in 1989, but this same amount of output was not directly comparable, because there were important quality and structural differences between what was delivered to the market then and what is being delivered to the market now. Moreover, these differences show up not only in the marketing of new models, new products, and new designs, but also in new technologies and new skills, geographical shifts in trade patterns, and other significant structural changes, including property rights (Table 9).

3.3. THE DRAWBACKS AND MERITS OF THE POSTSOCIALIST LEGACY

In the countries which undertook reform under the socialist order, the following political, social, and institutional factors have been particularly important for recovery and growth.

First, *a significant role has been played by pre-transition structural reforms such as partial price liberalization, limited foreign exchange liberalization, and the introduction of two-tier banking systems, antitrust laws, and bankruptcy regulations.* All these arrangements, though introduced to upgrade socialist systems, eventually facilitated market allocation and behavioural changes in line with the logic and values of the market system. In no case has there been any need to withdraw these arrangements; on the contrary, they have been reinforced.

Second, *the greater ability and flexibility of some entities—banks and financial agents, fiscal authorities, independent enterprises, local governments, trade*

Table 9 Structural changes in Poland, 1989–1997

	1989	1990	1991	1992	1993	1994	1995	1996	1997
Share of the private sector									
GDP[a]	28.6	30.9	41.7	47.2	51.9	52.2	57.9	60.1	64.1
Employment[b]	43.9	45.1	50.2	53.7	56.8	59.4	61.9	64.1	68.5
Industrial output[c]	16.2	18.3	24.8	28.2	34.6	39.4	46.9	52.4	61.7
Profitability of enterprises[d]									
Total	—	22.0	4.6	2.2	2.8	4.1	4.2	3.4	3.6
Public	—	—	—	3.0	3.7	5.2	4.8	3.1	3.5
Private	—	—	—	0.0	1.1	2.1	3.3	3.7	3.6
Direction of trade[e]									
Former Comecon	34.8	23.2	16.8	15.4	13.3	14.5	17.5	20.5	24.4
EU	32.1	44.3	55.6	58.0	63.2	62.7	70.0	66.2	64.0
Other	33.1	32.5	27.6	26.6	23.5	22.8	12.5	13.3	11.6
Share of exports in GDP[f]	5.8	9.2	13.3	13.3	13.6	16.0	18.0	18.4	20.1
Average tariff rate[g]	18.3	5.5	18.4	18.4	19.0	19.5	16.3	11.5	6.9
Share of administered prices in CPI basket[h]	19.0	11.0	11.0	11.0	10.6	12.0	12.0	11.6	10.6
Share of private banks									
Assets	—	—	—	—	13.0	18.6	26.9	27.9	
Capital	—	—	—	—	26.4	27.7	32.2	38.2	
Pension expenditure as a share of GDP[i]	7.1	8.1	12.2	14.7	14.9	15.8	15.4	15.2	15.2
Number of private businesses (000s)	830	1,171	1,473	1,698	1,944	2,071	2,061	2,356	2,539

[a] Since 1992, the share of the private sector in gross value added. [b] Annual average employment, including agriculture. [c] Industrial output sold; from 1993, excludes VAT. [d] Ratio of gross profit to total income (for 1992, the ratio of gross profit to total cost). [e] Share of exports to country groups in total exports; customs statistics (FOB). [f] Estimates based on balance of payments statistics; 1989–95 shares recalculated at 1996 real effective exchange rate. [g] Including free trade agreements. [h] Prices directly controlled by the government; end-year weights. [i] Including uniformed personnel and farmer pensions.

Sources: Central Statistical Office, Ministry of Finance, Central Planning Office, National Bank of Poland, author's estimates.

unions, and chambers of commerce—in adjusting to the new market rules have contributed to a more prompt positive supply response. Though weak, the market-oriented organizations designed to enhance the old system turned out to be the precursors of organizations which have proved indispensable in the true market environment. The decentralization of state sector management, the streamlining of local governments, and the more rigid financial constraints placed on state banks were all crucial in facilitating the continuity of economic processes and in supporting sustained growth.

Third, *the greater understanding of markets achieved among managers, bureaucrats, legal experts, intellectuals, and the news media rendered adjustment more effective.* Organizations and institutions can function well only when staffs are sufficiently knowledgeable to carry out the task of expansion under the market regime. In reformed economies the professionals were much better prepared to meet the forthcoming challenges. Their understanding of the principles and rules of the market economy and their practical ability to take advantage of this understanding in the design and management of initiatives have been crucial in guiding the course of the transition. In another apparent paradox, the destabilization caused by incomplete reforms and mistaken policies had an upside in the process of learning by doing. When the political environment changed, this experience could be used, this time to the full.

Fourth, *the existence of the more flexible private sector in agriculture provided an additional cushion against a severe fall in output.* Under socialism, agriculture and food processing were nationalized and collectivized. However, management and corporate governance in these areas were less rigid and less bureaucratic in some countries. Agriculture is still important in employment and output, particularly in relatively less-developed transition economies. Agricultural performance is vital in terms of urban household food expenditures and the consumption of food and thus also in terms of standards of living. In contrast to the advanced market nations, the average share of food in household expenditures in the European transition economies hovers between 35 and 55 per cent. Clearly, a fall in food production is no minor event. However, in general, the slump in agriculture was milder in countries with a relatively large private sector in farming and more decentralized state farming policies.[7]

Fifth, *the development of a small- or medium-size private sector and especially of small local companies in non-rural areas had a great impact on later business expansion.* The allocation of resources through markets tended to foster more growth if the entrepreneurial spirit already existed. The wider the scope of private sector activities during the socialist reform period, the stronger the push for profit-oriented expansion during the early transition.

---

[7] Nonetheless, agricultural sector restructuring in Poland, despite the fact that agriculture was mostly in private hands, was more difficult than this sort of restructuring in the Czech Republic or Hungary, where agriculture had been collectivized (see earlier).

In Hungary, Poland, and Yugoslavia in the 1970s and 80s and in China and Vietnam in the 90s, despite the limitations of the socialist regimes, the private sector took root and grew. In Poland in 1989, prior to the transition, 20 per cent of GDP was already being produced by the private sector, half of which (outside agriculture) was accounted for by small and medium ventures.

Sixth, *early foreign direct investment paved the way for greater inflows of capital that boosted the ability of the economy to grow.* Unlike the more recent situation in the Asian socialist countries, the foreign investment in Eastern European socialist countries was insignificant in value. However, it nourished new institutional arrangements and more flexible regulatory measures. Albeit quite limited, the concessions in favour of the liberalization of the foreign exchange regime and the decentralization in investment procedures facilitated foreign capital inflows, as well as domestic business. Special priorities and solutions first introduced exclusively for the sake of foreign investors were later expanded, thereby contributing to liberalization in other areas. Though this was never exercised as widely in Europe, not even in Hungary or Poland, as it has been in China (witness the experiment with special economic zones in that country), it was still quite important, particularly with respect to the quicker supply response at the onset of transition.

Seventh, *early membership in international financial organizations, especially the International Monetary Fund and the World Bank, led to acceptance of structural adjustment programmes backed by the additional financing provided by these organizations and other financial institutions, particularly investment and commercial banks.* Several Eastern European countries, including Hungary, Poland, Romania, and Yugoslavia, were members of the Bretton Woods institutions before the transition and could take advantage of this connection as long as the authorities were able to reach appropriate decisions about the necessary policies and as long as these organizations were not used by the industrialized countries as a lever for sanctions and restrictions.[8]

While it is true that the great output collapse which took place in the 1990s in the vast area from Central Europe to the western coast of the Pacific was closely tied to the transition from socialism, it is also true that the remarkable growth of the Asian socialist economies is closely linked to the comprehensive reform of socialism. No pattern can be clearly read from these developments, except that *neither the reforms, nor the transition can be*

---

[8] Such a lever was used against Poland for several years during the 1980s and then against Romania in the early 90s. Romania sought to forge agreements with the IMF, but prior to the radical attempt at reform in 1997 the relationship was often rather difficult. Assistance to the Romanian government was suspended or frozen several times. Romania obtained its first Compensatory and Contingency Financing Facility in March 1991 and its first Stand-by Arrangement the following month. Some republics of the former Yugoslavia, such as Croatia for a short time, and the new Yugoslavia also fit this category.

blessed or blamed for events in the economy; it is policies which have been crucial. There are examples of good policies and of bad policies in both cases, and there are also examples of growth and recession in both cases. Good development policies undertaken within the well-designed institutions of a market economy are certainly much better than bad development policies exercised within an unreformed socialist system. But comparing different combinations of good and bad features is like comparing apples and oranges. Bad development policies which are applied in an attempt to transform the old system into a better one (that is, the market economy) have sometimes produced even worse results than has the mixture of good development policies implemented exclusively within the framework of the old system of socialism.

It is obvious that the transition in Eastern Europe and the former Soviet republics has been linked to a severe output collapse lasting from three to eight years. But it is also true that the transition deserves credit for the recent acceleration in growth in the region and, hopefully, even better performance hereafter. Meanwhile, not socialism, but the comprehensive and wisely designed reform of socialism deserves credit for the sound growth of the Asian socialist economies. Likewise, not the socialist system, but the political inability to reform it in a timely way ought to be blamed for some of the barriers to economic expansion in countries which have since decided to transform the overall system as the only means to ensure sustainable long-term growth.

4

Transitional Recession: Expectations, Reality, Interpretations

4.1. LIBERALIZATION, STABILIZATION, AND THE GREAT SLUMP OF THE 1990s

The more severe the shortageflation syndrome, the greater the financial instability at the onset of the transition. Although it would have been much easier to liberalize the economy under conditions of equilibrium and relative balance between supply and demand, this option was not available. Some economies, like those of Czechoslovakia and the GDR, were more balanced than were others, like those of Hungary or Romania. The disequilibrium in Hungary was rendered evident mostly through open inflation, whereas in Romania the inflation was primarily repressed. In other nations, most spectacularly first in Poland and later in Russia, there were both types of imbalances—open and repressed inflation—at the same time.

Precisely because of such extremely unfavourable circumstances, overall liberalization became even more necessary. During the initial stage of postsocialist transition, thoroughgoing liberalization was a fundamental principle, together with privatization and new market institutions. One problem was the identification of the best method for controlling the impact of liberalization, especially in terms of output, employment, investment, and consumption. Whatever the rationale for change over the long run as regards the greater efficiency and better ability to expand of the liberal market regime, the change had to be guided through the difficult short and medium term.

For instance, because of the burden of repressed inflation and the potential for it to explode the moment prices were freed, the acceleration of inflation was rightly anticipated as an immediate consequence of liberalization. For obvious reasons, open inflation acts against efficiency, too. Under conditions of rapidly rising prices, it would have been close to impossible to improve the allocation of resources and facilitate growth. So, price liberalization in distorted postsocialist economies must be accompanied by stabilization if long-term efficiency is to be attained. Otherwise, one malaise is merely replaced by another. Repressed inflation is wiped out by open price-wage inflation, but the inefficiencies remain; only the mechanism is changed. No matter which sort of inflation there is, the price signals are still distorted, and investors and manufacturers are still being misled. The losers and the winners might be different with one or the other type of inflation, but the shift from one to the other would not have any positive effect on the overall propensity to save. The savings ratio might even be lower under open inflation than it is under repressed inflation which is accompanied by shortages.

It is therefore necessary first to liberalize prices and later to stabilize them. This is the only time when it makes sense to consider radicalism versus gradualism. Whereas privatization and institutional arrangements must last for years, liberalization measures and stabilization policy can be imposed for a short time if the political situation permits. The response to the policy choice between radicalism and gradualism is a function of the magnitude of financial instability and should be based on a government's capacity to carry out socially unpopular initiatives. The bigger the instability, the more justified are 'radical' stabilization measures, but the more radical the stabilization policy, the more severe is the following contraction. Furthermore, in such a case the radical stabilization policy is not only more justified, but also, for psychological and political reasons, more suitable. Of course, this is so only for a limited time, since, if the policy is effective, it will not be needed for long, and, if it is not effective and the first attempts at stabilization fail, society's resistance to the policy will start to rise. This was the situation in a number of postsocialist countries, and it made the transition exercise still more difficult.

The core tactic of a macroeconomic stabilization policy is the containment of excessive aggregate demand. If the stabilization policy is executed in a radical manner, then demand is going to contract in real terms. Real household income can be held down in various ways, including through strict administrative controls, despite the general orientation toward liberalization. In some circumstances, a standard wage-based taxation mechanism can be used as an instrument of wage control, especially in the state sector, which is characterized by more lenient wage discipline relative to the private sector. But the only way to control wage growth over the longer run is to impose hard budget constraints on both private sector and state sector enterprises. For the private sector enterprises the main tool is a fundamental change in the corporate governance of companies which have just been privatized. The new system of incentives, especially the responsibility of managers for the financial well-being of their companies, acts as an automatic check on wage expansion. For the state sector enterprises direct income policy instruments must be used, but also intermediate fiscal and monetary instruments.

Thus, putting a cap on aggregate demand during a period of liberalization calls for restrictive fiscal and monetary policies. Heavy taxation is used to remove excessive liquidity from companies and households. Very high (in real terms) lending rates are employed to the same end. In such an environment, the contraction in demand carries over into a contraction in supply. This had never occurred under the centrally planned system, where there were always shortages of almost everything—capital, labour, foreign exchange, raw materials, consumer goods—except money. Now, it seems as though there is an abundance of everything, and the only shortage is the shortage of money. The reaction to this crucial change is immediate; first aggregate demand, then aggregate supply go into sharp decline, and the economy enters recession. The greater the containment of excessive demand, the bigger the recession.

This is why stabilization and liberalization led to transitional recession, but it does not explain why output shrank by such a huge margin. It shrank so much because the stabilization policy overshot the mark. Indeed, *at least some of the contraction associated with the transition would have been avoided if severe policy mistakes had not been made in managing the liberalization and in the nature and the timing of the measures used to achieve macroeconomic stabilization.* The strongest argument in support of this thesis is the inflation itself. In every country it was higher than expected and lasted for a longer time than expected. The miscalculation of the rate of inflation was on a greater scale than even the underestimates of the amount of contraction in output. And the inflationary period is not over yet, since inflationary inertia is still very strong (Table 10).

Hence the roots of falling production are in macroeconomic stabilization policy, which, by aiming at the removal of shortages and the introduction of market clearing prices, generates a contraction in production as a negative offshoot of the demand constraints imposed for the sake of equilibrium under any system, but particularly when the point of departure is unfavourable.

This is especially so in postsocialist countries. It is inevitable that aggregate demand will be brought down to the level of supply, which is already shrinking, but in postsocialist countries nominal and real demand must initially be curtailed by a greater amount than would be the case under similar circumstances in a free market economy. In a free market economy, because of market clearing prices, the disequilibrium in the flows of aggregate supply and aggregate demand is the main challenge. This is so since, in a destabilized free market, there is no stock of forced savings, that is, no money is being held involuntarily. In contrast, under a centrally planned regime, such a situation occurs all the time. As a consequence, excess liquidity occurs, too.

Thus, under the centrally planned regime, there were imbalances in the flows and in the stocks of money. Accordingly, the amount of the reduction in effective demand had to be sufficient to eliminate the excessive liquidity created both by the flows (current nominal income) and the stocks

Table 10 Inflation in transition economies, 1991–1998
(% change in year-end retail and consumer price level)

	1991	1992	1993	1994	1995	1996	1997	1998
Albania	104.0	236.6	30.9	15.8	6.0	17.4	42.0	14.0
Armenia	25.0	1,341.0	10,896.0	1,885.0	32.0	5.8	21.9	13.0
Azerbaijan	126.0	1,395.0	1,293.8	1,788.0	84.5	6.7	0.5	4.5
Belarus	93.0	1,159.0	1,996.0	1,960.0	244.0	39.2	63.1	84.0
Bulgaria	339.0	79.4	63.8	121.9	32.8	310.8	578.6	17.0
Croatia	250.0	938.2	1,149.0	−3.0	3.8	3.4	3.8	5.0
Czech Republic	52.0	12.7	18.2	9.7	7.9	8.6	10.0	11.5
Estonia	304.0	953.5	35.6	42.0	29.0	15.0	12.0	11.0
Georgia	131.0	1,177.0	7,488.0	6,474.4	57.4	13.8	8.1	8.0
Hungary	32.0	21.6	21.1	21.2	28.3	19.8	18.4	14.0
Kazakhstan	137.0	2,984.1	2,169.0	1,160.0	60.4	28.6	11.3	8.5
Kyrgyzstan	170.0	1,259.0	1,363.0	95.7	31.9	35.0	14.8	12.1
Latvia	262.0	959.0	35.0	26.0	23.0	13.1	7.0	5.0
Lithuania	345.0	1,161.1	188.8	45.0	35.5	13.1	8.5	6.8
FYR Macedonia	230.0	1,925.2	229.6	55.4	9.3	0.2	4.6	5.0
Moldova	151.0	2,198.0	837.0	116.0	23.8	15.1	11.2	10.0
Poland	60.0	44.3	37.6	29.4	21.6	18.5	13.2	10.0
Romania	223.0	199.2	295.5	61.7	27.8	56.9	151.6	47.0
Russia	144.0	2,508.8	840.1	204.7	131.3	21.8	11.1	10.0
Slovakia	58.0	9.1	25.1	11.7	7.2	5.4	6.4	7.0
Slovenia	247.0	92.9	22.9	18.3	8.6	8.8	9.4	8.0
Tajikistan	204.0	1,364.0	7,344.0	1.1	2,133.0	40.5	165.0	19.3
Turkmenistan	155.0	644.0	9,750.0	1,328.0	1,262.0	446.0	21.5	50.0
Ukraine	161.0	2,730.0	10,155.0	401.0	182.0	39.7	10.1	19.0
Uzbekistan	169.0	910.0	885.0	1,281.0	117.0	64.0	28.0	35.0

Sources: EBRD 1998. Data for 1990–6 represent the most recent official estimates in publications of national authorities, IMF, World Bank, OECD, PlanEcon, and Institute of International Finance. Data for 1997 are preliminary, mostly official government estimates. Data for 1998 are EBRD projections.

(inflationary or monetary overhang). It was therefore easy inadvertently to restrain demand too much. Especially the IMF and orthodox monetarist economists were inclined to promote policies which wiped out not only excessive demand, but even some non-excessive demand. So, overshooting occurred in stabilization measures and in stabilization targets, with all the negative by-effects of too much contraction in demand and subsequently too much contraction in output (Kolodko, Gotz-Kozierkiewicz, and Skrzeszewska-Paczek 1992).

The situation varied from country to country (Bruno 1992, Blejer and Skreb 1997). In the stabilization programme of 1990 in Poland, not only was the devaluation of the exchange rate overshot, but also aggregate demand was reduced too much, and fiscal and monetary policies were too restrictive. It appears that in some postsocialist economies the primary budget balance was overshot, too (Table 11).

Table 11 General government balance in transition economies, 1990–1998 (% GDP)

	1990	1991	1992	1993	1994	1995	1996	1997	1998
Albania	−15.0	−31.0	−20.3	−14.4	−12.4	−10.4	−11.4	−17.0	−14.8
Armenia	—	−1.8	−8.1	−56.1	−10.1	−12.0	−9.3	−6.7	−5.6
Azerbaijan	—	—	2.8	−12.7	−11.4	−4.2	−2.6	−2.8	−3.0
Belarus	—	—	0.0	−1.9	−2.5	−1.9	−1.6	−2.7	−3.3
Bulgaria	—	—	−5.2	−10.9	−5.8	−6.4	−13.4	−2.7	−1.6
Croatia	—	—	−4.0	−0.8	1.7	−0.9	−0.5	1.4	2.1
Czech Republic	—	—	−3.1	0.5	−1.2	−1.8	−1.2	−2.1	−0.9
Estonia	—	5.2	−0.3	−0.7	1.3	−1.2	−1.5	2.3	1.7
Georgia	—	−3.0	−25.4	−26.2	−7.4	−4.5	−4.4	−3.8	−3.0
Hungary	0.4	−2.2	−6.8	−5.5	−8.4	−6.7	−3.5	−4.6	−4.9
Kazakhstan	1.4	−7.9	−7.3	−1.3	−7.2	−2.0	−2.5	−3.4	−4.5
Kyrgyzstan	0.3	4.6	−17.4	−14.2	−11.6	−17.2	−9.6	−9.2	9.0
Moldova	—	0.0	−26.2	−7.4	−8.7	−5.7	−6.7	−7.5	−7.5
Latvia	—	—	−0.8	0.6	−4.1	−3.5	−1.4	1.3	−0.4
Lithuania	5.4	2.7	0.5	−4.3	−5.4	−4.5	−4.0	−2.4	−3.0
FYR Macedonia	—	—	−9.6	−13.6	−3.2	−1.3	−0.4	−0.6	−0.8
Poland	3.1	−6.7	−6.6	−3.4	−2.8	−3.6	−3.1	−3.0	−3.0
Romania	1.0	3.3	−4.6	−0.4	−1.9	−2.6	−3.9	−4.5	−5.0
Russia	—	—	−21.6	−7.4	−10.4	−5.7	−8.2	−7.5	−6.0
Slovakia	—	—	—	−7.0	−1.3	0.2	−1.9	−3.4	−2.1
Slovenia	−0.3	2.6	0.2	0.3	−0.2	0.0	0.3	−1.5	−1.0
Tajikistan	—	−16.4	−28.4	−23.6	−10.2	−11.2	−5.8	−3.5	3.0
Turkmenistan	1.2	2.5	13.2	−0.5	−1.4	−1.6	−0.2	−0.5	−5.0
Ukraine	—	—	−25.4	−16.2	−7.8	−4.8	−3.2	−5.8	−4.0
Uzbekistan	−1.1	−3.6	−18.4	−10.4	−6.1	−4.1	−7.3	−2.3	3.0

Note: General government includes the state, municipalities, and extrabudgetary funds. Balances are reported on a cash basis except for Albania and Poland. Data for Armenia refer to the consolidated state government, for Croatia to the consolidated central government, and for Uzbekistan to state and extrabudgetary funds.

Sources: EBRD 1997a, 1998. Data for 1990–6 are the most recent official estimates in publications of national authorities, IMF, World Bank, OECD, PlanEcon, and Institute of International Finance. Data for 1997 are preliminary, mostly official government estimates. Data for 1998 are EBRD projections.

At the very early stage of structural adjustment, overly narrow fiscal policies led to unnecessary budget surpluses and simultaneous output declines (Kolodko 1992b). Unfortunately, only later, when the harm had already been done, was it recognized (though not by all the key actors) that the financial squeeze imposed on the state sector had been too severe and that this had contributed to an unnecessary drop in production. In 1992 the IMF admitted that 'In some Eastern European countries there were substantial budget and current account surpluses in the early stages of the reform programmes, which might, ex post, suggest that macroeconomic policies could have been less restrictive' (IMF 1992, p. 46). This conclusion should not have been reached 'ex post', since there was plenty of warning ex ante. Regrettably, the alarm bells went unheeded.[1]

Despite a belief common in some academic and financial circles, it is not true that there is no difference between fiscal deficits in the post-socialist economies and those in less-developed market economies. At the initial stage of stabilization, so-called 'perverse fiscal adjustment' began to produce results which were quite opposed to those anticipated, including additional falls, instead of rises, in tax revenue (Kolodko 1992c). The extraordinary one-time revenues which had been gained through the taxation of the windfall income accrued by companies through the unloading of inventory and the sale of appreciating spare foreign exchange had led to balanced budgets and even transitory surpluses. After a short period of improvement, however, a contraction generated a more rapid drop in revenues than in expenditures, and the deficit charged back up. This happened in several countries. For example, in Poland in 1992, after the lull, the deficit climbed to 6 per cent of GDP. A pro-inflationary, trade-protectionist import surcharge of 6 per cent was therefore imposed to raise extra revenues and face down the threat of further fiscal destabilization. This import tax was gradually eliminated in 1995–7.

Aside from the overshooting, if not sometimes the overkilling, of stabilization targets, there was another key factor in the drop in production. This was linked to trade liberalization (Rodrik 1990). Though liberalization does enhance growth in the long run, this was not the case over the short and medium term. Output fell more than was justified by the contraction in aggregate demand because domestic production was being replaced by imports. These imports were often subsidized by foreign manufacturers, who were looking for new opportunities to expand and thought they had found them in the postsocialist emerging markets. But because local companies were not yet ready to meet the challenge of trade liberalization and exposure to foreign competition, domestic output declined even further.

One must distinguish trade liberalization and the removal of quantitative barriers from the combination of tariff abatement and devaluation that they caused. While the pace of liberalization may have been right, the tariff abatement and devaluation were so excessive that there were reversals very early on, and tariffs and import surcharges had to be reintroduced. It became common for transition economies to lose thereby the easy access to regional markets that they had enjoyed prior to trade liberalization. Even close neighbours undergoing transition were crowded out of each other's markets by more developed competitors. The substitution of imports for domestic output beyond any economic rationale drove countries still more deeply into recession. Trade liberalization accompanied by the foreign

[1] Among others, see Kolodko 1989a, 1991, Frydman, Kolodko, and Wellisz 1991, Laski 1990, Nuti 1990, van Brabant 1990, Caselli and Pastrello 1991, Rosati 1991.

exchange undervaluation which had been enforced by the sudden opening had serious inflationary implications and led to worsening terms of trade. *The more radical the trade shocks, the bigger the contraction and the longer the recovery* (Roland and Verdier 1997).

In another typical situation in centrally planned economies, the shift away from monopolistic structures resulted in a long-lasting shortageflation syndrome, whereby it became very easy to sell everything, but quite difficult to buy anything. The idea of putting suitable domestic enterprises on a similar footing with foreign ones seemed to be correct from the point of view of the removal of shortages and encouragement for market balance. In fact, this did contribute to short-term stabilization, but it also contributed to output decline. Part of domestic output was replaced in the flood of imports. If this problem was tackled through an effective strategy of export-led growth, the threat diminished after a couple of years. But if export expansion was insufficiently facilitated, then a new set of problems emerged, especially with respect to trade and the current account balance (Roubini and Wachtel 1997, Tanzi 1997a, EBRD 1997b, IMF 1998a). Whereas Russia and Ukraine, enmeshed for so long in acute recession, have had trade and current account surpluses, the more successful economies, like the Czech Republic, Estonia, Hungary, Poland, Slovakia, and Slovenia, have reported growing deficits (Table 12).

The healthiest response would have been even stronger export-led growth and additional inflows of foreign direct investment. This sort of absorption of foreign savings is the best way to fill the gap between domestic savings and overall investments. Unfortunately, it is not easy to achieve in an early phase of transition. Export expansion calls for a rather mature ability to compete on global markets, and this in turn requires more trade liberalization and a certain amount of integration within the world economy.

However, there is a risk that mounting difficulties with current account sustainability may hinder this process and provoke an opposite policy reaction, that is, a resurgence in protectionism and the postponement of additional and appropriate liberalization measures. If this occurs, one can expect the rate of growth to slow again, although the current account deficit is brought temporarily under control. This type of tradeoff has been a clear alternative in development policy. It is a challenge in relatively more open economies which have decided to liberalize current accounts and deregulate capital flows. During the transition, before liberalization began yielding positive results (greater competitiveness, foreign market access, and inflows of foreign direct investment, along with new technologies, expertise, and managerial skills), the negative consequences of these reforms were more evident (that is, falling output and rising unemployment).

When the reality turned out to be so far from the promise, odd attempts were sometimes made to excuse the policy failures. The exceptional

Table 12 Current account and trade balance in transition economies, 1996–1997

	Current account balance, 1997	Merchandise trade balance, 1997	Current account balance, 1997	Merchandise trade balance, 1997	Change in current account balance, 1996–7	Change in merchandise trade balance, 1996–7
	($ millions)		(% GDP)		(% change in GDP share)	
Albania	−195	−415	−8.5	−18.0	0.8	−7.8
Armenia	−428	−559	−23.4	−13.8	−0.4	−6.1
Azerbaijan	−961	−569	−23.6	−8.0	0.2	−5.8
Belarus	−995	−1,497	−7.5	−11.2	−0.7	−1.3
Bulgaria	184	311	1.8	3.0	0.5	0.8
Croatia	−1,900	−4,800	−10.3	−26.1	−5.6	−6.7
Czech Republic	−3,156	−4,600	−6.1	−8.8	1.5	1.7
Estonia	−610	−1,188	−13.1	−25.6	−3.4	−1.6
Georgia	−318	−366	−6.2	−7.1	−1.3	0.8
Hungary	−987	−1,700	−2.2	−3.8	1.6	2.2
Kazakhstan	−1,000	−500	−4.8	−2.4	−1.4	−0.9
Kyrgyzstan	−187	−134	−11.5	−8.2	12.5	12.6
Moldova	−310	−275	−14.9	−13.2	−1.4	0.2
Latvia	−350	−887	−6.4	−16.3	−0.5	−0.4
FYR Macedonia	−254	−343	−8.1	−10.9	−0.8	−2.3
Lithuania	−945	−1,115	−10.3	−12.2	−1.0	−0.6
Poland	−4,300	−11,300	−3.2	−8.4	−2.2	−2.4
Romania	−1,900	1,414	−5.5	4.1	1.8	8.8
Slovakia	−1,500	−1,500	−7.9	−7.9	3.2	4.3
Slovenia	70	−770	0.4	−4.3	0.2	0.4
Russia	3,900	16,600	0.8	3.5	0.3	−0.4
Tajikistan	−15	−5	−1.3	−0.4	5.8	3.2
Turkmenistan	−596	−245	−26.1	−10.7	−28.0	−17.5
Ukraine	−1,500	−4,800	−3.1	−9.9	0.3	0.2
Uzbekistan	−754	−254	−5.2	−1.8	2.7	5.1

Note: Changes in the current account and merchandise trade balances in 1996–7 represent the difference between the ratios of the current account and merchandise trade balances to GDP in respective years. The current account balance for Armenia excludes transfers.

Sources: EBRD 1998. Data are the most recent official estimates in publications of national authorities, IMF, World Bank, OECD, PlanEcon, and Institute of International Finance.

dropoff in production was explained in every way possible except as a mistake in the policies of governments, central banks, or international organizations. This is how a link was made between 'external shocks' and the transitional recession.

Of course, external shocks can occur any place any time, and they were real troublemakers in the complicated situation in which the transition countries found themselves. However, the external shocks which have most frequently been assigned a leading role in the tremendous slump in post-socialist economies were all of a very specific nature. Aside from the often exaggerated impact of the 1991 Gulf War, which occurred at the onset of the transition, of great importance were the collapse of the old Comecon trading system that was felt especially in Cuba, Eastern Europe, Mongolia, and Vietnam and the disintegration of the Soviet Union that particularly affected the trade of the Baltic States and trade among the CIS countries.

There can be no doubt that these represented acute shocks for many industries in these nations. However, it should also be remembered that the disappearance of Comecon was actually a self-imposed shock. The authorities in these nations who, with the blessing of international organizations, dismantled Comecon disregarded possible intermediate solutions which could have provided an alternative to the old trade regime (van Brabant 1990). Temporary schemes for inter-CIS trade could have been worked out (indeed, some are being used now) so that these economies could have had breathing space before it was necessary to trade among themselves exclusively at world prices and solely in convertible currencies. As it was, the lack of a proper trade regime was a very significant factor in the decline in production capacity in the former Soviet republics.

The real reason for the contraction in the trade of the Baltic States and in trade among the CIS nations—sometimes as high as 90 per cent—was the significant domestic price distortions. Whereas the prices of the primary goods and raw materials traded among Comecon members had been set since the 1970s on the basis of the most recent five-year moving average of world prices, in the Soviet Union they were fixed by central government fiat, often with little concern for world prices. So, the trade between, say, Armenia and Lithuania relied on prices which were different from those used in the trade of the same goods between, say, Armenia and Hungary, or Hungary and Romania.

Overall, the Eastern European countries were more well prepared to open their economies to the world. Whereas over 90 per cent of the total exports of some Soviet republics, such as Estonia and Moldova, went to other Soviet republics, more than half the exports of some Eastern European nations, like Hungary and Poland, went to non-socialist economies.[2] In this case,

---

[2] A comparison of the trade of Canada's provinces and the trade of the Soviet Central Asian republics is striking. The export and import turnover relative to GDP was similar in

geopolitics was a positive factor. The more a country had traded with non-Comecon partners prior to the transition, the easier it was for that country to absorb the external shocks associated with the transition.

Among the nations outside Europe that were members of Comecon, but that had little to do with the dissolution of the trade bloc, the response to the (external) shock of the disappearance of Comecon was quite different. The worst was the reaction of Cuba, which did not apply any trade liberalization. Cuba's policies remained mainly inward oriented. Only later did the country change direction slightly, especially by permitting additional and much-needed foreign direct investment, which was aimed mostly at the vibrant and lucrative tourist industry. Nonetheless, Cuba was hampered at every step by the US-led sanctions, which were being enforced for political reasons.

With the keen technical assistance of liberal experts from New Zealand, Mongolia, in contrast to Cuba, lifted all trade tariffs and barriers and exposed itself completely to free trade. This remote Asian nation has thereby gone further with trade liberalization than any other postsocialist economy.

The example of a middle-of-the-road reaction is offered by Vietnam. After the dissolution of Comecon, an event which was an external shock for this country, too, Vietnam implemented a gradual, though determined liberalization of foreign trade and capital flows. This has turned out to be quite successful and, together with other structural reforms, has contributed to durable export-led growth.

Two conclusions are drawn here from these examples. First, the more rapid the liberalization of trade, the bigger the initial shock and the deeper the ensuing recession. Second, the more progress realized by the new trade regime and the more substantial the supporting policies, the stronger the ability to recover later on. However, was it really necessary to liberalize trade in such an extreme fashion for the sake of better performance later? Wouldn't it have been possible to launch export-led growth without provoking such a severe fall in production? The correct answer to these two questions is 'yes'. It should have been possible to expand trade and achieve growth in a more gradual way, especially vis-à-vis exports to developed market nations.

This time, it appears that the proper lessons were learned, if not immediately, then at least not too late. After first overshooting in trade liberalization, several countries turned to an approach which was more gradual. In no transition economy has the initial expansion in trade been sustained unless it has been supported later by well-designed industrial policies and policies aimed at export-led growth. After the first significant shifts in trade

both cases, but up to half the trade of Canada's provinces was sold outside Canada, while only about one-tenth of the Soviet Central Asian trade went outside the USSR. The bulk of this sliver of foreign trade was used in barter transactions with other Comecon countries or with less-developed countries closely linked to the USSR (Pomfret 1997).

structure toward the new markets and the subsequent strong export-push driven by domestic demand constraints, the rate of growth in exports started to decline. Only sound policies, together with (rather than instead of) deliberate liberalization and microeconomic measures targeting a rise in competitiveness, were able to respark export growth.

The initial great slump also stemmed from the liquidation of negative value added output.[3] Under the usual price controls employed in the central planning system, it was possible for output to be exported at prices fixed not only below world prices, but also below the world prices for the production inputs (McKinnon 1991). Sometimes, raw materials were supplied to manufacturers at subsidized prices and then used to produce export goods. Such export-boosting schemes were profitable for enterprises, although they were not so profitable from a macroeconomic perspective. After the adjustment of prices and the withdrawal of subsidies, export output had nowhere to go but down.

4.2. POLICY MISTAKES

Although a transitional recession was inevitable, the true cause of the collapse in output was not external shocks, the legacy of the past, or any other uncontrollable circumstances. The real driving force behind the great slump of the 1990s was policy mistakes. The most severe of all was the fact that *the mistaken policies were based on poor diagnoses and wrong economics.*

The postsocialist economic environment in Eastern Europe and in the former Soviet republics, despite frequent statements to the contrary, was not like the situation in Western Europe after the Second World War, nor were the transition economies like the distorted Latin American economies of the 1980s. Hence the policies applied for the sake of liberalization, privatization, structural adjustment, and new institutional arrangements should not have relied too much on the lessons from these experiences. But they did.

It is easier to act if there is a pattern, a benchmark, a point of reference which can be used as a guide. However, such a guide is not always available; sometimes the context is quite unique. This has certainly been the case of the postsocialist transition. Yet, many felt the need of an analogy, a model for comparison. This was too often true of experts, international organizations, and non-transition governments. Thus, for instance, their lack of understanding of the real legacy of central planning and the claim that the end of Soviet-style socialism meant the end of the cold war

[3] The real GDP of Eastern Europe and the CIS shrank by almost 24% in 1990–2, the first three years of transition: almost 21% in Eastern Europe and over 27% in the CIS (see Table 8).

combined to suggest to many of them the analogy of the aftermath of the Second World War (Eichengreen and Uzan 1992, Kiyono 1992, Wolf 1992).

Even the name of the new regional bank which was very quickly created (through the initiative of French President François Mitterrand) for the purpose of providing financial assistance to transition countries—the 'European Bank for Reconstruction and Development' (EBRD), in London —suggests not only the need for 'development' in the region, but also the need for 'reconstruction', presumably because there was a previous 'destruction'.[4] The other regional banks—the Inter-American (IADB) in Washington, the Asian (ADB) in Manila and the African (also known as ADB or AfDB) in Abidjan—are all merely 'development' banks.[5]

However, the analogy with the postwar period is quite misleading and inappropriate. *The socialist centrally planned economies had not been devastated and destroyed, nor had they gone bankrupt.* Increasing inefficiency and falling productivity meant that these economies were unable to compete with the rest of the world or to meet the growing demands of their own populations. Yet, unlike the situation in many places immediately following a war, these countries possessed healthy, well-educated, skilled, and intact human resources which could be used in a more purposeful manner if only the labour market could be made more flexible and the allocation system more innovative. Although there were sectoral labour shortages, there was no overall shortage of labour, only a sort of 'hidden' unemployment or overemployment. The other productive assets were also considerable, though they had not yet been put to the most effective use (due to price distortions, but also because of the cold war and the arms race). This was clear after the introduction of the new 'rules', when these assets were quickly shifted toward the production of the goods demanded by the market. Indeed, the instant these assets were privatized, prospective buyers emerged, including foreign ones. There was also an extensive infrastructure of roads, electricity grids, railroads, ports, and telecommunications networks.

In some countries there were vast shortages, and the 'quasi-markets' were regulated by central governments. In extreme cases, this may have reminded some people of the price controls exercised during wartime or under the traditional socialist command economy.[6] Nonetheless, these nations (perhaps with the exception of Romania under Ceauçescu) had been significantly reformed, and the economic mechanisms of the late 1980s had hardly anything to do with the 'war communism' of the early years of

---

[4] The influence of the transition countries on the decisions of the bank is rather minor. In this sense, these countries are the newsmakers rather than the decisionmakers.

[5] The official name of the World Bank is 'International Bank for Reconstruction and Development' precisely because it was founded especially to assist in 'reconstruction' after the Second World War.

[6] In Poland even the special decree imposing martial law in December 1981 referred to a 'state of war'. This was so because the constitution did not allow for a 'state of emergency'. Despite this, any analogy with a real war or with postwar reconstruction would be ridiculous.

the Soviet Union or even with the rigid central planning regime of the Stalinist era. Nor did the economic systems have much in common with 'war economies' or with the economies of Western Europe during postwar reconstruction (Charlesworth 1955).

It was therefore a mistake to speak of 'another Marshall Plan' or of the 'aftermath of the cold war', since this suggested that the policies implemented during the initial years of the postsocialist transformation should achieve the same sort of outcomes accomplished immediately after the Second World War, and this was unrealistic.[7]

Thus, the policy advice in a number of cases was based upon wrong assumptions and ignorance of the postsocialist reality (Sachs 1989). The conditions at the outset of the transition were very different from those affecting other types of distorted economies, so the remedies applied should have varied as well (Edwards 1992). Yet, instead of serious concern about the unique problems of transition countries, the policy analysis and the advice were based too much on orthodox economic thinking.

Before Fiat, the Italian carmaker, launched a new model aimed at emerging markets, the company contracted a team of engineers from countries like Brazil, Poland, and Turkey to design an automobile which would be suited to the poor road conditions in these countries. But before the West proposed policies for the postsocialist transformation, it did not create such a team. The policy blueprints for these nations were designed by outsiders who were not very familiar with the real issues and mostly ignored the suggestions of local economists and other local experts. Instead of an attempt to understand the peculiar circumstances in the distorted socialist economies, there was an insistence, sometimes even arrogant, that the proposed remedies represented the only option. No wonder the resulting vehicle produced such a bumpy ride on the transition motorway.

Only after several difficult years of profound change did the differences between Eastern Europe and South America or Southeast Asia start to evaporate. Meanwhile, the challenges were accumulating. Dealing with the rise in unemployment from nil to 17 per cent in Poland was not the same as dealing with the rise in unemployment from around 12 per cent to 17 per cent in a market economy like Argentina. A similar rate does not mean a similar difficulty. Whereas unemployment had not been seen in Poland for generations, in Argentina the problem was an old one, perhaps no less

---

[7] A misleading analogy of this sort could be heard in reference to German reunification, too (Akerlof et al. 1991). Nonetheless, the reincorporation of the five Länder of the 'late' GDR into a reunited Germany was quite a different kettle of fish from a postwar reconstruction, including the one which had taken place earlier in the western part of the country. Not surprisingly, the output collapse in the former GDR was greater than expected; the recovery came later than anticipated, and the costs of unification were much higher than planned. The institutional reforms, which were indeed 'radical' in this exceptional case, did not produce the predicted results.

damaging to society, but familiar nonetheless. Likewise, dealing with an increase in the share of the private sector in GDP from nada to about 80 per cent in the Czech Republic was not the same as boosting the share of the private sector in the GDP of Peru from 60 to 80 per cent. It is one thing to expand the private sector if one already exists, and quite another to develop one out of the blue.

That some of these early policies have eventually delivered welcome results, including recovery and growth, should not outweigh the fact that, though these policies may be effective now under changed conditions, they were not effective nine, six, or even three years ago. It was not necessary to experience a tremendous economic slump in order to reach a point where policies proposed years ago could finally start to work. They might have worked even better if transition had been managed in a better way and if the costs of transition had not been so harsh. Unfortunately, the price had to be paid, and it was paid. Naturally, the people of the nations in transition got the bill, since the consequences of policy are always borne by the people.

During the early stages of transition there were several substantial policy inaccuracies. The most important was *the mismanagement of the state sector*. One might have anticipated that, due to the rigidity of this sector toward relative price changes, there would be an initial lack of positive supply response to rapid and thoroughgoing liberalization, since this would initially mean further destabilization and the accelerated inflationary redistribution of the flows and stocks of capital and resources. The deflationary measures and overall liberalization were bound to lead to a negative reaction which would be reflected in an additional slowdown in already sluggish economic activity, rather than in an immediate restructuring of capacity and appropriate adjustments on the input side. Some orthodox liberal policymakers even believed that industrial policy should be abandoned altogether, but the attempts to do so had dreadful economic consequences.

The discriminatory fiscal tightness imposed on state enterprises, ongoing financial redistribution between profitable and loss-making firms through monetary instruments, and deficiencies in the corporate governance in state companies, including the failure to alter performance criteria or to establish growth-oriented systems for management evaluation, favoured resource misallocations, divestment, and falling output.

There was also a delay in the commercialization of public enterprises. For instance, commercialization was enforced in Poland only in 1996, and in some transition economies it has not yet been enforced. If it was not feasible to introduce such reforms at the time of the financial squeeze and before price and trade liberalization, at least they should be advanced as much as possible now.

Several mistakes have been linked to the *poor sequencing of policy measures*. Everything cannot be done at once, so it is always necessary to take some steps earlier, and some later. The sequencing of transition measures is no less important than the accurate design and appropriate implementation of the measures. Sometimes it is worse to take certain steps in the wrong sequence than not to take them at all.

First, *state companies should be formed into corporations at the onset of transition, that is, before privatization*. If corporatization and demonopolization are carried forward at the same time that hard budget constraints are imposed on state enterprises, this ought to force through microeconomic restructuring and accelerate improvements in competitiveness. Not surprisingly, the delay in implementing these reforms generated unnecessarily high price rises and additional income redistribution, while cutting into the ability to expand. Privatization which is carried out too soon can also tend to foster existing monopolies, since state assets are often sold before the demonopolization and restructuring take place.[8] The sequence should therefore be different because private monopolies are no better than state ones; actually, they are worse.

Second, *the regulation of capital markets should precede the liberalization of capital flows, and a system of bank supervision and deposit insurance should be introduced before the banks have been decentralized and privatized*. Unfortunately, in many countries the constant pressure to accelerate deregulation and privatization on the one hand and the exploitation of the naïve expectations of the public about the performance of the emerging capital markets on the other created serious difficulties in financial sector restructuring. Measures intended to stimulate the propensity to save and encourage capital formation sometimes caused people to lose their money and their good will. To recover the former, though very difficult, may be easier than reclaiming the latter.

Third, *fiscal reforms and adjustment should be sequenced carefully*. Thus, for example, measures to make the taxation of the private sector more efficient and to boost the collection of indirect taxes, like the value added tax, ought to be applied prior to or at least simultaneously with macroeconomic stabilization. Only then will it be possible to offset (of course, only more or less) the fall in the revenues so far provided mainly by the direct taxation of state enterprises.[9] Attempts at sound fiscal reform were undertaken (unsuccessfully) in Russia at the insistence of the IMF only in 1998, after the great economic slump and the 'great redistribution' had already taken their toll. Tax evasion had by then become endemic in the

---

[8] A good example of a bad sequence in these areas was the demonopolization in the Czech Republic of the electricity utility after privatization had been undertaken.

[9] In the socialist economic system there was no significant personal income tax. This sort of taxation was introduced only later during the transition.

private sector and even among big state companies. The lack of fiscal discipline and of a fiscal culture led to the edge of the financial brink after GDP had fallen by half and the constant fiscal deficit had come to mean that civil servants could not be paid and that the outlays for public sector services had to be postponed.

Fourth, *the sequencing was wrong for particular components of monetary policy, for instance interest rate adjustment and new exchange rate management.* The attempt to establish a positive real interest rate at the very outset of stabilization programmes caused a credit crunch which drove a number of firms into liquidity crises, non-performing inter-enterprise debt, and mounting arrears (Calvo and Coricelli 1992). At the same time, in several cases, real deposit interest rates were negative. Such lending ratios and deposit interest rates could not help overcome inflationary expectations. Exchange rate management was often inconsistent with the policy on interest rates, and, as the NBP, the independent central bank in Poland, proved in 1994–5 and again in 1997–8, the poor coordination of interest and exchange rate adjustments can cause a wave of short-term speculative investment. The rapidly growing foreign reserves fuelled inflationary pressure which in turn weakened government anti-inflation policy.[10]

The effort at stabilization was undertaken before privatization in several countries, including the Baltic States, Croatia, Hungary, Poland, and Slovenia and, under different circumstances, China and Vietnam. This is no mistake; to go the other way around would simply not be feasible. The claim that the initial great slump was caused by the delay in privatization (Sachs 1993), thereby implying that there was an alternative in the sequencing of stabilization and privatization, is incorrect. No matter how serious the commitment of a government may be to the rapid and comprehensive execution of privatization, the process is very complex and requires much more time than does stabilization. Of course, the privatization process may be pushed through more quickly and more extensively than has yet been the case, but this would not alter the proper sequence (Frydman, Rapaczynski, and Earle 1993). Over the short term, a formal programme of privatization (that is, the legal transfer of property rights to private entities) may represent the salvation of particular firms, but it cannot guarantee improvements in the macroeconomic situation, including the aggregate supply response and financial equilibrium.

---

[10] For the monetary policy of a central bank, rather than government fiscal policy, to cause inflation is quite bizarre. Early criticism of the NBP's poor management of monetary policy was disregarded. Only in May 1998 did the bank admit (indirectly) that its previous policy had been wrong. Despite the fact that the inflation rate was not falling (for the first time since the beginning of the transition, the inflation rate in the first half of the year was higher than it had been in December of the previous year), the NBP rightly decided this time that there was room for a decline in the interest rate so as to discourage any further pro-inflationary growth in foreign reserves.

4.3. THE FAILURE OF 'SHOCK THERAPY' AND 'CREATIVE DESTRUCTION'

It is now easier to understand why, contrary to expectations and promises, the biggest failures of the transition process so far have been meagre economic growth and the lack of a strong positive supply response. Profound systemic and political change has not delivered economic expansion and an improvement in living standards. It remains a hard truth that the post-socialist recession was extremely severe, despite attempts to massage the statistics, often in order to distort the picture and hide the real scope of the drop in output (Winiecki 1991).

Whatever the truth of the claims about the non-policy causes of the output collapse, the full extent of the decline in production cannot reasonably be explained only by such causes (Gavrilenkov and Koen 1994). D. Mario Nuti (1992b) rightly says that

this state of affairs is not a necessary concomitant of transition, nor a consequence of 'shock therapy' which might be eased by a more gradualist approach, but the totally unnecessary consequence of policy failures. . . . To a very great extent, these failures are linked with ideological totems and taboos, namely, obsession with mass free privatization and with instant free trade and prejudice against the state sector and any attempt at improvement and reorganization.

Ideologically and politically motivated endeavours have thus been undertaken to explain the great slump, and, not surprisingly, they try to minimize the dire consequences of the reliance on wrong economics and wrong policies. Confusion about the various processes—such as the shortage removal effect, the liquidation of negative value added output, and the elimination of unregistered economic activities—has sometimes led to weird opinions. Thus, because of the complexity of the changes, some argue that the contraction was better than growth would have been, that the decline in real wages was better than an increase, that the higher prices were more suitable for consumption than lower ones, and so on. For instance, Jan Winiecki tries to repeat his earlier assertions about the existence of improvements in standards of living and in the general economic situation despite the great slump, while suggesting in a curious way that

An Estonian who bought a packet of Western-made (and therefore reliable) condoms for $1 in 1991 was spending 3% of his monthly income. Now he is spending [after a contraction by one-third in GDP] less than 0.5%, so the relative price to him of these high-quality foreign goods has fallen steeply—a rise in his living standard that most measures would ignore. (Quoted in *The Economist* 1997b)

One now pays relatively less in real terms if incomes and prices are expressed in dollars, of course, but if they are denominated in the local currency, which happens after all still to be the legal tender, one pays much more. Besides, if only Western-made products are reliable in a nation aspiring to join the European Union after a decade of transition, then why has it been necessary to undergo a transition in the first place?

There are abundant reasons to be an ardent fan of the transition. It is not necessary to try to support it through mistaken declarations and trivial and vague arguments. While it is true that some products were poor in quality and that in a few extreme cases the value added during the manufacturing process was negative, such output was not so significant, nor has other production been substituted for it since its disappearance. So, whatever may have been the truth about the good or bad quality of the Trabant, the little jewel of the East German automotive industry, despite any negative value added involved in production, the car cannot be 'replaced' in GDP accounts by the current lack of a brand-new BMW.

It might be objected that the elimination of negative value added activities should raise rather than reduce GDP. But it has only been since price liberalization that the negative nature of many productive activities has been revealed. Cutting away negative value added activities raises GDP with respect to what it would have been without such a cut, but it still causes GDP to fall with respect to the earlier levels achieved when domestic prices diverged from the opportunity costs and from international prices. During the transitional contraction a great deal of output was wiped out in a radical way, without speedy replacement by other production. At most, the drop in output was substituted by a rise in imports. Some companies were crowded out of the market by the credit crunch, especially by the prohibitively high real interest rates imposed not only on new loans (a justified measure, considering the need for a financial squeeze for the sake of successful stabilization), but on old debt, too.

Another deluded attempt to overstate the volume of production involves pointing to unregistered economic activity. The more such activity was repressed under the socialist regime, the more it seemed to mushroom up immediately after the start of the transition. For this reason, the relative weight of the shadow economy at the outset rose more, for example, in Lithuania than it did in Hungary and more in Romania than in Croatia. Later, owing to the process of absorption, the relative importance of this segment of the economy declined, and the decrease was more rapid in the more advanced nations with healthier institutions and better regulation. The rates of the early expansion and of the later relative decline of shadow economies have varied, but the size of these economies are smaller now. Even if unregistered production now accounted for one-third or even one-half of official national income, certainly at the current stage of transition it would be growing much more slowly, not more quickly, than the reported portion of output.

By definition, unregistered economic activity cannot be measured precisely (Kaufmann and Kaliberda 1995). Only rough proxy estimates are feasible (*The Economist* 1997c).[11] However, this should not serve as an excuse to add non-existent goods and services to output. In any case, if the unreported slice of GDP were as big as is sometimes suggested, it ought to be (but is not) included in the baseline against which later contraction or growth is measured. In other words, while a shadow economy may puff up the level of real GDP, it does not necessarily affect the reported rate of growth or rate of decline. Moreover, transition must also be seen as the gradual process of the institutionalization of informal economic activities. In this sense, in relative terms the scope for these activities decreases as the market evolves. The more advanced the processes of liberalization, privatization, and institution-building, the smaller the scope for a shadow economy.

There have been some interesting assessments of the share of the shadow economy in transition nations. Kaufmann (1997a) estimates that in 1994 the share ranged from only 10 per cent in Uzbekistan and 15 per cent in Poland to as much as 40 per cent in Russia and 64 per cent in Georgia. According to Kaufmann, the unweighted average hovered around 30 per cent of GDP. After the initial surge at the beginning of transition, the share seems to have been falling, except perhaps in the more disintegrated (as opposed to the more deregulated) economies, like Russia and Ukraine, and in countries engaged in local conflicts, like Albania, Armenia, Azerbaijan, Bosnia-Herzegovina, and Tajikistan.[12]

For other reasons, the shadow economy is on the ascent in the distorted economy of Cuba, where rapidly growing parallel economic activity is a by-effect of the shortageflation syndrome. The attempts at limited liberalization, combined with the reforms undertaken lately by the Castro Government, also allow for some expansion of the shadow economy. However, the efforts to bring the shadow economy under control are not bearing

---

[11] This segment of the economy is estimated to contribute from 15% to 50% of GDP in certain less-developed countries. For advanced market economies, the GDP share of the shadow economy is estimated at around 15% for the European Union, and below 10% for the US. The situation in the postsocialist countries is anybody's guess. 'The Russian tax police First Deputy Director Vasily Volkovsky told *Nezavisimaya Gazeta* that one-third of Russian businesses are not paying any taxes, and a further 50% pay tax only occasionally. Volkovsky said in the next few years the authorities intended to aggressively scale down the grey economy to a level at which it ceased to pose *a threat to Russia's economic security*. He said the grey economy accounted for 45% of GDP in 1996' (quoted in IMF 1998b; emphasis added).

[12] In Russia the data have been further distorted by corrupt government statisticians who were seeking to help companies which had bribed them for the purpose of tax evasion. Yet, for some, every cloud seems to have a silver lining: 'In one sense, the scandal is good news. In effect, the officials are being accused of taking money to underestimate the production of Russian enterprises and therefore to help minimize the companies' tax obligations. That indicates that Russia's economy is larger than the Government's statistics suggest. The International Monetary Fund, for instance, has privately estimated that Russia's economic production is roughly 20 per cent greater than official estimates' (*New York Times* 1998, p. 3).

It appears that in Russia almost everything is becoming 'privatized', even the opinion of the IMF about the share of the informal economy.

fruit, so some of these activities are continuing without government monitoring or reporting and, of course, without the taxation of earned income. Similar phenomena occurred in several East European nations in the 1980s. Cuba seems poised to repeat the familiar sequence of liberalization accompanied by an expanding parallel economy, followed by a period of shrinkage in unregistered activities as they gradually become institutionalized.

In the reformed socialist economies of China and Indochina (Cambodia, Laos, and Vietnam) the parallel economy has grown more quickly in recent years than has overall production. This has occurred because thoroughgoing liberalization has been associated with poor fiscal administration. The shadow economy in China is believed to represent around 20 per cent of GDP, although some estimates—rather unrealistic—go as high as 50 per cent. For example, 'Jim Walker, an economist at Crédit Lyonnais, estimates that the underground economy is 20–30% of GDP in South Korea and Malaysia and 30–50% in China, Indonesia, and Thailand' (quoted in *The Economist* 1998a). Yet, it is rather inappropriate to call these types of activities 'underground', since they are taking place very much 'above ground'—directly on the streets—and are legal, even though they may not yet be reflected in official statistics or taxed.[13]

Under socialism there was justified criticism of so-called 'official optimism'. Strangely, this sort of optimism became widely practised during the first postsocialist years, even among international organizations, which took it to new heights. If this 'official optimism' had been more accurate, output would now be at least half again as much as it actually is. Unfortunately, year after year, the reality turned out to be less than the prediction. There has not been a single year in which a major international organization or respected research group has been able to predict the actual amount of economic contraction, and they are also all inclined to overestimate the rate of economic expansion in cases in which this is already occurring.

For instance, in the spring of 1991 the IMF predicted that the rate of GDP growth in Eastern Europe would be minus 1.5 per cent in 1991 and 2.8 per cent in 1992 (IMF 1991). In autumn 1992 the IMF re-estimated growth during these years at minus 13.7 per cent and minus 9.2 per cent, respectively (IMF 1992). So, instead of the anticipated cumulative growth of 1.3 per cent predicted earlier for these two years, the exceedingly optimistic forecasts were replaced by the expectation of an output collapse of

[13] This is a matter of definition, too. If the notion 'shadow' or 'parallel' economy is supposed also to include organized crime, then the higher estimates of the share in actual GDP may be proper, and the notion 'underground' would indeed be quite justified. Nonetheless, there is no good reason to include in such estimates the 'market' value of criminal activities like drug trafficking, illegal gambling, prostitution, kidnapping, extortion, contract killings, and so on. The concept 'shadow economy' is relevant only if it encompasses activities which contribute to the wealth of nations, whereas organized crime can hardly be said to do so.

22 per cent. Despite this experience with such a huge miscalculation (or was it a misconception?) and an actual contraction in 1991 of 11 per cent, the IMF rubbed on its smoky crystal ball once more and forecast growth of 2.4 per cent for 1993 (IMF 1991, 1992). Though 1993 turned out to be the first year of positive growth in Eastern Europe, actual GDP expanded only by a meagre 0.4 per cent, that is, sixfold less than the prediction.

While one may agree that during the transition it has been difficult to predict the future, it has apparently been no less difficult to foresee the past. For example, the EBRD (1997a) calculates the contraction in GDP for Eastern Europe in 1991 and 1992 at 11 per cent and 4.3 per cent, for a total of minus 14.8 per cent, but in a subsequent report (EBRD 1997b) it estimates the contraction at 10.6 and 4.2 per cent, respectively, for a cumulative rate of minus 14.4 per cent. As for the growth in 1993, it corrected the index downward from 0.7 to 0.4 per cent.

These are minor and therefore quite excusable differences which are probably due to methodological and technical factors. But sometimes the data are changed significantly ex post for political reasons. Presumably, the overall picture is being made to look more appealing to give the impression that there was not as much hardship as the critics of policy mismanagement dare to point out. For instance, several attempts have been made in Poland to discount the drop in output and the deterioration in the standard of living during the initial stage of transformation (Balcerowicz 1992, Gomulka 1996). A good (more precisely, a bad) example of this sort of exercise is the calculation which has reduced the estimate of the fall in GDP in Poland from 11.6 per cent in 1990 and 7 per cent in 1991 (EBRD 1997b), that is, from minus 17.8 per cent in 1990–1, to a more palatable minus 7 per cent during the entire period of transitional contraction (Czyzewski, Orlowski, and Zienkowski 1996). So, the outcomes of the disastrous year of 1990—the year of 'shock without therapy'—are being levitated from the record as if by magic.

According to Czyzewski, Orlowski, and Zienkowski (1996), the GDP reported in national statistics for 1989 was overestimated because of the high inflation (549 per cent at a yearly point-to-point rate), which meant that, according to the national income conventions of the time, the increase in the value of inventories because of inflation was being treated as income rather than being deducted from output.

These authors also introduce a novel methodology to evaluate the specific weight of factors contributing to shifts in gross industrial output in Poland during 1989–91. Seven factors are considered: the 'Comecon effect', 'other' changes in exports, import effects, the domestic spillover of Comecon effects (estimated by means of a 1990 input-output table elaborated by the Central Statistical Office for 32 areas of the economy), the domestic spillover of 'other' net export effects, the effect of stabilization (both of these last two by means of input-output analysis), and, finally, a 'structural effect'. The last factor is used to account for an otherwise unexplained residual, although quantitative structural changes are already fully covered in the analysis. This 'structural effect', it so happens, had in 1990 a greater negative weight than did stabilization, which made a positive contribution to average industrial output change in 1991.

While some of these arguments have no real substance, others are vastly overplayed. The 'search for goods' had been replaced by the search for jobs, with one giant queue of unemployed replacing the innumerable queues for goods, while the welfare of employed workers was worsened by job insecurity. Moreover, established national income conventions do not include 'consumer surpluses' derived from sheer access to markets and the broadening of consumer choice.

Another exercise (Berg and Sachs 1992) tries to argue that real consumption in Poland in 1990 fell only by about 4 per cent, despite the tremendous decrease in real wages of approximately 25 per cent. Of course, owing to the shortage removal effect, the fall in real consumption was smaller than the officially registered statistical decrease in real wages. Nonetheless, the difference was much less than suggested in this exercise. It is not merely misleading, but also rather smug to maintain that there was really only a slight deterioration in living conditions when unemployment was soaring and household consumption was plunging. The number of jobless jumped from zero to over one million in only one year, and in the same short time the highest ever decline was registered in real wages.

The advocates of the policy package which was actually implemented anticipated a shorter economic contraction, an earlier recovery, and more rapid growth. They were in the wrong on all three counts. The contraction lasted two or three times longer than expected; the output collapse was more distressing than the most distressing scenario, and the recovery, when it ultimately came, was only sluggish. When their unrealistic predictions did not materialize, the policymakers and their advisors, because they had been unable to modify the present, tried to modify the past. For their miscalculations, they blamed ex post not their erroneous policy assumptions, which had been based on wrong economics, nor their erroneous forecasts, which had been based on the wrong assumptions, but they blamed unfavourable, unforeseen circumstances. When their policies were criticized, they said not that the targets were overshot, but that the policies had not really been carried through.

In fact, even if they knew what the outcome was going to be like, the political leaders and ruling parties would never have dared to announce an economic programme involving a drop in output by one-quarter or one-half over the few years of their administration. If they had done so, not one of them would have survived for long under the emerging democratic system. They would have had no chance to push forward their structural adjustment policies if they had acknowledged publicly beforehand that the policies were going to lead to severe economic contraction and to a deterioration in living standards. Such an announcement, even if combined with a promise that the slump would be shortlived, would not have gained the desired political support.

A game is always being played between government, which has plans, and society, which has expectations, between international organizations, which exert pressure, and countries, which must tolerate tough adjustment programmes, between truth and the lies in a public debate, between good and bad intentions in a political tug-of-war.

In any case, it should not have been so difficult to analyse the circumstances correctly and to predict the miserable results of the policies actually adopted (Kolodko 1992b, 1993a, Nuti 1990, Laski 1990, Poznanski 1993). Truly, it would have made more sense to assume at the time that the conditions necessary for a decrease or an increase in production might not be forthcoming than to forecast the impact of the policies being applied under such volatile, unstable circumstances. If only some of the potential negative consequences of these policies had been viewed more seriously, it should have been possible to take precautionary steps. But this was not done.

The issue is not that there has been an intellectual inability to draw the right conclusions, but simply that there is no political commitment to do so on the part of political leaders. It seems as if authorities and politicians are not always keen to know the truth about the outcome of their policies because this truth may be uncomfortable for them. Sometimes it seems as though it is easier for them not to know the truth than to know the evil truth. In the end, perhaps this is not an intellectual debate over who is right and who is wrong, but a political fight over whose interests are going to be satisfied first and over which group of interests is going to be championed. Perhaps there are no errors of econometric forecasting, only tricks of political dealing.

In 1990 the Polish government embraced the false scenario that there would be a mild contraction of only 3.1 per cent. It did this partly because of myopia over its own policies, which were based on the wrong economics, and partly intentionally for the sake of misleading public opinion so as to garner, if not support, at least a neutral reaction to an unpopular outcome. The contraction was four times more severe than predicted.

This sort of experience should have offered a lesson. However, this has not been the case. There are many examples of similar miscalculations and unrealistic scenarios. For instance, in Bulgaria in 1997, when it should have been obvious that the government policy package was going to cause a serious contraction, the austerity programme was geared toward a decline in production of 'only' 4 per cent. In fact, the contraction turned out to be two times greater. A like course of events occurred in the Czech Republic in 1998.

The reasoning of influential international organizations has sometimes shown similar traits. The Bretton Woods institutions frequently seem overly optimistic about programmes they support. The basic argument is simple: the fruits are appetizing, so people should be eager to tighten their belts now to obtain some of the fruits later. However, it usually turns out that the fruits mature very slowly, not everybody gets some, and they are less tasty than advertised, but, oh well, belts have now already been tightened, so no harm has been done. Though their duty to society does not require it, government authorities, backed by news media and certain interest groups, for similar political reasons, often share this inclination and support the Bretton Woods institutions.

While some people among the political and social elites were already enjoying a much better present, a majority in society, with a great deal of naïveté, were anticipating a better future. There was a very pervasive, almost devout psychological need to believe the assumptions and the forecasts. Usually, it is difficult to argue with religious faith. Economic issues sometimes seem little different: one deeply believes more than one knows for sure. Of course, the new reality is treated by the faithful as if it were something better, whatever the facts, whatever the costs. But, really, the point is that it is not always enough to compare the costs and count the benefits, since often someone else pays the costs, and someone else gets the benefits. The casino makes a profit, no matter who the losers and who the winners, and no matter that the winners are few, while the losers are always many.

So, in transition economies there has been the politics of the optimistic future and of exaggerated expectations. This has been based on erroneous analysis at the point of departure, but also on a deliberately biased picture of what is to come. It will never be admitted officially, but the gap between the expectations and the reality cannot be satisfactorily explained without considering the existence of a combination of delusions, mistaken policies, insincere promises, and inaccurate predictions.

The systemic and development policies were wrong, and the market failed, though it was supposed to (and will) perform better than the plan. Policies can be wrong under the plan and under the market. During the later stages of the planned economy, the reality was worse than expected because the plan was wrong as a policy instrument and was doomed to underperform. Likewise, under the postsocialist market economy, the reality was worse than expected by an even greater margin because the redesigned system was wrong and was also doomed to underperform.[14]

Though the gap between the prognosis and the reality is no longer such a worrisome issue since the situation has improved and expectations have become a little more realistic, there is still this rather peculiar difference between the forecasts and the outcomes in the transition economies.

---

[14] The difference between two Soviet schools of economic planning, the teleological and the genetic (Nove 1992), comes to mind in this context.

Thus, in the spring of 1997 the EBRD predicted that the GDP growth rate for all 25 countries in which the bank operates would be 3 per cent that year (EBRD 1997a). This would reflect a 3.9 per cent growth rate in Eastern Europe and a 1.4 per cent growth rate in the CIS. Only six months later, in the fall of 1997, the forecast was revised downward (not surprisingly). GDP was now anticipated to increase by only 1.7 per cent for the whole group of countries, due to 3.1 per cent growth in Eastern Europe and a meagre 0.8 per cent growth in the CIS (EBRD 1997b).

The great slump in transition economies is a fact of history. This has been acknowledged by everyone, although some individuals, political parties, and organizations which deserve to be blamed for this misfortune are still trying to minimize the true scope of the event. Considering the unprecedented size of the output collapse, the postsocialist recession has been the most severe recession in peacetime ever. Despite the ongoing recovery in several nations for some years, there is still a long and rocky road to travel before the pre-transition level of output is regained. Only half the transition countries enjoyed positive growth in 1994–7. In 1997, five countries were still experiencing contraction. In four cases output was falling once more after a period of growth, and in one country there had not yet been any recovery, so that output had been decreasing for nearly a decade. The situation was not much better in 1998. In several nations the growth rate slowed, while in Russia, the largest of all transition economies, the contraction continued.

In the contemporary world, even when output has declined following a natural disaster or because of local military conflicts, the drop has not been so sharp and drastic as it has been in Eastern Europe and the former Soviet republics. The whole transition region lost almost one-third of its GDP during the first seven years of transition, and by no means will this wealth be recovered during the next seven years. In one of the worst cases of the second half of the 20th century, Chad's GDP contracted by about 50 per cent between 1960 and 1990. To achieve a similar result, Russia needed only seven years; the GDP of Russia halved between 1990 and 1996, similar to the case of Zaire, which suffered an average annual rate of contraction of more than 8 per cent during the same period. And Russia is not even the worst case among transition nations, since eight other countries endured a GDP fall in excess of 50 per cent (Table 13). Now, Russia is engaged with a second round of recession in the aftermath of the financial collapse of the summer of 1998. While other countries are already on the path of growth, Russia is headed toward several more years of output decline.

There have also been more positive episodes, for example the relatively better performance of Estonia in Eastern Europe and of Kyrgyzstan in Central Asia, or of Hungary and Poland outside the former Soviet Union, or of Croatia and Slovenia outside the former Comecon. However, this does not justify very many wide-ranging conclusions about the adequacy of early transition policies.

Table 13 Recession and growth in transition economies, 1990–1997

	Years of GDP decline	GDP fell after recovery?	Average annual GDP growth			1997 GDP index (1989 = 100)	Rank
			1990–3	1994–7	1990–7		
Poland	2	No	−3.1	6.3	1.6	111.8	1
Slovenia	3	No	−3.9	4.0	0.0	99.3	2
Czech Republic	3	No	−4.3	3.6	−0.4	95.8	3
Slovakia	4	No	−6.8	6.3	−0.3	95.6	4
Hungary	4	No	−4.8	2.5	−1.1	90.4	5
Uzbekistan	5	No	−3.1	−0.3	−1.7	86.7	6
Romania	4	Yes	−6.4	2.1	−2.2	82.4	7
Albania	4	Yes	−8.8	4.9	−2.0	79.1	8
Estonia	5	No	−9.7	4.1	−2.8	77.9	9
Croatia	4	No	−9.9	3.0	−3.4	73.3	10
Belarus	6	No	−5.4	−2.6	−4.0	70.8	11
Bulgaria	6	Yes	−7.4	−3.6	−5.5	62.8	12
Kyrgyzstan	5	No	−9.3	−2.4	−5.8	58.7	13
Kazakhstan	6	No	−6.7	−6.0	−6.3	58.1	14
Latvia	4	Yes	−13.8	2.2	−5.8	56.8	15
FYR Macedonia	6	No	−12.9	−0.8	−6.9	55.3	16
Russia	7	No	−10.1	−5.3	−7.7	52.2	17
Turkmenistan	7	No	−4.5	−12.5	−8.5	48.3	18
Lithuania	5	No	−18.3	0.5	−8.9	42.8	19
Armenia	4	No	−21.4	5.4	−8.0	41.1	20
Azerbaijan	6	No	−14.5	−5.7	−10.1	40.5	21
Tajikistan	7	No	−12.2	−8.4	−10.3	40.0	22
Ukraine	8	No recovery	−10.1	−12.1	−11.1	38.3	23
Moldova	7	No	−12.6	−10.2	−11.4	35.1	24
Georgia	5	No	−24.1	2.9	−10.6	34.3	25

Sources: National statistics, data from international organizations, author's calculations.

Likewise, there are no grounds for linking the success stories, including the most spectacular one, the case of Poland, with so-called 'shock therapy'. In fact, the Polish accomplishment has mainly been due to a shift from policies of shocks without therapy to policies of therapy without shocks. There should be no doubt about the inadequacy of the concept of 'shock therapy'. The Polish success has been achieved not because of it, but in spite of it, and the reasoning behind shock therapy and interventions based upon the concept must take much of the blame for the great slump.

The same might be said about the misuse of the concept of 'creative destruction'. More than a half-century ago Joseph Schumpeter (1942) described this concept. Schumpeter was referring to a vision of economic growth driven by a permanent commitment to accumulation and investment and to the creation of better business opportunities—not their destruction—on the foundations of a technical progress which has not fallen like manna from heaven, as in the orthodox neo-classical model, but which has grown out of a hard competitive struggle.

Schumpeter's 'creative destruction' was misconstrued early on during the transition (Gomulka 1991). It requires investment and innovation, and none of this happens automatically during transition. In postsocialism, because of the influence of an erroneous understanding of 'creative destruction', there have been a great many shocks without therapy and a great deal of destruction without creation. Instead of durable growth, this has led to prolonged slumpflation.

Schumpeter's notion of 'creative destruction' would make some sense in the transition only vis-à-vis institutional structures and only under the circumstances of a gradual (not shock-enduced) rearrangement of these structures. As long as there is a discontinuity between the institutions of the old system and those of the new system, there must be constant efforts to create institutions to support the new system and to dismantle ('destroy'?) institutions which serve the old system. Such dismantling might indeed be 'destructive', but it must be carried out by design and must not be chaotic.

In contrast, any destruction of the real economy, whatever the ideological reasoning behind such an escapade, must lead directly to a collapse in output. This should not seem surprising. What should amaze is the fact that this approach was the dominant one during the early stages of transition. It was not necessary. It was a mistake and a very costly one.

4.4. THE SYSTEMIC VACUUM: NEITHER PLAN NOR MARKET

The breadth of the transitional contraction can be explained by the existence of a systemic vacuum which lasted much longer than the supporters of 'shock therapy' expected. If certain interest groups had not succumbed to the temptations represented by a course which involved such enormous modifications in the structure of ownership ('Why not? It's "therapy"') and if the ultimately harmful course had not become such a fertile ground for experimentation, then it would not have been followed, and the contraction would not have been so severe. Instead, the situation became a nightmare in a number of countries caught on the fence between the plan and the market. Inherited problems and the mismanagement of transition were producing a hybrid system, and this added to the mounting difficulties.[15]

This systemic vacuum is very obvious in the second largest postsocialist economy, Ukraine, where production has been shrinking since the beginning of the 1990s and where the civil code has been inadequate for so long. Only in mid-1997 did

Ukraine's often recalcitrant parliament . . . [approve] the country's draft civil code . . . in a move which reformers said would create a legal foundation for the country's fledgling market economy. . . . Western lawyers said the civil code was a major step in Ukraine's efforts to replace its ungainly, Soviet-era laws with a Western legal system appropriate for a capitalist economy. (Freeland 1997b)

Ukraine is not the only case in which the creation of a proper legal framework is just the belated beginning of the lengthy process of institutional change and learning by doing that is required to achieve the market. The introduction of the civil code has turned out to be difficult in Ukraine, and the implementation of the fresh rules and development policies within the new institutional framework is going to be still more difficult.

The systemic vacuum first appeared in those countries using more radical methods to dismantle old institutions. The vacuum was an outcome of the radical, ideologically and politically driven overthrow ('creative destruction'?) of old institutions without the establishment of new arrangements to replace them.

In some economies, for instance in Hungary, Lithuania, Poland, and later in the Czech Republic, more successful policies were devised after the failures in the initial stages of transition. Thus, by the mid-1990s, 'interactive' economic policies aiming at gradual structural change and the involvement of society in the transition process were turning the Polish economy around (Hausner 1997). In this case, the early transition 'shock therapy' and 'creative destruction' which had led to mismanagement and to the systemic vacuum were replaced by 'gradual therapy' and 'creative construction'.

---

[15] Russia 'has Africa's subsistence economy, Pakistan's corruption, Brazil's wayward congress, Italy's Mafia, Canada's fissiparousness—and a Communist Party all its own' (*The Economist* 1997d). It has also taken on the most awful elements from the policies of other transition countries: 'Bulgarian stabilization, Romanian fiscal policy, Polish monetary policy, Czech privatization, Slovak restructuring, Hungarian debt management, Yugoslav inter-republican relations, and Albanian bank supervision' (Nuti 1997b).

During the early transition the delusion of a rapid recovery followed by robust growth was very strongly tied to the delusion that new institutions would emerge spontaneously. It was assumed that a 'feedback loop' would operate between these processes, and there had been an exaggerated expectation that market organizations and their institutional linkages would appear quite soon, if not immediately. There is such a feedback loop, but, unfortunately, it is negative, and the progress which was supposed to be furnished by creative forces unleashed by artificially imposed shocks turned out to be only a mirage. Instead, the systemic vacuum favoured more contraction, and the steady contraction made the elimination of the 'neither plan, nor market' syndrome still more difficult.

The old system of allocation, with all its inefficiencies, had been dismantled abruptly, but the new system—a performing market economy—had not yet been created. Blanchard (1997) calls this 'disorganization'. The natural continuity between economic development and institutional evolution had been broken. New institutions had not risen up as a result of social awareness, sensitive policy-management, and the containment of negative externalities and market failures. The 'bad part' of the market was now in charge of economic outcomes, and this was having an impact on economic efficiency (weak) and income distribution (unfair). Instead of an 'emerging market', a systemic vacuum emerged, and only a few were able to profit from the situation.

The best (or worst) example is again Russia.

Lack of efficiency and discipline in the government and civil service, exacerbated at all levels by venality, incompetence, and inexperience, contributed to an economic slump. . . . The resolve and the ability of any firm that wanted to do business honestly were undermined. The easiest way to survive in the 'new Russia' was to lie to the taxman; pay off the protection racketeers, bribe the local bureaucrats, barter for supplies, and pay workers months late, if at all. The system did not merely allow all of these things: in effect, it demanded them if companies were to survive. (Cottrell 1997)

This was not inevitable. Simply because an event has occurred should not be taken to signify that it must be accepted ex-post as justified and forgivable. In this case, we should not let bygones be bygones; the implications for the present and for the future are too serious.

In place of the bankruptcy of 'shock therapy' and 'creative destruction', active policy involvement in institution-building can shorten the period of transitional recession and encourage the onset of recovery.[16] The length of the recession depends on the inherited features of the economy (obviously,

---

[16] There would have been some transitional contraction even if the policy approach had been excellent. Popov (1998b) argues that, because of the serious structural distortions typical of such countries, recession was inevitable in any postsocialist country with a GDP over $3,000 per person. The question is: Why has it been so severe?

the more the system had previously been reformed, the better), but also on the extent of the systemic vacuum. The sooner the economy can start to recover, the sooner it can regain the pre-transition level of output, since the size of the transitional contraction is a function of the average rate of output decline, as well as the amount of time the recession has lasted.

Therefore, following the initial shock of liberalization, the process of shifting the economy back to the path of growth can be accelerated by appropriate policies, especially structural, industrial, and agricultural measures. Quite often, the 'wait-and-see' approach has contributed to a weak supply response and prolonged the recession unnecessarily. In Russia, where the increase in GDP was officially reported at a mere 0.4 per cent in 1997, output has been showing a falling trend. Recession has even reappeared in some countries, like Albania, Bulgaria, the Czech Republic, Latvia, and Romania. In others, growth has again slowed after a period of expansion. This will happen elsewhere if the appropriate lessons are not learned.

4.5. THE REVOLUTION IN PROPERTY RIGHTS AND THE DECLINE IN PRODUCTION

Transition cannot occur without privatization. If there is liberalization, but no substantial change in property rights, there may be reforms, but there is no transition. Some deregulation and decentralization took place under the socialist systems in Europe, and even more fundamental shifts are well under way in countries like China and Vietnam. Nonetheless, in these cases, though management structures are opened up, the state remains the owner of all crucial assets and the only major player in the economic game. However, an essential characteristic of the transition to a full-fledged market and the capitalist restoration is the transfer of property rights from the state to private entities.

Not surprisingly, to engineer the most significant denationalization in history is a tremendous challenge which entails quite innovative policy responses, as well as many great disappointments (Frydman and Rapaczynski 1991, Lavigne 1995, Uvalic and Vaughan-Whitehead 1997). There is a widely shared assumption that, to achieve sustained growth, it is necessary and sufficient to privatize state assets, the more and the more quickly, the better. According to this theory, privatization, together with liberalization and the imposition of hard budget constraints, will facilitate swift recovery and rapid, durable growth (World Bank 1996). But this scenario has not held up because even those nations which have been skilful at implementing the approach are not yet on the path to sustained growth.

The speed of growth (or of contraction) is not an accurate measure of progress in privatization (or the lack thereof). On such a basis, one could reach the false conclusion that, for instance, the approach in Belarus to the challenge of privatization is much better at facilitating growth than is the path Latvia has chosen, because the GDP of Belarus in 1998 has been estimated at 72.6 per cent of the pre-transition level, whereas the corresponding ratio for the GDP of Latvia in 1998 was only 58.4 per cent. Or one might decide on this basis that, since Uzbekistan and Hungary in 1998 were expected to reach about the same level of GDP relative to the output in 1989 (88.1 and 91.5 per cent, respectively), they undoubtedly took the same road toward privatization both before and after the collapse of socialism.

In fact, Poland has managed to privatize about the same share of state assets as has the Czech Republic, but it is doing much better in terms of growth. Relative to the pre-transition level, the GDPs of these two countries stood at around 119 and 99 per cent, respectively, in 1998. Advocates of the 'revolutionary' pace in privatization may be surprised to learn that the speed of output growth has been greater in Poland, which has adopted the more gradualist attitude toward denationalization. Obviously, the pace of privatization is not the key to growth.

More important is the environment for competition and for the corporate governance of assets, both the assets which have already been privatized and those which have not yet been privatized. Privatization undertaken by the state through the sale of assets in an emerging postsocialist market has a direct impact on allocation, efficiency, and growth, but this impact has varied from country to country depending on the environment.

By the same token, one cannot argue that a telecommunications company in Hungary is similar to one in Argentina merely because they both provide the same services, own similar physical assets, and use the same technologies and even the same management methods. There may be technical similarities, but real similarities are not that common in the social and political context. Neither at the outset of the transition, nor during the recent wave of denationalization was Hungary like Argentina, so one should not put an equals sign between these two nations.

In contrast to other economic systems, in the postsocialist countries privatization was launched as a means of creating capitalism without capitalists. This goal has definitely not existed in the case of any of the less-developed countries pursuing vast programmes of privatization and structural adjustment in the 1990s. These nations possessed stock exchanges, investment banks, and holders of capital seeking good investment opportunities. They had always possessed capitalists keen to take advantage of a privatization or a denationalization of assets. In the transition countries, there was a shortage of investment capital to finance privatization, and an entrepreneurial class was only emerging step-by-step within an alien economic and social structure.

The first major argument in favour of privatization stressed that *shifting resources from the state (assumed to be wasteful) to the private sector would be sufficient to improve allocative efficiency and therefore put the economy on the path of speedy, durable growth.* The argument was based on the assumption that, owing to the shortage removal effect, full capacity utilization could be achieved very quickly and that this in turn would boost growth in the short to medium term, even without new investment. It became very clear very soon, however, that the shift in property rights could achieve full capacity utilization only if it was supported by sound institutional arrangements, new market behaviours, and, especially, appropriate schemes of corporate governance. Otherwise, because of the chaos accompanying the transition before the new order has been established, capital allocation may be less efficient than it was prior to privatization, and this situation may last for a period of years. Even a 'big bang' in entrepreneurship may be neutral from the expansion viewpoint, since the meagreness of the legal, institutional, and behavioural environment, as well as the inadequacies in economic policy, can tame the process of competitive market allocation. While some resources will be utilized almost instantly in a more efficient way, others will be even more severely misallocated, or they will simply be wasted. They may now be more easily stolen or transferred abroad through capital flight and organized crime.

This malady in performance seems to affect early transition economies and nations with a weak state and ineffective policies. Among less-developed countries, Nigeria illustrates well the malady. It has a huge private sector with vast experience in entrepreneurship, but because of deficiencies in the state and in policy, Nigeria is unable to sustain economic growth.

The second argument in favour of privatization is that *radical trade liberalization should generate a rapid supply response and an immediate increase in output* (Sachs 1989). Unfortunately, the contrary has occurred. Because of weak competitiveness, structural inflexibility, and the dearth of experience with open markets, the supply response was immediately negative. The plan vanished, but the market did not instantly appear. Instead of the growth anticipated following rapid trade liberalization, there was deep recession. Over the medium term, those countries did much better that exercised gradual, but determined and steady-going liberalization.

The third argument in favour of privatization is that *macroeconomic stabilization, especially if it is enforced in a radical manner, will boost the propensity to save and thereby the ability to invest in efficient and competitive endeavours, particularly in the quickly emerging private sector.* The advance in overall performance should then be able to contribute to long-term sustainable growth. This seems true in principle, but in practice stabilization could not be achieved quickly enough. The initial by-effect of stabilization measures was a drastic decline in existing stocks of savings rather than the accumulation of new savings. This was so because in each nation the stabilization drive was followed by recession, and savings therefore fell, too. Only after a critical level of stabilization had been reached and only after real household incomes had grown did savings begin to rise substantially.

Table 14 Progress in institutional transition and GDP growth

	Aggregate EBRD index[a]	EU index, institutional development	EU index, political development	World Bank classification[b]	Private sector share in GDP, 1995 (%)	Change, 1969–95 (%)	Annual GDP growth, 1990–7 (%)	GDP rank, 1997 (1989 = 100)
Poland	3.1	3.3	3.3	4	60	31	1.6	1
Slovenia	2.9	3.4	3.5	4	45	37	0.0	2
Czech Republic	3.3	3.3	3.5	4	70	59	−1.1	3
Slovakia	3.0	2.7	2.5	4	60	50	−0.4	4
Hungary	3.3	3.3	3.5	4	60	45	−1.7	5
Uzbekistan	2.0	1.5	1.3	1	30	25	−2.0	6
Romania	2.2	2.2	2.0	3	40	27	−2.2	7
Albania	2.0	2.1	2.0	3	60	55	−2.8	8
Estonia	2.9	3.0	2.9	3	65	55	−3.4	9
Croatia	2.5	2.3	1.9	0	45	30	−0.3	10
Belarus	1.8	1.4	1.3	1	15	10	−5.5	11
Bulgaria	2.3	2.2	2.2	3	45	30	−4.0	12
Kyrgyzstan	2.5	1.8	1.7	2	40	35	−5.8	13
Kazakhstan	1.8	1.9	1.6	2	25	10	−8.9	14
Latvia	2.4	2.6	2.5	3	60	50	−6.9	15
FYR Macedonia	2.1	2.1	2.2	0	40	30	−6.3	16
Russia	2.3	2.3	2.1	2	55	50	−7.7	17
Lithuania	2.5	2.5	2.5	3	55	45	−9.8	18
Turkmenistan	0.8	1.4	1.3	1	15	10	−5.8	19
Armenia	1.8	1.9	1.9	0	45	37	−8.0	20
Azerbaijan	1.3	1.6	1.5	0	25	20	−10.3	21
Tajikistan	1.3	1.2	1.2	0	15	10	−11.4	22
Ukraine	1.9	1.8	1.9	1	35	30	−10.1	23
Moldova	2.3	2.1	2.1	2	30	25	−11.1	24
Georgia	1.7	1.8	1.8	0	30	12	−10.6	25
Bosnia-Herzegovina	—	1.4	1.4	0	?	?	?	26
Eastern/Central Europe[c]	3.1	3.2	3.3	—	63	46	—	—
CIS[c]	1.8	1.7	1.7	—	30	22	—	—

[a] EBRD classification is on a scale of 1–4.5. [b] World Bank classification: 4 = leading reformers, 3 = advanced reformers, 2 = intermediate reformers, 1 = slow reformers, 0 = affected by regional tensions. [c] Regional averages are unweighted.

Sources: EBRD 1996, 1997b, 1998, PlanEcon 1996, 1997b, 1997c, author's calculations.

Moreover, the shift in savings from the state sector to the private sector did not automatically promote the propensity to invest, nor did it secure the more effective allocation of savings straightaway. Such processes require a sound banking sector and a stable political environment. Not surprisingly, during the transition the political scene was even more lively than the economic one. Overnight political changes meant that priorities and economic policy tools were often transitory, and this had a significant influence on expectations and thus on the climate for business.

Although privatization facilitates the expansion of capital over the long term, in the short and medium term it is not a sufficient condition for the accumulation and competitive allocation of private savings. To sustain growth, savings must be able to seek the most productive use. Otherwise, they may become depleted or may be taken out of the country.

In other words, the wrong sequence in the application of liberalization measures and privatization may diminish the amount of disposable capital instead of increasing it. If this occurs in the midst of the institutional chaos accompanying the early phases of transformation, then privatization and liberalization will generate more recession than expansion. A weak financial system, particularly in the banking sector, has been a thorn in the side of transition efforts at capital accumulation. The financial system should therefore be overhauled before rather than after the start of privatization.

It is easier now to understand why there is not a direct, verifiable link in every case between the maturity of the institutional transition and the level of economic activity as expressed in the rate of growth (or contraction). Whatever criteria are used to gauge these phenomena (EBRD 1996), some countries, like the Czech Republic in 1997–8, are further along in the transition in terms of institutions, but are stagnating or showing only slow growth, while other countries, like Belarus or Georgia, are institutionally less mature, but are enjoying remarkably high rates of growth (Table 14). The average rate of growth in the Czech Republic in 1997–8 has been estimated at around 1.5 per cent, but it was 6 per cent in Belarus and 10 per cent in Georgia.

In sketching growth scenarios, one must take into consideration not only the size of the private sector and the extent of liberalization, but also the policies which may (or may not) be able to take advantage of the progress being made in these areas. After all, privatization and liberalization are only the means, not the ends of development, and in the very long run the better economic performance and the higher rates of growth will fall to the economies which are most advanced in transition (Ellman 1997). Then, the progress in the expansion of the private sector and in the maturity of the institutional arrangements is going to be decisive. Sustainable development can be achieved only through a steady and comprehensive advance in systemic transformation.

5

The Washington Consensus Revisited

5.1. POLICY WITHOUT GROWTH: MISSING ELEMENTS

At the end of the 1980s and the beginning of the 90s the so-called 'Washington consensus' was thought to represent the received wisdom on the proper way to step from stabilization to growth. According to the consensus a tough financial policy, accompanied by deregulation and trade liberalization, would be enough to eliminate stagnation and launch economic expansion. Although they had been developed mostly as solutions to problems in Latin America, the proposals for reform that were based on the Washington consensus were used to address structural crises in various regions (Williamson 1990, Dornbusch 1991, Selowsky 1991). Later, there was also a crossover effect, a process of learning by doing. This orientation in policy reform thus came to have an important impact on the course of the postsocialist transition.

John Williamson, who first called this set of policy proposals the 'Washington consensus' already in 1989, has highlighted the importance of the influential financial organizations involved. He finds that 10 points appear to have been agreed upon among these organizations, as well as leading professional economists and government policymaking bodies such as the US Treasury Department.

- Fiscal Discipline: Budget deficit . . . should be small enough to be financed without recourse to the inflation tax. . . .
- Public Expenditure Priorities: Expenditure should be redirected from politically sensitive areas . . . toward neglected fields with high economic returns and the potential to improve income distribution. . . .
- Tax Reform: Tax reform involves broadening the tax base and cutting marginal tax rates. The aim is to sharpen incentives and improve horizontal equity without lowering realized progressivity. . . .
- Financial Liberalization: The ultimate objective of financial liberalization is market-determined interest rates, but experience has shown that, under conditions of a chronic lack of confidence, market-determined rates can be so high as to threaten the financial solvency of productive enterprise and government. . . .
- Exchange Rates: Countries need a unified (at least for trade transactions) exchange rate set at a level sufficiently competitive to induce a rapid growth in non-traditional exports and managed so as to assure exporters that this competitiveness will be maintained in the future.

- Trade Liberalization: Quantitative trade restrictions should be rapidly replaced by tariffs, and these should be progressively reduced until a uniform low tariff in the range of 10 per cent (at most around 20 per cent) is achieved. . . .
- Foreign Direct Investment: Barriers impeding the entry of foreign firms should be abolished; foreign and domestic firms should be allowed to compete on equal terms.
- Privatization: State enterprises should be privatized.
- Deregulation: Governments should abolish regulations that impede the entry of new firms or that restrict competition and then should ensure that all regulations are justified by such criteria as safety, environmental protection, or prudential supervision of financial institutions.
- Property Rights: The legal system should provide secure property rights without excessive costs and should make such rights available to the informal sector. (Williamson 1997, pp. 60–1)

Later, the 'new agenda' was introduced. It was mainly shaped by the encounter with the difficulties of Latin American economies during the first half of the 1990s. It did take into consideration all the lessons which might have been learned in other regions, including especially Eastern Europe and the former Soviet republics. It contained obvious old points, but there were also new concerns. Ten major issues were again raised:

- increase saving by (inter alia) maintaining fiscal discipline
- reorient public expenditure toward (inter alia) well-directed social expenditure
- reform the tax system by (inter alia) introducing an eco-sensitive land tax
- strengthen banking supervision
- maintain a competitive exchange rate, abandoning both floating and the use of the exchange rate as a nominal anchor
- pursue intraregional trade liberalization
- build a competitive market economy by (inter alia) privatizing and deregulating (including the labour market)
- make well-defined property rights available to all
- build key institutions such as independent central banks, strong budget offices, independent and incorruptible judiciaries, and agencies to sponsor productivity missions
- increase educational spending and redirect it toward primary and secondary schools. (Williamson 1997, p. 58)

The policies of the Washington consensus were not drafted or initially proposed in order to solve the crisis in postsocialist countries entering a period of transition toward a market economy. The early consensus was actually aimed at economies which were already market economies and not in transition. Joseph Stiglitz, senior vice president for development and chief economist at the World Bank, while stressing the importance of governments as a complement to markets, clearly points out that the consensus achieved at the end of the 1980s and the beginning of the 90s among the US Treasury Department, the IMF, and the World Bank, as well as some influential research groups, was catalysed because of the experience of Latin America in the 80s (Stiglitz 1998a).

For this reason, nations facing other challenges have never found satisfactory answers to their most pressing questions in the Washington consensus. The consensus interpretation vis-à-vis the postsocialist transition economies suggests that it would be sufficient to fix the financial fundamentals and privatize the bulk of state assets. Subsequently, growth should occur and be sustainable. This is an oversimplification, and things have not turned out as expected or as promised.

For instance, the 'new agenda' correctly addresses the issues of institution-building, the protection of the natural environment, and investment in education. Still missing are several points of great importance not only, but especially, for transition economies. The main missing elements in this sense are the corporate governance of the state sector before it is privatized and the behavioural aspects of institution-building.

The briefest of the 10 points of the early Washington consensus, that is, 'Privatization: State enterprises should be privatized', is actually the most persistent policy challenge in transition countries in real terms. Even if there is—and this is not always necessarily the case—a sound commitment to privatize a great deal and quickly, this is not feasible for technical and political reasons. In addition, there are the problems of sequencing, pace, the distribution of costs and benefits, and the exercise of corporate governance in the most efficient way.

To build institutions in postsocialist transition economies, unlike in distorted developing market economies, it is not enough simply to establish the organizations, even the basic ones such as an independent central bank or a comprehensive tax administration. It is also necessary to engineer changes in institutional culture and behaviour and in the links among the new organizations so as to facilitate efficiency and growth.

Nonetheless, although the problems of transition countries seem not to have been a main concern in the policy reforms proposed by the Washington consensus, the policy attitudes toward the transition countries have had a significant influence on the mainstream line of thought that seems to dominate in Washington-based organizations, including the ones dealing with international economic and financial order. Moreover, the transition experience has certainly generated modifications in the policy proposals of the consensus. This interaction has had both merits and drawbacks.

Always there has been the question: Has the Washington consensus actually been achieved, or has there merely been a well-intentioned attempt? The latter is rather more the truth, since

There is no standard terminology for these sets of doctrines, and various practitioners advocated these doctrines with [a] varying degree of subtlety and emphasis.

The set of views is often summarized as the 'Washington consensus', though to be sure, there never was a consensus even in Washington (let alone outside of Washington) on the appropriateness of these policies. (Stiglitz 1998b, p. 58)[1]

In any case, the scope of the 'agreement' appears to have diminished in recent years, at least according to certain publications, declarations issued by the Bretton Woods institutions or under their auspices, and the policies counselled and supported by these organizations worldwide (World Bank 1993, 1996, IMF 1996, 1998c). Considerable differences among policy views came clearly to the fore during the lively debate about the causes of and the policy responses to the East Asian crisis of 1997–8.

Curiously, the serious difficulties and failures of the policy packages being implemented in transition nations for the last 10 years have not drawn so much attention as have the policy proposals in East Asia during a single year. It seems as though the importance attached to a crisis might depend not on the relative dimensions of the challenges, but on the relative dimensions of the financial investments.

But perhaps, after all, this is not so surprising. It has been estimated that growth in East Asia fell from minus 2 to minus 15 per cent in 1998, and the prospects for 1999 appeared gloomy, too. The capital flight from the five major crisis countries—Indonesia, Malaysia, the Philippines, South Korea, and Thailand—from the beginning of the downturn to mid-1998 has been valued at a staggering $115 billion. This represented about 10 per cent of the GDP of these nations. Meanwhile, over the same period, banking credits were reduced by $88 billion, another 8 per cent of GDP. The biggest difference between the crisis countries of East Asia and the transition countries seems to be that, unlike the East Asian 'contagion', the problems of Eastern Europe have not cut into the expansive potential of industrial nations.

However, there may be another factor—strictly political in nature—behind the delayed reaction to the postsocialist malaise. Eastern Europe and the former Soviet Union were always so constantly branded as the scapegoats for all misfortunes that one may now tend to think 'It's their own fault; they have only themselves to blame'. Even the new elites in Central and Eastern Europe are keen to take part in tracing all sins to the socialist past:

---

[1] Stiglitz looks to be right. On the eve of his departure for Moscow, during the period of constant turmoil on Russian financial markets, leading newspapers noted the ongoing debates and disagreements at the top levels of the IMF and the World Bank. The following cites comments of the World Bank: 'senior Russian officials said yesterday that the IMF has told the Russian Government that it needs to slash its budget deficit and overhaul its tax system if it wants to qualify for billions of dollars in extra loans. . . . the IMF and Russia are in intricate negotiations over terms of a new loan, on top of the $9.2 billion the Fund already has promised to Russia. The story says negotiations are so delicate that the World Bank considered preventing Joseph Stiglitz . . . from going to Moscow this week to give advice, approving the trip only after Stiglitz received a formal invitation from the Russians' (*Development News* 1998b).

it pays very well. Such a discourse is not possible in East Asia. For one thing, the political leaders there are the same people who were in charge of the economic 'miracle' in Asia. Moreover, these leaders, unlike those in postsocialist countries, are standing firmly against any 'whitewash'; they are taking some of the responsibility for what has happened, but they are also pointing fingers elsewhere, including at international financial organizations, foreign private investors, and the global capital market.

The worldwide public debate over economic development policy has focused on several regions, but the role the Bretton Woods institutions and the US government should play is always highlighted. Since Washington is such an important location for the debate (among other reasons for this, Bretton Woods institutions and other key bodies have offices there), this is the place the consensus must be reached, be it on the challenge posed by the structural crisis in Latin America in the 1980s, the transition crisis in Eastern European and post-Soviet economies throughout the 90s, the financial crisis in Asia in 1997–8, or the debt crisis among the 'highly indebted poor countries' in the late 90s.[2] It appears that, outside the well-developed market nations, only China remains relatively less exposed and less vulnerable to the influence of the 'Washington consensus'. Curiously, China seems to be doing quite well.

The Washington consensus has partially failed with respect to the transition economies because it has neglected the significance of institution-building even when the other fundamentals are by and large in order. This oversight explains why so many Western scholars did not at first properly understand the true nature of the challenge. Institutions can be changed only gradually, and they exert a very strong influence on economic performance. It was quite naïve to expect robust economic growth so soon after the fundamentals (but not the institutions) were in place. In fact, in real economic affairs, it is not possible to sustain fundamentals if they are not backed by solid institutions. Douglass C. North has written that, because

Western neo-classical economic theory is devoid of institutions, it is of little help in analysing the underlying sources of economic performance. It would be little exaggeration to say that, while neo-classical theory is focused on the operation of

---

[2] The early consensus had also to be worked out in Washington because of the debt issue. Latin America became so important in the policy debate not because inequity was increasing or because of spreading poverty, but because of the region's debt. It was not compassion for the suffering of the continent that stimulated the US government, international organizations, and financial interest groups to take action, but the desire to have the debt crisis resolved so that the debt could be repaid. Today, a decade later, there is no such enthusiasm for an international attempt to overhaul the African economy since Africa does not have so much outstanding debt as did Latin America in the 1980s. Also unlike Latin America, Eastern European countries (apart from Poland) had no outstanding debt, nor any rampant inflation (except for Poland and Yugoslavia). On the Latin American debt crisis, see Larrain and Selowsky 1991.

efficient factor and product markets, *few Western economists understand the institutional requirements essential to the creation of such markets since they simply take them for granted.* A set of political and economic institutions that provides low-cost transacting and credible commitment makes possible the efficient factor and product markets underlying economic growth. (North 1997, p. 2; emphasis added)

The problem is also that, if institutions should not be taken for granted in general, there is all the more reason why they must be taken seriously under the conditions of transition.

Rapid growth was anticipated because it was assumed that market institutions, if they did not appear out of thin air, would rise up quite spontaneously the 'day after' liberalization and stabilization. It was thought that policy need only secure a foothold for stabilization and lay the groundwork for the sound fundamentals. Thereafter, the economy would regain momentum on its own, and development would advance quickly.

However, the 'day after' liberalization and stabilization was even more depressing than the day before. Because of the 'neither plan, nor market' systemic vacuum, productive capacity was being employed even less; savings and investment were declining, and instead of rapid growth there was rapid recession. *The lack of appropriate institutions turned out to be the key element missing from the transition policies counselled by the Washington consensus.* Liberalization and privatization, unsupported by well-organized market structures, generated not sustained growth, but a lengthy period of contraction. This was not an inherited problem; it was the result of poor policy.

Under some circumstances, the reasoning of the Washington consensus may be relevant in dealing with the challenges faced by distorted, less-developed market economies. However, in these economies, market organizations have already been in place for years. The postsocialist economies possessed no basic market organizations, since such organizations had not existed under the centrally planned regime (Pohl, Jedrzejczak, and Anderson 1995). Therefore, because the absence of these organizations had apparently gone unnoticed until after the beginning of the transition, the market had no place to set roots and grow. Especially if the liberalization was rapid and the privatization radical, but in other cases, too, there could be no adequate and timely supply response. The misallocation of resources and of investments merely continued, although now for different reasons.

At the start, only the relatively well-developed portion of the market infrastructure could act as a foundation for commodity trading. Capital market structures were non-existent, or at best, in the most highly reformed nations, were only in infancy. Previously, the tasks performed by capital markets in full-fledged market economies had been conducted primarily through the state budget. Only a minor share of allocation occurred through 'unliquid' and limited 'quasi-markets' which were regulated by cooperative and state banks or 'grey' foreign exchange markets. The scarcity of financial intermediaries, including sound commercial and investment banks, discouraged accumulation and the allocation of any existing savings. Thus, immediately after the collapse of socialism the lack of the proper regulation of the emerging capital markets and the dearth of key organizations like investment banks, mutual funds, stock exchanges, and security control commissions caused distortions which could not be offset through liberalization and privatization alone.

In postsocialist economies, the creation of market organizations and institutional linkages could not possibly have occurred overnight. *The transition process must involve the retraining of many professionals to enable them to work effectively within the market environment.* This takes years, and it would clearly be much wiser to manage liberalization and privatization at a pace compatible with the speed of this necessary evolution in human capital. Otherwise, brute market forces are unleashed, and these alone will not propel an entire economy toward competitiveness, efficiency, and growth. In a number of countries trying to take a more radical tack toward transition, liberalization (rapid) and institution-building (slow) were occurring side-by-side, but in an uncoordinated, chaotic manner, so that, in terms of organizations and institutional linkages, 'creative destruction' was destroying more than it was creating.

The socialist nations enjoyed full or over-full employment (that is, there were labour shortages). No social security system protected against unemployment, since there was no unemployment.[3] The entire region had therefore to develop unemployment 'safety nets' from scratch.[4] But, in the meantime, before this change could be implemented, *on top of the misallocation of capital, the misallocation of labour began to occur.* The framework was inadequate for deregulating and policing a flexible labour market. If there was any sort of labour 'market' in the old system, it had been rather rigid owing to the weak political motivation of the authorities to make labour reply to any market-demand conditions, but even more because of the lack of labour mobility.[5]

The shortage of housing has been a serious barrier to labour mobility. It is thus not surprising that in transition countries the unemployed generally spend a very long time looking for work. The ratio between the highest and the lowest rates of unemployment among provinces is often in excess

[3] The only exception to this 'rule' was former Yugoslavia.

[4] The Chinese reforms in the late 1990s went quite a different route. China now accepts open unemployment, which was believed to exceed 4% of the labour force in 1998.

[5] In transition economies, with the exception of most of the former Soviet republics, the average membership in trade unions is lower than that in the European Union. According to the International Labour Organization, trade unions account for an average share of the total workforce ranging from only about 20% in Hungary to over 90% in Belarus. Yet, this is not the whole story either, since the unions in Hungary are much more independent than are those in Belarus, with all the obvious consequences in wage negotiations and so forth.

of five to one because of the concentration of obsolete industries in some areas, but also because of very weak labour mobility.

To resolve such labour market problems requires sound microeconomic restructuring of industrial capacity, years of gradual institution-building, and years of socially sensitive workforce redeployment and retraining.

Clearly, the Washington consensus underestimated the extent to which appropriate institutional arrangements were essential early on for a take-off in growth in postsocialist countries and in other economies going through a process of structural adjustment.

The economic policy orientation of the Washington consensus had a tremendous influence on the theory and practice in Eastern Europe and the former Soviet republics, as well as in the Asian socialist economies, but from the results it appears as though these nations did not all draw the same policy conclusions. A number of less-developed and transition economies realized quickly that there can be no sustained growth without sound fundamentals.

Lessons were eventually learned in Washington and London, too, and since the mid-1990s the Bretton Woods institutions have been paying more attention to the way market structures are organized and to the behavioural aspects of market performance. Now they know that liberalization and structural organization are both required for the market and economic growth. Because of the bitter experience of transitional contraction, but particularly because of the Asian crisis, it has become clear that there will be no sustained growth unless the sound fundamentals—a balanced budget, balance in the current account, low inflation, a stable currency, liberalized trade, and a vast private sector—are supported by appropriate institutional structures. There is now a consensus that the Washington consensus ought to be reconsidered, revised, and adjusted to reflect the lessons learned under real conditions (Williamson 1997, Stiglitz 1998a).

5.2. TOWARD A NEW CONSENSUS

The quest for consensus and for partners who can make the consensus a successful one is a constant process.[6] It is quite similar to the lifelong search for the recipe for a good life; one may take a step closer to the goal or further away from the goal, but one will never reach the goal and dis-

---

[6] The IMF organized a conference on 'Economic Policy and Equity' on 8–9 June 1998. Policymakers from the Bretton Woods institutions and the US Treasury Department and politicians, researchers, trade unionists, and clergy from all over the world participated in this interesting and important endeavour. However, if we need Washington to pierce equity issues and the Vatican to pierce efficiency issues, we may be better off doing things the old way. What about the Vatican's investment ethics? (Brother Ty, Buckley, and Tierney 1998).

cover the recipe. From time to time, as the situation changes and our knowledge evolves, new concerns and new vistas come to the fore.

A good example is the September 1996 IMF Interim Committee Declaration on 'Partnership for Sustainable Global Growth' (IMF 1996). This declaration may be seen as a modified version of the early Washington consensus. It contains 11 points. Point 1 stresses that monetary, fiscal, and structural policies are complementary and reinforce each other. Point 3 affirms that there is the need to create a favourable environment for private savings. Point 7 indicates that budgetary policies must aim at medium-term balance and at a reduction in public debt. Point 9 states that structural reform must show special attention to labour markets. Point 10 highlights the importance of good corporate governance. Point 11 emphasizes that banks must be monitored and that bank supervision must be strengthened so as to hinder corruption in the public sector and money laundering through the banking system. The other points are also relevant to sustainable development in transition economies. They address the issues of exchange rate stability (point 2), 'disinflation' (4), resistance to protectionist pressures (5), greater freedom for capital movement (6), and fiscal adjustment through adequate investment in infrastructure and the reduction of unproductive spending (8). These are all examples of the sorts of advice the postsocialist countries (and others) so very dearly needed during the first half of the 1990s, though at that time such advice was not necessarily on the front-burner among the IMF recommendations, and, still worse, even if the advice has more recently been offered, it has not always and everywhere been taken.

When gradual change and the more active involvement of the state in the design of institutions in postsocialist transition economies were first expounded (Laski 1990, Nuti 1990, Kolodko 1989a, 1991, 1993b, 1996, Poznanski 1993, 1996) and then implemented in Poland, they were considered unorthodox and controversial approaches in terms of the 'conventional' radical policy—though not necessarily therapy—of the Washington consensus. In fact, the Polish 'innovation' was the recognition not so much that change should be 'gradual', but that it is time consuming.

In 1997 and 1998, even in high-level international circles, there were many signs that a new consensus was emerging and that it is based on ideas tried in Poland in the mid-1990s. The policies being implemented in Poland at that time had to some extent been developed as an alternative to the mainstream early Washington consensus. Thanks to this 'multi-track approach', Poland avoided much of the adverse experience of other transition economies, such as the Czech Republic and Russia, which have 'ended up with cloudy, crony-dominated systems in which banks and company bosses keep each other comfortable, but create little value for shareholders'.[7]

---

[7] *The Economist*, 15 Feb. 1997.

On the subject of the first stages of the recession, Bob Mundell (1995), a dispassionate and authoritative voice, states unambiguously that 'early denials that the contractions were occurring have proven to be incorrect' and that in general these contractions were due to 'a bungle of economic policy on an unprecedented scale'.

An initial supporter of the Polish 1989–91 policy package and strong advocate of 'creative destruction' admitted that 'The percentage falls in total measured output in most transition economies . . . still remain formidable after reasonable corrections of the official data are made.' On the relatively minor importance of the privatization of state assets relative to the 'organic' growth of the private sector, he now accepts the view that 'the single most important factor underlying the considerable variation in the pace of recovery in the few countries which experienced it by 1995–6 has been, on the supply side, the initial size and the subsequent growth of the *de novo* private sector' (Gomulka 1996). Several other studies find that *de novo* private firms account for the major share of employment creation, although these firms represent a small fraction of existing employment. In this respect Poland has imitated a pattern familiar from the Chinese and Vietnamese experiences.

Why then the early rush 'creatively' to destroy the state sector or to give it away?

In the light of economic and financial events over the 1990s, Jeffrey Sachs eventually changed his opinion, too, and has acknowledged that his belief in shock treatment must be reconsidered. The experience of Eastern Europe—especially the aftermath of 'shock failure' in Poland in 1989–91 and the persistent Russian malaise—and the crisis in Asia in 1997–8 have led him this time to the right conclusion, that

Trade policy reform, in my view, should be quite [quick] because opening up the economy to trade gives a powerful stimulus [to] competition and market forces. Financial deregulation should proceed more gradually. . . . If the financial market reform lasts over a number of years, that would be fine and appropriate if it really moves forward step-by-step. (Quoted in Ravi 1998)

Albeit indirectly, this claim shares the outlook that radical liberalization is not feasible because of financial markets, which, unlike the trade regime, cannot be freed up so swiftly. Financial deregulation must be carried forward in a gradual manner, and due attention must be paid to the way it is implemented and to the goals of deregulation.

Why then was there such a push to liberalize and privatize almost everything overnight without heeding the warnings about the tremendous social costs of such an approach?

Opinions have changed so drastically that statements from the same source sometimes appear to come from widely disparate sources. The neoliberal weekly magazine *The Economist* was once very supportive of radical, rapid, and far-reaching liberalization and privatization in transition economies. For years it favoured free-market policies and praised Vaclav Klaus for the path he was taking. Then, it changed tack when the former Czech prime minister was already coming up against failure. Suddenly, *The Economist* noticed that

Mr Klaus has only himself to blame. . . . His hasty mass-privatization programme, which made ordinary Czechs the formal owners of most enterprises, but gave control to state-owned banks with no interest in improving them, created a crisis that culminated in a humiliating devaluation of the currency in May last year. Now unemployment and inflation are rising and real incomes are falling; the economy grew by just 1% in 1997 and will at best barely make 2% this year. (*The Economist* 1998b, p. 50)

Why then the earlier, extremely emphatic support for instant privatization and the equally imprudent support for the liberal policies of Czech centre-right governments?

After the Asian crisis had already achieved proportions beyond anyone's expectations, influential people in the international financial community began to change their minds, and doubts were finally raised about the rightness of the recipes being proposed for the emerging postsocialist market economies, especially Russia. Though there was not yet a new consensus, lessons were at last being learned. Now, it was being admitted that

The benefits brought by short-term international lenders are questionable: they do not provide new technology; they do not improve the management of domestic institutions, and they do not offer reliable finance [for the] current account deficit. In countries with high savings rates, they also increase already excessive investment rates. To manage the inflows, borrowers may have to accumulate huge reserves. . . . The Asian saga proves, once again, that liberalization of inadequately regulated and capitalized financial systems is a recipe for disaster. (Wolf 1998)

These are very accurate conclusions indeed. They had already been drawn elsewhere as well, for instance in Poland during that nation's tough negotiations on these subjects with the IMF and the Organization for Economic Cooperation and Development (OECD). But at that time these conclusions had not been the prevailing ones, and the subsequent policies in Poland were widely and heavily criticized.

A major problem has been the fact that the emerging markets in the transition economies are weaker and more vulnerable than are those in Asia and Latin America to swings in the flow of short-term speculative investments. Why then did *The Economist*, a leading journal with such close ties to international financial circles, exercise 'moral persuasion' for so long in favour of premature and risky liberalization in the access to postsocialist capital markets?

Meanwhile, the Bretton Woods institutions were always making their financial involvement contingent on the implementation of specific fiscal and monetary policies. Whether GDP was declining by 10 per cent or growing by 10 per cent, they were always exerting pressure on governments to bring the fiscal gap down and interest rates up. They imposed the requirement that fiscal and monetary tightness had to be maintained even if the budget deficit was smaller in a transition country than it was in the advanced industrial nations and even if the real interest rate was already so high that it was no longer possible to contain the deficit further because of the soaring cost of servicing public debt.[8] An interest rate which is 'overshot' through interest rate differentials facilitates the task of portfolio investors, but at the expense of the budget, that is, at the expense of the contributors to and the beneficiaries of the budget. In 1998 this requirement was still being imposed in Russia, where there was ongoing recession and the fiscal deficit stood at around 6 per cent of GDP during the first half of the year, and in Poland, where growth was almost 6 per cent and the deficit was only slightly over 2 per cent of GDP. So, this 'orthodoxy' is being applied as a fixed and fast rule, no matter the real causes of underlying problems or the unique conditions in particular countries.

Consider the crisis in Asia: 'a financial panic has caused—and is causing —greater damage than the underlying weaknesses of these economies could justify' (Wolf 1998).[9] Neither the fiscal deficit nor the public debt has led to the crisis. The private sector is at fault because it has been playing both ends against the middle. Private foreign lending institutions, especially banks and investment funds in the advanced market countries, were lending the money, and private domestic banks and corporations were borrowing it. The financing drive went too far, but to counteract it now is like fighting the use of drugs: one has to attack it from both ends, that is, the excessive supply in Medellin and the excessive demand in Miami must be addressed at the same time.

There are signs that, because of the gravity of the Asian crisis, the World Bank is starting to see the issues in a new light, perhaps even in a way which is different from the view of the IMF. Jean-Michel Severino, the World Bank vice president for East Asia and the Pacific, has said that the 'governments should initiate fresh spending on infrastructure and on social programmes to alleviate growing poverty, while *budget deficits should be allowed to widen, and interest rates should be kept down* if possible.'[10]

It is only a matter of time before there is a similar shift in the policy advice of World Bank and IMF experts to Russia, Ukraine, and other post-

---

[8] In other words, the cost of servicing the debt was so high not because of the nominal size of the debt, but because the real interest rate being paid on the debt was so high.

[9] If such a panic were to occur in Eastern Europe, it would not cause nearly so much harm. The exposure of the emerging postsocialist markets, including the biggest of them, to speculation by international capital is still slight. The amount of capital being invested in or pulled out of Eastern Europe is scanty compared to the capital flows in the ASEAN countries.

[10] Quoted in *Morning Press* (Washington, DC: External Relations Department, IMF), 16 June 1998; emphasis added.

socialist nations. It must be at last acknowledged that the circumstances there call for more, not less, state intervention. The government must step in, correct market imperfections vis-à-vis the allocation of capital, and provide financing in areas where the market cannot do so. Improvements in efficiency through sound corporate governance require patience and active government policies. Why for so long has there been such stubborn insistence on cuts in government spending and on higher interest rates? How is it still possible for anyone to believe that there can be efficient private ownership without a well-performing government?

In referring to Russia, Michel Camdessus, the managing director of the IMF, has said that 'No one measured the true depth of the collapse of all administrative structures, the decomposition of the state which accompanied the collapse of the communist system.'[11] Yet, Eatwell *et al.* (1995) and Poznanski (1996) already gave ample and prominent space to this issue (see also Kolodko and Nuti 1997). These studies assume not less government at any cost, but better government if possible.

US Secretary of the Treasury Lawrence H. Summers, a long-time fan of the mistaken approach toward assistance for the transition in Russia by the US and the IMF, has stated that

It is often said that governments today have less power, but in a sense they hold a society's fate in [their] hands more than ever before. The right policies are now better reinforced, and the wrong policies are more swiftly punished. Thus, *the impact of policies has never been greater.* The element of truth in this statement about the powerlessness of governments is that certain things, thought important for government to do, are becoming more difficult. (Summers 1998, p. 5; emphasis added)

Nicholas Stern, the EBRD chief economist, recognizes that

The building of institutions takes time. Clear examples are the financial and legal institutions. Banks depend on special skills, including accounting, credit analysis, and the like. These depend on the establishment of relationships, track records, and working methods. Legal systems have to be first established and then implemented. The analysis . . . of the 'Transition Report for 1995' shows that the implementation has been much weaker than the setting of legal structures themselves. Similar considerations apply to competition policy and, more generally, to the changing role of the state. (Stern 1996, p. 7)

The EBRD (1997a) now stresses that the 'Strengthening of existing institutions and policies, augmented by behavioural changes of private agents and authorities, is essential to yield sustained improvements in the investment climate of the region.' So, the attitude of important organizations such as the World Bank, the IMF, and the EBRD has changed under the sway of the new way of seeing the issues and thinking about the manner in which the issues ought to be addressed.

---

[11] Quoted in *Financial Times*, 10 Jan. 1997.

The importance of corporate governance—as opposed to the sheer transfer of property titles—is now being recognized even by the early keen supporters of massive, rapid privatization, such as Frydman and Rapaczynski (1991, 1994). Estrin (1996) reports that in the Czech Republic, Hungary, Poland, and Russia there is no clear evidence that privatized enterprises perform better than do state enterprises which have not yet been privatized and declares that effective corporate governance takes time to establish.[12] Stern (1996, p. 8) points to the process of restructuring, which 'itself will be a major and fundamental task involving investment, hard decisions, and dislocation. It will be much less painful if economic growth, effective corporate governance, and well-functioning safety nets are established.' Konings, Lehmann, and Schaffer (1996) rightly argue that, for recovery, good corporate governance is at least as essential as privatization and overall liberalization.

After the extreme laissez faire of the early transition, the values of cooperation and solidarity are being rediscovered. Even the billionaire financier George Soros in January 1997 did not hesitate to admit that,

Although I have made a fortune in the financial markets, I now fear that the untrammelled intensification of laissez-faire capitalism and the spread of market values into all areas of life [are] endangering our open and democratic society. . . . Too much competition and too little cooperation can cause intolerable inequities and instability. (Soros 1997)

Devoted to transition, *World Development Report 1996* emphasizes very strongly the need for social consensus. 'Establishing a social consensus will be crucial for the long-term success of transition—cross-country analyses suggest that societies that are very unequal in terms of income or assets tend to be politically and socially less stable and to have lower rates of investment and growth' (World Bank 1996).

It is now widely accepted that in economies which are still affected by structural rigidities, such as formal and informal indexation and sluggish supply responses, attempts at speeding up disinflation, once inflation has fallen below a threshold of about 40 per cent, would have significant, perhaps intolerable costs. In any case, the costs would be higher than those generated by the moderately falling inflation actually being experienced in some of the leading transition countries which have recently been following the path first adopted in Poland. What counts is that inflation should continue to fall steadily and noticeably and never accelerate again. Such a process of disinflation contributes to the credibility of the government and the monetary authorities, but also secures a certain predictability about

---

[12] Pohl, Djankov, and Anderson (1996) stress the positive impact of privatization, claiming that the performance of big enterprises restructured through privatization is superior. However, because there is an element of selection in the decision to privatize certain enterprises or not, such observations may not be conclusive.

developments in the economy, creates a better business environment, and encourages confidence on the international scene. Poland since the mid-1990s is a case in point.

The targeting of a positive real interest rate—an unwarranted dogma and a ruinous policy during the early transition—is now seen more comprehensively as a determinant of savings that is less significant than demographic trends, national pension policy, and overall fiscal and regulatory policies.[13]

A considerate neglect of real interest rates is displayed by Buiter, Lago, and Stern (1996), who illustrate the importance of the 'permanent income and life-cycle' hypothesis. According to this hypothesis, it is plausible that some 'target' savers may respond negatively to a higher interest rate, which in principle would allow them to achieve a given consumption transfer to the future at the cost of lower current sacrifice. This may be likely in an ageing society, as many Eastern European nations are, since people who are relatively older may be relatively less interested in achieving such a consumption transfer. In a situation of higher real incomes and falling inflation, the real interest rate required to boost savings is bound to be much lower.

The prerequisites for an enhanced savings ratio—that is, savings which are rising more quickly than income—are real income growth, stabilization, and optimistic expectations. Only against such a background can the propensity to save be nurtured.

Transition Report 1996 (EBRD 1996), which is devoted to infrastructure and savings, stresses the role of mounting government savings—particularly through the overhaul and reform of the social security and pension systems and through more broadly based taxation at lower rates—and the development of contractual long-term savings and life insurance. From this perspective, the early (and also the later) pressure on transition countries to maintain high and positive real interest rates was grossly misplaced. The fiscal and quasi-fiscal activities of central banks, notably in the emerging economies and especially in the postsocialist nations, have attracted considerable attention (Fry 1993). The costs of the sterilization policies required because of excessive interest rate differentials and undervalued currencies have thus come to the fore, for instance in the OECD country study of the Czech Republic (OECD 1996a). It turns out that for a considerable

---

[13] The dogma has cost Polish taxpayers a great deal, especially when interest rates were being maintained at an exorbitantly high level during the necessary real revaluations in 1996 and 1998. When at last this ill-advised policy was abandoned in Poland in mid-1998, the costs had already been borne. Of course, the losses of the taxpayers and of the national economy were someone else's gain, especially that of short-term speculative portfolio investors. Russian taxpayers have been required to pay an even heavier price for the failed attempts to enforce policies stemming from this erroneous dogma. Shortly before the 1998 financial collapse, with the approval of the IMF and international portfolio investors, the interest rate was fixed at 150%, while inflation remained below 10%.

time the central banks of both the Czech Republic and Poland were losing about 1 per cent of annual GDP through unfortunate sterilization policies (Nuti 1996).[14]

The Asian crisis and the positive Polish experience with the rejection of the 'radical' policies of the first Washington consensus offer numerous valuable lessons. The fact that certain observations and opinions are becoming more widely shared suggests that there may now be an opportunity to reach a new consensus about the conditions for sustained growth and about the policies which may create these conditions. The 'post-Washington consensus', if it ever comes, could help facilitate the application of policies which are oriented toward sustained growth, but which do not ignore crucial elements such as institution-building and the active role of the state.[15]

Any emerging consensus must have at least one more key feature. This time it must gather more partners to augment the leading role of the Washington-based organizations, especially the IMF and the World Bank. Other international organizations—the United Nations, the Organization for Economic Cooperation and Development, the World Trade Organization, the International Labour Organization, the European Bank for Reconstruction and Development—should have a larger part. Likewise, regional organizations, such as the Association of South East Asian Nations, the Central European Free Trade Agreement, and the Commonwealth of Independent States, should improve their ability to project their presence in the global forum and try to affect the process of change in the international financial and economic order. Some international non-governmental organizations ought to become more influential, too. The search for a revised consensus must rely on a quest not only for new policies agreed in Washington, but also for new policies agreed between Washington and other important actors in other areas of the global economy.

5.3. THE MEANS AND THE ENDS OF ECONOMIC POLICY

The lack of real success of the policies of the Washington consensus has also been due to a confusion between the means and the ends of policy. A sound fiscal

[14] What may have appeared to some outside observers as a challenge to the independence of the National Bank of Poland on the part of the Polish government, particularly the Ministry of Finance, was actually a well-founded disagreement over policy priorities (inflation versus unemployment) and policy instruments (interest rates versus exchange rates).

[15] In contrast, some of the partners in the first Washington consensus are still claiming, contrary to the evidence and to all logic, that the success of Poland has been due to a radical approach and to neoliberalism, just as the Russian malaise has been caused by the lack thereof. The fallacy of their point of view is clearly shown by the poor economic performance in Poland at the beginning of the 1990s and in Russia over the entire decade. If these actors continue to insist that countries must 'stay the course', as has been the case of the US government and, consequently, the IMF following Russia's default in late 1998, the realization of the 'post-Washington consensus' will be even more difficult.

stance, low inflation, stable exchange rates, and overall financial stabilization are only the means of economic policy, while sustained growth and healthier standards of living are the ends. Very important changes, such as privatization and liberalization, are merely instruments, not targets. One can easily lose sight of this fact and present 'instruments' or 'processes' as the core or final goal of economic policy, just as, under the socialist system, 'perfecting the central plan' was widely understood as the aim of policy rather than merely a tool, or just as reform was executed simply for the sake of reform. The identification of ways to improve efficiency and competitiveness is now often the main focus, though the real focus should be the ultimate outcomes of policy. This sort of bias leads to policy distortions and insufficient concern for the impact of policies on the real economy.

How could it have come about otherwise that orthodox neoliberalism embraced an intellectual oversimplification according to which there is no need to think very much about how to drive the machine, since at some point and under certain circumstances it can run for a while on its own? An extreme example is the idea that 'the best policy is no policy'.[16]

The distinction between the ends and the means should be obvious to anyone, but especially to people involved in economic research and policy-making. In fact, the confusion between the ends and the means is not really to be explained away by the naïveté and laziness of economists and politicians, who do work hard and are not so naïve. The intellectual misunderstandings result from political antagonisms. The arguments are more about conflicts of interest and less about alternative theoretical concepts and scientific explanations.

Naturally, policy mistakes also occur simply because of errors in knowledge and errors in policy advice, but more often they are due to obedience to a group of interests or to a 'theoretical school' which happens also to represent a group of interests. There are no leftist or rightist doctors and engineers, only leftist and rightist (and so on) economists and politicians.

John Williamson (1990) stresses the priorities and policy alternatives of 'political' Washington and of 'technocratic' Washington. However, the picture is more complex because there are other priorities and options beyond the purely 'political' or 'technocratic'. Some actors play both games. Moreover, the influence and policies of the Bretton Woods institutions, especially the IMF, have such serious implications for particular countries and regions, if not the global economy, that sometimes they determine— and decide—much more than purely 'technocratic' issues.

Williamson also considers differences through the prisms of theoretical arguments, which can lead to consensus, and normative values, where the

---

[16] 'The best policy is no policy' was an actual statement (and unfortunately also principle of action) heard within the Polish government during the period of 'shock therapy'. No wonder industrial output fell by about 40% in just two years.

differences are sometimes more substantial and more enduring. Thus, he tries to distinguish between 'the left' and 'the right':

the fundamental political divide [on economic issues] is not between capitalism and socialism, or between free markets and state intervention, but between those concerned to promote an equitable income distribution ['the left'] and those concerned to defend established privileges ['the right']. Note that this dividing line helps explain why it seemed natural for communist hardliners to be called right-wing in recent Soviet debates, while those seeking the transition to a market economy were called the left. (Williamson 1993, p. 1331)

But the situation is even more complicated, since, aside from the intellectual controversies and the various normative values, there are also political, economic, and financial interests. Otherwise, it would be impossible to understand how erroneous policies could have held sway so long, even after it had become obvious that they were wrong. This was the case, for instance, with early liberalization and stabilization in Poland in 1989–92, or with the negligence of corporate governance in the Czech Republic in 1993–6, or with the Russian privatization of 1994–8 that was executed with the active involvement of informal institutions having political ties or links to organized crime, or with the fraudulent financial intermediaries in Albania in 1995–7 who were tolerated until the economy collapsed like a house of cards.

These are examples of the confusion between the instruments and the targets of economic policy. Economic policy is not to be judged by the pace of privatization, but by the efficiency of privatization as measured first by the rise in competitiveness and in budget revenues and then by the increase in national income. The insistence by some on acceleration in the implementation of privatization has been due only to a desire to see the assets sold as cheaply as possible. The hope is not necessarily to be able to sell off the assets sooner, a motive often hinted at, but rather to be able to acquire them for less than would be possible through a more reasonable practice. Who sells fast, sells cheap. Society loses the potential budget revenue, but someone else profits.

Warnings, criticism, and intellectual and political opposition have been raised against these unwise polices, which have nonetheless been bullied through. Why? The answer is that they have been implemented not owing to a deficit in sound economic ideas or sound policy programmes, but because of the pressure of strong lobbies and interest groups. Apparently, policies are the correct ones as long as they fill the needs of these groups. It so happens that often the strongest support is behind not truth and logic, but money and power.

True reform leads toward the long-term target of sustained growth and thereby satisfies the interests of the many, not the special interests of the few. Failing that, 'progress' is not real, and the improvement in the overall economic situation is only theoretical. The overall situation is worse, not better, if the size of the private sector, the scope of trade liberalization, or the extent of the deregulation in capital transfers has become greater, but the contraction of the economy is severe, growth is sluggish, and the standard of living is deteriorating. Yet, frequently the situation as seen from the perspective of a particular group of interests is presented as though it were the overall economic picture. Thus, evaluations of the health of an economy and the appropriateness of a policy approach are often biased and should be examined with care to determine what has been evaluated, how the evaluation has been made, who has made it, and for what purpose. Obviously, the evaluations of, for example, Moody's and of Russian trade unions may be as different as are the interests of, say, Morgan Stanley Investment Bank and of miners in Siberia.

In each economy systemic changes ought to be judged according to the extent to which they enhance the competitiveness of the business sector and the standard of living of households. Just as it is clear that one must assure competitiveness and keep the real cost of labour under control, it would be absurd to allow a significant contraction of real wages to go on too long, as occurred in Poland, where real wages dropped altogether by about 25 per cent in 1990–1, or in Hungary, where they contracted by around 18 per cent in 1995–6.[17] It may happen that a temporary decline in wages appears to be necessary in order to sustain the long-term ability of the economy to compete, and to a degree this was the situation in Poland at the beginning of the 1990s and in Hungary in 1995–6. Yet, it is begging the question to claim that such a decline is evidence of sound economic policy.

Indeed, the contrary is more likely true. The long-run growth of real wages is a sign of a well-performing economy. This is even more the case during the transition to the market, at least so long as international competitiveness is not adversely affected. The postsocialist countries began the transition from a relatively backward position, and the process of reaching the level of the more well developed part of the world economy should be understood to involve a non-inflationary upward wage adjustment based on the long-term growth of labour productivity.

If one is able to distinguish between policy instruments and policy aims, then one can also understand that better economic performance is characterized by a higher rate of growth and not by higher bankruptcy rates, by higher real income and not by real wage falls, by mounting employment and not by more joblessness, and by efficient privatization and not by the precipitous sale of national assets at giveaway prices. The good policy

---

[17] In Poland, after the initial drop in 1990, real wages fell by a further 6% in 1991–3 and started to rise again only in 1994. In Hungary, after the slump of 1995–6, they recovered by about 6% in 1997 and continued to increase in 1998, though at a much slower pace (PlanEcon 1997b).

is not the one which is hard on large segments of society and favourable to small segments, but the one which is able to secure development and which leads to improvement in the living standards of all in society.

Apart from the confusion between the means and the ends of economic policy, *there is also a confusion between transition policy and development policy, and there is a confusion surrounding the nature of transition, which encompasses not only liberalization and stabilization, but also institutional change and microeconomic restructuring.* Liberalization and stabilization are separate from institutional and behavioural change, and all these areas must be addressed properly within the framework of a comprehensive transition policy (EBRD 1997a).

A high rate of GDP growth goes hand-in-hand with rising output, but leads only much later to an improvement in the quality of life, which is much more all-encompassing than the level of economic activity as reflected in GDP. The human development index (HDI) calculated by the United Nations Development Programme seems to be a more relevant measure of improvement in society than is GDP, although, in general, over the long run there is a strong positive correlation between the level of GDP per capita and changes in the HDI (UNDP 1997, World Bank 1997a, Ravallion 1997). The HDI is a composite indicator and takes into consideration accomplishments in areas of basic human capability such as life expectancy at birth, educational attainment, and income. Hence the HDI is a more suitable measure of change vis-à-vis the ultimate target of development policy.[18]

Not surprisingly, the ranking of the postsocialist economies according to the HDI is higher than the ranking of these economies according to GDP per capita. Moreover, the HDI ranking of these economies is in almost all cases relatively better than that of the developed market countries. The difference between the HDI ranking and the ranking according to real GDP per capita (on a purchasing power parity basis) in the case of the advanced countries varies from 19 positions for Spain and 15 for Finland and New Zealand to zero for Japan, minus 8 for Denmark and minus 12 for Switzerland. The difference in the corresponding rankings among the postsocialist countries (with the exceptions of Laos and Mongolia, the only countries with a negative value) varies from 3 positions for the Czech Republic, Romania, and Slovenia and 14 for Poland to over 30 for Georgia and Tajikistan (Table 15). This result is due to the positive legacy of the old system, which emphasized high educational standards, active cultural

[18] The HDI is described by the UNDP (1997, p. 44) as follows: 'The HDI value for each country indicates how far the country has to go to attain certain defined goals: an average life span of 85 years, access to education for all, and a decent standard of living. The HDI reduces all three basic indicators to a common measuring rod by measuring achievement in each as the relative distance from the desirable goal. The maximum and minimum values for each variable are reduced to a scale between 0 and 1, with each country at some point on the scale.'

Table 15 The human development index for transition countries, 1994

	HDI value	HDI rank	Real GDP per capita (PPP$), 1994	HDI rank minus GDP rank[a]
Slovenia	0.886	35	10,404	3
Czech Republic	0.882	39	9,201	3
Slovakia	0.873	42	6,389	12
Hungary	0.857	48	6,437	5
Poland	0.834	58	5,002	14
Belarus	0.806	62	4,713	13
Russia	0.792	67	4,828	7
Bulgaria	0.780	69	4,533	9
Estonia	0.776	71	4,294	8
Lithuania	0.762	76	4,011	8
Croatia	0.760	77	3,960	10
Romania	0.748	79	4,037	3
FYR Macedonia	0.748	80	3,965	5
Turkmenistan	0.723	85	3,469	12
Latvia	0.711	92	3,332	6
Kazakhstan	0.709	93	3,284	6
Ukraine	0.689	95	2,718	14
Uzbekistan	0.662	100	2,438	14
Albania	0.655	102	2,788	4
Armenia	0.651	103	1,737	24
Georgia	0.637	105	1,585	31
Azerbaijan	0.636	106	1,670	25
Kyrgyzstan	0.635	107	1,930	18
Moldova	0.612	110	1,576	28
Tajikistan	0.580	115	1,117	35
Mongolia	0.661	101	3,766	−10
China	0.626	108	2,604	3
Vietnam	0.557	121	1,208	26
Laos	0.459	136	2,484	−23
Cambodia	0.348	153	1,084	1
North Korea	0.765	75	3,965	10
Cuba	0.723	86	3,000	17

[a] A positive figure indicates that the HDI rank is better than the real GDP per capita rank (purchasing power parity dollars); a negative figure indicates the opposite.
Source: UNDP 1997.

institutions, and free universal health care. Consequently, for example, life expectancy at birth is generally longer in transition countries than it is in other nations at a similar level of GDP per capita.

It can be seen that the aims of development policy are still more comprehensive than are those of transition policy, and attitudes toward the two sets of aims have changed over time, including among the early partners of the Washington consensus, particularly the World Bank. *A stable economy, sustainable growth, and a high standard of living are serious and appropriate policy concerns, but so also should be equitable income distribution, the good health of the natural environment, and the sound state of democracy itself.*

'Our understanding of the instruments to promote well-functioning markets has . . . improved, and we have broadened the objectives of development to include other goals, such as sustainable development, egalitarian development, and democratic development' (Stiglitz 1998a, p. 1). Despite the bad reputation in this respect of banks generally, the World Bank has always been inclined to take social issues and the development of human capital a little more seriously than have other international financial institutions. It should be acknowledged that in many countries, including transition economies, the World Bank has been involved in projects which have served well the aim of raising standards of living and alleviating poverty.

Moreover, even the IMF is now claiming that it is keen to take up the call for a fairer distribution of the fruits of growth, if only the policies it counsels would deliver some. Being for a long time himself quite concerned about equitable growth, Stanley Fischer, the first deputy managing director of the IMF, has asked the question 'Why do equity considerations matter for the Fund?' and then answered it.

First, as a matter of social justice, all members of society should share in the benefits of economic growth. And although there are many important arguments about precisely what constitutes a fair distribution of income, we accept the view that poverty in the midst of plenty is not socially acceptable. But, second, there is also an instrumental argument for equity: adjustment programmes that are equitable and growth that is equitable are more likely to be sustainable. These are good enough reasons for the IMF to be concerned about equity considerations—whether it be poverty reduction or concerns about income distribution in the programmes the IMF supports. (Fischer 1998a, p. 1)

This would indeed be an approach whereby, for once, the means and the ends of policy would not be confused.

Whether it is the thorny path from contraction to growth in the post-socialist economies or the more well pruned path toward durable growth in the Asian reformed socialist economies (which did not follow the proposals of the early Washington consensus), the experience of transformation has undoubtedly contributed significantly to the shift in attitudes. This experience, together with the East Asian crisis, may yet be the catalyst for the emergence of a 'post-Washington consensus' as, in a similar way, the debt crisis in Latin America in the 1980s sparked the earlier Washington consensus. Yet, the distance is still great between an intellectual consensus and appropriate policy action.

The Journey

6

Transition Policy and Development Strategy

6.1. TRANSITION AS A PROCESS OF THE REDESIGN OF SYSTEMS

The ultimate success of transformation depends on the existence of a reliable institutional design. In the former Soviet republics, where the design process is more difficult than it is in Eastern Europe, basic institutions such as sovereign central banks, local currencies, and private ownership of the means of production were virtually unknown, and these and many other institutions have had to be built from the ground up. While institution-building—always slow by nature—has been more problematic in countries affected by overly radical liberalization and excessive withdrawal of the state from the regulation of economic activities, it has been moving steadily forward in the Asian reformed socialist economies. The institutional changes in these economies have been immense during the last decade.

Some of the postsocialist nations took a course of gradual liberalization and privatization, perhaps in certain cases overly gradual. Though this led to only relatively mild contraction, it was generally accompanied by delays in crucial structural reform, too. If the time permitted by gradual liberalization is used for appropriate institution-building, it can be fruitful; if it is wasted from the perspective of institutional reform, then the chance for long-term expansion will be small. Other countries chose the course of rapid change. Though the resulting contraction was more severe during the early stages, often the process of institution-building reached a more advanced level later.

In the long run, both general approaches have involved the bitter lesson that the market economy cannot expand without wise government-led development policy and well-designed institutions. The state management of institution-building is vitally important. Truly, this—and not liberalization—is the very essence and core of transition. Without adequate care for the institutional arrangements, liberalization and privatization will not deliver what societies expect from the economy. It has even been claimed that,

when pursued simultaneously, privatization may actually impede the transition process following market liberalization and reduce social welfare. . . . Compared to a fully functioning market in a mature economy, a market in transition is characterized by greater uncertainty regarding market conditions, including free market equilibrium levels of prices and quantities. Market participants must learn about these conditions through their participation in the market process. When the effects of learning are incorporated into the analysis, the optimal level of privatization decreases monotonically as the level of uncertainty increases. (Goodhue, Rausser, and Simon 1996)

Thus, if the state does not design a proper institutional set-up, then market failures prevail, and 'informal institutionalization' takes over (Stein 1993). Instead of sound markets, 'crony capitalism' emerges.

It is easy to identify institutional arrangements that work well: each partner does what it is supposed to do, there is good coordination [and] little conflict and the economy grows smoothly and rapidly. We can also recognize ill-functioning institutional arrangements: change is inhibited by bureaucratic requirements, or there is 'bandit capitalism' with pervasive corruption and deceit. (Stern and Stiglitz 1997, p. 20)

These institutional pathologies can arise as a result of transition-by-chance, as opposed to transition-by-design. Sometimes faulty transition policies have opened the door to systems in which 'only the stupid pay taxes', contracts are not executed as agreed, or bills and wages are not paid on time. Rather than a market economy, this is the chaos caused by institutional disintegration and the absence of organizations and mechanisms able to fix things and make them work the way they are supposed to work under a sound liberal regime. This chaos was a common feature of the early transition.

Without a vision of the way to establish a new system and without an understanding of the way it should work, one will not be able to realize the new system readily or easily. The transition protracts; the costs rise, and the outcomes are less than what they might have been: the recession lasts too long; recovery comes so late, and output expands only very slowly.

Thus, a paramount task is to create successful institutions during the transition, a task which is rendered even more difficult because of institutional discontinuity: the old arrangements (the Gosplan, say, or the branch ministries) don't work anymore, but the new ones (say, the investment banking sector and the stock exchange) are not yet in place.

Market capitalism requires the pre-eminence of private ownership, but also a competitive enterprise sector, functioning markets, and respect for the rules of market allocation. Well-performing financial intermediaries are necessary to facilitate trading and investment and to promote savings. The market also requires a proper legal environment which is able to enforce market rules and contracts and ensure the proper behaviour of economic agents, whether firms, households, organizations, or governments. In the most institutionally advanced nations, constitutional courts are sometimes big troublemakers because they throw out bad laws which have just been adopted in parliament at the insistence of the government majority. This does not make policy easier in the short run, but it definitely contributes to the rule of law in the long run.

Thus, good institutions matter a great deal for good economic perform-ance and sustainable development. According to the received wisdom, the better the market organizations and the more compatible these organizations and public services, the sounder will be economic and social development.

In a special issue of *World Development Report*, the World Bank has high-lighted the role of the state in the contemporary world and pointed to the need to distinguish between the means (institutions and state involvement) and the ends (growth and development). It has also stressed that

the state makes a vital contribution to economic development when its role matches its institutional capability. But capability is not destiny. It can and must be improved if governments are to promote further improvements in economic and social welfare. . . . Three interrelated sets of institutional mechanisms can help create incentives that will strengthen the state's capability. These mechanisms aim to:
• Enforce rules and restraints in society as well as within the state,
• Promote competitive pressures from outside and from within the state, and
• Facilitate voice and partnership both outside and within the state. (World Bank 1997b)

This is true in all economic systems, but especially in transition economies. In transition economies, the enforcement of new regulations and new types of behaviour among economic entities calls for very determined state involve-ment. Unfortunately, the transition state faces additional challenges com-pared to the state under socialism, as well as the state in traditional market economies with mature civic societies and well-functioning institutions. Moreover, the postsocialist state has been weakened by neoliberal policies, which have often received official support from the governments of lead-ing industrial market countries and the international organizations heavily influenced by them. It is difficult for the new state to regain some of the sovereign control which the old state lost through the chaotic process of liberalization.

Discussions in 1997–8 between the Russian government and the IMF and the repeated postponements in the payment of subsequent instalments of stand-by credit are a good case in point. The inability to collect taxes is a result of institutional collapse; hence the IMF insistence on sound improvements in budgetary revenues was in vain. The problem is not exclus-ively a matter of a lack of government commitment to fight tax avoidance and tax evasion. It is also a legacy of the mismanagement of the transi-tion and of structural adjustment policies which were implemented under agreements with the IMF and the World Bank. Now, the enforcement of the new rules—for example the payment of taxes and other contributions—is going to be a long and tough process. The greater the ill-advised shocks administered early on, the more difficult is the task of enforcing the new rules later.

Governments under the centrally planned regime often disregarded the need for consumer protection, and the shortageflation syndrome wiped out any possibility for true competition. During the early transition, because of the legacy of the old monopolistic structures and practices, there was also little competition. The creation of an institutional framework to ensure fair competition takes time. It calls for the development of numerous civic organizations.

But even if the appropriate structures, organizations, and legal system have already been established, the issue of the behaviour of producers must still be addressed. Sellers, distributors, and dealers must be taught to treat the market as a place to sell goods and provide services, not as a place to cheat one another, consumers, or the Treasury. Antitrust organizations and consumer protection agencies must therefore be established; a functioning banking and tax system must be constituted, and prudent fiscal policy must be in place.

The development of the partnership among the market players is precisely what gradual institution-building is all about. This partnership can eventually enhance the growth potential of an economy, but during the initial stages of transition the constant changes can destabilize the linkages among the partners involved in economic activities. The old ties have ceased to exist, but the new ones are only *in statu nascendi*. The state's involvement is thus essential, since market relations otherwise become more and more associated with haphazard events resulting from the conduct of interest groups and informal organizations, including organized crime.

6.2. TRANSITION AS AN INSTRUMENT OF DEVELOPMENT STRATEGY

The new institutional set-up must be founded upon organizations which did not exist (since they were not needed) under the statist economy. Transition requires a new legal system, but also new sorts of behaviour. Enterprises, banks, civil servants, the state bureaucracy, and even households must immediately abandon old ways and learn new ones. Who is supposed to enforce this changeover, and how is it supposed to be accomplished? We may know who the students in this class are and which subjects are to be taught in the course, but where are the teachers? Hands-on experience with the emerging market is a good teacher, but it is slow and generates enormous costs and a great many failures before its lessons can be learned.

The political leaders in postsocialist countries do not have 40 years, as Moses did, to lead their peoples to the Promised Land. To accelerate the process and cut the costs of institutional and cultural adjustment demand special training and education initiatives by the authorities, political and intellectual elites, and non-governmental organizations. The Bretton Woods institutions must contribute as well. Because of the meagre outcomes of the first years of transition, they are getting the message that help with the acquisition of new knowledge and skills is sometimes at least as important as lending the money, and they have started to pay much more attention to technical assistance and professional training.

In nations enjoying a relatively more liberal system under socialism, the learning process is much faster. If a private sector and the decentralized management of state companies already exist, the learning of new corporate governance methods is smoother. If a two-tier banking system is already in operation, the learning of sound commercial banking is easier. If there are already antitrust agencies, they may be quite useful if markets are well supplied (though they were not very useful when there was shortageflation).

In countries which had traditional centrally planned regimes until the late 1980s, the learning process is slower. This explains the differences in economic performance between neighbours such as Hungary and Romania. The faster the process of institution-building, the better the environment for business activities and for growth. Government guidance and intervention can hasten the process, but, if mismanaged, may spoil it instead. Nonetheless, this risk should not be an excuse for the withdrawal of the state. On the contrary, it means the state must counsel wisely and act rationally.

Over the long term, transition should be seen as the major instrument of development policy. Steps which do not lead toward durable growth and sustainable development do not make sense. However, some shifts may be ideologically or politically motivated and welcomed by certain groups which are unconcerned about the implications for society. Such a situation has occurred often during the period of postsocialist transformation, regardless of whether it is being carried out gradually or in a radical way. The special interest groups involved must not be ignored since they may be very strong. To counterbalance them, one must rely on other groups which are oriented toward progress and long-run development. However, this is not easy, since it requires the ability to restrain the significant pressure which can be exerted by particular groups. Moreover, *many groups use any means at their disposal to advance their own particular interests, but there are few groups keen to fight with determination in favour of long-term development and remote policy targets.*

However obvious it may be that systemic transition is not the ultimate goal, but only the tool of a more important aim, there is still some bafflement on these subjects. This applies most clearly to the interdependence of institutional change and real economic expansion. How can a system be considered perfect while growth is unsatisfactory? How can a system be praised if it produces little capacity for economic expansion? Even well-known and very competent professionals and the official publications of respected international organizations have lauded the reforms for their own sake rather than paying due attention to the real outcomes.

Important causes of the enormous economic contraction in Eastern Europe and the former Soviet republics have therefore been ignorance of development policy, exaggeration of the significance of transition as such, and a confusion of transition with liberalization and privatization. Policies have focused mainly on stabilization, trade liberalization, and privatization and little on the real economy as reflected in output, consumption, investment, and unemployment.

In contrast to this experience, close attention to development policy and to market-oriented reform as the means to reach successful development has contributed significantly to the high rates of growth in China and Vietnam (Montes 1997). This is revealing particularly because there has not yet been a similar flowering in the postsocialist economies. Reforms which have failed in Europe have worked in Asia. In Asia the distinction has been made between system design and policy guidance. In Asia it has been possible to rely on the advantages of the system, or, whenever necessary, adjust the system to new challenges for the sake of further growth. In Asia the system and modifications to the system have been used as a means of expansion, not as a target.

The system itself should not serve as a substitute for good policy. Sometimes—and this has usually been the case in the course of history—it is sufficient to improve policies without overhauling the system. Of course, economic policies during transition may be better or worse; government actions may be wise or less than wise, and the involvement of the international community may be generally beneficial or not.

In the very long term, the design of the system plays an instrumental role in expansion and development. The system must be flexible enough to meet emerging challenges and changing circumstances. It must be adjusted from time to time in line with its role of serving the long-term goals of growth and better standards of living. Thus, the entire transformation should be viewed only as an episode, which may serve development well if only policy will allow it to do so.

6.3. INSTITUTION-BUILDING: FROM SHOCK FAILURE TO GRADUAL THERAPY

It has been possible to decide to introduce the market through a postsocialist transition because so much experience and knowledge have been gained about market performance and the management and improvement of market institutions over the centuries. Nowadays, we know a priori what kinds of institutions a market economy requires. If to such knowledge one can add a close and accurate evaluation of the specific conditions in a given case, then one may take steps toward the market economy.

Yet, taking such 'steps' takes time. Institutions are being built, but in fact they must also be 'learned'.

Institutions and the way they evolve shape economic performance. Institutions affect economic performance by determining (together with the technology employed) the cost of transacting and producing. They are composed of formal rules, of informal constraints, and of their enforcement characteristics; while formal rules can be changed overnight by the polity, informal constraints change very slowly. Both are ultimately shaped by the subjective perceptions people possess to explain the world around them which in turn determine explicit choices of formal rules and evolving informal constraints. Institutions differ from organizations. The former are the rules of the game; the latter are groups of individuals bound together by a common objective function (economic organizations are firms, trade unions, cooperatives; political organizations are political parties, legislative bodies, etc.). (North 1997, p. 1)

In the real world, even institutions do not change overnight from a formal viewpoint. Or, more precisely, the law and the legal aspects of institutional arrangements must be overhauled before there can at last be such a night.

Whether in its abbreviated form in Poland, or in the long, drawn out version in Russia, 'shock therapy' has failed especially because of the systemic vacuum which followed the radical dismantling of the old institutional set-up and because of the huge recession. The process of postsocialist transformation has subsequently been managed more reasonably through deliberate measures and at a somewhat slower pace.

It has thus turned out that a transition from a centrally planned to a market economy must be executed by means of a gradual process of structural, institutional, and behavioural change. Because of the very nature of this long and complex process, it cannot be carried forward in a radical way. It requires time and is costly. It is risky and exposes populations to social and political tensions.

Only part of the multilayer transition process, namely, liberalization and stabilization, can be executed in a radical manner (if the political conditions permit). To carry out the liberalization and stabilization in a radical way is not normally an obligation, but only a policy choice which depends on the risk of monetary and fiscal imbalances and on the extent of social tolerance.

Structural adjustments, institutional reforms, and behavioural changes take at least several years whatever the conditions.[1] The postsocialist

---

[1] For example, in Eastern Europe pirated versions account for about 77% of the computer software used, while in the United States the figure is only slightly more than a quarter of

transition may seem very long to the populations and political leaders involved, but it is very short on the clock of history, especially considering the enormously complex and comprehensive changes which are taking place in structures, institutions, and behaviours. The establishment of well-performing market economies in the past took much more time than has the current transformation process in socialist and postsocialist countries. To overhaul an economy in 10 years is actually quite a feat.

There have been many hardships, however. The hardships have not been due to a lack of knowledge about how markets work. They have been due to a lack of knowledge about how to establish a market system in late-socialist economies in severe systemic and structural crisis. The most challenging problem has not been the target design of new organizations and institutions, but the very process of transition leading toward them. The most difficult question is not 'How should the institutions work once they are established?', but 'How do we get to there from here?'. To lecture on the methods used on the stock exchange on Wall Street would not have made much sense at the outset of transition, because at the time the need was desperate for an understanding of how to lay the foundation of a capital market, rather than about how a sophisticated one functions. To insist on copying the British model of privatization would have been folly in a situation in which almost all assets were owned by the state. It would have been a mistake to push for the radical liberalization of housing rents, when the skyrocketing prices might have caused a collapse in real incomes below a socially acceptable level.

As strange as it may seem, in the West there were studies on the emergency measures to be implemented in the aftermath of a large-scale disaster, but none on the immediate consequences of a collapse of the entire socialist economic system. Although Caspar Weinberger, a secretary of defence in the Reagan Administration, admitted frankly sometime in the 1980s that the biggest challenge for the United States would be how to manage the collapse of communism, it turned out that nobody was truly prepared for such a collapse. Under the sponsorship of the same Reagan Administration, a study was conducted on the prospects for economic recovery after a thermonuclear war (Hirshleifer 1987), but not on the problem of recovery after a transitional contraction, and this despite the fact that the most common opinion among the actors involved was that the postsocialist contraction was going to be very severe.

A remarkable amount of theoretical knowledge and technical skill had been employed in the West on stabilization policies and structural reforms,

this—around 20%. This can only be partially explained by more efficient law enforcement or better marketing. Essentially, it is a matter of the difference between market behaviour under weak institutional arrangements and market behaviour under mature institutions (although one might also point out that the market institutions in the US may be more sophisticated and mature, and the market culture may be older, but piracy is still piracy).

but in the context of another type of economy and to be implemented else-where in a quite particular institutional framework. Already, at the early stages of the stabilization efforts, alarm bells were being sounded (although somehow they were not heeded) about this subtlety that the policies being counselled might have been developed on another model. In reference to the transition, a prominent IMF economist has pointed out that

The reform of [the] tax system will take place under difficult economic, social, and political conditions. Successful tax reform is never easy, but, given the circumstances, it is likely to be especially difficult in these countries and to take longer than many observers have assumed. In taxation *there cannot be a 'big bang' solution* since required changes, even when mistakes are avoided, cannot be made overnight. Because of the different environment in which the tax reform will be enacted, there is no certainty that the final outcome will be as good as one would desire. (Tanzi 1991; emphasis added)

Clearly, influential scholars in the West and important international institutions possessed an insufficient understanding of the *differentia specifica* of the socialist centrally planned economies. They were unpleasantly sur-prised by the unexpected and unfamiliar intellectual and political challenge and were forced to take advantage of theories and measures developed for other situations. They had been shocked, but knew of only one kind of therapy, which was, however, not quite suited to the features and the goals of the transition. Their response was another illusion of economic thought, not a vision (Heilbroner and Milberg 1995).

The generally unsatisfactory level of knowledge among the profes-sionals about the available policy options meant that the transition was a fertile ground for experimentation with numerous theoretical concepts. Whereas in some countries the transition occurred more by chance, in others it was managed by design, though the designs were each quite dif-ferent.[2] Indeed, in some professional circles it seemed that economics had become a very entertaining experimental science.

'Sovietologists', with their vast library of economic and historical studies, were taken by surprise, too, and were totally unprepared to deal with the (in some senses) 'ultimate' challenge. They had been concentrating on thorough descriptions of the old system and focused a great deal of atten-tion on its inefficiencies and weaknesses (and on ways to make it even weaker), but never truly on the aftermath of an eventual systemic collapse. Paradoxically, for decades the main role of Sovietology was as a weapon in the struggle to destroy socialist ('communist') ideology and practice, but, when the system of 'real socialism' broke apart, the Sovietologists and their sponsors had no blueprints handy showing the path from a profound

---

[2] In this respect, economists in Hungary and Poland were in a relatively better position owing to the partial political liberalization and early market reforms which had already taken place in those countries.

socialist systemic crisis to a better democratic and capitalist future, although, of course, this had been the whole point of the struggle in the first place.

At the same time, however, 'shock therapy' and 'creative destruction' could not have caused any harm if they had not been implemented. The responsibility for the subsequent dire situation therefore rests squarely on the shoulders of the authorities in the transition countries. This is especially true since an alternative approach was available that might have mitigated somewhat the social hardships and accelerated the onset of recovery. Unfortunately, this approach, which consisted in gradual, yet comprehensive and determined reform, new institutional arrangements, and a redefined role of the state and which was later executed as 'the Polish alternative', was either not accepted initially, or applied only partially (Kolodko 1989a, 1992c, Laski 1990, Nuti 1990, Hausner 1997, Kolodko and Nuti 1997).

Meanwhile, the process of learning by doing has been taking place. In both the East and the West the theoretical explanations and pragmatic answers have been evolving quickly. Professionals in the transition countries now have a great deal more knowledge about market performance in a postsocialist environment. Enormously wide-ranging political and intellectual debates, training at home and abroad, and personal contact with the search for solutions to actual problems in transition economies have boosted tremendously the expertise and understanding of researchers, entrepreneurs, and political leaders. Professionals in advanced market nations, including government experts, the officials of international organizations, and business people, have become familiar with the specific circumstances of transition. They have been able to absorb much knowledge about postsocialist realities and have understood that one should attack the challenges in ways tailored to the local context. At long last, important lessons about the significance of institution-building for durable growth have been learned, and the proper policy conclusions seem to have been drawn.

However, this process of learning by doing has been very costly not for Western experts and professionals, but for the populations of the Eastern nations. Future growth will never make up for the hardships. Indeed, GDP contraction has been more severe in the transition economies than it was during the Great Depression in 1929–33. Moreover, the transition contraction could have been avoided to some extent, if only the signs and warnings had not been neglected and the adjustments in Western economic theory and practice had not taken so long. The early cures prescribed for the suffering postsocialist economies did not fit the disease.

Recently, there have been more well orchestrated attempts to implement a gradual, but steady process of institution-building, including the development of market organizations, appropriate linkages, and the expertise of the actors on the economic stage. The international assistance has also become much more sensitive and more well coordinated, and transition policies seem to be shifting in the right direction. New laws have been drafted and adopted, and new skills have been acquired. The differences between the Eastern Europe and, to a lesser degree, the former Soviet republics of the late 1990s and the region in the early 90s are incredible. And 'different' this time may finally mean 'better'.

7

Transition from Plan to Market: Concept and Implementation

7.1. PRIVATIZATION, THE NEW PRIVATE SECTOR, AND CORPORATE GOVERNANCE

During the lively debates about socialism, transition, and capitalism, the superiority of private property over state ownership and the supremacy of private management over state management were constantly pointed out. The conviction that allocation through a free market, unlike central planning, guarantees higher efficiency, rising output, and better living standards has been a driving force behind the desire to transform the socialist system. In fact, *the entire concept of transition is based on the correct assumption that the transfer of assets to the private sector would improve efficiency and foster growth.*

The private sector has been established through two parallel methods. First, as the market evolves, there is a natural tendency toward the expansion of existing businesses and the creation of new ones. Second, in the transition economies, property rights have been transferred from the state to private entities. Orthodox liberal economic theory stresses the significance of the second method—the rapid privatization or denationalization of state assets—as the key element in a successful transition toward durable growth. Indeed, in Eastern Europe and the former Soviet republics, in contrast to China and Vietnam, the importance of the first method—the grassroots expansion of the private sector, or so-called 'organic privatization'—was somehow overlooked during the initial stages of transition, whereas that of denationalization was exaggerated. Only later was the emerging private sector, not denationalization, recognized as the more critical determinant of business expansion.

The emerging private sector has been a decisive factor in postsocialist recovery and growth especially in Albania (before the crisis of 1997–8), Croatia, Estonia, Hungary, Lithuania (since 1996), Mongolia (since 1995), Poland, and Slovenia. In Poland, among the almost one million people who found jobs in 1994–7, the majority were employed in the new private sector, and in 1998 small- and medium-size private businesses supplied one-third of GDP and provided about 60 per cent of non-farm employment. In the CIS the new private sector, mainly small- and medium-size service companies, has contributed to the overhaul of economies. In the Baltic States and in the Central Asian republics of Azerbaijan, Kyrgyzstan, and Uzbekistan the new private sector has had a role in the recent recovery.

Overall liberalization (including the right of individuals to start enterprises), as well as monetary and fiscal policies which have encouraged the establishment and enlargement of private economic activities, has fostered a positive supply response. The new private sector has been flourishing because of independent capital formation, the growing propensity to save, and soaring entrepreneurship.

The ongoing accumulation and concentration of capital have led to the appearance of big new private companies capable of competing with their foreign counterparts and with the large state enterprises.

Following the liberalization of trade and capital transfers and because of favourable treatment of foreign direct investment, many new private entities owned entirely by foreign capital or created as joint ventures between foreign companies and local partners—either within the state sector, or emerging from the new private sector—began to operate.

Though most have been formed with investors from developed market nations, many of the joint ventures involve partners and capital in other postsocialist transition economies. For instance, in Russia in 1998, there were over 2,500 joint ventures with private capital from Poland, while in Ukraine there were about 800 such ventures. The significance of these postsocialist joint ventures is greater than may be judged solely on the basis of their contribution to trade turnover and overall output. This is so because, in the current context of growing international competition, they are serving as points of access to 'new' markets. Thus, for example, private Czech companies have become active in Kazakhstan just as state companies from Czechoslovakia might have 'cooperated' with state companies in the Soviet Republic of Kazakhstan 10 years ago, although the modalities of the involvement and the nature of the market are now completely different: Kazakhstan is the same but not the same. Moreover, pretty often the very same people are doing the deals, although they are acting according to new rules: the people are the same but not the same.

Crossborder commerce and trade are contributing to rising entrepreneurship in neighbouring countries. There is no doubt that the Poles—well known for their entrepreneurial spirit—have been able to transfer some of their expertise and market culture to neighbours like Belarus, Lithuania, Slovakia, and Ukraine. Hungarians have been assisting Bulgarians and Romanians. Firms in FYR Macedonia have been active in Albania. Chinese and Vietnamese have enhanced the business climate in Cambodia and Laos, while Chinese have also been operating in Mongolia, Tajikistan, and several other countries.

Despite the barriers of geography and distance, this entrepreneurial spirit has become evident throughout the region because of the positive impact of liberalization and the strong incentives to do business at one's own risk and on one's own account. Charter flights are now transporting business-men between remote places such as Baku on the Caspian coast of Azerbaijan and Rzeszow in southern Poland, or between Kaliningrad, the Russian enclave on the Baltic coast, and Tashkent in Uzbekistan in Central Asia.

The orthodox assumption was that the denationalization of state assets, the other main avenue for the expansion of the private sector, would generate a quick and remarkable improvement in allocative efficiency and therefore a positive supply response and GDP growth. For a number of well-known reasons this has not occurred. Despite the many attempts to make the centrally planned system somehow bear the blame for the deep economic contraction and the long recession, the manner chosen to carry out denationalization partly explains why it is taking so long to recover the pre-transition level of production and to restructure industrial capacity.

While it may be true that in the long run the private sector will prove superior to the state sector in terms of efficiency, it is clear that during the initial phases of transformation, when assets were being dragged through the hectic process of the transfer of property rights, the distortions induced in management and corporate governance were quite serious. Privatiza-tions which are politically driven, hurriedly executed, and not well planned intensify rather than reduce allocative inefficiency. The new capacity created by the investments already allocated by the market has not yet come on line, while much of the old capacity is no longer being fully employed. The delays due to the turbulence created by the revolution in property rights have been much longer than anticipated. Nonetheless, the process of denationalization has continued, and allocative efficiency has been rising slowly. In the meantime, the underutilization of capacity has driven production down unnecessarily.

Because of the inherited structure of the economy, *it would have been more beneficial and practical to conduct suitable industrial policies and to con-sider privatization only as an instrument of these industrial policies.* Of course, the state may mismanage its economic functions and execute the wrong set of industrial policies, but the panacea should never be no industrial policy at all, though this was the solution advised by hidebound free market fundamentalists. Industrial policy should not consist in the iden-tification of industries which are successful in the market and then the creation of support for them, but rather in export promotion and the dis-semination industry-wide of technological progress. It should also involve efforts to contain the risks for entrepreneurs through arrangements which ensure trade credits and foreign direct investment.

There are many examples of policies which have been successful because they have facilitated technological spillovers and encouraged competition through the promotion of export-led growth. However, a dilemma in transi-tion economies has been the fact that new industrial policies have had to be carried out by the old bureaucracy. This means that special programmes supported by governments and international organizations are required for the comprehensive retraining of the bureaucracy, as well as of private sector professionals.

During the early transition either the need for industrial policy was ignored by the free market zealots and the enemies of state intervention, for example during the Czech transformation under the Vaclav Klaus Administration, or the state bureaucracy overshot the goals of industrial policy. There was also the somewhat nostalgic 'look back' in Romania before the 1997 policy shift and in Belarus even at the end of the decade. Thus, a whole spectrum of opportunities has been missed for determined industrial policy interventions in the market for the sake of supporting and enhancing market forces.

The experience in a number of transition economies bears out the notion that *the better the corporate governance of the public sector, the more rapid the growth of former state firms after privatization* (Konings, Lehmann, and Schaffer 1996). Progress in the corporate governance of state companies should therefore have a key place in the effort to ease economic contraction and initiate recovery. This should be accomplished by turning state companies into corporations. This means that, before they become privatized and before the formal transfer of ownership, the companies should be subjected to market pressures and become exposed to normal competitive rules. Such a step requires the imposition of hard budget constraints and an alteration in legal status so that the state units formally become joint stock companies, with the shares still controlled by the state.

Moreover, if the care in the improvement of corporate governance is matched by sound industrial policy and the gradual denationalization of state assets, recovery comes earlier, and the subsequent growth is more robust. Evidence for this claim is offered through a comparison of the contraction in industrial output of about 40 per cent in Poland in 1990–1, the initial years of the transition there, and the remarkable growth of over 20 per cent in 1996–7. In the first two-year period not only was proper corporate governance lacking in the state sector, but state enterprises suffered from discrimination. Thus, additional credit restrictions existed in the state sector (including restrictions on lending from international financial organizations for even the most competitive and profitable enterprises), and special fiscal measures were applied exclusively to state companies. In the second two-year period, both the state sector and the private sector were treated the same. Therefore, while the new private sector and the recently privatized former state companies were adding to the soaring output, the improvement in efficiency and the increasing competitiveness of the state sector played an active role as well. Instead of being a burden on the budget, the state sector was contributing revenue and boosting employment and exports.

Hence corporate status should be assigned to state enterprises before they are privatized. This policy could become part of a wider effort at marketization that would also stress a profit orientation and a shift in management incentives: 'the conditions under which privatization can achieve the public objectives of efficiency and equity are very limited and are very similar to the conditions under which competitive markets attain Pareto-efficient outcomes' (Edlin and Stiglitz 1995).[1]

If, for instance, competition is lacking, creating a private, unregulated monopoly will likely result in even higher prices for consumers. . . . The differences between public and private enterprises are blurry, and there is a continuum of arrangements in between. Corporatization, for instance, maintains government ownership but moves firms toward hard budget constraints and self-financing; performance-based government organizations use output-oriented performance measures as a basis for incentives. Some evidence suggests that much of the gains from privatization occur before privatization as a result of the process of putting in place effective individual and organizational incentives. (Stiglitz 1998a, p. 21)

Therefore, *a substantial share of the credit for postsocialist expansion is due to the 'commercialization' of the public sector.* This lesson seems to have been noted in the Asian reformed socialist economies, which are attempting to use commercialization as the main vehicle of competition policy.

Some countries undertook efforts at commercialization before transition and then continued them later, despite vigorous political debates motivated by economic concerns, but also by political preferences. This tug-of-war was more about the control of the economy than about efficiency and growth. In any case, commercialization was sometimes even more successful than privatization in facilitating growth. The successes in Poland after 1993 are to be explained to quite a significant degree by the commercialization of the state sector, not by denationalization, which was also a factor in the progress achieved, though it played only a secondary role in the overall expansion. In Croatia, Estonia, Kyrgyzstan, Slovakia, Slovenia, and Uzbekistan the relatively mild contraction can be understood as a positive result of the commercialization of state enterprises and the attempt to impose hard budget constraints. Here, too, commercialization and the improvement in the corporate governance of the public sector contributed more to expansion than did the denationalization of the state sector.

It is not expedient to privatize all public assets in a short time. It is much wiser to attempt to manage the state sector according to sound market principles instead of subjecting it to unfavourable fiscal and monetary policies (Nuti 1997c). Thus, even though the well-known voucher privatization in the Czech Republic and Russia took about three years to be completed merely from the formal point of view, the experiment was not followed immediately by improvements in corporate governance and efficiency. On the contrary; the turmoil accompanying the privatization led to a decline

---

[1] Pareto-efficient outcomes are a situation of perfect market balance: sound equilibrium at full capacity utilization, full employment, and market clearing prices.

in overall efficiency in the Czech Republic for some time, while in Russia it fostered significant mismanagement, persistent crisis and the flight of capital. It was mistaken to believe that the neglect of reliable corporate governance and the postponement of microeconomic restructuring among state firms would accelerate privatization and raise allocative efficiency.

One apparently found it easier to rid the state of assets through a sort of managed bankruptcy. Unfortunately, the approach helped render the recession more severe than necessary and made the recovery more difficult. This was a good example of mismanagement. *The greater the mismanagement of the state sector, the more severe the transitional recession, and the more carefully administered the state sector, the earlier the recovery.* There are still lessons to be learned from these experiences (What has worked and why? What has failed and why?), and the issues of privatization and corporate governance will remain challenging for a long time to come.

7.2. INTEREST GROUPS AND THE FORMATION OF A GROWTH LOBBY

An evolution in interest groups is of the greatest importance in the formation of the public support required for sustained growth. In view of their origins, characteristics, and dynamics, the interest groups inherited from the socialist system are quite different from those needed for the expansion of the new system. One should not wait to see what sorts of interest groups emerge from the chaos of the transition, but appropriate actions aimed at shaping new and influential groups representative of society should be taken quickly. The appearance of a 'growth lobby' should not be made to depend on the assumption that certain groups will spontaneously begin vigorously supporting positive measures to expand the economy; this should be a matter of policy. Although liberalization and privatization did automatically set in motion the creation of some groups acting in favour of growth, the process ought also to be a deliberate one. Workers, farmers, academics, and the bureaucracy are not all able to join naturally together to take part in the growth lobby. The emergence of a special group of development leaders must be fostered during the wide-ranging restructuring of society and the overhaul of old institutions.

It is necessary to intervene because interest groups are themselves in transition. Moreover, there is a great deal of interaction between the shifts experienced by these groups and ongoing economic and political change. In extreme cases, either a new growth lobby will emerge to act as a decisive interest group, or the old bureaucracy will continue to lead economic events. In the worst case, new political elites with close ties to organized crime will come to exercise a significant role in the informal institutional set-up and thus in policymaking.

It may be thought that a growth lobby will emerge on its own out of the new middle class arising from liberalization and structural reform. Yet, if this process is to occur in a sensible and speedy way, there must be strong and determined political leadership. The growth lobby in a transition society consists initially of entrepreneurs, investors, managers, and reform-oriented politicians and economists. The legacy of the centrally planned regime—with its institutional, behavioural, and cultural dimensions—represents a hurdle for the appearance of the new lobby, since the market environment is fundamentally different.

The formation of a growth lobby is a slow and complex process which should be assisted as much as possible. Because it is linked to the fall of the old elites and the rise of new ones, it is also a conflict-prone process. First, the old elites seek to remain in control and to become the new elites. Second, the process takes place in the context of a series of sensitive privatizations and the restructuring of financial intermediaries, and this generates lively public debates about the best ways to realize the policies. Third, the process is also tied to and influenced by the democratization of political life and the emergence of democratic institutions. There is thus interaction between the economic power and the political position of particular individuals, groups, and parties, and this has an impact on the creation of interest groups.

Among those involved in such groups, be they entrepreneurs, managers, bankers, investors, politicians, trade unionists, civil servants, economists, lawyers, or journalists, some will act in favour of growth, but others will seek to bulldoze events toward their own particular ends, even at the cost of growth, that is, at the cost of society as a whole. Especially if the institutional environment is weak, some of these people will act against the law, will not respect the market rules, or will try to evade taxes, thereby undermining the potential for expansion. Their logic seems to be, the less they pay to the Treasury, the more they will be able to save and then spend including, of course, on their own affairs. They are not concerned that this behaviour has a negative effect on the fiscal balance by reducing the resources available for financing the public expenditures indispensable for sustaining growth.

If the entrepreneurial spirit is oriented mainly toward capital formation, investment, export expansion, the generation of new jobs, and fair competition, then the growth lobby can be strong. But if this spirit is directed toward the existing capital redistribution, mergers and acquisitions, tax evasion and tax avoidance, the exploitation of labour, and unfair competition, then there is a sort of 'capitalist populism', and the important lobbies tend to be 'antigrowth'.

The challenge for the political leadership is to enhance the emerging growth lobby and to coordinate policies, both macro and micro, in such a way that the groups desirous of real economic expansion will be able to check populist tendencies and limit the power of the conservative bureaucracy, while not becoming too strong themselves. Hence the coordination of transition and development policies involves passing between the Scylla of populism and the Charybdis of expansionism. *While populism stresses too heavily the importance of income distribution and consumption without proper attention to efficiency, expansionism emphasizes too much the significance of capital formation and growth without sufficient consideration for equity.*

Entrepreneurs and investors are taking the places vacated by the old party activists, the statist bureaucrats, and the directors of state companies. These are the people who are now expected to bear the risk and to take responsibility not only for their own decisions, but for the consequences on others of those decisions, too. Entrepreneurship and the readiness to take risks in investment are features of a certain sort of personality and reflect a certain kind of knowledge and technical skill. Whereas character traits and attitudes are a given, the expertise must be acquired. The government must therefore also foster technical and professional training among business people. Even if these people believe that they already know how to solve the mounting problems in risk assessment, marketing, and management, the state should not cease seeking to upgrade these precious abilities. The greater these abilities are, the greater also will be the rate of expansion.

For several years subsequent to the onset of transition, before staff-members begin to retire and be replaced by a new generation, the majority of the executives running the privatized and newly market-oriented companies are recruited from the old guard among the directors of former state enterprises. Not all these people are able to change old habits easily or to the degree necessary for business management in the market, which is so different from the old system. Transforming the director of a state enterprise who has functioned for so long within a closed statist economy into a manager of a private company operating on open competitive markets can be as difficult as converting an old-style politician into a new-era leader or a central planning zealot into a capitalist fanatic. In fact, the latter metamorphoses are much less difficult.

Under the command economy and the shortage phenomenon, the biggest department in a state factory was procurement. In privatized or newly market-oriented enterprises during transition, the trick is not in buying the inputs, but in selling the outputs on the open and competitive market. Even if the new managers are flexible and able to acquire the new skills (often the case), this takes time. Meanwhile, the postsocialist managers sometimes lose their way in the market; they make mistakes in microeconomic management, and this has an obvious negative impact on macroeconomic growth. Radical liberalization cannot work as a cure-all in this case.

While some managers are quick to devote themselves to expansion and are eager to take up the competitive challenge represented by the open market, others are keen to insist on the maintenance of the state tutelage which is so familiar to them. While progressive managers are ready to shoulder risks and are lobbying on behalf of fair competition, deregulation, and growth, others act conservatively and are lobbying only for subsidies and allowances, which influence the redistribution of income and cause distortions in market signals and, consequently, in allocative efficiency.

To be sure, in the long term the more deregulated the economy, the bigger the voice of profit-oriented managers and of the growth lobby. However, there is also a danger of going too far in this direction. Likewise, if it is too far-reaching and poorly designed, state involvement in economic matters, especially the supervision of corporate governance and microeconomic policy, can weaken the growth lobby.

7.3. INFORMAL INSTITUTIONS:
CORRUPTION AND ORGANIZED CRIME

The more the state is able firmly to coordinate systemic change through development policy, the more powerful the growth lobby can be. The more the state fails in this duty during the period of institutional underdevelopment, the more room there is for the spread of informal interest groups, including corrupt bureaucrats and organized crime.

Unfortunately, in many countries it is a common practice to bribe low-level bureaucrats or policemen for the sake of operating freely in the shadow economy or doing business at the limits of the law. So familiar in several less-developed market economies, this phenomenon is no longer unusual in postsocialist nations, especially those with relatively low income and weaker institutions, particularly those in the Balkans, the Caucasus, and Central Asia.

The transition economies, like other emerging markets with weak institutions and a poor market culture, generate additional temptations to bribe or to be bribed. However, corruption is apparently less extensive than it is in other economies at a similar level of development and no more extensive than it is in economies at a much higher level of GDP per capita, including the members of the OECD or the European Union.

International Transparency, an activist organization in the struggle against corruption, has studied the situation in a sample of 50 nations and developed a special indicator, the 'corruption perception index'. The index describes the extent of corruption by taking into account anecdotal evidence, the transparency of legal codes, the maturity of institutional arrangements, the range of overall liberalization, the amount of regulation of economic activities, the criteria for granting licences and permits for administratively regulated activities and businesses, the efficiency of the judiciary, the skill level of the bureaucracy, the efficiency and transparency of the fiscal system and tax administration, and the effectiveness and man-

Table 16 Corruption perception index in selected countries, 1997

Country	Corruption index	GNP per capita (PPP$)	Country	Corruption index	GNP per capita (PPP$)
Denmark	9.94	21,230	Belgium	5.25	21,660
Finland	9.48	17,760	Czech Rep.	5.20	9,770
Sweden	9.35	18,540	Hungary	5.18	6,410
New Zealand	9.23	16,360	Poland	5.08	5,400
Canada	9.10	21,130	Italy	5.03	19,870
Netherlands	9.03	19,950	Malaysia	5.01	9,020
Norway	8.92	21,940	South Africa	4.95	5,030
Australia	8.86	18,940	South Korea	4.29	11,450
Singapore	8.66	22,770	Uruguay	4.14	6,630
Luxembourg	8.61	37,930	Brazil	3.56	5,400
Switzerland	8.61	25,860	Romania	3.44	4,360
Ireland	8.28	15,680	Turkey	3.21	5,580
Germany	8.23	20,070	Thailand	3.06	7,540
UK	8.22	19,260	Philippines	3.05	2,850
Israel	7.97	16,490	China	2.88	2,920
US	7.61	26,980	Argentina	2.81	8,310
Austria	7.61	21,250	Venezuela	2.77	7,900
Hong Kong	7.28	22,950	India	2.75	1,400
Portugal	6.97	12,670	Indonesia	2.72	3,800
France	6.66	21,030	Mexico	2.66	6,400
Japan	6.57	22,110	Pakistan	2.53	2,230
Costa Rica	6.45	5,850	Russia	2.27	4,480
Chile	6.05	9,520	Colombia	2.23	6,130
Spain	5.90	14,520	Bolivia	2.05	2,540
Greece	5.35	11,710	Nigeria	1.76	1,220

Sources: Transparency International, World Bank.

agement of customs. Through conventional methods, all these factors are weighted to produce the overall indicator. The higher a country is on the index (on a scale from zero to 10), the less corruption there is (Table 16).

The transition economies included in the sample rank somewhere among the 'most corrupt' countries in the European Union and the 'least corrupt' among the developing nations. The rank of the Czech Republic, Hungary, and Poland is close to that of Belgium, Greece, Italy, and Spain. Romania is in much worse shape (between Brazil and Turkey), while in worse shape still is China (between the Philippines and Argentina). Once again, Russia is near the bottom of the list, this time between Pakistan and Colombia. Of course, such an index can only be considered a rough approximation of the actual situation, but it does provide some insight into the extent of the problem.

Some economists, leaving aside the moral issues, argue that under specific circumstances corruption can increase efficiency. They offer the example of import licences which are either sold by administrators to the highest bidder, or are distributed according to equitable criteria. In the first case, there is definitely more room for corruption, but there may also be more potential for efficiency improvements, since the producer who can afford to pay the most for a licence may, other things being equal, also be able to use the imported goods more effectively, thereby creating more output.

According to this argument, corruption in licensing may be 'good'. However, the economic analysis does not end here, and many questions remain. How does corruption affect growth and development? Is economic growth slower in countries with more corruption? Does slow economic growth encourage corruption?

Corruption works against growth and development in at least five ways. First, *corruption has a negative effect on allocative efficiency*. As an economic phenomenon, corruption can be described as a particular method to distribute income or allocate resources that does not follow normal market rules. Income is not distributed as compensation for a contribution to public wealth, nor in a manner which secures the highest rate of return on investment. Resources are transferred according to non-market signals, which may depend, for example, on the political or administrative position of a corrupt decisionmaker. The distribution of capital is distorted, and, at a given propensity to save, the investments are not as efficient as they would be through transparent market allocation. Tanzi and Davoodi (1997) point out that corruption induces an increase in public investment at the expense of productivity. So, even if an economy invests relatively more capital, it may invest less efficiently due to distortions caused by corruption.

Second, *corruption reduces the propensity to save*. Since the allocation of scarce capital is distorted by non-market signals, the rate of return on invested capital is relatively lower, and so is the average income. This in turn affects the propensity to save in a negative way. In addition, since the income stemming from illegal activity and bribes may not always be usable in transparent ways, it may be hidden or taken out of the country. This capital flight causes a drop in the savings ratio in the economy, although it may cause more savings elsewhere, that is, in the nations which absorb the capital flight by providing in exchange the service of money laundering.

However, one may argue that bribery boosts the propensity to save, since, though it is nasty, it is an efficient additional means of capital concentration. Since the savings ratio is generally higher among groups with more disposable income, the accumulation and concentration of wealth through corruption should enhance savings and consequently the pace of growth. This may be the case in transition economies, since some of the new financial elites have roots in the former state bureaucracy and the management of denationalized companies. If these people have collected bribes during liberalization and privatization and obtained some initial capital through corruption, they are now able to transform themselves into the new entrepreneurial class. After a time, *pecunia non olet*, and what began life as a bribe might attain maturity as a well-performing asset on an emerging market.

Thus, in this case, the outcome is a vector of the two contradictory events outlined above. Even if under certain circumstances at the initial stage of transition corruption may boost the propensity to save, in the long run the negative effects dominate, and the propensity to save declines.

Third, *corruption weakens motivation and hampers labour productivity*. If a share of income is due to illegal activities, including the acceptance of bribes, the motivation for sound effort and an increase in labour productivity is dampened. The consciousness that some income is transferred through corruption diminishes the commitment to work hard and to respect laws, including the ones normally observed on the labour market. Together with the desire to avoid taxation, this leads to a shift of some activities to the shadow economy. In the long run such an attitude can cause even more devastating results, for instance in the quality of human capital because of the loss in the motivation to invest in one's own skills. In a corrupt economy, human capital investment does not necessarily guarantee higher future wages; thus, corruption can discourage education and vocational training.

Fourth, *corruption raises political tensions and contributes to social disintegration*. If government authorities and government workers accept or exhort bribes, the overall attitude of the population toward economic and social policies is hardly going to be a positive one in the long run. The conviction that there is an inequitable distribution of national income and a practice of taking advantage of public jobs for private gain cuts away at the credibility of government policy and may even lead to action against the government.

Fifth, *corruption betrays expectations*. The lack of social integration and the strong political tensions destabilize expectations. This influences negatively the propensity to save and the overall efficiency of economic processes. In a climate of fragile expectations, outcomes become less predictable, so that investment decisions are often biased, and this slows the pace of growth or even drives the economy into decline.

The conviction is overwhelming that corruption must be fought for ethical reasons, but also because of its long-run negative influence on resource allocation, efficiency, and growth (Johnston 1997, Kaufmann 1997b, Mauro 1997, Rose-Ackerman 1997). This conviction is behind the growing commitment of international organizations, including the OECD, the IMF, and the World Bank, to resist the threat of corruption everywhere, including in transition economies. The World Bank and the IMF have also undertaken special initiatives to encourage anticorruption measures due to the fact that aid money and commercial lending which are designated for structural reform and regional development programmes are sometimes diverted to other purposes, mainly into the pockets of corrupt officials and bureaucrats (Pleskovic and Stiglitz 1997, Wedel 1998a). This has occurred in many developing countries, especially in Africa, so the transfer of these resources to the emerging postsocialist markets has to be carefully scrutinized, too. Although there is no evidence of such misbehaviour in the postsocialist economies so far (with the exception of Russia), the weak institutions and the unstable political climate could change the situation for the worse.

Transition economies possess particular features which may encourage corruption. Three of them are quite significant: privatization, deregulation, and the news media. Privatization is corruption-prone since denationalization is a vast process and hardly transparent, and the potential for illegal activities is great. The desire to execute privatization quickly and radically and the furious pace of the saleoff of state assets have represented additional opportunities for corruption. It has been said that *the sooner there is nothing left to privatize and the sooner the connection between the state bureaucracy and denationalization is cut, the easier it will be to contain corruption.* There is much truth in this.

A standout feature of transition economies is the large number of regulations left over from the over-regulated central planning regime. Of course, an overly regulated economy is corruption-prone since it is sometimes easier to pay or collect the bribes than to comply or force compliance with the regulations. Moreover, it takes time to deregulate and to re-regulate. And this offers opportunities to prey on old regulations which are still operative, though they will eventually be dismantled. At the more advanced stages of transition this threat diminishes, since more and more is being decided by market forces and less and less by the bureaucracy. The remedy for the threat over the long term is proper deregulation and re-regulation, with transparent institutional arrangements and a commitment to enforce the laws in vigour at the moment. This may be as important as the liberalization itself.

The debates about corruption are taking place publicly, with the lively engagement of the news media. While this involvement is understandable and desirable, it so happens that the news media may in a certain sense sometimes be corrupt, too. It is not uncommon for influential newspapers and leading television stations to be owned by, or at least linked to people who have vast interests in the way in which the economy is deregulated and the privatization of state assets is managed. Of course, these same symptoms can also be found in developing countries and in advanced market nations.[2]

If corruption is understood as an exchange of favours for money, then the news media may be at least as exposed to corruption as is the govern-

---

[2] For instance, *The Economist* (1997e) points to the lack of transparency in the links between some news media and industrial and financial groups in leading EU countries. While perhaps not 'corruption' as such, this certainly appears to be a questionable sort of lobbying power.

ment bureaucracy. The media can be used as a means to exercise 'moral persuasion' on government authorities and decisionmakers. The problem is very sensitive and difficult to tackle, since corrupt business circles may use the media for their own purposes, but there is no easy way to expose them to the judgement of public opinion because of the ties of the news media and the interest groups.

In quite spectacular cases, the media have manipulated political parties, thereby becoming political actors. In Albania, corrupt media organizations were closely involved in fraudulent financial pyramids. The media fuelled irrational expectations and attracted the savings of households into enterprises which were already bankrupt. In many countries, in exchange for indirect financial compensation, the media have contributed to shady stock market schemes. At the Kremlin in September 1997 Russian bankers were asked by President Yeltsin to stop their media campaign against reform-minded economists in the government. Some of the media were owned by the bankers.

The border between vigorous lobbying and discreet corruption is a 'grey zone', in which the good and the bad are not so clearly defined. It takes time and tremendous effort to eliminate wrongdoing in such situations, and this is impossible without democracy, a true civic society, and a culture of public interest.

If institutions are weak and not yet able to support the market economy fully, then the systemic niche may be filled by a 'particular' form of institutional arrangement, that is, organized crime. In this regard the transition economies are a special case because of the vacuum of 'neither plan, nor market'. When antitrust agencies, efficient tax and customs administration, sound financial intermediaries, and comprehensive legal and judiciary systems are lacking and when deregulation is not accompanied by an attempt to develop a reliable institutional framework for private business activities, then the opportunities for the expansion of organized crime become legion.

The naïve expectation that market forces alone can regulate economic activities within a context of changing values, structures, priorities, and economic, social, and political links can only disappoint. Thus, in Albania in 1997, the disaster following on the heels of the collapse of a crooked savings scheme brought the state to the verge of chaos. The international community did not act decisively until it was too late. Foreign military intervention was necessary, and it was much more costly than timely political action would have been (Kolodko 1997a).

According to some estimates, as much as 40 per cent of the economic activity in Russia can be linked to organized crime (Shelly 1997).[3] Organized criminal groups in Russia are involved in both legitimate and illegal

---

[3] These estimates have been publicized by the World Bank, which, under the leadership of James Wolfensohn, has paid great attention to the fight against corruption and criminal activity.

activities. This makes the challenge still more imposing.[4] Though the actual extent of the problem is being debated, it is clearly not minor and has infected the entire economy. Organized crime activities are concentrated mainly in banks, trade and distribution systems, and the lucrative energy sector. Mafia-like groups have been very active in a number of privatization schemes, and the vast process of denationalization has been a fertile ground for rampant speculation and illegal dealing on emerging capital markets. It has been admitted that

Some of the most significant entities in the Russian economy today were born of criminal origins. . . . We constantly observe the process by which individuals and businesses, which three or four years ago would by most international standards be regarded as criminal or semi-criminal, are transforming themselves, often with the assistance of public relations specialists, into paragons of civilized corporate and individual citizenry. (Quoted in *Financial Times* 1997a)[5]

Organized crime has become a very serious policy concern. Only one day after the IMF, under pressure from international financiers and investors and the governments of the G-7 group of industrial nations, decided to come once more (and in vain) to the rescue of the Russian financial system with a bailout of an additional $12.2 billion from mid-1998 through 1999, striking data on corruption, organized crime, and capital flight were revealed. Vladislav Selivanov, the head of the Interior Ministry's antiorganized crime division, said that

We have information that members of criminal structures and their patrons are located in both local legislatures and in the centre. According to this governmental body . . . about 9,000 criminal groups set up according to all the [standards] of the international organized criminal community operate in Russia today. They have . . . state-of-the-art weapons and means of communication, their own intelligence and counterintelligence services, and connections with corrupt officials and politicians (not only among the legislators). The shadow business profits eloquently show what a criminal monster is hovering over Russia. (Yermolin 1998)

Selivanov cited Swiss Federal Prosecutor Carla del Ponte in saying that approximately 40 per cent of the $40 billion kept by Russians in Swiss banks was of criminal origin. While the estimate may be open to doubt, it is certain that some of the money earmarked for loans or investment in the Russian economy has been recirculated through informal institutions and has left the country. Thus, a weakness in the bailout package put together

---

[4] No wonder Boris Nemtsov, the deputy prime minister in 1997–8, during his first days in office, was insisting that Russia must choose between 'bandit capitalism' and 'capitalism with a human face'. Unfortunately, the situation had not changed when he was forced to leave the government in August 1998. Indeed, some analysts were saying that 'bandit capitalism' had grown even more rampant.

[5] An opinion expressed by Richard Prior, associate managing director of Kroll Associates, a US investigation company.

in the summer of 1998 was the lack of proper institutional and policy checks to counteract the involvement of 'shadow businesses' in financial affairs and ongoing flights of capital.

1998 looks to have been yet one more year during which the amount of money involved in capital flights exceeded the amount of lending from international organizations. This vicious circle cannot be broken by injecting additional liquidity into the disorganized economy. Some of this money is being taken over by the informal sector through various redistribution schemes. If there were a strong commitment by international financial intermediaries, businesses, powerful interest groups, or leading Western governments (as in the case of the dormant Swiss bank accounts of Holocaust victims, the money laundered in Switzerland by the brother of Salinas de Gortari, the former Mexican president, or the capital transferred abroad by Ferdinand Marcos, the former dictator of the Philippines), at least an attempt to stop such practices could be made. However, part of the problem is this very lack of commitment.

The wealth being accumulated in a criminal manner often eventually finds its way into legal activities. This 'transitional laundering of capital' is much more important than traditional money laundering, since an important share of primary postsocialist capital accumulation has been taking place on this foundation. This may explain the somewhat lax response by international organizations and the governments of the advanced market nations.[6]

Organized crime is being strengthened because of the absence of proper regulations, the weak and inadequate judicial systems, and the limited effectiveness of law enforcement. Governments which change frequently, even if they are determined to fight organized crime (surely the usual situation), do not have the political leverage and technical capabilities to stand up to this disease. Often they are not supported by the news media, and there may be an ambivalent attitude on the part of the international community. This was the case during the initial stage of transition. Only more recently, owing to the improved institutional set-up and the more active engagement of international organizations, including the World Bank, the IMF, and the OECD, has it been possible to eliminate some of the laundering of capital and to contain organized crime activities more readily.

Conditions are quite different in China and Vietnam. In these countries privatization has not been carried out in the same way as it has been in transition economies. This has reduced somewhat the scope for corruption. Meanwhile, the law enforcement effort against crimes like corruption has been extremely harsh, especially in China.

---

[6] In 1997, on the insistence of the US authorities, several offshore banks owned by Russian financiers were closed on the Cayman Islands. However, the international community has not done very much else to stop the transitional laundering of capital.

In the majority of transition nations, particularly those in Eastern Europe (with the exception of Albania), the malady of corruption and transitional laundering of capital has not been as severe as it is in Russia and some other former Soviet republics. This is so because of the existence in the Eastern European countries of a relatively more advanced market culture and the greater attention paid to institutional changes at the beginning of the transformation. The geopolitical factor is also important. The neighbourly European Union has exerted pressure for adequate law enforcement in Eastern Europe, especially in the 10 countries associated with the EU, and the coordination at the international level of anticrime activities has also played a positive role.

These differences in the level of organized crime may at least partly explain why the recession was less severe in Eastern Europe than it was in the former Soviet republics and why the contraction has lasted relatively longer in the latter. Corruption and organized crime introduce similar types of distortions and false signals to the market. In each case, the accumulation and allocation of capital do not take place because of normal market forces, which are supposed to guarantee the optimal use of resources, but because of the desire of particular interest groups engaged in shady business to be able to maximize their profits and wealth without worrying about externalities.

However, as in the case of bribery, illegal businesses, even organized crime, may have a positive impact on economic growth under certain conditions. This is the situation in some less-developed economies, like Colombia or Jamaica, where so much wealth has depended on drug trafficking. When moral considerations are left to somebody else (which, unfortunately, so often occurs), capital can sometimes rather easily be accumulated in a dishonest way. Given the existence of slavery, the careless treatment of native Americans, and the free rein allowed to the 'robber barons', this sort of formula may in part explain the great economic expansion of the US in the 19th century. Likewise, as bad as they may be, illegal businesses may contribute to primary capital accumulation, and this capital, if invested wisely, may facilitate growth. More capital, whether criminal or not, comes to mean more growth.

Nonetheless, all the direct and indirect negative aspects of corruption and organized crime eventually lead to deteriorations in efficiency and to slower growth. They have also added to the persistence of the contraction. Both have a serious negative effect on the equitability of income distribution. They certainly hamper the course and the speed of institutional reform.

However, policymakers should be aware that some features of liberalization, privatization, and deregulation may spur the activities of informal groups linked to corruption and organized crime. This makes the fight against corruption still more complex and difficult. This fight requires the firm commitment of governments, the assistance of non-governmental and international organizations, and the support of truly independent news media.

8

Financial Reform and Policy

8.1. THE NEW FISCAL SYSTEM

An efficient system of resource allocation and a strong propensity to save are necessary for robust growth. The idea that growth would come quickly as a result of denationalization and deregulation ignored the fact that initially, because of shrinking GDP, savings decrease. A boost in the savings ratio—the ratio of capital formation over GDP—calls for rising real household incomes, a favourable tax system, reliable fiscal policy, appropriate financial intermediaries (particularly banks, stock exchanges, and investment funds), the adequate regulation of financial markets, and an understanding of the market rules and market performance. All these are important factors in the growth of savings, but none of them appears automatically.

On the contrary; the propensity to save diminishes at the beginning of transition because the policies facilitating savings and capital allocation under the centrally planned economy do not work anymore, and the new organizations serving these purposes in the market economy are still evolving. Real household expenditures drop, though more gradually than the slump in production, because investments are contracting more quickly than is overall GDP. In other words, capital formation declines more rapidly than does production, while consumption declines more slowly than does production. This phenomenon has elsewhere been called the 'rule of the retardation of consumption adjustment' (Pohorille 1982).

The transitional contraction was so severe that even a huge reduction in investments did not help maintain the pre-crisis level of consumption.[1] Yet, before consumption started to fall in absolute terms, the marginal

---

[1] In the business cycles typical of the market mechanism and in the growth cycles of the centrally planned economy the share of consumption in the absorption of GDP is always two to four times higher (say, 65% to over 80%) than is the corresponding share of investments (say, 35% to less than 20%). Yet to some extent a reduction in investments subsequent to a slowdown or a drop in the growth of national income may serve as a cushion against decreasing consumption. As long as investments are declining in absolute terms on a par with GDP, consumption does not decline. If, for instance, GDP slips from 100 to 95 units, and at the same time investments shrink from 30 to 25 units, consumption remains equal to 70 units in absolute terms. The structure of GDP absorption has changed, however. The investment rate has shifted from 30/100 to 25/95, while the rate of consumption has climbed from 70/100 to 70/95. Thus, the former has gone down from 30% to 26.3%, while the latter has gone up from 70% to 73.7%. The rate of consumption is therefore higher, though the absolute level of consumption is the same.

propensity to save flagged, and the amount of savings thus decreased even more than did real income. The 'death spiral' of plunging real income, the dwindling propensity to save, and a weakening ability to invest was set in motion. Later, when the economy ultimately bottomed out, the trends in production and GDP absorption began to recover. Then, capital formation was growing more quickly than GDP, whereas consumption was climbing at a slower rate. Thus, the savings ratio was again rising. As real income grows, the marginal propensity to save can increase as well if certain additional conditions are met.

Even the savings used for such reasonable purposes as children's education, better housing, a new car, or next summer's holiday on the coast cannot be accumulated as long as real income is shrinking, even if the central bank tries to maintain high real interest rates. The positive interest rates can act as an incentive for additional saving only if they succeed in discouraging households from spending a certain marginal portion of income for current consumption. Clearly, this can happen only when consumption is above a critical level.

During a long period of output decline and deteriorating living standards, it is virtually impossible to raise the savings ratio solely by manipulating the interest rate. First, households must earn the income which will allow them to save; second, they need a reason to wish to save; and, third, the savings must furnish a positive interest rate. If the real income of a household is barely sufficient to make ends meet and secure a basic standard of living (considered to be below the poverty line for the majority of people in several transition economies), then the interest rate may be set very high, but it still will not promote the overall propensity to save. People do not save because the central bank raises the interest rate, but because they have an income that permits money to be saved and because they have a goal for which to save.

Of course, it may be possible to convince even the people in a poor country that these conditions are met, as was the disastrous case of the savings pyramids in Albania or similar, though less serious fraudulent financial schemes in other countries. Such schemes turn out to involve a process of 'de-saving' rather than sound capital formation. Likewise, several post-socialist countries got caught up in the childish euphoria created by soaring capital markets, which led to a 'bubble economy'. Eventually, the bubble bursts, and households are often the losers. Such events contribute to tremendous redistributions of assets and savings to more fortunate speculators and are pretty devastating for the long-term propensity to save. Only after purchasing power has begun to rise once more and when nominal income is increasing more rapidly than are prices can household savings expand in a more stable manner.

The flow of savings is not motivated exclusively by the availability of sound and expanding sources of disposable income, but also by the existence of good reasons to postpone spending on current consumption. The decision to save now must have a chance of paying off later, when some positive return (in real terms) can be gained on a well-supplied market. The decision depends on a mix of motives, including the wish to be prepared for the future and a keenness to acquire greater purchasing power for desired goods, but also on the presence of well-performing financial intermediaries and confidence in government fiscal and monetary policies.

The path leading from the old savings system to the savings system required for a healthy market economy is winding. The savings ratio in the centrally planned economy was relatively high (definitely much higher than it was during transition), although it must be remembered that the high propensity to save in Eastern Europe and the former Soviet Union was essentially involuntary. This was not due to a problem in the level of development, nor was it a question of traditions or social custom; it was a feature specific to the economic and political system in these countries. Savings were forced because of the persistent shortages. The culture of saving was thus of a different sort than it is in a market economy, and the mechanisms for the absorption of savings were remarkably different, too (Kolodko 1986a, 1986b, Kornai 1980). This had serious implications for the transition process.

The statist economy had a special tax system, which was one of its main features. Government revenue was derived mainly from the taxation of state companies and through the indirect taxation of households. For this reason, the reform of the fiscal system has been a major element in the whole transition exercise (Tanzi 1992). This task is rendered more difficult because, as the new system is introduced, it must contribute immediately to the enhancement of capital formation. However, tax administration is weak; the financial culture is immature, and fiscal policy must overcome the hurdle of the resistance to taxation exhibited by the emerging middle class and others who have never paid taxes before. None of the postsocialist countries has yet completed the introduction of an effective tax system. Even the adoption of a new tax code requires several years, and much more time must pass before there is a change in the attitudes of both the taxman and the taxpayer.

A healthy public finance system calls for effective policies, which can be implemented only if there are effective institutions and the various economic actors behave according to the new rules. The actors must adjust to the standards of the market economy, and this takes time and much effort by the fiscal authorities, who must also adapt to the new circumstances (Blejer and Ter-Minassian 1997a, 1997b). The process is long and complex and is beset by many conflicts. The legal system must be adjusted, and the people involved in the fiscal system must learn about budgetary redistribution in a market economy. Since the new fiscal system alters the way in which people are affected by income distribution, important interests are at stake. This generates tensions and tough political struggles. Taxation comes to be discussed as widely and with as much heat as a spectacular sporting event. However, the final score of a football game is not usually decided in parliament, while the tax rate is, even several times in a single term.

The taxman is frequently seen by political parties and the news media they influence as an adversary who is trying to deprive entrepreneurs and households of their just income. The finance minister can easily become public enemy number one. The natural reluctance to pay taxes is exploited as a political weapon, as, for example, in Russia in 1997–8, when changes in the tax code were being debated and then adopted (with some flaws). The opposition usually claims that taxes are too high, no matter if the opposition, when it was in power, did not reduce them. So, taxes are always too high, and, of course, expenditures are always too low, and, to be sure, the fiscal deficit is always too big.

The dilemmas connected to taxation and capital formation in a transition economy are similar to the dilemmas in a market economy, but it is more difficult to tackle them. The optimal tax rate is as much a political issue as an economic one. Whereas among some policymakers there is always a temptation to raise taxes so as to generate more revenue and thus boost expenditures, the government can also overshoot the target and usher in the perverse effects of a tax rise. Instead of satisfying the fiscal needs of the state, an excessively high tax rate can harm the overall ability of an economy to invest and grow in the long term. Yet, an excessively low tax rate can destabilize the public financial system, since certain routine expenditures must then be paid for through deficit spending and public debt. This also harms the ability of an economy to expand.

The fewer the taxes collected at a given amount of public expenditure, the stronger the 'crowding out' effect. The public deficit must be financed in a non-inflationary way, that is, through government borrowings on the money market, but this elbows private businesses out of the market, since credit is now more expensive because of the higher interest rates. Actually, whether they are funded by taxes or by borrowing (a proposition known as the 'Ricardian equivalence of tax and debt'), or through monetary expansion, all government expenditures potentially crowd out all private expenditures. The subsequent inflation then cuts into the real value of the liquid assets of the private sector.

The identification of an optimal tax rate involves a compromise between economics and politics. From the viewpoint of economics, the optimal tax rate is a relative concept. The actual rate selected should depend on numerous structural and institutional factors, as well as on the current level of development. For instance, economic considerations suggest that there should be a different tax rate in, say, Armenia and Hungary, because the institutions in the second country are more advanced, but also because the first country is less developed.

The political motives behind the selection of a particular tax rate depend on the strength of social tensions and conflicts, the political structure of the society, the position of non-governmental organizations, and the maturity of democracy and of the mechanisms employed to conduct the public debate of issues. The traditions and the 'culture' of negotiations and bargaining among professional and worker groups, various segments of the population, and the government are especially important as a sort of 'intermediary' institution.[2]

A compromise between economic necessity and political feasibility is no more easily achieved simply because a nation is more developed or enjoys a higher growth rate. Indeed, if income is not growing, neither are public expenditures. So, in a poorer country, the structure of public outlays remains by and large the same from one year to the next. However, when there is an additional portion of income, as there is in a growing economy, then there is good cause to engage in a political fight over the extra slice of the cake. This is why discussions get so heated in European Union countries over monetary union, in the US over new budget spending, and in Japan over the management of fiscal packages to support the yen. No wonder such issues are the subject of serious political quarrels in the emerging democracies.

There may be room for a tax cut in the later stages of transition, but only if there is already a sturdy rising trend in production. If this is so, taxes should be reduced first in the business sector, although in some cases the tax burden of households may be eased as well. In Poland, under the government programme 'Package 2000', taxes were substantially lowered in both sectors (Kolodko 1996). Until 1996 the corporate income tax was set at a flat rate of 40 per cent, but since 1997 it has been cut by 2 percentage points each year, so that it will stand at 32 per cent by 2000 and is supposed to remain at that level thereafter. This should raise investments and, in the longer run, enhance international competitiveness. Meanwhile, the personal income tax was decreased in two stages. In the first stage, executed in 1997 after a political consensus had been reached in parliament, the three personal tax rates were each brought down by 1 point, to 20, 32, and 44 per cent. Later, in 1998, the rates were cut again, to 19, 30, and 40 per cent, respectively.

Constant and fervent political debate accompanied the attempts to introduce these changes. Strong resistance against the proposed schemes developed both within the ruling coalition and among its political opponents,

---

[2] In Poland a special tripartite permanent commission has been created. The commission is composed of representatives of trade unions (labour), private and state enterprises (management), and the government. Its main function is to negotiate the scale of the growth in wages for white-collar workers directly and for blue-collar workers indirectly (that is, through a wage guidance system). The commission must surmount great difficulties, given the ongoing processes of de-indexation and disinflation, but it works.

though for different reasons. Within government circles the argument against the corporate tax cut was that it would be better to expand the existing system of tax deductions to encourage new investments rather than to lower the tax burden on all enterprises. The opposition argued that it would be better to give up the system of tax deductions for investments altogether and to decrease the overall corporate tax rate even further.

The personal income tax and income dispersion system in Poland works in such a way that only people belonging to the top decile for at least some months must pay taxes according to either of the two upper rates, that is, 30 and 40 per cent since the cuts in 1998.[3] Among the parties support-ing the government, the major argument against the cuts was that they would favour the wealthy by providing them with a reduction in the nominal tax rate of 5 points, whereas for the overwhelming majority of the population it would be only 1 point. (It ought to be noted that personal income taxes had previously been raised by the same margins, that is up to 21, 33, and 45 per cent.) The attitude of the opposition liberal party was rather curious. Though they declared a strong pro-business orienta-tion, the party leaders really did not want a tax reduction plan to go through under a government controlled by the leftist party, which, according to their rhetoric, was supposed to be in favour of 'tax and spending'. Eventually, along with some other minor alterations (vis-à-vis tax deductions for human capital investments, especially in higher education), the tax cut on the lowest rate was raised to 2 points, and the scheme was implemented.

Many of the political difficulties facing such tax reduction schemes stem from the fact that, from the macroeconomic angle, it is much less costly (in terms of alternative budgetary revenues) to cut the upper tax rates than it is to cut the lower ones. The propensity to save inevitably starts to increase anyway, and so savings also rise. In the long term, this helps finance addi-tional investments and facilitates growth.

Not surprisingly, a few other countries, like the Czech Republic and Romania, are trying to follow this lead. In a healthy situation, the approach can foster domestic capital formation and may ease the dependency on foreign capital inflows, that is, the absorption of the savings of other nations. This will occur only if the tax system is stable and fiscal policy is trans-parent. The predictability and stability of fiscal policy instruments and targets are crucial. The better policy may be the one that maintains relatively higher tax rates for a little longer rather than reducing them too early and later being forced to raise them again.

The motivation behind these particular schemes is that an increase in the propensity to save can create the financial resources for a strong drive toward economic growth. It is hoped that more revenue will be forthcoming

---

[3] In 1996 more than 7% of all taxpayers had paid taxes at the rate of 33%, while only about 2% had paid the rate of 45%. These rates applied not for the entire year, but only for some months, depending on the income accrued on a cumulative basis.

at lower tax rates. This depends on progress in tax administration and a widening tax base, but mainly on tax-supply elasticity. According to this mechanism, which is described in the 'Laffer curve', tax revenues initially rise as the tax rate rises, but later, after some critical point has been reached, tax revenues begin to decline despite the rise in the tax rate. Up to a point, under certain conditions, the reverse is true, too: total revenues rise as the tax rate declines. Otherwise, a tax cut does not make much sense and, instead of favouring the prospects for capital formation and durable growth, may damage them.

8.2. SOCIAL SECURITY REFORM, SAVINGS, AND GROWTH

In the socialist economy the state provided pensions for the elderly. Pension funds like those employed in advanced market economies did not exist, and these useful tools for the accumulation and redistribution of household savings were thus unavailable. Pensions were covered entirely by the public finance system, and, if a deficit appeared in the social security account, the state budget came immediately to the rescue. Such deficits did sometimes occur in the late period of socialism because the share of the elderly in the population had begun to grow more quickly, and so social security expenditures were also rising rapidly, occasionally outstripping the ability to finance the necessary outlays through the state extrabudgetary pension funds. The ageing population and longer life expectancy were rendering the system less sustainable due to the additional pressure on public finance. The deficits being produced by the social security system were being transformed into central government deficits.

At the beginning of the 1990s the first attempts to upgrade the old pay-as-you-go (PAYG) public system through minor changes in revenues and expenditures, mainly cuts in benefits and higher payroll taxes, did not solve the problem and even worsened it somewhat by further eroding the capacity to provide at least a stable level of basic social protection. It now became necessary to find additional revenues to support the system. This meant the imposition of a big and ever-growing financial burden on the business sector, which, together with households, supplied the revenue required by the public finance system.

Other distortions have revolved around the lax eligibility requirements, the low retirement age, and the lack of transparency between the contributions paid into the system and the level of the pensions paid out through the system (Andrews and Rashid 1996). Growing arrears in unpaid pensions (as in Russia in 1996–8) and very high payroll taxes (for example, 52 per cent in Ukraine) prove that the system has reached its limits.

Because of demographic trends, early retirements, and vague regulations about the benefits for the disabled, the segments of populations that depend on transfers from the social security system have been growing quickly. Among the former Soviet republics, in 1990 the highest dependency ratios (the ratio of the number of pensioners to the number of people employed) were 47.4 per cent in Lithuania and 51.4 per cent in Ukraine. Already by 1996 these ratios had climbed to 53.8 and 65.3 per cent, respectively. In Eastern Europe between these two years the highest ratios jumped from 55 per cent in Bulgaria and 47 per cent in Hungary to 74.4 and 76.9 per cent, respectively. After five or so years of transition the only countries with comfortable dependency ratios seem to have been Turkmenistan (25.3 per cent), Tajikistan (27 per cent), and Uzbekistan (29.2 per cent), but this was so more because of the lack of social security coverage and pensions for some people than because these systems were healthy, which they definitely were not (Branco 1998).

Over the medium term, only the reduction of relative pension levels could bring the burden of the social security system on public finance under control, and the replacement rate (the ratio of the average pension to the average wage) declined in the majority of countries. It fell by more than 10 percentage points on average between 1990 and 1993 in Albania, Croatia, and Romania, but later it evolved along quite different lines in these three countries. In Croatia it continued to drop quickly, from 62 per cent in 1993 to 35.4 per cent in 1995. In Romania it rose back from 26 to 29.7 per cent in 1993–5. Between 1990 and 1996 only in five transition economies— Kyrgyzstan, Latvia, Moldova, Poland, and Turkmenistan—did the rate increase, while in the Czech Republic it remained unchanged. In 1996 it varied from 31.4 per cent in Bulgaria to twice that in Poland (61.3 per cent). In the former Soviet republics the range was relatively even bigger: from 23.7 per cent in Tajikistan to 53.3 per cent in Turkmenistan (Table 17).

The amount of the climb in the dependency ratio has been larger in countries where unemployment has increased significantly, since the ratio represents the proportion of retired people to the working part of the population and not to the entire labour force, including those who are idle. So, in the case of countries with rising unemployment, the numerator in the ratio has gone up, while the denominator has gone down.

There is a tradeoff between the financial implications of unemployment and the financial strains coming from a rapid advance in the number of pensioners. In some countries with relatively lower rates of unemployment (or even sectoral overemployment), such as the Czech Republic, the dependency ratio is lower than it is in countries with higher unemployment rates, such as Slovakia. In the Czech Republic in 1996 the unemployment rate was 3.5 per cent, and the dependency ratio was 61 per cent, while in Slovakia these ratios were 12.6 per cent and 46.1 per cent, respectively.[4]

---

[4] In 1997 and 1998 the unemployment rate was rising in the Czech Republic and falling in Slovakia.

Table 17 Public pension systems in transition countries, 1990–1996

	System dependency ratio[a] (%)			Average replacement rate[b] (%)		
	1990	1993	1996	1990	1993	1996
Armenia	33.8	43.7	44.1	44.6	30.7	24.3
Azerbaijan	38.8	42.9	41.6	42.3	21.2	29.2
Belarus	46.1	54.0	71.0	40.1	38.0	40.9
Bulgaria	55.0	80.0	74.4	42.8	40.2	31.4
Croatia	31.0	43.0	54.3	73.0	62.0	35.4
Czech Republic	42.0	51.0	61.0[c]	47.6	43.4	47.8
Estonia	45.3	47.9	55.9	—	—	29.4
Georgia	34.6	37.3	54.9	—	—	36.4
Hungary	47.0	66.0	76.9	49.7	47.3	41.4
Kazakhstan	31.9	43.7	57.1	38.5	39.3	34.0
Kyrgyzstan	34.6	38.0	34.0	44.8	38.4	48.5
Latvia	42.7	53.1	54.9	31.2	33.3	38.6
Lithuania	47.4	50.2	53.8	36.3	28.4	30.8
Moldova	34.6	46.9	50.2	38.6	32.1	40.1
Poland	40.0	53.0	61.3	59.0	76.8	61.3
Romania	34.0	49.0	52.3[c]	41.9	26.0	29.7
Russia	44.9	52.4	57.0	38.0	24.5	28.4
Slovakia	39.0	53.0	46.1	48.3	44.0	42.0
Tajikistan	27.3	32.9	27.0	47.8	45.9	23.7
Turkmenistan	25.4	28.0	25.3	41.1	47.5	53.3
Ukraine	51.4	60.5	65.3	41.6	26.9	32.7
Uzbekistan	29.9	33.1	29.2	45.1	29.9	40.9

[a] Number of pensioners relative to the number of people employed. [b] Average pension relative to the average wage. [c] Reflects data for 1995.
Source: IMF 1998c.

This variance is a clear result of the distinct strategies adopted in the two countries. Under socialism, the ratios were not so different in these two parts of the former Czechoslovakia. During transition, the Czech strategy has been to permit sectoral overemployment, thus raising the denominator (that is, the number of employed people). The Slovak strategy has been more radical and allows for a more quickly falling denominator (and higher unemployment). Nonetheless, owing to the slower growth in the numerator (that is, the number of pensioners), the Slovak strategy has not led to a big increase in the dependency ratio. While in the Czech Republic it soared by 19 percentage points in six years, in Slovakia the gain was only 7.1 percentage points.

In Poland, unfortunately, the worst of both worlds met. Due to the mismanagement of the early transition and a mistaken sequence in adjustment, the dependency ratio jumped by half, from 40 per cent in 1990 to 53 per cent in 1993 and 61.3 per cent in 1996. This occurred because hundreds of thousands of people were put on early retirement in 1990–3. This was supposed to be an antidote for rapidly growing unemployment, which had gone up anyhow to 16.4 per cent by the end of 1993. Whereas the number of working people was shrinking, the number of pensioners and disabled was growing by a significant amount.[5] Thus, the increase in the size of both groups—decisive for the dependency ratio—was more a function of policy mistakes than of objective demographic processes. Only later, when the new policy had accelerated growth and diminished unemployment by one-third, did the dependency ratio start to improve.

This points to a solution for other transition economies. If countries can take advantage of early retirement and lax disability pensions as a way to counteract surging unemployment, then falling unemployment during a period of fast growth will ease fiscal tensions because the contributions to the PAYG system will be rising rapidly as well. In the long run, this time due to demographic changes and not to policy, the problem with early retiree-pensioners will vanish, since this has been a one-ff solution. The remaining life expectancy within this group of the population is not long, so the relative share of this group among all retired and disabled people will decrease.

The roots of the crisis in the social security system do not lie in the previous system, but within the transition. First, the long and deep transitional recession led to falling contributions and rising costs in the system. Second, the lack of proper institutional arrangements meant that there was no possibility of adopting alternative measures. A growing share of the ageing population therefore had to rely on the deteriorating system. Third, the feeble commitment of political leaders to undertake adjustments in the existing system so as to confront economic and financial realities caused permanent inflationary pressure. Fourth, weak tax administration led to the inadequate collection of payroll taxes.

Not surprisingly, on the microeconomic side the individual pensions are often too low to meet the 'social minimum' standard of living, while on the macroeconomic side the entire system is out of balance. The public expenditure on pensions has become an intolerable burden on public finance and is adding to the deficit. Governments are trying to pay the pensions, but this is eating into other urgent expenditures for education, health care, and infrastructure development. The remaining gap is being covered through inflationary monetary expansion or by borrowing on capital markets, and this either fuels inflation, or strengthens the crowding-out effect. Both

---

[5] Many of the 'disabled' were actually still able to work, considering their age and their health.

Table 18 Public pension expenditure in transition countries,
1993 and 1996 (% GDP)

	1993	1996		1993	1996
Albania	6.5	6.8	Latvia	9.5	10.8
Armenia	2.5	3.1	Lithuania	4.8	6.2
Azerbaijan	6.7	2.5	FYR Macedonia	15.6	11.2
Belarus	7.6	8.4	Moldova	—	8.1
Bulgaria	14.1	9.5	Poland	13.4	14.4
Croatia	6.2	10.2	Romania	6.2	5.8
Czech Republic	7.3	8.4	Russia	6.1	4.5
Estonia	6.4	7.6	Slovakia	9.4	8.3
Georgia	—	1.7	Tajikistan	6.9	3.0
Hungary	10.6	9.7	Turkmenistan	2.3	—
Kazakhstan	4.4	5.3	Ukraine	8.3	8.7
Kyrgyzstan	—	7.7	Uzbekistan	10.0	6.4

Source: IMF 1998c.

act against efficiency and growth, and thus the situation for pensioners deteriorates still further (Table 18).

The crisis in the PAYG system is not exclusively a financial one. It is also a very serious political issue. As the dependency ratio has grown, so has the share of retired and disabled people in the electorate, with all the implications for politics. Perhaps this, even more than economic and financial considerations, makes the reform of the system so urgent. Still, the reform must be implemented through comprehensive changes in the law, and these changes must be accepted by parliaments in which the deputies are susceptible to voter opinion. Moreover, retirees have formed associations which have become influential by lobbying parliaments. Parliamentary majorities and ruling coalitions have sometimes had to depend on these groups for support, and government must listen to them in determining the policy toward pension system reform. The reform should ideally be aimed at smooth changes over a long time horizon. However, the present generation of pensioners is looking for current improvements in their standard of living and therefore immediate real growth in their pensions.[6] Yet, while running a government without the support of pensioners is extremely difficult, running a government against them would be impossible.

The dependency ratio generally ranges between 40 and 60 per cent in the transition countries, though in extreme cases it may be as low as 25 per cent or as high as over 75 per cent. A 50 to 75 per cent ratio means

[6] As John Maynard Keynes wrote 75 years ago in *A Tract on Monetary Reform*, 'Long run is a misleading guide to current affairs. In the long run we are all dead.'

that four working people must earn enough not only to meet their own needs and the needs of their families, but also at least some of the needs of another two or three people who depend on pensions provided within the PAYG. In this case, the pension system is clearly unsustainable. In fact, it has already broken down in some countries. The state is unable to meet its obligations, since it is unable to raise the revenues to pay the pensions. In some countries, like Azerbaijan, Georgia, Kyrgyzstan, Moldova, and Russia, the difficulties are very serious. Payroll tax collection is very poor, and the effective pension contribution rate has fallen below half the nominal rate of the pensions due (IMF 1998c). Consequently, the overhaul of social security arrangements in transition economies is a must. Further improvement of the PAYG system is also necessary, but this cannot be a substitute for a definitive solution to the problem.

Some countries have already initiated attempts to rebuild their systems. The sequence of the steps taken toward this end is important. Since the ongoing reforms are tending to rely on the introduction of private pension funds into the system, strong supervision and regulation must be secured. This requires proper organizations and institutional frameworks, since government must underwrite the entire system. The new structure must be credible, since otherwise it will not be able to attract and accumulate a sufficient amount of savings. It must also be supported by strong macroeconomic fundamentals and relatively established financial markets. The sequence is therefore clear. First, transparent regulations are needed. Then, private pension funds can be allowed to evolve. No doubt this can occur only in a context of economic growth.

The idea should be to replace the traditional but increasingly inefficient and conflict-ridden PAYG system with a 'multi-pillar' social security system. The system is actually three systems in one. First, there is still the old, though significantly downsized, PAYG pillar. This is maintained to provide pensions for elderly people who have already been receiving pensions through this very system for some time. So, these people are going to continue to be provided with a social safety net similar to the one which protected them in the past. The second pillar is a private yet mandatory system that is fully funded by contributions. This element aims at attracting the retirement savings of the active population and involves the investment of these savings into capital market funds. The third pillar consists of the entirely voluntary private schemes.

Supported by the technical and financial assistance of the World Bank, such systems are in various stages of implementation in Hungary, Kazakhstan, Latvia, and Poland. Several other countries, including Azerbaijan, Croatia, the Czech Republic, Estonia, Georgia, Lithuania, FYR Macedonia, Romania, Russia, and Slovenia, are preparing plans for such systems. Some of these nations have already established the legal and regulatory regime for the creation of private pension funds (Hemming 1998).

Kazakhstan has adopted a slightly more radical approach toward the establishment of such a three-tiered system whereby, as in Chile, all currently employed workers participate in the new privately managed schemes, while people who had already retired before these schemes were launched at the beginning of 1998 remain with the PAYG system.

Hungary, Latvia, and Poland have been taking a more gradual approach. In Hungary, only young people (currently below 20 years of age) who are now entering the labour force for the first time are obliged to save for retirement through the privately managed fully funded pillar. Other people who have not yet retired—no matter how long they have been working, even if only for a couple of years or even if they are facing retirement soon—have the opportunity to decide themselves to remain in the restructured PAYG pillar or to take advantage of the new scheme and save through private pension funds. People who have already retired remain with the PAYG system and are not affected by the reform.

In Latvia, discussions are continuing. For the time being the conventional PAYG pillar has been replaced by a 'notionally defined contribution' system. Under this scheme, each pension is calculated as the sum of the life-time contributions divided by the average life expectancy at the age of retirement. The latter is estimated at around 12 years for males and 17 years for females.

In Poland, people between the ages of 30 and 50 who are currently working can decide on their own which system they wish to join. For people under 30, the privately funded scheme is mandatory, and for those over 50 the PAYG system is still required, as it is, of course, for current pensioners (Office of the Government Plenipotentiary for Social Security Reform 1997, Gora and Rutkowski 1998, Hausner 1998).

These approaches have caused a great deal of misunderstanding among some people, since for a long time the entire discussion about social security reform focused so much attention on matters relating only to current pensioners, though, of course, the whole endeavour must be addressed mainly at future pensioners.

Like the second pillar, the third one—the entirely voluntary private schemes—ought to boost savings and therefore the ability of the economy to expand. This is the area where social security reform is directly linked with the development of the financial sector and with the policy target of raising the propensity of households to save. A special significance of this pillar is that it allows people to become personally involved in the pension decision. No longer does the faceless state alone determine the amount of money that is to be saved by an individual for his future retirement. Not only should this choice contribute to the propensity to save, but the effective, professional management of private pension funds ought to secure profitable investment opportunities for the accumulated savings, thereby augmenting both the efficiency of social policy and overall economic growth.

8.3. EXCHANGE RATE REGIMES

It may seem that monetary theory has found in the unique research laboratory of the transition economies a fertile ground for experimentation. Exchange rate management and the introduction of convertibility are good examples. The results of the experiments have been mixed.

In Poland at the beginning of 1990 the devaluation of the currency significantly overshot the mark, and the effort to use the exchange rate as a nominal anchor of the stabilization programme failed. The rate of inflation by the end of 1990 had reached about 250 per cent, although the government declared that within a couple of months the rise in the consumer price index would be remaining below 1 per cent per month, that is, 12 per cent or so per year. Unfortunately, this was not the case, and, after 16 months during which the nominal exchange rate was frozen at 9,500 zloty per dollar, another devaluation became unavoidable. In the meantime, prices kept going up by 3 to 5 per cent monthly, and output was shrinking rapidly. Similar was the course of events at that time in the former Yugoslavia. Later, there was a clear pattern of diversification in currency regimes and currency management.

In a market economy foreign exchange settlements serve various, sometimes contradictory purposes, so that conflicting policy targets can have an important impact on the foreign exchange regime and the system of currency management. Although in the long run the main objective of monetary policy is price stability, the policy cannot neglect the issues of growth and employment. So, the true aim of monetary policy should be the sustainability of growth, which also demands financial soundness and a stable currency. Yet, even in the leading industrial nations the exchange rate is sometimes treated as a policy instrument and sometimes as a medium-term policy target. The exchange rates among major currencies have fluctuated widely in recent years, for instance from about 140 yen to 80 yen and then back to 140 yen per dollar and from over 1.70 DM to 1.40 DM and back up to 1.85 DM per dollar in the case of the German currency. This is hardly 'stability'.

During transition an essential systemic change has been the move away from centrally planned international trade conducted by foreign-trade enterprises. These enterprises were state owned and specialized in the import and export of commodities under monopoly conditions and within the framework of the Comecon trade bloc. During transition they have been transformed to handle free, unrestricted trade and are open to ownership by any private enterprise or individual.

Moreover, the reintegration of the transition economies into the world trade regime has started, too. This process, which has involved the restructuring and redirection of trade flows, requires not only the dismantling of the foreign-trade monopoly through the transformation of the foreign-trade organizations and the regulation of any foreign-trade activities under-taken by entities, whether state or non-state, but also market access to the foreign exchange needed to pay for imports and the ability to use at will all currency earnings originating in exports.

In other words, it has been recognized that harvesting trade benefits demands the existence of a freedom among residents to be able to con-vert domestic currency to foreign currencies for current account purposes. In its fullest form, this 'internal convertibility' is defined by Article VIII of the IMF General Agreement. It is more than the convertibility of money into goods. It is the convertibility of money into foreign goods. This level of convertibility is simply a consequence of the nature of an open market economy.

In the old system, money was not even freely convertible into domestic goods, let alone into foreign currencies, which, like material goods, were underpriced. This was so because of the endemic shortages existing in goods (and currencies) at administered prices, as well as because of the frequent coexistence of shortages and inflation, or shortageflation. Hence the domestic currency was overvalued, scarce, and directly allocated to strictly authorized users according to the central plan.

In its simpler form, internal convertibility can be achieved easily by legalizing the black market for foreign exchange, as Poland did in February 1989, before the transition got under way, or as Russia did at the begin-ning of January 1992. In this case the exchange rate is a freely floating market-determined rate. There is no need for foreign currency reserves to be used to back a pre-fixed exchange rate. Trade competitiveness is automatically maintained by devaluing the currency as required, and the convertibility can be speedily introduced.

In the actual exercise, due to inflationary expectations generated by simultaneous price liberalization, the main disadvantage of such a solution was gross undervaluation of the domestic currency in terms of purchasing power and long-term equilibrium. This kind of undervaluation in turn can cause further inflation. However, it was not only inevitable, but also to a certain extent desirable during the liberalization and stabilization period, since corrective inflation happened to be an instrument of structural adjustment.

If convertibility is introduced without too much haste after inflationary expectations have been dampened and in the presence of significant central reserves, a pre-fixed exchange rate level or 'bands' can be aimed at, with potential advantages for price stability. In this case, the danger is that interna-tional competitiveness may erode unless unit wage costs can be contained by means of productivity growth, or wage restraint, or both.

The real issue therefore is not whether internal convertibility should or should not be introduced (since it is part and parcel of the market economy), but at what exchange rate level and under which exchange rate regime the introduction should be carried out. The choice between fixed and float-ing exchange rates is roughly a choice between the fight against inflation or the struggle against unemployment, with any mixture of policies rep-resenting a compromise between these two evils.

The exchange rate regimes under which convertibility has been intro-duced have varied enormously: from the floating rate (Russia, January 1992 through 1995) to the fixed rate (Poland, January 1990 to November 1991, with intermittent devaluation in May and November 1991), from the (theoretically) permanently fixed exchange rate of the currency boards (Estonia and Lithuania since 1992 and Bulgaria since 1997) to the inter-mediate regimes of sliding-crawling pegs (Poland, November 1991 to May 1995), and from crawling bands (Poland since May 1995) to fixed bands (Russia from 1996 to August 1998). The Czech Republic and Hungary have also had to adjust currency regimes to changing circumstances and new policy options, and lately they have settled on a kind of 'managed floating' exchange rate. The Czech Republic was obliged in the summer of 1997 to perform a de facto devaluation of the koruna by 10 per cent, and the relative weight of the dollar was changed in the basket of curren-cies against which the koruna was pegged.

Regardless of the exchange rate regime, the transition experience with currency has followed a fairly standard pattern. An initial severe under-valuation of the domestic currency with respect to purchasing power par-ities and other measures of competitiveness, accompanied by trade surpluses, has been followed by real revaluation. This has been achieved mostly through inflation differentials, often accompanied by trade balance deterioration, unless (as in Poland) competitiveness has been enhanced by large productivity gains which are more significant than wage growth, and (or) the real revaluation has been contained by nominal devaluation. The inflationary costs of undervaluation that are associated with early convertibility should be set against the advantages of the rapid shift and expansion in trade and the enhanced inducements for foreign investment. It has been argued that a modest level of tariff protection, temporary and non-discriminatory, might have mitigated the amount of devaluation required by convertibility and even raised government revenues, thereby alleviating the fiscal crisis (Tanzi 1997a).

The integration of transition economies into international markets also requires the achievement of current account convertibility. As demonstrated by the Czech koruna crisis of June 1997 and, to a much greater extent, by the subsequent East Asian contagion, current account convertibility involves significant vulnerability to speculative flows, especially through hedge funds.[7] It follows that, in the sequencing of transition reforms, this *fuller*

---

[7] Unregulated and often performing offshore, hedge funds aggressively seek juicy profits by supporting high-risk ventures.

convertibility should come only after stabilization has been consolidated into stability, government policies have established international credibility, and enterprise restructuring—financial and real—has been broadly realized. The effort is actually being made to follow this sequence, so full convertibility, including capital account convertibility at some later date, is not on the current agenda even in the countries which are most advanced in transition. These countries will have reached this stage by the time they join the European Union. Thus, these targets may be achieved in the near future.

The impact of currency regimes on overall economic activity and therefore on the amount of real output can vary. If currency policies have been well balanced and carried forward gradually with proper care for institutional arrangements, they can contribute to growth in trade and attract additional inflows of foreign direct investment. But the wrong sequence in the liberalization of the foreign exchange regime can hamper the capacity for growth. There are examples, like the stop-and-go-and-then-go-back-again policy in Uzbekistan. Such a chaotic approach to the currency regime inhibits foreign trade and discourages exports. The multiple exchange rate system for the Uzbek som that was reintroduced by the authorities in 1997 after an earlier partial liberalization and exchange rate unification definitely interfered with the flow of imports and foreign direct investment, and this in turn slowed exports and overall growth (Kolodko 1997b).

Thus, a sound evaluation of currency regimes and exchange rate policies must take into account the impact on the economy and on capital flows. In transition nations, as in other emerging markets, interest rate differentials and trends in exchange rates are of great importance. Whereas long-term capital investors, mainly foreign direct investors, are looking for long-run prospects, market potential, and chances to earn reasonable profits on invested money, the short-term capital is driven basically by interest rate differentials and expectations as regards exchange rate fluctuations. If these favour foreign capital, then obviously foreign capital is keen to flow into transition economies, as was the case in several countries in 1994–8 (UNECE 1998). Especially the Czech Republic, Estonia, Hungary, Poland, and Slovakia—and of course Russia—attracted significant injections of speculative capital. The differences between domestic real interest rates and the interest rates on global markets encouraged this type of investment. These factors also contributed to the significant vulnerability of new exchange rate systems. Thus, exchange rate policy remains among the most urgent and major issues on the transition and development policy agenda.

8.4. FINANCIAL SECTOR DEVELOPMENT

In the shortage economy the absorption of the excessive liquidity of households and the provision of financing for a production sector controlled by the central planning allocation mechanism were very critical problems. Only later, in the reformed economies of Eastern Europe and in China and Vietnam, were banks used as core institutions through which governments might try to impose hard budget constraints on state-owned and private enterprises.

A banking system which serves business and household economies efficiently is essential everywhere, and the structure of the banking system is very important. Sound commercial banks are a prerequisite in the effort to guarantee competition. *Privatization cannot succeed if it is not backed by a supportive competitive climate, which is not feasible as long as there is no solid banking system.*

The successful overhaul of the banking system calls for the privatization of state banks. The saleoff of assets to strategic domestic and foreign investors and deregulation permitting the operations of foreign banks may help, but they do not respond to the pressing need for bank recapitalization. Because of the contraction, banks were being stripped of their assets; and, as the economy shrank, there was no way to avoid severe losses in the banking sector. The process of consolidation and recapitalization is always costly for the budget; hence it ought to be initiated together with the reforms in the fiscal system. When these steps must be undertaken, output is still declining or has only recently begun to recover. Savings are scant; the adequacy ratio is too low, and capital is insufficient and 'deconcentrated'. The need to recapitalize in a situation in which capital is insufficient is another vicious circle which must be broken during transition.

In Russia in the mid-1990s there were about 2,500 banks, only a small portion of which could be considered reliable. Since then bank consolidation has been advancing speedily, particularly among the larger Moscow-based banks. A special bankruptcy law has been adopted by parliament, and many banks qualify for restructuring under this law. Since then, the process of bank restructuring has apparently been gaining momentum (Bernstam and Rabushka 1998).[8] However, this occurred too late to avert the spectacular crisis in the summer of 1998.

In Poland, due to a special government bank consolidation programme initiated in 1993, less reliable banks, of which there were many, began to disappear, and the relative number of more dependable banks grew. The quality of banking services for businesses and households rose as well. Gradual privatization and an orderly process of increasing openness toward foreign banks facilitated further enhancements and improved the corporate governance of banks and of companies to which banks were lending.

In the Czech Republic, the banking sector became caught up in crisis owing to the mismanagement of a mass privatization programme and the

---

[8] The OECD (1997b) survey on Russia is excellent on the then-current Russian banking system.

lack of proper banking regulations. Banks had been more involved in speculative acquisitions and mergers than in commercial lending or financial consultancy for the restructuring of privatized companies. Efficiency and output were not being raised, and the economy was losing momentum and was stagnating. Only in 1998 was an appropriate law adopted for the regulation of the financial sector.

In Bulgaria in 1996–7 the banking crisis was so severe that the whole course of transition policy had to be detoured. At the insistence of the IMF, several banks were closed, and a currency board was introduced. In January 1998, for the sake of transparency, a list of bad debtors was published.

The restructuring of portfolios of outstanding debt is important, too. These debt portfolios were not a legacy of the centrally planned economy, but appeared as a by-product of transition. Contraction and the attempts to stabilize the economy through austere monetary measures led to an increase in non-performing debt. Given that restrictive interest rates were imposed not only on new credit, but on old credit as well, it should hardly come as a surprise that many debt-ridden companies soon became insolvent. Later, they tried to save themselves by taking advantage of mounting inter-enterprise arrears (Selowsky and Vogel 1995). Many companies experienced a sudden switch from excessive liquidity to insufficient liquidity, and this had negative consequences for capacity utilization, employment, and output.

Recapitalization has been carried out in various ways. In Poland banks have been obliged to forgive, restructure, lend to, or bankrupt their debtors. In the Czech Republic loss-making enterprises have been assigned to an agency which then attempts to recover some of the bad loans. The Czech currency crisis of mid-1997 and its harmful influence on growth suggest that the Polish approach may have been more effective. Although in Poland the banking sector was far from perfect, it recovered. In contrast, in the Czech Republic not only the banking sector, but the entire capital market was driven back onto the ropes.

Meanwhile, in Albania, Bulgaria, and Romania the situation has been still more difficult. In Hungary there has been progress, though numerous major banks have become entirely dependent on foreign capital. Such dependency highlights the danger of excessive injections of foreign capital, which, however, may relieve the problem of recapitalization. This sort of dependency is a more sensitive issue in the banking sector than it is in non-financial sectors.

The road leading to the liquidity of the entire banking system and to healthy individual banks without a resurgence of inflation is very bumpy and not always very direct. Gradual privatizations, the upgrading of corporate governance, the injection of fresh capital, and Treasury-assisted debt-to-equity swaps between banks and companies do help, but the difficulties remain quite serious. One dilemma is the fact that bank recapitalization and the elimination of inter-enterprise arrears are only possible if there is sufficient capital. Unless it becomes available because the economy is already growing, such capital must be supplied from elsewhere. So far, foreign assistance—despite all the statements to the contrary—has been minor, although the banking sector (along with energy and telecommunications) is a favourite target of big foreign investors in transition economies.[9]

As bank consolidation advances and the economy begins to expand, commercial and investment banks are able to absorb growing savings. By borrowing for profitable ventures and investing in other financial inter- mediaries, these banks contribute to the efficient allocation of savings, and the savings add to capital formation.

Yet, the overhaul of the banking system is only part of the story of the development of the financial sector. Another important chapter is the establishment of capital markets.

Postsocialist nations have opted for a course whereby the core of the financial sector is being taken over by the banks. The stock exchange is of relatively minor significance. Even in the most advanced economies the capitalization of the stock exchange is rather limited. For example, in Hungary and Poland it does not exceed 10 per cent of GDP, although about three- quarters of the output of these two countries is being produced by the pri- vate sector. In the countries considered advanced in the transition process by the EBRD in 1998, that is, in Croatia, the Czech Republic, Estonia, Hungary, Latvia, Lithuania, Poland, Slovakia, and Slovenia, the share of foreign capital in the stock exchanges is 20 to 30 per cent (during a bull market, of course), in contrast to the situation in the whole economy, where the share of foreign capital is very small.

In Croatia and Estonia there is a structural bias on the stock exchange since the financial sector is 'overbanked', meaning that the banks listed on the stock exchange account for about one-third of overall capitalization. The activities of financial intermediaries are still limited in Georgia. In Russia banking regulations and bank supervision were enhanced in response to the East Asian crisis, but this came too late, and the banking sector went into severe crisis. In Bulgaria the first major bank was privatized only in 1997, and the stock exchange started to operate in October of that year. In Hungary over half of the banking sector is in foreign hands, and the stock exchange has been flourishing for several years already. In Poland the major banks are profitable and well capitalized. In Turkmenistan the banking sector is still burdened with non-performing loans. In Moldova

---

[9] One need only compare the total lending provided to transition economies by the Bretton Woods institutions and the EBRD (and the relatively small engagement of private capital in bank restructuring and recapitalization) with the remarkable sums invested in the attempt to bail out the Asian countries. The $10 billion provided gradually under tough conditionality by the IMF and the World Bank to Russia between 1991 and mid-1998 is dwarfed by the rescue package of almost $20 billion for Thailand, about $43 billion for Indonesia, and over $58 billion for South Korea.

higher minimum capital requirements for banking have been enforced since 1997. In Tajikistan asset liquidity continues to deteriorate (EBRD 1998). Thus, the health and regulatory environment of the banking sector in post-socialist economies are not like those in Ethiopia, nor are they like those in Switzerland. They remain in transition.

The stock exchange also functions as a useful vehicle for privatization schemes. In this role, it has significance for technical purposes, such as the saleoff of state assets through public offers, but also as a substantial means of demonstrating to people how capital and the market work. Yet, perhaps the cost of some of this educational process has been too dear, and perhaps not enough people are learning the lessons well. The huge price fluctuations—greater than any in developed market economies— have beguiled many individual investors and then ruined them, and the speculative manoeuvres of big investors, mainly the institutional ones, have sometimes rendered these markets too vulnerable.

9

The Redistribution of the Costs and Benefits of Transition

9.1. PRIVATIZATION: THE STRUGGLE OVER THE DISTRIBUTION OF WEALTH

There are two dangers involved in privatization. First, the need for budgetary revenue creates pressure to sell off assets quickly to the highest bidder. However, this actually encourages firesale prices and provokes an unhealthy tendency to sacrifice long-run improvements in corporate governance to the urge to boost current revenue rapidly. In trying to sell assets precipitously, governments may succumb to the temptation to sell them cheaply, and, aside from the direct financial loss, this opens up room for lightning profits among insider traders, permits major rent-seeking, and raises the risk of corruption.

The second danger is that one may be overly reluctant to privatize owing to the enormous difficulties, including social tensions and political controversies (Pitelis and Clarke 1993). There is a desire to slow the whole process down so as to lessen the hardships which usually accompany restructuring. Job cuts and big layoffs, retraining and labour redeployment, changes in management methods and technologies, the struggle for access to new markets, and growing competition are genuine challenges which privatization raises. Despite a growing consensus that in the long term privatization secures improvements in efficiency, one may choose to put it on hold until some restructuring has taken place, which may not be immediately.

Policy should seek to improve microeconomic effectiveness and raise budgetary revenues at the same time. While the former contributes to the potential for growth, the latter strengthens macroeconomic stabilization. A good policy approach is therefore to sail cautiously between the two dangers in privatization.

It appears as though the second danger—the postponement of privatization—gathers more media attention than does the first, though both have major implications for development and the success of transition. If one analyses this phenomenon through the prism of the 'public debates' in the news media, the conclusion might be drawn that there was much more public concern about the privatization of the tobacco industry than

about the fight against unemployment, or about a saleoff of telecommunications firms rather than about the alleviation of poverty. One should
remember that the unemployed and the poor do not lobby, and they do
not compensate the media for their support; wealthy industries do these
things.

The insistence on ever more rapid privatization—be it of gas fields in
Azerbaijan, commercial banks in Bulgaria, automobile plants in the Czech
Republic, telecommunications service providers in Hungary, the tobacco
industry in Poland, or energy companies in Russia—is not due merely to
the danger inherent in a postponement of privatization. Clearly, among
many people who have the most to gain from rapid privatization, the main
goal is not improved corporate governance, more fiscal balance, or higher
living standards, but the acquisition of very valuable assets at bargain prices.[1]
This is a bizarre situation: active advocates of an efficient free market
system spurring on the sale of 'goods' (extremely useful ones, since they
produce other goods and therefore profits) at below the 'real' value, that
is, below the market clearing price.

However, it is doubtful that rent-seeking alone is to blame (Åslund 1996).
Rent-seeking is nothing more than profit-seeking under non-competitive
conditions, and it is therefore due to bad institutions rather than bad
behaviour, since the institutions tolerate the rent-seeking and thus make
it possible.[2] The less mature the institutional side of the market, the more
room there is for rent-seeking.

While the wish to acquire assets at the lowest possible price may be
understandable, this time there is a serious political issue, too. If the political pressure is irresistible, and the privatization is conducted through an
everything-must-go sale, then the private sector will grow, but the public
debt will grow, too, and so will political tensions. For any government,
it is awkward to get rid of state property so quickly and equally quickly to
become saddled with such a large debt. Not governments, but nations own
both the assets and the debt.

Privatizations in the former GDR were carried out very rapidly, but
this should be an exception. There is no Federal Republic of Belarus and
no West Romania. In general, the privatizations should occur gradually.
The Treasury ought to be seeking to protect the interests of all citizens.
The denationalizations should therefore be conducted through transparent

[1] While minister of finance of Poland in 1994–7, the author was not asked even once by
a foreign investor or a foreign association to privatize a (presumably less attractive) state coal
mine, steel mill, shipyard, or tractor factory. Yet, constantly and with the very vigorous and
well-orchestrated support of certain political parties and interest groups, he was pressed to
accelerate the privatization of banks, telecommunications firms, and utilities, especially in the
energy sector.

[2] According to an old adage, if central planning were introduced into the Sahara, there
would soon be a shortage of sand. In this case, the adage might be: the moment one can
acquire wealth through bad behaviour, one begins behaving badly.

procedures under the watchful eye of public opinion. Privatization must be carried out so that the state simultaneously sells public assets and reduces public debt. Up to now there has been a strong negative link between these assets and debt, so there should now be a positive link between them during privatization. In a certain sense, *the public debt ought to be privatized together with the public assets.*

Owing to political instability and the systemic vacuum, it is possible in transition nations today to amass quantities of assets that are not justified by the relatively small effort applied or by the relatively small risk involved. Wealth today is not often due to hard work, an innovative approach to business, or a meaningful contribution to technological progress; it is coming from insider trading, smart dealing, and a crony's handling (or mishandling?) of a denationalization. Privatization is no longer exclusively an exercise in the transfer of state assets at a reasonable price into the hands of new owners who are expected to be able to manage the assets more effectively. Today, it is a way to get rich quick. Thus, there is a furious struggle over the redistribution of assets in the transition economies. The more rapidly and the more radically privatization is implemented, the easier it is to make bagloads of money, even though (or especially because) there is a severe drop in national income.

If some groups are making enormous profits, then something may be wrong. As long as there was no open crisis in the Czech Republic and as long as the bubble on the Russian stock market was blinding foreign analysts and their Russian partners, the policy was a 'success', and not much criticism was directed at the way privatization was being conducted. Nonetheless, it should have been obvious that the way it was being managed —the poor corporate governance exercised over privatized assets and the lack of an industrial policy—must ultimately lead to a breakdown. In the Czech Republic there was a short period of stagnation, but in Russia the collapse had extremely severe consequences even beyond the domestic economy. It should have been possible to predict these crises in privatization because of poor policies, just as it was possible in neighbouring countries to avoid such crises through good policies. However, the ability of politicians to detect early those policies which will lead to crisis—be it in the Czech Republic or Indonesia, or be it in Russia or Brazil—seems to be limited. Apparently, the interests of certain influential financial and political groups are stronger than rational argument, which seems to be heard and listened to only after the roots of crisis have taken hold and the crisis has already grown out of hand.

As long as privatization in Russia was favourable for well-established and influential domestic groups and equally well-connected foreign capital, there was not so much criticism. Though from time to time the words 'crony capitalism' were being whispered, rather a sympathetic tone dominated on the international scene. Indeed, additional financial speculation was being encouraged, and investment was often occurring in a context of ignorance about social realities and arrogance toward people and the importance of the physical assets changing hands through the lucrative deals. When the Russian capital market was bullish,

investors did not really seem to care where the companies they were buying were located and what exactly they were called, as long as they belonged to [a] hot sector such as telecommunications or electricity. As one US fund manager, on a visit to Moscow, put it: 'Honey, I don't pronounce 'em, I just buy 'em'. (Freeland 1998)

A delay in the privatization of an energy company can garner more attention than the postponement of the payment of pensions or wages. Whereas the former is considered a crucial problem in the distribution of wealth, the latter seems to be viewed as a secondary technical problem in the current cash flow. Meanwhile, though public assets are frequently being sold off at closeout prices, the liabilities of the state are growing. Odd, that.

Ultimately, when the necessity to take special policy action can no longer be avoided, the costs of the adjustment have gone higher. Although such costs are nowhere in Eastern Europe as high as they are in the bailouts in East Asia, the measures which must be applied are still very tough, and now they will cause even more hardship. In the aftermath of the Czech crisis it was remarked that

Analysts said public hostility to the austerity measures would be reduced only if combined with other reforms the government pledged to undertake. Key areas are an overhaul of the legal system and a crackdown on white-collar crime, which has enriched a tiny elite at the expense of thousands of investors in the vouchers-for-shares privatization drive. (Boland 1997)

Where were all these 'analysts' earlier, and what were they saying back then? What were the comments of the mass media during the 'privatization drive'? Why did the government not act on time? Why were the unfavourable policies which ultimately led to crisis actually backed by international organizations and institutional investors? Why were early warnings not taken seriously?[3]

Over and again, the answers to such questions revolve around economic interests and not simply economics theory. They all point to an underestimation of the importance of institution-building, especially the re-regulation, not deregulation, of capital and financial markets. Ill-advised neoliberal policies, so heavily supported for so long by the international

[3] For an early warning, see Komarek 1992. It was expected that the rate of GDP growth in the Czech Republic would be at least 4% in 1997, but later this estimate was revised downward several times until it had nearly reached nil. Instead of accelerated growth, there was stagnation, which continued into 1998. However, in the meantime, there were parliamentary elections, and the government—along with policies—changed, with a probable positive impact on future growth.

business and financial community, have been very significant, too. Such policies serve the interests of specific groups, but have had a negative impact on efficiency, growth, and income equity. The application of these policies was a mistake, and the price must now be paid in declining growth and deteriorating standards of living.

In an advanced market country it would be at least suspicious if the value of assets were to skyrocket in a very short time, as was happening in Russia. Robert Strauss, former US ambassador to that country, has been quoted as saying that 'If he had $100,000 and wanted to make $10 million, he would take it all to Russia. . . . And if he had $10 million and wanted to double it, he would still take $100,000 to Russia' (*Financial Times* 1997b).

The systemic vacuum, mainly the lack of effective regulations and controls, together with the neoliberal policy environment, has made such windfalls possible and within the law. There is no doubt that such sensational gains on capital investments can easily be realized through a privatization process which is carried out at less than market clearing prices. This has certainly been the case in many other countries besides Russia.

Because of very precipitous, if not chaotic, privatization, it is easy to take advantage of the weak policy commitment to counteract such transfers of state assets. Only at a later stage—and this is acknowledged openly—and in some of the more spectacular cases has proper action been taken. For instance, in the case of Russia's mighty Gazprom, it has been observed that 'buying shares on the local markets has been attractive because they are trading [at] about one-third the price of the stock offered to foreigners'. And, interestingly, it was a 'public secret' for a long time that the 'domestic market is closed to outside investors, but foreigners have bought shares through various grey funds, vehicles established by foreign fund managers to exploit local loopholes' (Freeland and Corzine 1997). This explains why there is such tremendous political pressure, including reports by local and international news media and well-paid experts, for a rapid and radical push for privatization and why so-called 'grey funds' have been tolerated. They will continue to be tolerated as long as they are needed and serve a purpose, that is, until the privatization drive is over.

Therefore, privatization must also be seen through the prism of the redistribution of wealth and not exclusively as a means of improving microeconomic efficiency. Indeed, the improvement of microeconomic efficiency has not necessarily even been the first goal among the two. The case of Russia is one good example. Others are the scandalous financial pyramids in Albania, the non-performing vouchers-for-shares investment funds which were so heavily publicized during the Czech privatization, and the sale of the major bank in Poland for a fraction of its real value.[4]

---

[4] When in 1993 the author asked a high-level official in the Ministry of finance in Poland why the shares of Bank Slaski were being sold at several times below the market clearing

9.2. EQUITY AND EQUALITY: EXPECTATIONS AND OUTCOMES

The distribution of income was generally more equitable in socialist countries than it is in market economies, and it was more equitably distributed in the socialist countries then than it is in the postsocialist countries now. The level of equitability also differed among the socialist countries, and it is possible to distinguish certain patterns among specific groups of countries in terms of the Gini coefficient.

Though 'the Gini' is not a perfect measure of income dispersion, it is the best single method we possess for such analysis (Sen 1992). The higher the Gini coefficient, the greater the inequality in income distribution, and the lower the index, the more equal the income distribution. If the Gini is '1', then income is distributed in an absolutely egalitarian way, and everybody receives the same portion of the cake. If it is '100', then one individual gets the entire cake, and everybody else gets nothing at all.

In Eastern Europe and the former Soviet Union during the late 1980s, the Gini index varied from a low of 20 in Slovakia to a high of 28 in Uzbekistan and stood mostly between 23 and 24. On average the index was six points lower in these countries than it was in Western Europe (with a somewhat special situation in the former Yugoslavia). Income distribution before transition was quite equitable in the socialist nations, which were similar in this regard to Finland, West Germany, the Netherlands, Norway, and Sweden. For the OECD nations Atkinson, Rainwater and Smeeding (1994) propose a division into four groups: countries with income inequality which is high (the Gini in the 33–5 range), average (29–31), low (24–6), and very low (20–2). From this perspective, all the former socialist nations would have been in the low or very low income inequality groups (Table 19).

Centrally planned economies possessed specific features in terms of income distribution and income inequality. In this sense, the distribution of primary nominal income and the mechanism of income redistribution have been important for transition policies.

In terms of primary income distribution, there were three key features. First, the state ownership of the means of production meant that the role of certain types of individual income, such as capital gains, profits, rents, and dividends, was marginal. Only in nations like Hungary, Poland, and Yugoslavia, with not insignificant private sectors, did these influence the income distribution among households, albeit still in no major way. Likewise, interest did not account for much income, due to a weak banking

price, he was told that the reason was simple: to provide the new owners with such extraordinary capital gains that they would soon be able to acquire yet another bank. And they were. The Bank Slaski shares, when quoted a couple of months later on the floor of Warsaw's stock exchange, were being traded at a price more than 13 times higher than that asked by the Ministry of finance. The state budget lost a great deal in this transaction, while a few investors gained a great deal.

Table 19 Income inequality indexes in Eastern Europe and
developed market countries, 1986–1987

	Gross earnings		Net disposable income	
	Gini coefficient	Decile ratio	Gini coefficient	Decile ratio
Czechoslovakia	19.7	2.5	19.9	2.4
Hungary	22.1	2.6	20.9	2.6
Poland	24.2	2.8	25.3	3.0
Soviet Union	27.6	3.3	25.6	3.3
Britain	26.7	3.2	29.7	3.9
United States			31.7[a]	
Germany			25.2[b]	
Australia			28.7[b]	

[a] 1987.   [b] 1981.

Sources: Atkinson and Micklewright 1992, Milanovic 1998.

sector and an absence of other financial intermediaries. Hence the bulk of
disposable income came from wages and pensions.

Second, wage settlements were centralized, and only in a handful of
countries did market reforms allow for a little bit more leeway in this area.
The social pressure for egalitarian distribution was strong and, together
with ideology, was a driving force behind the fact that the distribution of
primary income was more egalitarian than elsewhere, with all the obvious
effects on labour allocation and productivity.

Third, the state pension system was strictly linked to the wage structure, and the structure of the pensions accrued over the period of employment activity thus reflected the wage structure. Of course, on average the
pensions were lower than the wages, but the close relationship among the
pensions within particular strata was a consequence of a more or less
egalitarian wage policy.

In terms of income redistribution, there were likewise three key features
of centrally planned economies. First, the extensive range of subsidies was
of great importance.[5] Though the subsidies were directed mainly at the
poorer segments of society, the allocation contributed to a fairer income
distribution only to a certain extent. Subsidies were granted mainly for goods
and services with low income-elasticity, for example housing rents, electricity, water, home heating, public transport, and medicines. Such preferences were supposed to benefit especially groups with lower incomes.
Yet, they also favoured households doing relatively better. For example,

---

[5] In Poland in 1980 (the year of the greatest-ever labour protests in a socialist country)
subsidies accounted for 10% of national income.

subsidies were relatively high for people who lived in bigger apartments and travelled frequently.

Second, taxation did not have an important role, and direct taxes had only a marginal significance for income redistribution. For almost everyone, the gross remuneration was the same as the net compensation.

Third, the shortages had a tremendous impact on actual consumption, since true access to scarce goods was sometimes even more valuable than a relatively higher money income. Hence it is not really possible to evaluate real income dispersion on the basis of data referring exclusively to money income.

Under socialism the pressure for equitable distribution was very strong, and public dissatisfaction due to growing disparities in real income, including consumption in kind and the results of shortageflation, eventually began to appear. Undoubtedly, *one of the main causes of the postsocialist revolution was the public's conviction that income distribution had become unfair.*

It is difficult to ascertain to what degree people were concerned about the absolute level of their incomes and to what degree they were concerned about the way incomes were distributed. However, it is conceivable that the latter may have been the more important factor in the downfall of socialism. Indeed, at the onset of transition and even later in several countries there was not necessarily any clear desire to move away from relatively egalitarian planned socialism toward less egalitarian market capitalism. This desire emerged still later, and in some countries, including the two largest transition economies, Russia and Ukraine, does not seem to be particularly dominant even at the end of the 1990s.

The conviction that the advanced countries are rich simply because they have a market economy, not because of complex historical factors, was not uncommon even among political leaders. The belief that the amount of income would be higher in a market economy and that income distribution would become more equal was likewise widespread. It seemed to be confirmed in the ongoing political debates and by the demonstration effect of industrial market nations. Hence *most people anticipated that the transition would quickly generate higher incomes and a fairer distribution of the fruits of better performing economies.* But this was mostly a delusion.

One might understand and forgive unrealistic expectations and confusion among the public in terms of the equity and equality outcomes the transition is supposed to achieve, but the views of political leaders deserve more criticism. It was taken almost as a given that the price liberalization and the elimination of shortages which would accompany the introduction of the market system would lead to more equitable income distribution. It is still widely thought that reforms in the system of transfers, especially pensions, will not aggravate income inequality.

Unfortunately, these assumptions are not true for a number of reasons. Even if the very short-term effects of these measures were to contribute to more equal income distribution (in the same way that price liberalization expanded the access to goods which had been in short supply), other events related to transition, like rampant inflation, plummeting real wages, and swelling unemployment, cause income inequality and generate some poverty.

Yet, considering the political climate of the transition and the quest for the support needed to push forward difficult structural reforms, the politicians and the policymakers did not hesitate to take advantage of people's expectations of a fast improvement in living standards. In a sense, this was a policy of walking from one point-of-no-return to the next point-of-no-return. A recent illustration comes from Hungary, where in 1998, immediately after (not before) the election, won by the centre-right coalition, Viktor Orban, the new prime minister, declared that the main target of the government was to raise the standard of living up to the level in the European Union. However, he failed to add that this might be feasible— if high-speed growth could be achieved—in a generation at the earliest.

The faith was quite strong that mass privatization would generate egalitarian results. There was a populist expectation that postsocialism would evolve toward a sort of 'people's capitalism' because of the free distribution of the shares of denationalized assets. The disappointment has been as great as was the hope, especially among grassroots groups and populist political activists.

There is definitely nothing wrong with this type of redistribution if the people are not misled by politicians, if the 'rules of the game' are transparent, if the interests of the public are being protected properly, and if the changes in redistribution patterns contribute to sound development over the long term. A very pragmatic method might be to sell state property at market clearing prices to any investors able to pay. A more idealist method might involve the equitable distribution of the assets freely among all eligible citizens. The choice between these two extremes is not simple. A more 'unequal' privatization through the sale of assets to strategic investors ought to be more favourable for competitiveness and thus for growth and higher income levels in the long run, whereas in the short run a more egalitarian distribution of assets ought to foster more income equality, but not necessarily efficiency.

In the real world only a mixture of these two methods can be implemented, although even in neighbouring countries the 'mixtures' have been quite distinct. Hungary came closer to the 'investor' model; the Czech Republic tried to exercise something similar to the 'populist' model, and Poland went down the middle of the road. In small Estonia a big part was played in privatization by foreign capital. In Russia the huge redistribution of assets was managed through mass privatization, but also by non-transparent insider trading. In all cases the implications for corporate governance, microeconomic efficiency, and long-term income inequality have varied, too.

The populist mainstream in economics and politics suggests that mass privatization through a free distribution of shares can offset the hardships arising as a by-product of structural adjustment, especially growing unemployment and falling real income. This may be true, but only to an extent and solely as a transient compensation for the lost income. In fact, workers in several countries went on strike not against privatization, but in favour of it. They did so not because they are zealots of capitalism and the free market. For sure, they are not. They simply wanted more purchasing power in the form of 'pseudo-money', that is, the shares or the vouchers for the shares in redistributed assets. A situation in which a jobless individual, perhaps not even on the dole because of the unravelling safety net and now without ready access to social services, owns one or two shares is somehow bizarre.[6] This is neither the market economy, nor people's capitalism. It's merely poverty.

Certainly, it is an irony of history that there are relatively more stockholders today in the Czech Republic than there are in Austria, in Poland than in Germany, and in Russia than in the US.[7] Of course, not the number of 'capitalists', but the existence of high-performance capital and of an institutional environment which facilitates this high performance determines the presence of market capitalism. Indeed, the bulk of the shares distributed freely becomes concentrated in any case among institutional investors, including banks and other financial intermediaries. Thus, equitable privatization (or so-called 'enfranchisement') does not exclude the eventual concentration of capital. Actually, it renders such a concentration of capital possible. It is true that a great number of people obtained the shares free of charge, but it is also true that many of these people got rid of the shares quickly. Obviously, it was their choice to do so, but little by little, due to constant redistribution, the shares have been accumulated by a few investors who are oriented toward business and not by the masses who are oriented toward consumption.

There was also an expectation that regional differences would decrease. For numerous reasons, in the centrally planned economies there was significant diversity in income levels and living standards among regions. The biggest

---

[6] Juha Honkkila (1997, p. 6) claims that 'For individuals brought up in a communist society, the loss of safe employment or other social benefits provided by the state sector cannot be offset by minor opportunities to enjoy the personal ownership of assets.'

[7] A special programme of 'mass privatization' was carried out in Poland in 1995 after several years of debate and preparation. Over 500 state companies, with a book value of about 10% of all state assets before privatization, were transferred through 15 specially established 'national investment funds' to the population for a nominal fee equivalent to $7 each, or 2% of the average monthly wage at that time. Around 97% of the eligible citizens participated in the programme. Among the remaining 3% were, inter alia, the president and the deputy premier (who did not collect their certificates because they were very 'busy'). After trading on the secondary market, it is estimated that at most one-third of the participating citizens have retained the shares originally acquired, while two-thirds have sold their certificates to other entities for a price 5 or 6 times as high as the price at the primary market.

differences occurred in the former Soviet Union and Yugoslavia. Due to the dismantling of these states, the richer and the poorer former republics have become independent nations, and 'interregional' tensions have eased in the former Soviet republics between, for instance, Estonia and Tajikistan, or in the former Yugoslavia between Slovenia and FYR Macedonia.

In general, there have been two sets of contradictory expectations among regions. The backward regions have been looking for a fast improvement in standards of living and are pushing for still larger transfers in their favour. Meanwhile, the richer regions are looking to contain outward transfers, since they are afraid that, under market allocation, they may be forced to give up a part of their income to lagging regions. So the political tensions are growing.[8]

Income distribution has not evolved during transition in line with these expectations. Income inequality has been rising everywhere, as should have been anticipated, but was not. The changes in income, first falling and then rising, and the changes in the wage structure among different groups have led to more income dispersion than these societies had experienced in generations. The biggest shifts occurred at the early stage of transition, when real income contracted tremendously, though at a different pace for particular groups. In a matter of a couple of years, income shares changed significantly.

Milanovic (1998) divides postsocialist economies into three groups in this respect. In the first group, consisting of Hungary, Slovakia, and Slovenia (with almost 18 million people altogether), income distribution, measured in terms of quintile relations, did not change. None of the household quintiles gained or lost more than 1 percentage point in the share of total income received, so the shift in income did not occur among the quintiles, but within them. Moreover, the shift was rather minor, since the Gini coefficient went up in Hungary by 2 points (from 21 to 23) and in Slovenia by 3 points (from 22 to 25). In Slovakia an even more equal distribution was observed, since the Gini coefficient fell from 20 to 19 (Table 20).

In the second group, including Belarus, the Czech Republic, Latvia, Poland, and Romania (with a population of about 84 million), moderate regressive transfers were noticeable. The maximum loses were in the range of 1 to 2 points and occurred only among the three lower quintiles. At the same time, the gains of the top quintile varied from about 6 points in the case of the Czech Republic and Latvia to below 2 points in Poland. So,

---

[8] In Poland the most difficult problem emerged in traditional industrial centres (coal mining and steel) in Upper Silesia. The demands of this region for an adjustment in national income distribution were addressed in a special programme, 'A Contract for Silesia', adopted in 1995. The programme did not generate more beneficial income transfers, but it enhanced local industries and entrepreneurship, boosted the region's investment potential, raised the region's ability to absorb foreign direct investment, and more effectively coordinated regional policy. The tensions in the region subsequently eased.

Table 20 Changes in inequality during transition

	Gini coefficient (income per capita)[a]			Gini coefficient (income per capita)[a]	
	1987–8	1993–5		1987–8	1993–5
Kyrgyzstan	26	55[b]	Uzbekistan	28[d]	33
Russia	24	48[b]	Latvia	23	31
Ukraine	23	47[c]	Romania	23[d]	29[c]
Lithuania	23	37	Poland	26	28[e]
Moldova	24	36	Belarus	23	28[b]
Turkmenistan	26	36	Czech Republic	19	27[c]
Estonia	23	35[b]	Slovenia	22	25
Bulgaria	23[d]	34	Hungary	21	23
Kazakhstan	26	33	Slovakia	20	19

[a] For most countries the income concept in 1993–5 is disposable income. In 1987–8 it is gross income, since at that time personal income taxes were small, and so was the difference between net income and gross income. Income includes consumption in kind, except for Hungary and Lithuania in 1993–5.   [b] Quarterly.   [c] Monthly.   [d] 1989.   [e] Semi-annually.

Sources: UNDP 1996, Milanovic 1998.

only the highest quintile gained some benefits and then solely in the share in income, not the absolute level. Owing to very severe contraction, absolute real income was declining among all quintiles, although the higher the quintile, the lower the rate of decline. Within this group of countries, the Gini coefficient rose by only 2 points in Poland (from 26 to 28) and by a meaningful 8 points in the Czech Republic (from 19 to 27).

In the third group—Bulgaria, Estonia, Lithuania, Moldova, Russia, and Ukraine (the biggest group of all, with over 220 million people)—the alteration in the income structure was much greater. The income decline for the bottom quintile was 4 to 5 points, and the second and third quintiles lost similar margins from their earlier shares. Far-reaching changes took place in Russia, Ukraine, and Lithuania, where the fifth quintile gained 20, 14 and 11 points, respectively. The biggest shift occurred in Russia, where the share of the bottom quintile in total income was halved, from 10 to 5 per cent, and the share of the top quintile jumped from an already relatively high 34 per cent to 54 per cent. Meanwhile, the Gini coefficient increased by 11 points in Bulgaria and doubled in Russia and Ukraine, soaring from 24 and 23 to 48 and 47 points, respectively (Table 21).

Following all these changes, the income distribution in the first and second groups of countries was, on average, still more equitable than it is in developed market economies. In the third group, especially in the former Soviet republics, it had become less equitable than it is in the OECD nations.

Table 21 Changes in Gini coefficients, 1987/8–1993/5

Slovakia	−1	Romania	6	Moldova	12
Poland	2	Czech Republic	8	Lithuania	14
Hungary	2	Latvia	8	Russia	24
Slovenia	3	Turkmenistan	10	Ukraine	24
Belarus	5	Bulgaria	11	Kazakhstan	29
Uzbekistan	5	Estonia	12	Kyrgyzstan	29

Sources: Author's calculations based on UNDP 1996, Milanovic 1998.

Subsequently, the process has taken another turn. In an overwhelming majority of countries income inequality has been growing steadily (albeit at a much slower pace than previously), while in the rest it has stabilized. In recent years it appears to be hovering at around the same level of dispersion that emerged after the early shocks. Of course, the relative incomes of particular households and certain professional groups are still fluctuating, but the changes have not been as noteworthy recently as they were during the first half of the decade. Lately, they seem to be occurring within specific quintiles and deciles rather than among them.

However, these conclusions ought to be viewed with care because of the extensive shadow economy. Since the shadow economy involves unregistered economic activities, an estimate of the actual impact of income flowing from it is impossible. Nonetheless, income inequality and the way it evolves are certainly affected by this part of the economy.

There are many types of unregistered activities. Some should be eliminated, and others should be brought under the control of regulation. Moreover, because the parallel economy may encompass organized crime, it must be confronted aggressively. Mostly, however, it consists of a lot of small businesses in numerous sectors. These businesses produce goods, provide services, and deliver jobs. And they pay wages.

When people are told to take their fate into their own hands, many actually do so. By the same token, they may not be so eager to record their endeavours and pay taxes and social security contributions. It takes time to change such attitudes. In any case, for the moment this sort of entrepreneurship has come to represent a reasonable source of income. Thus, it should be tolerated and only gradually incorporated into the registered economy through the use of the 'carrot and the stick', that is, profits and taxation.

In the meantime, a large part of the income produced in the shadow economy is being redistributed through the parallel sector. The amount of this income and the range of the redistribution of this income are anybody's guess, but these 'corrections' of the distribution pattern definitely complicate the income picture. Many households counted among the lower income groups actually earn much more due to their participation in the shadow economy. This additional income is not formally recorded, not even in household budget surveys. The most important sectors involved are petty commerce, housing construction and maintenance, and certain traditional services. Likewise, the majority of the unemployed (if not all of them) are officially counted within the bottom quintile, but some are probably actually in the second quintile. Considering the size of the shadow economy and the methodological problems in estimating unemployment properly, it is obvious that a large share of the unemployed receive income outside the registered economy. Their true earnings are therefore not reflected in the data collected in official statistics or even in the expenditure data in comprehensive household budget surveys.

At the other end of the income dispersion spectrum, the official picture may be biased even more than it is for the poorer part of society. This is so because many of the activities being undertaken by the new entrepreneurs are not recorded in income data and are concealed from the taxman. Some people are therefore actually in higher quintiles and deciles, and this raises the ratio of total income in the highest decile. If account is taken of the income gained through the shadow economy, some of the 'new rich' must be reclassified from, say, the eighth or ninth decile to the tenth decile, and the individuals already in the upper extremities of the tenth decile must be elevated into heaven.

In countries experiencing ongoing recession, many people are seeking opportunities to earn extra income, including in the shadow economy, where, however, there are generally fewer jobs than in the official economy. When output is growing, more of those who are considered unemployed are actually making ends meet by working in the shadow economy rather than by remaining on the dole. Enterprises are also able to take greater advantage of the healthy shadow markets. At the same time, the weak regulations allow them to hide at least part of their actual income. The ultimate result of all these phenomena is rather a puzzle. Nonetheless, most (necessarily rough) estimates suggest that activities in the shadow economy tend to raise average incomes in the upper deciles more than they do those in the lower deciles.

The shadow economy adds to the average income, but it is impossible to tell precisely how it influences the final distribution of real disposable income. The informal sector fosters higher production and welfare as a whole, but it also transfers part of income from some groups of households to others. These income movements are complicated and often contradictory. The contours on the map of informal income transfers are not well enough known so that one can draw general conclusions and suggest viable policy options.

However, this is clearly not a zero-sum game. The income redistribution taking place within the parallel economy (as well as between it and the official one) can enhance the overall capacity for growth. In the longer run, it can contribute to higher standards of living throughout society. Nonetheless, it appears that, through its contribution to actual national income and its impact on income redistribution, the parallel economy expands inequality. The difference between the picture presented by official income distribution data and the actual dispersion of real income, including earnings from the shadow economy, also seems to be much bigger in transition countries than it is in advanced market countries.

9.3. THE MECHANISMS OF DISTRIBUTION

The transition has been irreversibly set in motion, though it is far from over. It is leading to an enormous intergenerational redistribution of wealth and income. The pattern of income distribution has already evolved considerably. The elimination of the 'rules of the game' under the centrally planned regime has been vital in this process (Kolodko 1998a).

First, *subsidies and allowances were cut radically.* The removal of many subsidies was considered necessary by international organizations, especially the IMF, which was prepared to back only structural adjustment policies involving the liquidation of subsidies. This conditionality contributed to domestic tugs-of-war, particularly between populists of the old left and the new right on one side and free market zealots on the other.

The way the subsidies were removed influenced income dispersion to varying degrees depending on the political situation and the path taken toward price liberalization. In general, the more radical the subsidy cuts, the greater the initial change in income distribution. Whereas the shortages in some cases disappeared rather quickly ('the shops were full of goods . . .'), the real income and savings of households shrank even more quickly ('. . . because the pockets of consumers were almost empty'). Consequently, though price liberalization and the slash in subsidies ultimately contributed to improvement in the fiscal balance and to the introduction of the market clearing mechanism, this was achieved in a context of high 'corrective' inflation and growing income inequality. This approach has generally paid off in the longer run.[9] The transparency of free market rules, the efficiency fostered by market clearing pricing, and the influence of this pricing on resource allocation and the elimination of distortions in distribution have all favoured better performance and greater competitiveness.

Subsidies remain an issue in Belarus, Bulgaria, Romania, and Ukraine. Rapid price rises are causing income redistribution due to the diversified price adjustments in specific product groups. Often, the cost of basic items is mounting. Food, housing, public transport, and utilities are becoming

---

[9] Some countries at an early stage of transition, like Turkmenistan, still have quite a way to go in this area of liberalization and adjustment.

more expensive more rapidly because they have also been the most heavily subsidized.[10] The market pricing of other substantial services (including health care) is generating additional growth in the cost of living.

Second, *the amount of redistribution depends on the indexation procedures used during stabilization.* While stabilization was calling for prices to increase more rapidly than wages and hence for a deeper fall in real income, the expectations of the public and political pressure were pushing governments toward more lenient adjustments. Against such a backdrop, indexation methods become a function of political compromise and not necessarily a logical consequence of strictly economic arguments. Some social and professional groups are able to bargain more effectively for compensation than are others. For instance, it is politically more expedient to compensate servicemen and workers (especially those in big industrial centres) before teachers or hospital personnel for the mounting cost of living. The relative shifts in the income of certain groups will occur without regard to changes in their contribution to national welfare (Gregory 1997). Since the process is ongoing, changes in relative wages will continue to generate political friction. However, these income shifts will not lead to substantial modifications in the existing pattern of overall income distribution, but will only alter the relative income position of particular professional groups.

Third, *inflationary redistribution affects household money balances.* Under the centrally planned system, a portion of disposable income could not be spent because of shortages. Despite forced substitution and parallel markets, households were left with residual income. Albeit 'disposable' it was not 'real', since it could not be used. So it was saved involuntarily. When prices were freed and raised to the market clearing level, the purchasing power of money balances, including bank savings, was indexed only partially.[11] Because of the poor health of the banking sector and of public finances, stabilization programmes did not allow for full compensation. So, money balances depreciated. Many people lost their life savings, while a relatively few were able to convert their liquid holdings into capital, which they increased during the wave of liberalization. This course of events has widened the inequality gap.

Fourth, *through early reforms the setting of wages within the state sector was liberalized.*[12] Whatever the initial pace of denationalization, in the majority

[10] In the most extreme case, shortages reappeared in Belarus in the spring of 1998 because of the government's attempts to apply direct price controls and because of the scope of the remaining subsidies. Owing to the overall state of the economy, especially the fiscal position of the government, the direct price controls could not be maintained for very long.

[11] The problem of the severe depreciation of accumulated savings still figured on the policy agenda in some countries in 1998, for example in Lithuania and, of course, in Russia.

[12] In countries which initiated market reform at the beginning of the 1990s, like the former Czechoslovakia and Romania, this led to more fundamental changes. In others which had undertaken reform and wage deregulation much earlier, like Hungary and Poland, the process was more rapid.

of economies more than half the workforce was still earning wages in the state sector in the mid-1990s. Under the socialist system the dispersion of wages was quite limited, but during transition a much wider differentiation is being accepted, and income has become more closely linked to job qualifications, experience, and performance. Thus, the transition has created a tighter relationship between past investment in human capital and current remuneration, and this has led to greater wage dispersion (Cornia 1996a). In the centrally planned economy the diversification in human capital was greater than that in wages. Thus, wage adjustments more in line with the market value of human capital have raised income inequality. At the same time income equity may have increased as well. This is true for blue-collar workers and white-collar workers alike.[13]

Fifth, *the shifts in labour from the state sector to the private sector and the growing share of labour engaged in the private sector have been substantial factors in the rise in income inequality*. Wage dispersion is greater in the private sector, and so is the average income. This is so because of the higher labour productivity in the private sector, not least because obsolete, non-competitive industries and a bulk of the poorly managed and relatively low-paying public services, like education and health care, remain in the hands of the state. Moreover, owing to the poor budgetary situation, the wages in the state sector cannot compete with those provided in industries which are performing profitably. Essentially, this is a reflection of a positive accommodation to the market valuation of labour quality. Nonetheless, in transition economies, where labour markets are still rigid, the wage structure remains distorted in favour of certain professional groups and certain regions.

Sixth, *the introduction of a comprehensive taxation system has altered income distribution outcomes*. The fiscal order in transition countries is hardly a masterpiece of public finance theory and practice, but is more the result of political compromise. Personal income taxes—an innovation in some nations—are always progressive, although the tax rates vary among countries and fluctuate from time to time. Since a higher income is usually taxed at a higher rate, taxation tends to decrease the gap between the net disposable incomes received by people at higher income and those of people at lower income. However, fiscal regimes and fiscal policies are not yet stable, and the equalizing effect of fiscal policy is therefore still unsteady, too.

Seventh, *in an economy moving from state socialism to market capitalism, the most revolutionary and fundamental change is the change in the ownership of assets*. Crucial systemic features in such an economy are denationalization, privatization, the restitution to the previous private owners of property which had been nationalized, the participation of foreign capital, and

---

[13] During the socialist era it was considered acceptable if the ratio of the wages paid by the state to unskilled workers and those paid to university professors did not exceed, say, 5 : 1. However, during transition a corresponding ratio in excess of, say, 15 : 1 is tolerated if the market so provides.

expansion among the financial intermediaries serving the private sector. These features also have important implications for income distribution. The transfer of assets from the state to private owners is accompanied by a shift in the way incomes are earned from these assets. The share of wages in total income thereby declines, while the share of capital gains—profits, dividends, interest, rents—climbs. This process has contributed considerably to growing income inequality and inequity. Moreover, if the assets are acquired unfairly through privatization, this may also raise inequity.

In general, especially in light of the 'equity and equality versus inequity and inequality' dilemma, these outcomes are quite serious. This is not so much because of the income distribution patterns in 1989–98 (though these patterns were affecting populations very significantly), but because of the irreversible changes in the fundamentals of income distribution for the future. The tempestuous and badly managed process of asset redistribution must bear much of the responsibility for this. While many people were lucky if their modest incomes (the current flows) were indexed even somewhat fairly, a few were quietly amassing enormous amounts of property (the accumulated stocks and, thus, future income).[14]

9.4. EQUITY ISSUES IN POLICYMAKING

At the heart of the transition is a desire to replace the central planning system with a market economy which is able to expand and compete on the international scene. Other issues, including the distribution of income and wealth, are sometimes seen as secondary targets of economic and social policy, or simply as the systemic features of change, or even as an important avenue for system overhaul in the sense that radical alterations in income distribution patterns can be an instrument for the additional wealth accumulation which is supposed to create the foundations of the new middle and upper classes required to support the market system. If not immediately, very quickly the message has been that there can be no restoration of capitalism without capital or without capitalists. The conclusion reached has seemed obvious: during transition income inequality will rise, and policy should aim at shaping this inequality so as to facilitate the success of transition.

The problem is first to design such a policy approach and then to implement it in the best possible fashion. This is more difficult than similar historical processes of primary accumulation because of the concurrent existence of severe contraction and perhaps even economic depression. Thus,

---

[14] While one individual might be in the highest tax bracket because of his very large income, another individual with only a small current flow of income might actually be much wealthier because he is the owner of accumulated stocks. Therefore, an analysis which takes into account only the flow of income cannot answer accurately any questions about the extent of inequality or about the pace or the direction of the evolution of inequality.

in considering the issue of inequality, the economic stages of contraction and growth must be distinguished.

From a social and a political standpoint, even in the best of times it is risky to permit a substantial shift in income from the poorest to the wealthiest. Certainly, it is quite dangerous to do so in a context of severe output collapse. If the average income is falling at a time when policy is favouring the emergence of a new middle class, then poverty must become more grinding. This is a characteristic of transition, since, during transition contraction, the redistribution mechanisms transfer a portion of income from the poorer segments of society to the richer ones.

This is how the picture might appear from the macroeconomic point of view. On the microlevel, however, the changing pattern in the flow of income reflects the shift in the contribution of particular population groups to GDP. From this perspective, the poor are becoming still poorer because their contribution to the shrinking national income is declining more rapidly than is the contribution of other groups. Obviously, a first general policy conclusion is that, *in addressing the issue of income inequality in transition nations, one must try to contain as much as possible the duration of this extremely difficult period and the depth of the drop in output.* 'To avoid' is not possible, but 'to react' is necessary.

Sooner or later transition economies will begin to grow, and at that point the issues of inequity and inequality can be addressed in a fresh way. During recession the question is: How can the loss in income be distributed? In a situation of expansion the question modifies: How can the rising income be distributed? Even in the most advanced market economies, policy intervenes to alter the way income is shared, since income distribution cannot be left exclusively to brute market forces. Government should exercise this power only to guarantee a reasonable compromise among the particular interests of income groups, while providing strong incentives for capital formation so as to facilitate future development and better standards of living for all (Tanzi and Chu 1998).

In a majority of transition economies unemployment has already peaked, but in some of them, for example Albania, the Czech Republic, Russia, and Ukraine, it is still bound to grow. This is a consequence of lagging microeconomic restructuring and a policy of countenancing excessive employment because of social concerns, including a fear that the dependency ratio of the social security system will increase too quickly. In the growing transition economies which have experienced vast microeconomic restructuring and high unemployment, many people, after being unemployed for a while, almost in all cases for the first time in their lives, are working again and, together with their families, have improved their absolute and relative income position. In this sense, income inequality is now being reduced. Hence a second general policy conclusion is that *only growth and declining unemployment can reduce income inequality.*

If it is to foster growth, the policy approach toward income and asset redistribution must favour capital accumulation, which is principally the domain of relatively richer individuals. But the probability seems greater that policy can succeed in this goal during a period of strong growth because there is a positive relationship—albeit only over the medium and long run—between growth and capital formation. Growth facilitates capital formation, and capital formation favours growth. Moreover, if capital formation has been set in motion in a context of positive events in the economy, including the financial sector, then it is easier to obtain public approval for the policy instruments employed. If some people are becoming richer while others are becoming poorer, which is the case during contraction, then there is no way to convince the public that they are better off. Yet, if some people, while still poor, are becoming a little less so, although other people are becoming a great deal richer, not at the expense of others, but while contributing to overall growth, then the situation may be accepted by a majority of the public.

Of course, such a policy will increase income dispersion. Surveys have measured public reactions toward trends in living standards and income dispersion in two transition economies in the 1990s: Poland and Russia. In Poland, the share of households assessing their own situation as 'good or very good' was slowly, but steadily increasing. It rose from a single digit per cent at the beginning of the decade to 12.2 per cent in 1995 and 13.1 per cent in 1997 (GUS 1997a). A small but growing number of households were therefore rather positive about both the higher absolute level of income and the changes in income distribution patterns.

Public opinion in Russia appears convinced that the transition has so far brought a plague of corruption and 'crony capitalism', which are associated in the public mind with constant recession and spreading poverty. The coexistence of mounting arrears in wages and pensions, insider privatization, lucrative deals on financial markets, and organized crime has contributed to expanding income inequality. The newly introduced economic system is blamed for the poverty by 82 per cent of the public; 88 per cent think that the main source of wealth is the 'right connections', and an astounding 76 per cent see dishonesty as the reason behind the wealth (Table 22). Cronyism, connections, cheating, and stealing are thought to be at the core of the current institutional arrangements, or the lack thereof. If an overwhelming majority of society is convinced that wealth depends on dishonesty and that poverty is directly caused by the economic system, then the future can not look very bright.

The negative opinions in Russia can certainly be linked to the growing inequality, which has gone up twofold and is still rising. In Poland, where households have a somewhat more positive attitude, the Gini coefficient has stabilized in recent years. According to an OECD study on Poland, after increasing from about 25 in 1989 to around 30 in 1994, the Gini

Table 22 Placing the blame in Russia: What are the reasons for poverty and wealth? (% of respondents citing each reason)

Poverty		Wealth	
Economic system	82	Connections	88
Laziness and drinking	77	Economic system	78
Unequal opportunities	65	Dishonesty	76
Discrimination	47	Good opportunities	62
Lack of effort	44	Talent	50
No talent	33	Luck	42
Bad luck	31	Hard work	39

Source: Interfax-AIF survey of a sample of 1,585 respondents, Moscow, Nov. 1997.

Table 23 Gini coefficients in Poland, 1993–1996

	Wages	Per capita income
1993	25.7	—
1994	28.1	33
1995	28.8	32
1996	29.5	34

Sources: Gini for wages: Jan Rutkowski, World Bank, Warsaw; Gini for per capita income (rounded to full point): Irena Topinska, University of Warsaw.

coefficient declined slightly to 29.4 in 1995 (OECD 1996b).[15] Estimates suggest that it may have remained close to this level or increased only modestly since then in terms of wage dispersion and perhaps a little bit more in terms of per capita income (Table 23).

Likewise, the ratio of the wages of the highest decile to those of the lowest decile (the 'decile ratio') increased in Poland to 3.03 in 1993 and 3.36 in 1994 and since then has stabilized or risen only slightly. More important changes have occurred within the top 5 per cent of the population due to wealth accumulation by the richest, but the actual income per segment of the population is unknown (World Bank 1995a). However, one must be careful in drawing conclusions from these observations. Especially at the top of the top decile the picture may be seriously biased, and the difference between decile ratios for wages and for overall income seems to be significant (Table 24).

[15] Estimates vary a little due to differences in methodology. Moreover, for the Gini coefficient, no matter how income is measured, whether through wages, per capita disposable income, or income expressed in equivalent units (for instance, food calories consumed), there is always a margin of statistical error of at least 1 point in either direction.

Table 24 Decile ratio for wages in Poland, 1993–1996

	Decile ratio
1993	3.03
1994	3.36
1995	3.38
1996	3.46

Source: Rutkowski 1997.

Not all indicators of income dispersion exhibit the same trends. While one measure of inequality might suggest that it is on the rise, another might suggest the opposite. For example, in Poland between 1994 and 1995 the Gini coefficient (in terms of wages) increased from 28.1 to 28.8. During the same period the decile ratio hovered steadily at around 3.4. This is important, since people often pay more attention to differences between the incomes of the rich and those of the poor than they do to the fact that their own individual incomes have risen over time.

Was the drive toward more equitable income distribution in Poland (an example of a more advanced transition country experiencing rapidly growing output) merely a coincidence or was it the result of deliberate policy? The answer is 'both'. On the one hand, market forces distribute income in fresh ways (Cornia and Popov 1998). The growing income has been shared out among almost all social strata in economies experiencing quickly expanding private sectors and the simultaneous restructuring of state industries. In Poland since 1995 the gains of the various decile groups in the flow of rising GDP have been rather proportional.

On the other hand, policymakers have felt that the more equitable distribution of income should be a distinct policy target, as well as a means to facilitate further economic growth. Identical arguments have more recently been put forward by the IMF as a rationale for its interest in more equitable growth worldwide (Fischer 1998a).

Initially, the shift in labour from the state to the private sector generated expanding wage inequalities. In Poland this trend was reinforced by discriminatory measures applied to the disadvantage of the state sector. At first, in a step that was considered essential in the early anti-inflation effort, tough, if not yet excessively restrictive wage-based tax instruments were adopted to contain nominal wages. Later, especially in 1991–3, the 'popiwek'—the wage-based tax tool designed to fight wage inflation by punishing excessive nominal wage growth—came to be used mainly as a lever to push state companies quickly toward privatization, though the ground had not been well prepared. While serving this purpose, however, it also allowed income disparity to widen and countered the incentive for more labour productivity in the public sector. When this instrument was ultimately abandoned at the beginning of 1995, state sector output started to soar. As a result, labour income growth in the state sector came to be on a par with that in the private sector. This suggests a third general policy conclusion: *it is unwise to exercise discriminatory measures favouring one sector at the cost of another even if this tends to accelerate privatization.* Such measures may at times act against competitiveness and lower growth not only in the state sector, but also throughout the economy.

Another important income policy challenge occurred at the initial stage of structural adjustment within an inflationary environment. During early stabilization there were attempts to contain aggregate demand through wage cuts among civil servants that were relatively larger than the fall in the income of industrial workers. Subsequent policy aimed at stimulating faster relative growth in the average compensation of civil servants. This sort of preference stemmed not only from the conviction that such a level of growth is fair, but also from the confidence that the additional investment in human capital would contribute to a higher capacity for growth. Thus, a connection has been made between boosting investment in human capital and higher earnings levels, a relationship which had been rather weak prior to and early on in the transition. Therefore, the fourth general policy conclusion is that, *whereas wages in the private sector should be left mostly to regulation by market forces, the remuneration of civil servants should be kept sufficiently close to the average industrial wage so as to facilitate human capital development.* Fiscal policy must serve this purpose in a stable and predictable way as well.

Transition policy shifts also raise the very difficult issue of the indexation of pensions and of benefits for the disabled. In Poland at the beginning of stabilization in 1990, instead of a cost-of-living adjustment, an indexation against nominal wages was established. This was another serious policy mistake. The approach was based on the idea that adjustments in real pensions should follow the path of the changes in wages. Accordingly, pensions fell quite steeply in line with the severe contraction in real wages. However, when wages started to increase owing to rising labour productivity, pensions increased as well despite the lack of financial resources to cover the increase.

It would have been more prudent to drop the level of real pensions at a slower rate than the decline in wages and then later allow pensions to climb back up also at a slower rate than the growth in wages. It turned out to be extremely difficult to modify the indexation method after the fact, although the government's attempts were eventually crowned with success. The index applied starting in 1996 allows for growth in real pensions, but within the limits of a non-inflationary level of financing. This has meant a certain amount of linkage between average salaries and pensions. Given the very high dependency ratio, these reforms have contributed to further financial stabilization, but have not had much effect on income dispersion.

Income policy during the transition has involved other tradeoffs as well. Whereas the drive to encourage the propensity to save suggests that there should be more lenient tax treatment for some types and sources of income, the growing income inequality suggests otherwise. The solution is precisely a matter of policy options. If the economy is expected to recover and expand rather more quickly, then there ought to be some fiscal preference for capital gains. Such an approach can be troublesome not only because the populist tendency may be quite strong, but also because it appears unfair, for example, to tax unemployment benefits, but not capital gains earned through speculation on the stock market. Yet, this sort of policy choice may be made for the sake of boosting the propensity to save. Capital gains through stock earnings, stock dividends, interest rates on bank deposits, and so on are mostly untaxed or taxed only modestly so as to foster capital formation and lift the national savings ratio. Of course, the approach enhances inequality, but it also facilitates growth through savings and investments, thereby raising the overall standard of living.

At the outset of the transition, especially during contraction, such policies worked only to the advantage of the more affluent part of the population, namely, persons with income available for savings or investment. Later, when the economy is healthier, more people are able to enjoy gains in real income as the expanding capital markets and better performing financial intermediaries, together with preferential fiscal policies, encourage an increase in savings among other income groups. Consequently, both the emerging middle class and the relatively poorer segments of society are able to save a greater share of earnings.

However, this policy approach can be quite controversial. In Poland in late 1992 and in 1993 the lack of taxation on earnings from stock market speculations and a general euphoria led to a bubble on the capital market. Rather typical of all emerging markets, postsocialist or otherwise, these events were accompanied by excessive enthusiasm in the mass media. Rates of return reached an unsustainably high level. So, particularly because the period was not proving very favourable for the rest of society, the insistent demands of other political actors for the taxation of these extraordinary profits seemed to be justified. Unfortunately, no appropriate steps were taken until it was too late. The bubble burst at the beginning of 1994, when the stock exchange index tumbled by about two-thirds. Thus, it no longer made any sense to tax capital gains. Only a neutral turnover tax of 0.2 per cent was imposed on short-term stock sale transactions, and even this was soon given up. In the government programme 'Package 2000', which is aimed at achieving sustained growth, it has been decided that capital gains should remain tax free at least until the end of the year 2000.

As a result of all these measures, the national savings ratio increased between 1993 and 1997 by about 4 per cent of GDP. A significant part of this increment came from higher domestic savings. If capital gains had been taxed, there would likely be a little less income inequality, but the growth would not have been so robust. Thus, the fifth general policy conclusion is that, *if there is a choice between less income inequality coupled with a lower rate of growth and more income inequality coupled with a higher rate of growth, then the priority ought to go to higher growth at the cost of greater income disparity.* In the end, the economy will be better off this way.

9.5. THE 'NOUVEAUX RICHES' VERSUS THE 'NOUVEAUX PAUVRES'

Under socialist central planning there were both rich and poor, though the number of each depended on when, where, and by what criteria one wished to count. Several years after the onset of the transition, it is unquestionable that there are more of both rich and poor. Nonetheless, while serious studies have been devoted to the subject, we do not really know much about the size of the population segment which can be considered as relatively or even absolutely rich.

Poverty has swelled significantly in Eastern Europe and the former Soviet republics in the course of the 1990s. As long as the decline in output can be linked to transition, the growing poverty is also going to be associated with this phenomenon. Only a lucky few among those people who were already poor under socialism have been able to rid themselves of the condition of poverty. In general the share of the poor in the population has expanded.

The situation varies from country to country, but it is possible to classify countries in distinct groups according to the level of poverty. Some countries exhibit 'very high poverty', which is defined to mean that more than half the population may be reckoned poor.[16] Other countries have 'low poverty', meaning that less than 5 per cent of the population may be deemed poor (Table 25).

Increasing inequality has had quite an important impact on poverty. Several studies have noticed that in some nations, for example in Bulgaria, Estonia, Poland, Romania, and Uzbekistan, the rise in poverty is due more to falling income equality than to falling income (UNICEF 1995, Honkkila 1997, Pomfret and Anderson 1997, Milanovic 1998). This phenomenon should be regarded as a very negative by-effect of transition (Table 26).

---

[16] It is estimated that soon after the climax of the Russian crisis in mid-1998 the share of the poor, defined as the population with income below $1 per day, jumped to over 40% and was rising. However, this was also due to the substantial devaluation of the rouble and thus a sharp drop in the income counted in dollars. Indeed, because of rampant inflation, real income declined to such an extent that a significant portion of the population was being driven rapidly into poverty.

Table 25 Income distribution according to the population share of the poor

	Gini, 1987–8	Gini, 1993–4
Low poverty (< 5%)		
Czech Republic	19	27
Hungary	21	23
Slovakia	20	20
Slovenia	24	28
Medium poverty (5–25%)		
China	35	38
Poland	26	31
Belarus	23	28
Latvia	23	27
High poverty (25–50%)		
Bulgaria	23	34
Romania	23	29
Estonia	23	39
Ukraine	23	33
Russia	24	48
Lithuania	23	36
Uzbekistan	28	33
Very high poverty (> 50%)		
Kazakhstan	26	33
Kyrgyzstan	26	35
Moldova	24	36
Vietnam	—	36

Note: The poverty classification used here for Eastern Europe and the former Soviet republics is from Milanovic (1996) and measures the share of the population—the percentages shown in the table—with an annual income of less than $120 (on a purchasing power parity basis). For China and Vietnam the concept of poverty is from UNDP (1994).

Sources: Deininger and Squire 1996, Honkkila 1997, Milanovic 1996, UNDP 1994, World Bank 1996.

It was impossible to contain the spread of poverty during the contraction, and other processes have also aggravated poverty. First, *there has been a regional factor in income redistribution*. Even if an economy is growing, some regions may still be experiencing expanding poverty. Unlike the central planning regime, through which the interregional redistribution of national income was enforced by political decisions and administrative measures, income redistribution through the public finance system has been relatively negligible under the emerging market. Market-led redistribution does not equalize average incomes among regions either; indeed, it presumably makes them still less equal. Meanwhile, due to the ongoing process of restructuring in industrial capacity, some regions are more affected by large income

Table 26 Increase in poverty and GDP decline during transition, 1987/9–1993/4

	Poverty relative to the country (% with 21–7% of average income)[a]			Poverty relative to the world (% with income < $120 PPP)		
	1989–90	1993–4	Increase	1987–8	1993–4	Increase
Azerbaijan	11.1	65.2	54.1	—	—	—
Belarus	—	—	—	1	23	22
Bulgaria	2.0	32.7	30.7	2	33	31
Czech Republic	0.2	1.4	1.2	0	< 1	0–1
Estonia	1.0	27.0	26.0	1	40	39
Hungary	1.1	4.0	2.9	< 1	3	2–3
Kazakhstan	—	—	—	5	50	45
Kyrgyzstan	—	—	—	12	84	72
Latvia	1.3	33.5	32.2	1	25	24
Lithuania	1.5	39.1	37.6	1	46	45
Moldova	2.4	40.6	38.2	4	65	61
Poland	5.8	10.9	5.1	6	19	13
Romania	7.0	25.3	18.3	6	39	33
Russia	—	—	—	2	45	43
Slovakia	0.1	5.1	5.0	0	< 1	0–1
Slovenia	4.5	6.1	1.6	0	< 1	0–1
Turkmenistan	—	—	—	12	57	45
Ukraine	—	—	—	2	41	39
Uzbekistan	—	—	—	24	47	23

[a] Poverty lines: 21% of average income for the Czech Republic and Slovenia; 24% for Estonia, Hungary, Latvia, Lithuania, Poland, and Slovakia; and 27% for Azerbaijan, Moldova, and Romania.

Sources: UNICEF 1995, Milanovic 1996.

falls. Bankruptcies, the closing of obsolete factories, and the elimination of entire non-competitive industries mean that in some regions output has dropped by as much as half and unemployment is several times above the national average. Within these regions cities are in extremely dire straits, particularly if they have traditionally depended on only one factory or on one industrial sector, which was often the case in socialist countries. This has been a typical situation from East Germany to East Siberia. In such regions and old industrial centres poverty is greater than average by a wide margin.

Second, *the transition has created a true labour market, and it has therefore generated unemployment*, which has been increasing additionally because of ongoing recession. The unemployed are being provided only with very modest benefits (if any), and many of them, notably those remaining jobless for a long period, are entering the ranks of the poor. The post-socialist countries were entirely unprepared to tackle unemployment, especi-ally long-term unemployment. Thus, while in some advanced market economies, like the United States, less than 5 per cent of the unemployed remain jobless for more than a year, the corresponding figure in countries like Slovakia is over one-third.

Third, *a majority of the population, including retired people with relatively low pensions, have been stripped of their savings* by rampant inflation and the lack of proper indexation mechanisms. In extreme cases, weak and inefficient financial intermediaries and policy negligence have sunk the life-time savings of many households. The fact that inflation accelerated when privatization was both creating many fortunes and rapidly impoverishing many individuals has had severe political implications and has weakened the support for transition, especially among older people.[17]

Fourth, *an ill-advised drive toward fiscal prudence has pushed some govern-ments to postpone the payment of pensions and the wages of civil servants.* This has created the illusion that budgets are healthier than they actually are, since current arrears are simply a hidden deficit, and accumulated arrears are simply public debt. Growing arrears, which are nominally equivalent to unpaid income, further decrease the standard of living. Curiously, whereas liberal economic policies, including the ones so strongly supported by the IMF and international financial circles, counsel with great determination the imposition of sanctions and additional interest for overdue loans, they never demand such compensation for overdue wages and pensions.[18]

Fifth, *the agriculture sector is still quite large.* In several postsocialist countries, including those most advanced in transition, a big part of the population is living in rural areas and working in agriculture. If one-third

[17] However, the elderly are not the poorest group. For example, in Poland only about 15% of retired people are poor or less well off on average than workers. A significant share of pensioners is found in the second and third quintiles. The poorest are most often the people in the largest households.

[18] In like manner, the *Financial Times* (1998) claims that, if the Yugoslav government pays off pensions and other arrears, it will lose the potential benefit of proceeds from privatiza-tion. Yet, whatever the sources of budgetary revenue, whether it comes through direct taxes or through the privatization of Sprska Telekom (the case mentioned in the *Financial Times* article), the state must meet its obligations. If it does not, the financial humbuggery can only result in a hidden deficit, more arrears, and growing public debt. Ultimately, it destabilizes the economy and works against transformation and growth. It has been a common feature of the Russian economy for many years, with all the negative consequences in terms of stunt-ing the transition and long-lasting recession. The problem of accumulated arrears must be solved properly. Though this is not easy, it has positive effects on stabilization and develop-ment and favours more openness in the economy and in economic integration with the global economy. So, all contracts should be enforced, including pensions and other arrears. This is what the market economy is all about, and it would be better to appreciate than to criticize the Yugoslav government's commitment to fulfil its responsibility in this case.

or even one-quarter of the people in a nation depend on farming and the sale of food and other agriculture products, a deterioration in working and living conditions in this sector will have an immediate impact on the overall standard of living. Many analyses disregard this fact and concentrate only on the living conditions of city dwellers. However, rapid trade liberalization and inflows of food imports from more competitive markets have driven many farmers into poverty and ruined numerous farms, both small family-farms and the big farms which used to be cooperatives or state owned.

These seem to be the crucial factors which have led to the emergence of the 'new poor' in postsocialist societies. This is partly the consequence of a series of unavoidable events, but it is also partly the outcome of policy mistakes. The output collapse and widening inequality have led to growing poverty. Homeless people have appeared on the streets for the first time in these countries, and crime has been rising as never before. Economically motivated migration has expanded, and grey markets are mushrooming. Life expectancy has declined, and mortality due to social stress has increased (Cornia 1996b, Paniccià 1997).

Per capita income did not fall in the immediate aftermath of the ravages of the Black Death in the 14th century. Indeed, the standard of living among the labouring classes improved, while the relative position of proprietors deteriorated. This was so because the income per person was higher, while the rents were lower. In contrast, in the worst cases of devastation connected with the transitional depression in the post-Soviet economies, the very opposite has occurred, with per capita income lower and rents higher in a context of extreme economic contraction.

With no Black Death, but because of poor policies, life expectancy in Russia and other former-Soviet republics like Latvia and Ukraine has gone down significantly (World Bank 1995b). Among men in Russia it dropped by a staggering six years between 1989 and 1995. It has been claimed that, due to this kind of demographic crisis in transition economies, around three million people have passed away sooner than otherwise would have been the case (UNICEF 1994, 1995, Cornia et al. 1996). This has been caused by the extraordinary hardships and other negative features of the transition. The deterioration in health standards owing to poor diets, the breakdown in water treatment, the worsening work safety conditions, and the rising mortality rates due to violence, suicide, cardiovascular disease, and stress have meant that in Russia in 1996 the number of deaths exceeded the number of live births by 60 per cent; the maternal mortality rate was five to ten times higher than in Western Europe, while the infant mortality rate was two to four times higher. The number of deaths from tuberculosis rose by 90 per cent in 1992–6 (Nuti 1997d, Twigg 1997).

Poverty has spread even in the transition economies which are the leaders in terms of systemic change and economic growth. This is due to the time-lag between economic recovery and the improvement in living standards among the poor. First, real output must revive; then employment grows. Only later does the healthier budget situation permit more financing to meet the social needs of the poor. Thus, poverty begins to decline only several years after the economy has recovered.

Such a sequence has been apparent in Poland, where, despite the resurgence in growth starting in the second half of 1992, the level of poverty did not begin to drop until at least 1995. Unemployment was rising until the summer of 1994, and wages in many sectors did not go up until 1995. The population share of the 'poor'—those people living below the 'relative poverty line' (defined as the equivalent of half the average monthly household expenditure)—climbed from 12 per cent in 1993 to 13.5 per cent in 1995 and 14 per cent in 1996 (GUS 1996, 1997a). Of course, this is a relative measure and does not mean that more people were being driven into absolute poverty; in fact, the opposite was true. The segment of the population that was enjoying the fruits of the expansion had been rising for several years. Thus, the proportion of households that described their situation as 'bad or very bad' declined from over half at the beginning of the 1990s to 32.5 per cent in 1995 and 30.3 per cent in 1997 (GUS 1997b).

Hence, while one may claim that the period of growing poverty is past, it is also true that the challenges are still tremendous. The next few years will be decisive. A single, uniform pattern in income distribution is not going to prevail in the transition economies. It will not be so easy to correct all the errors which have been made. Now that income inequality has widened, to reduce it significantly is going to be extremely difficult. The postsocialist genie has been let out of the lamp and is not going to go back in again.

The transition has also created a new class of rich people who are well educated, hard working, and capable not only of protecting their wealth, but of doing so while opening up fresh opportunities for their fellow citizens. Successful entrepreneurs have stepped forward in each of the emerging market economies. They are keen to take risks and invest their incomes in the new ventures on which overall expansion will depend. These entrepreneurs are the core of the new class of rich. Unfortunately, due to weak institutional arrangements and the poor market culture, there are also wealthy thieves, swindlers, and crooks.

As everywhere, people are becoming rich in many ways, but in transition economies there are distinctive factors which are rendering the whole process still more vast and dynamic. Throughout the entire region a major source of enrichment, although, contrary to a common misconception, not the most important one, is the very special postsocialist method of privatization, so-called 'self-enfranchisement'. A significant portion of the new middle class has emerged from among the managers and bureaucrats who were in charge of the same assets when these were still owned by cooperatives (mainly in the agricultural sector) or the state.

In some countries, like Russia, the main source of the new riches has not been only the redistribution of previously existing stocks, but also the accumulation of income from lucrative export deals and export subsidies, as well as from the subsidized credits extended at negative real interest rates. There has been a significant redistribution as well. No wonder the state now 'owns' a huge debt, while the 'tycoons' and a few among the new rich own the assets. Instead of a policy of the simultaneous privatization of state property and the reduction of state debt, the Russian road to the market has gone by way of an expansion in private property and a rise in public debt up to the very limits of default.

When the standard of living is falling during crisis and recession, the plight of the poor often grows worse for longer than does that of the rich. As the economy recovers, the needs of the rich have tended to be satisfied first; only later have improvements in the standard of living of the rest of society, including the poor, been considered. Following recession, the production sector requires more time to recover than do financial markets, which are soon back to full health. Episodes during which activity on the stock market is vigorous, but real output is simultaneously plummeting (as is employment) have not been rare under emerging market conditions. Such contradictory trends are possible because over the short and medium runs unique factors affect the stock market and GDP growth. Financial markets are susceptible to speculation and euphoria, while real output is not. In the most spectacular case, again Russia, the stock exchange index rose about fourfold (in dollar terms) in just over two years, in 1996–7, while GDP shrank by 5 per cent. There obviously had to be a day of reckoning, and indeed, after a time-lag, a financial collapse and a great crash in the capital market occurred in mid-1998.[19]

The extent to which societies differ in terms of income and wealth is a matter of historical process and past policies. History and policy have meant that income distribution is much more unequal in Latin America than it is in Asia. Enrique Iglesias (1998), the president of the Inter-American Development Bank, blames various structural and social factors for the extreme income inequality in Latin America, including the legacy of colonialism, although colonialism ended in that region so long ago. The Gini coefficient is very high in Latin America, ranging from 38.4 (Argentina) to 61.4 (Brazil). It has recently been estimated at 53 in Chile, 53.4 in Colombia, 54 in Mexico, and 47.2 in Venezuela (Londono, Spilimbergo, and Szekely 1997, Lustig and Deutsch 1998). Thus, income dispersion as measured by the Gini index is as unequal in Kyrgyzstan, Russia, and Ukraine as it is in Mexico. All other postsocialist countries show more equitable

---

[19] The Moscow stock exchange index soared from 100 to 571 between August 1995 and August 1997, but by August 1998 had plunged to the lowest level ever, a mere 37% of what it had been just 3 years before.

income distribution than does Argentina, the least inequitable Latin American country.

In Asia, the Gini varies significantly from country to country. Perhaps surprisingly, income distribution is relatively equitable in India (29.7 points) and Sri Lanka (30.1), which were colonies much more recently than were the Latin American countries. So, in this case the colonial legacy may have had a different outcome in terms of the strategies and policies being exercised. In Vietnam the Gini is not much higher and stands at 35.7, while in China it is already strikingly high (41.5), as it is in Malaysia (48.4) and Thailand (46.2) (World Bank 1998).

The way the transformation has been managed so far and the way the issues of growth and distribution are handled in the future will determine subsequent patterns in income distribution in postsocialist countries. Today, in terms of distribution, some of these nations remind us of South America, while others are more similar to South Asia.

9.6. INCOME DISTRIBUTION AND GROWTH

A policy which allows more income inequality during the implementation of a vast programme of privatization may foster growth if savings rates are high and corporate governance, including that in the state sector, is effective. Such a course ought to be at the top of the policy agenda. However, policies which intentionally aim in this direction can influence the capacity for growth in a negative way, too. This will depend on social and political circumstances which are often beyond the reach of policymaking over the short and even medium terms. Hence growth strategy and income policy must be very well balanced and should be re-examined frequently.

Inequality can slow the pace of growth if the income differences are perceived as too great, thereby fomenting social tensions and eroding the incentive for more labour productivity (Persson and Tabellini 1994). Regardless of the actual income distribution, this factor has played a substantial role in the postsocialist societies. Whatever the true income dispersion, the overwhelming majority of the population views it as unfair. To be sure, distribution may never be exactly right in the opinion of the public, especially during transition.

However, the temptation to favour more equal income distribution excessively, often augmented because of democratic processes, may cause a distortion in growth incentives, especially through higher taxes and bigger social transfers (Alesina 1997, Gordon and Li 1997). This seems to be the case in several transition economies in which parliaments are much keener to oversee the transfer of resources among segments of society than to engage in the struggle to maximize resources by favouring savings, capital formation, investment, and growth. The politics of growth in transition economies functions in such a way that the more reform-oriented members of governments must often clash with their own cabinets and parliamentary majorities in order to sustain the balance in public finance and stabilize the economy. If not for democratically elected parliaments, there would be less redistribution through public finance systems, and the cost of government would be lower. Thus, savings, investments, and, consequently, the pace of growth might be higher.

The young postsocialist democracies are very sensitive to fluctuations in social and economic conditions. Support for new political parties is quite dependent on positive changes in economic structures, but sometimes even more on patterns in income distribution and the way they evolve. For this reason, if reforms are to succeed, it may be crucial that income inequality does not surpass a certain critical mass, which is always unknown a priori. There is backing for the transition as long as the accompanying hardships are considered by the people to be relatively better than the drawbacks of the socialist economy and as long as the expectations of a better future offset current disappointments. Because of its newfound political freedom and the regeneration of civic institutions, the public is willing to put up with severe economic contraction and the subsequent deterioration in living standards that is associated with the transformation. However, if policy is not able to deliver some hope of coming improvement in living conditions and, simultaneously, if some groups are doing much better than others, then the terms of this 'social contract' may alter abruptly. Social tensions may boil over, and the favourable political climate indispensable for fundamental change in a democracy may evaporate.

Political instability stemming from socially unacceptable imbalances in income distribution clouds the climate for investment, competition, and economic expansion (Alesina and Perotti 1996). This is a particularly important factor in transition countries, because these are unstable by definition. When the system itself is in transition, then political institutions and political culture, laws and the ability to observe them, parliaments and governments, and policies and the expectations about their future route are all in a state of flux. A certain amount of uncertainty is therefore unavoidable. This must be reduced as much as possible, especially among entrepreneurs, investors, and consumers, thereby improving the chances for recovery and growth.

The final impact of these contradictory tendencies on the pace of growth seems to be a negative one over the short term, but it may become a positive one in the long term because of the steps to enhance the propensity to save and invest (Flemming 1998, Kolodko 1998b). Of great importance in this, however, are the pattern of income distribution and the public's perception of it. In a majority of nations this pattern is not favourable at the current stage of transition. A great deal of evidence and experience suggest that, despite growth in production and consumption, under some circumstances market forces tend to improve the relative position of the rich and consequently to worsen the relative position of the poor (Raiser 1997). Until now, this has clearly also been the case in the postsocialist economies.

The dual process of growing income inequality and spreading poverty is also a major challenge because there is a causal relationship between the two. The longer severe depression lasts, the more pressing this challenge becomes. Thus, for the 200 million people in Russia and Ukraine, growing income inequality is a political issue which has already provoked many tensions and conflicts, but it is also a serious economic problem which is raising obstacles to durable growth. A fair and socially acceptable level of equality in the distribution of income and wealth must therefore be a key long-run policy target.

Regardless of the policy intervention, income inequality rises during transition, but changes in equity—the fairness in the distribution of income and wealth and in the access to public services such as education and health care—can be controlled and managed to a much greater extent. The pace and scope of equity changes should not be left entirely to newly released market forces. However, in the real world, to accomplish this task and generate political support for it are sometimes quite difficult.

In a country attempting to catch up with more advanced nations, the choice between faster growth with greater inequality (but falling poverty) and slower growth with less inequality (but widening poverty) is clear: the first option is definitely more reasonable. *Economic policy ought first to facilitate sustained growth, and income policy must also support this superior aim.* In the longer term, there is then at least a chance that everyone's economic well-being will improve. After an initial, significant upsurge in inequality, it may even be possible—when the economy has recovered and is growing —to reduce income disparities without harming the capacity for further expansion. There have already been cases of such a sequence in transition countries. This is even more true of equity, since appropriate development strategies also serve the goal of fair income and wealth distribution. Therefore, the more transition progresses and the stronger the foundations for rapid and durable growth become, the less necessary it is to accept a tradeoff between equity and efficiency.

It must always be remembered that the aim of transition in postsocialist countries is not simply systemic change, but efficiency, competitiveness, durable growth, and sustainable development. This means that transition must lead to improvements in the standard of living of the overwhelming majority of the population. Otherwise, it makes no sense at all.

Arrival

10

Marketization and Democratization

10.1. THE COMPATIBILITY OF THE MARKET AND DEMOCRACY

Is it possible that at least for a while an economy can function well with-out democracy and the institutions of a civic society?[1] In the 20th century there are many examples, including the centrally planned economies from the 1950s to the 70s. Thus, Bulgaria enjoyed an average rate of growth of around 6 per cent from the early 50s to the late 80s. GDP was increasing in China during the third quarter of this century by an annual rate exceeding 5 per cent, that is, more quickly than any Western democracy at the time. Under the market reforms over the last 25 years, growth has been even much faster in China; in 1976–98 the annual growth rate was about 8 per cent. Yet, there has been no democracy.

This does not mean that there is a positive link between autocracy and growth and a negative one between democracy and development. Indeed, in the long run democracy facilitates growth and development. Well-known cases in which high-speed growth was achieved in the absence of democracy—Chile under Pinochet, Indonesia under Suharto, Spain under Franco, and Hong Kong, Singapore, South Korea, and Taiwan under various not-quite-democratic leaders and governments—are among the not so numerous exceptions to this general rule. The list of autocratic regimes which have failed to sustain growth is much, much longer. In the end all these countries are going to come to the conclusion, if they have not already done so, that in the contemporary global economy sustainable development needs the support of democracy.

Democratic organizations and practices have a multidimensional impact on economic activities and hence on growth capability (Nelson *et al.* 1994). There are at least three reasons for this. First and most important is the fact that *democracy means the freedom to get involved in business*. Free entry

---

[1] Some authors stress that democracy is not an indispensable characteristic of the market economy. Janos Kornai (1998, p. 49) points to the fact that investors favour either the stability of a consolidated democracy, or the stability of a dictatorship ruled with a firm hand. An unstable democracy repels them the most. This (along with the vast resources of oil and gas) explains why several Western governments and interest groups are eager to support the leaders of rather undemocratic regimes, such as those in Azerbaijan and Turkmenistan. This double standard leads one to wonder whether, for instance, President Lukashenka would be backed more energetically by Western governments if Belarus were a significant source of energy and possessed abundant raw materials.

and free exit in business signify that there is a mechanism which can bring entrepreneurs into the production sector or take them out if they happen not to find a niche. People who become entrepreneurs because they want to are more likely to be able to maximize their own profits and also to contribute something new to national product. Business associations and other business interest groups, though oriented toward their own survival, can galvanize the overall thrust toward economic growth if they have the support of democratic surroundings. The freedom to do business—to buy and sell, to produce and compete, to save and invest—is a driving force which, only by being well accepted, can stoke the growth of the whole economy. It can play an even bigger role in postsocialist countries because of the freshly released energy in favour of entrepreneurship that it represents in these countries.

Second, *democracy accommodates a framework for efficient economic policy*. Even the most sophisticated market mechanism cannot substitute for sound economic development policy because the two are complementary, not contradictory. Democratic order and market discipline are basic ingredients of a mixture which facilitates durable growth. Democracy means organizations and rules, but it also means culture and behaviour. All these factors, if sufficiently mature, promote transparency in market rules and predictability in market conditions. Democracy works on behalf of stability, and stability always spurs economic expansion.

Third, *democracy can enhance the capacity for expansion if politics does not take over from economics*. Democracy does not guarantee in each case that the choice of the electorate is going to be the optimum one for successful economic policy. The structure of contemporary civic society is such that socially motivated concerns can overcome economic reasoning. There are non-economic aspects of public life that sometimes matter more than production and trade or investment and consumption. There are diverse ideologies and opposing value systems. There are political, social, and cultural issues—abortion, minority rights, regional conflict, pollution, crime, classes in religion at schools, the attitude to the legacy of 'communism'—which during an election may prevail over economic arguments, no matter how rational these are.[2] Such processes can sometimes be devastating for economic policy and growth.

In the end, decisions on development strategy are taken by those who are supported by the majority, not by those who might know better how

---

[2] An illustration is offered by the outcomes of recent elections in two well-performing Central European economies. In an election in Poland in September 1997, the ruling left-centre coalition was forced to go into opposition despite its remarkable economic success. Non-economic factors turned out to be more important than the economic record of the outgoing government. Similar was the situation during a May 1998 election in Hungary when a new coalition was put in office despite the positive results of the sound economic policy of the previous government.

to tackle the issues. In transition countries the recession has been long, and democracy is only just emerging. The people who are in charge are not always the right ones. In particular, the lack of a sound and reasonable compromise vis-à-vis problems related to income distribution can hamper growth. Populist temptations are everywhere, even in the most advanced market nations.[3]

Even more important than the results of a free election is the mechanism by which important decisions are taken. For instance, taxation and the budget, two areas of tremendous consequence for stability and growth, are determined by democratic procedures, unfortunately often without solid economic reasoning. Debates on these issues always look as if they were discussions about the distribution of public resources. However, from a long-term perspective, the decisions taken even about a single annual budget have serious implications for growth. The 'long term' consists, after all, of a series of one-year periods.

Sometimes exaggerated conclusions are drawn about the relationship between the market and democracy or freedom and efficiency. Even many who are in favour of political democracy and the free market may believe that democracy constrains rather than enhances economic freedom. 'The evidence to date is that *democracy is incompatible with freedom*, at least in a form that the classical liberals might have recognized. . . . [A] lack of good alternatives makes its record no less disappointing and its prospects no less disturbing' (*The Economist* 1997f; emphasis added). This statement misses the point that the choice is not between democracy or no democracy, but between good policy and bad policy. Democracy does not automatically guarantee that policy will be wise or that the business environment will be healthy, nor does a lack of democracy automatically guarantee that policy and the business environment will be bad. An excellent example is the contrast between China and Russia in the 1990s.

The discussion should focus on the effort to identify good policies under democracy, not on the search for an alternative to democracy, because there is no positive alternative in the contemporary world. In 1960 only 37 governments and heads-of-state were freely and democratically elected; in 1998 there were 117 nations with democratically elected governments. Doubtless, there is a positive relationship between this impressive progress of democracy and the acceleration in economic growth during the last decades of the 20th century. Hence theoretical arguments, but also recent history support the thesis that democracy is compatible with well-performing markets, that is, with a growing economy, if not everywhere and at all times, then at least in a majority of cases over the long term.

---

[3] The French, German, and Italian struggles in 1996–8 to contain the fiscal deficit below the Maastricht criterion of 3% of GDP provide a good example.

10.2. THE FEEDBACK LOOP

Is all this relevant to the postsocialist countries, of which all but a few have freely elected governments, but in which so much is *in statu nascendi*? The general claim that democracy and the market are compatible does not inevitably mean that simultaneous democratization and marketization are compatible, since 'marketization' does not mean the same as 'market', and democratization is not an equivalent of democracy. The market and democracy are the economic and political goals of the systemic transition in postsocialist countries. Marketization and democratization are the processes leading to these goals.

The political systems in the socialist states differed in particulars as much as did the economic systems. Under socialism, countries like Hungary, Poland, and Yugoslavia enjoyed partial political decentralization and liberalization. Even in the Soviet Union in the 1980s, through the Gorbachev policies of glasnost and perestroika, there was some political liberalization. Meanwhile, authoritarian regimes dominated in Bulgaria, Czechoslovakia, the GDR, and especially Albania and Romania. Authoritarian regimes in Cuba and North Korea have already outlasted socialism in Eastern Europe and the former Soviet Union by a decade.

The point of departure for the process of democratization was therefore also more auspicious in some nations than it was in others. The same was true of the process of marketization. Not surprisingly, the climate for these two processes was more favourable in the same places, since the limited liberalization which took place under socialism was carried out in the same countries both in the economy and in political life.

While 'shock therapy' was ill advised from the very beginning as a means to introduce the market, the situation is quite the opposite for the introduction of democracy. Marketization and democratization both call for fundamental changes in institutional arrangements and behavioural patterns, but from a formal viewpoint democracy is easier to introduce than is the market. Much less time is required for the revolutionary process of altering a political group and disestablishing a form of government, even an authoritarian political system, than for the implementation of the market. It is therefore feasible to lay the legal foundations and establish the general framework of a democratic political system in a radical manner and rather quickly.

However, democracy and the market should not be seen exclusively through the prism of formal legal structures. It is not sufficient now merely to accept these words 'democracy' and 'market', so vilified for so long, and to translate them into new laws.[4] It is also necessary to modify culture

---

[4] Within 1 to 7 years after the onset of transition, new constitutions had been approved or the old ones thoroughly amended in all postsocialist nations. Revealing is the case of Poland, the country most advanced in transition; a new constitution was adopted there only in 1997.

and behaviour. The new political culture, unlike the new laws, cannot be enforced. It must be assimilated. This involves learning by doing. If it is to play its proper role, the new culture must be fathomed. Of course, this takes longer. Time is required to understand how democracy works and how to use it in favour of a well-performing economy and a healthy civic society. Democracy is a 'process', not an episode.

Some believe that entrepreneurship has been more vigorous in the Baltic States, for instance, than it has been in Belarus, Russia, or Ukraine owing to the relatively shorter existence of the Soviet-style planned economy in the former (Wolf 1997). Yet, this argument is not convincing because, even if the planned economy had lasted for three or four generations in the Baltic States as it did in other republics of the former Soviet Union, it probably would not have made a significantly greater difference. By the same token, the better economic performance of certain nations during the transition can probably be partly attributed to cultural factors. Thus, because of specific cultural features, Poles are said to be generally much more business oriented and entrepreneurial than are other peoples in Eastern Europe.

However, more enlightening is the case of Vietnam, where the north has benefited significantly from the experience of the active business community in the south, which had a lively market economy until only 10 years before the 'doi moi' reforms were launched in that country.[5] The truth is that countries like Hungary or Poland in Central Europe or Estonia among the former Soviet republics have gained from the fact that they implemented systemic reforms early on, during the socialist period. Although the reforms aimed only at adjusting the old system to new circumstances, they helped foster a spirit of entrepreneurship that gave these countries a headstart during the transition to market capitalism. The differences in market culture and business behaviour among postsocialist societies are therefore a matter not so much of older traditions or longer history as of earlier reform.

During the period of adjustment the relationship between democratization and marketization is also evolving. At first the relationship might be negative, but later it champions development. The shift of economic resources to the private sector encourages resource allocation patterns which are more efficient and growth prone, while grassroots 'organic privatization', occurring together with democratization, adds even more to growth than does the parallel process of denationalization. The recognition of the freedom of people to start up businesses is crucial to the effort to lift the economy from transitional recession and depression. It creates an opportunity for the most dynamic parts of society to contribute directly to economic

---

[5] Actually, the reforms were interrupted, and, strictly speaking, the 'doi moi' policies were applied only in 1986–9. Because these failed, radical stabilization policies (sometimes mistakenly called 'radical reforms' or even 'transition') were undertaken. In this sense, the 'doi moi' period is comparable to perestroika in the Soviet Union.

growth. Consequently, a vast number of new entities launch economic ventures which absorb an increasing share of capital and produce an increasing share of national income. The entrepreneurship of the new private sector becomes a driving force behind postsocialist recovery. Entrepreneurship was suppressed under the previous system, but democratization has revitalized it.

Due to democratization and economic liberalization, after depression there is recovery and a period of accelerated growth. Economic democratization provides a special boost for several years at the beginning of transition. Later, the growth continues, but at a slower pace. The period of extraordinary expansion has come to an end, not least because the initial enthusiasm over entrepreneurship has dampened. The impression that the free and open access to 'market opportunities' is something new, a kind of once-in-a-lifetime chance to exercise the entrepreneurial spirit, only lasts a little while, and so it can serve as a catalyst for growth for only a little while. Afterwards, when most of the fresh opportunities have already been taken up, then the catalyst begins to dissipate as more and more people realize that riches don't necessarily come easy in the market. (This is also because some of the most authentic and active 'entrepreneurs' have already been seduced from the high public places they once occupied to the high private sector positions they now enjoy.) In any case, for most people the private sector is not such a big deal anymore; the unusual is now the usual.

Democracy accommodates a framework for efficient economic policy. This is true over the long term in developed market economies and mature civic societies. To what extent is it true in the nations in transition? The answer is not simple. The experience of the first years of marketization and democratization seems to indicate overall that democratic institutions can promote reasonable economic policies. There are many positive examples of good policies adopted by the 'infant' democracies.

However, there are also many instances in which the economic policies adopted in the 'infant' democracies have not been good ones. Parliaments, democratically elected governments, and heads-of-state have sometimes taken the wrong decisions, and this has had a negative influence on growth. This was the case in Poland in 1989–91, when there was a drastic drop in production, soaring unemployment, and mounting inter-enterprise arrears. This was again the case in Poland when the country's first freely elected president, for political reasons, vetoed a new tax code aimed at the enhancement of capital formation. This was the case when democratically elected parliaments in Bulgaria and Romania made mistakes which led to very serious banking and financial crises and economic depression in 1992–5. This was the case with the Czech voucher privatization, which led directly to a deterioration in the competitiveness of industries and a decline in the rate of growth beginning in 1997. The Russian parliament and government administrations, also a product of infant postsocialist democracy, may serve as examples of freely elected bodies with horrible records in making economic decisions in that GDP collapsed by more than half between 1989 and 1998.

Are the transition economies a special case? Of course, they are. The political struggle has been much more intense during transition than it is in traditional democracies. What in the West is considered political extremism, in the East can have a rather routine influence on the course of events. This is a unique 'growing period', during which particular interest groups and the political parties they influence are not only fighting over current agendas, but are also seeking to take control over economic matters and the political negotiating process for a long time to come. The struggles are strategic and historical. Economic democracy alters the structure of society and the political balance in the state. The accompanying tugs-of-war make all political debates more aggressive. Tensions stemming from conflicts of interest are much more volatile.

To a certain extent, this should be accepted as a natural outcome of burgeoning political freedom. In emerging postsocialist democracies—more so in Eastern Europe, less so in the CIS—democratic procedures within such an environment generate odd political coalitions. Not infrequently, the economic polices of these coalitions, because they must be based on practical political compromises, may not always lead to the best outcomes. In fact, they lead there quite seldom. Often there is more discussion about the distribution of national product than about the best way to produce more of it. Sometimes it seems lucky if any problems are solved at all.

Politics and economics can become confused in a number of ways. In a situation in which so many things are changing so profoundly so quickly, there must be horsetrading between political realities and ideal economic solutions. Even if there is no direct link whatsoever between abortion law and income taxation, between election regulations and the structure of the budget, between bank privatization and military expenditures, or between housing subsidies and minority rights, in political negotiations indirect connections can appear between these issues. In real politics, owing to the permanent goal of shouldering forward one's own plank and the constant bargaining to win approval for pet projects, unrelated issues are always being put on the agenda together.

Democratization works in favour of growth if the political leaders who know how best to facilitate growth are in charge of policy. Of course, they must also be able to convince a majority of the electorate that they deserve to be trusted and elected. These two skills are not often coincident.

Nonetheless, economic democracy does not mean simply open access to business opportunities, although this may be the key to a surge in growth. It involves wide-ranging debates on ideological, cultural, political, and social issues. Democratization and democracy are autonomous values and aims in their own right. Democratization should also mean decentralization and employee participation in enterprise decisions and outcomes (Nuti 1998). It calls for a guaranteed minimum wage and a minimum income. So, it may even happen that a chance for economic expansion is sacrificed at the altar of democracy. However, the process is revolutionary enough that economic ideas and initiatives which at one time were not talked about openly now find their way before the public forum. The best approaches may not always be adopted, but now at least they are all aired.

Politics often wins out over economics because of populist temptations and unrealistic expectations. There is an urge to consume the fruits of the transition before a sufficient quantity can be harvested. The present is too often preferred over the future. Owing to tremendous social pressures, reinforced by political aims, there is a tendency to take decisions which are financially unrealistic. Later, when it is time to pay up, frustration becomes widespread, but the practice continues because the government is the same. And even if the government does not survive and is changed, the parliament may remain in the same hands so that ineffective institutional arrangements and policies may be retained although they do not foster economic growth or meet the other needs of society.

In some nations at the beginning of transition, along with the influence of free market zealots and of an extreme liberalism going beyond anything in traditional capitalism, there was a strong belief that the situation could be changed for the better by the power of political will alone. Inherited from the era of state socialism and the command economy, the conviction that things could be fixed through the simple expedient of the government's determination and central decisionmaking ability was widely held. Some politicians still nurse that conviction, although no executive order can force everyone to be wise, or honest, or both. According to this conviction, it is sufficient to shove ahead by the sheer power of will, this time by democratic means. The new political class quite often applies too liberally their ability to *divide et impera* and has a tendency to overlook the requirement to produce the goods and deliver the services first and then change habits, too.

Thus, a common malaise of economic policy under the previous system—the belief that policies can become successful merely because the authorities are deeply determined that they should be so—has persisted sometimes even during the transition. Yet, being in charge of policy does not necessarily mean the same thing as being in control of issues. This is so because there are many processes which by the very nature of the market and democracy are beyond government control, but also because the majority is not always strong enough to push forward to achieve everything it wishes.

It is not yet clear whether the democratic mechanism whereby the public can shift its support to an opposition party can function in a positive way in the transition context. In a democracy, if the electorate realizes after a year or two that it has made a mistake by selecting the wrong president or government, it must await the next election in two or three years' time to correct the mistake. If the head-of-government could be thrown out overnight what sort of democracy would it be? Likewise, democracy and the market (and democratization and marketization) function in such a way that 51 per cent of the vote is sometimes not enough. Society and the economy are not a stock company in which one can obtain the controlling number of shares. One should also be right. Likewise, it may not be enough to be right if one doesn't have the majority in parliament or the backing of the people.

In the local decisionmaking process, international pressure which is politically motivated sometimes gets the upper hand over domestic needs, and political considerations in the international arena sometimes run counter to sound domestic economic policies. The best example is the rapid privatization which was widely and extensively counselled in all transition countries by foreign governments and international organizations which beyond any doubt had first their own interests at heart and only thereafter the improvement of the socioeconomic situation. Thus, the British Know-How Fund and the American Overseas Development Council have accomplished at least as much for British and American investors, exporters, and merchants active in postsocialist nations as they have for the transition process through their efforts to upgrade the skills of local professionals.

The overall results of these tendencies and forces have been mixed. At the onset of the transition it was quite easy to blunder along with harsh policies even if they led inevitably to severe economic downturn. Taken by surprise by the speed of the revolutionary changes around them, people were ready to accept austerity measures because they believed what the new leaders and their advisors were saying, that austerity was essential. Under the unique political conditions it was not so difficult to spread the false idea that there was no alternative to policies which turned out to be not only wrong but counterproductive. Even if later the same democratic practices which had permitted such enormous mismanagement were able to uproot the bad policies, the economy had already been harmed; output had declined more than needed, and growth had accelerated less than might have otherwise been possible following recovery.

Good policies were implemented by the budding democracies, too. However, the task was not easy, since under democracy, unlike in an authoritarian system, many more entities must be convinced that the proposed policies are correct. The bureaucracy and the government, but also parliamentary caucuses, the president, the constitutional court, interest groups, civic organizations, and the news media (if truly independent), as well as the international establishment, especially the Bretton Woods institutions and the World Trade Organization, are involved in the process of turning the good ideas into practical solutions.

Thus, both good decisions and bad decisions have been taken in transition countries with the formal approval of democratic institutions. Although democratic procedures were not responsible for the goodness or the badness of the early policies, only during the more advanced stages of transition has democracy tended to work a little more against the threat of the supremacy of politics over economics. The infant democracy itself cannot guarantee that the majority will be right. However, democratization has now opened up the prospect of more suitable economic choices. This is very positive, since, after all, more could not have been accomplished without democracy. Even if there were a purely technical way to determine beforehand what is right and what is wrong, we would still need democracy. Democracy by itself is a valuable asset.

It is difficult to gauge precisely the impact of democratization on the overall economic situation in Eastern Europe and the former Soviet republics. However, there appears not to be much room yet for a positive finding, since democracy in a majority of countries is still associated with economic contraction rather than expansion, with recession rather than growth, with depression rather than development. Nonetheless, the impact is evident in several areas apart from the economy, and one must appreciate other changes which may yet facilitate growth and development. One must appreciate also the 'feedback loop'.

A close look at the nature, scope and pace of change leads one to the observation that democratization has truly enhanced marketization during the postsocialist transition and vice versa. The empirical evidence supports the thesis that these two processes are complementary.

A Freedom House survey (Shor 1997a, 1997b) has examined the entire range of systemic changes in political and economic structures in 25 countries. The review takes into account the political process and covers free elections and the conditions for political competition and popular participation in public activities. The maturity of civic society is measured through evaluations of the amount of freedom enjoyed by trade unions and professional organizations and the involvement of civic organizations in public affairs. The independence of the news media is examined through an analysis of the resistance of the media to the influence of governments and political parties. The rule of law is gauged in terms of the constitutional order and respect for ethnic minority rights. Legislative and executive transparency, together with government decentralization, is used as a yardstick for the quality of governance and public administration. In the evaluation of economic freedom, progress in privatization is judged qualitatively simply according to the share of the private sector in GDP; however, the evaluation of freedom in the economy itself is tested on the basis of the progress toward the creation of the foundations of a modern capitalist economy as embodied in property rights, central bank independence, and the free access of people to the business sector.

Ranking is on a scale of 1 to 7, with 1 representing the highest and 7 the lowest degree of achievement. So, the lower the score, the better the overall situation. Of course, the results of such a survey must be seen solely as a proxy. Nonetheless, they provide interesting insights (Table 27).

Using these measures, one can draw an overall picture of economic and political freedom in postsocialist nations and, therefore, an approximation of the level of democratization and marketization. As the result of such an exercise, transition economies have been ranked according to the progress accomplished so far (Table 28). They are divided into three groups: 'consolidated market economies' (seven countries), 'transitional economies' (fourteen countries), and 'consolidated statist economies' (four countries).

Unlike some other nations experiencing vast structural adjustment and economic liberalization, like Chile or Taiwan in the 1980s, the postsocialist economies are in transition to both democracy and the market. Countries like Chile are often pointed at to argue that under certain circumstances an authoritarian regime can serve economic growth better than can a democratic government. This argument is generally mistaken. However, it is not therefore automatically true that democratization can better serve this purpose than can autocracy.

A great deal of misunderstanding arises because of the confusion between the notions of 'democracy' and 'democratization'. While democracy and the market are compatible, the relationship between democratization and marketization is more complex. The more advanced the market system, the easier is the process of democratization. In this sequence the market system appears to be the foundation for the democratic state and civic society. But the relationship can also work the other way so that established democracy supports the introduction and development of the market economy (Williamson 1993).

It is also true that democratization can act as a cushion against contraction and depression during the early transition. Political and economic liberalization and emerging freedom appear to perform the function of a very special good which to some extent offsets the deterioration in the standard of living. Even severe impoverishment can be tolerated for a while, if only the people's need for profound change can be satisfied. Initially people are prepared to accept a worsening in their material well-being as a transitory episode. They view the experience as the price of pain that must be paid once and for all so as to obtain a better future.

The precedent is an ancient one, for the policy of *panem et circenses* was exercised long ago. Even though the hardships are severe and many, yet democracy is functioning and providing societies with a value which the economy has failed to supply, namely, the 'feel good' factor. However, a policy would be shortsighted that counted on this to work forever.

Table 27 Democratization in transition countries: Freedom House rankings, 1997

	Political process	Civil society	Independent media	Rule of law	Government and public administration (GPA)	Privatization	Economy	Private share of GDP (%)
Albania	4.3	4.3	4.8	4.8	4.8	3.8	4.3	75.0
Armenia	5.5	3.5	5.3	4.8	4.5	4.0	4.0	50.0
Azerbaijan	5.8	5.0	5.5	5.5	6.3	5.3	5.0	25.0
Belarus	6.0	5.3	6.3	6.0	6.0	6.0	6.0	15.0
Bulgaria	3.3	4.0	3.8	4.3	4.3	5.0	5.8	45.0
Croatia	4.0	3.5	4.8	4.8	4.0	4.0	3.8	50.0
Czech Republic	1.3	1.5	1.3	1.5	2.0	2.0	1.8	75.0
Estonia	2.0	2.3	1.8	2.3	2.3	2.3	2.0	70.0
Georgia	5.0	4.5	4.5	5.0	4.5	4.3	4.0	50.0
Hungary	1.3	1.3	1.5	1.8	1.8	1.5	1.8	70.0
Kazakhstan	5.5	5.3	5.3	5.0	5.5	4.3	4.5	40.0
Kyrgyzstan	5.0	4.5	5.0	4.5	4.3	4.0	3.5	50.0
Latvia	2.0	2.3	1.8	2.3	2.5	2.5	2.5	60.0
Lithuania	2.0	2.3	1.8	2.3	2.5	2.3	2.8	65.0
FYR Macedonia	3.5	3.8	4.0	4.3	4.0	4.0	5.0	50.0
Moldova	3.3	3.8	4.0	4.3	4.3	4.0	4.0	40.0
Poland	1.5	1.3	1.5	1.5	1.8	2.3	1.8	60.0
Romania	3.3	3.8	4.3	4.3	4.3	4.5	4.8	60.0
Russia	3.5	3.8	3.8	4.0	4.0	3.0	4.0	60.0
Slovakia	3.8	3.8	4.3	4.0	3.8	3.3	3.5	70.0
Slovenia	2.0	2.0	1.8	1.8	2.5	2.8	2.0	45.0
Tajikistan	6.0	5.5	6.3	6.3	7.0	6.3	6.0	20.0
Turkmenistan	7.0	7.0	7.0	6.8	6.8	6.8	6.0	20.0
Ukraine	3.3	4.0	4.5	3.8	4.5	4.3	4.3	40.0
Uzbekistan	6.3	6.5	6.5	6.5	6.0	6.3	6.3	40.0

Source: Shor 1997b.

Table 28 Marketization and democratization, 1997: an overall ranking

	Economy ranking	Democracy ranking	Overall ranking[a]
Consolidated market economies			
Hungary	1.6	1.4	1.5
Czech Republic	1.9	1.4	1.6
Poland	2.0	1.4	1.7
Estonia	2.1	2.1	2.1
Slovenia	2.4	1.9	2.1
Lithuania	2.5	2.1	2.3
Latvia	2.5	2.1	2.3
Transitional economies			
Slovakia	3.4	3.8	3.6
Russia	3.5	3.8	3.6
Moldova	4.0	3.8	3.9
Croatia	3.9	4.3	4.1
Ukraine	4.3	3.9	4.1
FYR Macedonia	4.5	3.9	4.2
Kyrgyzstan	3.8	4.8	4.3
Albania	4.0	4.5	4.3
Romania	4.6	3.9	4.3
Armenia	4.0	4.8	4.4
Georgia	4.1	4.8	4.4
Bulgaria	5.4	3.8	4.6
Kazakhstan	4.4	5.3	4.8
Azerbaijan	5.1	5.4	5.3
Consolidated statist economies			
Belarus	6.0	5.9	5.9
Tajikistan	6.1	6.0	6.1
Uzbekistan	6.3	6.4	6.3
Turkmenistan	6.4	6.9	6.7

[a] Overall ranking is an average of the economy and democracy rankings.

Sources: Shor 1997b, author's evaluations.

Actually, the 'feel good' factor has already ceased to be important in transition economies. There is not much room left for peaceful deterioration in living standards. In countries like Russia and Ukraine, if the economy does not start growing soon, the patience of the people will reach its limits, and there could be serious social unrest. To calm the situation then would be impossible by means of more games at the 'circus'. Only a policy of more 'bread' can work now. Durable growth must be restored.

When the economy begins to improve, it is easier to undertake to reinforce the relationship between democratization and marketization. This is already evident in a number of postsocialist nations. The decision-making process involved is very complicated, however. The arguments must be repeated often in order to convince, for their logic is not immediately understood nor accepted by all interest groups. When this has been accomplished, then more difficult reforms can be carried out. But if the economy is in a freefall driven by plunging real income, the dwindling propensity to save, and a weakening ability to invest, then the effort to advance democratization may appear hopeless.

Indeed, in this case, democratization can become an obstacle to marketization as people begin to long for the security they now think they felt under the authoritarian order. In backward low-income countries it is very difficult if not impossible to sustain a full-fledged democratic system. A rather high level of per capita income appears to be a crucial precondition for democracy (Barro 1996). But even more important seems to be relative income. An inordinate level of income inequality is not acceptable in a democratic environment and can generate a lot of problems in a poor country. Democracy is fine in, say, Canada, but what about Haiti? It works well in Australia, but maybe not so well in Papua New Guinea. Likewise, it already seems to be performing much better in the Czech Republic or Lithuania than in FYR Macedonia or Georgia.

Several transition economies of Central Asia (Armenia, Azerbaijan, Georgia, Kyrgyzstan, Mongolia, Tajikistan), Southeast Asia (Cambodia, Laos, Vietnam) and Southeastern Europe (Albania, FYR Macedonia) belong to the low-income group of countries, and their progress toward sound democracy has been significantly slower than that of other nations experiencing transformation. Actually, in Central Asia, only in Kyrgyzstan and Mongolia do democratic institutions seem to have evolved further. The Freedom House survey includes all the Central Asian countries among the less successful 'transitional economies' and 'consolidated statist economies' in terms of political and economic freedom. It is clear from this assessment that the richer and the more developed an economy, the more advanced is the process of democratization.

Despite the postsocialist malaise and the enormous costs of transition, democracy has not (at least not yet) been overthrown anywhere because of a re-emergence of authoritarianism. Whatever the desperate economic situation, democratization and marketization are enduring. At the worst, in some postsocialist democracies there have been postponements in the implementation of the institutional reforms crucial for improvement, but there has nonetheless been appreciable progress. This alone is a remarkable achievement.

10.3. THE DILEMMA OF THE
'POSTCOMMUNIST CONSTITUENCY'

It has been a severe mistake of Western governments and organizations to have overestimated the power and ability of right-wing parties to reform and overhaul economies and to have underappreciated the abilities of left-wing parties to do so. In transition societies the issue is not who is on the left and who is on the right, but who is left standing at the end and who has been right all along. Often, the left has been right, and the right has been wrong.

There is a clear correlation between political variables and institutional variables. Progress toward political and institutional stability facilitates growth, and the positive impact is stronger if the progress in the two areas, institutional and political, goes hand-in-hand. It has been observed that socio-political stability, the quality of government and institutions, and the maturity of democracy and of the socioeconomic characteristics of a country are interrelated. In transition economies these variables have special meaning since cabinets and government administrations are vulnerable to frequent reshuffling, and the political environment is not as stable as it is in older democracies. Policies change, and the institutional variables fluctuate. It is not uncommon for governments to face early elections or to fail to complete the full constitutional term (usually four years).

There were early elections in the otherwise politically stable Czech Republic in 1998. In Poland in the 10 years after the elections in June 1989 only one parliament completed a full four-year term (1993–7), and, even during those four years, there were three governments (although they were formed from the same coalition). President Boris Yeltsin in March 1998 fired the entire government; the main reason appears to have been the desire to prove by such an action that, contrary to the rumours, he was in charge. Then, only five months later, in August, he dismissed the next government in an effort to create scapegoats for the mismanagement of the transition and the resulting financial collapse. Such behaviour may be difficult to understand and consider normal in a country that has had regular presidential elections for more than 200 years, but it is not at all surprising in a country where there has only been one president elected in free balloting. This does make a difference.

The political debates over these issues, with all their implications for the business climate, are sometimes quite bizarre. For example, for four years, from September 1993 to September 1997, a great many alarm bells were being sounded about the threat of a 'postcommunist' government in Poland, especially by certain research and media organizations linked with investor interests and conservative (that is, 'liberal') parties and institutions. A similar suspicious tone was used in reference to other countries with left or centre-left governments, such as Hungary under Gyula Horn and, of course, the Primakov Administration in Russia.

In Western political circles and in Western public opinion, too, it is popular to speak of a 'postcommunist constituency', while in the transition countries mentioned in this context the governments in power are simply the governments which have been democratically elected.

This is a real problem. The traditional discord between the right and the left is casting a shadow over the course of postsocialism. Since important transition events quickly catch international attention, not much can be done without the involvement of key foreign, mainly Western, partners. Undoubtedly, this involvement helps the transition process a great deal. However, not surprisingly, the partners are not keen to support postsocialist governments which are associated with leftist alliances. Curiously, this seems to be the case even when the Western partner governments happen also to be of a leftist persuasion themselves. They think the so-called 'postcommunists' and their political parties cannot stand up to the challenges of a transition to a market economy and democracy.

The 'postcommunists' are also believed to be hostile to foreign investment and the acceptance of foreign bids in privatization deals. The fact that even the most 'leftist' among Western governments have preferred to lobby for such acceptance must mean that perhaps they are not so 'left' after all, but rather that they are firmly nearer the centre and hope to count on the support of their domestic business interests which wish to make the bids. Nonetheless, it is not true that the 'leftist' governments in Eastern Europe are not in favour of inward foreign investment. They are in favour of foreign investment (not least because of the potential for employment-creation), though they care much more about meeting national needs and the social implications of privatization than do many other (often 'liberal') governments.

A spectre is not haunting Europe. There is no spectre of 'postcommunism'. The myth of the existence of such a spectre only serves the needs of right-wing politicians who wish to manipulate the inexperienced new 'elites' and the public in the countries most advanced in transition. It may be true that in transition nations which are lagging behind in liberalization and the establishment of new institutional arrangements, the old habits seem to be dying hard. Yet, the supposed threat of 'postcommunism' is not very real in these nations.

The real threat is the resurgence of statism and left-wing populism. However, this threat is not constant, nor is it a function of ideological sentiments (or at least the ideological sentiments are only secondary). It stems from the inherited structure of the economy and the related social and demographic features of countries. Thus, instead of pointing a finger at policymakers in these countries for their 'postcommunist' sentiments, foreign partners ought to be providing still more political, technical, and financial assistance to scare away the real 'postcommunist' phantom.

This is essentially the situation in several former Soviet republics without much experience in market-oriented reform under the socialist economy and without any tradition of even limited political liberalization. Belarus and Turkmenistan seem to be the most exposed in this sense. Knowing how alive the legacy of the past still is in these countries, one ought to watch current policy outcomes closely.

The legacies are very similar; the threats are not. Whereas one country, like Kazakhstan, is less exposed to the threats, a neighbour, like Uzbekistan, is more exposed to them. Whereas the legacy is more distant in Kyrgyzstan, Tajikistan is still in its grip. These differences are also due to the strategies and policies which have been chosen and which reflect specific circumstances. One may not agree with the reasoning behind these choices, but the reasoning ought to be understood, and the circumstances carefully analysed.

A significant role in the persistence of the tendency toward statism and centralization in Turkmenistan and Uzbekistan is certainly played by cultural factors, such as the traditional respect shown for the position of males within the family, elders within the community, and strong leaders within the country. Both countries, unlike any other former Soviet republics, have rigid economic structures based on one or two essential resource sectors. In Turkmenistan it is gas and oil, in Uzbekistan cotton and gold. Who owns and manages the resources owns and manages the economy. Thus, the temptation is extremely strong for centralization and significant government-led regulation.

In Belarus, three specific structural factors have influenced the pace of transition in a negative way: the heavy dependence on a non-performing defence industry, a relatively huge share of non-competitive smokestack industries, and an extremely high dependency ratio in the social security system (71 per cent in 1996, up from 54 per cent in 1993). Of course, one may argue, the ponderous structural burden should have become an additional factor in favour of a 'radical' course of action involving a faster—not a slower—rate of denationalizations and less—not more—statism in the management of the economy. But someone else might just as easily argue the opposite and has obviously already done so, at least within the government. So, this second approach has been chosen as the option for the time being. Perhaps not surprisingly, this has won as much criticism from abroad (including other postsocialist countries) as it has applause from Belarusian workers and pensioners. And there are so many of them.

Still, in some Eastern European countries, as well as in the West, the 'risks' are exaggerated significantly for ideological and political reasons. Within the transition nations, policymakers, particularly those oriented toward systemic change, should be aware of the risks, but they must be aware, too, that the 'neoliberal bias' may harm the course of postsocialist transformation even more. *If there is any desire for a resurgence of statism and socialist populism, it is whipped up by liberalism which is too far-reaching, not by nostalgia for a lost past.*

If it is true that 'postcommunists' cannot build a market economy, then it must also be true that the people who are building it are not postcommunists. Has anybody ever seriously claimed that half a century ago 'post-capitalists' built the socialist economy in Central Europe? It's that simple. Some assume that the current reform-oriented and open-minded leaders are not able to work on behalf of the introduction of the market system. This is not true. The misconception that people (who anyway often were not communists under so-called 'communism') may now be accurately called 'postcommunists' is eagerly used in the West as a political weapon against real progress in the East. Practising anticommunism without communists and 'anti-postcommunism' without postcommunists is a weird political game and should be considered as ridiculous as the anticapitalist crusade in Eastern Europe half a century ago. Unfortunately, the implications are very serious for the ultimate success of the transition to the market.

Despite the additional hurdles raised by these ideological debates and political struggles, there are persuasive examples of cases in which 'leftist' parties (mainly 'postcommunist') have done much better than have their opponents from the right side of the political spectrum. At the end of the 1990s, this is being confirmed by the fact that the centre-left coalition government in the Czech Republic is doing better and the centre-right governments in Hungary and Poland are doing worse than their predecessors. In the Czech Republic, after the slowdown in 1997 and the first half of 1998, growth was accelerating, and disinflation was continuing. In Hungary growth was no more robust, and in Poland the pace of growth under the 'anti-postcommunist' government dropped by 2 percentage points in 1998 and fell further, to a meagre 3.2 per cent, in 1999. In both countries the effort at privatization is no more thoroughgoing now than it was under the previous governments. Curiously, since the election of September 1997, the Polish government, led once more by Solidarity, in coalition with Freedom Union, has been trying to explain away its failure to steam ahead with property restitution measures by claiming that the previous (centre-left) government privatized too much. In any case, there is little remaining to be privatized.

Deeds matter, not words. Due to the remarkable achievements of leftist governments, Hungary and Poland have taken a leading position among transition economies. It must be admitted (though for many this has a bitter taste) that at least in these cases the so-called 'postcommunists' have done a better job than has anybody else before or since. Moody's report on the state of the Polish economy on the eve of the parliamentary election in September 1997 claimed that

The dominance of this party [the SLD, the Left Democratic Alliance or, if one prefers, the 'postcommunists'] in the legislative and executive branches has done nothing to slow economic reforms. . . . The SLD electoral alliance is rapidly transforming itself into a conservative social democratic party, similar to the German SPD during the Helmut Schmidt years. . . . It speaks of the need to further develop the market economy while sharing the costs of the economic transformation of the country as fairly as possible. Simultaneously it supports tight fiscal and monetary policy. ('Moody's Report on Poland', Sept. 1997)

Moody's, the US rating agency, had become aware of 'extremely unfavourable policy developments that can threaten Poland's economic achievements registered to date', if Solidarity Electoral Action, the main opposition movement at the time, were to form the next government after four years of the successful economic policies of the SLD.[6] Hence practical success can overcome the prejudices expressed in public discussions about the means and the ends of economic policy. Hard facts speak and must be answered, and the messenger bringing the good (or is it the bad?) news must at least be heard.

In politics, one person's good news is always someone else's bad news. Although it is acknowledged (since in light of events it must be) that, 'As other emerging markets around the globe wrestle with crises, Poland is grappling with a very different problem: *managing success*. . . . Now Poland is racing to turn a model recovery into a modern economy' (Michaels 1998; emphasis added), no credit is given where credit is due. The real reason for this success was the medium-term transition and development programme, 'Strategy for Poland', executed by a government led by a 'leftist' or 'postcommunist' party (or at least so-called in the West and in certain opposition circles).

When the 'postcommunists' (the SLD), together with a small coalition partner, the centre peasants party (the PSL), took the reins of government in September 1993, they had faced a very different problem indeed: managing crisis. Unemployment was growing; the year-end rate of inflation was around 38 per cent; inter-enterprise arrears were soaring; a blueprint for the reform of the social security system had not yet been drafted; the inflow of foreign direct investment was below $1.8 billion; the lack of an agreement with the London Club of creditors was damaging the external financial position, and the currency was not even convertible for current transactions so that there was no access to international capital markets.

---

[6] It did so, but together with the liberal party, its enemy. Such a mixture of populism and liberalism has doomed this bizarre alliance to continue the policies of the previous government. This has turned out to be good for transition and development. Institutional changes continue; privatization proceeds, and foreign capital flows and the economy grow by and large along the lines set by the policies of the recent leftist government. Even the US rating agencies—not only governments and professors of economics—can be wrong.

The day after the 'postcommunists' had left the field, after four years of sound macroeconomic management, gradual systemic transition, and well-designed development policy, there appeared 'a very different problem: managing success'. Unemployment had been lowered by one-third (from 3 million to 2 million) and inflation by two-thirds (to about 13 per cent at the end of 1997). The arrears had been cleared, and convertibility had been introduced; a deal with the London Club had been signed in September 1994; an investment grading had been obtained from rating agencies (Moody's Investors Service, Standard and Poor's, and IBCA); a series of successful bond issues had been executed, and foreign direct investment had jumped over fourfold (to $6.6 billion in 1997 on a cash basis). No wonder Poland has joined the OECD, and the new Polish zloty has become the strongest among postsocialist currencies.

After the democratic election of September 1993 that brought the 'postcommunists' to power, The *Wall Street Journal*, a very respected newspaper, referred to a warning by the former minister of finance (who had been responsible for the early and not very successful stabilization policy) about an imminent 'creeping destruction'. This did not occur. Why did it not occur? And why is it so difficult to admit why it did not occur? Just as it is so easy to assign responsibility for the mismanagement of the early transition, it ought to be easy to assign responsibility for the subsequent successes.

The problem of the 'postcommunist constituency' is thus as much an issue for 'postcommunists' as it is for 'anti-postcommunists'. Whereas the former have a great deal yet to learn about the way the market economy and civic society work, the latter must at least learn to acknowledge that under the 'leftists' some things have changed for the better because of the real ability of the 'postcommunists' to manage certain issues. To eliminate dogmatism and hypocrisy is not easy in political debates about economic matters, but the sooner this happens, the better.

In the shaky and thus unpredictable circumstances of political and economic transition, the perception that a government may be replaced has an impact on the prospects for growth, even if ultimately the government stays on.[7] The expectation that there will be a new government raises the suspicion that economic, financial, and social policies will change, too. This created instabilities in planning and additional difficulties in the correct interpretation of economic events even in countries such as Britain, France, and Germany when government power shifted to the left

---

[7] Democracy sometimes seems to be an obstacle because it creates additional dangers and doubts. Thus, vis-à-vis certain emerging markets and young democracies, the World Bank 'has also outlined several risks that could lead to a deterioration of the situation, including the increasing corporate and banking stress, reduced foreign exchange reserves, continuation of regional turmoil, and the May 11 elections' (*Development News* 1998c). So, the elections are not necessarily a help.

in 1997–8. Consequently, on the basis of rumours and speculation, the inflow of investment or capital outflows may be reduced; the efficiency of resource allocations may deteriorate, and capacity may not be utilized to the full. This may occur even if the financial fundamentals are solid and structural reforms are succeeding. This time, the words may matter more than the deeds.

The professional and moral competence of the political leadership is a vital factor in the success of transition strategies. For several years, the 'new' political elites during transition are more or less the 'old' elites which governed before the transition. Transition strategies must therefore handle with great care the issue of the evolution of the political class, because there is a risk that a vacuum may appear. It is better to try to work with the 'new-old' elites, if there is not yet any sound replacement, than to fight them tooth and nail over political doubts and ideological anxieties. *The more comprehensive the international support for reform and the financial assistance facilitating reform, the stronger the determination of the new ('old') political elites to advance market arrangements and democracy.* And, to be sure, the stronger is this determination, the more comprehensive should be the support and the assistance. This is certainly true with respect to Russia since the crash of 1998. Instead of calling the Russian government '(post)communist' and battling against it, a much wiser course would be to offer it support in its attempts to overhaul the economy and help it to continue the necessary process of reform. Although the elites in postsocialist nations are 'domestic', the implications of their rises and falls are an international matter, too. So, this is another feedback loop affecting the path of marketization and democratization.

A key factor in the political and institutional environment is the quality of the state bureaucracy. Much more so than in the case of political elites, the state bureaucracy is a 'leftover' from the previous system. Indeed, after a dozen years or so the old political elites will have been entirely replaced by new ones, but the bureaucracy will still be largely the same. It is simply too big. This means that the ability to deal with the challenges of the market economy and the unfamiliar administrative issues must be acquired quickly by the bureaucracy for the sake of stability and to provide better services for the business sector and for households. An effective bureaucracy can foster growth directly through the proper management of public affairs, the reinforcement of market institutions, or the lack of corruption. The influence of the bureaucracy on economic performance thus also depends on the scope of government intervention in the market (World Bank 1995c). In turn, this is a function of the level of state ownership and state regulation of the market. Usually, the smaller the state sector, the less the influence of the bureaucracy.

However, even if the influence of the bureaucracy is relatively limited, which is more and more the case in transition economies owing to privatization and deregulation, the bureaucracy still has a consequential impact on economic matters. It is therefore important to assure that civil servants are properly trained and prepared to meet the new challenges of the market economy and civic society. It is sometimes very difficult to push through a reform not because of the obstacles created by democratic procedures, but because of bureaucratic barriers. Governments change, while the bureaucracy does not. It is also difficult to break old habits and old political ties. It is not enough to offer new incentives to improve performance. The skills and ways of thinking must also be modified. This takes time, since bureaucracies are often stubborn, inflexible, and not keen to change.

11

From Recovery to Sustained Growth

11.1. MARKET IMPERFECTIONS AND CRISIS

As the debate continues about the policies which should be used to shift from state socialism to the market economy and from stabilization to growth, it has become the generally accepted opinion—if not a truism—that none of this can happen without proper government engagement (Fischer, Sahay, and Vegh 1995). Even extreme neoliberal zealots in government—not at all a rare occurrence in Eastern Europe—exercise vast amounts of interventionism.[1] The laissez faire ideology remains where it belongs, in the world of words, in the sphere of ideas and illusions. In the world of real politics and true policymaking, laissez faire is not and cannot be a viable approach. The work of the market is being seconded by the active policies of government in financial, economic, and social matters (Kolodko 1998c).

Though arguing appropriately in favour of the market, some authors stress that until not so long ago government intervention played a very positive role in development. State control of the economy worked well for a long while in traditional capitalist countries. In reference to the statist policies adopted after the Second World War, Yergin and Stanislaw (1998, p. 128) ask,

Who could deny the success of the experiment? From the end of the Second World War until the oil crisis of the 1970s, the industrial world enjoyed three decades of prosperity and rising incomes that sparked aspiration and dreams. It was an extraordinary achievement.

And then they reach the conclusion (p. 129) that

By the end of the troubled 1970s, a new realization had gained ground: More than daily management, it was the entire structure of the economy that had reached its limits. It was imperative to rethink government's role in the marketplace.

---

[1] Some observers believe that the declared 'neoliberals' in Hungary and Poland, having already been taught by the experience of the early 1990s how the economy really works, are eager now to intervene in the market even more than the 'leftist' governments did (the leftists presumably having hesitated because they wished to prove that they were not 'postcommunists'). Though this is not true, the fact is that, whereas the gap between the words of the 'neoliberals' and the 'leftists' is like the Grand Canyon, the gap between their deeds is like a little ditch. Such pragmatism is a good sign for those who hope for the success of the transition.

If indeed the issue was the simple one of reaching the limits, then it is puzzling that almost the entire globe turned away from statism at almost the same moment, since at the time nations were at such varying stages of development.[2] But the world was also turning away from other old habits around then. Why? Simply because one must follow the leader. When changes are being undertaken in countries which are leading the course of events, soon afterwards they can (or must) be carried out elsewhere. If a step has already been accepted and executed by a leader, then it is much easier to push the case for such a step elsewhere. This is even more true in the midst of a vast process of globalization that is reaching well beyond economic and financial affairs alone. Thus, since a leader is getting rid of some old habits, during a period of globalization the old habits are being got rid of on a global scale. It is only a matter of time.

Of course, there is a world leadership, as well as local ones. The United States has unquestionably been leading the world since the end of the cold war, but there are also regional leaders taking steps which deserve to be followed. The social security reform implemented in Chile is catching on throughout South America. The way Poland has managed the transition is a model in Eastern Europe. Uganda is trying to find the path toward fast growth in Central Africa. The industrial policy of Singapore has imitators in East Asia.

If the impact of what is going on in the most advanced market economies is not always directly felt in the economies going through structural adjustment, then it is certainly very often felt indirectly. The best way to bring democracy and an open market economy to Paraguay is probably to do it via Chile, to Myanmar via Thailand, and to Belarus via Poland. This is well understood among world leaders, including the potential partners in the post-Washington consensus.

Aside from the geopolitical dimension, in trying to answer the important questions, one must take the historical perspective, too. For example, the United States has come to terms with the acknowledgement of the existence of minority rights quite late. Only a generation ago in some states there were still schools and other public institutions (including restaurants and public restrooms) 'for whites only'. So, the 1960s were not the best years for the US to complain and moralize about the civil rights of blacks in South Africa or about the treatment of the Hungarian ethnic minority in Czechoslovakia. On another topic, Joseph E. Stiglitz (1998b, p. 70) writes that

It is hard to escape the irony between early drug wars—Western powers trying to keep China open to the flow of drugs—and the more recent equally adamant stands [of the Western powers] trying to stem the flow of drugs into their own countries.

---

[2] This is also true of the former socialist economies. Hidden within the 'multi-republic' Soviet Union and the Yugoslav Federation were countries like Tajikistan with GDP per capita below $1,000 and countries like Slovenia with GDP per capita at 10 times that much.

Only the lapse of time—and lack of knowledge of these historical experiences—softens what otherwise seem[s] an intolerable level of hypocrisy.

Yet the hypocrisy is still there, even without the difference in historical periods.

After years of insistence on trade liberalization, the US House of Representatives—when a majority of emerging market countries in Latin America has finally accepted the idea and got keen to apply it—has denied the president the power to take the fast track in trade, and so trade has not turned out to be as free as the market zealots themselves have said it should be. Once more, it is a good idea to distinguish between the ideas and the words, the interests and the deeds.

And it is good to remember that hypocrisy exists, and that unfortunately it does matter in politics and politically motivated economic debates. In the real political world, including the international one, it so happens that the stronger partners really seem to expect the adage 'do what I say, not what I do' to be followed. If only what some are advising others to do were also being done by the advice-givers in their own countries, many problems would look quite different. For example, an upward adjustment of energy prices in the United States through the imposition of a special excise tax would have led to a decrease in the fiscal deficit several years ago. Likewise, if the advisers would only follow their own advice the EU bureaucracy in charge of agriculture policy would now be several times smaller than it actually is. Instead, today the energy prices in the United States are lower and the agriculture subsidies in Western Europe are higher than those in Eastern Europe.

When (or perhaps the question ought to be introduced by 'why') should one retreat from statism? It might be argued that the 'when' has arrived already, since the leaders of the global economy have already so decided and acted (albeit only to a degree). And they, for sure, know what they are doing and why. However, if state control has reached its limits in the advanced market economies (which is not certain), this is not necessarily the case in transition economies or in less-developed economies. Even at a time of deep structural crisis in Japan, one of the most developed countries, the most extreme of the neoliberal extremists have not expected markets to fix the problem, but have called on the government to do so.

In general, the state may retire from intervention in the economy when market mechanisms, market culture and behaviour, and proper institutional arrangements exist to carry out the functions it performs. There seem to be two criteria for the withdrawal (never complete) of the state from intervention in the economy. First, there must be a reliable mechanism to sustain long-run growth that is impervious to minor external shocks. Second, if there is nonetheless a crisis because of an unfortunate coincidence of external shocks, then there must be an automatic mechanism which corrects distortions so that the economy can remain on track toward development. Even in the most advanced market nations, including Germany and the United States, these criteria are not met.

If the involvement of the state in economic matters was justified in the past in the development of the countries which are currently most advanced, it is at least equally well justified in countries currently lagging behind with respect to development and market sophistication. There may be good arguments for significantly less government intervention in the economy in Belgium and Italy today, but they do not necessarily apply in, say, Bulgaria or FYR Macedonia. What may be reasonable in the United States under President Clinton may be irresponsible in Russia under President Yeltsin. Even what is now feasible in Hungary and Poland should not be attempted yet in Russia or Ukraine because of the institutional gap among these emerging market economies.

If the transition to the market is to succeed, governments must be energetic in a number of areas of the economy. Governments in the post-socialist nations must intervene to manage transition policy and development strategy so that production can start to increase. Active government intervention is especially required to steer the economy toward recovery, but it is needed to achieve sustainable growth, too. Government policy engagement must be maintained even when the economy is expanding, because nowhere—and this is particularly true during transition—is economic growth a given. It must be supported and managed. To sustain rapid growth—if it is to contribute to equity and not harm the environment—may even demand much more policy attention than the early stages of liberalization and stabilization. During the later stages of transition, in the aftermath of the postsocialist crisis, even more government involvement may be justified. When liberalization and stabilization are the priorities, the 'invisible hand' of the market can be relied upon more, but during the shift from stabilization to sustainable, environmentally friendly, and equitable development the 'visible hand' of the policymaker has more to do.

Few people like to go to the dentist, but the dentist is essential if we wish to monitor the health of our teeth properly. The dentist reduces the risks by cleaning, filling cavities, and sometimes doing a little drilling. But we would be wise to choose our dentist carefully. Likewise, if the government putters with the market, it may augment the distortions, but by intervening wisely it can prevent crisis. The government can inadvertently boost the effect of the imperfections in the market, or it can counteract them to enhance the strengths of the market.

Even in contemporary liberalized economies, governments and markets must complement each other.[3] All the more reason why this should be

---

[3] Obviously, the debate on this issue is far from over. For example, see Rodrik 1996, World Bank 1997b, *The Economist* 1997g.

so in postsocialist economies, where automatic mechanisms have not yet evolved sufficiently to enhance the institutional arrangements on which the market must depend if it is to function efficiently and contribute to the welfare of the nation.

Market imperfections, as well as governments, can cause serious economic problems and foster crisis. The expansion of the role of government is not a sure remedy for market imperfections, nor is the extensive liberalization of the market a sure remedy for the failures of government. The cure-all is a 'partnership' between the market and the policymaker. What is needed to mend market imperfections is not less market and more government, but a better and stronger relationship between the market and the government.

The collapse of state socialism was a result of the failure of the state for the simple reason that under state socialism there was no market. The Great Depression of 1929–33 was caused by the failure of both the market and the state. The Greater Depression of 1990–7 in postsocialist countries was likewise due to the fact that neither the state nor the market was able to clean up the mess. Now, in the aftermath of this depression neither the state alone, nor the market alone is going to be able to achieve recovery and sustainable growth. The transition is thus an ongoing search for the proper mix of market and government.

The market must evolve, and the government must assist in the process, but as the market evolves, so must the role of the government. Only a combination of these two regulatory systems, the one led by the market, and the other by the state, will be able to deliver sound supply responses. Market institutions must be designed by the state and then allowed to evolve in such a way that they promote efficiency and competitiveness. Meanwhile, as the market evolves, the state must redesign its interventions to correct market imperfections and assure equity and long-term development. Only coordination between these two processes can secure increased capital formation and growth.

The danger of excessively thoroughgoing government interventionism is especially high at the early stage of transition, when the burden of old policy instruments and weak institutions is greatest. The neoliberal solution is the withdrawal of government ('the best policy is no policy'). But then there is also no growth, or, if there is some, it is sluggish, unsustainable, and inequitable. Some segments of society benefit, but most people suffer more. Thus, the non-approach of 'the best policy is no policy' has been compromised (and not only in transition economies).

The constructive solution is a new style of engagement of the state, not the withdrawal of the state. A convincing argument in favour of this approach has already been provided through the experience of a number of growing economies, including reformed socialist economies and transition economies. The approach represents a foundation for the post-Washington consensus, and this is very important, for it can affect economic policies worldwide. Indeed, almost the entire globe is turning away from the neo-liberal bias and seeking a new role for the state, and the effort would have a better chance of paying off in Myanmar, Paraguay, or Belarus if it were well understood elsewhere, for instance among the potential partners of the post-Washington consensus.

The fact is that the contemporary world is so complicated because there are so many global links, and national economies need government-led policies and government intervention more than ever. Yet, the involvement must be of a different sort, especially in postsocialist countries. The core of the transition process is a liberalization which releases spontaneous market forces, but this should be matched by an effort to establish sound financial fundamentals, develop infrastructure, secure investments in human capital, introduce necessary structural reforms, and set new institutional arrangements. This effort should be serious enough that the state seeks to restructure its interventions in the economy, not eliminate them.

11.2. RECOVERY AND THE NEW ROLE OF THE STATE

In industrial nations the share of public spending in GDP jumped from about 12 per cent in 1913 and 18 per cent in 1920 to 28 per cent in 1960 and 45 per cent in 1990. There were several reasons for this phenomenon, but it would not have occurred if there had not been strong and constant political pressure and a good economic rationale for so much public expenditure. In part, it was also due to an evolution in social values, especially the growing conviction that development must be equitable and that the market system was unable to guarantee this equitability. The expansion seemed to be justified by traditional needs such as defence, infrastructure, and administration, but also by the widespread belief that only the state can furnish adequate education, health care, and social security for all. So, the new state and 'big' government emerged.

The insistence on an expansion in government spending can be reexamined only at a higher stage of development, when there are sufficient private resources to ensure that the requirements in education, health care, and social security can be reasonably met and when the institutions exist to manage these resources without direct state participation. The recent drive in advanced market countries to alter the decades-old tendency toward ever bigger government can be explained by the fact that they possess a positive alternative. Indeed, it may be necessary to contain or downsize big government for the sake of competitiveness, capital formation, and growth potential.

The situation is not the same in transition economies, and the same considerations are therefore not necessarily justified. The postsocialist nations are poorer, and their level of development is far from adequate. While the more advanced and the relatively rich among them have somewhat more resources, even these do not have private institutions able to provide the services only the state has supplied so far.

Because of the long experience in some regions it is being realized that development also depends on the 'visible hand' of the government rather than exclusively on the 'invisible hand' of market forces. In the mid-1960s the level of development was similar in Africa and East Asia. In 1990 Africa was still backward, but East Asia was 'newly industrialized'. Without appropriate state involvement and government policy backing, market forces in Africa have not been able to deliver durable growth. Paradoxically, the late 1990s Asian crisis, manageable neither exclusively by market forces, nor only by governments, is another argument in support of the claim that even at the *fin de millénaire* there is room for more and better government engagement, but not for government retirement.

The active role of the state must be redefined, not abandoned during systemic transformation, whether the reform of a socialist regime or the postsocialist transition. The process of privatization demands a different type of partnership between government and the private sector. The new circumstances call for a fresh regulatory environment, not only 'deregulation', but 're-regulation' (Stiglitz 1997). The government must take on the burden of a proper policy to encourage competition. It must fight monopolies. Even if just for this one cause, the old state may not be needed anymore, but the new one is very much required, at least until the competitive environment is established and efficient product markets appear.

During transition the state changes the scope of its activities and also the instruments it uses to implement its chosen strategies.

The market itself cannot deliver broad-based improvements in the standard of living without an active state which establishes the right conditions, responds to change, and which, together with the market, provides for the delivery of health, education, infrastructure, and social protection, which the market cannot provide by itself. The way in which the role of [the] state is defined, and in which services are delivered, is probably the most important determinant of the standard of living of the community over the long-run term. (Stern and Stiglitz 1997, p. 27)

These are still more important reasons because they are here being listed by the chief economists of the EBRD and the World Bank, and a successful shift from depression to recovery to sustained growth in the transition economies depends to a considerable extent on the financial and technical assistance of these organizations.

The world is so very diverse that it is quite strange that there is a tendency to draw general conclusions and give advice which is supposed to meet all challenges. What works under some circumstances is not necessarily appropriate in other circumstances. One size does not fit all. This is as true of shoes and socks as it is of the level of involvement of the state in managing recovery after a crisis. If the downturn in the business cycle in an advanced market economy is of the normal variety, then of course market forces and the government should react normally. But if there is long-lasting depression and extensive structural crisis, then a 'new deal' in government economic policy and in institutional responses may be required. This is true of the postsocialist transition and development, but also of the serious economic challenges being faced elsewhere in the world. The 'new state' is as much needed in Africa as it is East Asia.

According to the World Bank (1997b), there are five crucial functions which should be fulfilled by the state because the market and private institutions cannot perform them. These functions are related to legal foundations, the macroeconomic policy framework, investments in basic social services, in human capital, and in infrastructure, the comprehensive safety net for the vulnerable in society, and the protection of the natural environment.

The problem is that these five key functions are policy declarations or policy directives rather than conditions which are respected in the advice of international financial organizations and in the policies being executed in developing and transition economies. They have not really become performance criteria, and thus they are not considered so decisive in actual policy packages. Yet, financial and technical assistance would do well to focus greater attention on these five functions, which ought to be performed by the modern state in an emerging market economy.

Furthermore, lending by the World Bank and the EBRD should be based much more on conditionalities which recognize these five key domains of state activity and should definitely not support policies or programmes which may weaken or ignore them. This calls for a revision of the qualification procedures for financial assistance and especially a revision of the method of monitoring the countries being provided with lending by international organizations so that much more serious attention is paid to the fulfilment of these five essential state functions.

However, for the sake of fiscal prudence and monetary stability, policies which disregard these functions are being supported, too, especially stabilization and structural adjustment measures which, unfortunately, often lead to falling output and growing inequality and thus to spreading poverty, rising unemployment, divestment in human capital, a frazzling safety net, and weaker environmental standards.

There are contradictions between the means and the ends of policies, and there are thus also contradictions among the excessively numerous priorities on the agenda. So, the World Bank postulates firm financial reasons for one course of action, but these turn out to be secondary in the confrontation with the IMF over sound financial fundamentals.

Despite the significant structural and institutional changes of the 1990s, the redefined functions of the new state in transition economies are all quite similar. But 'similar' does not mean 'identical'.

It is often claimed that the shortest way to recovery and growth following transitional contraction is to diminish the role of the state. As proof of this, mainstream economists cite a few carefully selected examples of successful nations with small governments and fast growth. However, in light of experiences in the world economy, the supposed alternative between big government and a lower rate of growth or small government and a higher rate of growth does not really seem to be an entirely valid one. If there were such a clear choice, then small government might be a better option, even at the cost of a temporary dropoff in public services. In fact, in the real world, such a solution may sometimes be appropriate, but the opposite situation is more likely to emerge: a positive correlation between the size of government and the pace of growth.

In transition countries, 'small government', that is, a relatively lower amount of income redistribution through the public finance system and the relatively minor involvement of the state and the public bureaucracy in economic affairs, usually means that institutions are weaker and that the shadow economy is larger. Meanwhile, 'big government' means that the state is more active and redistributes a relatively larger chunk of income through the government budget.

Government expenditure can accelerate the pace of growth, particularly if it is directed at institution-building, the upgrading of infrastructure, and human capital investment, especially education, health care, and research and development. Government expenditure can hinder growth if the bulk of state expenditures flows toward the bureaucracy, defence, and subsidies for non-competitive activities. In short, outlays can be productive or non-productive; investments can be oriented toward the future or toward current consumption, and expenditures can be well targeted or miss the target. The trick is to determine the proper mix between management by the state and management by the market.

Orthodox neoliberal economics suggests that a reduction in the size of government facilitates growth. However, during the early transition something quite different happened. Owing to the complexity of the changes, it is not possible to identify exactly the nature of the correlation, but there can be no doubt that *during the early transition there was a causal relationship between the rapid shrinkage in the size of government and the significant fall in output*. The sudden withdrawal of subsidies caused a financial squeeze, and the radical stabilization measures led to a credit crunch. The initial shocks were thus followed by recession. Only later, after output is back on the path of growth, can the positive effects of the pruning in government be seen, if indeed they occur, for this depends more on the quality of development policy than on the pace and scope of the decrease in government expenditure.

Consequently, even if to some extent under certain conditions it may be true that smaller government can foster long-term growth, the issue is not really whether less government is better, but how to get from here to there and how long is 'long term'. Is it 15 years or 50? This is at least as important here as it is in a marriage. The challenge in transition economies is not the overall paring of government expenditures, but a change in the structure of government expenditures so that a greater portion of outlays contributes to faster growth and fairer income distribution.

It is almost impossible to prove that public services are more effective if there are fewer of them (that is, when government is smaller), but the attempt is still being made (*The Economist* 1997g). However, it is clear that the various components of government expenditure change during transition. Since the type of government is new, with new targets and instruments, new friends and enemies, and, especially, new sets of problems, expenditures in some areas must climb, but in others they decline. Nonetheless, an across-the-board reduction in the size of government by reining in expenditures, often those directed at infrastructure and human capital investments, can erode current levels of consumption and living standards, but also growth and the standard of living in the future. The belief that there is a strong inverse correlation between the size of government and the rate of economic growth can thus exert pressure for spending decreases which are too far-reaching not only in countries with unsustainable fiscal deficits, such as Russia and Ukraine, but also those with a sound fiscal position, such as the Czech Republic and Poland.

Analogous conclusions about the danger of excessive curbs on government expenditure have been derived from an extensive study conducted on the issue of humanitarian emergencies in a sample of 124 developing nations by the World Institute for Development Economics Research. The number of such emergencies rose from 20–5 per year in the early 1990s to 65–70 more recently.[4] 'External pressure by the World Bank, International Monetary Fund, and Western donors to cut the size of the state in order to encourage economic stability in practice triggered increased competition for governmental resources and ended up contributing to greater instability' (Nafziger 1998).

During the early transition, the share of GDP redistributed through the government budget dropped by 3 to 5 percentage points. This means that the participation of the state and its institutions in the absorption of national income diminished by a factor of about one-tenth and in some cases even more.

---

[4] Among transition economies there have been humanitarian emergencies in Armenia and Azerbaijan (due to the conflict over Nagorny Karabakh), Bosnia-Herzegovina, Cambodia, Georgia (due to the conflict over Abkhazia), and most recently in Albania and the Yugoslav province of Kosovo.

Table 29 Defence expenditure, 1985–1995 (% GDP)

	1985	1995	Change, 1985–1995		1985	1995	Change, 1985–1995
Croatia	3.7	12.6	8.9	Belarus	13.1	3.3	−9.8
Russia	13.1	7.4	−5.7	Latvia	13.1	3.2	−9.9
Tajikistan	13.1	6.9	−6.2	Romania	4.5	3.1	−1.4
China	7.9	5.7	−2.2	Ukraine	13.1	3.0	−10.1
Estonia	13.1	5.3	−7.8	Kazakhstan	13.1	3.0	−10.1
Azerbaijan	13.1	5.0	−8.1	Slovakia	8.2	2.8	−5.4
Armenia	13.1	4.4	−8.7	Czech Republic	8.2	2.8	−5.4
Vietnam	19.4	4.3	−15.1	Albania	5.3	2.8	−2.5
Moldova	13.1	3.7	−9.4	Poland	8.1	2.5	−5.6
FYR Macedonia	3.7	3.7	0.0	Mongolia	9.0	2.4	−6.6
Uzbekistan	13.1	3.6	−9.5	Lithuania	13.1	2.4	−10.7
Kyrgyzstan	13.1	3.5	−9.6	Turkmenistan	13.1	1.9	−11.2
Georgia	13.1	3.4	−9.7	Slovenia	3.7	1.5	−2.2
Bulgaria	14.1	3.3	−10.8	Hungary	7.2	1.4	−5.8

Note: Countries are in descending order according to the 1995 figure. The figure of 13.1 for all Soviet republics in 1985 is the GDP share of defence expenditure for the Soviet Union. For China, according to national statistics, the figures are 2.1 for 1985 and 1.6 for 1995 for a 'change' of −0.5.

Source: UNDP 1997.

At the end of the cold war, simply due to plummeting defence outlays, the share of public expenditure in GDP was slashed. This represented a very healthy form of government downsizing. Of the 28 countries involved in postsocialist transformations, only in one, Croatia, was defence expenditure increased, while in half it fell by about 10 percentage points (Table 29).[5]

The absolute and relative declines in defence spending and in subsidies, another major area of reduction, were one-time measures and cannot be repeated. They were executed in a radical manner, and this caused substantial modifications within the structure of public expenditures in a very short time. Meanwhile, the portion of public expenditures going for human capital and infrastructure investment rose, though the absolute level dropped significantly here, too. Whereas in 1991 military expenditures still exceeded combined education and health disbursements by 14 per cent in China and by 32 per cent in Russia, now these states invest more in human capital than they do in unproductive armaments.[6] The relatively

[5] To be sure, they also rose in Bosnia-Herzegovina and Yugoslavia, which are not included in this accounting.

[6] By comparison, in the same year military expenditure exceeded combined education and health care disbursements in Israel by 6%, in Pakistan by 25%, and in Iraq by 171% (UNDP 1997).

low military expenditures in China and Russia reflect a clear policy choice: defence has been subordinated to the reforms and to transition.[7] This is indeed an important shift in the pattern of income distribution through taxation and government spending. In the contemporary world there is no analogy for such a tremendous GDP redistribution in peacetime.

Yet, these quickly shrinking items (in absolute terms) on the expenditure side of the public finance balance sheet have been replaced by other quickly climbing items. A special burden is being imposed by the mushrooming costs of social security. The burst in unemployment and the mounting outlays to support the pension system are taking their toll. To maintain or curtail the relatively high levels of government spending is hardly a policy possibility as long as the reform of social security systems has not been completed. Only when an alternative method of financing pensions is in place can additional thinning out in overall government expenditures be considered. This will not be for quite some time.

Meanwhile, the public provision for social security will remain not only high, but must grow. Populations in the postsocialist countries are ageing (World Bank 1994). The share of people over 60 is expected to exceed 25 per cent by 2030 (IMF 1998c). However, by that time, pensions will no longer be financed through the old pay-as-you-go public systems, so relative government spending will have had (perhaps) an opportunity to diminish.

Government expenditures can also be trimmed across the board without so much attention to the composition and structure of the reductions, especially if the need is urgent or the external pressure is great. Often overlooked in such a situation is the lack of services or funding sources to replace those eliminated because of the cuts. What has so far been provided by the state through the budget is now supposed to be supplied by the private sector through market allocation. This is a very difficult part of the transition exercise, and through it the importance of the coordination between transition policy and development strategy can be clearly seen.

Only in a growing economy do households have a chance of finding alternatives to these services, and then only if they have enough income. To change the system is therefore only feasible if the economy is expanding; it is ill advised to push through the relevant structural reforms at a time when their implementation will lead to a deterioration in living standards.

A study prepared at the World Bank (Commander, Davoodi, and Lee 1996) finds that a country with a proper combination of small government and good institutions may be able to double GDP in about two decades, but that a country with a bad combination of big government and poor

---

[7] In the case of China, rapidly growing income means that there has been more flexibility in identifying spending priorities. In Russia the collapse of fiscal revenue has forced military expenditures downward, so that the 'choice' has been more like an economic constraint.

institutions would need two and a half centuries to accomplish the same thing. This sounds impressive, but it looks more like mumbo-jumbo than economics. Fortunately, no modern nation anywhere anytime has needed 250 years to double its GDP, and this is not going to happen in any of the transition economies either. Anyway, the transition is not going to last that long, so there will be no chance to run the experiment. Even if the relative size of their governments is bigger than that of some of the most advanced market countries, the leading transition economies may be able to double their output in a matter of just one decade.[8]

What the study does point to correctly is the strong correlation between the rate of growth on the one hand and, on the other, the size of government and the appropriateness of institutional arrangements. The unfavourable combination of big government and low-quality institutions is a serious threat in postsocialist economies, as it is in several less-developed market economies. Such a combination favours ill-advised interventions of the weak state bureaucracy in market affairs. This may lead to improper allocations of public expenditure. It can also delay the adoption of new laws and needed market regulations.[9] It can fuel corruption, which takes resources away from the official economy.

Regulations which are transparent—especially vis-à-vis financial and capital markets, banking, privatization, and public-sector procurements— should be introduced and enforced as soon as this is feasible. The implementation of effective regulatory measures requires the sound commitment of the government. It also calls for a strong, not a weak state, and such a state must have already been redefined and redesigned.

It may be that at least part of the debate about the role of the state stems from a confusion between small and big government on the one hand and strong and weak government on the other. A lot of the confusion—if it exists—may be due to a false supposition that 'big' means 'inefficient' and that 'small' means 'efficient'. In fact, for instance, Turkmenistan has a big, strong government, which, however, is not very efficient. Meanwhile, Croatia also has a big, strong government, but it happens to be rather efficient. Whereas Latvia has a small, strong, and efficient government, Albania has a small, weak, and inefficient one.[10]

---

[8] This is what the World Bank envisages in another forecast (World Bank 1997c). If a transition economy is able to enjoy a 7% GDP growth rate over two decades, this would not be a doubling in output, but would represent a growth of nearly four times over the 20 years.

[9] Catch-22 situations sometimes arise. In Ukraine in 1998 a budget amendment could not be adopted until the summer, although it was a crucial provision required for numerous structural reforms. This occurred not because of any inability to obtain the support of a majority for the reforms or the budget amendment, but because parliament could not agree on a speaker. It failed to choose one in 11 attempts: very democratic, but very counterproductive.

[10] From a purely mathematical viewpoint, leaving aside any nuances or subtleties in terms of the specific conditions within countries, there are eight possible combinations of the words 'big' or 'small' government, 'strong' or 'weak' government, and 'efficiency' or 'inefficiency'.

The best (worst) example is Russia in the 1990s with its informal institutions and very poor regulatory framework. From time to time the government makes very serious attempts to push through sound structural reform, but the attempts quickly fail. The problem seems to be not that the government is too big, but that there are too many of them. There is a lack of transparency. What is the role of the government? What is the responsibility of the Kremlin, that is, the President's Administration? What is the attitude of the parliamentary majority toward the executive branch? What indeed is the position of the informal institutions (starting with the financial and industrial 'tycoons' and the news organizations they seem to control), which often behave as though they were another government?

In short, the government must first be strong enough to carry out its new role, and this ability is not a simple function of its size. The real choice is between the kind of regulations and the range of budgetary redistribution in efficient countries, like Hungary or Slovenia, and those in inefficient countries, like Belarus or Romania. Hungary and Slovenia have shown that, even if they do not have small governments, they do have experience, good institutions, and wise policies, and they have enjoyed good overall economic performance and an early recovery. Thus, the main challenge for the nations lagging behind in growth and development is not a reduction in the size of government, but the need to overhaul government and put it in order. This may call for downsizing, or it may not. A government can be too big, or it can be too small, but it can never be too good.

11.3. THE SIZE OF GOVERNMENT, EQUITY, AND GROWTH

The issue is not the need to decrease state expenditures, but the need to improve the allocation and efficiency of these expenditures.[11] In several nations, because of the resistance of the government bureaucracy, financing for schools and health care has been pared instead of controlling the excessive outlays for the bureaucracy. In many cases, crusades aiming at containing the size of the bureaucracy have ended up by containing only the number of teachers and doctors or adding to the arrears in salaries owed to teachers and doctors. The impact of such policies on growth and equity must be taken very seriously.

---

[11] The belief which says that the remedy lies in lower expenditures dies hard. 'The IMF will press Kiev to slash some 1,000 tax exemptions as a key condition for handing over the loan to the cash-strapped government. . . . the Fund has also asked the government to cut planned expenditures in the remaining half of the year by 30 per cent, or $2.1 billion' (*Development News* 1998d). However, even in a situation of robust growth and healthy performance, it is extremely difficult to reduce expenditures by such a huge margin; to require this in such wretched circumstances is simply unrealistic.

If the public finance system needs reform, this should be accomplished in a way which contributes both to growth and to equity. If the approach favours growth over equity or equity over growth, then we are back with the debate between liberalism and populism, and we already know that both these adversaries are wrong. If the government curbs its expenditures and its revenues simultaneously, then it is downgrading its financial effort to meet the needs of some parts of the population while boosting the net incomes of other parts of the population. So, the public finance system is redistributing resources from some individuals and groups to others.

Basically, this is a redistribution by the state to the private sector with as many implications as the number and kinds of services being affected. It might help movie theatres, but it might fail to improve health care. It may do no harm to the circulation of newspapers, but lead to the elimination of symphony orchestras. It may be justified vis-à-vis reduced support for postgraduate university studies, but it may not be justified in terms of the fall in secondary school enrolments. Perhaps postgraduate university studies can and should seek to survive without state help, but secondary school enrolments will be able to rise again only after long and painful adjustments in education at the expense of the future.

If such policies are applied, perhaps the private sector will be able to expand more quickly, but those groups will suffer that cannot now afford to pay for the services which used to cost so little when they were provided by 'big' government. Hence, even before output has started to grow, inequity has already risen a great deal. The roots and the fruits of this sort of redistributive policy, undertaken merely because of a curbstone opinion about the role and the size of the state, represent serious political challenges, not strictly economic and financial issues.

If a 'big' government economy is defined as one with public spending exceeding half of GDP (like Belgium, Italy, the Netherlands, Norway, and Sweden), and a 'small' government economy is defined as one with public spending below one-third of GDP (like Australia, Japan, Switzerland, and the United States), then the two possess similar characteristics. In 1997, the per capita output (adjusted for purchasing power parity, PPP) in the five former nations was over $21,000 and in the latter four nations around $23,000. The average annual rate of growth in 1960–95 in both cases was almost identical and equal to about 2.5 per cent. Gross fixed capital formation is also about the same, that is, 20.5 per cent and 20.7 per cent of GDP, respectively. The rate of inflation does not differ by much and in 1986–94 was at 3.9 per cent in the first group and 3.7 per cent in the second. Life expectancy at birth is 78 years in the former and 77.8 years in the latter. The respective infant mortality rates are 6.7 and 6.4 per 1,000 live births. The secondary school enrolment rate is 92.8 per cent in the big government sample and 89 per cent in the small government sample.[12] According to the composite school-enrolment ratio calculated by the UNDP, the weighted share of children of various ages attending schools in the former is 85 per cent and in the latter 82 per cent (UNDP 1997). Illiteracy rates are similarly low in both groups.

With respect to the quality of human capital and the standard of living, the admittedly minor distinctions seem generally to favour the big governments. However, what really seems to distinguish these two groups of economies is not GDP level or rate of growth, but income distribution. The bigger the government, the more equitable seems to be income distribution, and the smaller the government, the larger the share of the income distribution going to the richer part of the population. The debate therefore seems once again to be more about different interests rather than different theoretical concepts. The claim that small government is efficient government is not only an abstract intellectual argument, but it protects the interests of favoured income groups, too. This last may even be the real aim of policies designed on the basis of the inaccurate statement that small governments better satisfy social needs and serve economic welfare. They satisfy social needs and serve economic welfare, but often mainly the needs and the welfare of the privileged in society.

The two poorest quintiles of the population receive 24.1 per cent of the income distribution in countries with big governments, but 20.8 per cent in countries with small governments (Tanzi and Schuknecht 1995, Tanzi 1997b). In countries with small governments the most affluent quintile receives approximately 44 per cent of the income, while the poorest quintile takes in only a little more than 5 per cent. At the other end of the spectrum, in countries with big governments the richest quintile gains about 37 per cent of total income, while the poorest quintile gets 7.4 per cent. Thus, in countries with small governments the ratio of the income of the richest quintile relative to the income of the poorest quintile is approximately 8.3, while in countries with big governments it is about 5. That does make a difference.

There would be nothing wrong with these various ratios if they more or less reflected the contribution of the quintiles to a nation's wealth. But this is by no means clear, since the significant expansion in income dispersion in recent decades is anyway the result of an unfair distribution and does not necessarily reflect the real value of the human capital involved.[13]

---

[12] The infant mortality and secondary school enrolment rates for countries with 'small' government refer to nations in which public expenditures are below 40% of GDP. This sample clearly includes the countries mentioned above (Australia, Japan, Switzerland, and the United States), but is not necessarily limited to them.

[13] Inequality is growing internationally, too. Similar to the situation within countries, this does not reflect actual changes in the contribution of nations to global wealth, but results from the redistribution of income, this time on an international scale. Worldwide the ratio of the income received by the richest quintile relative to that of the poorest quintile jumped from an already unseemly 30 to 1 in 1960 to a shocking 59 to 1 in 1989 (UNDP 1992).

Even this might somehow be acceptable, if the inequalities enhanced the ability of an economy to grow over the long term. However, the words of neoliberals notwithstanding, it does not work this way. The truth is that, whether they have big governments or small governments, the sample countries are growing at similar average rates. Thus, in terms of equity and in a context of growth-oriented policies, the best combination seems to be not small government and good institutions, but big government and good institutions.

In fact, *big or small, the only really 'good' government is a capable government which can assure robust economic growth and a fair distribution of the results.* There are examples of countries in which government involvement in economic and social affairs is relatively substantial and in which the quality of life is more favourable than it is in countries with less government intervention in these areas (Alesina 1998). This depends mainly on the structure of government consumption and is therefore essentially a function of the policies chosen. For instance, although Vietnam shows a lower level of income per capita than does Nigeria and has a relatively bigger government, life expectancy at birth in Vietnam is 15 years longer, the chance of children surviving to the age of 5 is twice as high, and the illiteracy rate is half that of Nigeria.[14] Not surprisingly, whereas the human development index for Vietnam is 0.557, with GDP per capita at $1,208 (in PPP terms), the Nigerian HDI is 0.393, with GDP per capita at $1,351 (PPP). Consequently, the HDI rank minus the rank according to GDP per capita (PPP dollars) is 26 in Vietnam (see Table 15) and 1 in Nigeria. China has a GDP per capita at only half the level in Brazil ($2,604 and $5,362, PPP, respectively), but life expectancy at birth is four years longer in China. The relevant differences between the HDI and GDP ranks are 3 and 0, respectively (UNDP 1997). This is so simply because countries like Vietnam and China spend relatively more via the public finance system on human capital than do other countries at similar levels of development.

Thus, the size of government should be a function of the purposes the government serves, not merely a function of general 'rules' which may identify what is better and what is worse regardless of complex local economic concerns and social reasoning. The size of government evolves according to many factors which tend in several directions at once. In fact, the composition of government spending itself reflects the development process in a complicated way. It may happen that big government is sometimes better for growth and development, or that small government is in some cases more appropriate for these purposes. In some nations, big government may turn out to be unsustainable because it is too costly, and it may have to be downsized only for this reason, even if the downsizing slows growth for a while. It may be that, even if a smaller (or bigger) government would

---

[14] Data refer to 1995 (World Bank 1995d).

under some circumstances promote faster and more equitable growth, an attempt at enlarging (or downsizing) it appreciably in the wrong manner and at the wrong time may cripple performance and thus harm equity and growth.

Nonetheless, there are upper limits to the effective size of government, just as there is a limit to the amount taxes can be raised without hobbling capital formation, investment, and expansion. *Beyond some maximum, a rise in public expenditures is no longer accompanied by an increase in the quantity or an improvement in the quality of services provided by government.* This 'maximum' is believed to hover around 40 per cent of GDP (Tanzi and Schuknecht 1995). Thus, the governments defined earlier as 'big' (with public spending exceeding half of GDP) are probably too big, while the 'small governments' (with public spending below one-third of GDP) may be too small. If a drive toward further state expansion is too aggressive, government spending may pass the threshold beyond which additional increments become inefficient and no longer contribute to welfare. In countries where this has occurred, the challenge is turned around: first, how to contain state expansion and, second, how to cut non-productive public expenditure without causing erosion in the standard of living or in future development.

This is certainly not the case in postsocialist economies, where, after the initial sharp reduction in the size of government at the onset of transition, enormous efforts were undertaken to continue the process. Even the notion 'government consumption' is now being exploited to suggest that the state bureaucracy, not society, gains from government spending. If this stubborn push to downsize had permitted the sprouting up of a private sector able to use more efficiently the resources being released by the withdrawal of the state, then it might have been appropriate. However, allocative efficiency was not necessarily improving, and the more limited redistribution of GDP and the restrained fiscalism, instead of producing a positive effect, tended to aggravate the contraction and make it last longer than would probably have otherwise been the case. Moreover, the supply of social services began to dwindle, and the divestment in human capital was weakening the long-run potential for growth.

Unfortunately, policymakers were being misled by the half-baked piece of advice according to which the sooner government becomes small, the sooner the market economy can begin to rise and expand. Instead of focusing attention on the ends of policy, they burned a lot of energy attempting to adjust one important policy instrument. Thus, Jeffrey Sachs (1993) expressed the conviction that 'markets spring up as soon as central planning bureaucrats vacate the field.' So, bureaucrats vacated the field and moved to business, to the shadow economy, to policymaking, to cushy consultancy jobs, to organized crime, to countries with better economies, but the markets did not 'spring up'.

Healthy markets can expand quickly within institutionally mature systems which have abandoned central regulations and which are guided by liberalized government industrial and trade policies. This could occur in a nation like Japan, for instance (though, no doubt, Japan possesses a big bureaucratic burden and a poor regulatory environment), but it has never happened in developing and transition economies with weak institutions. In transition economies, the problem is to furnish the new state with the ability to police the economy and develop market institutions, not instantly to liquidate central planning bureaucrats, no matter who the terminator may be.

12

The Internationalization of Postsocialist Economies

12.1. TRANSITION AND GLOBALIZATION: THE ISSUE OF COORDINATION

International organizations are playing a major part in the attempt to guide the transition endeavour on an international scale. Of special significance have been the Bretton Woods institutions, which have been involved in the transition since the beginning. Other organizations, mainly the European Bank for Reconstruction and Development, the European Union, the Organization for Economic Cooperation and Development, and the World Trade Organization, though their roles and attitudes to transition differ, have also been important in the course of the transformation.

These organizations do not act exclusively on their own account. They are also employed as a means of assisting in the transition by developed market nations, especially the G-7 group, consisting of the seven most advanced market economies: Canada, France, Germany, Great Britain, Italy, Japan, and the United States. The West European nations are engaged through the EBRD and the EU in overhauling the Eastern European economies. These countries are all keen to push the transition forward quickly toward free market systems, but also to integrate the transition nations with the world economy or, in the case of the 'eastbound' EU enlargement, to integrate leading transition economies with the rest of Europe. It is thus no wonder that key changes in these economies are occurring on terms influenced significantly by the priorities of the advanced market countries.

Surprisingly, there has been little coordination among the postsocialist nations as they implement structural and institutional change. These nations have established no formal mechanism or framework to serve as the focal point for the study and the exchange of views on the transition and on development policy in Eastern Europe and the former Soviet republics. And this is certainly not because there is no perceived need for coordination. On the contrary; it is truly desired within these countries, just as a similar mechanism to coordinate policy responses would be welcome among the crisis-torn Asian nations. Since nobody has been able to control the spread of the Asian contagion, it is only ex post that policy coordination has been proposed on a global scale through the IMF

Interim Committee, especially vis-à-vis capital flows and the performance of emerging markets. This committee may eventually be upgraded and enhanced through periodic meetings of the heads-of-state of the 24 participating countries.

There are two reasons for the negligence. First, according to the neo-liberal bias and market fundamentalism, coordination at the regional level is not at all necessary and would only interfere with transition, which is proceeding firmly forward without it. Liberalization and globalization will suffice. Moreover, any policy coordinating institution would presumably resemble the defunct Comecon.

This last is a particularly irrelevant argument since Comecon was dissolved for good reasons, and transition policies ought to be coordinated for another set of good reasons. In any case, there should at least be a periodic conference of key policymakers from those transition countries seeking closer cooperation and policy guidance. This would only help enhance policy efficiency and facilitate the exchange of experiences.

Second, it has been assumed that the coordinating role can be handled adequately by the EBRD and the Bretton Woods institutions. This assumption would be correct if three other conditions were fulfilled. First, the interests of these organizations must correspond closely to the interests of the transition economies. Second, the transition economies must be able to influence the transition policies of these organizations. Third, the transition economies must be able to use these organizations to coordinate their own efforts. None of these conditions has been met.

It would be naïve to expect the rich nations not to take advantage of the collapse of the socialist system. Their insistence that the transition economies should quickly become open must be seen as natural behaviour. The immediate liberalization of capital and financial markets and the rapid privatization of state assets, among other measures, are considered very suitable because they promote not only transition as such, but Western interests, too. As long as they are compatible with the interests of transition economies, then such measures are fine. The problem is that this is not always so.

The emerging middle and upper classes in the transition countries have a strong interest in the success of the liberalization and privatization processes. They support fast 'Westernization', but they are not paying attention to the needs at the other end of the social rainbow. They have too much to gain and so little time.

However, healthy Westernization in the positive sense of a well-performing market economy and an active civic society is not feasible if the expansion of the middle class and of its well-being is accompanied by spreading poverty. Poverty is unfair. It also threatens political stability. Anyway, under such circumstances the business climate is not going to be favourable for domestic entrepreneurs or foreign investors. Likewise, if income becomes too unequal and 'Westernization' is seen by the new poor as a cause of their impoverishment, then the atmosphere for foreign involvement in overhauling the postsocialist economy is going to be stormy.

Nonetheless, that the new rich are in favour of foreign participation, while the new poor are not, is not always true. It depends. Some new rich are against the participation of foreigners, because without it they can make better deals, for instance through insider trading and connections with cronies who still have influential positions in the state bureaucracy. Some new poor are in favour of growing foreign involvement if only because they can at least afford a little bit of the goods now so readily available without queuing, though not yet available without cash.

A judicious policy would assure that a wide spectrum of the people in transition societies are in favour of growing links with the world economy. To accomplish this, a balance is needed between sharing the costs and sharing the fruits of the transition not only within the societies, but internationally as well. Foreign capital and foreign governments, in sound accord with international organizations, ought to prefer long-term investment and reasonable technical assistance which facilitates transition and serves the purpose of ongoing globalization. This approach works on behalf of all the parties involved. It creates within transition societies, if not support for the internationalization of the economy, then at least a calm climate.

However, if the foreign partners are less interested in long-term investment, the upgrading of industrial capacity, and the provision of assistance in the process of labour redeployment and if they are more interested in quick profits in trade, speculative investment, and non-transparent privatization deals conducted with corrupt local officials and the new rich, then a majority of people, including some of the new middle class, will remain suspicious and resist the more thoroughgoing involvement of foreign partners in 'their' affairs.

It so happens that in the era of the global economy the transition economies are already not exclusively 'theirs' anymore. The opening up of these societies to myriad contacts with the outside world is generating a cultural revolution. This is true even in the more geopolitically remote former Soviet republics. Indeed, the level of 'globalization' is no longer measured in terms of the number of bottles of soft drinks drunk or the dimensions of the market for hamburgers. Nor is it measured by the penetration of the emerging and the developing market economies by industrial machinery from everywhere else. The level of globalization can be measured by the fact that the imported cars, home appliances, and electronic gadgets are threatening trade balances, which have swung from surpluses following early devaluation and stabilization to deficits, especially in quickly growing economies. The level of globalization can be measured by the fact that pension benefits in developed market countries may now depend at least in part on the rate of return from pension funds invested in postsocialist emerging market countries. And the level of globalization can be measured by the fact that sometimes a government in a transition economy may have to increase the pension arrears owed by its own social security system in order to service the mounting public debt due to the interest it must pay on the bonds it has sold to pension funds in developed market nations. Pensioners in Arizona or Florida, like pensioners in Siberia, are blissfully unaware of this, but the economists and policymakers ought to be aware of it.

The way an economy opens up to links with the outside world matters as much for the elites as it does for ordinary people. If the inflow of foreign capital creates new well-paying jobs and if, for some of the new income, one can buy more goods no matter who the buyer, who the seller, and who the producer, then the opening may be healthy. But if the shops are full of goods which have been imported or are made by local firms owned by foreign capital or foreign firms operating locally, and if only a few people can afford the goods anyway, then the opening may not be so sensible, including for the foreign investors.[1]

People in the West may be tempted sometimes to evaluate the efficiency of a country's transition policies not according to GDP growth or the satisfaction of the basic needs of the people, but by the way the downtown streets look in the capital city.[2] Quite often they look pretty good because, unfortunately, the streets everywhere else look pretty bad. Even respected journals publish elaborate accounts of the presumed achievements of infant Russian capitalism because there are now Western-style up-market shopping streets (a sort of Fifth Avenue for Muscovites). However, it should be made clear that the vast corruption and the salary and pension arrears are not on display in the shop windows. Moreover, not only the nice looking, pricey shops, but also the not so nice daily lives of ordinary citizens shape the political environment in which foreign participation in the transition process must occur.

12.2. THE ROLE OF INTERNATIONAL ORGANIZATIONS

Their attempts to join the World Trade Organization, the Organization for Economic Cooperation and Development, and the European Union have special meaning for the leading transition nations. Of less importance,

---

[1] In the aftermath of the financial crisis and the currency devaluation in Russia in 1998, the supply of consumer goods and real household consumption deteriorated rapidly. This occurred partly because a bulk of consumer goods were being imported or were being produced locally using imported intermediate goods. It is thought that prior to the crisis as much as 80% of the consumer goods available in Moscow and more than 40% of the consumer goods available in Russia had been imported.

[2] Asked to name the greatest achievement of the stabilization programme in Poland in 1991, an advisor to the government answered that one could now buy kiwi fruit in Warsaw.

though not negligible, especially in the aftermath of the turmoil on global financial markets, is the cooperation between the central banks of the transition countries and the Bank for International Settlement, particularly in the areas of banking sector supervision and transparent and prudent banking regulations. This organization can play an even bigger role in institution-building, especially in bank restructuring and consolidation. Healthy banking systems are crucial for stabilization and capital allocation.

The process of joining the World Trade Organization, or a desire to do so, has accelerated trade liberalization in several nations. It has also been used by the G-7 governments to push through systemic and policy changes which have had an impact on international trade and liberalization in some postsocialist countries. The discussions of the WTO and the G-7 with China and Russia have been very influential on the market transformations occurring in these two huge economies. As usual, politics is also involved in these discussions. Thus, non-economic factors, including the status of human and minority rights, have been cited as reasons for the delay in China's membership in the WTO, despite the enormous progress of China in economic liberalization.

Participation in the WTO for all members, including transitional economies, has obvious benefits. First, members have more secure access to global markets. The process of removing trade tariffs and non-tariff barriers enlarges the limits of these markets, thereby enhancing the ability of all open economies to expand.

Second, since member nations must observe the international rules of trade agreed within the WTO, they are more able to resist domestic protectionist pressures. In the effort to prod through unpopular domestic industrial and trade policy measures, it is sometimes very useful to have the ready excuse of international obligations.

Third, member countries, even the relatively weaker ones, may count on fair treatment in any trade disputes with fellow members (Michalopoulos 1997). If, despite the free market ideology and official political support for free trade, a weaker partner is discriminated against or taken advantage of by a stronger one, then WTO arbitrage can come to the rescue.

Fourth, WTO members possess greater credibility in the face of international investors and can thus attract larger inflows of badly needed foreign direct investments.

Membership negotiations with the Organization for Economic Cooperation and Development in 1994–6 led to a great deal of acceleration in liberalization in the Czech Republic, Hungary, and Poland, especially the regulation of capital transfers and foreign investments. The governments of these nations worked with the OECD Committee on Capital Movements and International Transactions, which is responsible for the implementation of and compliance with the organization's Codes of Liberalization of Capital Movements and Current Invisible Operations. The new members are going to adopt these principles, which are legally binding instruments accepted by OECD countries. Certain transitory reservations and exceptions on specific items apply to new members, including those from Eastern Europe, but there is an agreed commitment that these will be lifted in due course (meaning that there will be tough and complex negotiations before any 'lifting' occurs).

Progress toward the gradual liberalization of capital movements and invisible transactions has been achieved in other nations, too. Conscious of the OECD membership requirements, but essentially on their own behalf, the Baltic States, Slovakia, and Slovenia have taken steps to widen the scope of liberalization. An official statement issued by Russia in September 1997 concerning a commitment to apply for association (though this is impossible for the time being) should also be considered through the prism of the readiness to carry out economic liberalization in line with OECD regulations and standards. While Russia's was a political gesture rather than a formal bid for application, the Baltic States and Slovenia have decided not to approach the OECD at this stage of transition. Following the experience of the Czech Republic, Hungary, and Poland, they are aware of the hard conditions which must be met before accession is possible.

The most difficult transition issues negotiated with the OECD by the Czech Republic, Hungary, and Poland have revolved around the liberalization of capital flows and the regulation of foreign direct investments. These are serious issues as far as OECD development policy is concerned. Hence the OECD has insisted very firmly on the need for rapid and far-reaching liberalization and deregulation.

However, in the Baltic States and Slovenia there is some reluctance to lift restrictions on the acquisition of real estate. Rightly or wrongly, for a number of reasons, including political and sentimental ones, they are wary of foreigners making a run on choice properties. The same concern was raised rather loudly within Poland during its negotiations with the OECD. In Slovenia one hears this fear expressed in relation to Italians, and in the Baltic States it arises toward Germans and Russians.[3] There may be no solid economic rationale for these reservations, but they must not be neglected since they can easily shift from simple concerns into insurmountable political challenges.

Another sticking point is the OECD insistence on transparent regulations on bank secrecy. The OECD wants the transparency so as to make price transferring more difficult to use as a means of money laundering or of hiding otherwise taxable profits from tax authorities.[4] However, in transition countries and in many other emerging markets there is strong

[3] Even Denmark maintains restrictions on the sale of land to foreigners because of a fear that Germans would buy up much of the available real estate.

[4] 'Price transferring' is the manipulation of price and cost information through accounting tricks carried out on an international level.

opposition to such a step from banks and financial organizations with influence in the media and among political parties. To break down this opposition is not easy, and a certain amount of political will must exist to do so. In the case of Poland, if not for the significant pressure from the OECD, the relevant amendments would not have been enacted. Whenever the issue was brought up, there was an attempt to kill it by hostile lobbying, while the central bank hemmed and hawed rather than driving the reforms forward through all political obstacles.

Some nations are not yet ready to accept the OECD requirements regarding capital flows because they are afraid that liberalization would lead to financial destabilization, thereby exposing the economy to the risk of severe external shocks. They are right, since liberalization in this area requires sound financial fundamentals and a sophisticated institutional framework. In its negotiations over this issue with the OECD, the Czech Republic was keen to show a willingness to accept very liberal regulations in order to prove its determination to go to the free market as speedily as possible. However, quite soon, only a year and a half after it joined the OECD, the country experienced a currency crisis because it had not been sufficiently concerned about the medium-term effects of the liberalization on current account sustainability and currency fluctuations.

In contrast, Poland was able to negotiate a slightly more gradual path toward the liberalization of capital flows, and this was one reason it avoided a similar crisis. Actually, among new OECD members—Mexico (since 1994), Hungary and the Czech Republic (1995), Poland (1996), and the Republic of Korea (1997)—only Poland has been able to sidestep an economic emergency linked to the poor regulation of capital flows and weak banking supervision. In some countries, the instant the confidence of investors in the economy was shaken by unexpected events, a crisis erupted. This proves only that liberalization and openness to international capital movements can be positive if there is careful policymaking and institution-building.

The series of crises among new members seems to have played a part in the fact that the OECD now appears less eager to take on fresh candidates. Another important cause is the spreading concern about the future of an organization which includes nations at such different levels of development as the United States and Mexico, Japan and South Korea, or Germany and Poland. Even if the liberal regulatory environments are becoming similar in these countries thanks to OECD technical assistance and the leverage it exercises, the development gap remains very large, and real partnership and cooperation are not always so easy within the OECD.

Some countries have found a good reason to join the OECD in the fact that this represents a strong argument for acceptance in the European Union. Naturally, it is possible to join the EU without joining the OECD, as is likely to be the case of Estonia and Slovenia, but this can be a slightly more difficult route. If Bulgaria, Latvia, Lithuania, Romania, and Slovakia had joined the OECD before 1997–8, when the current list of applicants to the EU was determined, then they would have had a better chance of being included on this list. This is not because OECD membership necessarily carries with it a deciding influence, but simply because the procedure leading to OECD membership is an important additional catalyst for certain major structural reforms and institutional changes. In any case, for the Czech Republic, Hungary, and Poland, the process of approaching the OECD was part of the process of approaching the EU. The reforms implemented during that time facilitated the course of the transition to the market economy, as well as of integration with the EU.

12.3. THE SPECIAL MISSION OF THE IMF AND THE WORLD BANK

Conditions are such in the postsocialist nations that the position of certain international organizations is relatively stronger there than it is elsewhere. This is so for many reasons, but especially because of the rather weak penetration of private capital in this area of the global economy. The transition nations are cash starved, but the growth they are seeking needs plenty of capital. Foreign governments are anxious to see the political and economic systems change quickly in these nations, but they do not wish to become entangled in complicated financial, legal, and technical difficulties. This represents an ideal situation for international organizations able to supply capital, expertise on market economy performance, and an arena for the indirect involvement of foreign governments. Hopefully, they will never consider a deserved dose of constructive criticism always out of place, but for once it ought also to be admitted that the contribution of these international organizations has been significant and positive.

The governments of countries in transition have always turned first for money and advice to the International Monetary Fund and the World Bank.[5] Quite soon they realize that from these two they obtain less money than advice on the policies needed to generate more money (and less advice) in due time. Though often they may not apply the policies, the bargaining procedures and the lengthy discussions are very useful in the process of learning by doing. This alone has represented a unique investment in human capital. Owing to the rapid rotation of government officials and higher level civil servants and the fact that many of them have left to work as executives in the private sector, the quality of the state bureaucracy and of corporate governance throughout the economy has been upgraded through the contacts with these organizations.

[5] In contrast, the European Bank for Reconstruction and Development, for instance, mostly lends to the private sector or for projects enhancing privatization.

Likewise, the persuasion and insistence employed especially by the IMF, but also by the World Bank, to push through certain policies have been important. The arguments on the way structural adjustment policies ought to be framed and implemented have been instructive, and they have influenced policymaking.

Of course, the credit for the policy achievements, as well as the blame for the policy failures, ought to be laid squarely at the door of the governments and the policymakers, but it must be acknowledged that, without the active and capable participation of the Bretton Woods institutions, the transition to the market economy would be more difficult. Despite many false starts, meaningful steps toward a market economy have been taken in the transition region, and, though late in coming, there is a chance for durable growth. *Because of the significant involvement of the IMF and the World Bank, the systemic transition has made more overall progress, and sustainable development has become more likely.*

Nonetheless, membership in the IMF and the World Bank has not helped the transition countries much in the regional coordination of transition policies and development strategies. Initial discussions between IMF staff and the fiscal and monetary authorities of these nations—the ministries of finance and central banks—were typically a sort of one-way street, without too much attention being given by the former to the views of the latter. The participation of the representatives of the transition economies in the 'constituencies' of Bretton Woods institutions is designed in a way which limits the opportunities for comprehensive coordination among the economic policies of the transition countries, as well as among the policies of these countries toward the organizations. Only China and Russia have been able to afford to establish themselves as single-country constituencies, so that their position is relatively stronger.[6] As for the others, they have been dispersed among various groups, which are sometimes organized so that the transition nations, even if there is a number of them together, do not have much say in the formulation of proposals, let alone the design of policies. A group is usually led by an advanced market country, and the other group members have only a minor influence on the policies of the organization, including the policies toward them.

The most well composed constituency in terms of postsocialist countries is the one led by Finland, since it is established on a clearly regional basis. The other members are the Nordic advanced market countries (Denmark, Iceland, Norway, and Sweden) and the three Baltic States (Estonia, Latvia, and Lithuania, which are transition countries). But for the remaining postsocialist economies, there are no clear links between them and the leaders and other members of their constituencies. For example,

---

[6] France, Germany, Great Britain, Japan, Saudi Arabia, and the United States form the other single-country constituencies.

the constituency led by Switzerland contains Poland and five former Soviet republics (Azerbaijan, Kyrgyzstan, Tajikistan, Turkmenistan, and Uzbekistan). The constituency led by Belgium includes three other market economies (Austria, Luxembourg, and Turkey) and six transition nations (Belarus, the Czech Republic, Hungary, Kazakhstan, Slovakia, and Slovenia). The constituency led by the Netherlands consists of Cyprus and Israel, as well as a number of transition economies (Armenia, Bosnia-Herzegovina, Bulgaria, Croatia, Georgia, FYR Macedonia, Moldova, Romania, and Ukraine).

It would be more reasonable and desirable to put transition countries together according to geopolitical criteria so that neighbours are not separated. What may have somehow made sense at the beginning of the transition in 1990 is not necessarily a suitable solution for the situation in 2000. So, why not establish at least one strong and competent constituency, if not exclusively of transition economies, then led by them?

Yet, the postsocialist countries must agree that it should be this way, too. However, there is sometimes an atmosphere of competition and even rivalry among them based upon the false assumption that this is a better method to gain political and financial support. But now more than ever there is a real need for sound policy coordination among these nations.

In the absence of other appropriate institutional arrangements, the creation of task force groups working within the international financial organizations might be a good means to coordinate policies, monitor developments, and funnel advice to transition countries. If it is considered natural that the US executive director in IMF can be called to appear before a Congressional hearing in Washington on support for American interests and policies within the IMF Board, why should it not be possible for Eastern European and CIS governments to have an organizational means to express their views in a coordinated way? If they are too small and too weak to act separately within the Bretton Woods institutions, this is all the more reason for them to seek to act together so that they are neither so small, nor so weak.

The composition of the 24 constituencies in each of the Bretton Woods institutions is determined on the basis of quotas in 'special drawing rights' (that is, according to the value of contributions to the institutions). Thus, an individual nation cannot join a constituency as it pleases (unless, of course, it contributes sufficiently to form a single-country constituency). However, a constituency could still be led by a transition country, just as less-developed countries now lead several existing constituencies. For instance, Mozambique currently leads the constituency of 22 sub-Saharan countries, including much stronger and more developed South Africa and Zimbabwe.[7]

---

[7] The other 19 countries are: Angola, Botswana, Burundi, Eritrea, Ethiopia, the Gambia, Kenya, Lesotho, Liberia, Malawi, Namibia, Nigeria, Seychelles, Sierra Leone, Sudan, Swaziland, Tanzania, Uganda, and Zambia.

Kuwait leads a constituency of countries in the Middle East and North Africa.[8] The Philippines heads up a group of countries in South America and the Caribbean.[9] Finally, Bolivia leads a constituency composed of several Latin American countries.[10] In these last two cases, the constituency leadership rotates, so that before the Philippines and Bolivia, the leaders were Brazil and Argentina, respectively. Hence the architecture of particular groups is not solely a matter of financial quotas, but political preferences play a role as well, and there could be a constituency led on a rotating basis by, for example, Estonia, Hungary, or Poland, or by the Czech Republic, Kazakhstan, or Ukraine. This would help in the formulation of regional policy and might raise the efficiency of the responses the Bretton Woods institutions address to these countries.

There are reasons for the current constituency structure. It was more comfortable for the IMF and the World Bank to spread the transition countries out among various constituency leaders. Moreover, several serious attempts on the part of these organizations to enhance the cooperation among the transition nations failed because of the lack of interest of these nations, which appear to share only the conviction that there is much more to be learned from the experience of the developed and developing market economies than from each other's failures and achievements.

The process of learning by doing has therefore occurred through an intermediary, since the IMF and the World Bank have not been able to provide sufficient institutional platforms for direct contacts among experts and policymakers from transition countries. Despite the flaws, however, knowledge and experience have been acquired. Moreover, the process of learning by doing is taking place within the Bretton Woods institutions, too, so that these organizations are becoming the international financial intermediaries of the transition, but also the international intermediaries of transition knowledge.

Yet, before these institutions could absorb the lessons, the questionable structural adjustment policies they had framed and proposed were tending to worsen the situation in postsocialist economies. Across Eastern Europe and the former Soviet republics, the once distorted centrally planned economies were becoming 'Latinized', so that the differences between them and distorted developing market economies, mainly those of Latin America, were shrinking. At the onset of the 1990s, these differences were substantial. Now, these two groups of economies, so diverse in background, are a little less distinct. The Russian economy of today recalls not the Russian

---

[8] Besides Kuwait, this constituency consists of Bahrain, Egypt, Jordan, Lebanon, Libya, Maldives, Oman, Qatar, Syria, United Arab Emirates, and Yemen.
[9] The constituency includes Brazil, Colombia, Dominican Republic, Ecuador, Haiti, Suriname, and Trinidad and Tobago.
[10] In this constituency are also Argentina, Chile, Paraguay, Peru, and Uruguay.

economy of the beginning of the decade, but the Brazilian economy of the late 1980s. The two differed substantially back then. This is no longer so. The same can be said of a number of other 'Latin-transition' pairs, say, Chile and the Czech Republic, Argentina and Poland, Uruguay and Latvia, or Nicaragua and Georgia.

Two groups of economies that were different at the end of the 1980s and the beginning of the 90s have become similar because the Washington consensus erroneously thought that the transition group required similar policy solutions. A shoulder-numbing shot of good anti-distorted-developing-market-economy vaccine was given to the wrong patient, and, in one of those ironies of nature, the patient has acquired the symptoms of a highly-distorted emerging market economy. Indeed, why not compose a new IMF and World Bank constituency from Latin American, Eastern European, and CIS nations?

The Bretton Woods institutions are normally perceived as lending institutions. For obvious reasons, the lending is subject to 'conditionalities' and is tied to numerous structural reforms. Therefore, what matters is how much money is being lent, but also the conditions which apply and the purposes of the reforms.

Whereas the IMF is concerned basically with financial fundamentals such as sound fiscal stance, a balanced current account, a stable currency, and low inflation, the focus of the World Bank is the restructuring of industrial capacity, infrastructure upgrading, and human capital investment. Thus, the IMF aims at stabilization, while the World Bank aims at growth. Each is also involved in structural reform and institution-building, the IMF being oriented to equilibrium and financial stabilization, and the World Bank to long-term development. For these reasons it may be a mistake to put both institutions on the same footing or to speak their names in the same breath, as one might say 'Marx and Engels'.

The financial support provided by the IMF to government budgets and the current account balance and the lending supplied by the World Bank for retraining and manpower redeployment, social security reform, health care upgrading, hard infrastructure, and environmental protection have been remarkably useful to the transition economies. Throughout the region during the early transition, as well as now in several countries with only limited access to private resources, a bulk of the external financing has been provided by these two organizations. Becoming active somewhat later, the EBRD has been helpful, too. Bilateral assistance, though more important for certain countries, has been relatively minor.

It should be remembered that the money comes in loans, not grants. The money is supposed to be allocated efficiently to foster systemic transition and socioeconomic development, but it takes the form of credits which must be paid back and which bear interest. So, the relationship is a business (and political) one, not charity.

The lending is always conducted through phased 'tranches' of credit that are to be used for specific purposes which have been agreed upon beforehand. The release of the tranches is usually well publicized. The government authorities take care of the publicity themselves. The conditions for the lending of the Bretton Woods institutions are known to be tough. Of course, in the age of the liberal global economy, a government capable of meeting tough conditions is a good government. If the government is good, everyone should know about it.

This mechanism also operates in another direction. The IMF performance criteria, which are used to assess the fiscal and monetary profile of an economy, are always linked to fiscal stance, the monetary aggregates, and the external financial position. They are well publicized, too, so that, similar to the situation with the credit tranches, there is always much more public debate over meeting or missing the criteria than the issue actually deserves. Often it is difficult to satisfy the criteria, but a government can nonetheless become exposed to strong pressure to succeed. If the government does not succeed, it can still succumb to the temptation to blame the criteria or the policies imposed by the 'outsiders'.

If subsequent tranches of stand-by credit are not urgently needed, it may be better to take them anyway and try to meet the performance criteria. This is so for three reasons. First, during the troublesome period of structural adjustment the demand for external financing is great, but if a transition economy has no access to private capital markets it can acquire the financing only through the IMF. Then, after achieving some progress in stabilization and structural reform, the country may apply for a credit evaluation, usually to the American rating agencies Moody's or S&P, or the British agency IBCA. Only with a proper grading is there a chance to approach international capital markets and try to borrow at commercial rates through the Eurobond or global bond issues. Thus, without a good relationship with the IMF, there is little likelihood for a good relationship with capital markets.

Second, reaching an agreement with the IMF is a seal of approval for prudent policies and thus opens up access to additional credits from the World Bank, the EBRD, and private commercial banks. In the early 1990s no postsocialist country could hope to acquire a major foreign commercial bank lending without the endorsement of its economic policies by the IMF. Even today, such a relationship is understood to be necessary.

Third, the IMF performance evaluation is a strong point in favour of or against a government's policies. If the evaluation is positive, this strengthens the government's position and credibility in dealing with other issues. If it is negative, the government's standing is weakened. The effort to fulfil the performance criteria is monitored by the IMF, the business community, and international investors and financiers, but also by the political opposition waiting in the wings. This can render policymaking even more difficult.

There is no doubt that the IMF and the World Bank had more say with governments during the early transition. The paradox is that they had much less of value to say at the time because of their lack of experience with the unique problems of the postsocialist nations. Later, though the Bretton Woods institutions gradually came to learn more through their monitoring functions and to understand which policy proposals had a better chance of working, their influence began to decline, particularly in transition economies doing relatively well. If structural reform has made sound progress, then the technical advice and financing assistance of these institutions, though still sought, are less critical.[11]

Economic recovery and growth encourage more inflows of foreign private investment and commercial lending from the private sector. As growth gains momentum, official lending begins to fall, and private investment and credit begin to increase. Simultaneously, the influence of private entities (investment banks, hedge funds, rating agencies, consulting firms, research establishments) on economic matters is expanding, while that of individual foreign governments and international organizations is shrinking.

There can also be turnarounds the instant another severe crisis occurs. The extent to which this is true can be gauged by the shift in relative power between the private sector and official institutions during the Asian crisis. While the crisis was caused mainly by the private sector, it must now be solved mainly by governments and international organizations. There has been a similar, though opposite shift especially in the more successful transition economies, where less and less is depending on governments and more and more on the private sector.

Clearly, *if a country is confronted by a deteriorating economy, then the sway of the IMF and the World Bank becomes stronger.* Only then is the government obliged—like it or not—to seek assistance; only then is it obliged to listen to the recommendations of outsiders, and only then does it not consider blaming the outsiders for intervening in its internal affairs. Thus, the Bretton Woods institutions have a greater say (and, more importantly, a greater power of decision), for example, in Russia than in China. In 1997–8 they were much more influential in Albania, Bulgaria, and Romania than they were in Hungary, Poland, or Slovenia.

---

[11] One might call the technical advice 'soft' not only because it is abstract, but also because it is always easier to give advice ('tighten your belt', 'cut expenditure', 'withdraw subsidies', 'close state companies', 'fire superfluous workers') than it is to apply it. In the same spirit, 'hard' (because tangible) financial assistance is more difficult to come by. There is always an excessive supply of easy advice and an insufficient supply of hard financing, but this is especially true during early transition, when the economy is weaker and more vulnerable.

12.4. INTEGRATION WITH THE WORLD ECONOMY

The amount of a country's openness toward, and the range of its integration with, the world economy have a significant impact on its ability to expand. Likewise, *the more integrated a country is into the world economy, the more its development will follow the overall trend in growth of the global economy*. This may not always be good news because of sluggish economic performance occurring from time to time in other regions or among the most advanced market nations. By the same token, because transition countries are trying to catch up with the developed market economies, they may end up growing at a faster rate than these economies, and, owing to ongoing integration, this can favour sustained growth in the global economy, too. Such a phenomenon may already be on the near horizon, since the transition economies are still expanding despite the East Asian contagion and the Japanese recession.

Integration with the world economy has fundamental implications for a country's expansion in trade and capital absorption. Rising exports and imports provide access to new markets, and foreign competition fosters technological and managerial upgrading. The greater openness also promotes the inflow of much-needed capital, which must be attracted for the purpose of closing the gap between the amount of domestic savings and the demand for new investments. The call for fresh capital is so intense in the transition economies that Eastern Europe alone will absorb at least another $150 billion during the first decade of the 21st century. The bulk of this inflow will be supplied by the private sector, and the relative influence of international financial institutions will therefore decline further. Substantial capital will be invested in the CIS if economic reform and political stabilization endure.

The leading transition economies will also be able to integrate rather rapidly with the world economy. Some Eastern European countries will have the option of joining the European Union. Socioeconomic development in the former Soviet republics in Central Asia could be as remarkable as that of South Korea between the 1960s and the 90s. Certain among these countries may eventually join ASEAN or join together in a new association, and for all of them there is the prospect of becoming members of the World Trade Organization fairly soon.

Since the collapse of the Soviet system and the dismantling of the Soviet Union and of Comecon, there has been much unravelling of regional structures, but there have also been new—and sometimes strange—forms of regional 'reintegration'. Four former Soviet republics, Belarus, Kazakhstan, Kyrgyzstan, and Russia, have created a 'common market'; these four countries belong to three different constituencies in the IMF and the World Bank. A socioeconomic union, with a commitment to eventual monetary unification, has been established between Belarus and Russia (two different constituencies). Georgia, Ukraine, Armenia, and Moldova have instituted the GUAM group of countries (a single constituency). In Eastern Europe the Central European Free Trade Agreement is active in the establishment of smooth trade arrangements. Other new regional and subregional organizations will certainly appear to facilitate growth, regional economic integration, and international economic cooperation.

However, such efforts at integration among these nations are not the real answer to the challenge of sound regionwide cooperation. More important at the current stage of development is regional policy coordination vis-à-vis other governments (which do coordinate their policies), other regions, international relations, and the global economy. There is no need for Central Europe to seek close economic ties, lavish trade, and integration with emerging markets in Central Asia, since these have more natural economic partners, but there is a true need to coordinate transition and development policies among all the emerging market countries.

In Denver in June 1997, Russia participated for the first time in a summit of the G-7 group of the world's largest economies. This exercise was repeated at the Birmingham summit in 1998. The invitation to Russia to participate in the economic policymaking deliberations has been forthcoming more because of political factors than because of economic ones. In the not too distant future China may also be invited to participate. However, all this is quite artificial. As long as there was only the G-7, the 'who's who' of the global economy was evident. Now, it is only a matter of time and political opportunity before the G-7 becomes the 'G-9', and the signals become jumbled. Neither Russia, the relative importance of which in the global economy is declining rapidly, nor China, which is enhancing its international economic standing day by day, are suited to the G-7 formula. (The same is true of Brazil and India.) They may be huge economies, but Russia and China are definitely not developed, nor will they be for at least several more decades. In fact, the old G-7 group is still quite alive; it is merely trying out another method to manipulate the course of the global economy according to its preferences and interests. The participation of Russia has been only minor and will not be sufficient to allow that country to influence global issues to any very great extent.

There is a sort of pattern that transition nations follow in becoming integrated in the world economy. They have first joined the Bretton Woods institutions.[12] Several of them, having proceeded rapidly with trade liberalization, have then become members of the World Trade Organization. Among the 135 members of the WTO are Bulgaria, the Czech Republic, Estonia, Hungary, Kyrgyzstan, Latvia, Mongolia, Poland, Romania, Slovakia,

---

[12] Some were already members of the IMF and the World Bank prior to the transition, for example Romania since 1972 and Hungary since 1982.

and Slovenia (as well as Cuba, which was a founder-member of the General Agreement on Tariffs and Trade, the predecessor of the WTO).

Once more, countries which undertook precocious market reform during the central planning period have had an advantage. Thus, their previous participation in the General Agreement on Tariffs and Trade has helped Hungary, Poland, and Slovenia to become members of the WTO without much difficulty.

Even countries which are lagging behind in the transition are finding their way to this institution. Among the 30 applicants to the WTO in 1998 were Albania, Armenia, Belarus, China, Croatia, Estonia, Georgia, Kazakhstan, Lithuania, Moldova, Russia, Ukraine, Uzbekistan, Vietnam, and Yugoslavia. The membership of China and Russia (and to a lesser extent Ukraine) is contingent on conditionalities which are similar to those for the early post-socialist members. Unlike the IMF and the World Bank, in which all post-socialist members have been admitted unconditionally, the WTO imposes economic and political conditions, such as further political liberalization in the case of China or a solution to local conflicts in the case of Croatia.

For some Eastern European countries, success in the attempt to join the European Union is most important. Joining is a long and difficult process, but certainly a most encouraging endeavour in terms of the progress in economic and political transition that can be achieved (Eatwell et al. 1997). *The ambition to join the EU undoubtedly arouses efforts to transform economic and political systems.*

By 1996, 10 transition countries—Bulgaria, the Czech Republic, Estonia, Hungary, Latvia, Lithuania, Poland, Romania, Slovakia, and Slovenia— were associated with the EU (Tables 30 and 31). The Czech Republic, Estonia, Hungary, Poland, and Slovenia started negotiations for full membership in March 1998, and there is a chance that they will join sometime after 2003. One may safely assume that in due course there will be a follow-up for the remaining associate countries, Bulgaria, Latvia, Lithuania, Romania, and Slovakia. Considering its progress with systemic transition, Croatia also deserves to be seen as a future member no less than, say, Bulgaria or Romania.

In inviting the Czech Republic, Estonia, Hungary, Poland, and Slovenia to discuss the terms of integration, the EU stressed that the first round of candidates had been selected on the basis of 'complete objective criteria. . . . The prerequisites for entry include a functioning market economy, the existence of democratic institutions and respect for ethnic minorities, the ability to compete in the single market, and reasonable public administration' (Barber 1997). Marketization matters, but democratization is important, too. The eastbound enlargement of the EU is as much an economic endeavour as it is a political venture.

In some cases, there are problems with certain aspects of the introduction of a full-fledged civic society in the EU aspirants. For instance, the

Table 30 Population and GDP in the EU and EU-associated
Eastern European economies, 1996

	Population (millions)	GDP per capita	
		EU average	PPP Ecu
All EU members	372.1	100	17,300
Austria	8.0	110.4	—
Belgium	10.1	110.8	—
Britain	58.1	95.6	—
Denmark	5.2	115.1	—
Finland	5.1	95.7	—
France	58.1	106.0	—
Germany	81.6	109.0	—
Greece	10.4	65.4	—
Ireland	3.5	96.9	—
Italy	57.2	103.3	—
Luxembourg	0.4	166.4	—
Netherlands	15.5	106.6	—
Portugal	9.8	67.3	—
Spain	39.6	76.4	—
Sweden	8.8	99.4	—
EU-associated countries	108.2	100	5,500
Bulgaria	8.5	18.6	4,200
Czech Republic[a]	10.3	50.9	9,100
Estonia[a]	1.5	24.8	3,900
Hungary[a]	10.1	32.1	6,300
Latvia	2.5	16.8	3,100
Lithuania	3.7	18.1	3,900
Poland[a]	38.6	32.1	5,300
Romania	22.7	23.6	4,100
Slovakia	5.3	39.1	7,100
Slovenia[a]	1.9	34.6	10,100

[a] Countries already negotiating terms of accession.

Sources: European Commission and OECD data.

treatment of the tiny gypsy minority in the Czech Republic or the attitude toward the large Russian minority in Estonia rubs the wrong way. However, the long process leading to membership by all means contributes to better and faster resolutions of these sorts of problems.

Among the other five nations associated with the EU, only Bulgaria and Romania are lagging behind substantially in the prospects for EU

Table 31 Agriculture in EU-associated economies, 1995

	% GDP	Share of exports to EU (%)
Bulgaria	13.0	56.0
Czech Republic	5.0	58.1
Estonia	7.1	63.1
Hungary	6.0	39.5
Latvia	8.5	59.2
Lithuania	9.5	48.7
Poland	6.6	62.2
Romania	20.0	48.4
Slovakia	5.6	40.3
Slovenia	4.8	68.3
EU 15	2.3	65.0

Source: European Commission.

membership, especially with respect to marketization. Slovakia, albeit taking a more radical path toward economic reform and usually reckoned among the nations most advanced in transition (see Table 14), has been omitted from the first round of membership negotiations. So have Latvia and Lithuania, both of which are ranked almost as high as Estonia and Slovenia in terms of institutional transition and GDP growth (see Tables 14 and 28).

One suspects that the selection process has also been inspired by other political and geopolitical considerations which have not been announced openly. The five countries invited to join the EU share borders with members.[13] Among the other postsocialist nations, Slovakia has a common border with Austria, while three Balkan states—Albania, Bulgaria, and FYR Macedonia—have short borders with Greece (which, together with Portugal, is the poorest EU member). In fact, though it is never admitted, the geopolitical factor is of special consequence for the integration of part of Eastern Europe with the European Union, and it has influenced decisions taken by the European Commission on the shadings to be used on the map of Europe should the EU negotiations and the overall transition process be crowned with success. Thus, even if, for example, Moldova were in better political and economic shape than Estonia, it would not necessarily be invited to undertake membership negotiations with the EU.

[13] Assuming—as the Estonians and Finns do—that the narrow lane of water in the Gulf of Finland is equivalent to a border.

Meanwhile, many factors have motivated the decision to include Estonia and Slovenia in the earliest wave of negotiations. Estonia and Slovenia are very small countries, with populations of about 1.5 million and 2 million, respectively. It is easier to manage the transition and integration of a small nation than to do so for a large one, say, Romania, with almost 23 million inhabitants. The small size and small population are important elements in view of the EU budget, especially since it has already also been determined (finally) that the common agriculture policy and the EU regional aid policy must be reformed before eastbound enlargement can proceed. Slovenia is the only republic of the former Yugoslavia to be invited, and it was the smallest of them all, too. Likewise, if it can fulfil the agreed conditions, Estonia will be the only former Soviet republic with a chance to join the EU in the foreseeable future. By including this country, the smallest among the former Soviet republics, the EU cannot be accused of abandoning the Baltic States to the Russian sphere of influence. Perhaps most significantly, nonetheless, both these tiny countries are relatively well developed. Estonia is the most developed among the former Soviet republics, and Slovenia is the most developed of all postsocialist economies (Table 32).

The evaluation of GNP or GDP on a PPP basis varies for well-known methodological reasons. *Agenda 2000*, presented in 1997 by Jacques Santer, the president of the EU, to the European Parliament, shows per capita GDP data for the associate countries that are different from those in Table 32. For instance, the EBRD estimates the per capita GDP of Poland in 1995 at $5,400, while the EU sees it closer to 5,300 ecu (about $5,800–$5,900 at the time). Another evaluation suggests that in 1997 per capita GDP was nearer to $7,000. This seems more reliable, especially considering the growth of about 14 per cent in 1996–7 and the fluctuations in domestic prices relative to international ones. After some tendency toward decline, particularly in 1995, when it fell from above 2 down to about 1.8, the ratio of the official exchange rate over the PPP exchange rate hovered in the range of 1.77 to 1.82 in 1996 and increased again to 1.9 or so in 1997 (PlanEcon 1997c).[14] This sort of problem with the evaluation of GDP on a PPP basis also occurs for all other countries.

Accomplishing the enlargement of the EU may be more difficult than merely accommodating the first five applicants, despite the likelihood that in future the other transition country aspirants will be even better prepared for integration than was the first round in 1998. There will always be questions about the effective limits of eastbound EU expansion and about the point at which adding members might become a disadvantage. So far,

---

[14] An evaluation at the end of 1998 gave the GDP per capita on a PPP basis at $5,033 for Estonia, $6,540 for Poland, $7,400 for Hungary, $10,521 for Slovenia, and $10,820 for the Czech Republic (*The Economist* 1998d).

Table 32 GNP per capita in transition economies and share in regional GNP

	Population (millions)	GNP per capita, 1995 (PPP$)		GNP (million PPP$, World Bank Atlas)	% regional GNP	% regional population
		World Bank Atlas	OECD			
Albania	3.3	—	—	—	—	0.8
Armenia	3.8	2,260	—	8,588	0.6	0.9
Azerbaijan	7.5	1,460	—	10,950	0.7	1.9
Belarus	10.3	4,220	—	43,466	2.8	2.6
Bulgaria	8.4	4,480	4,867	37,632	2.4	2.1
Croatia	4.8	—	—	—	—	1.2
Czech Republic	10.3	9,770	—	100,631	6.6	2.6
Estonia	1.5	4,220	4,053	6,330	0.4	0.4
FYR Macedonia	2.1	—	—	—	—	0.5
Georgia	5.4	1,470	—	7,938	0.5	1.3
Hungary	10.2	6,410	6,578	65,382	4.3	2.5
Kazakstan	16.6	3,010	—	49,966	3.3	4.1
Kyrgyzstan	4.5	1,800	—	8,100	0.5	1.1
Latvia	2.5	3,370	3,271	8,425	0.5	0.6
Lithuania	3.7	4,120	4,021	15,244	1.0	0.9
Moldova	4.3	—	—	—	—	1.1
Poland	38.6	5,400	5,482	208,440	13.6	9.6
Romania	22.7	4,360	4,309	98,972	6.4	5.7
Russia	148.2	4,480	—	663,936	43.2	37.0
Slovakia	5.3	3,610	7,371	19,133	1.2	1.3
Slovenia	2.0	—	10,509	—	—	0.5
Tajikistan	5.8	920	—	5,336	0.3	1.4
Turkmenistan	4.5	—	—	—	—	1.1
Ukraine	51.6	2,400	—	123,840	8.1	12.9
Uzbekistan	22.8	2,370	—	54,036	3.5	5.7
Regional total	400.7	4,060	—	1,536,345	100.0	100.0

Sources: World Bank 1997d, OECD 1997c.

Table 33 Transition economy membership in international economic
or financial organizations, 1998

	IMF and WB	WTO	EU association	OECD	EU invitation	Rank
Albania	★					★
Armenia	★					★
Azerbaijan	★					★
Belarus	★					★
Bulgaria	★	★	★			★★★
Croatia	★					★
Czech Republic	★	★	★	★	★	★★★★★
Estonia	★	★	★		★	★★★
FYR Macedonia	★					★
Georgia	★					★
Hungary	★	★	★	★	★	★★★★★
Kazakhstan	★					★
Kyrgyzstan	★	★				★★
Latvia	★	★	★			★★★
Lithuania	★		★			★★
Moldova	★					★
Poland	★	★	★	★	★	★★★★★
Romania	★	★	★			★★★
Russia	★					★
Slovakia	★	★	★			★★★
Slovenia	★	★	★		★	★★★★
Tajikistan	★					★
Turkmenistan	★					★
Ukraine	★					★
Uzbekistan	★					★

Source: Author's compilation based on data of various international organizations.

geopolitical position (which does not depend on policy) and OECD
membership (which depends exclusively on wise reform and policy) have
played key roles in the integration process.

From the viewpoint of membership in international economic, trade,
and financial organizations, only three transition economies, the Czech
Republic, Hungary, and Poland, have been 'five star' performers (Table 33).
These countries belong to the Bretton Woods institutions, the WTO, the
OECD, and also the North Atlantic Treaty Organization. During the Madrid
summit in the summer of 1997, official invitations were extended to the
three nations to join NATO in 1999. NATO membership has been much
easier to achieve than EU membership is going to be. The entry into

NATO can facilitate the process of the economic integration of these three nations with the EU, as well as with the global economy, inter alia through the positive impact on business confidence and foreign direct investment.

The forthcoming integration with the European Union should be seen as a partnership between the 15 old members and the five new ones, which must make their institutions conform to the demands of the EU and must also upgrade infrastructure and overhaul industries. The whole endeavour is going to be quite costly and must be paid for mainly from the pockets of taxpayers in the new member countries.[15] Before this tax effort can bear fruit, it will cause tensions. However, if these adjustments are not carried out at this stage of transition and integration, the costs may be even higher in the long run anyway.

Vietnam became a member of ASEAN in 1995, and Laos joined in 1997. Because of political turmoil in Cambodia in the summer of 1997, ASEAN has been forced to postpone a decision on that nation's entry into the organization. Membership in ASEAN is important for these countries, especially considering the wide development gap between them and the more advanced members of the association. The size of the gap depends on the yardstick used, but it is certainly enormous. For example, if calculated in PPP dollars, the figure for the GDP per capita for Vietnam is about four times higher than it is if calculated according to the market exchange rate. For Singapore, the PPP figure is lower by about 25 per cent. Thus, the ratio of the income per head in Singapore and that in Vietnam shrinks from a shocking 100:1 according to current nominal cross exchange rates to a still immense 20:1 according to purchasing power comparisons (Table 34).

The only way to close such a giant gap is by boosting the rates of growth in the less-developed countries past the rates among the richer nations. A significant means for accomplishing this is increased regional integration, accompanied by trade liberalization, freer capital flows, and the coordination of structural policies. Despite the crisis of 1998–9, or because of it, ASEAN plans to negotiate the Asian Free Trade Agreement and work on a programme called 'vision for the year 2020'. No mere illusion that the free market can solve all problems, the 'vision' is a very long-term horizon for the coordination of development strategies at the regional level. This is the sort of decisive approach which has enhanced the ability of Asian economies to sustain high rates of growth for so long. The recent profound crisis does not negate this conclusion. These economies can hardly fail to rebound. Such a vision is needed in Central Asia, Eastern Europe, and Russia, too.

---

[15] Assistance for upgrading infrastructure is also being provided by the European Investment Bank. This financial arm of the EU has already supplied significant credits (over 3 billion ecu by 1998) for infrastructure development in Central and Eastern Europe.

Table 34 Population and GDP per capita in ASEAN
countries and Cambodia, 1996

	Population (millions)	GDP per capita ($)
Indonesia	196.9	1,150
Vietnam	75.5	311
Philippines	69.8	1,200
Thailand	61.3	2,980
Malaysia	20.6	4,260
Singapore	3.0	30,860
Brunei	0.3	16,427
Laos	4.9	377
Myanmar	45.6	107[a]
Cambodia	10.7	292

[a] At the market exchange rate.
Source: Economist Intelligence Unit.

Will the process of the enlargement of ASEAN contribute to the acceleration of market reform and ultimately the transition to a full-fledged market in the socialist and postsocialist countries of Indochina?[16] In Vietnam price and trade liberalization, as well as a regulatory environment favourable to capital markets and foreign direct investment, have already been pushed forward by the membership in ASEAN, which has therefore had a positive effect on the pace of reform. If a country becomes a member before the economy has been brought up to speed with the association's standards, as was the case of Laos and Vietnam and probably is going also to be the case of Cambodia, then gradual liberalization must follow.

This is the advantage of joining early. (From this angle, it is never too early.) The structural and institutional changes are thus enforced by the membership, which has a strong influence on the policies exercised by the country. The early membership serves to help break down any ideological, political, or bureaucratic resistance to the necessary reforms. Contrary to the WTO, which requires that most reforms be carried out before a country is admitted, ASEAN membership is not based on political and institutional conditionality, but itself is understood as the cornerstone of change. Once a nation is a member, there will always be the time and the means to insist on reforms and adjustments.

Is the coming process of liberalization and regional integration going to mean that growth will be more rapid in the less-developed markets of ASEAN

---

[16] This question is even more relevant vis-à-vis Myanmar, which joined ASEAN in 1997. Though poorer than Vietnam and not a transition economy, Myanmar must take a similar road of political and economic liberalization in order to achieve development.

than it is in the developed ones? Despite the 1997–8 East Asian crisis and its impact on close neighbours, economic growth rates among the new ASEAN members have not decelerated significantly. In the long run the membership in ASEAN will also promote economic stability. One may therefore anticipate that, if there is continued cooperation and if the political dilemmas in Cambodia are solved, then the Indochinese economies will grow quickly. This will occur because these economies will become more open to foreign investment and technology transfers, but also because these processes will open up new markets for Cambodia, Laos, and Vietnam. This combination of the greater absorption of foreign capital and improved access to new markets will enable these economies to allocate resources better and expand through export-led growth.

12.5. THE TWO FACES OF EMERGING MARKETS

The markets in all postsocialist nations are 'emerging' in two senses. First, *these markets are in statu nascendi and can be considered as 'emerging' because they are rooted in the centrally planned economy and are gradually becoming part of the integrated world market economy.* This means that policymakers must be determined to foster mature market behaviour and institutional arrangements so that the market system can evolve in a healthy fashion.

Second, the postsocialist nations possess *financial and capital markets which are 'emerging' because they are opening up to the world economy and thereby represent fresh investment opportunities* (Mobius 1996). These opportunities are being keenly taken up, mainly by rich countries with extra savings which are not being absorbed by domestic investment. The propensity to save and the capacity for capital formation in these rich countries surpass their current domestic investment needs. Some savings therefore flow out in search of opportunities in other nations. Whereas in mature markets the supply of capital exceeds the demand, in emerging markets the demand for capital outstrips the supply. Since capital tends to flow from places where it is abundant to places where it is scarce, the spare capital is invested in emerging markets, where there is a chance of obtaining unusually high profits (and where the risks are also unusually high).

In 1997, the year before the crash, the shares traded on stock markets in emerging market economies were worth a very significant $2.7 trillion, or 14 per cent of the $19.3 trillion traded worldwide. The stock markets in the more advanced transition countries—the Czech Republic, Hungary, and Poland—had a higher turnover than did the stock market in Russia, but this time first place in the league of transforming countries was definitely held by China. The stock market turnover in China represented about 230 per cent of that nation's market capitalization, which means that the average share changed hands between two and three times. Along with

South Korea and Taiwan, China was therefore among the most active emerging markets in 1997. In terms of activity, Poland and Hungary, with turnover close to 80 per cent, were, respectively, between the United States and Brazil and between Malaysia and Greece. Russia was close to the bottom of the league, with turnover at about 25 per cent of market capitalization, placing it between Israel and South Africa.

A unique feature of the small infant postsocialist stock markets is the fact that they have provided remarkable profits to portfolio investors even when output within the economies has been severely contracting. These people may be considered to have taken greater risks in order to reap greater profits, but from a macroeconomic viewpoint there has simply been an outward transfer of part of national income to the accounts of foreign investors. The profits have not always been due to increased productivity resulting from the investments, and often they have not been reinvested locally, but have been quickly moved elsewhere.

A majority of transition economies have been able to attract healthy inflows of foreign direct investment, and emerging financial and capital markets generally facilitate capital formation and allocation, thereby contributing to postsocialist recovery and growth. However, in some countries the level of capital flight has risen above that of foreign lending and investment, including private capital inputs and the financial assistance of governments and international organizations. This would not have been possible had appropriate regulations been adopted. Instead there has been deregulation and a renunciation of the tools available for controlling cash flows. This occurred not because no one knew how to regulate capital flows, but because of weak political commitment and the lack of the courage necessary to carry out the reforms. No wonder the markets in some of these economies have emerged in a very awkward manner. In nations such as Albania and Russia for quite some time the interests of informal institutions were preferred over the needs of stabilization and national economic development, and the emerging markets were used as instruments to favour these interests.

Policies should therefore focus on guiding foreign capital inflows into long-term, preferably direct investments. These sorts of outlays encourage microeconomic restructuring and competitiveness and thus contribute to recovery and growth, which help both the foreign investors and the local recipients of the capital flows. If this policy approach is not adopted, the liberalization of financial and capital transfers may generate capital drain-off instead of more capital injection.

The best example of this last scenario is the Russian economy, which shrank in 1996 by 6 per cent, bringing GDP down to about 50 per cent of the pre-transition (1989) level. Simultaneously, the rate of return in dollar terms on the Russian stock market was 113 per cent. This trend continued through 1997. During that year the drop in GDP did not bottom out, while the rate of return was still a recklessly high 111 per cent. The

Table 35 Stock market rates of return: postsocialist markets
and selected developed markets

	1996, % change on 29 Dec. 1995	1997, % change on 31 Dec. 1996	1996–7, % change on 29 Dec. 1995
Emerging markets			
China	77.1	30.7	131.5
Czech Republic	10.0	−27.7	−20.5
Hungary	121.4	53.6	240.1
Poland	57.6	−16.8	31.1
Russia	112.6	110.2	346.9
Average[a]	75.7	30.0	128.5
Developed markets			
United States	24.0	22.8	52.3
Germany	15.2	26.5	45.7
Britain	17.3	20.6	41.5
Italy	14.6	36.2	56.1
Japan	−8.2	−29.5	−35.3
World[b]	10.0	13.8	25.2

[a] Unweighted average.   [b] Morgan Stanley Capital International index includes the
OECD markets, except for Greece, Mexico, Portugal, South Korea, and Turkey, and
except for the Czech Republic, Hungary, and Poland, which, although members of
OECD, are included in the emerging markets group.

Sources: Stock exchanges, national statistics, Reuters.

gains available in other emerging markets, including the leading transition
economies, were not so spectacular, but they were still large and in most cases
much greater than those accruing in advanced market countries (Table 35).

Then reality struck; the pendulum started to swing in the opposite direction after the onset of the Asian crisis, and the investors feeding off emerging markets worldwide began to panic. In the first half of 1998 the index
for the Moscow stock exchange fell by 63.3 per cent, meaning that in dollar terms the value of shares had plunged by nearly two-thirds in the space
of six months. By the end of the year the index had dropped by a staggering 96 per cent. How extremely hectic the stock market was can be seen by
the drop of 18.2 per cent in just one week in June. Indeed, Russia's has
become a 'gambling casino' economy. Many investors, including renowned
foreign investment banks and hedge funds, have lost substantial sums.

Nonetheless, the blame for Russia's stock market swoon ought not to
be directed at foreign investors and speculators, who were not acting out
of character, but at government macroeconomic mismanagement and
malfunctioning structural reform policies, mainly in privatization and corporate governance (Kolodko 1998d).

For several years the government had been selling assets below the market clearing price. Nonetheless, the increase in the stock market index by around 450 per cent in just two years, 1996–7, was irrational. Only to a certain extent was it due to a natural catching-up process involving the search for and the re-establishment of stable market value levels. The gap between the nominal prices on the primary market and the real value and profitability of the physical assets as expressed in the long run on the secondary market was closing, but most of the great leap skywards on the stock exchange was due to a bubble which was being pumped up by constant speculation and even intentionally by some investors, especially by insider traders. In turn, the bubble encouraged senseless expectations about the capacity for further growth. That the bubble would burst—that is, that the capitalization of the stock market would bring the market back down to the level it should have been at because of the performance of the real economy—was inevitable. Whereas real output halved in six years, it took only six months for the average value of stocks on the capital market to plummet by half.

While those six months were very bullish on stock markets in the advanced countries (the Dow Jones average on Wall Street rose by 14.4 per cent, and the Morgan Stanley Capital International index, which included the 23 most developed countries during that period, increased by 17.4 per cent), it was a very bearish six months for all but a few markets elsewhere. Over the same six-month period, the losses varied from 56.9 per cent in Indonesia and 49.6 per cent in Venezuela to 6.2 per cent in Brazil and 0.9 per cent in South Korea. On the major postsocialist markets, the losses were from 8.6 per cent in Hungary to 1.7 per cent in the Czech Republic. Only five of the 'smaller' markets registered positive returns from investments on the stock exchange during the first half of 1998: the three older markets of Greece (a gain of 50.9 per cent), Israel (5.2 per cent), and Portugal (39.5 per cent), and the transforming markets of China (11 per cent, despite a decline of 6.1 per cent in the last week of June) and Poland (9.6 per cent), the most stable and steadily growing emerging capital market.

China and Poland demonstrate that relatively firm macroeconomic fundamentals and well-designed structural adjustment policies do make a difference. They show that it is possible for an emerging market—whether in a reformed socialist economy or in an open postsocialist economy—to avoid financial crisis if only liberalization, stabilization, and institution-building are properly managed. China and Poland can continue this sort of performance in the future if the liberalization and deregulation of capital flows remain subordinate to development strategies, not the other way around.

In the case of Russia, the greed of portfolio investors for quick profits—regardless of financial instability, growing inequality, and spreading poverty—and the weak fundamentals, the inadequate regulation, and the inconsistent policies of the government created a bubble, which was readily burst by a market panic. The consequences were certainly negative for the real economy, output, and living standards. The only way to have avoided the bursting of the bubble was to have avoided the bubble. But the only way to have done that would have been to step on the toes of the financial interest groups. In effect, the 'tycoons' have not wanted the government to regulate capital flows and take care of adjustment properly, also because for some time there has been a little bit of fog surrounding the tycoons and the government. It is not surprising that there was a bubble which could burst and a severe crisis waiting to happen. In the meantime, there was an enormous redistribution of stocks and capital flows nationally, as well as internationally. Once more, the few became richer, and many became very poor.

The evaluation of the profits earned on emerging stock markets depends on the time span examined. For instance, in 1996, although the capitalization of stock markets in transition economies was relatively quite low, the real rate of return on these markets was more than seven times higher than the corresponding rate on developed markets. However, the index of emerging stock markets, including those in transition economies, compiled by the International Finance Corporation fell by 15 per cent in dollar terms between the end of 1993 and September 1997. Over the same period, the capitalization of Wall Street, that is, the Dow Jones average, more than doubled. Whereas from 1990 until September 1997 the average annual rate of return on all emerging markets was a mere 3.5 per cent, Wall Street yielded around 13 per cent. The postsocialist markets were more profitable until the bearish year of 1998.

The emerging capital markets have clearly been more profitable, but more chaotic and unpredictable, too. To a certain extent, this has been due to the advice coming from people in developed market nations. For quite some time, nobody on Wall Street had any sound understanding of how the Russian capital market ought to be developed from scratch and what the regulatory environment should be like. Still worse, *the knowledge which has been applied has been more useful for the exploitation rather than the protection of the emerging markets*. Even official aid designated for technical assistance in carrying out privatization and the establishment of capital markets has sometimes been redirected toward other, less socially justifiable purposes (Blasi, Kroumova, and Kruse 1997, Wedel 1998b). According to USAID, the US government agency which administers American foreign aid, some American advisors to Russia's privatization programme 'used information gained from their programme activities . . . to make further private investments in the Russian securities market' (*The Economist* 1997h). Unfortunately, insider trading, sometimes also involving foreigners, is quite common in transition economies. However, because of the participation of influential, well-connected investors with media contacts, cases of conflicts of interest and the use of confidential information for private gain have not received much public attention and the notoriety and criticism they deserve.

The emerging markets and the postsocialist economies should not be seen only as a field of action for financial speculation for international investors. Yet, owing to the foreign capital inflows they facilitate, these investors are important for transition countries, all of which possess insufficient domestic savings resources. Thus, a key to the development of these countries is the ability to attract as much long-term foreign investment as possible. In this respect, the situation in transition economies is very dynamic, since foreign direct capital investments, unlike the portfolio transactions, are expanding all the time.

12.6. ECONOMIC AID, DIRECT INVESTMENT, AND FOREIGN CAPITAL

At the onset of transition, the main source of foreign capital was international organizations, especially the IMF, the World Bank, and the EBRD. However, in the long run it will be the private sector. Initially, aid provided by the governments of advanced market countries also played a relatively larger role, though not everywhere. The recipients of the highest relative amounts of economic aid were Albania, Kyrgyzstan, and Poland. Relatively high per capita assistance was also received by the Baltic States (Table 36).[17]

The explanation for the preference for these countries is simple. Except for Poland, these are all small economies. To provide aid at $100 per head in Estonia in three years' time is about 35 times less costly than to deliver the same level of aid to Ukraine. Whereas aid worth about $33 per person per year over 1994–6 would have amounted altogether to around $150 million for Estonia, in Ukraine the same level of aid would have cost over $5 billion. The aid of over $50 per person in Albania and Kyrgyzstan may seem impressive in comparison to the meagre $2 or $3 for much bigger Kazakhstan and Uzbekistan, but in fact the total aid sent to these latter two dwarfs that received by the two former nations. Once more we see that, in regard to transition, 'small is beautiful'. It is cheaper to give many dollars to a few than to give a few dollars to the many.

Poland is an exception. A significant debt reduction was the reward to Poland for its pioneering role in the transition and in overhauling the

---

[17] This does not include military assistance, which, though 'unproductive', appreciably increases the aid figures, particularly for countries involved in local conflicts, such as Armenia, Azerbaijan, Georgia, and Tajikistan.

Table 36 Economic aid in transition economies, 1994–1996

	% GDP	Per capita ($)	Openness
Hungary	−0.1	−3	1
Uzbekistan	0.3	2	0
Kazakhstan	0.2	3	0
Turkmenistan	0.6	6	0
Ukraine	0.4	6	0
Romania	0.6	9	1
Russia	0.5	11	0
Tajikistan	3.2	11	0
Moldova	1.5	13	1
Czech Republic	0.4	14	1
Belarus	0.8	16	1
Bulgaria	1.3	16	1
Slovakia	0.6	16	1
Azerbaijan	3.4	17	0
Latvia	1.0	22	1
Estonia	1.2	33	1
Lithuania	1.8	33	1
Georgia	8.2	35	0
Kyrgyzstan	7.4	51	1
Albania	8.5	53	1
Armenia	8.7	54	0
Poland	2.6	72	1
Croatia	—	—	1
Slovenia	—	—	1
FYR Macedonia	—	—	1

Note: 'Aid' is defined as official development assistance grants, plus lending, minus repayments from OECD sources. Figures in the 'per capita' column are annual averages for 1994–6. '1' indicates an open economy' '0' a closed economy.

Source: Burnside and Dollar 1997.

socialist system.[18] If the postsocialist revolution had started in Hungary, then the debt of that country might have been lightened, while Poland would be choking under an unmanageable debt burden for years. Yet, Poland happened to be the first to start to turn the wheel of history.

Already in 1991 the Paris Club of official creditors took an initial decision regarding the outstanding debt of Poland, but the debt reduction scheme

[18] Contrary to what was being claimed at the time, the Gulf War in 1990–1 helped the transition in a certain sense, at least in Poland. The debt reduction for the benefit of Poland that was agreed with Western governments in 1991 was catalysed by the decision to cut by half the debt of Egypt. For strictly political reasons, it was virtually impossible to forgive Egypt's debt without doing the same for Poland, considering the crucial role the latter had played in the overthrow of the socialist system.

continued for several more years. The second major cut was agreed with the creditors from the London Club in 1994. In both cases the debt was pared by 50 per cent, and the deal was contingent on the strict conditionality of further progress with structural reform. Because this progress was achieved, the debt was forgiven. In this sense, among all postsocialist countries, Poland has obtained by far the largest amount of financial assistance from the developed market nations.[19]

One might view this assistance to Poland not only as a reward, but also, given the relative health of the emerging Polish market, as a good investment. Likewise, in terms of the economic rationale of the allocation of international aid among transition economies, *assistance has been mainly forthcoming for countries which are more advanced in or at least committed to structural reform and which exhibit a better record with reform*. For several years now, these countries have been enjoying stronger economic growth than have other emerging markets. This is good not simply for the sake of the nations receiving the assistance, but also for those providing it, for this means that the climate is favourable for investors from these nations. If, for example, assistance has been supplied to support institution-building, then the new market organizations which are established serve not only local businesses, but also foreign investors.

This sort of give and take is well known from the experience with technical and financial aid in the less-developed countries. It is easier to get foreign aid (or, shall we say, a 'foreign indirect investment') to finance feasibility studies, privatization schemes, stock exchanges, the training of banking personnel, or the purchase of computer hardware manufactured in the aid-giving country than it is to get foreign aid to finance poverty alleviation programmes, job creation schemes, cultural institutions, the training of hospital personnel, or the development of a local computer industry. There are no relevant studies, but anecdotal evidence suggests clearly that much more foreign aid has been channelled into the development of the financial sector than into antipoverty programmes. Assistance should therefore not be seen as charity, but as an investment, often in human capital. In fact, this bias can help the country absorbing the extra capital recover sooner and grow more quickly, so that the country may be able to gather independent resources to meet its needs in other areas, such as poverty alleviation, at a later date.

Like commercial lending from international financial institutions, the foreign aid is often conditional. The transfers of capital are frequently subject to the implementation of certain specified programmes or particular reforms. This sort of conditionality is rigorously practised by the EU, which

---

[19] Without this assistance, the prospects of Poland would not have become so bright since 1993. An overwhelming burden of unpayable debt—whether in Poland or Russia—renders successful transition impossible. For this reason, much of the outstanding debt of Russia should also be written off (Kolodko 1998e).

sometimes cancels planned aid allocations because of it. For instance, over
34 million ecu in grants to Poland under the PHARE initiative were rescinded
in 1998 because the government could not meet certain requirements.[20]
The fact that this kind of conditionality is tied to progress in structural
reform and institution-building partly explains why nations which are further along in transition are able to absorb more aid. It also shows why
more aid tends to help transition go forward more smoothly in these nations.
Aid cannot be used more efficiently in these nations than in lagging countries because the former possess more effective institutions. *Foreign aid has
a positive influence on economic policy, and, even if the amounts are small, they
can accelerate growth if they are mainly employed for investments rather than
for consumption* (Blustein 1997).

Before the collapse of its economy in 1997, this was the case of Albania,
the most backward country in Europe. The politics and economics of foreign aid had functioned in such a way that, due to the progress it had
achieved in stabilization and liberalization, Albania was for a time the recipient of the most foreign aid both as a share of GDP and on a per capita
basis. Since then it has continued to benefit from relatively important assistance despite policy failures, mainly the mismanagement of institutional
reform in the financial sector and in capital markets. However, this has
been the exception which has proved the rule, since the significant aid is
now being provided for geopolitical reasons linked to the fighting in the
Balkans, religious-ethnic considerations, and the Albanian immigrant
problem in neighbouring countries. In the case of the best performing small
former Soviet republics of the Baltic region and Central Asia, the link between
aid and reform is unmistakable: more aid is supplied to the countries more
advanced in institutional transition. And here, too, there is a positive feedback loop between the level of foreign capital inflows, including aid, and
overall economic attainment.

It is a fortunate historical coincidence that the postsocialist transition is
occurring during a period of swelling savings in developed market economies. With more than one and a half billion people, the emerging markets
in Europe and Asia represent a vast potential arena for foreign investment
and the expansion of market capitalism. In a certain sense, they are fulfilling
a function for global capitalism that is similar to the one performed for
European capitalism by the New World after 1492. Likewise, even in the
early 1990s the postsocialist region seemed *terra incognita* for the major
investment banks and investment funds.

---

[20] PHARE was created in 1989 specifically as a way to furnish financial and technical assistance to Hungary and Poland in the reform process. Hence the acronym, which stands for
'Pologne et Hongrie Action pour la Reforme Economique' ('Poland and Hungary: Action
for Economic Reform'). PHARE was eventually expanded, and it is now being run in a majority of postsocialist countries.

However, the foreign investors were quick to set up shop. The investors are of various sorts, but the major sorts are the investment banks and the aggressive hedge funds which are managing mutual and pension funds. Unlike the postsocialist economies, which still rely heavily on the old pay-as-you-go public pension systems, in the advanced economies social security arrangements have evolved mostly toward market-based, funded systems. According to InterSec Corporation, a research company, the total value of the world's pension assets grew by almost 60 per cent, from $5.4 trillion to $8.5 trillion, between 1991 and 1996. It was being anticipated that these assets would at least double over the next five years and exceed $17 trillion in 2001, although this may be exaggerated in light of the stock bubble in the developed market countries (except Japan) in 1995–7 and the turmoil on capital markets worldwide during 1998. During the second half of 1998 pension assets were depreciating owing to the corrections on these markets. In any case, because they represent so many additional investment opportunities for these assets, the transition nations, together with other emerging markets, have seemed like a newly discovered America.[21]

If there had been no capital in search of markets, the situation would have been even more difficult for the transition countries. As it is, the rapid changes taking place simultaneously in other regions of the world —especially in Latin America and Asia, but also in Africa—mean that the transition economies must compete for foreign investment. The Washington-based Institute for International Finance, a research group of private commercial and investment banks, estimates that net private capital flows to major emerging market economies dropped to $261 billion in 1997 from a record high of $281 billion in 1996. This was mainly the result of a contraction in the flow of investment into Asia by about $35 billion (from $142 billion down to $107 billion) and a decline of about 10 per cent in Latin America, while the capital flows to economies in transition continued to expand. In 1998 private capital flows were still falling and, because of the Russian 'syndrome', were beginning to affect negatively the postsocialist emerging markets, too.

Nonetheless, the postsocialist nations are clearly capable of competing for the attention of world capital markets. A new stage in this competition was reached in 1998 owing to the crisis in East Asia. As part of this competition, the postsocialist economies are trying to become viewed as 'emerging markets' by foreign investors and, moreover, to be referred to in this way. In 1995–6 Poland was the only postsocialist economy to be included on the list of the so-called 'Big Ten emerging markets' (Garten 1998).[22] This was a US government initiative to draw more American investors and exporters toward these markets.

[21] This time, hopefully, not so many Indians will be wiped out.
[22] The other nine 'big' markets on the list are Argentina, ASEAN, Brazil, China, India, Mexico, South Africa, South Korea, and Turkey. Russia is noteworthy for being absent.

The portfolio investors turned out to be the most active, followed by the direct investors, then the exporters, and only at the very end the importers. A more healthy sequence for the transition economies would have been the direct investors, followed by the importers, and then the exporters, with the portfolio investors bringing up the rear. Then growth would likely have been more robust, the current account deficits smaller, and the cumulative profits of foreign investors larger.

Transition economies have also started to compete among themselves to gain the biggest possible piece of the pie. The heads-of-state of transition countries eagerly attend vast numbers of conferences, gatherings, and other events to push the advantages of their markets. They entertain international bankers and fund managers and encourage them to invest in their countries. Such meetings were first organized mainly in relatively advanced Eastern European nations, but soon other countries, including the bigger economies among the former Soviet republics, also joined this 'club' of the emerging markets. They were launching vast privatization programmes and issuing Eurobonds and global bonds to finance their fiscal deficits. As a consequence, not only their markets 'emerged', but also their current account deficits, since the exports from these countries to advanced market nations were not growing quickly enough, while the portfolio investment flows in the opposite direction were growing too quickly.

On a cumulative basis, foreign direct investments in the transition economies of Eastern Europe and the CIS reached over $60 billion between 1989 or 1990 and the end of 1997 and $90 billion to $100 billion by the end of 1998. Around two-thirds of this was absorbed by Eastern Europe, and the other one-third by the CIS. This is quite a small amount relative to the needs of these countries and to the level of direct investment in other emerging markets.

Overall (not cumulative) foreign direct investments in 1996 totalled $349 billion according to the United Nations Conference on Trade and Development, but the share going to the transition economies was estimated by the EBRD at only about $15 billion, a meagre 4 per cent of the total. Most went to developed market economies, although the share received by developing nations, especially those in Asia and including China and Vietnam, was rising.

China was the largest recipient of foreign direct investment among emerging markets in terms of both flows and stock. It had taken in $169 billion on a cumulative basis through 1996.[23] In 1996 alone China received $42.3 billion, that is, about three times more than Eastern Europe and the former Soviet republics combined. However, since there are more than 1.2 billion Chinese, this otherwise remarkable inflow adds up to only

---

[23] The recipient of the next largest amount among the emerging markets was Brazil, which had absorbed $108 billion through 1996.

about $35 per person, which was comparable to the per capita share for the transition economies that year.

The following year (1997) the per capita average for the transition countries was $43, of which $86 per head went to Eastern Europe and $26 to the CIS. By the end of 1997 cumulative foreign direct investments in China had exceeded $200 billion. Approximately 230,000 enterprises backed by foreign capital had received authorization to operate in China, and 145,000 of them had started business. Enterprises supported by foreign capital employed 17 million people and accounted for more than 10 per cent of the industrial and commercial taxes collected by fiscal authorities and for about 40 per cent of China's total exports.[24] All these achievements resulted from a steadily growing commitment, since foreign direct investment, unlike portfolio flows, cannot pack up and go in the aftermath of shocks or radical local policy shifts.

Yet, the amount of money being invested in particular countries sometimes fluctuates significantly from year to year, since, for example, a privatization programme in a single industry can alter the picture substantially. The link between privatization and the foreign direct investment absorbed is not always obvious. Even if the overall pace of privatization is slow, significant injections of foreign direct investment can be attracted if the incentives to undertake new ventures and green field projects are strong enough. Usually this sort of equation involves foreign capital penetration in natural resources and large individual investment projects in the energy sector. Big privatization schemes in the banking sector, energy, and telecommunications have caused particular economies to move up on the list of the recipients of the most foreign direct investment. Thus, in 1997 Poland surpassed Hungary in terms of the Eastern European nation receiving the most cumulative foreign investment (Table 37).

Among the former Soviet republics and the countries of Eastern Europe, Russia is bound to lead in this respect eventually, considering the enormous sums to be invested, for example, in the energy sector, which has yet to be privatized. Although the investment per capita is relatively small, only about $13 and $26 in 1996 and 1997, respectively, Russia absorbed around $6 billion altogether during that time. This is still less than the total investment in Poland in 1997 alone ($6.6 billion), but almost three times as much as that in Kazakhstan in 1996 and 1997, where average per capita inflows were three times higher (about $73 and $76, respectively).[25] In Eastern Europe at the end of 1997 the stock of foreign direct investment per capita was highest in Hungary ($1,519), followed by the Czech Republic ($726), and Estonia ($557). In Russia and Ukraine, the

[24] Based on data in *Jie Fang Daily* (Beijing), 8 Sept. 1997.
[25] According to current account statistics, foreign direct investments in Russia in 1997 were valued at $3.9 billion, which was the highest inflow in any postsocialist country. Calculated on the same basis, the absorption in Poland was $3 billion (see Table 37).

Table 37 Foreign direct investment[a]

	1991	1992	1993	1994	1995	1996	1997[b]	Cumulative FDI inflows, 1989–97		FDI inflows per capita, 1997 ($)
								Total	Per capita ($)	
Albania	—	32	45	65	89	97	33	369	115	10
Bulgaria	56	42	40	105	82	100	575	1,000	121	69
Croatia	—	13	72	95	83	509	500	1,276	267	105
Czech Republic	511	983	517	749	2,526	1,388	1,275	7,473	726	124
Estonia	—	58	160	212	199	111	131	809	557	90
Hungary	1,459	1,471	2,339	1,097	4,453	1,986	2,100	15,403	1,519	207
Latvia	—	43	51	155	244	379	415	1,287	515	166
Lithuania[c]	—	—	30	31	72	152	327	612	165	88
FYR Macedonia	—	—	—	24	13	12	16	65	31	8
Poland[d]	117	284	580	542	1,134	2,741	3,044	8,442	218	79
	305	662	1,775	1,846	3,617	4,445	6,600	19,250	497	171
Romania	37	77	94	347	404	415	998	2,389	106	44
Slovakia	—	100	156	203	183	177	150	912	912	169
Slovenia	41	113	112	128	176	186	321	1,074	538	161
Eastern Europe	2,184	3,216	4,196	3,753	9,657	8,252	9,885	41,111	357	86

Armenia	—	—	—	—	3	22	26	70	19	7
Azerbaijan	—	7	20	22	284	661	1,006	1,993	262	132
Belarus	50	7	18	10	7	75	100	267	26	132
Georgia	—	—	—	8	6	25	65	104	19	12
Kazakhstan	—	—	473	635	859	1,100	1,200	4,267	272	76
Kyrgyzstan	—	—	10	45	96	46	50	247	54	11
Moldova	—	—	14	18	73	56	71	249	58	17
Russia	—	700	400	584	2,021	2,040	3,900	9,743	66	26
Tajikistan	—	8	9	12	17	20	20	86	14	3
Turkmenistan	—	11	104	103	233	129	108	652	139	23
Ukraine	—	170	200	100	400	526	700	2,096	41	14
Uzbekistan	—	9	73	73	−24	50	60	216	9	3
CIS	50	905	1,321	1,613	3,991	4,750	7,306	19,900	70	26
Total	2,234	4,121	5,517	5,366	13,648	13,002	17,191	61,100	153	43

[a] Net inflows recorded in the balance of payments. In millions of dollars unless otherwise indicated. [b] Estimated. [c] FDI figures for Lithuania are only available from 1993. For 1993–4, figures cover only investment in equity capital. For 1995–6, equity and reinvested earnings are covered, but inter-enterprise debt is excluded. [d] The second series for Poland supplements the data with information from a survey of foreign enterprises that was provided by the State Agency for Foreign Investments. The differences arise, in part, from investments in kind and reinvested earnings.

Source: EBRD 1998.

Table 38 Foreign direct investment in transition economies, 1989–1997

	Cumulative, % total investment, 1989–97	% GDP, 1997
Hungary	25.2	4.7
Russia	15.9	0.8
Poland	13.8	2.3
Czech Republic	12.2	2.4
Kazakhstan	7.0	5.7
Romania	3.9	2.9
Ukraine	3.4	1.4
Azerbaijan	3.3	24.4
Latvia	2.1	7.6
Croatia	2.1	2.7
Slovenia	1.8	1.8
Bulgaria	1.6	5.6
Slovakia	1.5	0.8
Estonia	1.3	2.8
Turkmenistan	1.1	4.7
Lithuania	1.0	3.6
Albania	0.6	1.4
Moldova	0.4	3.4
Kyrgyzstan	0.4	3.1
Belarus	0.4	0.7
Uzbekistan	0.4	0.4
Georgia	0.2	1.3
Tajikistan	0.1	1.8
Armenia	0.1	1.6
FYR Macedonia	0.1	0.5

Sources: EBRD 1998, Economist Intelligence Unit.

biggest countries in terms of population, the per capita stock was $66 and $41, respectively.

The best measure of relative foreign direct investment is not the amount per capita, but the share of GDP. According to this measure, Azerbaijan and China lead the way in Asia. It is believed that in 1997 foreign direct investment in Azerbaijan represented a remarkable 24.4 per cent of GDP (Table 38). In Eastern Europe, the most was absorbed by Latvia (7.6 per cent) and, despite the severe contraction there, Bulgaria (5.6 per cent). At the other end of the scale were Uzbekistan (0.4 per cent) in Central Asia and FYR Macedonia (0.5 per cent) in Eastern Europe.

Because of the generally positive outcomes produced by foreign investment, the earlier fears and the reluctance of certain political circles have waned. This shift in attitude is also due to the changed environment, since a portion of the political class is now tied to foreign capital, whether through the endeavours of individual entrepreneurs, financial intermediaries, or direct investors in green field projects or joint ventures. There has been a significant change in public opinion, too. More and more people are in favour of the absorption of foreign capital. Contrary to what they were led to believe during the socialist era, they generally experience these investments not only as harmless, but also as the means for the supply of new products and services and even as a chance for skill upgrading and eventually well-paying jobs. Thus, they are coming to perceive these investments as beneficial to overall economic performance at the workplace and to the standard of living at home.

12.7. OPENNESS, CAPITAL FLOWS, AND FOUR POLICY DILEMMAS

Governments are still hesitant to open up all industries and sectors to the unbridled penetration of foreign capital. This is the case of the automobile industry in China, banks in the Czech Republic, tourist services in Hungary, the energy sector in Russia, land in Slovenia, and so on. There are many concerns, depending on the time and the place and what segment of public opinion and the political spectrum one has in mind. There are also certain policy dilemmas with significant financial and economic implications and important political, psychological, and moral consequences. Four are worth particular note: the risk of dependent capitalism, the instability of portfolio investments, the redistribution of global wealth and income, and capital flight.

The first dilemma is *the risk of 'dependent capitalism'*. How are the governments of transition economies to hand over national assets to foreigners without handing over the independence and freedom of action of their countries, too? Postsocialist economies are often short on resources, and vast privatization therefore means that a significant portion of assets will be acquired by foreign capital. Unlike the case in other economies, the middle class and even the very wealthy often have no meaningful outward foreign investments and do not usually possess property in other countries. Thus, while people in other nations may come to own a growing part of the economy's assets, nationals of the transition country own little or nothing in the other nations. If the scales tip too far, then the transition country may become subject to a sort of 'dependent capitalism', with all the negative political implications.

Vis-à-vis capital flows there is also a risk of asymmetry between the usually stronger foreign partner who brings the capital and the transition economy governments, industries, and domestic financial intermediaries, which, being in need of cash, are usually the weaker partners. Of course, the ideal policy response is to prefer the formation of national capital, but this takes more time, and an ever-growing share of extremely important activities is meanwhile being oiled by foreign capital, which therefore is also working on behalf of national welfare. However, predator foreign investors may attempt to take control of certain industries by acquiring assets—which the transition nation sells off for the purpose of microeconomic restructuring and to sustain employment—and then crushing any local competition by using the assets to introduce to the domestic market the products they manufacture elsewhere.

The hedge funds aim at speculative profits. In a situation of financial instability, they may therefore be very vigorous. By allowing profits which are sufficiently high to maintain aggressive competition, but not too high to permit a net transfer of national wealth, governments must try to use the hedge funds on behalf of financial stability.

International financial institutions work on behalf of global financial stability and liquidity, but they must also take into account the expectations and interests of the largest and strongest economies. Less influential nations and their governments must nonetheless try to employ these institutions to attract reasonable amounts of long-term capital which is not too dear.

An indispensable part of any financial deal, conditionality is a trump card in the possession of the supplier of the capital and thus a means to guarantee the realization of his targets. However, the recipient of the capital flow must stand tough in the negotiations. The investor may have far-reaching preferences such as tax holidays, fiscal allowances, or customs duties which must be imposed on competitive imports, but the government must not accept awkward concessions exposing consumers and other producers to unfair competition and the state budget to unnecessarily low revenues.

From this perspective, the government should favour foreign direct investment because this type of capital inflow is subject to national laws, as well as regulations and policies, albeit in a roundabout way and only to a limited extent. Moreover, foreign direct investments are usually long term and stable and can therefore enhance the economy's growth potential by contributing to the restructuring of industrial capacity, which in turn supports competitiveness. Foreign direct investments are oriented not only toward the domestic market. Indeed, often foreign direct investors are seeking to take advantage of competitive local labour costs in order to produce for export. This can foster export-led growth, which in the longer run is beneficial for all concerned.

There is a strong and positive feedback loop between the scope and pace of privatization and the amount of foreign capital investments in a transition economy. It is true that the more rapidly state assets have been privatized, the more cheaply they have been sold off. However, this has also usually meant that a relatively larger amount of foreign capital is quickly injected into the economy. If the privatization programme is accompanied by steady progress in institution-building and financial stabilization, then the feedback loop can facilitate significant growth.

All in all, wise liberalization policies and the establishment of effective institutions are more important for recovery and growth than is privatization or foreign investment linked with denationalization. Yet, if all these elements are at work at the same time, then the risk of 'dependent capitalism' is greatly reduced, and transition growth can be accelerated. Privatization and liberalization encourage foreign investment. When supported by maturing institutional arrangements, this process can boost growth. The growth then secures increased domestic capital formation and additional absorption of portfolio investments and foreign direct investments. This stimulates more privatization and streamlines liberalization. Growth which is high quality, that is, fast, durable, and equitable, thereby gains momentum.

The existence of this interrelationship among liberalization, privatization, foreign investment, and institution-building explains why countries with relatively larger private sectors and relatively greater absorption of foreign capital can show a lower rate of growth (or higher rate of contraction) than countries with smaller private sectors and relatively less foreign capital.

A simple comparison, for instance between the Czech Republic and Slovenia in Eastern Europe or between Russia and Uzbekistan in the CIS, supports this claim. In the Czech Republic in 1994–8 the average rate of GDP growth was below 3 per cent, while in Slovenia it exceeded 4 per cent. In Russia during the same period GDP was shrinking annually by an average 4.2 per cent, while in Uzbekistan it was growing by an average 0.7 per cent. Yet, the share of the private sector in the economy was greater in the Czech Republic than it was in Slovenia, and it was greater in Russia than it was in Uzbekistan. Likewise, the stock of per capita foreign direct investment at the end of 1997 was higher by almost half in the Czech Republic than it was in Slovenia ($726 and $538, respectively), while it was over seven times higher in Russia than it was in Uzbekistan ($66 and $9, respectively).

The second dilemma is *the instability of portfolio investments*. This can persuade even the most liberal governments and policymakers to be reluctant to permit foreign capital free access to all sectors. The liquidity of portfolio investments is much greater than that of direct investments. Portfolio investments are thus more 'easy come, easy go'. It is prudent not to let them flow in too easily, since later it may be very difficult, if not impossible, to prevent them from doing damage by flowing out equally readily. Unlike direct investments, which are tied to fixed assets, portfolio investments, because of the liberal regulation of capital markets, can be pulled out with shocking speed.

Furthermore, secondary capital deficits (financial 'holes' left after the escape of capital which was invested and circulating in the economy) impair performance much more than do primary capital deficits (shortages of capital for planned investment and reform projects). Secondary capital deficits lead to more underutilization of existing capacity and thence to contraction in national income and the spread of poverty. Primary capital deficits mean only that industrial capacity cannot be raised. Therefore, they do not necessarily generate a reduction in economic activity, which is unavoidable in the case of the withdrawal of capital. In other words, the economic consequences and policy implications of each type of capital deficit are different. Portfolio capital may later return and often does (though still later it may again be pulled out). This is why portfolio capital investments represent a risk in terms of continuity and stability in the process of capital formation and hence the sustainability of growth. It was precisely the sudden flight of portfolio capital that has turned this risk into disaster in East Asia, where, instead of fresh foreign investment, there was a massive foreign divestment.

Thus, policy should focus not only on attracting investment capital, but also on keeping it in the country as long as possible. The more reinvestment there is of speculative capital and the profits earned from it, the more growth becomes stable and durable and the more development becomes sustainable. Sound fundamentals, attractive interest rate differentials, and a stable financial and political climate can encourage speculative capital to become long-term capital. So, transition countries should aim at constant institutional improvements, circumspect structural policies, and the consolidation of stabilization into stability. Then they will earn the growing confidence of international partners, including portfolio investors.

Of course, policy is handicapped in this endeavour. Owing to the speculative nature of portfolio investments, they often fluctuate and flow in and out in any case. The young postsocialist markets, being more volatile and chaotic, are more vulnerable to such fluctuations. Their financial and capital markets and other market institutions are still emerging, and so they have relatively weaker fundamentals and less effective regulations and cannot easily resist a capital market panic (though even mature capital markets sometimes panic, such as Wall Street in 1987).

If the investors panic, no official policy statement or significant economic argument is going to calm them down immediately. Since the market itself has no appropriate emergency mechanism, investors will tend to follow the herd. If worse comes to worst, capital will begin to flow out of the economy like water out of a sieve, and neither the market, nor the government is going to be able to plug the holes. Even the IMF (presumably nearer the angels) will be helpless.

There was the 'tequila effect' of the Mexican crisis and then the East Asian 'contagion', but there has not yet been a distinguishable 'vodka effect' from the turmoil on Russian markets, although there have been negative repercussions in several transition countries. In some nations, for instance in Poland, the government tried to draw political advantage from the Russian crisis by blaming it for the slowdown in growth, even though this was due to deliberate government policy.[26]

Meanwhile, in Estonia in 1998 growth slipped by about 1.5 percentage points in the aftermath of the events in Russia. Unfortunately, in the era of globalization, it may happen that other countries, even those with relatively healthy and mature fundamentals, institutions, and policies, will not be entirely immune to a similar 'effect'. All the more reason for transition economies to be attentive in the liberalization of foreign capital flows. If it is possible to launch a speculative attack on an exposed economy (and the postsocialist nations definitely belong in this category), then one will be launched, very much as wolves will attack sheep at any opportunity.

Nonetheless, in seeking profits on volatile markets, hedge funds and institutional investors also add liquidity to these markets, and this tends to reduce unpredictability and lessen the chances for speculation. Moreover, for the time being, there is a need for these funds on both the supply side and the demand side. They contribute to the development of world financial markets and to the market fluctuations which are part of the global financial and economic game.

Though the hedge funds will not be driven out of the market altogether since they are too powerful and enjoy the strong support of influential interest groups in the most advanced countries, at least the risk they represent to market stability may diminish. Yet, this will happen only if they are subjected to the sort of regulation applied to investment banks. Despite the sense of urgency due to the world financial crisis in 1998, a consensus has still not been reached (in Washington, of course) on how the re-regulation ought to occur.

It has been claimed that 'The hedge funds legitimize the role of the IMF in the eyes of its obstinate clientele. The hedge funds, in turn, depend on the IMF as a clean-up brigade' (Götz-Richter 1997). Hedge funds and the globalization of financial markets have certainly not lessened the role of the IMF. Indeed, they have enhanced it, including in the transition economies. Private financial intermediaries alone are clearly not capable of acting as watchdogs over capital flows on emerging markets. There are even cases in which these particular watchdogs have taken from the pantry.

Greed and the desire for big profits are powerful among some investors. If this causes problems, to shout at the market does not accomplish anything, but to deal with it wisely can be helpful. The governments of emerging market countries are looking increasingly to international financial

---

[26] The government mistakenly assumed that the economy was overheated and—almost a year before the crash in Russia in August 1998—decided to contain domestic demand. As a result the rate of growth dropped from an average 6.4% in 1994–7 to 4.8% in 1998 and was expected to fall further, to around 3.2%, in 1999.

institutions, like the IMF and the Bank for International Settlement, and to regional development banks, such as the EBRD, the Asian Development Bank, and the Inter-American Development Bank. Nations faced with the instability of capital inflows and outflows rely on these organizations for assistance.

Besides sound fundamentals and wise policies, cooperation with international financial organizations is the only remedy for the attacks of speculators that is available to transition nations, which must continue to open up to the global economy and accept the impact on their markets of global capital transfers. In fact, these organizations represent the market as much as they do governments, and there is no way to bring governments and the market together without their (official or secret) mediation. The influence of these organizations can make the task of hostile speculators more difficult.

Ironically, one outcome of transition has been an entirely unplanned interdependence among the once centrally planned economies. What is happening in Hungary or Poland depends to a certain extent on what is happening in Russia or Ukraine, the core republics of the former Soviet Union. The emerging capital markets are linked, and the turmoil among the biggest former Soviet republics is generating storm-clouds in other markets. Of course, this is at least as true of Hungary or Poland as it is of Argentina or Brazil. Without the worldwide coordination of policies toward financial and capital markets that is promoted by international financial organizations, a single country may be unable to resist market pressures, even if the fundamentals and the policies are sound.

The third dilemma is related to *the redistribution of global wealth and income*. Together with globalization, labour mobility, advanced information networks, and wise government policies (often guided by international organizations), the emerging markets may be viewed as buffers for the richer part of the world against the severe effects of sharp fluctuations in the business cycle (Weber 1997). Policies designed by the rich countries from this perspective may tend to ignore the impact of the global economy on working and living conditions elsewhere, thereby 'instrumentalizing' the transition economies. If transition economies are merely cushions against the business cycle for the advanced market countries, what does this say about the significance of the business cycles in the transition economies? How much does it matter? Who cares? The lack of a sound partnership might mean that, for example, the Czech economy could be used as a backup for German business whenever the German economy slows down, but that the German economy would never be available to Czech business in a like circumstance.

If this sort of arrangement is a logical consequence of the relative value of particular economies in international terms, then all the more reason it should be an issue in international policy discussions. This is yet another demonstration of the usefulness of the leading international economic and financial organizations. Without the support of these organizations, the transition economies cannot be sufficiently protected from exploitation by other players, be they hedge funds, investment banks, or foreign governments.

If the efforts of transition countries to establish a market economy and achieve high-quality growth are only a means to boost the well-being of people in other countries, then something is wrong with the world system. The problem is more serious than merely the success or failure of a raid by speculators on the peso or baht, ringgit or koruna, forint or rouble. Emerging capital markets, which the cash-poor economies wish to rely on as a stable instrument for the absorption of foreign savings and for capital formation, may be used by rich-country investors and governments as vehicles to transfer assets and income to themselves from emerging markets, including the transition nations. What starts out as investments in the poorer countries by a richer one ends up as capital divestment or asset stripping. As a result, income inequality increases, but this time the global economy is the scene of the 'old rich' taking from the 'new poor'. This is a serious challenge for international policy coordination.

The fourth dilemma is *capital flight*. Due to the denationalization of state assets, capital liquidity is rising. If this is accompanied by poor financial fundamentals and the flimsy regulation of capital transfers, then capital flight may be facilitated. The money is not always taken out of the economy because of a lack of prospects for profitable local investments or because the prospects are better elsewhere, but rather because of political and economic instability and unpredictability and sometimes simply because of the shadowy if not plain indecent way the assets have been accumulated, including illegal activities in the parallel economy, corruption, and organized crime.

Though it is impossible to gauge precisely the amounts of capital that have been transferred out of transition economies, they have certainly been large. Jacques de Larosière, the former managing director of the EBRD, claimed at the 1997 annual meeting of the bank that, with respect to Russia and other former Soviet republics, 'In 1996 alone the outflow of capital from the region probably exceeded the total invested by the EBRD since its creation' (*Financial Times* 1997c).

The Russian case is an extreme one, if it is possible to believe that $60 billion or $70 billion (*The Economist* 1997d) or even (up to the end of 1998) as much as $150 to $180 billion has left the country. These sums surpass the total foreign direct investment in Eastern Europe and the CIS over 1990–7. While capital flight and crossborder transfers have occurred elsewhere, too, they have not been of the same orders of magnitude as in Russia. It may be too much to believe (as an estimate of Deutsche Morgan Grenfell suggests) that in 1996 alone the capital outflows reached about $22 billion and therefore exceeded the amount of foreign direct investment absorbed by a factor of 10, but it does seem possible that the average level of capital flight has hovered around $12 billion annually since the onset of the transition.

If so much capital has been pulled out of Russia, one may ask whether the rates of return on investment were too high. The answer is that not all investors have acted the same. Some domestic investors, though not ready to take the risks foreign investors have taken, have kept their money in the country.[27] Of course, often domestic investors have simply lacked sufficient capital to bid for privatization deals. Many have lost money through financial intermediaries, including pyramid schemes, and this money has been transferred abroad as someone else's profits anyway.

A significant portion of the outflowing capital has been illicit money which could not be recirculated in the country without first being laundered somewhere else. By the same token, a small fraction of the foreign direct investment in Russia has been money in need of 'washing'. Poor regulation and inadequate commitment to fight money laundering make such activities possible. At least some of the capital leaving the country certainly finds its way back in, whether or not it left for laundering. A not negligible share of the inflows of both portfolio and direct investments (especially investments from the Cayman Islands, Cyprus, and Switzerland) is believed to be returning capital (Robinson 1997). In the meantime, the ownership of assets has changed, and privatization has continued. The capital and market position of the financial intermediaries who have transformed the capital from dirty domestic savings into clean foreign investments has been transformed, too.

So, in Russia, ill-advised privatization and organized crime have been the main sources of capital flight. Meanwhile, in Albania financial pyramids have been directly responsible. On the input side was a massive (and naïve) investment of savings in these fraudulent schemes. On the output side were the attempts to channel the money abroad. Inadequate regulations and weak institutions, as well as the inability if not unwillingness of the government to put a stop to the course of events, allowed the pyramids to grow so big that they were bound to collapse. Estimates of the losses vary, but according to the most credible ones about one-third of GDP was funnelled out of the pyramids. Obviously, a great deal of this money has flown out of the country. None of these financial pathologies—not the Russian, not the Albanian, not any other—would have been possible without the active participation of third (foreign) parties.

It is very bad that such indecent methods of capital accumulation, capital concentration, and capital transfer have been tolerated by these countries, foreign governments, and international financial circles, or at least that they have not been halted by appropriate means in a timely way.

[27] Often such 'investors' have not invested all their money or even put all of it to productive use. Most estimates place the amount of hard currency 'under the mattress' in Russian households at around $40 billion.

International organizations, influential media professionals, research entities, and advisors have not reacted promptly even to diminish the losses once the problem has become visible. In each case too little came too late (though this is clearly not the view of those reaping the profits).

In a rather bizarre way, this financial hocus pocus has helped post-socialist countries accelerate primary capital accumulation and improve the links to global capital markets. The creation of a new class of entrepreneurs has been catalysed; capital has become more concentrated, and international ties have been established. However, the negative political and psychological effects have damaged the goodwill which is so important to the transition. Some may believe that liberalization, privatization, and internationalization have been accelerated, but institution-building, behavioural change, and the development of market culture have been delayed. In the end, this sort of redistribution of capital may have led to the emergence of new 'capitalists' and the concentration of assets, but it has also handicapped the formation of financial and human capital. It should have been possible to achieve more of both.

The Future

13

The Long-term Perspectives

13.1. ALTERNATIVE PATHS: STAGNATION, GROWTH, SUSTAINABLE DEVELOPMENT

The prospects for recovery and growth are too uncertain to permit reliance on easy forecasts. Time and again even short-run predictions have proved false. The examples from the early transition, when so much was unknown, are more numerous, such as the case of Poland, where in 1990, instead of the anticipated decline of 3.1 per cent, GDP fell by four times that amount.

Now, it is a little more difficult to excuse such errors. Yet, as late as December 1996 it was being forecast that the GDP of Bulgaria would drop by around 1 per cent in 1996–8, due to a contraction of 6 per cent in 1996, a recovery of 0.4 per cent in 1997, and growth of 4.8 per cent in 1998 (PlanEcon 1996). However, already in October 1997 it was being said that GDP would shrink in 1998 to about 85 per cent of the 1995 level, this time owing to a decline in 1996 of 10 per cent, a further decline in 1997 of 7 per cent, and only a very modest growth in 1998 of 1.5 per cent (EBRD 1997b). From December 1996 to October 1997, only 10 months, three respected organizations—the Washington-based PlanEcon, the London-based EBRD, and the ING Barings Bank, Emerging Europe Division—changed their predictions about the 1997 GDP growth of Bulgaria from plus 0.4 per cent down to minus 7 per cent.

Even extremely short-term estimates of GDP growth, such as those for one relatively uneventful year, can vary widely. Some of the differences in the predictions for particular countries shown in Table 39 are quite significant. Forecasting errors are rather more understandable in the case of conflict-torn Tajikistan, but appear curious in the case of a peaceful country like Kyrgyzstan, for which the EBRD in February 1997 had envisaged GDP growth of 8 per cent (a 'boom'), but the Economist Intelligence Unit expected only the more conservative increase of 3.2 per cent. For Romania the difference between the most optimistic scenario (5.4 per cent growth according to PlanEcon) and the most pessimistic one (minus 2.5 per cent according to the EBRD) was a whopping 8 percentage points. The corresponding difference in the case of Lithuania was over 4 percentage points in that the United Nations anticipated a weak recovery of 1.5 per cent, while PlanEcon foresaw energetic growth of 5.8 per cent. The spread in

Table 39 A comparison of GDP growth forecasts for 1997 (%)

	EBRD, Feb. 1997	UN survey, Jan. 1997	EU, Oct. 1996	PlanEcon, Dec. 1996	Economist Intelligence Unit, Jan. 1997
Eastern Europe					
Albania[a]		6.0	—	7.7	6.0
Bulgaria	−4.0	0.0	−3.1	0.4	−1.0
Croatia	5.5	—	—	4.9	6.0
Czech Republic	4.0	5.0	5.3	4.8	4.0
Estonia	4.0	3.0	4.5	5.4	3.5
Hungary	2.5	2.0	2.7	3.9	3.0
Latvia	4.0	1.7	2.2	5.2	3.0
Lithuania	4.0	1.5	2.7	5.8	3.7
FYR Macedonia	5.0	—	—	4.5	5.0
Poland	5.5	5.2	5.1	5.5	5.3
Romania	−2.5	4.0	4.2	5.4	4.0
Slovakia	5.0	5.0	4.6	5.5	4.4
Slovenia	4.0	—	4.1	5.2	4.0
Average	3.1	3.3	3.2	4.9	3.9
CIS					
Armenia	7.0	—	—	4.7	4.5
Azerbaijan	5.0	—	—	7.4	4.0
Belarus	0.0	—	—	−0.5	3.0
Georgia	10.0	—	—	8.2	6.0
Kazakhstan	2.8	1.5	—	1.2	2.5
Kyrgyzstan	8.0	—	—	5.2	3.0
Moldova	5.0	—	—	6.0	5.0
Russia	1.5	−1.0	2.5	0.9	1.0
Tajikistan	−3.0	—	—	−5.0	−10.0
Turkmenistan	5.0	—	—	2.2	5.0
Ukraine	−2.0	−2.2	−2.0	−2.1	−3.0
Uzbekistan	1.0	—	—	4.5	1.0
Average	3.4	−0.6	0.3	2.8	1.8

[a] No EBRD projections were made for Albania due to the significant uncertainty over developments there.

Source: EBRD 1997a.

the estimates for Tajikistan might be explained by the regional conflict, but for other countries the uncharted waters of transition are the only excuse. The lesson to be drawn from this exercise is that even short-run forecasts should be treated with great care. Especially in transition economies nothing is forever or for sure.

Nonetheless, while one should not be too eager to rely on predictions and despite the difficulties of the initial years of transition and the frustration owing to the great slump, the conviction has been growing recently that the transition economies have 'bottomed out' and can now finally begin to gather momentum for further growth. This applies even in nations which, after some years of recovery, have experienced a second wave of contraction. Between 1990 and 1997 this occurred in Albania, Bulgaria, Latvia, and Romania (see Table 13).

Disregarding Belarus, for which PlanEcon sees an annual growth rate of only 0.7 per cent over 1998–2002, for another 25 transition economies the forecasts range from 3.8 per cent for Slovakia and 4 per cent for Ukraine to 9.3 per cent for Georgia and 9.7 per cent for Azerbaijan. On average, according to these estimates, the GDP growth rate should stand at about 4.9 per cent for 11 countries in Eastern Europe (omitting Bosnia-Herzegovina) and at around 4.3 per cent for the 15 former Soviet republics. Hence *the average weighted rate of growth of GDP among transition economies for the next few years is expected to be around 4–6 per cent.* However, by 2002 only one-third (nine) of these economies are anticipated to have recovered the pre-transition level of output. Of these, only two—Estonia and Uzbekistan—are former Soviet republics (Table 40).

Yet, there still must be doubts, particularly in the aftermath of the Russian financial crisis in the summer of 1998. Immediately after the de facto devaluation of the rouble by one-third in August 1998, PlanEcon revised its forecast for Russia downward, predicting a fall in GDP of 2.5 per cent in 1998 and 4 per cent in 1999, with a chance for the drop to bottom out only in 2000. Inflation was expected to accelerate significantly, and it was being anticipated that capital formation would decline further, with the obvious implications for medium- and long-term growth. A couple of months later, at the end of 1998, the government was already making much bleaker forecasts, predicting a GDP drop of 3 per cent for 1998 and of from 5 per cent to as much as 9 per cent for 1999 (Dolgov 1998).

Instead of predictions, 'possible scenarios' might be more judicious. A moderately positive scenario for 1999–2002 might be based on the likelihood that there will be recovery and growth in the average postsocialist economy over the medium term (see the Statistical Appendix, part two). Taking into consideration the differences between the rates of GDP growth (measured in various ways) and the rates of growth in the absorption of GDP through private consumption and investments, one might develop various hypotheses (Table 41).

First, as a result of ongoing economic liberalization and openness, this time in a context of growth, the gap between GDP counted in constant prices in the domestic currency and the estimates of GDP on a purchasing power parity basis will tend to decrease. This is a strong tendency, as shown by the 'A' indexes (see Table 41), which measure the ratio of the average annual rate of per capita GDP growth at market exchange rates

Table 40 Forecast of economic growth in transition economies, 1998–2002

	GDP index, 1997 (1989 = 100)	Rate of growth					Average, 1998–2002	Ranking[a]	GDP index, 2002	
		1998	1999	2000	2001	2002			1997 = 100	1989 = 100
Poland	111.8	6.5	5.9	5.8	5.8	6.1	6.0	7	133.9	149.8
Slovenia	99.3	4.1	4.1	4.8	4.2	4.9	4.4	20	124.1	123.3
Albania	79.1	10.2	9.7	10.6	8.6	3.7	8.6	4	150.6	119.1
Slovakia	95.6	4.0	2.3	2.5	5.0	5.0	3.8	22	120.2	114.9
Czech Republic	95.8	1.4	3.3	4.3	4.5	4.7	3.6	24	119.5	114.5
Hungary	90.4	5.4	4.6	4.5	4.8	4.5	4.8	19	126.2	114.1
Uzbekistan	86.7	5.8	4.3	4.9	4.5	4.5	4.8	16	126.4	109.6
Estonia	77.9	6.4	5.5	5.9	5.6	5.9	5.9	8	132.9	103.6
Romania	82.4	-2.1	3.3	5.8	5.5	4.9	4.9	21	118.4	97.6
Croatia	73.3	5.5	3.4	5.4	5.4	4.9	4.9	15	127.1	93.2
Kyrgyzstan	58.7	6.5	6.8	6.0	5.5	5.6	6.1	6	134.3	78.8
Bulgaria	62.8	3.5	5.4	5.7	4.4	4.0	4.6	18	125.2	78.6
Yugoslavia	62.7	3.7	2.3	3.9	5.0	6.0	4.2	9	122.7	76.9
Kazakhstan	58.1	4.4	3.8	4.9	7.0	7.0	5.4	11	130.1	75.6
Latvia	56.8	6.0	3.9	4.6	5.8	5.7	5.2	12	128.8	73.2
Belarus	70.8	-7.1	-1.5	2.7	3.7	5.5	0.7	26	102.8	72.8
Turkmenistan	48.3	4.7	12.1	16.0	3.5	4.2	8.1	3	146.8	70.9
FYR Macedonia	55.3	2.8	3.4	3.4	4.9	5.0	3.9	17	121.1	66.9
Azerbaijan	40.5	7.1	9.0	10.7	11.2	10.7	9.7	1	159.1	64.4
Armenia	41.1	6.6	6.5	6.7	7.8	6.9	6.9	5	139.6	57.4
Lithuania	42.8	5.0	5.0	5.7	5.1	4.9	5.1	13	128.5	55.0
Georgia	34.3	10.2	10.1	9.3	9.1	7.6	9.3	2	155.7	53.4
Tajikistan	40.0	4.5	5.1	5.7	6.0	6.1	5.5	10	130.6	52.2
Russia	52.2	-3.8	-4.7	-1.8	1.4	3.1	-1.2	25	94.1	49.1
Ukraine	38.3	1.2	3.0	4.8	5.2	6.0	4.0	23	121.8	46.7
Moldova	35.1	1.2	6.6	5.0	6.3	5.8	5.0	14	127.4	44.7

[a] Ranking is according to the average rate of growth in 1998–2002 and the 2002 GDP index.

Sources: PlanEcon 1998a, 1998b, author's calculations based on Table 13.

Table 41 Indexes of structural change, 1999–2002

	A	B	C	D	E
Albania	1.134	1.020	1.496	0.931	0.982
Armenia	1.388	1.016	1.156	0.887	1.057
Azerbaijan	1.386	1.047	1.503	0.817	0.964
Belarus	1.581	1.016	1.127	0.934	1.005
Bulgaria	1.411	1.011	1.181	1.009	1.000
Croatia	1.166	0.995	1.112	0.946	0.929
Czech Republic	1.508	1.006	0.979	1.030	0.962
Estonia	1.391	1.009	1.020	0.958	0.975
Georgia	1.346	1.022	1.367	0.839	0.897
Hungary	1.177	1.005	1.087	0.977	0.984
Kazakhstan	1.188	0.998	1.236	0.998	0.963
Kyrgyzstan	1.124	1.057	1.379	0.931	0.981
Latvia	1.149	0.981	1.288	0.942	0.963
Lithuania	1.195	1.003	1.067	0.965	1.000
FYR Macedonia	1.092	1.027	1.138	0.955	0.981
Moldova	1.118	1.008	1.744	0.977	0.990
Poland	1.240	1.004	1.021	0.977	0.904
Romania	1.237	0.991	1.157	0.970	0.981
Russia	0.798	0.985	1.129	1.045	0.958
Slovakia	1.110	1.003	0.939	0.990	1.002
Slovenia	1.074	0.994	1.094	0.960	0.981
Tajikistan	1.460	1.083	1.155	1.057	0.963
Turkmenistan	1.533	1.054	0.849	1.201	0.964
Ukraine	1.269	0.998	1.139	0.972	0.973
Uzbekistan	1.508	1.113	0.956	0.994	0.981
Yugoslavia	1.224	1.016	1.362	0.939	0.962

Note: A = Ratio of the per capita GDP growth rate at market exchange rates to the per capita GDP growth rate at purchasing power parities. B = Ratio of the real per capita GDP growth rate to the per capita GDP growth rate at PPP. C = Ratio of the growth rate of gross fixed investments to the real GDP growth rate. D = Ratio of the growth rate of private consumption to the real GDP growth rate. E = Ratio of the growth rate of average real wages to the real GDP growth rate.

Source: Author's computation based on Statistical Appendix, pt. 2.

over the average rate of per capita GDP growth at PPP during the period 1999–2002. In each case, with the exception of Russia, about which any forecast must be taken with great reservation, the index is greater than unity, and the difference is meaningful. If this trend occurs, then *the market exchange rate and the purchasing power parity exchange rate will move closer*, and the current gap between these rates, usually between 1.5 and 2, will steadily diminish.

Second, the 'B' indexes, which measure the ratio of the average real GDP growth rate (in domestic currency, at fixed prices) over the average GDP growth rate at PPP, reveal two likely tendencies in shifts in relative exchange rates. *In a number of countries the process of the real appreciation of national currencies will continue*, contributing to the closing gap between the value of national income as expressed on a PPP basis and its value as expressed in constant prices in the national currency. If this index is higher than unity, then the relative efficiency of the economy is growing, and therefore the competitiveness of the economy is improving, too. If it is less than unity, the relative efficiency and competitiveness are declining.

The index of only about one-third of the transition economies is anticipated to be (slightly) below '1', indicating that there may be a limited depreciation in the national currencies. With an index significantly lower, only 0.985, the Russian economy, which was forecast before the financial crisis in the summer of 1998 to grow at a rate of 4.1 per cent over 1999–2002 (in terms of real GDP at constant prices in 1998 roubles), should still grow, but due more to extensive than to intensive factors. In any case, both tendencies mean that the integration of these countries with the world economy should continue.

Third, the 'C', 'D', and 'E' indexes indicate a growth tendency in all but a few of these nations. The 'C' indexes, which measure the ratio of the average rate of growth of gross fixed investments over the real GDP growth rate, show that the process of capital formation should gather speed. This will result from an increasing propensity to save and thus a declining marginal propensity to consume, both of which are apparent in the 'D' and 'E' indexes. If these indexes are below '1', then *capital formation should rise more quickly than consumption and GDP, and this should create a strong foundation for more growth.* For rapid and sustained expansion, domestic capital formation is always more decisive than the inflow of foreign savings. Only for the Czech Republic, Slovakia, Turkmenistan, and Uzbekistan are the 'C' indexes forecast to remain below '1', which means that consumption is going to increase more quickly than investment. If this does happen, then 'eating the fruits of the future' may take place, and the rate of growth may slow after 2002.

Another reason for the confidence in the sustained growth of postsocialist nations has been the fact that the developing market economies, including the transition economies, were expected to register rapid growth rates. In 1997 the World Bank (1997c) forecast an average rate of growth of 5–6 per cent for this group of economies over the next 25 years, while it expected the advanced market economies to expand by only 2.5 per cent (Table 42). The rate of GDP growth for the 'Big 5' (Brazil, China, India, Indonesia, and Russia) was anticipated to be 5.8 per cent per year.[1] China and Russia

---

[1] Coincidentally, soon after the World Bank began to turn so much of its attention on the 'Big 5', they became bigger headaches for the world economy.

Table 42 Annual average world growth and shares in world GDP, 1974–2020 (%)

Country or group	Real GDP[a]				Capital stock, 1992–2020	Total factor productivity, 1992–2020	Share of world real GDP[a]	
	1974–82	1982–92	1992–5	1992–2020			1992	2020
World	2.6	3.0	2.4	2.9	3.6	0.5	100.0	100.0
High-income economies	2.3	3.1	2.2	2.5	3.3	0.3	84.2	70.9
OECD	2.2	2.9	2.0	2.4	3.1	0.3	81.5	66.7
Newly industrialized economies[b]	8.0	8.7	7.4	4.9	6.0	1.3	2.3	3.8
Hong Kong	7.7	9.3	7.8	4.0	4.0	1.1	0.3	0.4
Developing countries	3.7	2.6	3.1	5.4	6.0	1.3	15.7	29.1
Big 5[c]	4.4	2.7	3.3	5.8	7.2	1.7	7.8	16.1
China	6.5	10.3	12.5	7.0	9.5	2.2	1.4	3.9
India	4.4	5.4	5.5	5.8	6.7	1.9	1.0	2.1
Brazil	4.3	1.8	4.8	4.6	4.6	1.1	1.7	2.5
Indonesia	6.8	7.1	7.6	6.9	6.9	1.9	0.6	1.5
Economies in transition	3.8	–0.7	–5.4	5.5	7.0	1.7	3.2	6.0
ASEAN 3[d]	6.3	5.6	7.7	7.1	6.7	2.0	0.8	2.4
Rest of South Asia	5.3	5.2	4.0	5.2	5.7	1.4	0.3	0.6
Rest of Latin America and Caribbean	3.0	2.0	2.2	4.2	4.0	0.9	2.1	2.9
Sub-Saharan Africa	2.2	2.0	2.1	4.2	3.4	0.8	1.2	1.7
Middle East and North Africa	2.2	2.0	2.1	4.2	4.1	0.3	2.3	3.1
Rest of the World	3.3	2.4	2.6	5.6	5.8	1.4	1.2	2.3

[a] Constant 1992 dollars using market exchange rates.   [b] Singapore, South Korea, and Taiwan.   [c] Brazil, China, India, Indonesia, and Russia.
[d] Malaysia, the Philippines, and Thailand.

Source: World Bank 1997c.

were obviously supposed to play an important role, given their relatively significant weight in the global economy. Altogether, according to the World Bank, the share of the Big 5 economies in global output would rise from 8 per cent in the mid-1990s to about 16 per cent by 2020. The share of the Big 5 in total worldwide exports would increase appreciably, from 9 to 22 per cent, of which almost half (around 10 per cent) would be accounted for by China alone.

However, only one year later all these forecasts had to be revised. Aside from the irrelevant methodological assumptions behind them, the march of events had changed the situation substantially. Because of the East Asian contagion and the ongoing crisis in Russia, the level of optimism in 1998 was already a notch below that in 1997, and the policies of governments and international organizations had to be reconsidered and altered.

Following nuclear tests in India and Pakistan, the G-7 (and, unfortunately, on the insistence of the United States, also the World Bank) imposed economic sanctions. However, these were soon lifted, though not because of any worry that economic growth in India and Pakistan might slow, but mainly due to the concern that opportunities might be lost for export expansion in the markets of these countries.

It had been thought that in 1997 the robust growth in Indonesia would continue, but by 1998 the World Bank was predicting a contraction of 10 to 15 per cent for that year alone, and an additional 50 million Indonesians are estimated to have been driven below the poverty line (defined as an income below $1 per day), inter alia owing to a staggering increase of 20 million in the number of the unemployed. If appropriate reforms and the structural adjustment measures agreed with the Bretton Woods institutions were carried forward, it was hoped that there could be a recovery of between 2 and 4 per cent in 2000 after a further recession of 2 per cent in 1999. In the aftermath of the East Asian crisis, Indonesia was expected to follow the 'model' of Mexico, where, after the December 1994 devaluation of the peso, GDP dropped by 7 per cent, before springing back by the same 7 per cent. Yet, in East Asia, because of the unprecedented capital outflows, economic contraction may last longer, and recovery may come later.

Thus, a good chance of becoming a leading performer in the Big 5 seemed to belong to Brazil, which, however, began to exhibit structural tensions and a negative impact from the turmoil on global capital markets and also did not expand as much as expected. Substantial short-term debt and the associated very high interest rates were imposing an additional burden on the state budget. With an eye to the experience of the Indonesian crisis and the Russian malaise, the IMF and the US government decided to bail out the Brazilian economy. For this purpose a special emergency financial package of about $41.5 billion—that is, almost twice as much as in the case of Russia, which had been in much worse straits—was put together in November 1998. This time, however, not only the fate of the Brazilian economy is at stake, but also the prestige of the IMF and the US Treasury. While some have been blaming the Indonesian crisis and the Russian malaise on cronyism and the socialist legacy, a severe setback in Brazil could mean that the bulk of that country's huge foreign debt, mainly owed to creditors in the US, would not be repaid, and these losses would prompt a search for the deeper causes of the crises. In other words, it would become extremely difficult to continue to argue that the wrong policies are the right ones.

Meanwhile, for the transition economies between 1992 and 2020, the World Bank (1997c) in 1997 had predicted an average GDP growth rate of 5.5 per cent, which was less than the estimate for Indonesia (6.9 per cent) and three other ASEAN countries, namely, Malaysia, the Philippines, and Thailand (7.1 per cent). Although the World Bank forecast was 'long term', it also had to be revised after only a single year, as the transition nations moved to the top of the list of the most quickly growing economies. Unfortunately, this occurred not because of a sudden acceleration in growth, but simply because the Big 5 and the ASEAN economies had moved down on the list.[2]

In any case, even the World Bank prediction for the transition economies seems to have been overoptimistic. In 1992–6 these economies were shrinking by 5.1 per cent annually, and in 1997–8 their combined GDP expanded by only 2 per cent per year (see Table 8). Yet, the World Bank expected the output of these countries to increase an average 7.6 per cent per year in 1999–2020. This means that production would have to jump fourfold, and that the share of these countries in global GDP would have to nearly double, from a mere 3.2 per cent in the late 1990s to 6 per cent by 2020.[3]

But is it feasible for the transition economies to achieve and sustain such a high rate of GDP growth for so long? Moreover, since it is unlikely that all these nations would experience the same high growth rate, this would mean that in some of them the rate would have to be even higher, say, close to 10 per cent per year. However, there will certainly be more cases of a growth rate below the overly optimistic 7.6 per cent per year than above it. Once more, the World Bank (together with the IMF) was apparently a victim of its own excessive optimism and cheerful visions of the future.

Optimism may be a good quality, but excessive optimism can be misleading, especially in the case of development policy. While it may be gratifying to be able to believe that two dozen countries will expand more

[2] Indonesia belongs to both the Big 5 and ASEAN, but is included in Table 42 only in the forecast for the Big 5. Likewise, Russia, which belongs to the Big 5 and is also a transition economy, is counted in Table 42 only among the transition countries.

[3] It should be remembered that the loss by about one-third in national income during the transitional contraction of 1990–6 brought down the share of these countries in global GDP by about 1 percentage point, from over 4% in 1989 to 3.2% in 1996.

quickly than ever before for more than 20 years, such a belief verges on
the unrealistic. At most only a handful of the best-performing postsocialist economies actually have a chance of reaching anything like this remarkable level of growth over a short time. One or two may even enjoy it over
the full 20 years.

Usually countries are grouped according to geopolitical or systemic
criteria, but the postsocialist transition economies cannot be seen as a
homogeneous group from the point of view of their long-term growth. These
countries will enter the 21st century along different paths. For some it may
be stagnation, and for others it may be sustainable development and
durable growth.

13.2. ROSY FORECASTS, BLACK SCENARIOS, AND WISE POLICIES

Less than one year after the World Bank released its most-optimistic-ever
evaluation of the world economy and promised a brighter future, Robert
Reich, the former secretary of labour in the first Clinton Administration,
was already seeing things in a different light. In reaction to the response
to the East Asian crisis being adopted by the Bretton Woods institutions
and international financial circles, as well as his former colleagues at the
US Treasury Department, Reich warned that events could take a different
and decidedly unpleasant turn.

Consider the big picture: an East Asia of toppling currencies and bank insolvency;
rising unemployment in Latin America's largest economy and falling real wages
[in] the region; stagnation and unemployment in Europe; a rapidly approaching
limit to the capacity of US consumers to take on more debt. As the global economy slows, social unrest threatens. (Reich 1998)

Curiously, the risk of crisis in China is not mentioned. As for Eastern
Europe and the CIS, they were certainly not thought to be headed toward
success, but they may have been omitted from this scenario because of a
conviction about their minor significance in the world economy. However,
if one is painting a sad picture of the global economy, one should not exclude
a priori and unconditionally the potential negative contribution of the
transition countries, even if this appears to be less than that of the crisis
in East Asia.

In contrast, in 1998 one began hearing comparisons between the crisis
in East Asia and the situation in the transition economies. The similarities were frequently exaggerated and overemphasized, but the differences
were somehow ignored or overlooked. In Kiev in May 1998, at the annual
EBRD meeting, there was a good example of this.

Several speakers noted similarities between Asia and the countries of Central
and Eastern Europe and the former Soviet Union. . . . The similarities included

the widening of current account deficits in several countries and problems of corruption and corporate governance. In particular, speakers urged countries in the region to act quickly to strengthen their financial systems. Acting EBRD President Charles Frank said investors in the region encountered problems such as excessive bureaucracy, poorly designed and administered tax systems, and high levels of crime and corruption. Among regional companies, there was a disregard of shareholders' rights, a lack of transparency and adequate disclosure, insensitivity to conflicts of interest, and a willingness to pay and receive bribes. (IMF 1998a)

Such analogies should not be disregarded, but they should not be exaggerated either. Prior to the crisis the current account and the fiscal budget had looked healthier in East Asia than they do in transition economies. Moreover, the East Asian economies have had two or three decades of impressive high-speed growth, while the postsocialist nations have had nearly a decade of the great slump.

Nonetheless, though their recent experiences are quite distinct, they may face a similar next few years in terms of struggling to achieve long-term growth. East Asia must overcome its contagion, and the transition countries must progress further with institutional reform and structural adjustment.

A financial and economic crisis could also occur in transition economies. Thoroughgoing liberalization during a period of expansion in the global economy not only offers postsocialist countries a chance to grow, but also exposes them to the threat of becoming caught up in the turmoil of crises elsewhere. No group of economies has ever opened up as quickly to the outside world as the postsocialist countries have been doing. After a decade of transformation, many of them are more open to all sorts of transactions and dealings than are dozens of the less-developed market economies in Africa, Asia, and Latin America.

Thus, as a result of the coexistence of transition and globalization, *the fate of a majority of transition nations now hangs on factors which cannot be controlled solely, if at all, by the governments of these nations, including fiscal and monetary authorities.* Occurrences on capital markets in Moscow or Prague, Tashkent or Ljubljana, Bucharest or Bishkek depend less and less on local parliaments, presidents, governments, and central banks and more and more on global financial markets, especially in London or New York, Frankfurt or Tokyo. An extremely important consideration is the amount of short-term foreign capital involved in an emerging economy and hence the level of reliance of the economy on jittery investors. A worldwide deflation (in similar fashion to stagflation) could trigger a resurgence of crisis in the transition economies. If the big markets are not re-regulated under the auspices of international financial institutions in a manner which takes into account the interests of relatively weaker economies, these economies may be not able to meet the challenge.

From time to time, there are certainly going to be financial and economic crises, though it is difficult to know beforehand where and when. If there is a crisis in tiny Albania or Estonia, the repercussions will be less severe because small nations are involved, but mainly because there is less risk of contagion. However, if the crisis takes place in Poland, Russia, or Ukraine, then it will be everyone's problem. Likewise, a crisis in a big transition economy would definitely be much more significant for the region and for the global economy if it followed on the heels of an East Asian crisis than it would be if it occurred during a period of relative global calm.

Yet, the probability that something bad will happen becomes greater if one does not vigilantly try to avoid the worst. A good way to do this is to develop an understanding of possible scenarios and to take steps to forestall the unpleasant ones. 'Black scenarios' were actually discussed and preventive plans developed from time to time during the implementation of the 'Strategy for Poland'. Undoubtedly, the success of economic policy in that country in 1994–7 was at least partly due to this approach.

Nonetheless, crises are occurring not because of any lack of theoretical knowledge about how to evade them, but because of an inability to solve conflicts of interest before these lead to misfortune. Conflict management is an extremely important component of crisis management. There must be open discussion about confrontational issues, the methods of lobbyists (especially informal ones), and the real or potential interests of influential groups on the domestic and international scene, including the tycoons, the government bureaucracy, political parties, researchers and advisors, the media, or the ideologues. It is not true that everybody is unselfishly working on behalf of a healthy economy in a civil society. Many actors are merely seeking profitable advantage. This is yet another reason for a sound long-term overview of development goals that, together with current government policies, can lead to outcomes which serve the authentic needs of the economy and of society.

Economic turmoil or a financial or production crisis in Eastern Europe or the CIS alone are not likely to generate a worldwide recession. Although the involvement of the private sector in these economies is growing, the inflow of portfolio and direct investments increasing, and the role of international trade expanding, the exposure of the global economy in Eastern Europe and the former Soviet republics is still rather limited. After all, *the collapse of the central planning system and the great slump did not explode into world recession.* Indeed, they gave an additional boost to capitalism and to the expansion of the world economy.

However, if China were severely affected by an East Asian contagion, or if China should become subject to a crisis of its own, the consequences for the global economy would be much more drastic.[4] The linkages between China and the rest of the world are much stronger, and they are

---

[4] In fact, the East Asian crisis is reverberating in China because of that nation's significant exposure through trade with the crisis countries. Chinese exports grew by only 7.6% during the first six months of 1998. During the same period in 1997 they had soared by 26.2%. The drop was due principally to the falling demand for Chinese goods in East Asia.

still growing. China has become a very important market for the exports of the advanced countries, and it accepts significant foreign direct investment. No capable export producer or financial intermediary would want to ignore an emerging market with one-fifth of the world's population, and no capable economist would want to ignore the consequences of a potential crisis in such a huge market.

If the centrally planned economies of the late 1980s had been as tightly integrated with the world economy as China is in the late 90s, then the collapse of 'real socialism' would have provoked a worldwide recession. The industrial countries would have lost markets and the room they represented for their outward investments. Their exports to these countries would have fallen, and output and employment would have declined, as would have the capital gains and profits being accrued by international investors.

However, this did not happen, because the socialist 'markets' were almost entirely closed to Western penetration. Unlike the recent *fin de siècle* gold rush in the 'Wild East', the lack of convertibility and the political concerns about the course of the market reforms were keeping foreign banks, multinational corporations, and investors at arm's length. So, when output collapsed in the command economies, it was somebody else's output and somebody else who had few financial, trade, and production connections with the global economy.

For many corporations in the West and the Far East this was an opportunity: one person's misery was another person's fortune. Some were able to take more advantage than were others. Since then, there have been many more opportunities to sell products and invest capital in these emerging markets. General liberalization (including the introduction of currency convertibility) and the shift in the demand structure have boosted imports and foreign investment in the entire transition region.

In coming years the relative position of socialist and postsocialist economies will begin to change. Events in the biggest former Soviet economies, especially Russia and Ukraine, but also Kazakhstan, Turkmenistan, and Uzbekistan, will then become more crucial. A quarter of a billion people will be manufacturing and trading as never before, absorbing increasing amounts of imports, and producing mounting levels of exports. The immense natural resources (with the potential to shift world supply patterns appreciably in numerous sectors) will attract the ever greater attention of transnational corporations. Portfolio and direct investments will continue to pour in to satisfy the insatiable demand for capital. The biggest former Soviet economies will start to resemble China and Vietnam a few years ago, while the changes in the Central Asian transition economies may be even more dramatic and dynamic, so that the relative significance of particular countries may shift somewhat in favour of the former Soviet republics.

The postsocialist economies appear now to be involved in a long process of catching up with the most advanced countries. Starting from a relatively lower level of output, with per capita GDP somewhere between $3,000 and $10,000 in Eastern European and between $1,000 and $3,000 in Central Asia, they now have a chance to grow more quickly than most of the rest of the globe.

For this reason, transition economies are sometimes described as 'developing countries', and, indeed, there are several arguments in favour of this view. In fact, they are treated this way in some of the data assembled by the United Nations, the OECD, and the WTO. Structural adjustment, the inflow of foreign investments, trade and capital market liberalization, growing investments in infrastructure and human capital: all these are common features of both groups of countries. The pattern of growth, along with the possible pace of expansion, is a function of these characteristics. It is no coincidence that the GDP growth rate for both groups for the first two decades of the 21st century is forecast at 6 per cent for developing countries and 7 per cent for transition economies. These predictions are based on the assumption that capital stocks will increase by 7 per cent per year between 1992 and 2020, while total factor productivity will grow by 1.7 per cent.

The World Bank 'baseline scenario 2020'

is one in which the forces propelling global integration in the 1980s and early 1990s have had free play for another thirty-odd years. There is assumed to be considerable trade liberalization over and above the Uruguay Round. . . . Within this increasingly open world trading and investment environment, most developing countries and regions are assumed to achieve sustained progress across a broad range of structural and macroeconomic reforms, resulting in aggregate growth for developing countries in the period to 2020 running at 2–3 percentage points higher than in the past twenty-five years. (World Bank 1997c)

These trends seem to be feasible given the growing propensity to save and the results of structural adjustment, both enhanced furthermore by the inflow of foreign direct investments. Policy should therefore work to realize this positive though difficult and ambitious scenario. There are many reasons to expect even higher growth in total factor productivity. The market allocation of financial resources, raw materials, and labour, as well as technological progress, should facilitate a significant upward surge in overall productivity. Consequently, the capacity for sustainable and high-speed growth could be boosted. However, this will be true only for the most successful transition economies. Not everyone is going to be a winner.

Some studies on development and transition stress that trade liberalization and greater openness in postsocialist economies should contribute to improvements in efficiency and competitiveness and hence to higher rates of growth. Indeed, at least in the countries which are more advanced in transition, policies are aiming at export-led growth. International trade is viewed as the vehicle for growth acceleration and is expected to expand much more quickly than is overall output. It is anticipated that in these nations the long-term rise in exports will exceed the GDP growth rate by 0.7 percentage points and the growth in the share of world trade by 0.8 percentage points. For imports, the corresponding spread is estimated at only 0.4 and 0.5 percentage points, respectively.

Unlike the case with its forecasts of GDP growth, this time the World Bank estimates of the expansion in the trade of transition economies seem too conservative. Exports and imports may begin to expand much more rapidly in several countries. This is so because of the sequence in adjustment in transition economies. First, trade volume falls before overall output and by a bigger margin; then it recovers before GDP does, and later, being one of the engines of growth, it rises at a faster pace than national income. So, the share of transition economies in global trade in 2020 might be expected to go even higher than the World Bank figures of 3.6 per cent for exports, up from 3 per cent in 1992, and 3.9 per cent for imports, up from 3.4 per cent in 1992 (Table 43).

How all this fits into the Global Trade Analysis Model, on which the whole matrix of the long-term forecast for the global economy is founded, is another matter. It appears that the impact of trade expansion on the growth of production has been underestimated, while the significance of non-trade factors which facilitate growth, for instance the increase in labour productivity and the improvements in allocative efficiency due to liberalization and privatization, has been overestimated. In short, the World Bank prognosis seems to be overly pessimistic about the prospects for growth in trade and overly optimistic about the rise in GDP. It might be better if the World Bank were wrong the other way around.

In view of the variety of geopolitical, financial, and cultural characteristics, it would be a big mistake to expect all transition economies to expand in a uniform manner. Although it may be awkward especially for international organizations to try to identify in advance the countries which are going to do well and those which are not, one can readily assume that some postsocialist economies (we do not yet know which ones) will experience stagnation, if not a more serious economic plight. There will be periods when some nations enjoy fast expansion, and others when they suffer crisis. Contrary to the expectations of many experts, this has already happened with the Czech Republic (rapid growth up to 1997 and crisis in 1997–8), as well as Albania, Bulgaria, and Romania, though much less markedly. Overoptimistic forecasts have been bandied about again and again for Russia, which seems to be trapped in a systemic vacuum and was unable to launch growth again most recently in 1997–9 (contrary to widespread predictions formulated before the August 1998 crash).

Table 43 Trade growth and market shares, 1992–2020 (%)

Country or group	Exports growth, 1992–2020[a]	Share of world exports		Imports growth, 1992–2020[a]	Share of world imports	
		1992	2020		1992	2020
World	5.5	100.0	100.0	5.3	100.0	100.0
High-income economies	4.0	76.5	51.6	4.3	74.3	56.6
OECD	3.5	67.8	40.4	4.0	65.3	45.3
Newly industrialized countries	6.5	7.4	9.7	6.3	7.2	9.4
Hong Kong	6.0	1.3	1.5	5.7	1.8	1.9
Developing countries	8.1	23.5	48.4	7.3	25.7	43.3
Big 5[b]	8.9	9.0	22.0	8.5	8.7	20.1
China	10.0	3.0	9.8	10.2	2.8	9.9
India	12.0	0.7	3.9	11.0	0.8	3.2
Brazil	7.2	1.2	1.9	6.8	0.9	1.3
Indonesia	8.8	1.1	2.7	7.8	0.9	1.8
Economies in transition	6.2	3.0	3.6	5.9	3.4	3.9
ASEAN 3[c]	9.6	2.8	8.4	8.6	3.0	7.0
Rest of South Asia	8.0	0.5	0.9	6.8	0.6	0.8
Rest of Latin America and Caribbean	6.7	2.8	3.9	5.4	3.5	3.5
Sub-Saharan Africa	6.7	1.7	2.4	5.3	2.1	2.1
Middle East and North Africa	6.4	5.2	6.6	5.4	5.9	6.0
Rest of world	9.4	1.5	4.2	8.1	1.9	3.9

[a] Exports and imports in constant 1992 dollars.   [b] Brazil, China, India, Indonesia, and Russia.   [c] Malaysia, the Philippines, and Thailand.

Source: World Bank 1997c.

In reality, unlike in the forecasts, we continue to see periods of sluggish economic performance in countries and subregions. In any case, by 2020 the transition region's GDP will certainly not have grown by a factor of four. A more realistic estimate would be that the total GDP of 28 transition economies (Mongolia and the 27 postsocialist countries of the CIS and Eastern Europe) may double over the next two decades.

However, if the GDP of a country contracts at a certain rate over a certain number of years and then expands at the same rate for an equal amount of time, this does not mean that the expansion necessarily offsets the contraction, particularly in the situation of a shift from pre-transition output to post-transition growth. It is a question of simple arithmetic. For example, the GDP decline in Russia over the eight years between 1990 and 1997 was an average 8.3 per cent per year. This represented a fall of 50 per cent with respect to the pre-crisis 1989 level of GDP. Yet, to match the 1989 level, the Russian economy must now grow an average 7.2 per cent per year for an entire decade, or an average 9.1 per cent over a similar eight-year period. But if the rate of growth is the same as the rate of contraction (that is, 8.3 per cent), then to reattain the pre-crisis level of GDP will require nine years, not eight. Similarly, in Poland in 1990–1 GDP fell by 18 per cent, or an average 9.4 per cent per year. The same rate applied to growth would mean that the 1989 output level would be fully recovered not in two years, but in two years plus a couple of months. Actually, it took the Polish economy about three and a half years at an average annual rate of growth of 5.8 per cent to reach again the pre-transition level of output. Going down is easier than going up.

If one can foresee annual growth rates over the next quarter century in the range of 7 to 8 per cent for the leading transition countries, which will enjoy relatively more favourable external conditions and have the luck to be governed by wise policies, one ought also to have enough imagination to foresee that for the next 25 years a more likely average annual weighted growth rate for transition economies is something like 4 to 5 per cent. Still, this should exceed the rate of expansion of the global economy, so the share of transition economies in global production will be climbing as well, albeit hardly to 6 per cent by 2020.

Already from 1992—the beginning of the period of the World Bank forecast—to 1997 and 1998, the average annual rate of GDP growth was much lower than the average predicted for the entire period 1992–2020. The World Bank foresaw a 5.5 per cent annual growth rate for the period, but the average weighted GDP growth for the 25 countries in the sphere of operations of the EBRD was only 1.6 per cent in 1997 and was expected to be 2.5 per cent in 1998 (see Table 8). In 1995–7 only a few countries enjoyed the sort of high-speed growth in the optimistic World Bank forecast. Even Poland recorded 'only' a 6.4 per cent expansion in real GDP in 1994–7, and it would be a great achievement if this outstanding performance were to continue very long (Kolodko 1997c). Under these circumstances, the World Bank forecast is going to have to be revised downward yet again.

The World Bank and other institutions and influential analysts are going to continue making inaccurate forecasts of GDP growth. There is nothing wrong with this. After all, the forecasts are only 'educated' guesses and can become reality only if the assumptions behind them also prove accurate. But this is not going to be the case of the World Bank predictions about transition economies, although no one knows beforehand when or why the growth will take an unexpected turn. The World Bank predictions are simply too rosy. Likewise, no one in, say, 1988 or even 1996 foresaw that there would be a severe crisis in four ASEAN countries. There is no reason to complain too much about inaccurate forecasting. After all, policymaking, not forecasting, has been at fault.

By the same token, if the economy is healthier than expected, this does not necessarily mean that the forecasts have been bad. It may be that policymaking has been better than anticipated. Actual growth rates are not determined exclusively by the initial conditions or by well-known and thus more well understood patterns of growth. They are also affected by external shocks (or lack thereof), by sudden turns in the development path of particular nations, and, of course, by the policies exercised by governments, central banks, and international organizations. Conditions change; priorities change; and policy instruments evolve. So, the pace of growth can change, too. There is no reason to think that policy failures will never occur in transition economies, and this alone should be sufficient cause for caution in making predictions.

The relative weight of a particular country in the world economy depends on the country's contribution to world GDP. From this angle, Russia carries the most weight among the transition economies. Despite the profound recession there, Russia still contributes more than 40 per cent of the total GDP of postsocialist economies. The next most important country is Poland, with a GDP share of around 14 per cent. Due to the great slump in Russia and the very quick growth in Poland, the relative positions of these two economies, crucial for the expansion of many other postsocialist economies, have changed significantly. While the ratio of the GDP of Russia to that of Poland was close to 7 to 1 (in PPP dollars) in 1990, in 1998 it was at most 3 to 1. Geopolitically, this shift in the economic weight of the two countries is more important than is Poland's invitation to join NATO.

The fluctuations in the rate of growth in transition economies in the future will be very different from the cyclical oscillations in the positive economic growth in centrally planned economies. They will be more like the ups and downs of the business cycle typical of a contemporary market economy. There will be fluctuations in growth because of supply and demand factors.

There will be growth cycles due to labour market performance. Unemployment will sometimes keep wages down and profits up, and, through cyclical fluctuations, this will generate accumulation which will lower unemployment (Blanchard 1997). For both internal and external reasons, there are thus going to be periods of accelerated growth and periods of slow growth, stagnation, or even brief contraction.

Without doubt, however, *the postsocialist economies are going to be growing economies*. Growth rates in production and national income are probably going to follow patterns similar to the ones in the 1950s or 70s (see Table 7) rather than to the ones in the 90s (see Tables 8 and 13). There will be shifts between a more rapid and a slower pace of growth, but these shifts should not damage the long-run ability of the economies to compete and expand. Hence the transition will generate much greater changes in the type of growth than in the amount of growth. The type of growth will be different mainly because of enhancements in the quality of products and services and thus in international competitiveness. As the integration of the transition economies progresses, the appearance of larger cyclical fluctuations will depend more and more on growth trends in the world economy. Nonetheless, the ultimate pattern of growth, including the pace and any periodic fluctuations, will be determined mainly by domestic policies and not by external events. This will therefore represent as much a chance as a challenge.

13.3. DETOURS AND DEAD-ENDS

The art of transition management and economic policymaking is to seek a balance in satisfying the expectations of the public for improvements in living standards and the expectations of the business community. Only in the long run and only if managed carefully can these two tendencies support each other, and under such circumstances growth can become durable. But if there is a bias toward an unsustainable increase in household incomes (that is, an increase which is too rapid and too significant relative to the potential of the economy), then instability will boil away any chance for real improvement in living conditions and turn society against the transition. If there is an opposite bias, this time toward too far-reaching concessions to domestic and international investors and financial circles, the result would be very similar. Only an integrated approach toward the needs of the working, consuming, saving, and investing segments of society and the expectations of the international business and financial community can facilitate high-quality growth.

It is very difficult to manage such an approach, since there are many conflicting interests involved in the transition process, and these interests are reflected in the various possible transition strategies and policies. In the political arena, it is sometimes difficult to distinguish between the good ideas and the ideas which solely further particular interests. The whole process of transition is multi-track and multidimensional, and the particular features of the process evolve each according to its own logic. A proper understanding of the many roots of the process is essential. If the changes being implemented are not paced and coordinated efficiently (for instance, privatization and the establishment of financial intermediaries, or price liberalization and the creation of a social safety net, or trade liberalization and the policy toward competition), then a crisis may result that is even more persistent than the one accompanying the fading central planning era.

Transition to a market economy is as much a management challenge as it is an economic one. The process is very dynamic, and each case is unique, so that there is a temptation among research economists and other experts to generalize and propose single theoretical frameworks to explain this process entirely in all its complexity. Actually, the proper approach within each country should be more like that of a manager who nearly every day must confront fresh problems and find responses to new questions. *The transition process, including the structural and institutional aspects, involves such rapid and frequent shifts that the theoretical generalizations are often of little practical relevance or usefulness.* Some situations are in such rapid flux that trying to apply the theory is a little like trying to take a photo of the passing landscape from the window of a speeding train.

One may gather a fairly accurate idea of the efficiency of an anti-inflation policy in a timely fashion through the analysis of the appropriate monthly data; if inflation is growing month after month, it is possible to see this and to act quickly. However, the punctual identification of poverty trends is much more difficult. Thus, it may be possible to realize that inequality and poverty were growing in 1998 only in, say, 2001, but by then it may be too late to apply specific remedies.

A good policy implemented at the wrong time can become a bad policy. Likewise, there is often no proper policy response to a fait accompli. If one-time events are not managed appropriately, a theoretical evaluation of this may have no reasonable further policy application. For instance, if it becomes evident that the privatization of certain assets is being handled badly, it may not be easy or even useful to try to restore the status quo ante by reversing the relevant political, financial, and legal steps which have already been taken. In such situations, the only feasible reaction may be to shrug one's shoulders and push on ahead anyway.

Given these practical barriers to effective problem-solving, many economists and policymakers tend to rely on theories and remedies which already exist, although often these are not appropriate for the current challenges. The researchers are looking for benchmarks, for reference points. The advisors are trying to use the expertise they have gained in other contexts.

Yet, the postsocialist transition—as researchers and advisors have been learning at their cost—is not following any well-understood historical or theoretical precedent, be it the postwar European experience, orthodox neo-liberal doctrines, the Washington consensus, or old bureaucratic methods of government intervention. For this reason, transition policies must be creative, innovative, and flexible. Transition policymakers should certainly rely on the knowledge, experience, and advice available in other systems and regions, but they must be able to effect quick adjustments as circumstances require and to learn from mistakes and the achievements of other countries in transition. Any given policy may sometimes work and sometimes not. It may work within a single country at different periods or in different countries at the same period.

Unsuitable doctrines and poor advice have had too much negative influence on transition policymaking and have led several postsocialist countries into detours and dead-ends. After several years of transition and despite all the hardships they have gone through, there has not yet been a sign that Albania, Belarus, Bosnia-Herzegovina, Turkmenistan, and Yugoslavia are close to becoming healthy economies. This is also true of the largest postsocialist nations, Russia and Ukraine.[5]

Advisors, governments, and organizations continue to support policies which are mistaken. Countries must be wary of poor advice and of conditionalities which have nothing to do with local circumstances. They should examine transition experiences elsewhere to seek ways to avoid the dead-ends and unnecessary detours. For smaller countries, a great deal can be learned from the case of Slovenia. Even remote Kyrgyzstan can provide examples of fruitful policies which may be relevant for small- or medium-size former Soviet republics. Poland offers many lessons.

In general, the accomplishments of Eastern Europe, the former Soviet republics, China, and Vietnam in the effort to establish a market economy and achieve economic growth must be acknowledged. Even in the countries experiencing serious bouts of economic depression and institutional disarray, many of the changes, including new organizations and the evolution of market behaviour, have been very positive. The seeds of the market economy have been sown, though in some places the harvest may still be a long time coming.

---

[5] The differences between Poland and Ukraine with respect to economic liberalization and market culture were already large in 1989 owing to the thoroughgoing reforms in Poland and the virtual lack of reform in Ukraine. At the end of the 1990s the differences are even greater, and one more major difference has appeared: a tremendous development gap. In 1998 the total GDP of Poland was around 120% of the 1989 level in that country, while the GDP of Ukraine was less than 40% of the corresponding 1989 level. The share of Poland in the total GDP of Eastern Europe and the former Soviet Union stood at about 8% in 1989, while that of Ukraine was about 12–13%. These proportions have been reversed, with 13.6% accounted for by Poland, and 8.1% by Ukraine. The ratio between the two shares swung from 5 : 3 in favour of Ukraine in 1989 to 5 : 3 in favour of Poland a decade later.

There is a growing similarity between the challenges facing the leading transition countries of Eastern Europe and the problems in the EU economies. Indeed, transition is unlikely to eliminate persistent unemployment, the fiscal difficulties linked to ageing societies, inequalities and inequities in income distribution, and the vulnerability of capital markets. In addressing such issues, no nation is bound to succeed or doomed to fail.

Yet, though seemingly obvious, only lately has it been widely and openly admitted that the involvement of government through active transition and development policies and the management of economic events—and not free market forces—is the determining factor behind success in transition. In this respect, the main approach of some leading international organizations started to change comprehensively only in 1997, undoubtedly because of the ongoing economic depression and the increasing criticisms not only of the transition governments themselves, but also of such diverse institutions as the Vatican and Yale, Moody's and UNESCO, the Institute for International Finance and the International Labour Organization. All the major international organizations have finally begun to underline the crucial significance of government policy (World Bank 1997b, OECD 1997d, EBRD 1997b, IMF 1998c).

Whereas these organizations once assumed that spontaneous market forces would lead the transition economies toward durable growth, the pendulum has started to swing in the opposite direction owing to the discouraging results of the old attitude. Thus, for instance, the most successful transition economy, Poland, has shown in numerous ways that innovative policies can produce results which surpass even the most optimistic forecasts and that the liberal 'wait and see' approach is not nearly as effective as active and wise government involvement.[6] Given the experiences of both contraction and growth during the early transition in numerous countries, 'In 1996, it became even more apparent that success in transformation owes much to the credibility and consistency of government policy' (OECD 1997d).[7]

The point is not that government is better than the market, but that good government is better than bad government or no government. *Only*

---

[6] This is one more argument in favour of the view not that the widespread belief of the early 1990s in fast recovery and robust growth was bad, but that policies were wrong (Kolodko 1997d, PlanEcon 1997d).

[7] Of course, despite all the criticism aired so far concerning the policies of the early 1990s, the success of Poland would not have been possible if not for many of the changes executed at all stages of the transition. The relatively more favourable point of departure of Poland in the transition, the early policy of accelerated liberalization, the sound commitment to build institutions from scratch that could facilitate the development of capital markets, and especially the launching of true privatization: all these were major factors leading to the eventual membership of Poland in the OECD. Indeed, the greatest achievement of the early transition, the removal of the shortage phenomenon, which was having such a devastating effect on the overall performance of the economy, was accomplished in a rapid and comprehensive manner at the onset in 1990. The credit for this positive result goes to the approach adopted at that time by the government and the central bank.

the government which actively favours creative market forces deserves to be called a good one. A mix of the free market and government policy seems to be the best recipe for transition to succeed and for sustainable development. Wise government can use the market to attain economic policy targets, but market forces are not capable of moulding government for such a purpose. The achievement of high-quality growth is not feasible as long as a balance between government and the market is lacking. This is another lesson of the early transition, when a number of countries failed precisely for this reason.

13.4. IS THERE A HAPPY ENDING?

Socioeconomic and cultural development will continue even after the shift from the old institutional arrangements to the new ones is completed. Economic systems will always be evolving, while the transition is only an episode of history. There will be an end to the transition process, though there may be no end of history.[8]

The decolonization of the 'Third World' and the rise and fall of the socialist system, the 'Second World', have been extremely significant historical processes of the 20th century. The repercussions of the fall of socialism will continue to be felt in the global economy well into the 21st century.

Although the transition began in the countries of Eastern Europe and in the former Soviet Union at approximately the same time, the process will obviously come to an end in particular countries at different times. Just as it is possible to point to countries which have not initiated transition (such as Cuba), it is also possible to point to countries which are further along in transition (for example, Hungary) and to countries which are less so (like Armenia). This judgement relies mostly on the size of the private sector, although the amount of openness and integration with the global economy is also an important criterion.

It has been said that in the long run marketization must be accompanied by democratization. This is the most likely and most welcome scenario. Nonetheless, a non-democratic, market-friendly regime could undertake structural reform and institutional and cultural change to a sufficient degree to achieve a transition to the market without establishing a full-fledged democracy or a civic society. This has already happened in the less-developed world, and such a scenario is quite imaginable for several former Soviet republics, especially those in Central Asia.

---

[8] Barring the collision of the earth with a giant asteroid (such as the one expected to pass close to Earth in 2028), causing perhaps less mental anguish than the transition has done.

The geopolitical position of a country will affect the outcome of the transition process. Some countries, like the Czech Republic, Estonia, Hungary, Poland, and Slovenia, will become similar to the developed market economies of the European Union. This will probably also eventually be true of Bulgaria, Croatia, Latvia, Lithuania, Romania, and Slovakia. Although Albania, Bosnia-Herzegovina, FYR Macedonia, and Yugoslavia may undertake to follow this path, they will certainly not be joining the EU any time soon. The economies of some nations, like Kazakhstan and Uzbekistan, are probably going to resemble those of Iran or Turkey. Still others, such as Georgia and Kyrgyzstan, may come to have many features in common with Lebanon or Syria. Vietnam, already a member of ASEAN, will probably follow an economic development track similar to that of Thailand.

These analogies may not all fit. Indeed, the transition itself may create a wholly new type of market economy with, in some cases, a special post-socialist or post-Soviet 'flavour'. After all, countries as different as Hungary and Mongolia or Slovakia and Turkmenistan share a common past linked to their membership in Comecon. Nonetheless, the differences between Poland and Tajikistan, for instance, likely will become only more evident. Poland is in Central Europe, has joined the OECD, and is involved in negotiations to become a member of the EU. Tajikistan is in Central Asia, is a former Soviet republic, and has already experienced a serious local military conflict. Though they were both members of Comecon and the Warsaw Pact and though they now belong to the same constituency in the IMF and the World Bank, they probably do not share a similar destiny in terms of institution-building or economic and cultural development.

Because of the influence of Russia over the republics of the former Soviet Union and the influence of the Soviet Union over the socialist countries, there was a constant process of systemic uniformization under the previous order. Institutional arrangements, policies, and economic structures became quite similar from one nation to the next. Economically, only China in Asia and Yugoslavia in Europe, though still socialist, evolved in a markedly different way. On the political side, Albania and to a certain extent Romania attempted to remain somewhat separate and to tackle issues in a distinct manner. Albania and Yugoslavia stayed outside Comecon and the Warsaw Pact. Romania belonged to both, although it often took a unique stance in international affairs.

As a result of the historical process of transformation, a new convergence is taking place. Already in the past, market capitalism adopted and absorbed certain socialist values. This time, the postsocialist economies are taking on the characteristics of capitalism. Yet, like immigrants who maintain something from the old country while assimilating in the new one, the emerging market institutions are retaining some socialist features. A commitment to equity, attention to human capital development, loyalty to the larger community and to the nation, social solidarity, the expectation that government policy will exercise its responsibility toward the well-being of all: these are the values which for a generation will continue to shape the face of capitalism in the postsocialist countries.

The transition nations are also tending to assimilate some of the special arrangements and market behaviours of their nearest capitalist neighbours because of a strong demonstration effect and because they frequently rely on the experience and advice of these neighbours. This will eventually lead to additional differences between countries like Bulgaria and Mongolia or Lithuania and Tajikistan despite their uniformity during the common socialist past. In due time, Uzbekistan is going to be more like Turkey than Bulgaria, which in turn may become more like Greece. Estonia in many respects is already more like Finland than Azerbaijan, which in turn is now no longer so dissimilar to the west of Iran. To believe that the transition countries are headed toward a common future is simply one more illusion.

Meanwhile, China and Russia are developing new sorts of market economies. They will become even more unlike each other in the future, though these large and very significant countries will take on features similar to those of other big countries like Brazil, India, and Indonesia. Yet, more and more China will become the 'new China', and Russia will become the 'new Russia'. As they grow over the coming decades and the relative position of both countries rises in the world economy, China will take the lead. So far it is clear that China has been the winner in the competition between these two nations in terms of success with reform and development policy in the course of transformation.

After 40 years of confrontation between these countries over the best road to 'real socialism', we have entered a new era as they pursue two distinct paths toward a viable market economy and the capitalist system. A half century ago there was a certain parallelism in the institutional arrangements and development policies of these two nations. In the foreseeable future, the performance of these economies will become more and more alike, but the differences in institutional arrangements, economic structures, the cultural environment, and geopolitical positions will furnish plenty of material for comparative studies. China and Russia should not now be put into the same slot any more than they should have been in the past.

For the time being Russia is caught up in a systemic vacuum, with neither the plan, nor the market, but there may eventually be debate about whether this important country has completed the transition process (Åslund 1996). This is already happening with China. One has begun to hear the opinion that China is now a market economy. It is surely a matter of definition, but, judged according to the various criteria presented here, China and Russia, for different reasons, cannot yet be considered market economies.

In their studies and surveys on the global economy, as well as through their policies, which is even more significant, certain international organizations distinguish among 'advanced', 'developing', and 'transition' economies. A number of postsocialist countries, especially those belonging to the OECD or the Central European Free Trade Agreement, may eventually be included among the advanced economies; others may be counted as developing nations, and still others may be considered market economies 'in transition'—even after the process of transition has been completed—because of specific structural features, institutions, or patterns of performance.

In 1997, after a quarter-century of rapid economic growth and sound restructuring, four high-income nations—Hong Kong, Singapore, South Korea, and Taiwan—started to be counted among the 'advanced economies' by the World Bank and the IMF (IMF 1997). In contrast, at the end of the 1990s some OECD nations, for example South Korea, and even EU members like Greece and Portugal were still being treated by some organizations, especially investment banks and rating agencies, as 'emerging' markets.

How long does it take to 'emerge'? From a formal viewpoint, membership in the OECD and in the EU should be considered a seal of approval that the transition process has been completed. Nonetheless, from a practical standpoint, even if a country has been accepted into these organizations, there may still be a great deal to do before it has a full-fledged market economy and a civic society. Behavioural and cultural changes require an especially long time, perhaps even an entire generation. Indeed, *at least a generation is probably needed to complete a successful transition from a postsocialist economy to a market economy.*

Just as there were several types of socialist centrally planned economies, various types of postsocialist market economies are going to emerge. The complex process of postsocialist transformation must constantly be reviewed and adjusted according to the unique features in each nation. The process is not a uniform one. Policies which work in one place will not work in another. Different legacies and challenges and different aims and opportunities, together with the unique transition experience, signify that each country will undergo a special pattern of change.

Moreover, the market system has many faces, too. Thus, no one says that Turkey is 'in transition'; it is a member of the OECD and NATO, and so it is a market economy. Yet Turkey bears many 'transition-like' features. Many economies which everyone counts among the market economies actually possess much larger public sectors than do the postsocialist nations. There are 'market economies' with GDP per capita below $500, and there are economies 'in transition' with GDP per capita exceeding $10,000.

Parts of Eastern Europe are already catching up fast. Even in their current transitional state, the postcommunist economies are arguably no worse-governed than

Greece and no sleazier than Italy; their labour markets are no more inflexible than Spain's, and their taxes no more job destroying than Belgium's. Their schools score is higher than Britain's. And aside from inflation, . . . their public finances come closer to meeting Maastricht criteria than those of many of the first-round members of [the European Monetary Union]. Poland's agriculture is awkward, but for the same cultural and historical reasons as France's. The productivity leap many postcommunist businesses will have to make is huge, but the same was true, say, in Portugal when it joined the EU. (*The Economist* 1997c)

The criteria for determining which countries are and are not market economies are therefore fluid. For the time being, one might agree that membership in the OECD is not a sure sign that the transition has been completed. However, full-fledged membership in the European Union should be seen as evidence that the transition has come to a conclusion. In any case, ex ante what matters most is not the formal criteria, but the constant progress toward durable growth.

The debates about transition will continue, but it should be remembered that the introduction of market forces into postsocialist economies is supposed to be aimed at fostering sustainable development. Otherwise, though history may decide that the transition process is over, the whole exercise will not have been worthwhile or even sensible.

In short, countries do have a choice.

14

Doubts and Conclusions

14.1. POLICYMAKING AND THE POST-WASHINGTON CONSENSUS

Policies derived from the Washington consensus have greatly influenced the direction of systemic reform and the course of change in postsocialist economies. However, the transformations have also had a significant counter-impact. The policies have not generated the anticipated results, and this has led to a search for alternative measures. As the postsocialist markets have emerged, so have fresh issues, problems, and concerns. The reactions to these have differed, and new approaches have been evolved. Twelve major policy conclusions have been identified here.

First, *institutional arrangements are the most important factor in the achievement of durable growth*. They should be established through a process directed by government (by design) rather than spontaneously (by chance). In those nations in which government has been committed to this approach, recovery has come sooner, growth has been more robust, and there are more prospects for sustainable development. Those countries in which government has relied on the spontaneous appearance of new institutions have not been able to manage this complex process adequately and are lagging behind in the transition.

Second, the *size of government is less important than the quality of government policies and the manner in which change is realized*. In transition economies a profound restructuring of the public finance system is more important than is downsizing government. Fiscal transfers should be redirected from non-competitive sectors toward institution-building (including behavioural and cultural changes) and investments in human capital and hard infrastructure. Attempts to downsize government through expenditure cuts can do more harm than good in terms of recovery from transitional recession and the achievement of sustainable growth. Even if one believes that small government is better than big government, to downsize may lead to economic contraction and deterioration in standards of living. Despite the neoliberal, monetarist conviction, creative downsizing of government should be undertaken only in an environment of economic expansion. Otherwise, expenditures should not be cut for the sake of the illusion of fiscal prudence, but should be restructured.

Third, *institution-building must be a gradual process*. The effects of specific inputs in this process must be constantly monitored, and policies must be regularly adjusted and corrected. One should not depend on the experiences in distorted market economies, but should understand the special features of the emerging postsocialist markets. This is especially true in privatization and the development of capital markets.

Fourth, if institutional arrangements are neglected and left to spontaneous processes and liberalized market forces, then *there will be a systemic vacuum and 'informal institutionalization' will occur*. Spreading corruption and organized crime are extreme examples of informal institutionalization. These are the two principal diseases in countries in which liberalization and privatization have taken place under weak government. Governments may sometimes be too weak because they are too big, but in transition economies they are often too weak because they have been downsized too soon, before the emerging market was able to take over relevant functions of the state. Even if the aim of the downsizing is to reduce the scope of fiscal redistribution so as to encourage capital formation and hence investment and growth, one must not overlook the fact that the struggle against informal institutions is costly in fiscal terms, too. A prematurely or too thoroughly downsized government may not be strong enough to lead in this struggle, and the market may quickly expand within the informal sector, while the difficulties are mounting in the official economy. Thus, profits will accrue to the informal sector, while revenues drop in the official sector. Profits are thereby 'privatized', while loses are 'socialized' in a politically unsustainable process full of negative consequences for the budget and for social policy.

Fifth, in transition economies *policies must aim at transforming and streamlining the legal system so that it can serve the market economy*. The establishment and development of new laws—trade and tax codes, capital market regulations, the protection of property rights, antitrust regulations, banking supervision, consumer protection, environmental protection—are extremely important and ought to be addressed before state assets are privatized. The establishment of a legal framework which is appropriate for the market economy should be much higher on the agenda of international financial organizations. It must be a more urgent and important issue than liberalization and privatization, since these latter can contribute to sound growth only if the former has been assured.

Sixth, *a shift in functions from the central government to local governments is necessary for deregulation in the postsocialist economy*. This means that some decentralization must be undertaken in the public finance system and that local governments must be given more fiscal autonomy. The process of taking functions away from the central government must be matched by reinforcing local governments. Both levels of government must be seen as two parts of a single entity which is essential for gradual institution-building. If local governments are not strengthened as the central government is reduced, then healthy market forces cannot be supported by new institutional arrangements, and liberalization and privatization are less likely to improve capital allocation and raise efficiency.

Seventh, *the development of non-governmental organizations must be accelerated.* More significant international technical and financial assistance must be channelled into the effort to empower non-governmental organizations. Along with the private sector and the state, these organizations are an indispensable pillar of the contemporary market economy and civic society. A wide range of non-governmental organizations active in various areas of public life is needed to ease the constant tension between the state and society. The expanding private sector cannot adequately fill this gap. Certain areas of public life can rely neither on the state, nor on the business-oriented private sector. Without the institutional infrastructure provided by non-governmental organizations, successful systemic change and high-quality growth become more problematic, the infant market economy and democracy in postsocialist nations cannot evolve properly, and the transition will remain incomplete.

Eighth, *income policy and equitable growth are very important for the success of the transition.* Because increasing inequity is unavoidable during the initial years of transition, the state, through fiscal and social policies, must play an active role in managing income dispersion. Beyond a certain limit, income disparities inhibit the expansion of economic activity, stunt economic growth, and delay recovery. Substantial inequities hamper crucial institutional and structural reform.

Ninth, the postsocialist transition to the market is taking place in a context of worldwide globalization. Hence integration with the world economy is an indispensable part of the process. This must be managed carefully. *Special attention must be paid to short-term capital liberalization, which must be monitored and controlled by fiscal and monetary authorities and supported by international financial institutions.* It is better to liberalize capital markets later rather than sooner. Institution-building must first be sufficiently advanced, and stabilization ought already to be consolidated into stability. Only then should financial markets be liberalized in a gradual manner. Otherwise the populations in the young and emerging democracies will not back the introduction of market mechanisms or integration with the world economy and may even become hostile to these steps.

Tenth, *international organizations should not only encourage regional integration and cooperation, but should insist upon them.* Rapid and durable growth requires export expansion, which depends on strong regional linkages. In turn, this calls for institutional support through import-export banks, commodity exchanges, credit insurance agencies, and so on. This should be the main focus of the institution-building effort of the EBRD through its direct lending and technical assistance. This sort of market infrastructure is now underdeveloped in transition economies, and regional trade and direct cross-country investment are lagging behind in the process of change. What should be a driving force behind sustainable growth is actually now a major obstacle.

Eleventh, the Bretton Woods institutions should reconsider their policy approach toward transition economies. While the IMF should emphasize financial liquidity, currency convertibility, and fiscal and monetary stabilization, the World Bank should focus mainly on realizing equitable growth and sustainable development. These two areas of economic policy are frequently at odds. Too often, policies in line with the IMF orientation are stressed excessively. Thus, there is a tendency to confuse the means and the ends of policy, to favour short-term stabilization over long-term development. The belief that this can work is an illusion, and the record of transition so far has shown this clearly, for, where there is not much development, there is not yet stability either. *Hence decisionmakers should not rely only on stabilization policies, but should seek a proper balance between stabilization policies and medium- and long-term development strategies.* Fiscal and monetary policies must be subordinated to development policy, not the other way around. The World Bank performance criteria for socioeconomic development are needed as much as are the IMF fiscal and monetary criteria. There should always be an eye on the impact of financial policies in terms of growth, capital allocation, income distribution, and the social safety net. The World Bank should not support policy initiatives which, while aiming at financial stabilization in keeping with IMF proposals, may lead to social destabilization because of the lack of growth, the spread of poverty, increasing inequality, and divestment in human capital.

Twelfth, the interactive processes of 'learning by monitoring' and 'learning by doing' will continue. If there is any chance for the emergence of a 'post-Washington consensus' (as indeed there seems to be), this consensus will have to be understood as a process. *Any eventual post-Washington consensus must involve many more partners than merely the important organizations based in Washington.* Policies agreed on only in Washington may not always be able to deliver sufficient results. This may not yet be obvious in the era of globalization. Nonetheless, policies must be revised as conditions change and challenges appear. The quest for a comprehensive and achievable policy consensus which facilitates sustainable growth must be ongoing.

14.2. BLIND FORCES AND SUSTAINABLE DEVELOPMENT

Why has the transition occurred? Why now rather than earlier or later? Why was the transition launched in Poland, although the roots of the failure of the socialist system were elsewhere? It may be disappointing for an economist to come at last to the realization that political factors were much more decisive than economic ones in changing the course of history, but this is so: in the answers to these questions, political factors are more important than economic ones.

'Real socialism' possessed many drawbacks, but also many merits, which should not be disregarded or forgotten. It might have lasted longer, and systems might have been more gradually adapted to changing circumstances if not for the reckless policies of the Soviet Union, which wasted a great deal of effort and vast resources on an ill-advised attempt at outward expansion instead of internal reform and development. A costly military complex, involvement in distant regional conflicts, political and financial support for foreign regimes, an inflexible stance toward systemic diversity in other socialist countries, a long and hostile rivalry with China: these were the key non-economic factors which undermined the adaptability of the system to new challenges.

Without these policies and despite the growing weakness of the leading socialist superpower, the other problems of the socialist system, including the most important economic ones, might have been resolved. Even the malaise of 'shortageflation', itself a result of structural flaws and macro-economic mismanagement, would not alone have led to the end of the system throughout the region, since it was not that serious in several countries, for instance Czechoslovakia and the GDR. However, the strong demonstration effect and the political pressure radiating from outside the region sparked a chain reaction. If healthy economies like Austria or Switzerland had been practising state socialism at the time, even they would have collapsed.

Still, despite these circumstances, the transition would not have occurred when it did if not for the brave political decision taken in the summer of 1988 by General Wojciech Jaruzelski, the Polish leader, to initiate historic roundtable negotiations with the opposition, which had been illegal for so long. If not for the success of these negotiations during the spring of 1989, the beginning of the exodus of families from the GDR would not have been possible the following summer. Then, in the autumn, from the moment the Hungarian government permitted the first East German families to pass freely through to Austria on their way to West Germany, the critical decision taken by Mikhail Gorbachev, the Soviet leader, to tear down the Berlin Wall became inevitable. The next winter turned out to be the last for the old socialist system, and then there was the 'spring' of new postsocialist nations.

Only this 'domino effect' of significant events could have led to the transition from state socialism to a market economy. In the long run, the negative economic consequences of Soviet expansionism and the inability of the system to adjust to changing global economic conditions were crucial. In the short run, the transition was triggered by the success of the Polish roundtable negotiations and the fall of the Berlin Wall in 1989. The long-run causes were decisive in the sense that, without them, the transition would not have occurred. The immediate causes were decisive because they determined when it occurred. Once it had begun, the process was bound to continue and expand in terms of both geography and systemic change.

The transition was accompanied by a major collapse in output from 1989 until the mid-to-late 1990s. Most postsocialist economies are now seeking to initiate sustained growth. For this to materialize, the state must play a stronger role, since major structural problems remain to be resolved and the infant market forces are unable to meet the challenge alone. Thus, these countries should not repudiate the state; they should redesign it through the reform of government administration, the commercialization of state enterprises, and the promotion of private ownership through appropriate institutional arrangements and market regulation.

The transition is a generation-long process of change. By definition, almost everything is *in statu nascendi*: institutions and structures, laws and regulations, governance and behaviour, culture and political life. Additional difficulties arise from the confusion between transformation and development, systemic transition and market reform, conflicts of ideas and conflicts of interest, and the means and the ends of economic policy. The confusion occurs both in theoretical considerations and in practical dealings. There may be no adequate remedies at hand for tackling specific issues. Nonetheless, there may also be no time for experimentation with alternative approaches. The ability readily to distinguish the essence of an issue is therefore basic to solving problems. And there are still so many problems.

It is essential to design transition policies and development strategies which can support each other. The aim of transition is to introduce market forces which can foster sustainable development, but it should be obvious that the market will not be able to do the job alone. The logic of this thesis is clear: market forces should not be relied upon as the instrument to achieve a certain type of market system, that is, one which is development oriented. If this market system already exists, then the transition has been completed; if not, then there is still a transition. The market is supposed to foster the achievement of the target (sustainable development) and should not itself become the target. Thus, government policy must guide the market and always aim at high-quality (that is, balanced, rapid, and equitable) growth.

Stanley Fischer, the first deputy managing director of the International Monetary Fund, in a special address to the 10th World Bank Conference on Development Economics, admitted that

For a long time, even after WDR91 [*World Development Report 1991*, World Bank] was published, I believed that there was an elixir of growth, a magic ingredient that was missing from the set of policies listed in the WDR, and that if included would make a miracle—even an East Asian miracle—possible. I no longer believe that. Or rather, I believe that I know the missing ingredient. It is hard work. For it is a long and arduous task, a matter of many people doing many things right, over many years, to make a country grow. (Fischer 1998b, p. 16)

A missing ingredient may indeed be hard work over many years, perhaps even generations, though to some this affirmation may sound Marxist. In any case, without wise policy, hard work—though certainly necessary—may be wasted, whether it is that of a Chinese peasant, a Russian teacher, a Polish coal miner, or an IMF first deputy managing director. Policies make the 'miracles', and policies make the crises. One must acknowledge that, for instance, in the ASEAN countries, people work very hard. So did many people in Eastern Europe prior to the transition. Yet, the hard work must be managed and organized in ways which favour growth, not merely the pocketbooks of speculators and investors, including foreign ones. The hard work must secure higher standards of living among all the people, not only among the ruling elites and the tycoons. Nor should all the fruits of the people's labour be transferred elsewhere through sophisticated international financial and capital networks. If this occurs, problems will not be solved; they will only become more numerous and severe.

The market alone cannot organize and manage the hard work. In fact, the tendency of the market to distort the outcomes desired through hard work is one more reason—perhaps the main one—that the 'free' market must be firmly regulated and controlled.

The recent Asian crisis was caused mainly by market failure. This must be understood if similar crises are to be avoided in other places, including the postsocialist region. Any neglect of the need to make the emerging markets act according to reasonable rules would be a mistake.

The true missing ingredient, the true 'elixir of growth' is therefore the appropriate involvement of 'wise' government in the formation and allocation of physical and human capital and in well-orchestrated cooperation with international organizations. Not only the people, but especially governments and international organizations must work harder. Among the tasks is the mining of the rich experience in socioeconomic affairs in order to understand the failures and the successes. This is possible and within the reach of researchers and policymakers. An even more difficult task is to resolve the conflicting interests which hinder the achievement of sustainable development. This may not be feasible and is much further beyond the abilities of most politicians and financial groups.

Alan Greenspan, the chairman of the US Federal Reserve, has come to the opinion that 'only free-market systems exhibit the flexibility and robustness to accommodate human nature and harness rapidly advancing technology to consistently advance living standards' (quoted in *The Economist* 1998c, p. 29). Greenspan may be correct if he is referring only to the 'free market' model in the United States. But what about China? What about

Russia? Is Greenspan's supposition valid there, too, considering the legacy of the socialist system, the current situation, and the future challenges in these countries? Certainly not.

Just as Greenspan's opinion may be correct in a specific case, an observation once made by Jawaharlal Nehru, the late prime minister of India, is not wrong if it is understood in the proper historical context. Several decades before Greenspan's remark about the free market, Nehru said that 'The idea of planning and a planned society is accepted now in varying degrees by everyone' (quoted in Muravchik 1998, p. 77). At the time Nehru said it, the statement was true. In a sense, it is still pretty true today. There is no important actor on the economic scene who is not planning his next moves all the time. Of course, this is very distinct from the kind of planning that was meant by Nehru, the kind exercised under the socialist system or in countries keen to take advantage of central planning, such as India in the 1960s and 70s. Yet, in fact, corporations and governments and even the 'Fed' under Alan Greenspan 'plan' whenever they try to shape the world to meet their targets. Central planning and state socialism are gone with the wind. Strategic and indicative planning as a means of realizing sound social and economic policies is still with us in our businesses and our governments.

Transition should not mean that society must leave its fate solely to the blind forces of the 'free' market. The market can be free only to the extent that it is mature and unflawed. Barring that, it must be effectively guided by policy. It is not true that a completely uncontrolled ('free') market serves the best interests of a free society. Indeed, there is nowhere a market that is entirely free in this sense. The state must intervene to subordinate market forces to the needs of society. Market forces must serve society, not the other way around.

In 1848 Marx and Engels wrote *The Communist Manifesto*. A century later, in 1948, George Orwell wrote *1984*. After another half century, in 1998, the postsocialist nations of Europe and Asia are moving from shock to therapy, from the great postsocialist slump to sustained growth, from seclusion from world markets to integration with the global economy, from autocratic regimes to the construction of civic society. Is there a happy ending? No, because there is no end of challenges. What is the future going to be like? How will the economic, social, and political landscape look in another half century, in 2048? We do not know, but it may be better. This will depend on the next generation.

STATISTICAL APPENDIX

Because of the difficulties in data collection and for methodological reasons, data supplied in the main text and in this appendix may differ in a very few instances. In certain parts of certain tables no data are offered owing to a lack of reliable sources. Although the data which are supplied are the most reliable available, they should be viewed with caution, especially those for Albania, former Soviet republics, and former Yugoslavia. Data on GDP absorption may not always be consistent with data on GDP changes because the relevant time series have been derived from different sources. Even data published by international organizations on the same categories, countries, and years sometimes vary considerably.

The data for 1990–7 represent official estimates of outcomes as reflected in publications of national authorities, the International Monetary Fund, the World Bank, the Organization for Economic Cooperation and Development, the International Labour Organization, PlanEcon, and the Institute of International Finance. Data for 1998 are projections and evaluations based partly on information from these same organizations and found in EBRD 1998. The forecasts for 1999–2002 are based on predictions in PlanEcon 1998a, 1998b, and, in certain cases regarding 1999–2000, the author's own forecasts.

Data on registered unemployment are year-end unless indicated otherwise. Data on per cent changes in real wages are from EBRD 1998, PlanEcon 1998a, 1998b, and the author's own calculations using data on nominal wages provided through national sources and data from the International Monetary Fund and the European Bank for Reconstruction and Development on inflation.

General government includes the state, the municipalities, and extrabudgetary funds.

Data on trade balance and merchandise exports and imports are from balance-of-payments statistics.

Data on reserves reflect the reserves of monetary authorities, excluding gold.

PPP stands for purchasing power parity. The estimates are measured in 1995 dollars and come from PlanEcon 1997b, unless stated otherwise. In the computation of these estimates, the country's nominal GDP per capita in local currency has been divided by the PPP, defined as the number of units of the country's currency required to buy the same amount of goods and services in the domestic market as one dollar would buy in the United States. Considering the large differences in the PlanEcon estimates and the estimates found in OECD 1997e for the Baltic States, a second estimate is supplied of GDP in PPP dollars, according to the latter source.

PART 1

Selected economic indicators, 1990–1998

Albania: selected economic indicators, 1990–1998

	1990	1991	1992	1993	1994	1995	1996	1997	1998
Output (% change)									
GDP at constant prices	-10.0	-27.7	-7.2	9.6	9.4	8.9	9.1	-8.0	10.2
Private consumption	—	—	—	—	4.2	8.2	-0.6	-8.9	9.5
Public consumption	—	—	—	—	6.7	8.9	2.5	-18.4	6.4
Gross fixed investment	—	—	—	—	22.7	21.4	3.5	-31.2	32.6
Industrial gross output	-14.2	-42.0	-51.2	-10.0	-2.0	2.0	8.7	-11.5	13.0
Agricultural gross output	-5.4	-17.4	18.5	10.4	6.5	10.0	6.0	0.5	4.0
Composition of output (% GDP)									
Industry (1990 constant prices)	39.8	32.1	16.9	13.9	12.4	11.5	—	—	—
Agriculture (1990 constant prices)	37.0	42.5	54.2	54.6	55.1	55.9	—	—	—
Unemployment (% labour force)	9.5	9.5	27.0	22.0	18.5	13.1	12.1	14.0	13.8
Prices and wages (% change)									
Consumer prices, annual average	0.0	35.5	193.1	85.0	21.5	8.0	12.7	38.0	32.0
Consumer prices, end-year	0.0	104.1	236.6	35.6	15.0	6.0	17.4	42.1	19.0
Average wage	—	-15.0	-14.1	-1.9	26.5	8.9	10.1	-5.0	9.7
Government sector (% GDP)									
General government balance	—	-20.7	-17.0	-9.3	-11.3	-6.6	-11.0	-10.9	-7.0
General government expenditure[a]	62.1	61.9	44.0	34.9	31.2	30.8	29.0	25.7	—
Monetary sector (% change)									
Broad money, end-year	23.4	104.4	152.7	75.0	40.6	51.8	43.8	41.3	—
Domestic credit, end-year	—	100.1	68.0	27.7	16.5	-22.0	39.0	38.6	—
Broad money (% GDP)	33.0	69.1	54.1	40.2	37.7	47.8	55.0	63.2	—

Interest and exchange rates (% per year), end-year									
Deposit rate, one year[b]	1.0–2.0	5.0–8.0	32.0	23.0	16.5	13.8	19.1	27.5	—
Lending rate, one year[c]		8.0–12.0	39.0	30.0	20.0	21.0	28.8	31.0	—
Lek per $									
Exchange rate, end-year	10.0	24.0	102.9	102.0	94.7	93.0	104.5	148.9	152.6
Exchange rate, annual average	8.0	14.6	75.1	102.1	94.7	92.8	105.9	150.0	153.6
External sector ($ millions)									
Current account	-122	-249	-434	-365	-284	-181	-249	-195	—
Trade balance	150	208	454	490	460	474	711	497	829
Exports	231	73	70	112	141	205	210	141	162
Imports	381	281	524	602	601	679	921	638	991
Foreign direct investment, net	—	8	32	45	65	89	97	33	50
Gross reserves	199	1	72	147	204	240	280	300	—
External debt stock	377	628	769	877	960	667	753	815	—
In months of current account expenditures, excluding transfers									
Gross usable reserves, end-year	5.9	0.0	1.4	2.3	3.2	3.7	3.3	5.1	—
% current account revenues, excluding transfers									
Debt service		33.0	5.6	27.7	23.7	6.6	6.1	6.7	—
Current account/GDP		-22.1	-61.3	-29.7	-14.3	-7.5	-9.3	-8.5	-10.5
External debt/GDP		55.7	108.6	71.5	48.4	27.6	28.1	35.4	—
External debt/exports		860.3	1,098.6	783.0	680.9	325.5	329.0	447.8	—
Memorandum items									
Population (millions)	3.3	3.3	3.2	3.2	3.2	3.2	3.2	3.2	3.2
GDP (lek, billions)	17.0	16.5	53.2	125.3	187.9	224.7	281.0	345.2	—
GDP per capita ($)	210	210	330	400	640	800	660	730	1,019
GDP per capita (PPP$)		1,179	1,062	1,153	1,241	1,340	1,441	1,321	1,449

[a] 1996 figures for the first half of 1996.   [b] Until 1995 the floor of the band set by the central bank, then average interest rates on 12-month deposits.   [c] Until 1995 the guideline rate of central bank, then average interest rates for 12-month loans.

Armenia: selected economic indicators, 1990–1998

	1990	1991	1992	1993	1994	1995	1996	1997	1998
Output (% change)									
GDP at constant prices	-7.4	-17.1	-52.6	-14.8	5.4	6.9	5.8	3.3	6.0
Private consumption	—	—	13.6	-27.6	5.3	10.0	8.4	5.0	0.7
Public consumption	—	—	-11.3	7.7	-3.3	-8.2	-2.4	3.0	-1.3
Gross fixed investment	—	—	-87.2	-8.7	44.8	-17.3	11.1	15.0	9.1
Industrial gross output	—	—	-52.5	-5.3	13.5	1.5	1.2	0.9	6.0
Agricultural gross output	—	—	-8.9	-1.9	3.2	4.7	1.7	-6.0	1.3
Composition of output (% GDP)									
Industry	—	46.5	36.0	25.8	29.1	24.3	23.8	—	—
Agriculture	—	23.6	28.4	49.1	43.5	42.8	38.3	—	—
Unemployment (% labour force)	—	—	3.5	6.2	5.6	8.1	9.7	11.0	10.8
Prices and wages (% change)									
Consumer prices, annual average	10.3	274.1	1,346	3,732	5,273	176.7	18.7	14.0	22.5
Consumer prices, end-year	—	25.0	1,341	10,896	1,885	32.0	5.6	21.9	23.4
Average wage	—	—	-48.6	-53.2	-50.7	9.9	7.3	4.5	5.3
Government sector (% GDP)									
General government balance[a]	—	-1.8	-16.0	-11.8	-6.1	-4.7	-4.8	-2.5	-5.6
General government expenditure[a]	—	7.3	12.3	59.5	28.4	23.7	19.7	24.4	—
Monetary sector (% change)									
Broad money, end-year	—	—	—	—	684.0	68.7	35.1	20.6	—
Domestic credit, end-year	—	—	—	864.8	1,437	66.4	27.6	8.2	—

Exchange rates (dram per year)								
Exchange rate, end-year	—	—	75.0	405.5	403.3	435.1	495.6	561.9
Exchange rate, annual average	—	—	75.0	288.4	405.7	419.2	490.7	592.6
External sector ($ millions)								
Current account, excluding grants	-1,382	-195	-315	-231	-483	-425	-559	—
Trade balance	-1,382	-114	-166	-192	-402	-467	-559	—
Exports	2,904	220	206	209	271	290	239	798
Imports	4,286	334	372	401	673	757	798	—
Foreign direct investment, net	0	0	0	3	19	22	26	—
Gross reserves, end-year	0	0	32	107	168	219	200	—
External debt stock	—	—	200	371	614	798	798	—
In months of imports of goods and services								
Gross reserves, end-year	—	—	0.7	1.6	2.2	2.8	—	—
% exports of goods and services								
Debt service	—	—	3.0	20.6	18.7	22.0	—	—
Current account/GDP	-71.2	-35.5	-37.6	-26.6	-27.0	-23.1	—	—
External debt/GDP	—	—	30.7	28.9	38.4	50.4	—	—
External debt/exports	—	—	95.5	136.9	211.7	333.9	—	—
Memorandum items								
Population (millions)	3.7	3.7	3.7	3.7	3.7	3.7	3.7	3.7
GDP (dram, millions)	—	80	295	3,898	187,049	522,285	660,311	778,000
GDP per capita ($)	—	—	173	343	418	418	438	438
GDP per capita (PPP$)	—	2,345	2,097	2,199	2,343	2,470	2,535	2,620

a Consolidated state government.

Azerbaijan: selected economic indicators, 1990–1998

	1990	1991	1992	1993	1994	1995	1996	1997	1998
Output (% change)									
GDP at constant prices	-11.7	-0.7	-22.6	-23.1	-18.1	-11.0	1.3	5.0	7.0
Private consumption	—	—	11.5	-24.9	-22.2	-0.3	8.2	0.2	2.5
Public consumption	—	—	50.5	1.2	-5.6	-16.6	6.2	-0.3	0.5
Gross fixed investment	—	—	-41.0	-39.0	-48.0	-72.0	77.4	24.1	39.7
Industrial gross output	—	-7.5	-18.2	-21.4	-24.7	-21.4	-6.7	0.3	5.3
Agricultural gross output	—	-2.6	-25.1	-16.3	-12.8	-5.0	3.0	-5.0	5.0
Composition of output (% GDP)									
Industry	22	30	26	25	25	22	23	—	—
Agriculture	26	39	27	30	30	31	30	—	—
Unemployment (% labour force)	—	—	0.2	0.7	0.9	1.1	1.1	1.2	2.6
Prices and wages (% change)									
Consumer prices, annual average	7.8	106	616	1,130	1,664	411.7	19.8	3.6	5.5
Consumer prices, end-year	—	126	1,395	1,294	1,788	84.5	6.7	0.5	4.5
Average wage	—	—	-23.7	-38.5	-60.2	-25.1	0.3	20.0	6.1
Government sector (% GDP)									
General government balance	—	—	2.8	-12.7	-11.4	-4.2	-2.6	-2.8	-3.0
General government expenditure	—	—	46.3	46.1	36.0	19.5	18.8	20.8	—
Monetary sector (% change)									
Broad money, end-year	—	—	—	685.9	486.1	122.2	25.8	14.3	—
Domestic credit, end-year	—	—	968.6	421.6	750.7	113.5	40.0	30.0	—
Broad money (% GDP)	—	—	37.5	45.0	39.0	14.8	13.3	12.6	—

Interest and exchange rates (% per year), end-year									
Deposit rate, one month	—	—	22	60	1,355	101	26	10	—
Lending rate[a]	—	—	75	332	502	147	33	29	—
Manat per $									
Exchange rate, end-year	—	—	45	238	4,318	4,440	4,095	3,888	3,964
Exchange rate, annual average	—	—	120	1,149	1,457	4,416	4,305	3,985	3,984
External sector ($ millions)									
Current account	—	153	488	2	–121	–318	–811	–961	—
Trade balance	—	60	489	–5	–163	–275	–549	–569	—
Exports	—	295	1,275	716	682	680	789	825	—
Imports	—	336	786	721	845	955	1,338	1,395	—
Foreign direct investment, net	—	—	—	20	22	284	661	1,006	—
Gross reserves, end-year	—	—	0	0	2	119	214	457	—
External debt stock	—	—	—	—	89	420	560	567	—
In weeks of exports of goods and services									
Gross reserves, end-year	—	—	0	0	0	5	8	15	—
% exports of goods and services									
Debt service	—	—	—	—	—	7.9	9.7	8.7	—
Current account/GDP	—	—	233.3	1.2	–6.6	–11.5	–23.6	–23.4	–28.6
External debt/GDP	—	—	—	—	4.8	15.1	16.3	13.8	—
External debt/exports	—	—	—	—	13.0	61.8	71.0	68.8	—
Memorandum items									
Population (millions)	—	—	7.3	7.4	7.4	7.5	7.6	7.6	7.7
GDP (manat, billions)[b]	1.5	2.1	25.1	191.0	2,685	12,264	14,807	16,399	—
GDP per capita ($)	—	—	364.0	223.0	246.0	368.0	451.0	541.1	555.2
GDP per capita (PPP$)	—	—	3,027	2,306	1,837	1,604	1,602	1,677	1,777

[a] Average lending rate for private enterprises. [b] GDP figures in roubles for 1990–1991 have been converted at the rate of 10 roubles per manat.

Belarus: selected economic indicators, 1990–1998

	1990	1991	1992	1993	1994	1995	1996	1997	1998
Output (% change)									
GDP at constant prices	-3.0	-1.2	-9.6	-7.6	-12.6	-10.4	2.6	10.0	2.0
Private consumption	—	—	-7.9	-1.5	-13.4	-12.8	28.5	13.3	—
Public consumption	—	—	-15.3	-10.5	-3.0	-2.9	—	-13.7	—
Gross fixed investment	—	—	-18.1	-15.4	-17.2	-29.6	-5.0	20.0	—
Industrial gross output	—	1.0	-5.2	-10.5	-18.9	-10.6	3.0	17.6	—
Agricultural gross output	—	-3.2	-14.5	-10.4	-14.9	-7.4	1.9	-5.0	0.5
Composition of output (% GDP)									
Industry	—	28.6	40.4	30.9	30.8	31.4	35.3	37.4	—
Agriculture	—	18.2	23.8	18.3	15.0	17.7	15.9	15.0	—
Unemployment (% labour force)	—	0.0	0.5	1.4	2.1	2.7	3.9	2.3	—
Prices and wages (% change)									
Consumer prices, annual average	—	84	969	1,187	2,221	709	54.1	63.9	95.3
Consumer prices, end-year	—	93	1,559	1,996	1,960	244	39.2	63.1	117.7
Producer prices, annual average	—	150	2,330	1,495	2,171	499	37.8	89.7	81.0
Producer prices, end-year	—	—	3,275	2,316	1,867	140	32.1	90.8	—
Average wage, gross	—	—	-12.3	-6.2	-30.9	-5.0	4.5	14.7	-14.3
Government sector (% GDP)									
General government balance	—	—	0.0	-1.9	-2.5	-1.9	-1.6	-2.7	-3.3
General government expenditure	—	—	46.1	56.2	50.0	44.6	43.6	44.6	—
Monetary sector (% change)									
Broad money, end-year	—	—	—	954.0	1,818	173.7	52.4	111.4	—
Domestic credit, end-year	—	—	—	—	2,031	157.4	58.5	83.0	—
Broad money (% GDP)	—	—	—	34.6	36.8	15.0	15.2	17.9	—

Interest and exchange rates (% per year), end-year								
Deposit rate, one year	—	—	—	65	90	101	32	16
Lending rate, one year	—	—	—	72	149	175	64	32
Belarusian roubles per $								
Exchange rate, end-year	—	—	15	699	10,600	11,500	15,500	30,700
Exchange rate, annual average	—	—	17	269	3,666	11,529	13,292	26,300
External sector ($ millions)								
Current account	—	—	—	−1,113	−641	−254	−909	−995
Trade balance	—	—	377	−1,051	−710	−528	−1,335	−1,497
Exports	—	—	3,580	2,812	2,641	4,621	5,404	7,147
Imports	—	—	3,203	3,863	3,351	5,149	6,739	8,644
Foreign direct investment, net	—	50	7	18	10	7	75	100
Gross reserves, end-year	—	—	—	91	101	377	469	394
External debt stock	—	—	—	1,014	1,251	1,513	947	970
In months of imports of goods and services								
Gross reserves, end-year	—	—	—	0.3	0.4	0.9	0.8	0.6
% exports of goods and services								
Debt service	—	—	—	0.5	4.5	3.9	2.1	2.0
Current account/GDP	—	—	—	−3.1	−13.2	−2.4	−6.7	−8.7
External debt/GDP	—	—	—	2.8	25.7	14.6	7.0	7.3
External debt/exports	—	—	—	36.1	47.4	32.7	17.5	13.6
Memorandum items								
Population (millions)	10.3	10.3	10.3	10.4	10.3	10.3	10.2	10.2
GDP, Belarusian roubles (billions)	—	86	914	9,776	17,815	119,813	179,820	351,043
GDP per capita ($)	—	5,199	3,508	470	1,013	1,311	1,257	1,054
GDP per capita (PPP$)	—	6,845	6,081	5,304	4,762	4,903	5,407	5,007

Bosnia-Herzegovina: selected economic indicators, 1990–1998

	1990	1991	1992	1993	1994	1995	1996	1997	1998
Output (% change)									
Real GDP	−9	−20	—	—	—	32	50	30	30
Industrial gross output, 1991 = 100[a]	112	100	50	4	2	10	19	32	—
Retail prices, annual average (% change)	—	114	73,109	44,069	780	4	−25	12	10
Monetary sector (% change)									
Broad money, end-year[b]	—	—	—	—	—	33	110	—	—
Dinar per DM									
Exchange rate, annual average[c]	—	—	—	—	—	100	100	100	—
Government sector (DM millions)									
Consolidated government balance[d]	—	—	—	—	−339	−9	−177	−161	−150
Consolidated government expenditure[d]	—	—	—	—	896	1,051	2,173	2,755	—

External sector ($ millions)									
Current account	—	—	—	—	-177	-193	-748	-1,046	—
excluding official transfers	—	—	—	—	-492	-570	-1,306	-1,545	—
Exports[e]	1,990	2,120	495	7	91	152	336	570	—
Imports[e]	1,953	1,673	429	60	894	1,082	1,882	2,199	—
of which humanitarian aid in-kind	—	—	—	—	561	459	260	360	—
Gross official reserves[a]	—	—	—	—	92	213	459	684	—
In months of merchandise imports									
Gross official reserves[a]	—	—	—	—	1.2	2.4	2.9	3.5	—
Current account/GDP[f]	—	—	—	—	-25.1	-26.4	-39.3	-34.7	—
Memorandum items									
GDP ($ millions)	10,471	8,670	—	—	1,964	2,157	3,327	4,455	—
Population (millions)[g]	4.4	4.4	4.2	4.1	4.1	4.1	4.0	4.0	3.9
GDP per capita ($)	2,396	1,979	—	—	547	607	815	—	—

[a] Until 1995 data for only the Bosniak-majority area, Federation area thereafter.
[b] Figures for 1996 refer to the first 9 months.
[c] Bosnia-Herzegovina has a currency board. The currency is pegged to the DM.
[d] Cash basis, including grants. Data for 1996 are estimates for the first 9 months from different sources and are not consistent.
[e] Data for 1992–1993 are based on limited customs data for the Bosniak-majority area; 1994–1996 data are rough estimates for the whole territory of Bosnia-Herzegovina.
[f] Excluding official transfers.
[g] Data include refugees abroad.

Bulgaria: selected economic indicators, 1990–1998

	1990	1991	1992	1993	1994	1995	1996	1997	1998
Output (% change)									
GDP at constant prices	-9.1	-11.7	-7.3	-1.5	1.8	2.1	-10.9	-7.4	3.5
Private consumption	0.3	-15.3	-1.0	-3.6	-4.5	-2.9	-11.9	-6.5	2.0
Public consumption	3.2	-7.8	-9.3	-15.0	-16.9	-2.2	-31.8	8.1	-10.4
Gross fixed investment	-29.8	-16.6	-7.3	-17.5	1.1	8.8	-13.5	-15.6	12.7
Industrial gross output	-12.5	-21.0	-6.4	-6.2	6.0	1.7	-8.3	-13.0	3.0
Agricultural gross output	-3.7	4.3	-14.8	-30.2	9.5	16.3	-18.1	26.2	4.1
Composition of output (% GDP)									
Industry	—	39.6	39.0	32.7	29.9	31.1	31.6	—	—
Agriculture	—	15.4	11.6	9.9	11.5	12.8	11.4	—	—
Unemployment (% labour force)	1.6	10.5	13.2	16.3	14.1	11.4	11.1	14.2	14
Prices and wages (% change)									
Consumer prices, annual average	26	334	85	73	96	62	123	1,083	28
Consumer prices, end-year	72.5	338.9	79.4	63.9	121.9	32.9	310.8	578.6	14.0
Producer prices, annual average	—	296	56	27	75	53	138.0	887	21.0
Average wage, gross	5.3	-24.7	7.2	-8.8	-23.8	-4.6	-20.3	-6.9	3.5
Government sector (% GDP)									
General government balance	-12.7	-14.9	-5.2	-10.9	-5.8	-6.4	-13.4	-2.7	-2.0
General government expenditure	65.9	45.6	43.6	48.1	45.7	43.0	47.6	34.3	—
Monetary sector (% change)									
Broad money, end-year	17.0	110.0	53.6	47.6	78.6	39.6	124.5	359.3	—
Domestic credit, end-year	26.0	148.0	51.8	56.0	37.1	15.7	219.9	255.5	—
Broad money (% GDP)	—	76.0	79.0	78.3	79.5	67.2	78.9	35.7	—

Interest and exchange rates (% per year), end-year									
Deposit rate, one month	—	57.7	45.3	53.6	72.3	25.3	211.8	3.0	—
Lending rate, less than one year	—	83.9	64.6	83.7	117.8	51.4	480.8	6.7	—
Leva per $									
Exchange rate, end-year	2.8	21.8	24.5	32.7	66.0	70.7	487.4	1,776.5	1,760.4
Exchange rate, annual average	2.6	17.9	23.3	27.6	54.2	67.2	175.8	1,676.5	1,802.4
External sector ($ millions)									
Current account	-1,180	-406	-801	-1,386	-203	-59	117	184	224
Trade balance	—	404	-212	-885	-17	120	209	311	215
Exports	2,534	2,734	3,956	3,727	3,935	5,345	4,890	4,974	5,517
Imports	3,086	2,330	4,169	4,612	3,952	5,224	4,703	4,662	5,302
Foreign direct investment, net	—	56	42	40	105	82	100	575	300
Gross reserves, end-year	—	331	935	655	1,002	1,236	483	2,484	—
Gross external debt	10,000	11,802	12,548	13,890	11,411	10,229	9,660	9,977	9,644
In months of current account expenditures, excluding transfers									
Gross reserves, end-year	—	0.8	1.9	1.2	2.1	2.2	0.9	3.5	—
% current account revenues, excluding transfers									
Debt service	64.8	24.1	38.1	33.7	19.3	15.4	19.3	15.5	—
Current account/GDP	-2.8	-5.4	-9.3	-12.8	-2.1	-0.5	1.3	1.8	1.7
External debt/GDP	—	157.4	145.6	128.3	117.5	79.2	103.5	97.0	—
External debt/exports	—	431.7	317.2	372.7	299.0	191.4	197.5	200.6	—
Memorandum items									
Population (millions)	8.7	8.6	8.5	8.5	8.4	8.4	8.4	8.3	8.3
GDP, market prices (leva, billions)	45	136	201	299	526	868	1,660	16,875	—
GDP per capita ($)	1,939	880	1,009	1,278	1,187	1,558	1,209	1,319	1,593
GDP per capita (PPP$)	4,648	4,275	4,006	3,984	4,063	4,179	3,721	3,462	3,579

Croatia: selected economic indicators, 1990–1998

	1990	1991	1992	1993	1994	1995	1996	1997	1998
Output (% change)									
GDP at constant prices	-6.9	-20.6	-11.7	-0.9	0.6	1.6	4.3	5.5	5.5
Private consumption	—	—	-1.1	-7.0	16.4	8.9	5.7	4.8	1.0
Public consumption	—	—	—	-3.2	30.5	12.4	10.5	9.7	4.4
Gross fixed investment	—	—	—	0.5	6.4	8.1	18.1	9.2	9.0
Industrial gross output	-11.3	-28.5	-14.6	-5.9	-2.7	0.3	3.1	5.4	5.0
Agricultural gross output	-2.9	-7.0	-13.0	5.0	-2.5	-2.6	2.7	2.2	4.8
Composition of output (% GDP)									
Industry	26.0	23.4	22.6	21.5	20.8	20.5	20.3	—	—
Agriculture and fishing	8.3	9.6	9.5	10.0	9.6	9.5	9.2	—	—
Unemployment (% labour force)	9.3	14.9	17.2	16.8	16.7	16.7	18.2	17.0	14.4
Prices and wages (% change)									
Retail prices, annual average	610.0	123.0	665.5	1,517.5	97.6	2.0	3.6	3.6	6.7
Retail prices, end-year	136.0	250.0	938.0	1,149.0	-3.0	3.7	3.5	3.4	7.5
Producer prices, annual average	455.0	146.0	825.2	1,512.4	77.6	0.7	1.4	2.4	5.0
Producer prices, end-year	—	412.0	1,079.0	1,076.0	-5.5	1.6	1.5	1.6	—
Average wage, to 1994 gross, then net	—	-24.2	-46.6	-2.7	20.0	31.4	7.2	3.1	3.5
Government sector (% GDP)									
Government balance[a]	—	—	-4.0	-0.8	1.7	-0.9	-0.5	-2.7	-2.9
Government expenditure[a]	—	—	37.2	32.6	41.6	46.7	47.2	48.5	—
Monetary sector (% change)									
Narrow money (M1), end-year	—	—	—	—	111.9	24.6	37.9	20.9	—
Domestic credit, end-year	—	—	—	—	9.1	10.9	1.0	15.5	—
Broad money (M4), end-year (% GDP)	—	—	—	24.0	20.5	25.9	35.3	44.5	—

Interest and exchange rates (% per year), end-year									
Average deposit rate	—	—	434.5	27.4	5.0	6.1	4.2	4.4	—
Average lending rate	—	—	2,333	59.0	15.4	22.3	18.5	14.1	—
Kuna per $									
Exchange rate, end-year	0.01	—	0.80	6.56	5.63	5.32	5.54	6.3	6.0
Exchange rate, annual average	—	0.02	0.26	3.59	5.99	5.23	5.43	6.16	6.10
External sector ($ billions)[b]									
Current account	1.1	-0.6	0.8	0.6	0.8	-1.3	-0.9	-1.9	-2.1
Trade balance	-1.2	-0.5	-0.3	-1.0	-1.3	-3.2	-3.7	-3.1	-3.3
Merchandise exports	4.0	3.3	3.1	3.9	4.3	4.6	4.5	4.6	5.1
Merchandise imports	5.2	3.8	3.4	4.9	5.6	7.9	8.2	8.7	8.6
Foreign direct investment, net	—	—	0.0	0.1	0.1	0.1	0.5	0.5	0.6
Gross reserves, end-year	0.0	0.0	0.2	0.6	1.4	1.9	2.3	2.5	2.8
External debt stock, end-year	—	—	3.0	2.7	2.6	3.1	3.7	4.8	6.9
In months of imports of goods and services									
Gross international reserves, end-year	—	—	—	0.0	0.4	1.2	2.5	2.8	—
% exports of goods and services									
Debt service	—	—	12.3	8.9	6.5	4.2	6.2	8.3	10.1
Current account/GDP	—	-3.5	8.3	0.9	0.7	-9.5	-7.6	-10.3	-10.1
External debt/GDP	—	—	17.7	27.5	22.6	21.5	20.2	25.4	34.3
External debt/exports	—	—	90.5	87.5	67.6	72	79	106.6	154.1
Memorandum items									
Population (millions)	4.8	4.8	4.8	4.8	4.8	4.8	4.8	4.8	4.8
GDP (kuna, billions)	0.3	0.4	2.6	41.8	85.3	94.6	103.6	113.2	—
GDP per capita ($)	5,106	3,510	2,079	2,440	2,980	3,786	3,993	3,846	4,356
GDP per capita (PPP$)	—	7,064	6,245	6,193	6,235	6,342	6,614	6,957	7,349

[a] Consolidated central government.   [b] Data for 1990–1992 exclude trade with the republics of former Yugoslavia.

Czech Republic: selected economic indicators, 1990–1998

	1990	1991	1992	1993	1994	1995	1996	1997	1998
Output (% change)									
GDP at constant prices	-1.2	-11.5	-3.3	0.6	3.2	6.4	3.9	1.0	1.4
Private consumption	6.7	-28.5	15.1	2.9	5.3	6.9	7.0	1.6	-0.5
Public consumption	0.9	-9.0	-3.1	-0.1	-2.3	-2.0	4.1	-2.1	-1.5
Gross fixed investment	-2.1	-17.7	8.9	-7.7	17.3	21.0	8.7	-4.9	-1.1
Industrial gross output	-3.5	-22.3	-7.7	-5.6	2.9	8.6	6.8	4.5	6.4
Agricultural gross output	—	-8.9	-12.1	-2.3	-6.0	5.0	-1.4	-5.9	1.6
Composition of output (% GDP)									
Industry	—	—	40.2	34.9	33.6	34.1	33.8	34.9	—
Agriculture	8.4	6.0	6.1	6.5	3.8	5.3	5.1	5.1	—
Unemployment (% labour force)	0.8	4.1	2.6	3.5	3.2	2.9	3.5	5.2	6.7
Prices and wages (% change)									
Consumer prices, annual average	10.8	56.6	11.1	20.8	10.0	9.1	8.8	8.5	11.9
Consumer prices, end-year	18.4	52.0	12.7	18.2	9.7	7.9	8.6	10.0	10.8
Producer prices, annual average	4.4	70.4	10.0	13.1	5.3	7.6	4.8	7.5	10.9
Producer prices, end-year	—	—	9.3	11.4	5.6	7.2	4.4	5.7	—
Average wage	-5.7	-26.3	10.2	3.7	7.7	7.7	8.5	3.1	0.4
Government sector (% GDP)									
General government balance	-1.8[a]	-1.9	-3.1	0.5	-1.2	-1.8	-1.2	-2.1	-0.9
General government expenditure	—	—	—	41.9	43.3	42.8	41.8	41.6	—
Monetary sector (% change)									
Broad money, end-year	0.5[a]	26.8[a]	20.7	19.8	19.9	19.8	9.2	10.1	—
Domestic credit, end-year	—	—	14.6	18.5	15.4	6.4	8.4	5.0	—
Broad money (% GDP)	—	—	69.4	70.3	73.9	75.6	72.2	73.8	—

Interest and exchange rates (% per year), end-year									
Deposit rate	—	—	6.3	7.0	6.9	6.9	6.7	8.1	—
Lending rate	—	—	13.3	14.1	12.8	12.7	12.5	13.9	14.4
Koruna per $									
Exchange rate, end-year	28.0[a]	28.9[a]	28.7[a]	29.0	28.2	26.6	27.4	34.6	32.5
Exchange rate, annual average	18.0[a]	29.5[a]	28.3[a]	29.2	28.8	26.6	27.1	31.7	33.3
External sector ($ billions)									
Current account	-1.1[a]	0.3[a]	-0.3[a]	0.1	0.0	-1.4	-4.3	-3.2	-2.3
Trade balance[b]	-0.8[a]	-0.5[a]	-1.9[a]	-0.3	-0.9	-3.7	-5.9	-4.6	-3.3
Exports[b]	5.9[a]	8.3[a]	8.4[a]	13.0	14.0	21.5	21.7	22.5	24.7
Imports[b]	6.5[a]	8.3[a]	10.4[a]	13.3	14.9	25.1	27.6	27.1	28.0
Foreign direct investment, net	—	0.5[a]	1.0[a]	0.5	0.7	2.5	1.4	1.3	—
Gross reserves, end-year	0.2	0.7	0.8	3.9	6.2	14.0	12.4	9.8	—
External debt stock, convertible currency	6.0	6.7	7.1	8.5	10.7	16.5	20.8	21.4	23.5
In months of imports of goods and services									
Gross reserves, end-year	0.3	0.8	0.8	2.7	3.9	5.6	4.2	3.6	—
% exports of goods and services									
Debt service	—	—	12.4	6.5	13.1	9.3	10.4	15.9	—
Current account/GDP	-2.9[a]	1.2	-1	0.3	-0.1	-2.7	-7.6	-6.1	-4.1
External debt/GDP	—	26.4	23.7	24.7	26.9	32.8	36.9	42.3	—
External debt/exports	—	80.8	83.8	65.4	76.3	77.1	96.1	97.6	—
Memorandum items									
Population (millions)	10.3	10.3	10.3	10.3	10.3	10.3	10.3	10.3	10.3
GDP (koruna, billions)	579	750	847	1,002	1,143	1,339	1,533	1,650	—
GDP per capita ($)	3,126	2,466	2,899	3,326	3,862	4,921	5,476	5,050	5,418
GDP per capita (PPP$)	8,856	8,554	8,596	8,873	9,447	9,826	9,933	10,056	

[a] Data refer to former Czechoslovakia.   [b] For 1990–1992 the Czech Republic's share of the total for Czechoslovakia.

Estonia: selected economic indicators, 1990–1998

	1990	1991	1992	1993	1994	1995	1996	1997	1998
Output (% change)									
GDP at constant prices	-8.1	-7.9	-14.2	-8.5	-1.8	4.3	4.0	10.0	5.5
Private consumption	—	—	-19.6	-5.5	1.5	1.4	9.5	12.5	2.0
Public consumption	—	—	-17.0	15.5	8.9	7.5	-8.3	12.0	0.0
Gross fixed investment	—	—	-13.5	4.8	6.7	0.3	4.0	9.2	3.7
Industrial gross output	—	—	-35.6	-18.7	-3.0	1.9	2.9	13.4	10.5
Agricultural gross output	—	—	-18.6	-7.7	-14.2	-1.2	-3.2	6.6	4.1
Composition of output (% GDP)									
Industry	—	—	27.5	22.0	21.1	20.2	18.9	—	—
Agriculture	—	—	12.6	9.8	9.0	7.1	6.4	—	—
Unemployment (% labour force)	—	—	—	5.0	5.1	5.1	5.6	5.4	5.3
Prices and wages (% change)									
Consumer prices, annual average	23.0	210.5	1,076.0	89.8	48.0	29.0	23.0	11.0	12.0
Consumer prices, end-year	—	303.8	953.5	35.6	42.0	29.0	15.0	12.0	11.0
Producer prices, annual average	—	—	1,208.0	75.0	36.3	25.6	14.8	8.8	6.7
Producer prices, end-year	—	—	—	—	32.8	22.0	9.9	7.7	—
Average wage in industry, gross	—	—	—	1.8	16.4	5.2	0.4	8.9	5.9
Government sector (% GDP)									
General government balance	—	5.2	-0.3	-0.7	1.3	-1.2	-1.5	-2.3	1.7
General government expenditure	—	—	34.9	40.3	38.3	40.8	40.4	—	—
Monetary sector (% change)									
Broad money, end-year	—	—	71.1	86.5	31.0	30.5	36.6	40.4	—
Domestic credit, end-year	—	—	29.6	61.4	40.1	63.1	100.6	87.3	—
Broad money (% GDP)	—	—	—	—	26.2	25.0	27.0	30.7	—

Interest and exchange rates (% per year), end-year[a]									
Deposit rate, over 12 months[a]	—	—	—	—	10.13	7.21	7.48	10.4	—
Lending rate, 1–3 years	—	—	—	21.90	19.08	16.82	17.23	11.9	—
Kroon per $									
Exchange rate, end-year	—	—	12.9	13.9	12.4	11.5	12.4	14.2	13.6
Exchange rate, annual average	—	—	—	13.2	13.0	11.5	12.0	13.9	13.6
External sector ($ millions)									
Current account	—	—	—	36	23	-166	-166	-424	-610
Trade balance	—	—	—	-90	-145	-356	-674	-1,046	-1,188
Exports	—	—	—	461	812	1,329	1,857	1,789	2,096
Imports	—	—	—	551	957	1,684	2,531	2,835	3,283
Foreign direct investment, net	—	—	—	58	160	212	199	111	131
Gross reserves, end-year	—	—	—	170	386	443	579	679	776
External debt stock, end-year	—	—	—	—	161	187	287	407	563
In months of current account expenditures, excluding transfers									
Gross reserves, end-year	—	—	—	2.8	3.7	2.5	2.3	2.0	2.2
% exports of goods and non-factor services									
Debt service	—	—	—	—	1.4	0.4	0.5	0.8	—
Current account/GDP	—	—	—	1.3	-7.1	-4.6	-9.7	-13.2	-9.2
External debt/GDP	—	—	—	—	9.7	8.0	8.0	9.3	12.1
External debt/exports	—	—	—	—	19.8	14.1	15.5	22.8	28.8
Memorandum items									
Population (millions)	1.6	1.6	1.5	1.5	1.5	1.5	1.5	1.5	1.4
GDP (kroon, millions)	—	—	13,054	21,918	30,268	41,279	52,379	64,536	—
GDP per capita ($)	—	—	663	1,101	1,563	2,439	2,996	3,203	3,728
GDP per capita (PPP$)	—	—	7,635	7,076	7,021	7,398	7,765	8,569	9,168
GDP per capita (PPP$)[b]	—	—	3,957	3,785	3,842	4,138	4,431	—	—

[a] Time deposit rate for 1994 and 1995, which also includes deposits with up to 3 and 3–12 month maturities.　　[b] According to an evaluation from OECD 1997e.

Georgia: selected economic indicators, 1990–1998

	1990	1991	1992	1993	1994	1995	1996	1997	1998
Output (% change)									
GDP at constant prices	-12.4	-20.6	-44.8	-25.4	-11.4	2.4	10.5	10.0	10.0
Private consumption	—	—	-8.4	-32.7	-0.4	-0.7	7.7	10.5	6.4
Public consumption	—	—	-40.0	-70.4	-5.4	58.9	-13.6	8.5	4.4
Gross fixed investment	—	—	-55.0	-62.0	-0.5	2.0	1.6	17.4	19.6
Industrial gross output	-30.0	-24.4	-43.3	-21.0	-39.7	-9.8	6.7	8.1	13.0
Agricultural gross output	62.0	-10.1	-34.2	-42.0	11.6	13.4	12.0	6.0	8.2
Composition of output (% GDP)									
Industry	—	—	12.6	6.3	21.3	14.5	14.2	—	—
Agriculture	—	—	54.5	67.7	28.7	38.0	32.6	—	—
Unemployment (% labour force)	—	—	0.9	1.4	3.6	3.4	2.3	2.6	—
Prices and wages (% change)									
Consumer prices, annual average	3.0	79.0	887.4	3,125.4	15,606.5	162.7	39.4	8.0	8.0
Consumer prices, end-year	5.0	131.0	1,176.9	7,487.9	6,474.4	57.4	13.8	8.1	8.0
Average real wage in industry	—	—	—	-36.4	49.1	-15.5	14.2	—	—
Average nominal wage in industry	—	—	—	1,950	23,315	121.9	59.2	—	—
Government sector (% GDP)									
General government balance	—	-3.0	-25.4	-26.2	-7.4	-4.5	-4.4	-3.8	-3.0
General government expenditure	—	33.0	35.7	35.9	24.2	12.3	13.9	13.9	—
Monetary sector (% change)									
Broad money, end-year	—	—	464.0	4,319.0	2,229.0	146.4	41.9	29.0	—
Domestic credit, end-year	—	—	724.0	2,048.0	3,448.3	84.6	59.6	54.5	—
Broad money (% GDP)	—	—	38.5	19.2	5.3	4.9	4.5	4.9	—

Exchange rates (lari per $)								
Exchange rate, end-year	—	—	0.10	1.28	1.24	1.28	1.30	1.33
Exchange rate, annual average	—	—	—	1.10	1.29	1.26	1.30	1.32
External sector ($ millions)								
Current account								
with official transfers	—	—	−248	−354	−278	−215	−220	−318
without official transfers	—	—	−319	−485	−448	−404	−360	−366
Trade balance	—	—	−378	−448	−365	−335	−293	−379
Exports	—	—	267	457	381	358	417	466
Imports	—	—	645	905	746	693	710	845
Foreign direct investment, net	—	—	—	8	6	25	65	65
Gross reserves, end-year	—	—	95	1	41	157	158	150
External debt stock	—	—	—	597	1,002	1,223	1,373	1,565
In months of merchandise imports								
Gross reserves, end-year	—	—	0.0	0.0	0.7	2.7	2.7	2.1
% exports of goods and services								
Debt service[a]	—	—	—	—	—	7.3	9.8	9.2
Current account/GDP	—	—	—	−22.3	−7.5	−4.8	−6.2	−6.1
External debt/GDP[a]	—	—	35.6	130.6	80.2	42.7	30.2	30.4
External debt/exports[a]	—	—	—	263.1	341.6	329.3	335.8	335.8
Memorandum items								
Population (millions)	5.4	5.4	5.4	5.4	5.4	5.4	5.4	5.4
GDP (lari, millions)	—	—	0.2	16.4	1,373	3,694	5,724	6,800
GDP per capita ($)	—	132	214	245	378	577	669	787
GDP per capita (PPP$)	—	2,366	1,677	1,508	1,552	1,671	1,858	2,041

[a] Following debt restructuring.

Hungary: selected economic indicators, 1990–1998

	1990	1991	1992	1993	1994	1995	1996	1997	1998
Output (% change)									
GDP at constant prices	-3.5	-11.9	-3.1	-0.6	2.9	1.5	1.3	4.3	5.4
Private consumption	-3.6	-5.6	0.0	1.9	-0.2	-7.1	-2.1	0.1	3.0
Public consumption	2.6	-6.7	4.9	27.5	-12.7	-4.1	-5.4	0.1	4.0
Gross fixed investment	-7.1	-10.4	-2.6	2.0	12.5	-4.3	6.3	8.2	12.0
Industrial gross output	-9.3	-18.3	-9.7	4.0	9.6	4.6	3.4	11.1	12.0
Agricultural gross output	-4.7	-6.2	-20.0	-9.7	3.2	2.6	4.9	-0.6	-2.0
Composition of output (% GDP)									
Industry	28.8	26.7	24.4	23.2	22.8	23.9	—	—	—
Agriculture	9.6	7.8	6.5	5.8	6.0	6.4	—	—	—
Unemployment (% labour force)	1.9	7.8	13.2	12.1	10.4	10.4	10.7	10.4	8.7
Prices and wages (% change)									
Consumer prices, annual average	28.9	35.0	23.0	22.5	18.8	28.2	23.6	18.3	15.6
Consumer prices, end-year	33.4	35.0	23.0	21.1	21.2	28.3	19.8	18.4	14.2
Producer prices, annual average	22.0	32.6	12.3	10.8	11.3	28.9	21.8	19.4	13.2
Producer prices, end-year	39.3	23.5	18.8	10.3	19.9	30.2	20.1	19.5	—
Average wage	-1.8	-1.7	-4.0	-5.1	5.5	-12.2	-5.0	4.9	6.4
Government sector (% GDP)									
General government balance	0.4	-2.9	-6.8	-5.5	-8.4	-6.7	-3.5	-4.6	-4.0
General government expenditure	53.5	55.4	59.4	60.6	60.9	53.9	50.9	49.7	—
Monetary sector (% change)									
Broad money, end-year	29.2	35.7	27.3	15.7	13.0	20.1	22.5	19.4	—
Domestic credit, end-year	—	17.6	11.4	0.5	20.9	18.0	12.7	12.1	—
Broad money (% GDP)	—	54.8	59.2	56.8	52.2	49.8	49.0	48.0	—

Interest and exchange rates (% per year), end-year

Deposit rate, one year	28.5	29.4	16.1	16.6	22.9	24.4	18.6	16.6	—
Lending rate, one year	32.1	35.5	28.8	25.6	29.7	32.2	24.0	20.7	18.6
Forint per $									
Exchange rate, end-year	61.5	75.6	84.0	100.7	110.7	139.5	164.9	203.5	204.9
Exchange rate, annual average	63.2	74.7	79.0	92.0	105.4	125.7	152.6	187.6	201.7

External sector ($ billions)

Current account	0.1	0.3	0.3	-3.5	-3.9	-2.5	-1.7	-1.0	-1.1
Trade balance[a]	0.3	0.2	0.0	-3.2	-3.6	-2.4	-2.7	-1.7	-1.7
Exports[a]	—	9.3	10.0	8.1	7.6	12.8	14.2	19.6	21.4
Imports[a]	—	9.1	10.1	11.3	11.2	15.3	16.8	21.4	23.1
Foreign direct investment, net	0.3	1.5	1.5	2.3	1.1	4.5	2.0	2.1	2.1
Gross reserves, end-year	—	3.9	4.3	6.7	6.8	12.0	9.8	8.4	—
External debt stock	—	22.6	21.4	24.6	28.5	31.7	27.6	26.3	27.9

In months of current account expenditures, excluding transfers

Gross reserves, end-year	1.3	3.8	3.6	5.2	5.1	7.0	5.3	3.6	—

% current account revenues, excluding transfers

Debt service[b]	48.2	33.9	34.4	43.2	54.8	47.3	50.4	23.3	—
Current account/GDP	0.4	0.8	0.9	-8.9	-9.4	-5.7	-3.8	-2.2	-3.3
External debt/GDP	—	67.8	57.5	63.6	68.7	72.4	61.6	54.0	—
External debt/exports	—	244.5	213.8	303.4	374.6	247.2	194.9	123.7	—

Memorandum items

Population (in millions)	10.4	10.3	10.3	10.3	10.3	10.2	10.2	10.1	10.1
GDP (forint, billions)	2,089	2,498	2,943	3,548	4,365	5,494	6,845	8,446	—
GDP per capita ($)	3,186	3,229	3,604	3,739	4,040	4,359	4,393	4,462	5,016
GDP per capita (PPP$)	7,612	6,719	6,522	6,500	6,710	6,831	6,943	7,275	7,695

[a] Data from balance of payments. Customs-based trade data, excluding trade from free export zones, show considerably higher trade growth in 1994, but lower growth in 1995–1996. [b] Debt service in 1996 includes prepayments ($1.687 billion) to international financial institutions and commercial creditors.

Kazakhstan: selected economic indicators, 1990–1998

	1990	1991	1992	1993	1994	1995	1996	1997	1998
Output (% change)									
GDP at constant prices	-0.4	-13.0	-2.9	-10.4	-17.8	-8.9	1.1	1.8	2.7
Private consumption	—	—	-13.3	-5.2	-15.9	-19.6	20.2	4.0	2.5
Public consumption	—	—	-4.8	-2.8	-3.8	—	19.2	1.0	1.5
Gross fixed investment	—	—	-30.0	-39.0	-31.8	-25.7	-39.9	19.0	11.7
Industrial gross output	-1.0	-1.0	-14.0	-14.0	-27.5	-8.2	0.3	4.0	6.5
Agricultural gross output	16.0	-9.0	28.7	-6.9	-21.0	-24.4	-5.0	-2.0	4.0
Composition of output (% GDP)									
Industry	41.5	38.0	34.7	28.7	29.1	23.4	21.3	20.2	—
Agriculture	28.1	29.0	30.4	16.4	14.9	12.1	11.9	9.2	—
Unemployment (% labour force)	0.0	0.0	0.5	0.5	8.0	11.0	13.0	13.5	14.5
Prices and wages (% change)									
Consumer prices, annual average	105	79.0	1,381	1,662	1,892	176	39.1	17.7	13.5
Consumer prices, end-year		137	2,984	2,169	1,160	60.4	28.6	11.3	8.5
Average wage	—	—	11.8	-11.1	-31.5	0.4	2.9	7.4	3.4
Government sector (% GDP)									
General government balance	1.4	-7.9	-7.3	-1.3	-7.2	-2.0	-2.5	-3.4	-4.5
General government expenditure	31.4	32.9	31.8	25.2	25.9	20.7	18.5	19.9	—
Monetary sector (% change)									
Broad money, end-year	—	211.0	391.0	692.0	576.0	103.8	14.7	12.9	—
Domestic credit, end-year	—	289.0	1,343.0	653.0	710.0	-22.5	-12.0	—	—
Broad money (% GDP)	—	—	45.0	20.9	25.9	11.5	4.4	—	—

Interest and exchange rates (% per year), end-year								
Deposit rate, one year	—	—	—	—	—	53.3	30.0	12.6
Lending rate, one year	—	—	—	—	—	58.3	39.4	22.9
Tenge per $								
Exchange rate, end-year	—	0.8	6.1	54.3	64.0	73.3	75.8	81.4
Exchange rate, annual average	—	0.4	1.9	36.0	61.0	67.3	75.6	79.9
External sector ($ billions)								
Current account	—	-1.3	-1.9	-0.4	-0.9	-0.7	-0.7	-1.0
Trade balance	—	-3.2	-1.1	-0.4	-0.9	-0.2	-0.3	-0.5
Exports	—	10.2	3.6	4.8	3.3	5.2	6.3	6.8
Imports	—	13.4	4.7	5.2	4.2	5.4	6.6	7.3
Foreign direct investment, net	—	—	—	0.5	0.6	0.9	1.1	1.2
Gross reserves, end-year	—	—	—	0.6	1.2	1.7	2.0	2.1
External debt stock	—	—	1.5	1.9	2.7	3.4	3.9	4.3
In months of imports of goods and services								
Gross reserves, end-year[a]	—	—	1.5	3.5	3.2	3.5	—	4.2
% exports of goods and services								
Total debt service	—	4.3	1.4	3.3	8.0	5.5	7.0	—
Current account/GDP	—	-38.0	-2.4	-7.2	-3.9	-3.4	-4.8	-4.8
External debt/GDP	—	29.6	11.0	21.8	19.3	18.7	18.7	—
External debt/exports	—	41.1	38.5	82.4	66.0	61.7	63.2	—
Memorandum items								
Population (millions), end-year	16.6	16.7	16.9	16.7	16.5	16.4	15.7	15.5
GDP (tenge, billions)	—	2	32	450	1,086	1,416	1,700	—
GDP per capita ($)	—	322	981	785	1,079	1,278	1,343	1,533
GDP per capita (PPP$)	—	3,245	2,929	2,573	2,405	2,442	2,499	2,650

[a] Foreign exchange reserves of monetary authorities in months of merchandise imports until 1995.

Kyrgyzstan: selected economic indicators, 1990–1998

	1990	1991	1992	1993	1994	1995	1996	1997	1998
Output (% change)									
GDP at constant prices	3.0	–5.0	–19.0	–16.0	–20.0	–5.4	5.6	10.4	5.9
Private consumption	—	—	–40.4	17.8	–30.6	–1.2	15.8	7.4	3.8
Public consumption	—	—	–17.3	–20.7	–22.0	–18.8	–14.1	6.4	2.8
Gross fixed investment	—	—	–35.0	–31.0	–28.3	56.6	10.6	–35.3	24.7
Industrial gross output	–0.6	–0.3	–26.1	2.4	–28.0	–17.8	8.8	46.8	12.0
Agricultural gross output	1.3	–10.0	–5.0	–10.0	–15.0	–9.0	13.1	10.7	3.4
Composition of output (% GDP)									
Industry	26	27	32	25	20	16	12	—	—
Agriculture	32	35	37	39	38	40	47	—	—
Unemployment (% labour force)	—	0.0	0.1	0.2	4.1	5.7	7.8	7.5	—
Prices and wages (% change)									
Consumer prices, annual average	—	85.0	855.0	772.4	228.7	52.5	30.4	25.4	11.7
Consumer prices, end-year	—	170.0	1,259.0	1,363.0	95.7	31.9	35.0	14.8	12.1
Average wage	—	—	–36.0	–25.9	–11.4	9.3	–3.0	0.7	5.9
Government sector (% GDP)									
General government balance	0.3	4.6	–17.4	–14.2	–11.6	–17.2	–9.6	–9.2	–9.0
Government expenditure, net lending	38.3	30.3	33.9	39.1	28.6	30.2	23.3	22.4	—
Monetary sector (% change)									
Broad money, end-year	—	84.0	428.0	180.0	125.0	76.7	22.4	19.9	—
Net domestic assets	—	—	761.0	307.0	83.5	96.8	21.1	14.4	—

Interest and exchange rates (% per year), end-year, minimum/maximum

Deposit rate, three-month	—	—	—	—	—	20/50	15/40	—	—
Lending rate	—	—	—	—	—	35/140	45/120	—	—
Som per $									
Exchange rate, end-year[a]	1.7	1.7	414.5	8.0	10.7	11.0	17.0	17.4	17.9
Exchange rate, annual average[a]	1.8	1.8	222.0	6.0	10.8	10.8	12.1	17.2	17.6
External sector ($ millions)									
Current account balance	—	—	—	-61	-162	-124	-242	-418	-187
Trade balance	—	—	-41	-74	-166	-119	-179	-363	-134
Exports	—	—	3,845	258	335	340	409	531	671
Imports	—	—	3,886	332	501	459	588	894	805
Foreign direct investment, net	—	—	—	—	10	45	96	46	50
Gross reserves, end-year	—	—	—	—	46	96	123	129	184
External debt stock	—	—	—	—	290	414	585	753	934
In months of imports of goods and services									
Gross reserves, end-year	—	—	—	—	1.1	2.5	2.5	1.8	2.7
% merchandise exports									
Debt service	—	—	—	—	0.6	5.0	19.5	12.9	6.0
Current account/GDP	—	—	-18.3	-18.5	-11.3	-16.2	-24.0	-11.5	-9.5
External debt/GDP	—	—	—	—	33.0	37.5	39.1	43.2	57.3
External debt/exports	—	—	—	—	86.5	121.7	143.0	141.7	139.3
Memorandum items									
Population (millions)	4.4	4.4	4.5	4.5	4.5	4.6	4.6	4.6	4.6
GDP (som, millions)	—	—	43	741	5,355	12,019	16,145	22,468	28,700
GDP per capita ($)	93	—	155	199	250	336	413	397	—
GDP per capita (PPP$)	—	3,046	2,537	1,920	1,796	1,870	2,021	2,125	—

[a] Roubles per dollar until 1992, som per dollar thereafter.

Latvia: selected economic indicators, 1990–1998

	1990	1991	1992	1993	1994	1995	1996	1997	1998
Output (% change)									
GDP at constant prices	2.9	-10.4	-34.9	-14.9	0.6	-0.8	2.8	6.0	6.0
Private consumption	—	-26.0	-43.3	-7.4	3.2	3.9	2.5	14.2	4.7
Public consumption	—	-4.9	5.6	1.6	-0.9	3.1	3.5	22.7	3.7
Gross fixed investment	—	-63.9	-28.7	-15.8	0.8	12.6	5.0	8.9	15.2
Industrial gross output	—	-0.3	-34.6	-38.1	-9.5	-6.3	1.4	6.1	7.0
Agricultural gross output	—	-1.1	-15.6	-22.2	-20.6	-6.2	-0.9	3.4	3.9
Composition of output (% GDP)									
Industry	38.3	39.9	29.8	30.8	25.4	25.3	27.8	—	—
Agriculture	21.9	17.6	11.8	9.5	9.8	9.8	9.1	—	—
Unemployment (% labour force)	—	—	2.3	4.7	6.4	6.3	7.2	6.7	7.3
Prices and wages (% change)									
Consumer prices, annual average	10.5	172.0	951.2	108.0	35.9	25.0	17.6	8.4	6.0
Consumer prices, end-year	—	262.4	959.0	35.0	26.0	23.0	13.1	7.0	5.0
Producer prices, annual average	—	—	1,310.0	98.1	17.0	12.0	13.8	4.3	4.7
Producer prices, end-year	—	—	—	—	—	—	—	—	—
Average wages in industry, gross	—	—	—	5.8	10.6	1.8	-4.6	11.3	4.9
Government sector (% GDP)									
General government balance	—	—	-0.8	0.6	-4.1	-3.5	-1.4	1.3	-0.4
General government expenditure	—	—	28.2	35.2	38.2	40.5	40.2	38.2	—
Monetary sector (% change)									
Broad money, end-year	—	153.0	169.9	84.1	47.7	-23.1	19.9	38.7	—
Domestic credit, end-year	—	91.0	303.8	146.0	65.7	-25.4	6.0	25.0	—
Broad money (% GDP)	—	—	—	31.5	33.6	22.3	22.7	25.6	—

Interest and exchange rates (% per year), end-year									
Deposit rate, less than one year	—	—	—	28.4	18.8	15.0	10.0	—	—
Lending rate, less than one year	—	—	—	70.8	36.7	31.1	20.3	—	—
Lats per $									
Exchange rate, end-year	—	—	0.84	0.60	0.55	0.54	0.56	0.56	0.59
Exchange rate, annual average	—	—	0.67	0.67	0.56	0.53	0.55	0.55	0.58
External sector ($ millions)									
Current account	—	—	—	25	151	−86	−159	−350	−350
Trade balance	—	—	—	−215	−160	−378	−579	−798	−887
Exports	—	—	—	831	998	997	1,368	1,488	1,745
Imports	—	—	—	1,046	1,158	1,375	1,947	2,286	2,632
Foreign direct investment, net	—	—	—	43	51	155	244	379	415
Gross reserves, end-year	—	—	—	—	432	545	506	654	691
External debt stock, end-year	—	—	—	43	225	362	429	432	486
In months of imports of goods and services									
Gross reserves, end-year	—	—	—	1.5	4.4	4.6	3	2.9	2.7
% exports of goods and services									
Debt service	—	—	—	0	2	5	3	5	—
Current account/GDP	—	—	1.7	3.1	−1.2	−2.4	−3.6	−7.0	−6.4
External debt/GDP	—	—	—	2.9	10.3	9.9	9.6	8.6	8.9
External debt/exports	—	—	—	5.2	22.5	36.3	31.4	29.0	27.8
Memorandum items									
Population (millions)	2.7	2.7	2.6	2.6	2.5	2.5	2.5	2.5	2.5
GDP (lats, millions)	62	143	1,005	1,467	2,043	2,349	2,768	3,152	—
GDP per capita ($)	—	—	578	848	1,443	1,779	2,026	2,318	2,573
GDP per capita (PPP$)	—	—	6,062	5,242	5,348	5,365	5,629	6,076	6,491
GDP per capita (PPP$)[a]	—	—	3,451	3,070	3,204	3,291	3,484	—	—

[a] According to an evaluation in OECD 1997e.

Lithuania: selected economic indicators, 1990–1998

	1990	1991	1992	1993	1994	1995	1996	1997	1998
Output (% change)									
GDP at constant prices	−5.0	−13.4	−37.7	−17.1	−11.3	2.3	5.1	5.7	5.5
Private consumption	—	—	—	−30.6	2.1	1.0	6.4	6.7	3.2
Public consumption	—	—	—	−10.5	8.4	14.2	−2.2	3.7	1.2
Gross fixed investment	—	—	—	−42.1	−17.3	9.5	−0.9	9.1	5.5
Industrial gross output	—	—	−28.6	−34.4	−26.6	5.5	3.6	−0.9	4.9
Agricultural and forestry gross output	−9.0	−5.0	−24.0	−8.0	−18.0	16.3	16.7	5.7	4.8
Composition of output (% GDP)									
Industry	32.8	55.7	39.4	30.4	25.8	29.0	28.3	—	—
Agriculture and forestry	27.6	19.2	11.6	11.0	7.3	9.3	11.4	—	—
Unemployment (% labour force)	—	0.3	1.3	4.2	3.8	6.1	7.1	5.9	5.8
Prices and wages (% change)									
Consumer prices, annual average	8.4	224.7	1,020.5	410.4	72.1	39.5	24.7	8.9	6.4
Consumer prices, end-year	—	345.0	1,161.1	188.8	45.0	35.5	13.1	8.5	6.8
Producer prices, annual average	—	148.2	1,517.4	397.7	44.7	28.3	16.5	4.0	4.4
Producer prices, end-year	—	—	2,407.1	131.6	33.8	20.6	12.8	0.8	—
Average wage in industry, gross	—	—	—	−34.8	5.8	2.5	5.1	6.0	5.0
Government sector (% GDP)									
General government balance	−5.4	2.0	0.5	−4.3	−5.4	−4.5	−4.0	−2.4	−3.0
Government expenditure, net lending	49.1	38.7	31.7	28.3	29.4	28.8	26.0	24.6	—
Monetary sector (% change)									
Broad money, end-year	55.0	143.0	245.3	100.4	62.9	28.5	−3.5	34.1	—
Domestic credit, end-year	—	—	—	—	—	16.6	2.0	37.6	—
Broad money (% GDP)	—	—	—	23.4	25.9	23.6	17.5	19.9	—

Interest and exchange rates (% per year), end-year								
Deposit rate[a]	—	17.0	110.0	39.3	8.9	8.0	—	—
Lending rate[a]	—	38.0	—	88.3	29.8	23.9	16.0	11.5
Litai per $								
Exchange rate, end-year[b]	—	—	379.0	4.4	4.0	4.0	4.0	4.0
Exchange rate, annual average[b]	—	—	177.0	3.9	4.0	4.0	4.0	4.0
External sector ($ millions)								
Current account	—	—	203	-86	-94	-614	-723	-945
Trade balance	—	—	101	-155	-205	-698	-896	-1,115
Exports, merchandise	—	—	1,142	2,026	2,029	2,706	3,413	4,174
Imports, merchandise	—	—	1,041	2,180	2,234	3,404	4,309	5,289
Foreign direct investment, net	—	—	10	30	31	72	152	327
Gross reserves, end-year	—	—	45	350	525	757	772	999
External debt stock, end-year	—	—	59	325	529	845	1,189	1,787
In months of merchandise imports								
Gross reserves, end-year	—	—	0.5	1.9	2.8	2.7	2.2	2.3
% merchandise exports								
Debt service	—	—	—	0.4	2.7	4.5	8.7	19.1
Current account/GDP	—	—	1.1	-3.3	-2.2	-10.3	-9.3	-6.4
External debt/GDP	—	—	311.0	12.4	12.5	14.2	15.3	19.5
External debt/exports	—	—	5.2	16.0	26.1	31.2	34.8	42.8
Memorandum items								
Population (millions)	3.7	3.7	3.7	3.7	3.7	3.7	3.7	3.7
GDP (litai/litai equivalent, millions)	129	382	3,387	11,420	16,837	23,768	31,009	36,600
GDP per capita ($)	265	511	705	1,138	1,602	2,090	2,473	2,799
GDP per capita (PPP$)	—	—	4,879	3,407	3,556	3,710	3,935	4,135
GDP per capita (PPP$)[c]	—	—	5,174	4,049	4,471	4,766	—	—

[a] Weighted average rate of commercial banks.   [b] Roubles per dollar for 1990 and 1991; talonai per dollar for 1992, and litai per dollar thereafter.   [c] According to an evaluation in OECD 1997e.

FYR Macedonia: selected economic indicators, 1990–1998

	1990	1991	1992	1993	1994	1995	1996	1997	1998
Output (% change)									
GDP at constant prices	-9.9	-12.1	-21.1	-8.4	-4.0	-1.4	1.1	1.0	2.8
Private consumption	—	-13.6	-7.3	-9.9	-7.5	-0.6	-2.4	-3.5	1.9
Public consumption	—	0.6	-17.2	-10.9	-16.4	-1.6	-3.4	-4.8	2.0
Gross fixed investment	—	-4.4	8.4	-20.2	-15.1	-5.0	-3.0	7.5	8.0
Industrial gross output	—	-17.2	-15.6	-13.8	-10.5	-10.7	3.2	2.0	4.0
Agricultural gross output	—	31.3	-14.7	-21.5	37.0	4.0	-4.0	3.0	3.5
Composition of output (% GDP)									
Industry, including mining	48.0	45.6	44.7	44.4	42.8	39.3	—	—	—
Agriculture	10.3	13.8	16.8	15.8	16.5	17.8	—	—	—
Unemployment (% labour force)	—	19.2	19.8	18.7	20.7	23.7	24.9	30.0	—
Prices and wages (% change)									
Retail prices, annual average	608.0	110.8	1,511.0	362.0	128.3	15.7	3.8	4.4	5.1
Retail prices, end-year	121.0	229.7	1,925.2	73.3	54.2	10.3	-0.6	4.0	4.5
Producer prices, industry, average	394.0	112.0	2,198.2	258.3	88.9	4.7	-0.3	4.2	4.9
Producer prices, industry, end-year	42.0	281.5	2,148.6	176.1	28.6	2.2	-0.6	8.4	1.8
Average wage	—	-14.9	-34.9	28.6	-10.2	-4.3	0.5	0.2	
Government sector (% GDP)									
General government balance	—	—	-9.6	-13.6	-3.2	-1.3	-0.4	-0.6	-0.8
General government expenditure	—	—	48.2	54.5	54.2	46.5	44.7	43.0	—
Monetary sector (% change)									
Broad money, end-year	—	—	—	—	—	0.3	0.5	8.0	—
Domestic credit, end-year	—	—	—	—	—	-22.3	-6.4	5.0	—
Broad money (% GDP)	—	—	—	25.6	17.1	16.2	16.4	16.5	—

Interest and exchange rates (% per year), end-year									
Deposit rate, 3–6 months	—	—	435–885	322–418	32–49	9–21	9–21	9–21	—
Lending rate, one year	—	—	—	275–368	77–81	25–30	19–30	17–27	—
Denar per $									
Exchange rate, end-year	—	—	—	44.5	40.6	38.0	41.4	55.4	51.0
Exchange rate, annual average	19.7	—	—	23.6	43.3	37.9	40.0	50.0	51.3
External sector ($ millions)									
Current account	-400	-262	-19	-87	-213	-230	-268	-404	-414
Trade balance	-418	-225	-7	-171	-186	-235	-317	-549	-539
Exports	1,113	1,150	1,199	1,056	1,086	1,204	1,147	1,201	1,268
Imports	1,531	1,375	1,206	1,227	1,272	1,439	1,464	1,816	1,892
Foreign direct investment, net	—	—	—	—	24	13	12	16	—
Gross reserves, end-year	—	—	—	105	149	257	249	254	—
External debt stock	—	744	812	873	898	1,115	1,176	1,131	—
In months of current account expenditures, excluding transfers									
Gross reserves, end-year	—	—	—	1.0	1.4	2.1	2.1	1.9	—
% current account revenues, excluding transfers									
Debt service	—	—	—	13.0	15.7	10.3	9.5	8.7	—
Current account/GDP	—	—	—	-3.5	-6.8	-6.1	-7.3	-12.9	-12.6
External debt/GDP	—	—	—	768	749	858	927	877	—
External debt/exports	—	64.7	67.7	82.7	82.7	92.6	102.5	92.3	—
Memorandum items									
Population (millions)	2.1	2.2	2.2	2.2	2.1	2.1	2.1	2.1	2.0
GDP (denar, millions)	507	920	11,791	59,161	136,033	143,597	147,554	154,246	—
GDP per capita ($)	1,077	911	771	753	1,931	1,864	1,565	1,637	—
GDP per capita (PPP$)	3,328	3,038	2,750	2,867	2,808	2,807	2,823	2,886	—

Moldova: selected economic indicators, 1990–1998

	1990	1991	1992	1993	1994	1995	1996	1997	1998
Output (% change)									
GDP at constant prices	-2.4	-17.5	-29.1	-1.2	-31.2	-3.0	-8.0	1.3	1.0
Private consumption	—	—	-38.4	-5.5	-5.8	-0.9	6.9	8.5	2.5
Public consumption	—	—	-26.4	19.9	-31.8	16.1	-7.8	6.5	0.5
Gross fixed investment	—	—	-26.0	-44.0	-51.0	-17.0	-15.0	-6.0	10.7
Industrial gross output	—	-21.0	-27.1	0.3	-27.7	-3.9	-6.5	-2.3	0.6
Agricultural gross output	—	-28.0	-15.0	5.9	-22.2	3.6	-10.0	9.0	1.6
Composition of output (% GDP)									
Industry	—	30	31	29	25	22	25	—	—
Agriculture	—	33	38	46	48	49	—	—	—
Unemployment (% labour force)	—	—	0.1	0.7	1.1	1.4	1.4	1.7	—
Prices and wages (% change)									
Consumer prices, annual average	4.0	98.0	1,109	1,614	486.4	29.9	23.5	11.8	11.8
Consumer prices, end-year	—	151.0	1,670	2,706	104.6	23.8	15.1	11.1	12.2
Producer prices, annual average	—	—	1,211	1,291	438.0	48.0	21.2	20.0	10.6
Producer prices, end-year	—	—	—	6,947.0	207.0	47.0	—	—	—
Average wage in industry, gross	—	—	-38.7	-62.3	-40.8	1.7	4.5	6.5	0.9
Government sector (% GDP)									
General government balance	—	0.0	-26.2	-7.4	-8.7	-5.7	-6.7	-7.5	-7.5
General government expenditure	—	24.7	56.6	29.4	40.6	39.2	39.1	43.3	—
Monetary sector (% change)									
Broad money, end-year	—	—	361.7	320.2	115.7	65.2	15.3	25.7	—
Domestic credit, end-year	—	—	550	333.8	116.6	55.8	18.5	31.9	—
Broad money (% GDP)	—	69.5	43.3	15.8	13.0	16.3	16.4	18.8	—

Interest and exchange rates (% per year), end-year							
Deposit rate, one year	—	—	—	—	20.6	25.4	—
Lending rate, one year	—	—	—	—	41.6	36.7	—
Lei per $							
Exchange rate, end-year[a]	0.0	0.4	3.6	4.3	4.5	4.7	4.6
Exchange rate, annual average[a]	—	0.2	3.7	4.1	4.5	4.6	4.6
External sector ($ millions)							
Current account	—	-39	-182	-82	-149	-256	-310
Trade balance	—	-37	-180	-54	-70	-254	-275
Exports	—	868	451	618	739	802	725
Imports	—	905	631	672	809	1,056	1,000
Foreign direct investment, net	—	17	14.0	18	73	56	71
Gross reserves, end-year	—	—	89	179	257	315	324
External debt stock	—	16	255	503	670	795	969
In months of imports of goods and services							
Gross reserves, end-year	—	—	1.7	2.9	3.0	3.0	3.0
% exports of goods and services							
Debt service	—	—	—	2.4	9.4	6.5	22.7
Current account/GDP	—	-3.0	-11.9	-5.8	-8.9	-14.9	-15.5
External debt/GDP	—	1.3	16.7	35.3	40.0	41.8	46.5
External debt/exports	—	1.9	56.4	81.3	90.7	99.2	133.6
Memorandum items							
Population (in millions)	4.4	4.4	4.3	4.4	4.3	4.3	4.3
GDP (lei, millions)	26	192	2,210	5,780	7,636	8,748	9,585
GDP per capita ($)	—	232	137	326	391	452	523
GDP per capita (PPP$)	4,412	3,281	3,250	2,243	2,203	2,038	2,091

[a] Russian roubles per dollar until August 1993; Moldovan roubles per dollar until November 1993; Moldovan lei per dollar thereafter.

Poland: selected economic indicators, 1990–1998

	1990	1991	1992	1993	1994	1995	1996	1997	1998
Output (% change)									
GDP at constant prices	−11.6	−7.0	2.6	3.8	5.2	7.0	6.1	6.9	6.5
Private consumption	−15.3	6.3	2.3	5.2	4.3	4.5	8.7	7.0	4.9
Public consumption	0.5	10.2	6.4	3.8	2.8	2.9	3.4	1.8	1.0
Gross fixed investment	−10.6	−4.4	2.3	2.9	9.2	18.5	20.6	21.9	16.2
Industrial gross output	−24.2	−8.0	2.8	6.4	12.1	9.7	9.2	10.2	9.0
Agricultural gross output	−2.2	−1.6	−12.7	6.8	−9.3	10.7	0.3	0.8	0.5
Composition of output (% GDP)									
Industry	44.9	40.2	34.0	32.9	32.2	28.9	—	—	—
Agriculture	7.4	6.8	6.7	6.6	6.2	6.6	—	—	—
Unemployment (% labour force)	6.3	12.2	14.3	16.4	16.0	14.9	13.6	10.5	9.6
Prices and wages (% change)									
Consumer prices, annual average	585.8	70.3	43.0	35.3	32.2	27.8	19.8	14.5	12.2
Consumer prices, end-year	249.0	60.4	44.3	37.6	29.4	21.6	18.5	13.2	10.0
Producer prices, annual average	622.4	48.1	34.5	31.9	30.1	25.4	12.1	12.5	8.0
Producer prices, end-year	192.8	35.7	31.5	37.0	27.9	18.9	11.2	11.6	—
Average wage in industry, gross	−31.3	−0.3	−2.7	−2.9	0.5	3.0	5.7	6.8	5.2
Government sector (% GDP)									
General government balance[a]	3.1	−3.8	−6.0	−2.8	−2.7	−2.6	−2.5	−1.4	−1.0
General government expenditure	39.8	49.0	50.4	50.5	49.6	49.9	49.2	48.1	—
Monetary sector (% change)									
Broad money, end-year	160.1	37.0	57.5	36.0	38.2	35.0	29.3	29.6	—
Domestic credit, end-year	183.5	158.7	55.6	44.2	30.1	20.1	29.7	27.5	—
Broad money (% GDP)	32.2	31.6	35.8	35.9	36.7	36.5	37.5	39.5	—

Interest and exchange rates (% per year), end-year									
Deposit rate	53.0	36.0	32.0	25.0	26.0	22.0	18.3		—
Lending rate	61.0	40.0	39.0	35.0	31.0	24.0	23.3	24.5	22.0
Zloty per $									
Exchange rate, end-year[b]	0.95	1.10	1.58	2.13	2.44	2.47	2.88	3.52	3.64
Exchange rate, annual average[b]	0.95	1.06	1.36	1.81	2.27	2.43	2.70	3.28	3.56
External sector ($ billions)									
Current account	0.6	-2.0	0.9	-0.6	2.3	5.5	-1.3	-4.3	-5.6
Trade balance[c]	2.2	0.1	0.5	-2.3	-0.8	-1.8	-8.2	-11.3	-12.4
Exports[c]	10.9	12.8	14.0	13.6	17.0	22.9	24.4	27.2	30.3
Imports[c]	8.6	12.7	13.5	15.9	17.8	24.7	32.6	38.5	42.7
Foreign direct investment, net	0.0	0.3	0.7	1.8	1.8	3.6	4.4	6.6	—
Gross reserves, end-year	4.5	3.6	4.1	4.1	5.8	14.8	17.8	20.7	—
External debt stock	49.0	48.0	47.6	47.2	42.2	43.9	40.4	38.1	40.4
In months of current account expenditures, excluding transfers									
Gross reserves, end-year	3.8	2.5	2.9	2.6	3.2	6.1	5.8	5.7	—
% current account revenues, excluding transfers									
Debt service	53.7	68.9	19.3	20.1	14.3	6.7	7.6	5.7	
Current account/GDP	1.2	-2.6	1.1	-0.7	2.5	4.6	-1.0	-3.2	-4.7
External debt/GDP	—	61.5	56.4	54.9	45.6	36.9	30.0	28.3	—
External debt/exports	—	375.0	340.0	347.1	248.2	191.7	165.6	139.7	—
Memorandum items									
Population (millions)	38.2	38.3	38.4	38.5	38.6	38.6	38.6	38.7	38.8
GDP (zloty, billions)[b]	59.0	82.5	114.9	155.8	210.4	288.7	362.8	440.0	—
GDP per capita ($)	1,630	2,033	2,195	2,230	2,400	3,061	3,478	3,510	3,811
GDP per capita (PPP$)	—	4,948	5,062	5,242	5,504	5,887	6,238	6,667	7,095

[a] Excluding privatization receipts.   [b] For the period prior to 1 January 1996, the figures represent the old zloty. The new zloty, reflecting a denomination by a factor of 10,000, was introduced on that date.   [c] Balance of payments data rely on banking statistics and are presented on a settlements basis. According to customs questionnaires, exports are virtually the same as on a settlements basis, while imports are higher (about 20% in 1994–1996).

Romania: selected economic indicators, 1990–1998

	1990	1991	1992	1993	1994	1995	1996	1997	1998
Output (% change)									
GDP at constant prices	-5.6	-12.9	-8.7	1.5	3.9	7.1	4.1	-6.6	-2.1
Private consumption	—	—	-7.5	0.9	2.6	19.2	6.2	-5.6	-3.6
Public consumption	—	—	5.2	2.8	10.9	-9.7	-8.6	-11.0	-4.8
Gross fixed investment	—	—	11.0	8.3	20.7	8.6	4.5	-15.9	1.7
Industrial gross output	-23.7	-22.8	-21.9	1.3	3.3	9.4	9.9	-5.9	-4.0
Agricultural gross output	—	-8.6	-13.3	10.2	0.2	4.5	-3.3	3.1	1.5
Composition of output (% GDP)									
Industry	40.6	37.9	38.3	33.8	35.6	34.6	36.0	34.5	—
Agriculture	21.8	18.9	19.0	21.0	19.8	19.9	19.1	20.7	—
Unemployment (% labour force)	—	—	8.2	10.4	10.9	9.5	6.4	8.8	10.5
Prices (% change)									
Consumer prices, annual average	5.1	161.1	210.4	256.1	137.1	32.2	38.7	154.2	57.2
Consumer prices, end-year	37.7	222.8	199.2	295.5	61.7	27.8	56.9	151.4	35.4
Government sector (% GDP)									
General government balance	1.0	3.3	-4.6	-0.4	-1.9	-2.6	-3.9	-4.5	-5.0
General government expenditure	38.7	38.7	42.0	34.2	33.9	34.5	33.6	31.4	—
Monetary sector (% change)									
Broad money, end-year	22.0	101.2	79.6	141.0	138.1	71.6	66.0	48.9	—
Domestic credit, end-year	7.5	121.8	34.9	131.3	114.4	92.4	88.0	66.3	—
Broad money (% GDP)	59.6	46.7	28.9	9.1	21.5	25.4	28.9	24.9	—

Interest and exchange rates (% per year), annual average									
Deposit rate, one year	—	—	38	52	62	38	47	60	—
Lending rate, one year	—	—	53	129	83	59	71	70	—
Lei per $									
Exchange rate, end-year	34.7	189.0	460.0	1,276	1,767	2,578	4,035	7,850	11,290
Exchange rate, annual average	22.4	76.3	308.0	760.0	1,667	2,034	3,093	7,158	10,336
External sector ($ millions)									
Current account	−1,656	−1,181	−1,518	−1,239	−516	−1,732	−2,571	−2,486	−2,263
Trade balance	−1,743	−1,254	−1,373	−1,130	−483	−1,605	−2,494	−1,414	−2,915
Exports	3,364	3,241	4,286	4,882	6,067	7,882	8,061	8,540	8,980
Imports	5,107	4,495	5,659	6,012	6,550	9,487	10,555	9,875	11,894
Foreign direct investment, net	18	37	77	94	347	404	415	998	1,500
Gross reserves, end-year	524	695	826	995	2,086	1,579	2,103	3,436	—
Total external debt stock	1,140	2,131	3,240	4,249	5,509	6,710	8,480	9,200	9,631
In months of current account expenditures, excluding transfers									
Gross reserves, end-year	1.0	1.5	1.5	1.7	3.6	1.9	2.2	3.6	—
% current account revenues, excluding transfers									
Debt service	0.2	2.3	8.9	6.2	8.7	11.5	14.8	—	—
Current account/GDP	−4.4	−4.1	−7.8	−4.7	−1.6	−4.9	−7.1	−6.6	−5.7
External debt/GDP	—	7.4	16.6	16.1	17.5	18.8	23.9	30.2	—
External debt/exports	65.8	75.6	87.0	90.8	85.1	105.2	121.8	—	—
Memorandum items									
Population (millions)	23.2	23.2	22.8	22.7	22.6	22.6	22.6	22.6	22.5
GDP (lei, billions)	858	2,204	6,029	20,036	49,768	72,560	109,515	249,750	—
GDP per capita ($)	1,257	1,187	859	1,159	1,314	1,573	1,567	1,671	1,753
GDP per capita (PPP$)	—	3,220	2,939	2,988	3,108	3,336	3,485	3,262	3,201

Russia: selected economic indicators, 1990–1998

	1990	1991	1992	1993	1994	1995	1996	1997	1998
Output (% change)									
GDP at constant prices	-4.0	-13.0	-14.5	-8.7	-12.6	-4.0	-4.9	0.4	-0.4
Private consumption	—	—	-3.0	-13.4	-7.8	7.7	-1.8	-1.2	0.8
Public consumption	—	—	-9.9	32.1	-5.8	-23.6	-4.4	4.0	-4.0
Gross fixed investment	—	10.1	-37.1	-21.1	-29.3	-6.0	-15.0	-5.0	-1.0
Industrial gross output	-0.1	-8.0	-18.1	-14.1	-20.9	-3.3	-4.0	1.9	-0.5
Agricultural gross output	-4.0	-3.7	-9.4	-4.4	-12.0	-8.0	-7.0	0.1	1.9
Composition of output (% GDP)									
Industry	—	45.9	42.2	40.6	37.6	39.0	39.3	—	—
Agriculture	—	13.8	7.3	7.5	8.7	8.6	8.6	—	—
Unemployment (% labour force)[a]	0.0	0.0	4.8	5.7	7.5	8.8	9.3	9.0	9.8
Prices and wages (% change)									
Consumer prices, annual average	5.6	93.0	1,533.0	881.0	322.0	196.0	47.8	14.7	9.0
Consumer prices, end-year	—	144.0	2,525.0	847.2	223.6	131.4	21.8	11.0	9.5
Producer prices, annual average	3.9	193.0	3,916.0	1,149.0	347.0	243.0	52.2	15.0	6.7
Producer prices, end-year	—	345.0	3,274.9	927.7	233.9	174.7	25.6	7.4	—
Average wage	—	-3.0	-33.0	0.4	-8.0	-26.0	5.0	4.3	1.5
Government sector (% GDP)									
General government balance[b]	—	—	-21.6	-7.4	-10.4	-5.7	-8.2	-7.5	-6.0
General government expenditure	—	—	65.8	43.3	45.0	37.7	38.7	38.2	—
Monetary sector (% change)									
Broad money, end-year	17.6	125.9	568.1	425.8	197.5	127.5	33.7	30.0	—
Net domestic assets, end-year	—	—	—	770.0	359.8	70.3	80.9	14.0	—
Broad money (% GDP)	70.1	68.4	32.3	19.1	16.0	13.6	13.1	14.4	—

Interest and exchange rates (% per year), end-year									
Central bank refinance rate	—	6–9	80	210	180	160	48	28	—
Roubles per $									
Exchange rate, end-year[c]	1.7	169	415	1,247	3,550	4,640	5,560	5,958	6,578
Exchange rate, annual average[c]	1.7	67	222	933	2,205	4,557	5,123	5,785	6,360
External sector ($ billions)									
Current account[d]	—	—	—	2.6	10.4	4.5	2.2	3.9	—
Trade balance[d]	—	—	—	9.5	21.1	17.4	17.0	16.6	—
Exports[d]	—	—	—	58.3	69.6	90.2	88.8	—	—
Imports[d]	—	—	—	44.2	48.5	64.0	73.9	72.2	—
Foreign direct investment, net	—	—	0.7	0.4	0.6	2.0	2.0	3.9	—
Gross reserves, end-year	—	—	1.9	5.8	4.0	14.4	11.3	17.8	—
External debt stock[e]	61.1	67.0	107.7	112.7	119.9	120.4	125.0	131.9	—
In months of imports									
Gross reserves, end-year	—	—	—	1.7	1.2	2.4	2.0	2.2	—
% current account revenues, excluding transfers									
Debt service due	—	—	—	29.6	24.4	19.6	14.5	10.2	—
Current account/GDP	—	—	—	1.4	3.8	1.3	0.5	0.8	-0.4
External debt/GDP	—	321.1	124.6	61.3	43.3	33.7	28.4	27.8	—
External debt/exports	—	—	—	193.3	172.3	147.7	138.6	148.5	—
Memorandum items									
Population (millions)	148.3	148.9	148.3	148.2	149.0	148.1	147.7	147.2	147.0
GDP (roubles, trillions)	0.6	1.4	19.2	171.5	611	1,630	2,256	2,740	—
GDP per capita ($)	—	—	577	1,249	1,885	2,410	2,985	3,132	3,127
GDP per capita (PPP$)	—	—	6,131	5,609	4,904	4,701	4,486	4,499	4,513

[a] Estimates based on the ILO definition.   [b] 'General government' includes state and local budgets, extrabudgetary funds, and unbudgeted import subsidies for the period 1990–1994.   [c] Since 1998, the new rouble.   [d] Data from the consolidated balance of payments, which covers transactions with CIS and non-CIS countries.   [e] Since 1992, including debt to former Comecon countries.

Slovakia: selected economic indicators, 1990–1998

	1990	1991	1992	1993	1994	1995	1996	1997	1998
Output (% change)									
GDP at constant prices	-2.5[a]	-14.6	-6.5	-3.7	4.9	6.8	6.9	6.5	4.0
Private consumption	—	-18.5	-2.3	-1.5	0.0	3.4	7.2	5.7	4.7
Public consumption	—	-23.8	23.9	-2.2	-10.5	1.6	24.2	3.1	3.7
Gross fixed investment	—	-8.6	-15.7	-4.2	-5.1	5.8	33.3	10.2	-1.2
Industrial gross output	-3.6	-19.4	-9.2	-3.8	4.9	8.3	2.5	4.0	4.6
Agricultural gross output	-7.2	-7.4	-13.9	-8.1	4.8	2.4	2.7	5.0	2.5
Composition of output (% GDP)									
Industry	—	—	32.0	29.2	28.7	28.6	26.3	—	—
Agriculture	—	—	6.2	6.6	6.6	5.6	5.2	—	—
Unemployment (% labour force)	—	11.8	11.4	12.2	13.7	13.8	12.6	13.0	13.0
Prices and wages (% change)									
Consumer prices, annual average	10.8	56.0	10.0	23.2	13.4	9.9	5.8	6.1	7.3
Consumer prices, end-year	18.4	58.3	9.2	25.1	11.7	7.2	5.4	6.4	7.5
Producer prices, annual average	4.4	68.8	5.3	17.2	10.0	9.0	4.1	4.5	—
Producer prices, end-year	—	50.6	6.1	18.8	9.4	7.1	4.7	4.4	—
Average wage	-6.9	-25.3	8.7	-3.6	3.0	4.1	7.1	7.5	3.5
Government sector (% GDP)									
General government balance	-1.8[a]	0.6[a]	-0.5[a]	-7.0	-5.2	-1.6	-4.4	-5.7	-4.4
General government expenditure	—	—	—	51.2	47.7	46.9	48.9	45.3	—
Monetary sector (% change)									
Broad money, end-year	—	—	—	16.8	20.1	19.2	16.5	8.9	—
Domestic credit, end-year	—	—	—	—	9.2	7.8	14.4	3.1	—
Broad money, end-year (% GDP)	68.0	73.0	64.3	67.5	67.9	69.3	71.6	70.7	—

Interest and exchange rates (% per year), end-year									
Discount rate	8.5	9.5	9.5	12.0	12.0	9.8	8.8	8.8	—
Average lending rate[b]	—	—	—	14.1	14.4	14.8	13.2	16.0	—
Average deposit rate	—	—	—	8.7	9.2	8.2	6.2	9.0	—
Koruna per $									
Exchange rate, end-year	28.0ᵃ	27.8ᵃ	28.9ᵃ	33.1	31.3	29.7	31.7	34.5	38.6
Exchange rate, annual average	18.0ᵃ	29.5ᵃ	28.3ᵃ	30.8	32.1	29.7	30.7	33.6	35.1
External sector ($ billions)									
Current account	-1.1ᵃ	0.3ᵃ	-0.3ᵃ	-0.6	0.7	0.4	-2.1	-1.3	-1.7
Trade balance	-0.8ᵃ	-0.5ᵃ	-1.9ᵃ	-0.9	0.1	-0.2	-2.3	-1.4	-1.6
Exports	5.9ᵃ	8.3ᵃ	8.4ᵃ	5.5	6.7	8.6	8.8	8.8	10.0
Imports	6.5ᵃ	8.3ᵃ	10.4ᵃ	6.4	6.6	8.8	11.1	10.2	11.6
Foreign direct investment, net	—	—	0.1	0.2	0.2	0.2	0.2	0.2	0.3
Gross reserves, end-year	—	—	—	0.4	1.7	3.4	3.5	3.3	—
External debt stock	—	—	—	3.4	4.7	5.7	7.7	10.7	12.0
In months of imports of goods and services									
Gross international reserves, end-year	—	—	—	0.7	2.5	3.8	3.2	3.2	—
% exports of goods and services									
Debt service	—	—	—	8.6	8.7	9.3	10.8	17.4	—
Current account/GDP	-2.9ᵃ	—	—	-4.8	5.2	2.3	-11.1	-6.7	-8.2
External debt/GDP	—	—	—	28.1	33.8	32.8	40.4	52.5	—
External debt/exports	—	—	—	62	69.1	66.1	86.9	113.7	—
Memorandum items									
Population (millions)	5.3	5.3	5.3	5.3	5.3	5.4	5.4	5.4	5.4
GDP (koruna, billions)	258	320	332	370	441	515	581	647	—
GDP per capita ($)	2,710	1,798	2,214	2,253	2,570	3,232	3,526	3,620	3,837
GDP per capita (PPP$)	—	6,965	6,568	6,290	6,574	7,013	7,486	7,958	8,259

ᵃ Data refer to former Czechoslovakia.   ᵇ Excluding loans at zero interest rate since 1995.

Slovenia: selected economic indicators, 1990–1998

	1990	1991	1992	1993	1994	1995	1996	1997	1998
Output (% change)									
GDP at constant prices	-4.7	-8.9	-5.5	2.8	5.3	4.1	3.1	3.3	4.1
Private consumption	—	-11.0	-6.5	13.9	4.1	9.0	1.8	3.8	2.9
Public consumption	—	0.3	8.5	5.8	2.1	2.5	4.7	-1.4	1.9
Gross fixed investment	—	-11.5	-14.9	8.8	12.5	17.1	6.9	10.8	7.5
Industrial gross output	-10.5	-11.6	-12.6	-2.5	6.6	2.3	1.2	1.3	3.0
Agricultural gross output	1.6	-2.5	-6.7	-4.2	4.2	1.6	1.7	0.7	2.0
Composition of output (% GDP)									
Industry	38.0	36.0	32.1	29.3	30.4	28.6	27.8	27.1	—
Agriculture	4.7	5.2	5.2	4.5	4.0	3.9	3.7	3.8	—
Unemployment (% labour force)	4.7	8.2	11.6	14.6	14.5	14.0	13.9	14.4	13.8
Prices and wages (% change)									
Retail prices, annual average	549.7	117.7	201.3	32.3	19.8	12.6	9.7	9.1	9.1
Retail prices, end-year	105.0	246.7	92.9	22.9	18.3	8.6	8.8	9.4	8.2
Producer prices, annual average	390.4	124.1	215.7	21.6	17.7	12.8	6.8	6.1	7.0
Producer prices, end-year	44.0	311.8	21.6	18.6	17.7	12.8	6.8	6.1	—
Average wage, gross	-25.9	-10.9	-8.9	13.3	3.6	4.4	4.9	3.2	2.2
Government sector (% GDP)									
General government balance	-0.3	2.6	0.2	0.3	-0.2	0.0	0.3	-1.5	-0.8
General government expenditure	49.6	41.1	45.8	46.7	46.1	45.7	44.9	46.5	—
Monetary sector (% change)									
Broad money, end-year	—	—	131.6	64.2	50.7	30.2	19.4	22.6	—
Domestic credit, end-year	—	—	90.1	101.4	27.1	35.1	12.5	12.0	—
Broad money (% GDP)	—	—	28.1	32.8	38.3	42.2	44.6	47.0	—

Interest and exchange rates (% per year), end-year									
Deposit rate, one year and over	—	—	53.8	33.9	32.2	24.4	13.6	16.6	—
Lending rate, short-term working capital	—	—	72.2	42.6	38.5	28.0	18.3	20.3	—
Tolar per $									
Exchange rate, end-year[a]	10.7	56.7	98.7	131.8	126.5	126.0	141.5	169.2	169.3
Exchange rate, annual average[a]	11.3	27.6	81.3	113.2	128.8	118.5	135.4	159.7	168.5
External sector ($ billions)[b]									
Current account	0.5	0.1	0.9	0.2	0.6	0.0	0.0	0.0	-0.1
Trade balance	-0.6	-0.3	0.8	-0.2	-0.3	-1.0	-0.9	-1.0	-1.1
Exports	4.1	3.9	6.7	6.1	6.8	8.3	8.4	8.4	9.2
Imports	4.7	4.1	5.9	6.2	7.2	9.3	9.2	9.4	10.3
Foreign direct investment, net	—	0.0	0.1	0.1	0.1	0.2	0.2	0.3	0.4
Gross reserves, end-year	—	0.1	0.7	0.8	1.5	1.8	2.3	3.3	—
External debt stock	—	1.9	1.7	1.9	2.3	3.0	4.0	4.1	4.5
In months of current account expenditures, excluding transfers									
Gross reserves, end-year	0.6	0.4	1.2	1.2	2.1	2.0	2.5	3.7	—
% current account revenues, excluding transfers									
Debt service	—	7.0	5.2	5.5	5.4	6.9	8.6	8.5	—
Current account/GDP	—	1.0	7.4	1.5	4.2	-0.1	0.2	0.2	-0.4
External debt/GDP	—	14.7	13.9	14.8	15.7	15.8	21.3	23.2	—
External debt/exports	—	48.2	26.1	30.8	33.1	35.6	47.9	49.7	—
Memorandum items									
Population (millions)[c]	2.0	2.0	2.0	2.0	2.0	2.0	2.0	2.0	2.0
GDP (nominal)[c]	197	349	1,018	1,435	1,853	2,221	2,553	2,873	—
GDP per capita ($)	8,671	6,334	6,275	6,368	7,205	9,348	9,471	9,028	9,673
GDP per capita (PPP$)	12,392	11,268	10,680	11,008	11,602	12,086	12,437	12,940	13,497

[a] For the period prior to 8 October 1991 (the date of the introduction of the tolar), measured as the multiple of 10,000 dinars that would buy $1. The tolar was introduced at an exchange rate of 10,000 dinars per tolar.   [b] Data for 1990–1991 exclude transactions with former Yugoslav republics.   [c] In 10 trillions of dinars in 1990, in billions of tolars thereafter.

Tajikistan: selected economic indicators, 1990–1998

	1990	1991	1992	1993	1994	1995	1996	1997	1998
Output (% change)									
GDP at constant prices	-1.6	-7.1	-29.0	-11.0	-18.9	-12.5	-4.4	2.2	4.4
Private consumption	—	—	-25.3	-45.4	-5.5	-3.4	-22.9	3.4	6.3
Public consumption	—	—	-5.1	-61.7	-7.7	-4.5	-23.9	2.3	5.2
Net investments	—	—	-55.8	383.8	-50.1	-19.5	-26.0	7.7	10.5
Industrial gross output	—	-5.6	-19.9	-23.8	-18.8	-5.1	-23.9	-2.5	3.5
Agricultural and forestry gross output	—	-4.4	-27.8	-33.7	-31.2	-24.0	-18.0	4.0	3.3
Composition of output (% GDP)									
Industry	—	31.6	36.4	32.8	22.1	35.3	20.5	19.5	—
Agriculture	—	26.1	27.1	21.0	19.0	15.3	27.7	27.6	—
Unemployment (% labour force)	—	—	0.3	1.1	1.7	1.8	2.8	4.7	5.7
Prices and wages (% change)									
Consumer prices, annual average	4.0	112.0	963.1	1,484.5	239.0	1,079.9	502.4	71.7	78.3
Consumer prices, end-year	—	204.0	1,364.0	7,344.0	—	2,655.2	40.6	141.1	48.3
Producer prices, annual average	—	163.0	1,320.0	1,080.0	327.8	1,080.0	452.1	78.0	70.5
Producer prices, end-year	—	184.0	5,926.0	5,996.0	302.0	628.0	78.0	—	—
Average wage	5.7	-22.6	-47.2	-46.6	-36.3	-82.3	-36.4	67.2	—
Government sector (% GDP)									
State budget balance	—	-16.4	-28.4	-23.6	-10.2	-11.2	-5.8	-3.5	-3.0
State budget expenditure	—	49.6	55.5	50.7	54.8	26.5	17.9	15.1	—
Monetary sector (% change)									
Broad money, end-year	—	68	579	1,429	159	413	144	112	—
Domestic credit, end-year	—	—	—	—	125	393	164	192	—
Broad money (% GDP)	—	—	—	9.1	8.6	24.5	10.7	8.5	—

Interest and exchange rates (% per year), end-year								
Deposit rate, one year[a]	30	30	30	30	100	85	118	—
Lending rate, one year[a]	30	30	30	30	500	124	136	—
Tajik roubles per $								
Exchange rate, end-year[b]	1.8	415.0	1,247.0	3,550.0	284.6	320.0	747.0	781.7
Exchange rate, annual average[b]	1.7	222.0	930.0	2,204.0	86.1	302.3	533.5	754.0
External sector ($ millions)								
Current account	—	53	-208	-169	-54	-74	-15	—
Trade balance	—	-55	-204	-148	-41	-38	-5	—
Exports	—	—	456	559	839	770	727	—
Imports	—	—	660	707	880	808	732	—
Foreign direct investment, net	—	8	9	12	17	20	20	—
Gross reserves, end-year	—	0	2	1	4	14	41	—
External debt stock	—	—	509	760	817	868	893	—
In months of merchandise imports								
Gross international reserves, end-year	—	—	0.0	0.0	0.0	1.0	0.7	—
% merchandise exports								
Debt service	—	—	5.7	9.7	25.5	32.6	12.5	—
Current account/GDP	—	18.1	-27.4	-21.0	-11.2	-10.1	-2.8	-3.3
External debt/GDP	—	0.0	66.9	93.8	170.1	83.9	82.9	—
External debt/exports	—	—	111.6	136.0	97.4	112.7	122.8	—
Memorandum items								
Population (millions)	5.5	5.6	5.7	5.8	5.9	5.9	6.0	6.0
GDP (nominal)[c]	10,540	64,760	707,060	1,786,490	64,843	308,474	631,900	—
GDP per capita ($)	—	52	131	137	130	173	171	219
GDP per capita (PPP$)	—	1,574	1,300	997	861	705	707	727

[a] Interest rates were set by parliament until June 1995.   [b] Roubles per dollar until 1994, Tajik roubles per dollar thereafter.   [c] In millions of roubles until 1994, in millions of Tajik roubles thereafter.

Turkmenistan: selected economic indicators, 1990–1998

	1990	1991	1992	1993	1994	1995	1996	1997	1998
Output (% change)									
GDP at constant prices	2.0	−4.7	5.3	−10.0	−18.8	−8.2	−8.0	−25.0	12.0
Private consumption	—	—	−28.3	−12.4	−12.1	−16.2	15.7	5.9	8.4
Public consumption	—	—	−31.4	−13.4	−13.1	−17.2	14.7	−2.1	4.4
Gross fixed investment	—	—	20.0	45.0	−38.2	−8.4	−6.1	−8.8	−2.7
Industrial gross output	—	4.8	−14.9	5.4	−25.0	−7.0	17.9	−29.2	8.3
Agricultural gross output	—	—	−8.5	15.7	−17.6	−17.5	−32.8	5.4	2.8
Composition of output (% GDP)									
Industry	—	20.0	59.0	55.1	73.2	52.2	50.0	—	—
Agriculture	—	46.0	19.0	11.5	9.0	30.3	17.5	—	—
Unemployment (% labour force)[a]	2.0	2.0	—	—	—	3.0	—	—	—
Prices and wages (% change)									
Consumer prices, annual average	4.6	103	493	3,102	1,748	1,005	992	83.7	33.0
Consumer prices, end-year	—	155	644	9,750	1,328	1,262	446	21.5	50.0
Average wage in industry, gross	—	—	3.1	−11.0	−72.6	−42.2	−3.5	68.1	3.7
Government sector (% GDP)									
General government balance[b]	1.2	2.5	13.2	−0.5	−1.4	−1.6	−0.2	−0.5	−5.0
General government expenditure	43.6	38.2	42.2	19.2	11.9	14.0	15.7	29.0	—
Monetary sector (% change)									
Broad money, end-year	—	—	—	—	984	448	429	82	—
Domestic credit, end-year	—	—	—	—	915	403	1,388	26	—
Broad money (% GDP)	—	—	—	22.0	15.8	11.4	8.6	12.0	—

Interest and exchange rates (% per year), end-year									
Deposit rate, one year	—	—	—	50	206	80	130	42	—
Lending rate, one year	—	—	—	108	300	70	200	70	—
Manat per $									
Official exchange rate, end-year	—	—	—	2	75	500	5,200	5,300	8,450
Official exchange rate, annual average	—	—	—	—	17	195	3,472	5,300	7,769
External sector ($ millions)									
Current account	−249	590		776	84	23	43	−596	—
Trade balance[c]	151	1,238	1,140	1,100	485	441	159	−245	—
Exports[c]	400	648	2,149	2,693	2,176	2,084	1,691	759	—
Imports[c]	—	—	1,009	1,593	1,691	1,644	1,532	1,004	—
Foreign direct investment, net	—	—	11	104	103	233	129	108	—
Gross reserves, end-year	—	—	—	818	927	1,170	1,172	1,285	—
External debt stock	—	—	—	168	371	515	668	1,248	—
In months of current account expenditures, excluding transfers									
Gross reserves, end-year[d]	—	—	—	6.2	5.1	6.3	7.9	10.4	—
% current account revenues, excluding transfers									
Debt service	—	—	—	0	1.8	12.6	16.6	24.8	—
Current account/GDP	—	—	—	16.5	3.8	0.9	2.2	−33.8	−15.8
External debt/GDP	—	—	—	3.6	16.6	20.5	34.5	70.7	—
Current account/GDP	—	—	—	16.5	3.8	0.9	2.2	−33.8	−15.8
External debt/exports	—	—	—	6.2	17.0	24.7	39.5	164.4	—
Memorandum items									
Population (millions)	3.7	3.8	4.0	4.1	4.3	4.4	4.6	4.7	4.8
GDP (manat, billions)	—	—	—	9.4	141	1,072	7,608	9,446	—
GDP per capita ($)	—	—	386	1,098	188	193	278	432	399
GDP per capita (PPP$)	—	—	4,896	4,823	3,377	3,135	2,987	2,506	2,589

[a] Official unemployment does not exist. These figures are household survey estimates. [b] Until 1997, most quasi-budgetary expenditures of sectoral ministries fell outside the budget, and several off-budget funds were in operation. [c] From 1996, exports of gas are recorded FOB, and transit costs are added to imports. The current account on a cash basis (excluding the flow accumulation of gas payment arrears) was in deficit over 1993–1996. [d] The ratio is to imports only. Current account expenditures up to 1996 included gas transit fees. Thus, the later figures cannot be compared. Including transit fees, the ratio of reserves was around 6.6 per cent.

Ukraine: selected economic indicators, 1990–8

	1990	1991	1992	1993	1994	1995	1996	1997	1998
Output (% change)									
GDP at constant prices	-3.4	-11.6	-13.7	-14.2	-23.0	-12.2	-10.0	-3.2	1.0
Private consumption	—	—	-9.0	-30.1	-17.1	-15.1	-6.0	-0.4	1.0
Public consumption	—	—	-9.1	-27.3	-11.3	-13.1	-5.0	-4.4	0.0
Gross fixed investment	—	—	-37.0	-10.0	-25.0	-14.7	-19.8	-9.1	3.8
Industrial gross output	-0.1	-4.8	-6.4	-8.0	-27.3	-12.0	-5.1	-1.8	2.5
Agricultural gross output	-4.0	-13.0	-8.3	1.5	-16.5	-3.6	-9.5	-2.0	0.4
Composition of output (% GDP)									
Industry	34.7	45.8	43.5	29.9	39.0	34.6	31.0	34.0	—
Agriculture	24.4	24.4	20.3	21.6	16.0	14.9	6.7	6.0	—
Unemployment (% labour force)	0.0	0.0	0.3	0.4	0.4	0.5	1.6	2.9	4.0
Prices and wages (% change)									
Consumer prices, annual average	4.2	91.0	1,210	4,700	891	377	80.0	16.0	18.0
Consumer prices, end-year	—	161	2,730	10,155	401	182	39.7	10.1	19.0
Producer prices, annual average	4.5	125	2,384	2,453	1,134	593	59.0	7.5	—
Producer prices, end-year	4.5	163	3,828	9,668	774	172	17.3	5.0	—
Average wage in industry, gross	—	—	—	-46.4	-10.7	-13.8	-21.5	0.7	1.0
Government sector (% GDP)									
General government balance	—	—	-25.4	-16.2	-7.8	-4.8	-3.2	-5.8	-4.0
General government expenditure	—	—	58.4	54.5	51.5	43.9	40.4	43.2	—
Monetary sector (% change)									
Broad money, end-year	—	—	—	758	573	117	35	28	—
Domestic credit, end-year	—	—	2,400	1,529	583	166	38	31	—
Broad money (% GDP)	—	—	—	31.8	26.2	12.7	11.6	13.1	—

Interest and exchange rates (% per year), end-year									
Average deposit rate	—	—	82	216	140	62	26	43	—
Average lending rate	—	—	77	295	205	156	76	19	—
Hryvnia per $									
Exchange rate, end-year[a]	—	—	638	12,610	108,855	179,497	1.889	1.895	2.1832
Exchange rate, annual average[a]	59	174	275	4,533	49,860	147,308	1.829	1.862	2.13
External sector ($ billions)									
Current account	—	-2.9	-0.6	-0.8	-1.4	-1.2	-1.1	-1.5	—
Trade balance	-12.7	-3.4	-0.6	-2.5	-2.6	-2.7	-4.3	-4.8	—
Exports	74.6	50.0	11.3	12.8	13.9	14.2	15.5	15.3	—
Imports	87.3	53.4	11.9	15.3	16.5	15.9	19.8	20.1	—
Foreign direct investment, net	—	—	0.2	0.2	0.1	0.4	0.5	0.7	—
Gross reserves, end-year	—	—	0.5	0.2	0.6	1.1	2.0	2.2	—
External debt stock	—	—	0.5	3.7	7.7	8.1	9.2	10.2	—
In weeks of imports of goods and services									
Gross reserves, end-year	—	—	—	0.1	1.8	2.3	3.7	5.2	5.6
% exports of goods and services									
Debt service	—	—	—	1.3	12.1	9.3	6.0	6.7	—
Current account/GDP	—	—	—	-5.8	-3.8	-3.2	-2.5	-3.0	-2.4
External debt/GDP	—	—	—	26.6	20.4	22.0	20.8	20.5	—
External debt/exports	—	—	4.4	28.9	55.3	57.0	59.6	68.0	—
Memorandum items									
Population millions	51.8	51.9	52.0	52.1	51.9	51.7	51.3	50.9	50.6
GDP (hryvnia, millions)	2	3	51	1,483	12,038	54,516	80,510	92,500	—
GDP per capita ($)	—	—	351	627	463	724	870	961	953
GDP per capita (PPP$)	—	—	4,652	3,984	3,073	2,751	2,500	2,426	2,462

[a] Auction rate. Roubles per dollar until 1991; karbovanets per dollar until 1995; hrynia per dollar thereafter.

Uzbekistan: selected economic indicators, 1990–1998

	1990	1991	1992	1993	1994	1995	1996	1997	1998
Output (% change)									
GDP at constant prices	1.6	−0.5	−11.1	−2.3	−4.2	−0.9	1.6	2.4	2.0
Private consumption	—	—	−28.5	23.6	7.5	−17.6	5.2	8.1	3.6
Public consumption	—	—	−14.1	19.3	−17.3	−2.7	−22.9	7.1	2.6
Gross fixed investment	—	—	−32.0	−5.0	−0.1	25.1	1.7	8.1	3.7
Industrial gross output	—	−3.8	−6.7	3.6	1.6	0.2	6.0	6.5	7.0
Agricultural gross output	—	−0.4	−6.0	1.0	−8.0	−3.0	−5.4	3.2	3.3
Composition of output (% GDP)									
Industry	22.7	26.3	26.6	22.4	17.0	17.1	17.4	16.3	—
Agriculture	33.4	37.3	35.4	27.9	34.5	28.1	22.5	27.5	—
Unemployment (% labour force)	0.0	0.0	0.1	0.3	0.4	0.4	0.4	0.5	0.7
Prices and wages (% change)									
Consumer prices, annual average	3.1	82.2	645	534	1,568	305	54.0	59.0	24.0
Consumer prices, end-year	—	169.0	910	885	1,281	117	64.0	28.0	35.0
Producer prices, annual average	7.2	147.3	3,275	2,545	1,428	499	64.0	—	—
Producer prices, end-year	—	311.0	1,300	1,120	1,070	830	57.6	45.2	23.8
Average wage	—	−17.1	−10.2	6.7	−40.0	8.5	1.1	4.8	5.3
Government sector (% GDP)									
Consolidated state balance[a]	−1.1	−3.6	−18.4	−10.4	−6.1	−4.1	−7.3	−2.3	3.0
Consolidated state expenditure	46.1	52.7	43.4	38.8	33.3	37.6	36.2	32.8	—
Monetary sector (% change)									
Broad money, end-year	—	—	468.0	784.0	680.3	158.0	100.0	34.6	—
Domestic credit, end-year	—	—	—	854.4	239.0	58.3	258.8	79.7	—
Broad money (% GDP)	—	—	69.4	53.5	32.8	18.1	19.6	16.4	—

Interest and exchange rates (% per year), end-year								
Deposit rate, one year	—	7	10	60	90	40	39	—
Lending rate, one year	—	—	—	100	105	60	59	—
Som per $								
Exchange rate, end-year[b]	2.0	415.0	1,247	25.0	36.0	54.7	69.8	108.0
Exchange rate, annual average[b]	0.6	222.0	1.0	10.0	30.5	38.0	62.3	88.9
External sector ($ millions)								
Current account	7,225	−238	−429	118	−49	−1,075	−800	—
Trade balance	688	−236	−378	213	208	−931	−300	—
Exports	11,829	1,424	2,877	2,940	3,806	3,781	3,700	—
Imports	11,141	1,659	3,255	2,727	3,597	4,712	4,000	—
Foreign direct investment, net	—	9	73	73	−24	50	60	—
Gross reserves, end-year[c]	—	1	1,273	2,917	2,013	2,221	1,200	—
External debt stock	0	65	948	1,101	1,782	2,331	2,594	—
In months of imports of goods and services								
Gross reserves, end-year[c]	—	0.6	3.8	5.9	6.2	4.7	3.5	—
% exports of goods and services								
Debt service	—	0.4	0.7	10.5	15.8	9	9.8	—
Current account/GDP	—	—	−8.4	2.1	−0.5	−7.9	−5.5	−3.5
External debt/GDP	—	—	18.6	19.3	17.8	17.1	18.0	—
External debt/exports	—	4.6	33.0	37.4	46.8	61.7	70.1	—
Memorandum items								
Population (millions)	20.5	20.9	21.3	22.0	22.7	23.1	23.6	24.0
GDP (som, millions)	32.4	61.5	447	5,095	64,878	302,787	560,147	962,000
GDP per capita ($)	—	95	254	117	374	446	532	446
GDP per capita (PPP$)	1,706	2,746	2,621	2,455	2,384	2,368	2,430	2,504

[a] Includes extrabudgetary funds.   [b] Roubles per dollar until 1993; som per dollar thereafter.   [c] Including gold.

Yugoslavia: selected economic indicators, 1990–1998[a]

	1990	1991	1992	1993	1994	1995	1996	1997	1998
Output (% change)									
GDP at constant prices	—	-8.2	-26.1	-27.7	6.5	6.6	5.8	8.8	3.7
Private consumption	—	-15.3	-22.3	-35.8	31.8	13.0	3.0	9.0	0.2
Public consumption	—	-0.8	-8.5	-36.8	19.0	12.0	2.0	8.0	-0.8
Gross fixed investment	—	-9.4	-37.3	-35.0	-7.5	-5.0	4.0	9.8	11.1
Industrial gross output	—	-17.8	-22.1	-37.5	4.0	4.0	8.0	10.0	5.0
Agricultural gross output	—	10.0	-18.0	-3.0	6.0	3.0	-3.0	6.2	3.5
Unemployment (% labour force)	—	21.4	22.8	23.1	23.1	24.7	26.1	25.5	24.0
Prices and wages (% change)									
Consumer prices, annual average	—	122	8,926	—	3	79	93	18	46
Producer prices, annual average	—	124	9,093	—	8	58	90	20	91
Average wage	—	-5.0	-49.0	-61.1	200.9	41.7	-12.4	16.9	2.7
Exchange rates (dinars per $)[b]									
Exchange rate, end-year	—	19.7	750.0	1,776	1.6	4.7	5.0	5.9	11.6
Exchange rate, annual average	—	19.6	2,467	—	1.6	2.0	5.0	5.6	10.8
External sector ($ millions)									
Current account	—	-536	-935	—	—	—	-1,863	-2,062	-1,115
Trade balance	—	-844	-1,320	—	—	—	-2,266	-2,447	-1,527
Exports	—	4,704	2,539	—	—	—	1,831	2,406	2,547
Imports	—	5,548	3,859	—	—	—	4,097	4,853	4,074
Memorandum items									
Population (millions)	—	10.4	10.4	10.4	10.5	10.6	10.6	10.7	10.7
GDP (new dinars, millions)[b]	—	—	—	—	16,147	38,760	68,980	88,984	134,196
GDP per capita ($)	—	—	—	—	952	1,856	1,299	1,479	1,164
GDP per capita (PPP$)	—	4,919	3,619	2,607	2,769	2,938	3,093	3,352	3,462

[a] Serbia and Montenegro.   [b] In dinars until 1993, thereafter in 'new dinars' (equalling 1,000 old dinars).

PART 2

The forecast for 1999–2002

Albania: forecast for 1999–2002

	1999	2000	2001	2002	Average, 1999–2002	Index 2002 (1998 = 100)
GDP per capita						
PPP$	1,581	1,741	1,881	1,941	1,786	134.0
Market exchange rate ($)	1,143	1,296	1,449	1,548	1,359	151.9
Annual growth rate (%)						
GDP	9.7	10.6	8.6	3.7	8.2	136.6
Private consumption	6.9	8.1	7.4	2.5	6.2	127.2
Public consumption	5.9	7.1	6.4	1.5	5.2	122.5
Gross fixed investment	28.1	26.7	13.6	10.9	19.8	204.5
Industrial output	15.0	10.0	9.7	8.7	10.9	150.8
Agriculture	4.5	5.8	6.0	5.0	5.3	123.1
Real wages	9.2	10.1	8.1	3.2	7.7	134.1
Inflation (CPI, %)	16.6	13.5	12.2	11.0	13.3	164.8
Unemployment rate (%)	12.9	12.1	11.7	11.3	12.0	—

Armenia: forecast for 1999–2002

	1999	2000	2001	2002	Average, 1999–2002	Index 2002 (1998 = 100)
GDP per capita						
PPP$	2,782	2,951	3,136	3,367	3,059	128.5
Market exchange rate ($)	508	584	672	781	636.3	178.3
Annual growth rate (%)						
GDP	6.6	6.5	6.7	7.8	6.9	130.6
Private consumption	2.9	3.0	3.4	5.7	3.8	115.8
Public consumption	2.9	3.0	3.4	5.7	3.8	115.8
Gross fixed investment	11.0	10.6	9.7	12.1	10.9	151.0
Industrial output	8.4	8.8	9.3	9.7	9.1	141.4
Agriculture and forestry	3.6	3.0	3.0	3.1	3.2	113.3
Real wages	8.1	8.0	8.2	9.3	8.4	138.1
Inflation (CPI, %)	19.4	16.5	15.2	13.9	16.3	182.5
Unemployment rate (%)	10.6	10.4	10.1	9.9	10.3	—

Azerbaijan: forecast for 1999–2002

	1999	2000	2001	2002	Average, 1999–2002	Index 2002 (1998 = 100)
GDP per capita						
PPP$	1,914	2,095	2,304	2,522	2,208.8	141.9
Market exchange rate ($)	661	778	924	1,092	863.8	196.8
Annual growth rate (%)						
GDP	9.0	10.7	11.2	10.7	10.4	148.5
Private consumption	3.8	1.3	10.8	4.1	5.0	121.3
Public consumption	1.8	−0.7	8.8	2.1	3.0	112.3
Gross fixed investment	33.0	34.2	15.7	8.1	22.8	223.2
Industrial output	10.9	14.5	13.8	13.1	13.1	163.4
Agriculture	4.8	4.6	4.5	4.4	4.6	119.6
Real wages	8.0	9.7	10.2	9.7	9.4	143.2
Inflation (CPI, %)	9.4	9.9	9.0	8.0	9.1	141.5
Unemployment rate (%)	3.0	3.6	4.3	5.2	4.0	—

Belarus: forecast for 1999–2002

	1999	2000	2001	2002	Average, 1999–2002	Index 2002 (1998 = 100)
GDP per capita						
PPP$	4,913	5,023	5,190	5,452	5,144.5	108.9
Market exchange rate ($)	1,149	1,337	1,572	1,815	1,468.3	172.2
Annual growth rate (%)						
GDP	−1.5	2.7	3.7	5.5	2.6	110.7
Private consumption	−6.6	2.5	3.5	4.3	0.9	103.3
Public consumption	−6.6	2.5	3.5	4.3	0.9	103.3
Gross fixed investment	−2.2	7.1	8.0	10.3	5.8	124.8
Industrial output	−4.2	1.6	4.3	7.0	2.2	108.6
Agriculture	6.7	3.1	1.9	2.4	3.5	114.8
Real wages	−3.1	5.4	3.5	5.2	2.8	111.2
Inflation (CPI, %)	59.9	36.2	32.6	29.3	39.5	373.4
Unemployment rate (%)	8.0	10.0	9.0	8.6	8.9	—

Bulgaria: forecast for 1999–2002

	1999	2000	2001	2002	Average, 1999–2002	Index 2002 (1998 = 100)
GDP per capita						
PPP$	3,769	3,982	4,137	4,282	4,043	119.6
Market exchange rate ($)	2,009	2,344	2,541	2,689	2,396	168.8
Annual growth rate (%)						
GDP	5.4	5.7	4.4	4.0	4.9	121.0
Private consumption	5.8	5.9	4.4	4.3	5.1	122.0
Public consumption	1.2	−3.3	−4.2	−3.0	−2.3	90.9
Gross fixed investment	11.3	10.8	9.2	6.1	9.4	142.9
Industrial output	5.7	6.3	4.7	4.0	5.2	122.3
Agriculture	3.6	2.1	2.5	2.5	2.7	111.1
Real wages	5.4	5.7	4.4	4.0	4.9	121.0
Inflation (CPI, %)	16.0	14.0	14.0	12.0	14.0	168.8
Unemployment rate (%)	13.0	12.0	10.0	8.7	10.9	—

Croatia: forecast for 1999–2002

	1999	2000	2001	2002	Average, 1999–2002	Index 2002 (1998 = 100)
GDP per capita						
PPP$	7,610	8,030	8,473	8,898	8,252.8	121.1
Market exchange rate ($)	4,970	5,388	5,798	6,151	5,576.8	141.2
Annual growth rate (%)						
GDP	3.4	5.4	5.4	4.9	4.8	120.5
Private consumption	1.0	4.5	4.2	3.7	3.4	114.0
Public consumption	0.6	4.0	3.7	3.3	2.9	112.1
Gross fixed investment	−0.6	10.0	11.1	10.3	7.7	134.0
Industrial output	4.0	6.0	6.3	6.1	5.6	124.3
Agriculture	3.2	3.1	3.0	2.2	2.9	112.0
Real wages	1.4	3.4	3.8	2.9	2.9	112.0
Inflation (CPI, %)	7.3	5.8	4.8	3.5	5.4	123.1
Unemployment rate (%)	11.9	9.3	8.9	8.5	9.7	—

Czech Republic: forecast for 1999–2002

	1999	2000	2001	2002	Average, 1999–2002	Index 2002 (1998 = 100)
GDP per capita						
PPP$	10,369	10,800	11,271	11,786	11,057	117.2
Market exchange rate ($)	6,316	7,364	8,473	9,575	7,932	176.7
Annual growth rate (%)						
GDP	3.3	4.3	4.5	4.7	4.2	117.9
Private consumption	5.3	6.7	4.3	3.6	5.0	121.4
Public consumption	1.2	5.0	5.2	3.4	3.7	115.6
Gross fixed investment	3.2	4.6	3.2	3.6	3.7	115.4
Industrial output	5.2	5.5	5.7	6.1	5.6	124.5
Agriculture	1.5	2.5	2.4	2.3	2.2	109.0
Real wages	2.3	3.3	3.5	3.7	3.2	113.4
Inflation (CPI, %)	9.8	8.9	8.3	7.9	8.7	139.7
Unemployment rate (%)	7.0	6.8	6.5	6.3	6.7	—

Estonia: forecast for 1999–2002

	1999	2000	2001	2002	Average, 1999–2002	Index 2002 (1998 = 100)
GDP per capita						
PPP$	9,695	10,282	10,876	11,352	10,551.3	123.8
Market exchange rate ($)	4,457	5,086	5,752	6,422	5,429.3	172.3
Annual growth rate (%)						
GDP	5.5	5.9	5.6	5.9	5.7	124.9
Private consumption	2.3	3.8	5.3	7.1	4.6	119.8
Public consumption	0.3	2.8	4.3	6.1	3.4	114.1
Gross fixed investment	4.8	7.2	5.6	7.4	6.3	127.4
Industrial output	9.5	9.0	8.6	8.1	8.8	140.1
Agriculture and forestry	1.4	1.3	0.8	0.7	1.1	104.3
Real wages	4.8	5.4	5.1	4.9	5.1	121.8
Inflation (CPI, %)	8.6	7.7	6.9	6.2	7.4	132.8
Unemployment rate (%)[a]	3.8	3.7	3.6	5.0	4.0	—

[a] Annual average.

Georgia: forecast for 1999–2002

	1999	2000	2001	2002	Average, 1999–2002	Index 2002 (1998 = 100)
GDP per capita						
PPP$	2,338	2,440	2,643	2,822	2,560.8	138.3
Market exchange rate ($)	927	1,087	1,271	1,465	1,187.5	186.1
Annual growth rate (%)						
GDP	10.1	9.3	9.1	7.6	9.0	141.3
Private consumption	7.1	6.2	2.3	1.9	4.4	118.6
Public consumption	7.1	6.2	2.3	1.9	4.4	118.6
Gross fixed investment	24.3	24.1	12.5	11.3	18.1	193.1
Industrial output	12.0	11.4	10.8	10.3	11.1	152.5
Agriculture	8.4	8.0	7.2	6.7	7.6	133.9
Gross personal income	8.9	8.3	3.9	3.4	6.1	126.7
Inflation (CPI, %)	10.1	8.4	8.3	8.1	8.7	139.7

Hungary: forecast for 1999–2002

	1999	2000	2001	2002	Average, 1999–2002	Index 2002 (1998 = 100)
GDP per capita						
PPP$	8,043	8,430	8,818	9,170	8,615	119.2
Market exchange rate ($)	5,493	5,986	6,509	7,037	6,256	140.3
Annual growth rate (%)						
GDP	4.6	4.5	4.8	4.5	3.9	119.7
Private consumption	5.0	4.5	4.0	2.5	4.0	117.0
Public consumption	3.8	3.9	3.4	1.9	3.3	113.6
Gross fixed investment	9.5	6.9	6.2	4.7	6.8	130.2
Industrial output	7.0	6.0	5.0	4.7	5.7	124.7
Agriculture	1.9	3.5	2.4	2.0	2.5	110.2
Real wages	4.0	4.3	4.5	3.9	4.2	117.8
Inflation (CPI, %)	11.8	10.4	9.4	8.9	10.1	147.0
Unemployment rate (%)	8.1	7.6	7.0	6.8	7.4	—

Kazakhstan: forecast for 1999–2002

	1999	2000	2001	2002	Average, 1999–2002	Index 2002 (1998 = 100)
GDP per capita						
PPP$	2,766	2,899	3,098	3,311	3,018.5	124.9
Market exchange rate ($)	1,669	1,826	2,038	2,275	1,952	148.4
Annual growth rate (%)						
GDP	3.8	4.9	7.0	7.0	5.7	124.7
Private consumption	1.1	2.0	4.6	5.6	3.3	113.9
Public consumption	0.1	1.0	3.6	4.6	2.3	109.6
Gross fixed investment	9.8	10.3	12.6	13.0	11.4	154.1
Industrial output	5.0	6.0	8.0	7.5	6.6	129.2
Agriculture	8.8	9.3	11.6	12.0	10.4	148.6
Real wages	2.8	3.9	6.0	6.0	4.7	120.0
Inflation (CPI, %)	8.6	6.8	6.7	6.6	7.2	131.9
Unemployment rate (%)	15.5	14.6	13.8	13.0	14.2	—

Kyrgyzstan: forecast for 1999–2002

	1999	2000	2001	2002	Average, 1999–2002	Index 2002 (1998 = 100)
GDP per capita						
PPP$	2,239	2,342	2,437	2,535	2,388.3	119.3
Market exchange rate ($)	509	543	578	614	561	134.1
Annual growth rate (%)						
GDP	6.8	6.0	5.5	5.6	6.0	126.1
Private consumption	4.2	3.4	4.4	4.4	4.1	117.4
Public consumption	3.2	2.4	3.4	3.4	3.1	113.0
Gross fixed investment	22.5	19.6	9.0	8.9	15.0	173.9
Industrial output	10.8	8.1	8.9	9.0	9.2	142.2
Agriculture and forestry	3.3	3.2	3.0	2.9	3.1	113.0
Real wages	6.3	5.6	5.0	5.0	5.5	123.8
Inflation (CPI, %)	11.4	10.2	9.1	8.2	9.7	144.9

Latvia: forecast for 1999–2002

	1999	2000	2001	2002	Average, 1999–2002	Index 2002 (1998 = 100)
GDP per capita						
PPP$	6,783	7,128	7,574	8,039	7,381	123.8
Market exchange rate ($)	2,642	2,928	3,277	3,660	3,126.8	142.2
Annual growth rate (%)						
GDP	3.9	4.6	5.8	5.7	5.0	121.5
Private consumption	3.5	2.7	2.1	5.5	3.5	114.5
Public consumption	2.5	1.7	1.1	4.5	2.5	110.1
Gross fixed investment	−0.5	12.6	25.0	11.8	12.2	156.6
Industrial output	6.0	6.0	7.0	6.7	6.4	128.3
Agriculture	2.8	2.7	2.3	1.9	2.4	110.1
Real wages	2.9	3.6	4.8	4.8	4.0	117.1
Inflation (CPI, %)	10.4	9.4	8.4	6.9	8.8	140.0
Unemployment rate (%)	7.0	6.5	6.5	6.5	6.6	—

Lithuania: forecast for 1999–2002

	1999	2000	2001	2002	Average, 1999–2002	Index 2002 (1998 = 100)
GDP per capita						
PPP$	4,339	4,583	4,813	5,047	4,695.5	122.1
Market exchange rate ($)	3,093	3,433	3,781	4,082	3,597.3	145.8
Annual growth rate (%)						
GDP	5.0	5.7	5.1	4.9	5.2	122.4
Private consumption	2.9	5.0	5.1	4.0	4.3	118.1
Public consumption	0.9	3.0	3.1	3.0	2.5	110.4
Gross fixed investment	7.3	5.2	5.9	9.2	6.9	130.5
Industrial output	6.6	7.4	6.7	6.7	6.9	130.3
Agriculture and forestry	4.1	3.9	1.9	1.2	2.8	111.5
Real wages	5.0	5.7	5.1	4.9	5.2	122.4
Inflation (CPI, %)	5.6	5.2	5.0	3.8	4.9	121.1
Unemployment rate (%)	5.7	5.7	5.6	5.5	5.6	—

FYR Macedonia: forecast for 1999–2002

	1999	2000	2001	2002	Average, 1999–2002	Index 2002 (1998 = 100)
GDP per capita						
PPP$	2,966	3,046	3,173	3,310	3,124	114.7
Market exchange rate ($)	1,774	1,854	1,951	2,051	1,908	125.3
Annual growth rate (%)						
GDP	3.4	3.4	4.9	5.0	4.2	117.8
Private consumption	2.2	1.5	4.0	4.2	3.0	112.4
Public consumption	2.5	2.5	2.0	2.0	2.3	109.3
Gross fixed investment	8.1	7.4	7.4	7.5	7.6	134.0
Industrial output	5.0	6.0	7.0	7.0	6.3	127.4
Agriculture	3.5	3.0	3.0	3.0	3.1	113.1
Real wages	2.9	2.9	4.4	4.5	3.7	115.5
Inflation (CPI, %)	4.1	3.6	3.4	3.3	3.6	115.2

Moldova: forecast for 1999–2002

	1999	2000	2001	2002	Average, 1999–2002	Index 2002 (1998 = 100)
GDP per capita						
PPP$	2,224	2,330	2,473	2,611	2,409.5	124.9
Market exchange rate ($)	612	656	718	782	692.0	139.6
Annual growth rate (%)						
GDP	6.6	5.0	6.3	5.8	5.9	125.9
Private consumption	5.7	3.6	6.3	5.7	5.3	123.0
Public consumption	3.7	1.6	4.3	3.7	3.3	114.0
Gross fixed investment	31.5	31.8	12.8	12.3	22.1	219.5
Industrial output	5.3	3.5	5.5	5.3	4.9	121.1
Agriculture	6.3	4.5	4.5	4.3	4.9	121.1
Real wages	6.3	4.7	6.1	5.5	5.7	124.6
Inflation (CPI, %)	10.7	8.5	8.2	7.8	8.8	140.1

Poland: forecast for 1999–2002

	1999	2000	2001	2002	Average, 1999–2002	Index 2002 (1998 = 100)
GDP per capita						
PPP$	7,508	7,939	8,396	8,889	8,183	125.3
Market exchange rate ($)	4,198	4,638	5,238	5,922	4,999	155.4
Annual growth rate (%)						
GDP	5.9	5.8	5.8	6.1	5.9	125.8
Private consumption	4.8	4.9	5.1	6.4	5.3	122.9
Public consumption	2.4	3.4	3.5	3.7	3.3	113.6
Gross fixed investment	6.6	6.5	6.1	6.6	6.5	128.4
Industrial output	7.4	6.8	7.5	7.0	7.2	131.9
Agriculture	0.1	0.3	1.2	1.2	0.7	102.8
Real wages	3.0	3.8	2.2	4.0	3.3	113.6
Inflation (CPI, %)	9.1	7.4	6.2	5.0	6.9	130.7
Unemployment rate (%)	9.0	8.5	8.0	7.1	8.2	136.8

Romania: forecast for 1999–2002

	1999	2000	2001	2002	Average, 1999–2002	Index 2002 (1998 = 100)
GDP per capita						
PPP$	3,315	3,515	3,717	3,908	3,614	122.1
Market exchange rate ($)	1,907	2,131	2,379	2,648	2,266	151.1
Annual growth rate (%)						
GDP	3.3	5.8	5.5	4.9	4.9	121.0
Private consumption	−0.3	5.8	6.4	4.5	4.1	117.3
Public consumption	−1.4	4.7	5.8	3.4	3.1	112.9
Gross fixed investment	5.1	11.4	11.8	6.9	8.8	139.9
Industrial output	5.0	7.2	6.5	6.4	6.3	127.5
Agriculture	1.8	1.7	1.6	1.2	1.6	106.4
Real wages	2.8	5.3	5.0	4.4	4.4	118.7
Inflation (CPI, %)	33.4	24.7	19.4	16.5	23.5	231.4
Unemployment rate (%)	10.5	10.0	9.4	9.2	9.8	—

Russia: forecast for 1999–2002

	1999	2000	2001	2002	Average, 1999–2002	Index 2002 (1998 = 100)
GDP per capita						
PPP$	4,122	4,044	4,189	4,349	4,176	99.3
Market exchange rate ($)	2,023	1,879	2,052	2,269	2,864	79.2
Annual growth rate (%)						
GDP	−4.7	−1.8	1.4	3.1	−0.5	97.8
Private consumption	−12.2	−5.6	12.3	9.8	1.1	102.2
Public consumption	−12.7	−6.1	6.2	9.3	−0.8	95.2
Gross fixed investment	−6.4	−0.8	10.4	7.8	2.8	110.5
Industrial output	−4.8	−1.5	1.0	2.5	−0.7	97.1
Agriculture	−1.2	1.1	1.9	1.7	0.9	103.5
Real wages	−13.2	−6.8	11.1	4.3	−1.2	93.7
Inflation (CPI, %)	10.6	11.2	10.3	9.7	10.5	148.8
Unemployment rate (%)	12.3	12.8	13.1	12.2	12.6	—

Slovakia: forecast for 1999–2002

	1999	2000	2001	2002	Average, 1999–2002	Index 2002 (1998 = 100)
GDP per capita						
PPP$	8,435	8,638	9,062	9,522	8,914	115.3
Market exchange rate ($)	3,814	4,133	4,498	4,912	4,339	128.0
Annual growth rate (%)						
GDP	2.3	2.5	5.0	5.0	3.7	115.6
Private consumption	2.7	−1.1	6.0	6.3	3.5	114.4
Public consumption	−0.2	−2.6	4.6	4.8	1.7	106.6
Gross fixed investment	−6.4	4.4	5.3	5.5	2.2	108.6
Industrial output	3.0	6.0	4.8	4.5	4.6	119.6
Agriculture	3.2	3.4	3.0	3.1	3.2	113.3
Real wages	2.8	2.4	4.9	4.9	3.8	115.8
Inflation (CPI, %)	10.7	8.2	7.4	5.9	8.1	136.2
Unemployment rate (%)	12.4	11.7	11.3	10.9	11.6	—

Slovenia: forecast for 1999–2002

	1999	2000	2001	2002	Average, 1999–2002	Index 2002 (1998 = 100)
GDP per capita						
PPP$	14,085	14,299	15,465	16,200	15,012	120.0
Market exchange rate ($)	10,659	11,779	13,066	12,472	11,994	128.9
Annual growth rate (%)						
GDP	4.1	4.8	4.2	4.9	4.5	119.2
Private consumption	3.0	4.6	2.8	3.4	3.5	114.5
Public consumption	2.0	3.6	1.8	2.4	2.5	110.2
Gross fixed investment	8.1	8.7	5.5	5.2	6.9	130.4
Industrial output	4.0	5.0	4.5	5.5	4.8	120.4
Agriculture	3.7	4.6	4.1	5.1	4.4	118.7
Real wages	3.6	4.3	3.7	4.4	4.0	117.0
Inflation (CPI, %)	7.6	6.8	6.1	5.5	6.5	128.6
Unemployment rate (%)	13.2	12.5	11.8	11.1	12.2	158.2

Tajikistan: forecast for 1999–2002

	1999	2000	2001	2002	Average, 1999–2002	Index 2002 (1998 = 100)
GDP per capita						
PPP$	749	776	806	839	792.5	115.4
Market exchange rate ($)	284	314	340	369	326.8	168.5
Annual growth rate (%)						
GDP	5.1	5.7	6.0	6.1	5.7	124.9
Private consumption	6.6	7.1	7.6	7.5	7.2	132.1
Public consumption	5.5	6.0	6.5	6.4	6.1	126.7
Gross fixed investment	10.5	10.7	8.7	8.5	9.6	144.3
Industrial output	4.0	4.5	5.2	5.7	4.9	120.8
Agriculture and forestry	3.9	4.8	5.0	4.2	4.5	119.1
Gross personal income	4.1	4.7	5.0	5.1	4.7	120.3
Inflation (CPI, %)	36.2	24.5	18.3	16.4	23.9	233.5
Unemployment rate (%)	6.7	6.8	7.0	7.1	6.9	—

Turkmenistan: forecast for 1999–2002

	1999	2000	2001	2002	Average, 1999–2002	Index 2002 (1998 = 100)
GDP per capita						
PPP$	2,865	3,279	3,350	3,445	3,234.8	133.1
Market exchange rate ($)	524	713	759	814	702.5	204.0
Annual growth rate (%)						
GDP	12.1	16.0	3.5	4.2	9.0	140.2
Private consumption	18.4	23.9	6.7	7.6	14.2	168.4
Public consumption	13.4	15.9	3.7	5.1	9.5	143.2
Gross fixed investment	5.5	9.6	1.0	1.9	4.5	119.0
Industrial output	32.3	44.7	2.1	2.9	20.5	201.1
Agriculture	3.7	2.1	2.5	3.0	2.8	111.8
Real wages	11.1	15.0	2.5	3.2	8.0	135.1
Inflation (CPI, %)	19.4	16.5	15.2	13.9	16.3	182.5
Unemployment rate (%)	10.6	10.4	10.1	9.9	10.3	—

Ukraine: forecast for 1999–2002

	1999	2000	2001	2002	Average, 1999–2002	Index 2002 (1998 = 100)
GDP per capita						
PPP$	2,542	2,665	2,810	2,969	2,746.5	120.6
Market exchange rate ($)	1,057	1,169	1,304	1,458	1,247.0	153.0
Annual growth rate (%)						
GDP	3.0	4.8	5.2	6.0	4.8	120.4
Private consumption	2.2	4.5	4.7	4.6	4.0	117.0
Public consumption	1.2	3.5	4.3	3.6	3.2	113.2
Gross fixed investment	6.9	7.4	7.7	10.9	8.2	137.1
Industrial output	3.5	6.0	7.2	8.0	6.2	127.0
Agriculture	2.6	2.9	2.1	3.0	2.7	111.0
Real wages	2.4	4.3	4.8	4.6	4.0	117.1
Inflation (CPI, %)	12.8	11.0	9.0	7.7	10.1	147.0
Unemployment rate (%)	6.0	8.0	8.0	7.5	7.4	—

Uzbekistan: forecast for 1999–2002

	1999	2000	2001	2002	Average, 1999–2002	Index 2002 (1998 = 100)
GDP per capita						
PPP$	2,544	2,597	2,641	2,688	2,617.5	107.3
Market exchange rate ($)	483	523	631	722	589.8	161.9
Annual growth rate (%)						
GDP	4.3	4.9	4.5	4.5	4.6	119.5
Private consumption	2.4	4.3	6.3	4.6	4.4	118.8
Public consumption	1.4	3.3	5.3	3.6	3.4	114.3
Gross fixed investment	2.5	5.9	0.8	4.4	3.4	114.2
Industrial output	6.0	6.3	6.0	5.7	6.0	126.2
Agriculture	3.0	2.7	2.9	3.1	2.9	112.2
Real wages	3.8	4.4	4.0	4.0	4.1	117.2
Inflation (CPI, %)	34.2	28.2	25.1	22.6	27.5	263.9

Yugoslavia: forecast for 1999–2002

	1999	2000	2001	2002	Average, 1999–2002	Index 2002 (1998 = 100)
GDP per capita						
PPP$	3,528	3,651	3,817	4,030	3,757	116.4
Market exchange rate ($)	1,333	1,420	1,525	1,658	1,484	142.4
Annual growth rate (%)						
GDP	2.3	3.9	5.0	6.0	4.3	118.3
Private consumption	−0.2	1.2	4.4	5.4	2.7	111.1
Public consumption	−1.2	0.2	3.4	4.4	1.7	106.9
Gross fixed investment	9.8	19.3	10.5	11.3	12.7	161.1
Industrial output	2.5	4.0	5.0	6.0	4.4	118.6
Agriculture	4.1	2.5	2.9	2.4	3.0	112.4
Real wages	1.3	2.9	4.0	5.0	3.3	113.8
Inflation (CPI, %)	36.4	29.1	23.3	18.6	26.9	257.5
Unemployment rate (%)	21.0	18.0	15.0	14.0	17.0	187.2

REFERENCES

Akerlof, G., A. Rose, J. Yellin, and H. Hessinus. 1991. 'East Germany in from the Cold'. *Brookings Papers on Economic Activity*, 1, 1–87.

Alesina, Alberto. 1997. 'The Political Economy of High and Low Growth'. In Boris Pleskovic and Joseph E. Stiglitz (eds). *Annual Bank Conference on Development Economics*. Washington, DC: World Bank.

—— 1998. 'Too Large and Too Small Governments'. Conference paper presented at 'Economic Policy and Equity', International Monetary Fund, Washington, DC, 8–9 June.

Alesina, Alberto and Roberto Perotti. 1996. 'Income Distribution, Political Instability, and Investment'. *European Economic Review*, 40, 1,203–28.

Andrews, Emily and Mansoora Rashid. 1996. 'The Financing of Pension Systems in Central and Eastern Europe'. *World Bank Technical Papers*, 339 (October).

Åslund, Anders. 1995. *How Russia became a Market Economy*. Washington, DC: The Brookings Institution.

—— 1996. 'The Russian Economy: Where is It Headed?'. *The Ernest Sturc Memorial Lecture*, 7 November. Washington, DC: Paul H. Nitze School of Advanced International Studies, Johns Hopkins University.

Atkinson, Anthony B. and John Micklewright. 1992. *Economic Transformation in Eastern Europe and the Distribution of Income*. Cambridge, UK: Cambridge University Press.

Atkinson, Anthony B., Lee Rainwater, and Timothy Smeeding. 1994. 'Income Distribution in Advanced Economies: Evidence from the Luxembourg Income Study'. *Working Papers*, 120 (December). Luxembourg: Luxembourg Income Study, CEPS/INSTEAD.

Balcerowicz, Leszek. 1992. *800 Dni: Szok kontrolowany (800 Days: Controlled Shock)*. Warsaw: BGW.

Barber, Lionel. 1997. 'EU may Widen Membership Talks: EC Says Estonia and Slovenia should be Included in Enlargement Negotiations'. *Financial Times*, 8 July.

Barro, Robert. 1996. 'Democracy and Growth'. *Journal of Economic Growth*, 1, 1–27.

Bauer, Tamas. 1978. 'Investment Cycles in Planned Economies'. *Acta Economica*, xxi, March, 243–60.

Berg, Andrew and Jeffrey Sachs. 1992. 'Structural Adjustment and International Trade in Eastern Europe: The Case of Poland'. *Economic Policy*, 14 (April), 117–55.

Bernstam, Michael S. and A. Rabushka. 1998. *Fixing Russia's Banks: A Proposal for Growth*. Stanford, CA: Hoover Institution Press.

Blanchard, Olivier. 1997. *The Economics of Post-Communist Transition*. New York: Oxford University Press.

Blasi, Joseph R., Maya Kroumova, and Douglas Kruse. 1997. *Kremlin Capitalism: Privatizing the Russian Economy*. Ithaca, NY: Cornell University Press.

Blejer, Mario I. and Marko Skreb. 1997. *Macroeconomic Stabilization in Transition Economies*. Cambridge, UK: Cambridge University Press.

Blejer, Mario I. and Teresa Ter-Minassian. 1997a. *Fiscal Policy and Economic Reform: Essays in Honour of Vito Tanzi*. London: Routledge.

—— 1997b. *Macroeconomic Dimensions of Public finance: Essays in Honour of Vito Tanzi*. London: Routledge.

Blustein, Paul. 1997. 'Foreign Aid that doesn't Seem to Persuade'. *Washington Post*, 22 May.

Boland, Vincent. 1997. 'Czech PM's Cliffhanger Victory Fails to Dispel Survival Fears'. *Financial Times*, 12 June.

Branco, Marta de Castello. 1998. 'Pension Reform in the Baltics, Russia, and Other Countries of the Former Soviet Union'. *IMF Working Papers*, 98/11 (October).

Brother Ty, Christopher Buckley, and John Tierney. 1998. *God is My Broker: A Monk-Tycoon Reveals the 7–1/2 Laws of Spiritual and Financial Growth*. New York: Random House.

Bruno, Michael. 1992. 'Stabilization and Reform in Eastern Europe: A Preliminary Evaluation'. *IMF Working Papers*, 92/30 (June).

Brus, Wlodzimierz. 1988. 'The Political Economy of Reforms'. In Paul Marer and Wladyslaw Siwinski (eds). *Creditworthiness and Reform in Poland*. Bloomington, IN: Indiana University Press.

Brus, Wlodzimierz and Kazimierz Laski. 1989. *From Marx to Market*. Oxford: Oxford University Press.

Buiter, Willem H., Ricardo Lago, and Nicholas Stern. 1996. 'Promoting an Effective Market Economy in a Changing World'. *CEPR Discussion Papers*, 1,468 (October). London: Centre for Economic Policy Research.

Burnside, Craig and David Dollar. 1997. 'Good Policies are Needed to Make Aid Effective'. *Transition*, June.

Calvo, Guilermo and Fabrizio Coricelli. 1992. 'Stabilizing a Previously Centrally Planned Economy: Poland 1990'. *Economic Policy*, 14 (April), 175–211.

Caselli, G. P. and G. Pastrello. 1991. 'The 1990 Polish Recession: A Case of a Truncated Multiplier Process'. *Most*, 3, 51–68.

Cassidy, John. 1997. 'The Next Thinker: The Return of Karl Marx'. *The New Yorker*, 20 and 27 October.

Charlesworth, H. K. 1955. *The Economics of Repressed Inflation*. London: University Press of America.

Commander, S., H. Davoodi, and V. Lee. 1996. 'The Causes and Consequences of Government for Growth and Well-being'. Washington, DC: World Bank.

Cornia, Giovanni Andrea. 1996a. 'Transition and Income Distribution: Theory, Evidence, and Initial Interpretation'. *Research in Progress*, 1 (March). Helsinki: UNU/WIDER.

—— 1996b. 'Labour Market Shocks, Psychological Stress, and the Transition's Mortality Crisis'. *Research in Progress*, 4 (October). Helsinki: UNU/WIDER.

—— 1997. 'In Search of a Transition Theory'. Conference paper presented at 'Transition Strategies, Alternatives, and Outcomes', UNU/WIDER, Helsinki, 15–17 May.

Cornia, Giovanni Andrea and Vladimir Popov. 1998. 'Transition Strategies, Growth, and Poverty'. Conference paper presented at the critical authors' meeting for the UNDP report 'Poverty in Post-Communist Societies', United Nations Development Programme, New York, 10 January.

Cornia, Giovanni Andrea, Juha Honkkila, Renato Paniccià, and Vladimir Popov. 1996. 'Long-term Growth and Welfare in Transition Economies: The Impact of Demographic, Investment, and Social Policy Changes'. *WIDER Working Papers*, 122 (December). Helsinki: UNU/WIDER.

Cottrell, Robert. 1997. 'Russia: The New Oligarchy'. *The New York Review*, 27 March.

Csaba, Laszlo. 1995. *The Capitalist Revolution in Eastern Europe: A Contribution to the Economic Theory of System Change*. Brookfield, VT: Edward Elgar.

Czyzewski, Adam B., Witold M. Orlowski, and Leszek Zienkowski. 1996. 'Country Study for Poland: A Comparative Study of Causes of Output Decline in Transition Economies'. Paper presented at 'Third Workshop on Output Decline in Eastern Europe', Prague, 12–13 April.

Deininger, Klaus and Lyn Squire. 1996. 'A New Data Set Measuring Income Inequality'. *World Bank Economic Review*, x, 3, 565–91.

De Melo, Martha, Cevdet Denizer, and Alan Gelb. 1996. 'From Plan to Market: Patterns of Transition'. Washington, DC: World Bank.

Development News. 1998a. 'Hanoi in Dilemma over Cost of Economic Reform', 16 June.

—— 1998b. 'Russia Secretly Borrows $200 Mln: G-7 Promises Vague Support', 11 June.

—— 1998c. 'Daily Summary', 29 April.

—— 1998d. 'After Russian Bailout, IMF Turns Attention to Ukrainian Ills', 23 July.

Dodsworth, John R., Ajai Chopra, Chi D. Pham, and Hisanobu Shishido. 1996. 'Macroeconomic Experiences of the Transition Economies in Indochina'. *IMF Working Papers*, WP/96/112 (October).

Dolgov, Anna. 1998. 'Russia: Economy may Shrink 9 per cent'. *Johnson's Russia List*, 2,476 (13 November).

Dornbusch, Rudiger. 1991. 'Policies to Move from Stabilization to Growth'. In World Bank. *Proceedings of the World Bank Annual Conference on Development Economics, 1990*. Washington, DC: World Bank.

Eatwell, John, Michael Ellman, Mats Karlsson, D. Mario Nuti, and Judith Shapiro. 1995. *Transformation and Integration: Shaping the Future of Central Eastern Europe*. London: Institute for Public Policy Research.

—— 1997. *Not 'Just Another Accession': The Political Economy of EU Enlargement to the East*. London: Institute for Public Policy Research.

EBRD. 1996. *Transition Report 1996: Infrastructure and Savings*. London: European Bank for Reconstruction and Development.

—— 1997a. *Transition Report Update*. London: European Bank for Reconstruction and Development.

—— 1997b. *Transition Report 1997: Enterprise Performance and Growth*. London: European Bank for Reconstruction and Development.

—— 1998. *Transition Report Update*. London: European Bank for Reconstruction and Development.

EC. 1990. *Stabilization, Liberalization, and Devolution: Assessment of the Economic Situation and Reform Process in the Soviet Union*, December. Brussels: European Commission.

The Economist. 1997a. 'Cheer Up, Europe', 21 June.

—— 1997b. 'Now You See It, Now You Don't', 22 November.

—— 1997c. 'Recasts Itself: A Survey of Business in Eastern Europe', 22 November.

—— 1997d. 'Russia: The Survey', 12 July.

The Economist. 1997e. 'European Industry and Its Press', 11 October.
—— 1997f. 'The Future of Liberty', 20 September.
—— 1997g. 'The Future of the State: A Survey of the World Economy', 20 September.
—— 1997h. 'Foreign Aid: Profs in a Pickle', 24 May.
—— 1998a. 'Asia Goes on the Dole', 25 April.
—— 1998b. 'Left Turn?', 13 June.
—— 1998c. 'Too Triumphalist by Half', 25 April.
—— 1998d. 'Widening the European Union, but not too Fast', 7 November.
Edlin, Aaron and Joseph E. Stiglitz. 1995. 'Discouraging Rivals: Managerial Rent-seeking and Economic Inefficiencies'. *American Economic Review*, lxxxv, 5, 1,301–12.
Edwards, Sebastian. 1992. 'Stabilization and Liberalization Policies for Economies in Transition: Latin American Lessons for Eastern Europe'. In C. Clague and G. C. Rausser (eds). *The Emergence of Market Economies in Eastern Europe*. Oxford: Blackwell.
Eichengreen, B. and M. Uzan. 1992. 'The Marshall Plan: Economic Effects and Implications for Eastern Europe and the Former USSR'. *Economic Policy*, April, 13–75.
Ellman, Mark. 1986. 'Economic Reform in China'. *International Affairs*, lxii, 3, 423–42.
—— 1997. 'The Political Economy of Transformation'. *Oxford Review of Economic Policy*, xiii, 2, 23–32.
Estrin, Saul. 1996. 'How to Privatize', mimeo. London: London Business School.
Estrin, Saul and Giovanni Urga. 1997. 'Convergence in Output in Transition Economies: Central and Eastern Europe, 1970–1995'. *Discussion Papers*, DP 09–97 (March). London: Centre for Economic Forecasting, London Business School.
Fan, Gang. 1997. 'Growing into the Market: China's Economic Transition'. Conference paper presented at 'Transition Strategies, Alternatives, and Outcomes', UNU/WIDER, Helsinki, 15–17 May.
Feuchtwang, S. and A. Hussain (eds). 1983. *The Chinese Economic Reforms*. New York: St Martin's Press.
Financial Times. 1997a. 'Organized Crime Revenues at $900m', 14 April.
—— 1997b. 'Observer', 28 May.
—— 1997c. 'Investors Give E Europe a Miss', 15 April.
—— 1998. 'The True Significance of Kosovo', 9 March.
Fischer, Stanley. 1998a. 'Opening Remarks'. Conference paper presented at 'Economic Policy and Equity', International Monetary Fund, Washington, DC, 8–9 June.
—— 1998b. 'ABCDE: Tenth Conference Address'. Conference paper presented at 'Knowledge for Development', World Bank, Washington, DC, 20–1 April.
Fischer, Stanley, Ratna Sahay, and Carlos A. Vegh. 1995. 'Stabilization and Growth in Transition Economies: Early Experiences'. Washington, DC: International Monetary Fund.
Flemming, John. 1998. 'Equitable Economic Transformation'. In Vito Tanzi and Ke-young Chu (eds). *Income Distribution and High-Quality Growth*. Cambridge, MA: MIT Press.
Freeland, Christia. 1997a. 'Bleak Answer to Russia's Riddle'. *Financial Times*, 19 June.
—— 1997b. 'Ukraine Parliament Backs Draft Civil Code'. *Financial Times*, 6 June.

—— 1998. 'Testing Times for Investors in Russia'. *Financial Times*, 25 May.

Freeland, Christia and Robert Corzine. 1997. 'Yeltsin Changes Gazprom Share Rules'. *Financial Times*, 29 May.

Fry, Maxwell. 1993. 'The Fiscal Abuse of Central Banks'. *IMF Working Papers*, 93/58.

Frydman, Roman and Andrzej Rapaczynski. 1991. 'Privatization and Corporate Governance in Eastern Europe: Can a Market Economy be Designed?'. In Georg Winckler (ed.). *Central and Eastern Europe: Roads to Growth*. Vienna: International Monetary Fund and Austrian National Bank.

—— 1994. 'Is Privatization Working?'. *Open Society News*, summer.

Frydman, Roman, Grzegorz W. Kolodko, and Stanislaw Wellisz. 1991. 'Stabilization in Poland: A Progress Report'. In E. M. Classen (ed.). *Exchange Rate Policies in Developing and Post-Socialist Countries*. San Francisco: ICS Press and International Centre for Economic Growth.

Frydman, Roman, Andrzej Rapaczynski, and John S. Earle. 1993. *The Privatization Process*. Prague: Central European University Press.

Gallup, John Luke and Jeffrey Sachs. 1998. 'Geography and Economic Growth'. Conference paper presented at 'Knowledge for Development', World Bank, Washington, DC, 20–1 April.

Gardner, Stephen. 1998. *Comparative Economic Systems*. Philadelphia: The Dryden Press.

Garten, Jeffrey. 1998. *The Big Ten: The Big Emerging Markets and How They will Change Our Lives*. New York: Basic Books.

Gavrilenkov, Evgeny and Vincent Koen. 1994. 'How Large was the Output Collapse in Russia?'. *IMF Working Papers*, WP/94/154 (December).

Gomulka, Stanislaw. 1991. 'The Causes of Recession Following Stabilization'. *Comparative Economic Studies*, xxxiii, 2, 71–89.

—— 1996. 'Causes of Output Decline, Sources of Recovery, and Prospects for Growth in Transition Economies', mimeo (December). London: London School of Economics.

Goodhue, Rachael E., Gordon C. Rausser, and Leo K. Simon. 1996. 'Privatization, Market Liberalization, and Learning in Transition Economies'. *University of California Working Papers*, May. Berkeley, CA: University of California.

Gora, Marek and Michal Rutkowski. 1998. 'The Quest for a New Pension System: Poland's Security through Diversity', mimeo (August). Washington, DC: World Bank.

Gordon, Roger H. and David D. Li. 1997. 'Government Distributional Concerns and Economic Policy during the Transition from Socialism'. *Discussion Papers*, 1,662 (June). London: Centre for Economic Policy Research.

Gorski, Marian and Dariusz Jaszczynski. 1991. 'Inflation in the Transition from the Centrally Planned to the Market Economy: The Polish Experience'. *Working Papers*, 14. Warsaw: Research Institute of Finance.

Götz-Richter, Stephan. 1997. 'Blood Brothers: What do George Soros and the International Monetary Fund have in Common?'. *Weekly Wire*, 33 (8 September). Washington, Frankfurt, and Brussels: Trans Atlantic Futures.

Grant, Jeremy. 1997. 'Vietnam Reforms Run into Heavy Weather'. *Financial Times*, 9 June.

Gregory, Paul R. 1997. 'Transition Economies: Social Consequences of Transition', November. New York: United Nations Development Programme.

Gregory, Paul R. and Robert Stuart. 1992. *Comparative Economic Systems*. Boston: Houghton Mifflin Company.

—— 1994. *Soviet and Post-Soviet Economic Structure and Performance*. New York: Harper Collins College Publisher.

Gruszczynski Marek and Grzegorz W. Kolodko. 1976. 'Regularnosc wahan tempa wzrostu gospodarczego' ('Regularity of Fluctuations in Economic Growth'). *Gospodarka Planowa (Planned Economy)*, xxx, 7–8, (July-August), 421–30.

GUS. various years. *Rocznik Statystyczny (Statistical Yearbook)*. Warsaw: Glowny Urzad Statystyczny (Central Statistical Office).

—— 1988a. *Rocznik Statystyczny Handlu Zagranicznego 1988 (Statistical Yearbook of Foreign Trade 1988)*. Warsaw: Glowny Urzad Statystyczny (Central Statistical Office).

—— 1988b. *Rocznik Statystyczny 1988 (Statistical Yearbook 1988)*. Warsaw: Glowny Urzad Statystyczny (Central Statistical Office).

—— 1996. *Ubostwo w swietle badan budzetow gospodarstw domowych (Poverty in View of Household Budget Surveys)*. Warsaw: Glowny Urzad Statystyczny (Central Statistical Office).

—— 1997a. *Monitoring warunkow zycia ludnosci (Monitoring the Living Conditions of the Population)*, 15 September. Warsaw: Glowny Urzad Statystyczny (Central Statistical Office).

—— 1997b. *Wskazniki ubostwa w swietle badan budzetow gospodarstw domowych (Poverty Indicators in Household Budget Surveys)*. Warsaw: Glowny Urzad Statystyczny (Central Statistical Office).

Harding, H. and Ed A. Hewett. 1988. 'Reforms in China and the Soviet Union'. *The Brookings Review*, spring, 13–19.

Hausner, Jerzy. 1997. 'The Political Economy of Socialism's Transformation'. Conference paper presented at 'Transition Strategies, Alternatives, and Outcomes', UNU/WIDER, Helsinki, 15–17 May.

—— 1998. 'Security through Diversity: Conditions for Successful Reform of the Pension System in Poland'. Paper prepared for 'Focus Group on the Interaction of Politics and Economic Policy in the Post-Socialist Transition'. Budapest: Collegium Budapest.

Heilbroner; Robert and William Milberg. 1995. *The Crisis of Vision in Modern Economic Thought*. Cambridge, UK: Cambridge University Press.

Hemming, Richard. 1998. 'Should Public Pensions be Funded?'. *IMF Working Papers*, 98/35 (March).

Hirshleifer, Jack. 1987. *Economic Behaviour in Adversity*. Brighton, UK: Wheatsheaf Books.

Honkkila, Juha. 1997. 'Privatization, Asset Distribution, and Equity in Transitional Economies'. *Working Papers*, 125 (February). Helsinki: UNU/WIDER.

Iglesias, Enrique. 1998. 'Income Distribution and Sustainable Growth: A Latin American Perspective'. In Vito Tanzi and Ke-young Chu (eds). *Income Distribution and High-Quality Growth*. Cambridge, MA: MIT Press.

IMF. 1991. *World Economic Outlook*, May. Washington, DC: International Monetary Fund.

—— 1992. *World Economic Outlook*, October. Washington, DC: International Monetary Fund.

—— 1996. 'Partnership for Sustainable Global Growth: Interim Committee Declaration', 29 September. Washington, DC: International Monetary Fund.

—— 1997. *World Economic Outlook: Globalization, Opportunities, and Challenges*, May. Washington, DC: International Monetary Fund.

—— 1998a. 'Asia's Financial Crisis Loomed Large over the EBRD Annual Meeting'. *Morning Press*, May 14. Washington, DC: External Relations Department, International Monetary Fund.

—— 1998b. 'Russia, IMF Agree on 1998 Economic Programme'. *Morning Press*, 13 April. Washington, DC: External Relations Department, International Monetary Fund.

—— 1998c. *World Economic Outlook: Financial Crises, Causes, and Indicators*, May. Washington, DC: International Monetary Fund.

Johnston, Michael. 1997. 'What Can be Done about Entrenched Corruption?'. In Boris Pleskovic and Joseph E. Stiglitz (eds). *Annual Bank Conference on Development Economics*. Washington, DC: World Bank.

Kaufmann, Daniel. 1997a. 'Why is the Ukrainian Economy—and Russia's—not Growing?'. *Transition*, April.

—— 1997b. 'Corruption: The Facts'. *Foreign Policy*, 107 (summer), 114–31.

Kaufmann, Daniel and Daniel Kaliberda. 1995. 'Integrating the Unofficial Economy into the Dynamic of Post-socialist Economies: A Framework of Analysis and Evidence'. Conference paper presented at 'Economic Transition in the Newly Independent States', Kiev, 16 August.

Kiyono, K. 1992. 'Postwar Industrial Policy of Japan: A Brief Economic Perspective'. Conference paper presented at 'Industrial Policy', Ministry of Industry and Trade and Japanese External Trade Organization, Vienna, 25–6 May.

Kolodko, Grzegorz W. 1976. 'Economic Growth Cycles in the Centrally Planned Economy: The Case of Poland'. *Working Papers*. Warsaw: Institute for Economic Development, Warsaw School of Economics (SGPiS).

—— 1979. 'Fazy wzrostu gospodarczego' ('The Stages of Economic Growth'). *Gospodarka Planowa (Planned Economy)*, March, 137–43.

—— 1986a. 'Economic Growth Cycles in the Centrally Planned Economies: A Hypothesis of the "Long Cycle" '. *Faculty Working Papers*, 1,280 (September). Champaign-Urbana, IL: College of Commerce and Business Administration, Bureau of Economic and Business Research, University of Illinois.

—— 1986b. 'The Repressed Inflation and Inflationary Overhang under Socialism'. *Faculty Working Papers*, 1,224 (February). Champaign-Urbana, IL: College of Commerce and Business Administration, Bureau of Economic and Business Research, University of Illinois.

—— 1987. 'Development Goals and Macroeconomic Proportions'. *Eastern European Economics*, xxv, 3, 72–85.

—— 1989a. 'Reform, Stabilization Policies, and Economic Adjustment in Poland'. *WIDER Working Papers*, WP 51 (January). Helsinki: UNU/WIDER.

—— 1989b. 'Economic Reforms and Inflation in Socialism: Determinants, Mutual Relationships, and Prospects'. *Communist Economies*, i, 2, 167–82.

—— 1991. 'Inflation Stabilization in Poland: A Year After'. *Rivista di Politica Economica*, 6 (June), 289–330.

—— 1992a. 'Stabilization, Recession, and Growth in Postsocialist Economies'. *IF Working Papers*, 29. Warsaw: Research Institute of Finance.

—— 1992b. 'Economics of Transition: From Shortageflation to Stagflation, the Case of Poland'. In Armand Clesse and Rudolf Tökes (eds). *Preventing a New*

East-West Divide: The Economic and Social Imperatives of the Future Europe. Baden-Baden: Nomos Verlagsgesellschaft.

Kolodko, Grzegorz W. 1992c. 'From Output Collapse to Sustainable Growth in Transition Economies: The Fiscal Implications', December. Washington, DC: International Monetary Fund.

—— 1993a. 'From Recession to Growth in Postcommunist Economies: Expectations versus Reality'. *Communist and Post-Communist Studies*, xxvi, 2, 123–43.

—— 1993b. 'A Strategy for Economic Transformation in Eastern Europe'. *Most*, iv, 1, 1–25.

—— 1996. *Poland 2000: The New Economic Strategy*. Warsaw: Poltext.

—— 1997a. 'Albania Pays a Heavy Price'. *The European*, 6–12 March.

—— 1997b. 'Exchange Rate Liberalization Policy and Growth in Transition Economies'. *IF Working Papers*, 57. Warsaw: Research Institute of Finance.

—— 1997c. 'Change of Government will not Hurt Polish Economy'. *Financial Times*, 6 October.

—— 1997d. 'Poland's Path to a Strong Economy'. *The Journal of Commerce*, 9 May.

—— 1998a. 'Equity Issues in Policymaking in Transition Economies'. Conference paper presented at 'Economic Policy and Equity', International Monetary Fund, Washington, DC, 8–9 June.

—— 1998b. 'Comments on John Flemming's "Equitable Economic Transformation" '. In Vito Tanzi and Ke-young Chu (eds). *Income Distribution and High-Quality Growth*. Cambridge, MA: MIT Press.

—— 1998c. 'Economic Neoliberalism became Almost Irrelevant . . .'. *Transition*, ix, 3 (June), 1–6.

—— 1998d. 'Russia should Put Its People First'. *The New York Times*, 7 July.

—— 1998e. 'The Kolodko Seven-Point Plan for Russia'. *Johnson's Russia List*, 2,469 (10 November).

Kolodko, Grzegorz W. and Walter W. McMahon. 1987. 'Stagflation and Short-ageflation: A Comparative Approach'. *Kyklos*, xl, 2, 176–97.

Kolodko, Grzegorz W. and D. Mario Nuti. 1997. 'The Polish Alternative: Old Myths, Hard Facts, and New Strategies in the Successful Transformation of the Polish Economy'. *Research for Action*, 33. Helsinki: UNU/WIDER.

Kolodko, Grzegorz W., Danuta Gotz-Kozierkiewicz, and Elzbieta Skrzeszewska-Paczek. 1992. *Hyperinflation and Stabilization in Postsocialist Economies*. Boston: Kluwer.

Komarek, Valtr. 1992. 'Shock Therapy and Its Victims'. *The New York Times*, 5 January.

Konings, Jozef, Herbert Lehmann, and Mark E. Schaffer. 1996. 'Job Creation and Job Destruction in a Transition Economy: Ownership, Firm Size, and Gross Job Flows in Polish Manufacturing, 1988–91'. *Labour Economics*, 3, 299–317.

Kornai, Janos. 1980. *Economics of Shortage*. Amsterdam: North Holland.

—— 1986. 'The Hungarian Reform Process: Visions, Hopes, and Reality'. *Journal of Economic Literature*, xxiv, 4, 1,687–737.

—— 1993. 'Transformational Recession: A General Phenomenon Examined through the Example of Hungary's Development'. *Economie Appliqué*, xxxxvi, 2, 181–227.

—— 1998. 'From Socialism to Capitalism: What is Meant by the "Change of System"?'. *Papers*, 4 (June). London: Social Market Foundation for Post-Collective Studies, Profile Books.

Kosta, Jiri. 1987. 'The Chinese Economic Reform: Approaches, Results, and Prospects'. In Peter Gey, Jiri Kosta, and Wolfgang Quassier (eds). *Crisis and Reform in Socialist Economies*. Boulder, CO: Westview Press.

Larrain, Felipe and Marcelo Selowsky (eds). 1991. *The Public Sector and the Latin American Crisis*. San Francisco: ICS Press and International Centre for Economic Growth.

Laski, Kazimierz. 1990. 'The Stabilization Plan for Poland'. *Wirtschaftspolitische Blätter*, 5, 444–58.

Lavigne, Marie. 1995. *The Economics of Transition: From Socialist Economy to Market Economy*. Chatham, Kent: Macmillan.

Lee, Keun. 1997. 'The Road to the Market in North Korea: Projects, Problems, and Prospects'. Conference paper presented at 'Transition Strategies, Alternatives, and Outcomes', UNU/WIDER, Helsinki, 15–17 May.

Londono, J., A. Spilimbergo, and M. Szekely. 1997. 'Income Distribution, Factor Endowments, and Trade Openness'. *Working Papers*, 356. Washington, DC: Office of the Chief Economist, Inter-American Development Bank.

Lustig, Nora and Ruthanne Deutsch. 1998. *The Inter-American Development Bank and Poverty Reduction: An Overview*. Washington, DC: Inter-American Development Bank.

Mauro, Paolo. 1997. 'The Effects of Corruption on Growth, Investment, and Government Expenditure: A Cross-Country Analysis'. In Kimberley Ann Elliot (ed.). *Corruption and the Global Economy*. Washington, DC: Institute for International Economics.

McKinnon, Ronald. 1991. 'Foreign Trade, Protection, and Negative Value-added in a Liberalizing Socialist Economy'. In Ronald McKinnon (ed.). *The Order of Economic Liberalization: Financial Control in the Transition to a Market Economy*. Baltimore: Johns Hopkins University Press.

Michaels, Daniel. 1998. 'Poland's Strong Economic Turnaround Raises Challenges of Managing Growth'. *The Wall Street Journal*, 18 June.

Michalopoulos, Constantine. 1997. 'Economies in Transition and the WTO'. *Transition*, July, 22–4.

Milanovic, Branko. 1996. 'Income, Inequality, and Poverty during Transition'. *Research Papers*, 11. Washington, DC: Transition Economics Division, Policy Research Department, World Bank.

—— 1998. *Income, Inequality, and Poverty during the Transition from Planned to Market Economy*. Washington, DC: World Bank.

Mobius, J. Mark. 1996. *On Emerging Markets*. London: Pitman Publishing.

Montes, Manuel. 1997. 'Vietnam: Is There a Socialist Road to the Market?'. Conference paper presented at 'Transition Strategies, Alternatives, and Outcomes', UNU/WIDER, Helsinki, 15–17 May.

Mundell, Robert A. 1995. 'Great Contractions in Transition Economies'. Conference paper presented at 'First Dubrovnik Conference on Transition Economies', Dubrovnik, 8–9 June.

Muravchik, Joshua. 1998. 'Why Lenin? Why Stalin?'. *The American Spectator*, May, 77–8.

Nafziger, E. Wayne. 1998. 'Root of Human Suffering'. *Financial Times*, 21 January.

Nelson, Joan M., Jacek Kochanowicz, Kalman Mizsei, and Oscar Munoz. 1994. *Intricate Links: Democratization and Market Reforms in Latin America and Eastern Europe*. New Brunswick, NJ: Transaction Publishers.

Nelson, Lynn D. and Irina Y. Kuzes. 1995. *Radical Reform in Yeltsin's Russia: Political, Economic, and Social Dimensions*. Armonk, NY: M. E. Sharpe.

The New York Times. 1998. 'Moscow Statisticians Accused of Aiding Tax Evasion', 10 June.

North, Douglass C. 1997. 'The Contribution of the New Institutional Economics to an Understanding of the Transition Problem'. *WIDER Annual Lectures*, 1 (March). Helsinki: UNU/WIDER.

Nove, Alex. 1992. *An Economic History of the USSR*, 6th edition. Harmondsworth, UK: Penguin.

Nuti, D. Mario. 1989. 'Hidden and Repressed Inflation in Soviet-type Economies: Definitions, Measurements, and Stabilization'. In Chris Davis and Wojciech Charemza (eds). *Models of Disequilibrium and Shortage in Centrally Planned Economies*. London: Chapman and Hall.

—— 1990. 'Crisis, Reform, and Stabilization in Central Eastern Europe: Prospects and Western Response'. In *La Grande Europa, la Nuova Europa: Opportunità e Rischi*, November. Siena: Monte dei Paschi di Siena.

—— 1992a. 'Market Socialism: The System that Might Have Been but Never Was'. In Anders Åslund (ed.). *Market Socialism or the Restoration of Capitalism?*. Cambridge, UK: Cambridge University Press.

—— 1992b. 'Lessons from Stabilization and Reform in Central Eastern Europe'. *CEC Working Papers*, 92 (May). Brussels: Council of the European Community.

—— 1993. 'Teaching Materials on Comparative Economics Systems'. Rome: Economics Department, Università di Roma 'La Sapienza'.

—— 1996. 'Exchange Rate and Monetary Policy in Poland 1994–96, or the Case for Privatizing the National Bank of Poland'. Conference paper presented at 'Transition Strategies, Alternatives, and Outcomes', UNU/WIDER, Helsinki, 15–17 May.

—— 1997a. 'Comparative Economics after the Transition', mimeo. Aiessec Xi Biannual Meeting, Roundtable Discussion, Università di Roma 'La Sapienza', Rome, 25–6 September.

—— 1997b. 'On Russia's Transition to a Market Economy'. Lecture presented at Cambridge University, Cambridge, UK, 13 April.

—— 1997c. 'Employee Ownership in Polish Privatizations'. In Milica Uvalic and Daniel Vaughan-Whitehead (eds). *Privatization Surprises in Transition Economies: Employee Ownership in Central and Eastern Europe*. Aldershot, UK: Edward Elgar.

—— 1997d. 'Farewell Welfare?', mimeo. Background note for 'Social Welfare in the Transition', Stockholm, 5–6 September.

—— 1998. 'Stocks and Stakes: The Case for Protecting Stakeholders' Interests'. *Economic Analysis*, i, 1, 7–16.

OECD. 1996a. 'Czech Republic 1996'. *OECD Economic Surveys*. Paris: Organization for Economic Cooperation and Development.

—— 1996b. 'Poland 1997'. *OECD Economic Surveys*. Paris: Organization for Economic Cooperation and Development.

—— 1997a. *Sustainable Development: OECD Policy Approaches for the 21st Century*. Paris: Organization for Economic Cooperation and Development.

—— 1997b. 'Russia 1997'. *OECD Economic Surveys*. Paris: Organization for Economic Cooperation and Development.

—— 1997c. 'Short-term Economic Indicators: Transition Economies, 1/1997'. Paris: Centre for Cooperation with the Economies in Transition, Organization for Economic Cooperation and Development.

—— 1997d. *OECD Economic Outlook*, 61 (June). Paris: Organization for Economic Cooperation and Development.

—— 1997e. 'Short-term Economic Indicators: Transition Economies, 3/1997'. Paris: Centre for Cooperation with the Economies in Transition, Organization for Economic Cooperation and Development.

Office of the Government Plenipotentiary for Social Security Reform. 1997. 'Security through Diversity: Reform of the Pension System in Poland', June. Warsaw: Office of the Government Plenipotentiary for Social Security Reform.

Paniccià, Renato. 1997. 'Short- and Long-term Determinants of Cardiovascular Mortality: An Econometric Assessment of the Working Age Population in Russia, 1965–95'. *Research in Progress*, 14 (June). Helsinki: UNU/WIDER.

Pastor, Manuel. 1997. 'The Coming Cuban Transition?: Possibilities and Prospects for a Postsocialist Cuba'. Conference paper presented at 'Transition Strategies, Alternatives, and Outcomes', UNU/WIDER, Helsinki, 15–17 May.

Perkins, Dwight H. 1988. 'Reforming China's Economic System'. *Journal of Economic Literature*, xxvi, 2, 601–45.

Persson, Torsten and Guido Tabellini. 1994. 'Is Inequality Harmful for Growth?'. *American Economic Review*, lxxxiv, 3, 600–21.

Pinto, Brian, Marek Belka, and Stefan Krajewski. 1992. 'Microeconomics of Transformation in Poland: A Survey of State Enterprise Response'. Conference paper presented at 'The Second European Association for Comparative Economic Studies Conference on Problems of Transforming Economies', Groningen, Germany, 24–6 September.

Pitelis, Christos and Thomas Clarke. 1993. 'The Political Economy of Privatization'. In Thomas Clarke and Christos Pitelis. *The Political Economy of Privatization*. London: Routledge.

PlanEcon. 1996. *Review and Outlook for Eastern Europe*, December. Washington, DC: PlanEcon, Inc.

—— 1997a. *Review and Outlook for the Former Soviet Union*, September. Washington, DC: PlanEcon, Inc.

—— 1997b. *Review and Outlook for Eastern Europe*, December. Washington, DC: PlanEcon, Inc.

—— 1997c. *Review and Outlook for the Former Soviet Union*, March. Washington, DC: PlanEcon, Inc.

—— 1997d. 'Key Monetary and Fiscal Policy Decisions could Assure the Polish Economy a Smooth Ride'. *Polish Economic Monitor*, xiii, 19–20 (9 July).

—— 1998a. *Review and Outlook for the Former Soviet Union*, March. Washington, DC: PlanEcon, Inc.

—— 1998b. *Review and Outlook for Eastern Europe*, July. Washington, DC: PlanEcon, Inc.

Pleskovic, Boris and Joseph E. Stiglitz (eds). 1997. *Annual Bank Conference on Development Economics*. Washington, DC: World Bank.

Pohl, Gerhardt, Simeon Djankov, and Robert E. Anderson. 1996. 'Restructuring Large Industrial Firms in Central and Eastern Europe: An Empirical Analysis'. *World Bank Technical Papers*, 332 (August).

Pohl, Gerhardt, Gregory T. Jedrzejczak, and Robert E. Anderson. 1995. 'Creating Capital Markets in Central and Eastern Europe. *World Bank Technical Papers*, 295 (August).

Pohorille, Maksymilian (ed.). 1982. *Tendencje rozwoju konsumpcji. Postulaty i uwarunkowania.* (*Trends in the Growth of Consumption: Priorities and Determinants*). Warsaw: Panstwowe Wydawnictwo Ekonomiczne (Polish Economics Publisher).

Pomfret, Richard. 1997. 'Reform Paths in Central Asian Transition Economies'. Conference paper presented at 'Transition Strategies, Alternatives, and Outcomes', UNU/WIDER, Helsinki, 15–17 May.

Pomfret, Richard and Kathryn H. Anderson. 1997. 'Uzbekistan: Welfare Impact of Slow Transition'. *Working Papers*, 135 (June). Helsinki: UNU/WIDER.

Popov, Vladimir. 1998a. 'Investment in Transition Economies: Factors of Change and Implications for Performance'. *Journal of East-West Business*, iv, 1/2.

—— 1998b. 'Is Russia's Economy Likely to Get on the Fast Growth Track?'. *Communist Economies and Economic Transformation*, 4.

Popov, Vladimir and Nikolai Shmelev. 1990. *The Turning Point: Revitalizing the Soviet Economy.* New York: Doubleday.

Portes, R. 1981. 'Macroeconomic Equilibrium and Disequilibrium in Centrally Planned Economies'. *Birkbeck College Discussion Papers*, 161. London: Birkbeck College.

Poznanski, Kazimierz. 1993. 'Poland's Transition to Capitalism: Shock and Therapy'. In Kazimierz Poznanski (ed.). *Stabilization and Privatization in Poland.* Boston: Kluwer Academic Publishers.

—— 1996. *Poland's Protracted Transition: Institutional Change and Economic Growth.* Cambridge, UK: Cambridge University Press.

—— 1997. 'Comparative Transition Theory: Recession and Recovery in Post-Communist Economies'. Conference paper presented at 'Transition Strategies, Alternatives, and Outcomes', UNU/WIDER, Helsinki, 15–17 May.

Quassier, Wolfgang. 1987. 'The New Agricultural Reform in China: From the People's Communes to Peasant Agriculture'. In Peter Gey, Jiri Kosta, and Wolfgang Quassier (eds). *Crisis and Reform in Socialist Economies.* Boulder, CO: Westview Press.

Raiser, Martin. 1997. 'Destruction, Diversity, Dialogue: Notes on the Ethics of Development'. *Journal of International Development*, ix, 1, 39–57.

Ravallion, Martin. 1997. 'Good and Bad Growth: The *Human Development Reports*'. *World Development*, xxv, 5, 631–8.

Ravi, N. 1998. 'Opening Up Gradually to Global Finance'. *The Hindu* (New Delhi), 10 January.

Reich, Robert. 1998. 'Deflation: The Real Enemy'. *Financial Times*, 15 January.

Robinson, Anthony. 1997. 'Surge in Capital Flight from Russia'. *Financial Times*, 21 March.

Roca, Sergio G. 1988. *Socialist Cuba: Past Interpretations and Future Challenges.* Boulder, CO: Westview Press.

Rodrik, Dani. 1990. 'Premature Liberalization, Incomplete Stabilization: The Ozal Decade in Turkey'. *NBER Working Papers*, 3,300 (March). Cambridge, MA: National Bureau of Economic Research.

—— 1996. 'Understanding Economic Policy Reform'. *Journal of Economic Literature*, xxxiv, March, 9–41.

Roland, Gerard and Thierry Verdier. 1997. 'Transition and the Output Fall'. *Discussion Papers*, 1,636 (May). London: Centre for Economic Policy Research.

Rosati, Dariusz. 1991. 'The Transition from Central Planning to the Market: The Polish Experience'. *Thames Papers in Political Economy*, 2. London: Thames Polytechnic.

—— 1994. 'Output Decline during Transition from Plan to Market'. *Economics of Transition*, ii, 4, 419–42.

Rose-Ackerman, Susan. 1997. 'Corruption and Development'. In Boris Pleskovic and Joseph E. Stiglitz (eds). *Annual Bank Conference on Development Economics*. Washington, DC: World Bank.

Roubini, Nouriel and Paul Wachtel. 1997. 'Current Account Sustainability in Transition Economies'. Conference paper presented at 'Third Dubrovnik Conference on Transition Economies', Dubrovnik, 25–7 June.

Rutkowski, Jan. 1997. 'Labour Markets, Welfare, and Social Policy during Economic Transition in Poland', mimeo (15 October). Warsaw: World Bank.

Sachs, Jeffrey. 1989. 'My Plan for Poland'. *International Economy*, 3 (December 1989–January 1990), 24–9.

—— 1993. *Poland's Jump to the Market Economy*. Cambridge, MA: MIT Press.

Schumpeter, Joseph A. 1942. *Capitalism, Socialism, and Democracy*. New York: Harper & Brothers Publishers.

Selowsky, Marcelo. 1991. 'Comments on "Policies to Move from Stabilization to Growth", by Dornbusch'. In World Bank. *Proceedings of the World Bank Annual Conference on Development Economics 1990*. Washington, DC: World Bank.

Selowsky, Marcelo and Matthew Vogel. 1995. 'Enterprise Credit and Stabilization in Transition Economies: Present Experiences and Stabilization in Transition Economies'. Conference paper presented at 'First Dubrovnik Conference on Transition Economies', Dubrovnik, 8–9 June.

Sen, Amartya. 1992. *Inequality Reexamined*. New York: Russel Sage Foundation.

Shatalin, Stanislav *et al.* 1990. *Perekhod k Rynku: Kontseptsiya i Programma (Transition to the Market: Concept and Programme)*. Moscow: Government printer.

Shelly, Louise I. 1997. 'The Price Tag of Russia's Organized Crime'. *Transition*, February.

Shevtsova, Lilia. 1995. 'The Two Sides of the New Russia'. *The Journal of Democracy*, vi, 3 (July), 25–40.

Shor, Boris (ed.). 1997a. 'Nations in Transit 1997: Civil Society, Democracy, and Markets in Eastern Europe and the Newly Independent States'. New York: Freedom House.

—— 1997b. 'Nations in Transit 1997: Freedom House Rankings'. *Transition*, vii, 3 (June).

Simonia, Nodari. 1997. 'The Lessons of the Chinese and South-Korean Reforms for Russia', mimeo (September). Moscow: Institute of World Economics and International Relations, RAS, Slavic Research Centre, Hokudai University.

Soros, George. 1997. 'The Capitalist Threat'. *Atlantic Monthly*, February.

Stein, H. 1993. 'Institutional Theories and Structural Adjustment in Africa'. Conference paper presented at 'The Relevance of Public Policy Choice Theory for the Third World', Department of Economic History, London School of Economics, London, September.

Stern, Nicholas. 1996. 'The Transition in Eastern Europe and the Former Soviet Union: Some Strategic Lessons from the Experience of 25 Countries over Six Years'. Conference paper presented at 'OECD/CCET Colloquium', Paris, 29–30 May.

Stern, Nicholas and Joseph E. Stiglitz. 1997. 'A Framework for a Development Strategy in a Market Economy: Objectives, Scope, Institutions, and Instruments'. *EBRD Working Papers*, 20 (April).

Stiglitz, Joseph E. 1995. *Whither Socialism?*. Cambridge, MA: MIT Press.

—— 1996. 'Some Lessons from the East Asian Miracle'. *World Bank Research Observer*, xi, 2, 151–77.

—— 1997. 'An Agenda for Development for the Twenty-First Century'. In Boris Pleskovic and Joseph E. Stiglitz (eds). *Annual Bank Conference on Development Economics*. Washington, DC: World Bank.

—— 1998a. 'More Instruments and Broader Goals: Moving toward the Post-Washington Consensus'. *WIDER Annual Lectures*, 2 (January). Helsinki: UNU/WIDER.

—— 1998b. 'Economic Science, Economic Policy, and Economic Advice'. Conference paper presented at 'Knowledge for Development', World Bank, Washington, DC, 20–1 April.

Summers, Lawrence H. 1998. 'Equity in a Global Economy'. Remarks presented to the conference 'Economic Policy and Equity', International Monetary Fund, Washington, DC, 8–9 June.

Tanzi, Vito. 1991. 'Tax Reform and the Move to a Market Economy: Overview of the Issues'. In OECD. *The Role of Tax Reform in Central and Eastern European Economies*. Paris: Organization for Economic Cooperation and Development.

—— 1992. *Fiscal Issues in Economies in Transition*. Washington, DC: International Monetary Fund.

—— 1997a. 'The Fiscal Implications of Trade Liberalization in Transition Countries'. Conference paper presented at 'Third Dubrovnik Conference on Transition Economies', Dubrovnik, 25–7 June.

—— 1997b. 'Reconsidering the Fiscal Role of Government: The International Perspective'. *American Economic Review*, lxxxvii, 2 (May), 164–8.

Tanzi, Vito and Ke-young Chu (eds). 1998. *Income Distribution and High-Quality Growth*. Cambridge, MA: MIT Press.

Tanzi, Vito and Hamid Davoodi. 1997. 'Corruption, Public Investment, and Growth'. *IMF Working Papers*, 97/139 (October).

Tanzi, Vito and Ludger Schuknecht. 1995. 'The Growth of Government and the Reform of the State in Industrial Countries'. *IMF Working Papers*, 95/130.

Twigg, Judith L. 1997. 'Russian Health Care in Critical Condition'. *Transition*, iv, 3 (August).

UNDP (United Nations Development Programme). 1992. *Human Development Report 1992*. New York: Oxford University Press.

—— 1994. *Human Development Report 1994*. New York: Oxford University Press.

—— 1996. *Human Development Report 1996*. New York: Oxford University Press.

—— 1997. *Human Development Report 1997*. New York: Oxford University Press.

UNECE. 1998. *Economic Bulletin for Europe*, 47 (March). Geneva: United Nations Economic Commission for Europe.

UNICEF (United Nations Children's Fund). 1994. 'Crisis in Mortality, Health, and Nutrition'. *Regional Monitoring Reports*, 2. Florence: UNICEF International Child Development Centre.

—— 1995. 'Poverty, Children, and Policy: Responses for a Brighter Future'. *Regional Monitoring Reports*, 3. Florence: UNICEF International Child Development Centre.

Uvalic, Milica and Daniel Vaughan-Whitehead (eds). 1997. *Privatization Surprises in Transition Economies: Employee-Ownership in Central and Eastern Europe*. Aldershot, UK: Edward Elgar.

van Brabant, Josef. 1990. *Remaking Eastern Europe: On the Political Economy of Transition*. Boston: Kluwer.

Walker, Tony. 1997. 'Unbinding China'. *Financial Times*, 11 September.

Wang, Shan. 1994. *The Third Eye*. Beijing: Shanxi People's Press.

Weber, Steven. 1997. 'The End of the Business Cycle?'. *Foreign Affairs*, lxxvi, July–August, 65–82.

Wedel, Janine R. 1998a. *Collision and Collusion: The Strange Case of Western Aid to Eastern Europe 1989–1998*. New York: St. Martin's.

—— 1998b. 'The Harvard Boys do Russia'. *The Nation*, 1 June, 11–16.

Wilczynski, Jan. 1972. *Socialist Economic Development and Reforms*. London: Macmillan.

Wiles, Peter. J. 1977. *Economic Institutions Compared*. Oxford: Basil Blackwell.

Williamson, John. 1990. 'What Washington Means by Policy Reform'. In John Williamson (ed.). *Latin American Adjustment: How Much has Happened?*. Washington, DC: Institute for International Economics.

—— 1993. 'Democracy and the "Washington Consensus"'. *World Development*, xxi, 8, 1,329–36.

—— 1997. 'The Washington Consensus Revisited'. In Louis Emmerij (ed.). *Economic and Social Development into the XXI Century*. Washington, DC: Inter-American Development Bank.

Winiecki, Jan. 1991. 'Costs of Transition that are not Costs: On Non-welfare-reducing Output Fall'. *Rivista di Politica Economica*, 6 (June), 85–8.

Wolf, Holger C. 1992. 'Miracle Prescriptions: Postwar Reconstruction and Transition in the 1990s'. In Centre for Economic Policy Research. *The Economic Consequences of the East*. London: Centre for Economic Policy Research.

—— 1997. 'Transition Strategies: Choices and Outcomes', mimeo (December). New York: Stern Business School.

Wolf, Martin. 1998. 'Ins and Outs of Capital Flows'. *Financial Times*, 16 June.

World Bank. 1993. *World Development Report 1993: The East Asian Miracle, Economic Growth, and Public Policy*. Washington, DC: World Bank.

—— 1994. *Averting the Old Age Crisis: Policies to Protect the Old and Promote Growth*. Washington, DC: World Bank.

—— 1995a. *Understanding Poverty in Poland*. Washington, DC: World Bank.

—— 1995b. *Poverty in Russia: An Assessment*. Washington, DC: Human Resources Division, Europe and Central Asia Country Department III, World Bank.

—— 1995c. *Bureaucrats in Business: The Economics and Politics of Government Ownership*. Washington, DC: World Bank.

—— 1995d. *World Development Report 1995*. New York: Oxford University Press.

World Bank. 1996. *World Development Report 1996: From Plan to Market*. New York: Oxford University Press.

—— 1997a. *World Development Indicators*. Washington, DC: World Bank.

—— 1997b. *World Development Report 1997: The State in a Changing World*. New York: Oxford University Press.

—— 1997c. *Global Economic Prospects and the Developing Countries*. Washington, DC: World Bank.

—— 1997d. *World Bank Atlas 1997*. Washington, DC: World Bank.

—— 1998. *World Development Indicators*. Washington, DC: World Bank.

Wydawnictwo 'Rzeczpospolita'. 1988. 'Program realizacyjny drugiego etapu reformy gospodarczej' ('Programme for the Implementation of the Second Stage of Economic Reform'), February. Warsaw: Wydawnictwo 'Rzeczpospolita'.

Yergin, Daniel and Joseph Stanislaw. 1998. *The Commanding Heights: The Battle between Government and the Marketplace that is Remaking the Modern World*. New York: Simon & Schuster.

Yermolin, Vladimir. 1998. 'Police Know Where Thieves are: Russian Criminals have Strong Patrons in Political Community'. *Rusky Telegraf* (Moscow), 22 July.

Zhang, Yuan. 1989. 'Economic System Reform in China'. *WIDER Working Papers*, WP 55 (March). Helsinki: UNU/WIDER.

INDEX